Interdisciplinary Encyclopedia of Marine Sciences

Interdisciplinary Encyclopedia of Marine Sciences

EDITED BY

James W. Nybakken, Editor in Chief

William W. Broenkow and Tracy L. Vallier

Volume 1
A–F

GROLIER ACADEMIC REFERENCE, AN IMPRINT OF SCHOLASTIC LIBRARY PUBLISHING
DANBURY, CONNECTICUT

Published by Grolier Academic Reference, an imprint of Scholastic Library Publishing, Danbury, Connecticut

© 2003 by The Moschovitis Group, Inc.
339 Fifth Avenue, New York, New York 10010

Library of Congress Cataloging-in-Publication Data

Interdisciplinary encyclopedia of marine sciences / edited by James W. Nybakken, William W. Broenkow, Tracy L. Vallier.
    p. cm.
    Includes bibliographical references and index.
    ISBN 0-7172-5946-3 (set : alk. paper)
    1. Marine sciences–Encyclopedias. 2. Oceanography. I. Nybakken, James Willard. II. Broenkow, William W., 1939-III. Vallier, T. L. (Tracy L.)

GC9 .I58 2002
551.46'003–dc21

                    2002192707

Printed and Manufactured in the United States of America

Table of Contents

∼

VOLUME 1

Editorial and Production Staff

The Moschovitis Group, Inc.
Valerie Tomaselli: *Executive Editor*
Stephanie Schreiber: *Senior Editor*
Eleanora von Dehsen: *Editorial Consultant*
Sonja Matanovic: *Associate Editor*
Joseph J. Bizzarro: *Assistant to James W. Nybakken*
Nicole Cohen, Jessica Rosin, Colleen Sullivan: *Editorial Assistants*
Erin Anzelmo, Natalie Gerber, Alison Quito Ziegler: *Researchers*
Annemarie Redmond: *Design and Layout*
Richard Garratt, Grant Jerding: *Illustrations*
Gillian Speeth: *Photo Research*
K. Nura Abdul-Karim, Rashida Allen: *Production Assistants*
Zeiders & Associates: *Copyediting*
Carole Campbell, Lynn L. Lauerman, Paul A. Scaramazza: *Proofreading*
Appleton Ink: *Index*

Grolier Academic Reference
Mark Cummings: *Vice President and Publisher, Grolier Reference*
Donna S. Sanzone: *Editor in Chief, Grolier Academic Reference*
Cheryl Clark: *Senior Project Editor, Grolier Academic Reference*
Valerie Plue-Eriquezzo: *Vice President, Manufacturing/Supply Planning*
Christine L. Matta: *Director, Reference, International and Children's Publishing*
Donna L. Roberts: *Production Manager*
Diane C. Foster: *Production Assistant*

Preface

∾

The *Interdisciplinary Encyclopedia of Marine Sciences* is intended to offer the nonspecialist an introduction to the science and technology of the world's oceans. It presents articles on all the major subdisciplines of oceanography—biological, chemical, geological, and physical—as well as articles on the marine life, ecology, and economics of the ocean, major figures in the history of marine sciences, important technologies used to explore and understand the ocean environment, and parts of the ocean and geographic places within it.

In order to make the marine sciences accessible to as wide an audience as possible, the writers and editors have made every effort to develop articles that are clear and straightforward. Whenever possible, a life span has been included at the first mention of a person in an article; if not cited, the information was not available.

Descriptions of difficult technical and scientific concepts have been crafted carefully to offer the simplest explanations possible, and parenthetical definitions are provided whenever appropriate. Cross-references have been listed in a Related Articles section at the end of each article that will link readers to concepts explored more fully in other articles.

Illustrations, maps, charts, and photographic images illuminate many of the concepts presented in the articles. The illustrations range from schematic diagrams and cross sections of biological, geological, and chemical processes, for instance, to original drawings of marine life.

Locator maps are included for many of the geographic places and parts of the ocean featured in the encyclopedia. These highlight some of the most important features of these places, as well as offering the user a key to the location of a place. Other maps illustrate specific processes or physical conditions; for instance, a map is used to show the processes and effects of El Niño. Photographs accompany articles for a range of purposes: to represent interesting marine environments, to illustrate underwater technology, to bring the exotic beauty of marine specimens to life.

A Further Reading section is included after the text of each article to refer readers to the most important literature on the subject. This may include books, journal articles, and textbooks, as well as Web sites in some cases. Although it may have been desirable to limit the suggestions for further reading to nontechnical material, this was not possible, since some of the most critical literature on each topic is more advanced in nature. However, the authors and editors have also made attempts to list works that will be accessible to less technically advanced readers. The user will therefore find a wide range of material in these lists. Articles on individuals are augmented by Selected Writings lists when appropriate, so that readers have a guide to the most important literature contributed by that person.

Appended at the end of the book is a directory of important marine science research centers and educational institutions. This material will be useful for those interested in finding establishments that offer specialized studies and sponsor research programs in the various fields of oceanography and marine sciences. A bibliography is also included that offers readers a compendium of key resources in the major subdisciplines of marine sciences. It will be a valuable research tool for students and researchers who need a general introduction to these subfields.

The titles of encyclopedia articles on marine life have been given in the Latin form. For instance, *Asteroidea* is the scientific term for sea star, so a user will find this article listed under that title. However, if the animal is widely known under a different name, the article will appear with the more common name. For example, the article on sharks is titled "Shark" rather than Selachii, the name of the order.

Abreviations are used for standard terminology. Examples include ONR for Office of Navel Research and USN for United States Navy.

Measurements are given in metric units first, followed by their English equivalents in parentheses. Often, measurements are simple estimates, and both metric and English conversions are presented as approximations. The English conversion for measurements of speed, such as in many physical oceanography articles dealing with the speed of currents, has been provided in knots (nautical miles per hour) rather than in statute miles per hour since this is traditional in the field. Also, the salinity of seawater had previously been expressed in parts per thousand (‰). However, the new term, *practical salinity unit* (psu), is used throughout the encyclopedia.

Introduction

~

The oceans cover 71 percent of the surface of Earth and make up the largest and least explored part of our planet. As the last true frontier of our world, they have in recent decades attracted increasing attention from humans seeking not only to explore and learn more about them, but also to exploit them as a source of food, drugs, and petroleum to fuel our expanding population and as a possible ultimate repository for much of our waste. Additionally, the media's coverage of the recent failure of many ocean fisheries, our destruction of 25 percent of the world's coral reefs, the expanding areas of anoxic waters, and the increase in toxic algal blooms means that many more people are now aware of the oceans' problems and limitations. At the same time, as interest in the oceans has increased, no encyclopedia has been published that covers marine sciences comprehensively at the introductory level for high school and college students or the general public. Instead, most reference works on oceanography are too advanced for such an audience and are often accessible only in research libraries. It was to fill this gap that this encyclopedia was written.

Scope of Coverage

The encyclopedia covers the major subdisciplines in academic oceanography (biological, chemical, geological, and physical oceanography), as well as areas that would probably not appear in a traditional high school or college course in oceanography, such as ecology, technology, and the economics of the oceans. This broad focus creates a more comprehensive coverage than is encompassed by the major academic subdisciplines.

Biological oceanography in this encyclopedia encompasses the myriad of living marine organisms and their structure and function. Examples of these articles include "Algae," "Bacteria," "Cetacea," and "Coral." Chemical oceanography is concerned with the various chemical elements and compounds that are found in seawater and their distribution in the water column and interaction with each other and the surrounding environment and organisms. Examples of chemical oceanographic articles include "Biogeochemical Cycle," "Chemical Tracer," and "Oxygen Minimum Zone." Geological oceanography is concerned with the structure of the seafloor and the topographical features covered by the world's oceans as well as the processes that create such features. Examples of geological oceanographic articles include "Abyssal Plain," "Continental Margin," and "Subduction Zone." Physical oceanography deals with the movement of the water masses and their changes in temperature and density, as well as their interactions with the seafloor, adjacent geological structures, and the atmosphere. Examples of these articles include "Diurnal and Semidiurnal Tide," "Ocean Current," "Thermocline," and "Upwelling."

The encyclopedia also includes articles on economics, historical figures, parts of the ocean, places, technology, and ecology. Economics was included so that the value of various ocean products and the significance of particular treaties among seafaring countries could be better understood. "Fisheries," "Guano," and "Madrid Environmental Protocol" are examples of these articles. Similarly, we included articles on historical figures so that key marine scientists of the past and their accomplishments could be recognized. Deciding which individuals to include was difficult due to space limitations; we could not include many well-known marine scientists and have purposefully left out all living scientists. Some scientists included are "Roald Amundsen," "Rachel Louise Carson," and "Auguste Piccard." Parts of the ocean is a category that deals with the named currents, underwater topographic features, and special regions of the world's oceans. Examples include "Aphotic Zone," "Bay," "Continental Shelf," "Fjord," "Gulf Stream," and "Oceanic Island." We also included articles on geographic places, such as the various named seas and island arcs. Examples of these articles include "Arctic Ocean," "Great Barrier Reef," and "India Plate." We included articles on technology because this area is vital to understanding how oceanographers obtain their knowledge of the oceans. Examples include "Autonomous Underwater Vehicle," "Navigation," and "Underwater Communication." Finally, the category of ecology deals with the interactions of the marine organisms with each other and with the surrounding physical, chemical, and geological environment. Examples include "Biodiversity," "Estuary," and "Mangrove Forest."

Ecological Approach

This encyclopedia takes an overall interdisciplinary approach in that it focuses on the physical, chemical, geological, and biological processes and interactions that serve to structure the world's oceans. This is basically an ecological approach. In its broadest sense, marine ecology is the study of interactions and interrelationships that exist among marine organisms and between the organisms and their environment. Therefore, marine ecology is the most comprehensive of the subdivisions of oceanography because to understand how organisms exist and interact to form functioning biological communities and ecosystems, one must have a knowledge of all the subdisciplines of oceanography. Such an ecological approach is particularly relevant to the oceans because the world's oceans make up a contiguous mass of water in which the living organisms are suspended for at least some part of their lives. They must therefore interact not only with other organisms but also with the chemical, physical, and geological parameters of the medium in order to persist. This medium is much more changeable than the air that bathes the terrestrial environment. Furthermore, the bathing air does not itself contain permanent living communities as does the ocean.

The significance of this interdisciplinary, ecological approach can be better appreciated with an example. Coral reefs, for instance, are one of the most complex communities and contain the highest diversity of organisms in the sea. Coral reefs exist only under certain chemical and physical conditions. They must have temperatures above 18°C (64°F), they must have salinity of 32 to 35 practical salinity units (psu), and are limited to depths where the light intensity is not below 1 to 2 percent of surface intensity. In addition, the reefs thrive in areas of moderate wave action and do poorly where there is insufficient water circulation. They also are limited in upward growth by exposure to air and are killed by excessive amounts of silt or sediment in the water. Reefs, however, are limited by biological conditions as well. The major biological factor is that reefs are formed only by corals that have symbiotic algae in their tissues. If this symbiosis does not develop or is destroyed, the reefs will cease to exist. Additionally, the corals are outcompeted for space by many species of fast-growing algae and are therefore dependent on various algae–eating fish and invertebrates to keep the algae in check and support their existence. Thus, this entire coral ecosystem is maintained by a complex series of physical, chemical, geological, and biological interactions.

History of Oceanography

Oceanography is a comprehensive scientific discipline that is most simply defined as the study of the oceans: physical, chemical, geological, and biological. As a scientific discipline it is relatively young. While other scientific and technological disciplines, such as engineering and medicine, may go back thousands of years, oceanography had its beginnings in western Europe only in the eighteenth and nineteenth centuries. The first truly oceanographic expedition was that undertaken by the British HMS *Challenger* from 1872 to 1876. This was followed by a large number of oceanographic expeditions in the late nineteenth and early twentieth centuries by several western European nations as well as the United States. There are many reasons why oceanography developed so late, but the major ones were the vastness of the subject, the large amounts of money required to begin the study, and the lack of technology available to sample the depths of the oceans. It is only in the last half of the twentieth century that we finally perfected the technology to transport instruments and humans to the deepest parts of the ocean.

Early Technological Advances

Prior to World War I, much of our knowledge of the oceans, particularly the deep sea, was the result of a relatively few major expeditions mounted by the countries of western Europe or the United States. At that time no sonar, satellite navigation, or remotely operated vehicles equipped with photographic or video cameras existed. Following World War I came the devel-opment of sonar for depth sounding, which was intended to be used for the detection of submarines. After World War II, Jacques Cousteau and French engineer Emile Gagnan invented the aqualung, which permitted humans to enter the shallow nearshore environment and remain underwater for enough time to observe sea life in its natural state. This device became popular not only with scientists but also with the public and led to huge advances in our knowledge of the structure and function of nearshore biological communities such as kelp forests, coral reefs, and rocky reefs. For the first time, researchers could conduct experiments and test various ideas and theories. For example, diver-scientists could set up experimental plots in kelp forests, sea grass beds, and coral reefs, replicate them, subject them to different treatments, and then return at periodic intervals to assess the results of the treatments over time, something that had been done by terrestrial scientists for decades but never before done in the sea. It might even be said that the science of marine ecology was derived from the aqualung, now referred to by its modern name, *scuba* (self contained underwater breathing apparatus). This, however, left the vast majority of the world's oceans, that volume below about 30 to 50 meters (about 100 to 150 feet), still inaccessible to human observation and scientific exploration and experimentation.

Perhaps William Beebe made the first attempts to penetrate the deep sea with his bathysphere, a heavy metal sphere with a thick glass porthole used to observe life in the deep waters of the Atlantic Ocean in the early 1930s. Although he made some fascinating discoveries, Beebe was unable to descend beyond 600 to 700 meters (about 2000 feet) in the bathysphere, barely penetrating the deep sea.

The first photos of the deep sea were taken in the 1950s and 1960s by special cameras modified to withstand the tremendous pressures of the deep sea. These cameras were either towed by ships and synchronized with special lights or they were dropped into the deep sea with an attached bait to attract and photograph deep-sea organisms. A special link to an anchor kept the camera, lights, and bait on the bottom for a given period of time until the link was eroded by the seawater. This released the camera unit from the anchor and an attached buoy carried the entire apparatus back to the surface, where a beacon would broadcast its location for pickup. Although these cameras did emerge with some interesting photos of the sea bottom, there were still virtually no in situ photos of deep-sea animals living in the water column.

Perhaps the next technological breakthrough came with the development of deep submersibles, crewed submarines designed to penetrate well into the deep sea. In 1960, Lieutenant Don Walsh, USN, and the Frenchman Jacques Piccard (the son of Auguste Piccard) made the first successful dive with the French-designed *Trieste* into the deepest part of the ocean, to about 11,000 meters (about 36,000 feet) in the Challenger Deep in the Marianas Trench. Since that time several human-operated submersibles have been produced by the United States, Russia, and Japan that have been used to explore various deep-sea areas around the world.

RECENT TECHNOLOGICAL BREAKTHROUGHS

The most recent and most important technological advances that have enabled us to learn more about the oceans have been the development of remote-operated vehicles (ROVs), side-scan sonar, and satellite navigation. These devices have come into widespread use in the last two decades of the twentieth century. ROVs are large or small vehicles that usually carry a video camera, a photographic camera, or both; a mechanical device or devices for collecting samples; a set of lights; and motors for maneuvering in the water column. The cameras are tethered to the mother ship by a fiber-optic cable that carries the video signal back to the ship. The signal is displayed on the ship's television monitors along with any other signals from other sensors mounted on the vehicle that monitor such parameters as temperature, depth, pressure, and salinity. Such vehicles can be used to explore both the water column and the bottom. Because ROVs are steered by an operator on the mother ship, concerns about the safety of personnel that plague crewed submersibles, such as the need to provide an air supply for the crew, are not an issue.

Side-scan sonar is a high-resolution sonar that is able to map the ocean floor in fine three-dimensional detail, giving us much greater information about the objects on the bottom than was possible with ordinary depth-sounding sonar. A major advantage of side-scan sonar is that it can see long distances through murky water, thus permitting mapping of large areas in much shorter time. Satellite navigation can detect the location of any given point on the ocean's surface within a few meters, thus ensuring that we are able to locate any geographical location with an accuracy that was unheard of even a decade or two ago.

Even with all the advances in technology to help us study and understand the ocean environment, all is not well in the oceans. The original belief that the oceans are too vast for humans to damage has now been proven wrong, and we must consider our actions carefully in the future, to ensure the integrity of this last frontier and, perhaps, our own future.

The editor in chief of this encyclopedia is primarily a marine ecologist, and to the extent that there is any bias in the book, it is ecological. However, I would suggest that this bias is appropriate: Since the oceans are the largest ecosystem on the planet, any attempt to understand them must be grounded in ecological principles.

James W. Nybakken
Moss Landing Marine Institute
Moss Landing, California
October 2002

Alphabetical List of Entries

~

Interdisciplinary Encyclopedia of Marine Sciences

Abyssal Gigantism

Abyssal gigantism is a rare phenomenon occurring in deep-ocean waters in which certain species are larger than related shallow-water species. Abyssal gigantism is present in some deep-water invertebrates, animals without backbones, including amphipods, copepods, ostracods, isopods, and mysids. For example, *Gausia princeps,* a copepod, grows to a size of 10 millimeters (0.39 inch) in abyssal waters, whereas shallow-water copepods measure about 1 millimeter (0.039 inch).

Researchers suggest different explanations for gigantism. Some hypothesize that the significant pressure of abyssal waters may affect the metabolism of these invertebrates; others suggest that cold temperatures and limited food sources slow the rate of growth and delay sexual maturity. The result of these factors is a larger body size, which may provide an organism with an increased chance of survival. Larger animals typically produce larger offspring that can then feed upon a wider variety of prey, which is important in an environment where food sources are limited. Another benefit of larger body size is the ability to cover a wider area when searching for food and mates. Abyssal gigantism is uncommon; most deep-sea organisms are small, as one would expect in an environment with such limited resources.

Erin O'Donnell

FURTHER READING
Idyll, C. P. *Abyss.* New York: Crowell, 1964; rev. ed., 1976.
Menzie, Robert J., Robert Y. George, and Gilbert T. Rowe. *Abyssal Environment and Ecology of the World Oceans.* New York: Wiley, 1973.
Nybakken, James W. *Marine Biology: An Ecological Approach,* 5th ed. San Francisco: Benjamin Cummings, 2001.

RELATED ARTICLES
Copepod

Abyssal Hill

The deep ocean (abyss) lies between the continental margins and the mid-ocean ridge. The deep ocean is divided into three groups: abyssal provinces, consisting of abyssal hills and abyssal plains; oceanic rises; and seamounts and seamount groups.

Abyssal hills are volcanic features that rise from the ocean floor to a height of less than 1000 meters (3300 feet). Sometimes called *seaknolls,* abyssal hills average about 200 meters (660 feet) in height. If they exceed 1000 meters (3300 feet), they are called *seamounts.* Abyssal hills are less than 10 kilometers (33,000 feet) wide and the flanks are less than 15°. These volcanic features are often rounded, abundant, and cover a large part of the ocean floor. They are of basaltic composition, similar to other submarine volcanic features.

Extensive regions of the ocean floor are dominated by abyssal hills that occur between the mid-ocean ridge and the edge of the abyssal plains; these areas are called Abyssal Hill Provinces. Abyssal hills cover about 80 percent of the Pacific Ocean floor and about 50 percent of the Atlantic and Indian Ocean floors. Most abyssal hills originate at mid-ocean ridge spreading centers, where tectonic and volcanic processes form a very irregular seafloor that has relatively high relief. This relief is mitigated as the seafloor moves away from the spreading centers and subsides.

Abyssal hills are covered in many parts of the oceans by turbidite and abyssal brown clay deposits that may form an *abyssal plain*. Abyssal clay is a red-brown to buff-colored clay derived from the continents that is carried to the deep ocean by wind and ocean currents. Together with cosmic and volcanic dust, abyssal clay settles slowly to the ocean floor and covers the underlying volcanic features. Abyssal clay accumulates slowly at a rate of 1 millimeter (0.04 inch) per 1000 years. Many abyssal hills are buried or at least partly covered beneath a layer of sediment that is slightly thicker in the valleys than on the hills. This partial burial is more common in the Indian and Atlantic Oceans than in the Pacific Ocean. There is less sediment cover in the Pacific Ocean, due in part to the convergent plate margins. Trenches form at these margins and tend to trap sediment carried from the continent before it can reach the ocean floor.

David L. White

FURTHER READING

Gross, M. Grant. *Oceanography.* Columbus, Ohio: Charles E. Merrill, 1967; 7th ed., Upper Saddle River, N.J.: Prentice Hall, 1996.

Kennett, James. *Marine Geology.* Englewood Cliffs, N.J.: Prentice Hall, 1982.

Thurman, Harold V. *Essentials of Oceanography.* Columbus, Ohio: Charles E. Merrill, 1983; 6th ed., with Alan P. Trujillo, Upper Saddle River, N.J.: Prentice Hall, 1999.

Abyssal Plain; Deep-Sea Sediment; Mid-Ocean Ridge; Seamount; Turbidite

Abyssal Plain

The abyssal plain is a depositional surface that extends seaward from the continental rise along passive margins or from the ocean trench along active margins. Abyssal plains are flat and have less than 1° of slope; these are some of the flattest features on the planet. Abyssal plains cover a large part of the ocean floor and their surfaces range in depth from about 4500 to 6000 meters (15,000 to 20,000 feet). They are found in the Pacific, Atlantic, and Indian Oceans, and in the Mediterranean Sea, the Gulf of Mexico, and the Caribbean Sea. Abyssal plains may verge with deep-sea fans of the continental rise and may be eroded by channels that originate from submarine canyons. Light does not penetrate to the abyssal plain, and the water temperature is generally less than 3°C (37°F). The pressure ranges from 300 to 500 kilograms per square centimeter (4270 to 7110 pounds per square inch). Sediment is mudlike and there is little food for organisms, which limits the deep-sea biomass.

Abyssal plains form primarily from the deposition of turbidite deposits in the deep ocean. Other secondary sources of sediment include fine windblown particles (abyssal clay) that slowly settle to the bottom of the sea. The development of an abyssal plain is influenced by processes that occur along the continental margin. Along passive margins, the continental-derived turbidite sediment travels directly down the continental slope and is deposited on the abyssal plain.

Continental-derived sediment travels directly along the floor and adds to the total sediment load. The sediment covers, and ultimately smooths out, irregularities and uneven surfaces on the ocean floor. Abyssal plains are best

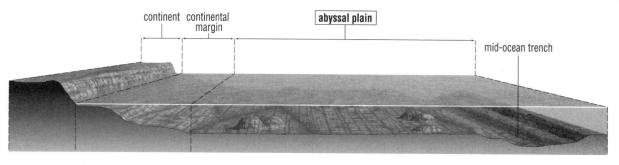

Cross section of an abyssal plain.

developed off major drainage systems of passive continental margins such as those that drain into the Atlantic and Indian Oceans. In the northwest Atlantic, the Sohm, Hatteras, and Mares abyssal plains smooth an originally irregular seafloor. Between the mid-ocean ridge and the African and European continents are the Biscay, Iberian, Tagus, Horseshoe, Madeira, and Cape Verde abyssal plains.

Along active margins, trenches are present. Sediment derived from the continent is initially deposited along the slope and is then transported and deposited in the trench. The trench is a sediment trap and prohibits the seaward movement of sediment. Therefore, abyssal plains are poorly developed in the Pacific, which has active margins. Abyssal plains of the Pacific are narrow and restricted to fringes along the North American continent. Tectonic activity may increase the rate of trench filling by uplift of coastal mountains, thus increasing erosion and trench filling by turbidites. In some places these trench sediments override the outer trench and form thick sediment covers.

The rate of abyssal plain formation increased during the late Cenozoic Era (about the last 5 million years). The widespread glacial events and the lowering of sea level caused an increase in erosion and turbidite deposition. Little new material appears to be added to abyssal plains at present, but evidence suggests that bottom currents are reworking the relict sediment in place.

David L. White

FURTHER READING

Gross, M. Grant. *Oceanography.* Columbus, Ohio: Charles E. Merrill, 1967; 7th ed., Upper Saddle River, N.J.: Prentice Hall, 1996.

Kennett, James. *Marine Geology.* Englewood Cliffs, N.J.: Prentice Hall, 1982.

Thurman, Harold V. *Essentials of Oceanography.* Columbus, Ohio: Charles E. Merrill, 1983; 6th ed., with Alan P. Trujillo, Upper Saddle River, N.J.: Prentice Hall, 1999.

RELATED ARTICLES
Abyssal Hill; Continental Margin; Deep-Sea Sediment; Turbidite

Abyssopelagic Zone

The abyssopelagic zone lies beneath the base of the bathypelagic zone at about 4000 meters (13,120 feet) and extends down to the top of the hadal zone, which is usually considered to be at a depth of 6000 meters (19,680 feet) or the seabed. Because nearly 53 percent of Earth's surface is covered by water deeper than 3000 meters (9840 feet), the abyssopelagic zone is one of the most extensive and voluminous habitats on the planet, yet it is probably among the least known. It is an environment that is totally dark except for occasional flashes of bioluminescence produced by its inhabitants. It is a cold environment in which the global range of temperature is 3 to -1.9°C (37 to 29°F), but in any one locality it is almost invariant.

The zone is very remote from the source of primary production that supplies it with organic material, which arrives as particles sinking through the water. Because the organic content of these particles is constantly being reduced by bacteria breaking it down, most of the easily digested (labile) material has been used up by the time it reaches abyssopelagic depths. Large corpses of fish and marine mammals will still contain large quantities of labile organic material, but they sink so rapidly that the inhabitants of the abyssopelagic zone have very little opportunity to feed on them. Consequently, the standing crop of animals that inhabit this zone is extremely low (about 1 percent of that found close to the surface).

Life in the abyssopelagic zone often involves waiting for something to appear because the chances of successful food foraging are exceedingly low. Animals can basically feed in only two modes; they can either consume detrital particles sinking from the upper layers or eat any other animals that they encounter by chance. The fish that live at such depths typically have mouths with enormous gaps and large curved teeth. They can swallow other fish as large as themselves. The teeth prevent prey from escaping once swallowing starts—an important attribute because if the prey does escape it may be capable of turning around and swallowing its attacker. Prey is often lured with luminous baits. Since there is little if any active chasing, the body muscles are weak and watery, so metabolic rates are low. Because of the low rates, abyssopelagic animals are incapable of sustained high-speed swimming.

In terms of diversity, abyssopelagic communities are not particularly rich in species. However, their physiological adaptations to the extreme conditions, particularly the low and unpredictable food supplies, provide us with key insight into the flexibility and adaptability of physiological systems.

Martin Angel

FURTHER READING
Childress, James J. "Are There Physiological and Biochemical Adaptations of Metabolism in Deep-Sea Animals?" *Trends in Ecology and Evolution,* Vol. 10 (1995), pp. 30–36.
Marshall, Norman B. *Developments in Deep-Sea Biology.* Poole, England: Blandford Press, 1979.
Ormond, Rupert F. G., John D. Gage, and Martin V. Angel. *Marine Biodiversity: Patterns and Processes.* Cambridge and New York: Cambridge University Press, 1997.
Randall, David J., and Anthony P. Farrell. *Deep-Sea Fishes.* San Diego: Academic Press, 1997.

RELATED ARTICLES
Bathypelagic Zone; Bioluminescence; Hadal Zone; Primary Productivity

Acanthocephala

Acanthocephalans (phylum Acanthocephala) are small parasitic worms, usually less than 20 centimeters (8 inches) in length, that live in the intestines of fish and other vertebrates. They are also known as *spiny-headed worms* because their snouts bear tiny hooks that enable the worms to fasten themselves to their hosts' intestines.

There are more than 700 known species of spiny-headed worms, all of which are parasites. Most parasitize freshwater fish, but they have also been found in amphibians, reptiles, birds, and mammals. They seldom infect humans. The worms have simple bodies, with no digestive system, no circulatory organs, and no respiratory organs. Nutrients and oxygen are absorbed through the thin skin from the fluid surroundings in the host's body. A simple nervous system allows the worms to sense touch and other stimuli, and muscles enable them to wriggle and retract the spiny snout (proboscis).

Spiny-headed worms have a complex life cycle. The sexes are separate, and males and females mate inside the intestines of the host. The female releases shelled larvae called *acanthors*, which pass out of the host with the feces. If an acanthor is swallowed by a crustacean or mollusk, it burrows into the new host's body cavity, where it grows into a second larval stage known as an *acanthella*. The acanthella is similar to an adult spiny-headed worm, but it is smaller and does not live in the host's intestine. When the acanthella has grown large enough, it develops into a resting stage called a *cystacanth*. This can infect fish or other vertebrates that eat the invertebrate, thus completing the life cycle.

The larvae of spiny-headed worms are often passed from one invertebrate to another before finding a suitable vertebrate host. When this happens, they remain as larvae but retain the ability to infect vertebrates and turn into adults. Some species are thought to influence the behavior of their invertebrate hosts so as to make them more likely to be eaten by a predator.

Ben Morgan

FURTHER READING
Brusca, Richard C., and Gary J. Brusca. *Invertebrates*. Sunderland, Mass.: Sinauer, 1990.
Margulis, Lynn. *Five Kingdoms: An Illustrated Guide to the Phyla of Life on Earth*. San Francisco: W. H. Freeman, 1982; 3rd ed., New York: W. H. Freeman, 1998.
Pechenik, Jan A. *Biology of the Invertebrates*. Boston: Prindle, Weber and Schmidt, 1985; 4th ed., Boston: McGraw-Hill, 2000.

RELATED ARTICLES
Parasitism

Acanthodii

The acanthodians are an extinct class of ancient, jawed fishes, present in the fossil record from the Lower Silurian to Lower Permian Periods, or between approximately 440 and 280 million years ago. Their Latin name refers to the stout median and paired fin spines evident in most fossils. In addition to these pronounced spines, acanthodians are characterized by cartilaginous skeletons, small nonoverlapping scales covering the body, a large head and eyes, and a tail with a longer upper than lower lobe (heterocercal). Although their maximum length is estimated at about 2.5 meters (about 8 feet), most species were less than 20 centimeters (about 8 inches) long. The earliest acanthodian remains are primarily from marine deposits, but by the start of the Devonian Period (408 million years ago), acanthodians had become common in fresh water as well. The acanthodians are considered to be the oldest jawed fishes and are often referred to as *spiny sharks*. However, this designation is misleading, since acanthodians are not closely related to sharks, although they share some similar anatomical features.

Despite their early appearance in the fossil record, most acanthodians were already somewhat specialized, and conflicting views exist regarding the taxonomic relationships of this group. Scientists have proposed that this group is (1) most closely related to the elasmobranchs (sharks, skates, and rays); (2) a sister group to the chondrichthyans (cartilaginous fishes), placoderms (an ancient, "plate-skinned" group of fishes), and osteichthyans (referring to the extant bony fishes); or, as is most widely subscribed to, (3) a sister group of the bony fishes (classes Sarcopterygii and Actinopterygii). This last grouping is due primarily to anatomical similarities, including the presence of otoliths ("ear bones"), three semicircular canals, and neural and hemal vertebral arches. There are three extinct orders of acanthodians (Climatiiformes, Acanthodiformes, and Ischnacanthiformes), consisting of nine families with about 60 total genera. The Climatiiformes were characterized by up to six rows of paired spines between the pectoral and pelvic fins in most taxa. The Acanthodiformes lacked teeth and had well-developed gill rakers, probably for filter feeding. The Ischnacanthiformes had teeth fixed to strong jaw bones, indicating that they were fierce predators.

Acanthodians were probably mid- and surface-water feeders. This has been inferred by their streamlined bodies, fin placement, and reduced bony armor as compared to the ostracoderms, a heavily armored group of jawless fishes that preceded them and may be related to the agnathans. The reduction in weight and increased mobility afforded by their physical characteristics enabled the acanthodians to occupy the water column, a habitat previously unexploited by fishes, and limited competition with bottom-dwelling ostracoderms. Within the group, acanthodians are believed to have displayed diverse diets and feeding habits. Some fed on small, planktonic organisms, whereas others were probably highly predaceous. This group of fishes was very successful, outlasting the major ostracoderm groups by 100 million years.

Joseph J. Bizzarro

FURTHER READING

Bond, Carl E. *Biology of Fishes.* Philadelphia: W. B. Saunders, 1979; 2nd ed., Fort Worth, Texas: Saunders College Publishing, 1996.

Carroll, R. L. *Vertebrate Paleontology and Evolution.* New York: W. H. Freeman, 1988.

Helfman, Gene S., Bruce B. Collette, and Douglas E. Facey. *The Diversity of Fishes.* Malden, Mass.: Blackwell Science, 1997.

Long, John A. *The Rise of Fishes: 500 Million Years of Evolution.* Baltimore: Johns Hopkins University Press, 1995.

Moyle, Peter B., and Joseph J. Cech. *Fishes: An Introduction to Ichthyology.* Englewood Cliffs, N.J.: Prentice Hall, 1982; 4th ed., Upper Saddle River, N.J.: Prentice Hall, 2000.

Nelson, Joseph S. *Fishes of the World,* 3rd ed. New York: Wiley, 1994.

RELATED ARTICLES

Actinopterygii; Chondrichthyes; Elasmobranchii; Fins; Gnathostomata; Osteichthyes; Otolith; Placodermi; Ray; Sarcopterygii; Shark; Skate

Accretionary Prism

Accretionary prisms form along convergent plate boundaries. Rocks of the igneous crust plunge down into the mantle as oceanic plates are subducted. Overlying layers of sedimentary strata, because of their relatively low strength and density, get scraped off the subducting plate and transferred to the toe of the overriding plate. This process of frontal offscraping is analogous to buildup of snow in front of a plow. Sediments also accumulate slowly above the accretionary prism, largely as aprons of fine-grained mud. In addition, at greater depths, rocks from the descending plate can accrete to the bottom of the upper plate, through a process known as *underplating.* Our knowledge of these complicated geologic systems is based largely on interpretations of seismic-reflection profiles, together with direct sampling by deep-ocean drilling.

Accretionary prisms exist where rates of terrigenous sedimentation are high and sediments entering the subduction zone are thicker than several 100 meters (more than 1000 feet). Notable examples include Cascadia (offshore Washington and Oregon), the Aleutian Trench (North Pacific), Nankai Trough (Philippine Sea), Middle America Trench (offshore Mexico), Chile Trench (southeast Pacific), Sunda Trench (Indian Ocean), and Barbados Ridge (west-central Atlantic). However, some subduction margins grow very little through time, and still others appear to be erosional. Changes in convergence rate, convergence direction, and/or sediment supply will force adjustments in rates of accretion.

A simple view of structural architecture begins with the plate-boundary fault at the accretionary prism's base. This master fault is referred to as the *décollement* (detachment structure). Rocks above and below the detachment experience independent styles of deformation. Understanding how material properties, fluids, and mechanical behavior change along the entire three-dimensional extent of a décollement is vital because they are sites of the world's most violent earthquakes.

Geologic materials above a décollement become highly deformed as two converging plates squeeze past one another. Smaller faults splay off the décollement and govern the prism's internal structure by folding, tilting, and shearing nearby strata. Disruption also can occur in the form of mud volcanoes. Long histories of deformation result in very complicated seafloor morphology, with numerous ridges, mounds, scarps, benches, and troughs. Rugged physiography is complicated further by deep incision of submarine canyons and large-scale mass wasting events.

Faults within accretionary prisms usually display a reverse sense of slip, which means that rocks above a given fault surface move up during displacement. This sense of motion is characteristic of systems under horizontal compression. Most reverse faults dip toward land at angles of 30° or less (i.e., in the same direction as the plate boundary). Networks of reverse faults form imbricate (shingled) patterns, similar to what a person might observe along the side of a tilted stack of books. Although large earthquakes are unlikely along such faults, offsets of the seafloor can create destructive tsunamis (seismic sea waves).

In a static snapshot of subduction, the seaward edge of an accretionary prism coincides with the landward edge of the flat trench floor, but this line of intersection migrates seaward with time. Sediment is constantly being added to the trench, largely through the action of turbidity currents. At the same time, motion of the two converging plates is continuous, typically at rates of 5 to 10 centimeters (2 to 4 inches) per year. The décollement propagates into, or beneath, the trench sediment to keep pace with plate motion. As each new reverse fault splays off the décollement, it slices upward through the trench sediment. With each added slice of trench sediment, the accretionary prism grows. Thus, over millions of years of time, this orogenic (mountain building) process provides one of the principal mechanisms of continental growth.

Michael B. Underwood

FURTHER READING

Karig, Daniel E., and George F. Sharmann III. "Subduction and Accretion in Trenches." *Geological Society of America Bulletin*, Vol. 86 (1975), pp. 377–389.
Moore, J. Casey, and Neil Lundberg. "Tectonic Overview of Deep Sea Drilling Project Transects of Forearcs." *Geological Society of America Memoir*, Vol. 166 (1986), pp. 1–12.
Moore, J. Casey, Asahiko Taira, and Greg Moore. "Ocean Drilling and Accretionary Processes." *GSA Today*, Vol. 1 (1991), pp. 265–270.
Scholl, David W., Roland von Huene, Tracy L. Vallier, and David G. Howell. "Sedimentary Masses and Concepts About Tectonic Processes at Underthrust Ocean Margins." *Geology*, Vol. 8 (1980), pp. 564–568.
Underwood, Michael B., and Gregory F. Moore. "Trenches and Trench-Slope Basins." In Cathy J. Busby and Raymond V. Ingersoll, eds., *Tectonics of Sedimentary Basins*. Cambridge, Mass.: Blackwell Science, 1995; pp. 179–219.

RELATED ARTICLES
Aleutian Arc; Cascadia; Convergence; Convergent Plate Boundary; Mud Volcano; Seismic Sea Wave (Tsunami); Subduction Zone; Submarine Earthquake; Trench

Acidity and Alkalinity

An *acid* is a hydrogen-containing compound that sets hydrogen ion(s) (H^+) free when dissolved in water, thus increasing the total concentration of free hydrogen ions per unit of water mass. A *base* is a hydroxide-containing compound that sets hydroxide ion(s) (OH^-) free when dissolved in water. A strong acid releases its hydrogen ions readily in a dilute solution. Similarly, a strong base readily releases its hydroxide ions in a dilute solution. Basic solutions can also be referred to as *alkaline*.

Water is made up of hydrogen and hydroxide ions that are constantly dissociating and re-forming via the reaction: $H_2O \leftrightarrow H^+ + OH^-$. Although pure water contains both hydrogen and hydroxide ions, it is a *neutral* species (neither acidic nor alkaline) because there is no excess of either ion—they are always found in equal concentrations. The pH of a substance is an indication of its acidity or alkalinity. The pH scale runs from 0 to 14 (no units) and is inversely proportional to the concentration of free hydrogen ions. The pH equals the negative log of the concentration of free hydrogen ions, or

$$pH = -\log [H^+]$$

where the bracket notation indicates concentration. Neutral species such as water have a pH of 7. Acidic solutions contain more free hydrogen ions and therefore have a pH value below 7 (pH is *inversely* proportional to hydrogen ion concentration), whereas alkaline solutions contain more free hydroxide ions than free hydrogen ions and have a pH value greater than 7. For example, if one added hydrochloric acid (HCl) to a beaker of pure water, the amount of free hydrogen ions would increase (due to the breakup of HCl into H^+ and Cl^- ions), thus lowering the pH of the solution. On the other hand, addition of sodium hydroxide (NaOH) to a beaker of pure water would increase the amount of hydroxide ion (due to the breakup of NaOH into Na^+ and OH^- ions), thus raising the pH of the solution (i.e., more free hydroxide ions than free hydrogen ions).

An ocean "controls" its pH through reactions with carbon dioxide (CO_2) from the atmosphere and carbonate ion (CO_3^{2-}) from the dissolution of solid calcium carbonate ($CaCO_3$). Atmospheric carbon dioxide enters the ocean and forms carbonic acid:

$$H_2O_{(liquid)} + CO_{2(aqueous)} \leftrightarrow H_2CO_{3(aqueous)}$$

Carbonic acid has two hydrogen ions that it can lose, and therefore it has a lower seawater pH value. The loss of one hydrogen ion results in bicarbonate ion (HCO_3^-) plus a free hydrogen ion. Bicarbonate can lose an additional hydrogen ion, resulting in carbonate ion (CO_3^{2-}) plus one free hydrogen ion:

$$H_2CO_{3(aqueous)} \leftrightarrow HCO_{3(aqueous)}^- + H_{(aqueous)}^+$$

$$HCO_{3(aqueous)}^- \leftrightarrow CO_{3(aqueous)}^{2-} + H_{(aqueous)}^+$$

A solution of pure water and carbon dioxide is acidic; it has a pH of about 5. However, the ocean is slightly alkaline; on average it has a pH of approximately 8. The dissolution of solid calcareous ($CaCO_3$) tests or shells serves to keep the ocean slightly alkaline. Once an organism that creates a calcareous shell (e.g., foraminifera) has died, the shell sinks through the water column and is deposited on the seafloor. When enough acid (in the form of carbon dioxide or otherwise) is added to the ocean, carbonate ions fall below saturation levels and solid calcium carbonate dissolves spontaneously:

$$CaCO_{3(solid)} \rightarrow Ca^{2+}_{(aqueous)} + CO_3^{2-}_{(aqueous)}$$

This introduces an excess of basic carbonate ions, which raises both the alkalinity and pH (decreases the acidity) of the ocean. The ocean can thus "regulate" its pH and alkalinity through formation and dissolution of calcium carbonate. This regulatory process is known as *buffering*. The enormous amount of solid calcium carbonate in sediments and sinking shells provides the ocean with a basically unlimited buffering capability. The calcium carbonate buffer system is crucial for keeping seawater slightly alkaline and at steady state for millions of years. The slight alkaline nature of the ocean is favorable for complex organic reactions to take place and is thought to have enabled life to form in the ocean over 3 billion years ago. The pH value of seawater varies from 8.1 to 8.3 in ocean surface waters and decreases to values around 7.8 in the oxygen minimum zone in the open ocean. In tide pools during periods of high photosynthesis, the pH can rise to 8.4 or even greater. In anoxic waters such as in the Black Sea and some fjords high in CO_2, concentrations allow the pH to fall to 7.5 or less.

Daniel Schuller

FURTHER READING

Millero, Frank J. *Chemical Oceanography.* Boca Raton, Fla.: CRC Press, 1992; 2nd ed., 1996.

Open University Course Team. *Seawater: Its Composition, Properties, and Behavior.* Oxford: Pergamon Press/Milton Keynes, England: Open University, 1989; 2nd ed., rev. by John Wright and Angela Colling, Oxford and New York: Pergamon Press, 1995.

Pinet, Paul R. *Invitation to Oceanography.* Minneapolis/St. Paul, Minn.: West Publishing, 1996; 2nd ed., Sudbury, Mass.: Jones & Bartlett, 1998.

Thurman, Harold V. *Introductory Oceanography.* Columbus, Ohio: Charles E. Merrill, 1975; 9th ed., with Elizabeth A. Burton, Upper Saddle River, N.J.: Prentice Hall, 2001.

RELATED ARTICLES

Calcium Carbonate Compensation Depth; Carbon Dioxide; Foraminifera; Seawater, pH of

Acoustic Doppler Current Profiler

The acoustic Doppler current profiler (ADCP) is an instrument that measures the speed and direction of ocean currents at a series of depths. This instrument transmits short pulses of sound at a single frequency and then listens for echoes from small particles and plankton that reflect the transmitted sound back to the source. Because small particles and plankton float freely in the ocean, they tend to move along with the same speed and direction as the prevailing flow. The apparent frequency of the sound waves transmitted by the ADCP is altered slightly when the pulses are reflected from moving objects. The frequency of the sound waves approaching a reflecting object that is moving toward the ADCP appears to be higher by an amount that is related directly to the speed of the current. Conversely, the frequency of the sound waves reflected from an object that is moving away from the source appears to be lower by an amount that is again directly related to the current speed. This

apparent change in frequency, referred to as the *Doppler shift,* is similar to the sound of a whistle on a moving train that first approaches the listener and then fades away as the train passes by. It is thus possible to measure the speed of the current at a given depth by measuring the Doppler shift of the reflected sound waves.

To determine the flow direction, the sound is pointed in specific directions, producing directional sound beams. After these directed sound pulses are reflected by various scatterers, they are processed by the ADCP to extract the easterly (x) and northerly (y) components of the flow. To obtain both components of the flow in the horizontal plane, two sound beams are required. To obtain all three components of the flow field (two horizontal components and one vertical component), the ADCP actually uses four acoustic beams. The fourth beam provides an estimate of the uncertainty or error in the measurement.

To measure the flow at different depths, the reflected sound beams are grouped according to the time it takes for the sound to go out and be reflected back to the source. Echoes from greater distances from the source correspond to deeper levels in the water column. By selecting specific time intervals for the reflected signals to arrive, specific depth ranges can be assigned to each time interval. As distance from the source increases (i.e., as depth increases), the reflected signals get weaker and a limiting depth is reached beyond which the signals are too weak to process. Finally, by averaging the data from the ADCP over many pulses at a given depth, it is possible to reduce the uncertainty that naturally arises in measuring currents using this approach.

Ocean currents are important for many applications, including search and rescue missions conducted by the U.S. Coast Guard and Navy for which information on the expected drift of downed planes or disabled vessels is required. An understanding of ocean currents is needed to track the movement of oil and toxic chemical spills and to predict the fate of harmful algal blooms such as the red tide. Ocean currents are important in determining optimum ship routes for vessels crossing the ocean and are needed to better understand the migration patterns of living marine resources. Ocean currents also exert forces on offshore structures such as oil rigs and other fixed platforms; therefore, a knowledge of the maximum expected currents is required to design these structures properly.

Laurence C. Breaker

FURTHER READING

Pinkel, R. "Acoustic Doppler Techniques." In F. Dobson, L. Hasse, and R. Davis, eds., *Air–Sea Interaction Instruments and Methods.* New York and London: Plenum Press, 1980; pp. 171–199.

RD Instruments. *Acoustic Doppler Current Profilers, Principles of Operation: A Practical Primer.* San Diego: RD Instruments, 1989.

RELATED ARTICLES

Acoustic Oceanography; Ocean Current

Acoustic Oceanography

Acoustic oceanography involves using sound to study the ocean. Just as bats use sound to "see" on land and doctors use ultrasound to image the inside of the human body, oceanographers can use sound to explore parts of the oceans they cannot readily see. Acoustic techniques have proven invaluable for understanding ocean processes, from the way currents circulate to the way temperatures are affected by global warming. Acoustics also offers a convenient method of studying marine creatures remotely, for example, as a means of counting fish stocks or monitoring whale populations. The many practical applications of acoustic oceanography range from submarine navigation to oil exploration.

Sound Propagation in the Sea

Due to strong absorption of visible light by water and phytoplankton, sunlight is *attenuated* (reduced in intensity) quickly in the sea. Virtually no sunlight penetrates beyond a depth of about 1000 meters (3300 feet). By contrast, sound is transmitted much more efficiently in the oceans than on land, and it is this property that makes it so useful to oceanographers.

Sound travels through seawater at a speed of about 5400 kilometers (3360 miles) per hour, or roughly four times faster than in air. The speed of sound increases as temperature and pressure increase. In the ocean, temperature decreases and pressure increases with depth. As a result, sound waves travel fastest near the ocean surface (where the temperature is greatest) and at the ocean bottom (where the pressure is greatest). Sound travels slowest at middepths [around 1000 meters (3300 feet)]. Both sound and light waves bend toward regions of minimum velocity. The region of minimum sound speed is known as the *sofar* (sound fixing and ranging) *channel*. Sound waves bend (refract) toward the middle of the sofar channel and travel along it for hundreds of miles, similar to the way that light travels along a fiber-optic cable. First recognized and used for military purposes during World War II by U.S. geophysicist Maurice Ewing (1906–74), the sofar channel has since become one of the most important features of sound propagation in the ocean.

Major Applications of Acoustic Oceanography

Acoustic oceanography has many practical applications. Among the most familiar are echo sounding (measuring the depth of the ocean by timing the reflection of a sound wave from the seabed) and sonar (sound navigation end ranging), the method by which submarines navigate underwater. The sofar channel was invented in 1943 as a means of locating ships and aircraft in wartime distress. If a craft sent out emergency signals through the sofar channel using explosive charges, it could be located by measuring the time it took for the signals to reach two or more receivers a known distance away, a navigation process known as *triangulation*. After World War II ended, the U.S. Navy established its Sound Surveillance System (SOSUS) antisubmarine warfare system, a comprehensive network of carefully positioned hydrophones on the seafloor connected to onshore receiving stations. The system is so sophisticated that it can detect the submarine type, the number of propellers on the submarine, and whether it is conventionally or nuclear powered—and it works across much of the northern hemisphere. Since October 1990, this highly sensitive apparatus has been used for a variety of oceanographic research.

Some of acoustic oceanography's most important applications are in geophysics (the use of physics to probe Earth's geology). Techniques such as seismic reflection (profiling) and seismic refraction enable geologists to study the structure of Earth beneath the seabed by transmitting and

receiving sound waves from ships; they are among the most important methods of offshore oil exploration. Acoustic techniques such as side-scan sonar enable geologists to study the nature of sediments and how they are transported on continental shelves and slopes. Since 1991 geologists and oceanographers have used the SOSUS antisubmarine array (and an independent array of hydrophones fitted in 1996) to monitor underwater seismic processes, such as the geological activity of ridge systems in the eastern Pacific; the system detected its first underwater volcanic eruption in 1993.

Studying Ocean Circulation with Sound

Many ingenious acoustic techniques have been used to study the properties of the ocean and the way it flows. *Swallow floats,* named for their British inventor J. C. Swallow, are scientific instruments that sink to a predefined depth and

An aviation machinist monitors the towing of a Q-14 side-scanning sonar device used to detect mines by a MH-53 helicopter aboard USS Tarawa. *(U.S. Navy photo)*

then follow the current flow. Using an onboard sound transmitter (pinger), they regularly signal their progress to a ship that trails hydrophones (sensitive underwater microphones) in the water. Sofar floats are more highly engineered versions of Swallow floats. Using the sound-carrying property of the sofar channel to transmit over both longer distances and greater timescales, their main purpose is to allow the study of deepwater circulation. Another important technique, the *acoustic Doppler current profiler,* measures properties of currents using a combination of the Doppler effect and sonar, much like a police radar speed gun.

Sound has proven equally useful for studying surface-water processes. Acoustic instruments have been used to study how the atmosphere and oceans interact, for example, how winds drive the surface circulation and make ocean waves break and how the atmosphere–ocean interaction works more precisely through the formation of bubbles and the exchange of gases. All of these processes can be studied through the sounds they generate. Other surface processes that generate noise, such as the breakup of sea ice, can also be studied with acoustic techniques.

Acoustics is not useful just for studying the long timescale processes of deep-ocean circulation and the short-timescale processes of surface currents. A technique called *ocean acoustic tomography* (OAT) has proved particularly valuable for understanding intermediate, *mesoscale* phenomena, such as ocean mixing and climatic events. *Acoustic tomography* is the ocean equivalent of a medical ultrasound scan. It involves using a set of combined transmitters and receivers, each of which sends coded signals to all others over distances of hundreds or thousands of miles through the sofar channel. Because these sounds are speeded up or slowed down by changes in temperature, density, salinity, or currents, measurements of the sounds' rate of travel between different transmitters and receivers can be processed to produce three-dimensional images of the ocean's interior. One of the most important current applications of this technique is a project called *Acoustic Thermometry of Ocean Climate* (ATOC), which studies how global warming is affecting ocean temperatures.

Acoustic Studies of Marine Creatures

Cetaceans use sound for a variety of purposes. Both whales and dolphins navigate using echolocation, and whales are believed to communicate over entire ocean basins by making their haunting moans in or near the sofar channel. One early concern about the ATOC project was that transmitting long-range acoustic thermometry signals through the same channel might disrupt long-range whale communications and even kill cetaceans. The techniques of acoustic oceanography have been used to probe this and other potential threats to marine mammals from noise pollution, such as seismic oil exploration and military activities. But some human activities, at least, are now proving beneficial to marine mammals. The U.S. Navy's antisubmarine SOSUS, originally constructed to listen for enemy submarines, has been used since 1992 to count and monitor whale populations.

Increasing concern about declining global fish stocks has prompted the development of new acoustic methods for monitoring fish. High-frequency side-scanning sonar (in which two sound beams are emitted at an angle rather than a single beam) have been used, for example, to estimate stocks of herring and track migrating salmon. The basic technique involves measuring how much an individual fish of a certain species scatters a sound beam. If scientists know what type of fish is likely to be present in a particular area, they can then estimate the population of fish present by measuring how much the sound beam is changed by the entire school of fish and dividing by the known effect of a single fish.

Chris Woodford

FURTHER READING

Antony, Joseph, and Ehrlich Desa. "Acoustic Remote Sensing of Ocean Flows." In S. P. Singal, ed., *Acoustic Remote Sensing Applications.* Berlin and New York: Springer-Verlag, 1997.

Blondel, Philippe, and Bramley Murton. *Handbook of Seafloor Sonar Imagery.* Chichester, England, and New York: Wiley, 1997.

Brekhovskikh, L. M., and Y. P. Lysanov. *Fundamentals of Ocean Acoustics.* Berlin and New York: Springer-Verlag, 1982; 2nd ed., 1991.

Buckingham, Michael J., John R. Potter, and Chad L. Epifanio. "Seeing Underwater with Background Noise." *Scientific American,* February 1996, p. 40.

Spindel, Robert, and Peter Worcester. "Ocean Acoustic Tomography." *Scientific American,* October 1990, p. 62.

RELATED ARTICLES

Acoustic Doppler Current Profiler; Acoustic Tomography; Navigation; Seismic Profiling; Seismic Refraction; Sofar; Sonar

Acoustic Tomography

Ocean acoustic tomography uses precise measurements of acoustic travel time to determine the physical character of the ocean through which the sound field has propagated. Although similar to medical computerized axial tomography (CAT) and the seismic use of earthquake-generated waves to study the interior of Earth, ocean acoustic tomography focuses on resolving the temporal changes in the distribution of water temperature, which control the speed of sound and the path of sound rays in the ocean. In turn, the distribution of temperature tells oceanographers much about ocean currents and storage of heat, thus helping to resolve global temperature change.

Since the speed of sound [1500 meters per second (3000 knots)] vastly exceeds that of a research vessel [10 meters per second (20 knots)], synoptic surveys of 1000-kilometer (about 620-mile) regions are possible using tomographic techniques. Measurements are made between each source (S) and receiver (R) in an array, so data return is increased (S × R) over traditional moored point measurements (S + R). Tomography complements satellite techniques by providing depth and time resolution for ocean measurements.

Ocean acoustic tomography exploits the physical character of the propagation of sound in the ocean. Consider the propagation of sound between a source and a receiver. The travel time of the acoustic pulse is a function of the temperature and the water velocity between the source and the receiver. When temperature and pressure increase, so does sound speed, and the result is a shorter travel time. Because the ocean is nearly transparent to low-frequency (10 to 300 hertz) sound, it does not take much energy (about 15 watts) to ensonify 1000-kilometer (about 620-mile) acoustic paths. This is in part due to the existence of a naturally occurring sound channel at about 1 kilometer (about 0.62 mile) depth over the world's tropical and subtropical oceans. Finally, as the sound propagates through the ocean, it is refracted by the sound speed gradient to turn toward lower sound speed.

As the receiver listens to the arrival of the sound pulse, a number of distinct arrivals are heard, which crescendo to a final cutoff. These correspond to the arrival of sound along individual rays. Even though they travel slightly farther, the rays with the steepest initial propagation path arrive first because they spend more time in a region of the water column where the sound speed is higher. The last sound pulse that arrives is that which travels along the direct line between the source and the receiver. The sound speed variations along each ray path are integrated by the travel-time measurement. This suppresses spot measurements of phenomena such as mesoscale eddies or internal waves that contaminate traditional shipboard measurements.

Forward Problem

The first step in tomography is to construct a pattern of the time of arrival for the sound traveling from the source to the receiver along individual rays for given ocean conditions. This is called the *forward problem*. It allows a given arrival to be *identifiable*, meaning that the arrival is associated with a specific ray path. Tomography also requires that received signals be stable and resolvable. *Stable* means that the arrivals show up consistently in repeated transmissions over an extended period. *Resolvable* means that rays that arrive at about the same time do not overlap one another, so that each can be clearly resolved. The magnitude of the travel time variations is about 100 milliseconds, so a timekeeping precision of about 1 millisecond is required. When arrivals are identifiable, stable, and resolvable, accurate path integral relationships can be established between the travel time data, unknown sound speed, and temperature variations.

Inverse Problem

The final step in tomography, known as the *inverse problem*, involves using the temporal variations in the times of arrival of individual rays to deduce the variation in the temperature of the ocean. The inverse solution is constructed as a minimum mean-square-error estimate with a specified (a priori) solution and noise variances. This step is mathematical and often not straightforward, but oceanographers can use additional information to help find the correct solution. For example, if shipboard or satellite observations are available for the ensonified region, they can be used to help solve the problem. The physics of many ocean processes is understood well enough that numerical ocean models can also be used.

Current Measurement

In many applications of ocean acoustic tomography, reciprocal transmissions are made between sources. The difference in travel time between the reciprocal transmissions is due to the flow of water along the acoustic path between the sources. This allows direct measurement of water velocities and is sometimes referred to as *velocity tomography*. A triangular or circular array of transponders can provide direct measurements of vorticity, which is a measure of the rate of rotation of a column of water. This is key to understanding many dynamic processes.

Application

Tomography, first introduced in 1979, has been used since to study a number of important ocean problems. These include mapping of mesoscale eddies, convection in the Greenland Sea and the Gulf of Lion, vorticity, and tides and internal tides. In situ measurements of sound speed have helped to improve the *equation of state for seawater* (the relationship between density, temperature, salinity, and pressure). Despite this progress, tomography has not become the universal tool that was envisioned when originally proposed. Part of the problem is that the instruments are complex and not easy to use. Additionally, when researchers proposed using acoustic measurements to measure ocean warming [the Acoustic Thermometry for Ocean Climate or (ATOC) project], concerns arose about the effect of the acoustic signals on marine mammals. Although subsequent studies have not shown any effect of tomography transmissions on marine mammals, public concern remains.

Curtis A. Collins

FURTHER READING

Munk, W. "The Heard Island Experiment." *Naval Research Reviews*, Vol. 42 (1990), pp. 2–22.

Munk, W., and C. Wunsch. "Ocean Acoustic Tomography: A Scheme for Large Scale Monitoring." *Deep-Sea Research*, Vol. 26 (1979), pp. 123–161.

Munk, W., P. Worcester, and C. Wunsch. *Ocean Acoustic Tomography.* New York: Cambridge University Press, 1995.

Ocean Tomography Group. "A Demonstration of Ocean Acoustic Tomography." *Nature*, Vol. 299 (1982), pp. 121–125.

RELATED ARTICLES

Acoustic Oceanography; Sound, Propagation and Speed of

Actinopterygii

The Actinopterygii (the ray-finned fishes, from the Greek *actino*, ray, and *pteryx*, fin) is one of two extant classes of bony fishes, the other being the Sarcopterygii (lobe-finned fishes). The Actinopterygii is an astonishingly successful vertebrate group, with almost 24,000 described species, about 50 percent of all living vertebrates. The range of body forms among living actinopterygians is highly diverse, ranging from seahorses to flatfishes, with most forms being a variation on the finned, torpedo-like shape (known as *fusiform*) that is the popular notion of a fish.

The earliest actinopterygians are known from freshwater deposits dating from the late Silurian and early Devonian Periods (about 410 million to 400 million years ago). Most were small, less than 25 centimeters (about 10 inches) long. These early ray-finned fishes (subclass Chondrostei, from the Greek *chondros*, cartilage, and *osteon*, bone) were heavily armored with ganoid scales (thick scales composed of ganoin, a silvery enamel, overlying bone) and had functional gills as well as lungs. The tail was heterocercal (the vertebral column upturned at the tail and the upper lobe of the caudal fin larger than the lower). By the beginning of the Carboniferous Period (some 345 million years ago) chondrosteans had become the dominant fresh water fishes and had begun their invasion of the seas. Today, only about 36 chondrostean species remain: the order Acipenseriformes, containing the sturgeons (24 species) and paddlefishes (two species), and the order Polypteriformes, containing the reedfish (one species) and the African bichirs of Africa (at least nine species). All live in fresh water or brackish water.

By the Permian Period (290 million to 248.2 million years ago), forms were emerging that had nearly homocercal caudal fins (upper and lower lobes of similar size) and a reduced number of bony rays supporting the fins. Along with these changes went a reduction in body armor, suggestive that fishes were now faster moving and were able to evade predators rather than relying on body armor for protection. These neopterygians (from the Greek *neos*, new, and *pteryx*, fin) are today represented by two lineages: the nonteleosts and the teleosts.

Nonteleost neopterygians (formerly known as holosteans, the Holostei) are today represented by the seven species of gar, genera *Lepisosteus* and *Atractosteus* (order Semionotiformes), and the North American bowfin *Amia calva* (order Amiiformes)—all live entirely or predominantly in fresh water. The teleosts (Teleostei, from the Greek *teleos*, perfect, and *osteon*, bone) are the major neopterygian lineage. The status of the Teleostei and its subdivisions varies according to the authority reporting. In *Fishes of the World* (1994), Joseph S. Nelson has the group containing 38 living orders, 426 families, and nearly 24,000 species. Most of the food fish with which we are familiar—anchovies, bass, cod, salmon, sardines, trout, and flatfishes, for example—are teleosts.

Several evolutionary developments have laid the foundation for the phenomenal success of teleosts. Fishes have progressively lost their heavy armor and increased internal ossification. Teleosts have thin, flexible scales offering weight reduction and hydrodynamic efficiency, enabling faster speeds and greater maneuverability. In some forms, such as catfishes and sculpins, scales have been secondarily lost. The jaw and its suspension have become more flexible and complex, enabling sucking as well as biting movements in many species. This opens up the possibility for a wider range of feeding strategies and dietary choices. The modification of the primitive fish lung into a hydrostatic swim bladder enables teleosts to maintain neutral buoyancy at different depths. This economizes on energy expenditure, since the fish does not need to swim to maintain its vertical station in the water. Coupled with highly flexible fins, it also enables delicate movements. Such developments, along with physiological advances, have helped facilitate the teleost invasion of a multiplicity of aquatic habitats and all zones of the marine water column to a recorded depth in excess of 7 kilometers (about 4 miles).

Trevor Day

FURTHER READING
Long, J. A. *The Rise of Fishes.* Baltimore: Johns Hopkins University Press, 1995.
Moyle, Peter B., and Joseph J. Cech. *Fishes: An Introduction to Ichthyology.* Englewood Cliffs, N.J.: Prentice Hall, 1982; 4th ed., Upper Saddle River, N.J.: Prentice Hall, 2000.
Nelson, Joseph S. *Fishes of the World.* New York: Wiley, 1976; 3rd ed., 1994
Paxton, John R., and William N. Eschmeyer, eds. *Encyclopedia of Fishes.* San Diego: Academic Press, 1994; 2nd ed., 1998.
Pough, F. Harvey, Christine M. Janis, and John B. Heiser. *Vertebrate Life,* 3rd ed. New York: Macmillan/ London: Collier Macmillan, 1989; 5th ed., Upper Saddle River, N.J.: Prentice Hall, 1999.

RELATED ARTICLES
Acanthodii; Buoyancy; Chondrostei; Fins; Fish Propulsion; Ichthyology; Neopterygii; Osteichthyes; Sarcopterygii; Sea Horse; Swim Bladder; Teleostei

Advection

The term *advection,* which refers to the transport or transfer of properties through sustained motions that occur in the ocean or the atmosphere, is used in both oceanography and meteorology. By way of contrast, the transfer of properties within a liquid or gas can be accomplished through the process of diffusion where the molecules themselves are in continuous motion and interact with one another. Any property that is carried bodily by the movement of waters in the ocean or by the air above is said to be advected. Advection can take place horizontally or vertically. Sustained motions associated with oceanic waters are usually referred to as *currents.* Because the density of ocean waters increases rapidly with depth, water motions or currents are largely confined to the horizontal plane. In the equations that govern the motion of liquids and gases (i.e., fluids), any of the terms that are multiplied by the velocity of the fluid are called *advective terms* because the net effect is to transport whatever quantity is involved in the direction of the flow. Through advection, ocean currents provide an important mechanism for transporting heat from lower latitudes in the tropics or subtropics to higher latitudes. The Gulf Stream off the U.S. east coast and the Kuroshio off Japan are examples of major ocean currents that transport warm water from lower latitudes to higher latitudes through the process of advection.

Laurence C. Breaker

FURTHER READING
Neumann, Gerhard. *Ocean Currents.* Amsterdam and New York: Elsevier, 1968.
Von Arx, William S. *Introduction to Physical Oceanography.* Reading, Mass.: Addison-Wesley, 1962.

RELATED ARTICLES
Gulf Stream; Kuroshio; Ocean Current

Aegean Sea

The Aegean Sea, named for Aegeus, a legendary Athenian king, is a gulf of the Mediterranean Sea bordered by the islands of Crete and Rhodes to the south, Greece to the west, and Turkey to the east. With southern access to the Mediterranean and northern access to the Sea of Marmara through the Straits of the Dardanelles, the Aegean enabled early mariners to navigate the waters and establish important trade routes. These routes, together with a favorable climate for agriculture and the discovery of bronze, gave rise to the Cretan civilization, the first of many European civilizations that flourished in this area.

Well known for its sparkling blue color, numerous bays, and irregular coastlines, the Aegean Sea is dotted with the islands of the Grecian Archipelago, which include the Cyclades, Delos, the Dodecanese, Euboea, Evvoia, Khios, Lesbos, Samos, the Sporades, and Thasos. Most of these islands belong to Greece, along with the leading mainland ports of Piraeus and Thessaloniki. Another major port city, Izmir, is located in Turkey.

The Aegean is approximately 610 kilometers (380 miles) long and 300 kilometers (186 miles) wide. Its total area is close to 214,000 square kilometers (83,000 square miles). The Aegean has an average depth of 362 meters (1188 feet) but plunges to 3544 meters (11,627 feet) off northern Crete.

Although low nutrient content limits marine life in the Aegean, many species of fish from the Black Sea use warmer Aegean waters as a breeding ground. Of these fish, sardines are the most important commercial catch. Sponges are also harvested. In addition, the Aegean is believed to hold oil, natural gas, mineral, and chemical deposits in its limestone seabed. Commercial development in these areas has been hampered by considerable political tension between Greece and Turkey since the 1970s.

Roger McHaney

FURTHER READING
Bahcheli, Tozum, T. A. Couloumbis, and P. Carley. *Greek–Turkish Relations and U.S. Foreign Policy: Cyprus, the Aegean, and Regional Stability.* Washington, D.C.: U.S. Institute of Peace, 1997.
Denham, H. M. *The Aegean: A Sea-Guide to Its Coasts and Islands.* New York: W. W. Norton, 1976.

RELATED ARTICLES
Black Sea; Mediterranean Sea

Agassiz, Alexander Emmanuel Rodolphe
1835–1910
Engineer, Coral Reef Researcher, and Director of the Museum of Comparative Zoology at Harvard College

Alexander Agassiz became director of the Museum of Comparative Zoology at Harvard College after the death of its founder, his father Louis, in 1873. Alexander Agassiz used his personal fortune to finance basic research in marine biology. He applied his engineering skills to improve equipment for collecting specimens from the deep sea and conducted extensive research into the nature of coral reefs and atolls.

Alexander Emmanuel Rodolphe Agassiz was born on 17 December 1835 in Neuchâtel, Switzerland, to Louis and Cécile Braun Agassiz. Louis Agassiz (1807–73) had become a well-known naturalist (specializing in geology and paleoichthyology) and professor at the College of Neuchâtel. In 1847, after the death of Cécile, Agassiz's father moved to Cambridge, Massachussetts, to assume a professorship at the new Lawrence Scientific School at Harvard. Agassiz followed shortly thereafter, in 1849. He became close to his new stepmother, Elizabeth Cary, who encouraged him to pursue a scientific career. Agassiz earned several degrees, including one in engineering (1857) and in zoology (1862), both from the Lawrence Scientific School.

Agassiz's father had become a famous zoologist as well as a well-connected and influential member of the American scientific community. In 1859, Louis Agassiz founded the Museum of Comparative Zoology (MCZ) at Harvard, which became the leading center for zoological training in the United States for two generations of scientists. Alexander Agassiz worked for the MCZ for the rest of his life, especially after his father's death in 1873, serving chiefly as director. Like his father,

Agassiz struggled to balance his own research interests with the time-consuming minutiae of museum administration.

In 1860, Agassiz married Anna Russell, who belonged to a wealthy Boston family. These connections, among others, combined with Agassiz's engineering background, led him to undertake management of and invest in copper mining ventures in northern Michigan in the mid-1860s. The Calumet and Hecla mines eventually made him a multimillionaire and gave Agassiz the financial independence to pursue oceanographic research on his own terms.

Marine biology at the MCZ greatly benefited from the relationship that Agassiz's father had established with the U.S. Coast Survey from the late 1840s. Alexander Agassiz furthered this relationship by serving the Coast Survey briefly in 1859, and then participating, as did his father, on a number of Coast Survey expeditions off the east coast of Florida. These excursions allowed Agassiz the opportunity to dredge for marine specimens. He was especially interested in echinoderms (starfish, brittlestars, sea urchins, and the like), publishing a "Revision of the Echini" between 1872 and 1874.

Agassiz built a relationship with the U.S. Fish commission, a rival government institution of the Coast Survey, formed in 1871. The Fish Commission was more explicitly interested in marine biological research (rather than coastal charting) and established a laboratory at Woods Hole, Massachusetts, that frequently coordinated with the MCZ, as well as with a private laboratory set up by Agassiz in Newport, Rhode Island. Agassiz later sailed aboard the commission's *Albatross*, the first American vessel built explicitly for deep-sea research. In 1904, Agassiz financed the refitting of the *Albatross* for further research.

Agassiz's work with echinoderms brought him to the attention of Charles Wyville Thomson (1830–82) and John Murray (1841–1914), the chief naturalists involved in the famous 1872–76 voyage of the British research vessel HMS *Challenger*. Agassiz was asked to prepare a *Report of the Echinoidea* (1881) based on specimens dredged during the expedition, as part of the 50 volumes that ultimately constituted the *Challenger* Report. The expedition set an international example as a model of naval and civilian cooperation in the interests of scientific research, and Agassiz himself believed that it provided an outline for all future scientific marine explorations.

Between 1877 and 1880, Agassiz directed three dredging cruises aboard the *Blake*, a steamer belonging to the Coast Survey (restructured as the U.S. Coast and Geodetic Survey in 1878). With the help of the vessel's captain, Charles Sigsbee (1845–1923), Agassiz applied his knowledge of mining technology (ore-hauling equipment) to redesign the ship's dredging, trawling, and sounding apparatus so that they could use wire rope instead of the bulkier and weaker hemp lines that had been commonplace. Agassiz recovered fauna from deep-sea areas in the Caribbean and off America's east coast and collected extensive amounts of other marine data. The results of these excursions were published in 1888 in the *Bulletin of the Museum of Comparative Zoology* and were considered to be nearly as valuable as the *Challenger* results. Despite Agassiz's technological improvements for dredging the seafloor, it was still difficult to recover specimens from the intermediate ocean depths with any assured precision. Until the end of his life, Agassiz himself supported a theory of an azoic, or lifeless, zone in the middle depths, which maintained that only the uppermost and lowest ocean regions contained organisms in significant amounts.

During the *Blake* cruises Agassiz began in earnest to turn his attention to a study of coral reef formation. Two competing theories existed, one put forth by Charles Darwin (1809–82) in 1842, the other by John Murray in 1880. Darwin's theory relied upon the geological subsidence of volcanic islands as a general principle. As the islands slowly sank, Darwin thought, the fringing corals continued to grow upward, maintaining a constant depth below the surface. Murray, on the other hand, was a pioneer in the study of seafloor deposits, and he believed that layers of sediments accumulated atop existing underwater mountains. These gradually built up to a depth at which coral would grow after being colonized by larvae. In Murray's theory, a form of elevation, rather than subsidence, was the key factor.

The controversy directly stimulated Agassiz's reef and atoll research, as he could not accept the universality of Darwin's theory, based on his own personal experience. From the mid-1890s on, Agassiz personally financed and conducted numerous reef explorations around the globe, leading him to become the world's foremost authority on the subject. He was often accompanied by assistants from the MCZ. In 1896–97, Agassiz investigated the Great Barrier Reef and reef structures among the Fiji Islands, towing for coral larvae, taking soundings, and making photographs of island geology. Between 1900 and 1902, he spent extended periods of time among the South Sea Islands and the Maldives in the Indian Ocean. Agassiz had even conducted some limited drilling and boring operations, although these were not very successful and were quite expensive. Reports of these trips were published through the MCZ, but Agassiz never produced a general work on reefs unifying the data he had collected. If anything, by the end of his career, he had come to accept the extreme difficulty of generalizing any principles of reef formation. To him, there seemed to be exceptions to any rule.

By the turn of the century, the federal government's financial support for basic ocean research, marine biology particularly, had dwindled significantly. The coasts had been mapped, and Congress saw little that was of immediate practical value to marine biology. Agassiz's independent wealth, in many respects, allowed oceanography

to continue as a form of scientific practice in the United States. On 27 March 1910, while making his way to the United States from England, Agassiz died at sea.

Agassiz made notable scientific contributions to the development of oceanography, principally through his echinoderm and coral reef research. Under his direction, the Museum of Comparative Zoology continued operating as an important zoological training center, with considerable emphasis on marine biology. Just as important, perhaps, was Agassiz's willingness to invest his personal wealth in oceanographic research.

J. Conor Burns

BIOGRAPHY
- Alexander Emmanuel Rodolphe Agassiz.
- Born on 17 December 1835 in Neuchâtel, Switzerland.
- Earned degrees in engineering (1857) and zoology (1862) from Lawrence Scientific School, Harvard College.
- In 1866, he undertook management of the Calumet and Hecla mines in Michigan.
- He became director of the Museum of Comparative Zoology after his father's death in 1873 and directed three dredging cruises aboard the *Blake*, 1877–80.
- Died at sea, 27 March 1910.

SELECTED WRITINGS
Agassiz, Alexander. "Revision of the Echini." *Illustrated Catalogue of the Museum of Comparative Zoology at Harvard College*, Vol. 7 (1872–74).
———. *Report of the Echinoidea, Dredged by H.M.S. Challenger during the Years 1873–1876.* Challenger Expedition. Report on the Scientific Results of the Voyage of H.M.S. *Challenger*, Vol. 3. London: Longmans, 1881.
———. *Three Cruises of the United States Coast and Geodetic Survey Steamer "Blake" in the Gulf of Mexico, in the Caribbean Sea, and along the Atlantic Coast of the United States, from 1877 to 1880*, 2 vols. Boston: Houghton Mifflin, 1888.

FURTHER READING
Deacon, Margaret. *Scientists and the Sea, 1650–1900: A Study of Marine Science.* London and New York:

Academic Press, 1971; 2nd ed., Aldershot, England and Brookfield, Vt.: Ashgate, 1997.

Schlee, Susan. *The Edge of an Unfamiliar World: A History of Oceanography*. New York: Dutton, 1973; London: Hale, 1975.

Winsor, Mary P. *Reading the Shape of Nature: Comparative Zoology at the Agassiz Museum*. Chicago: University of Chicago Press, 1991.

RELATED ARTICLES

Agassiz, Jean Louis Rodolphe; Coral; Coral Atoll; Coral Reef; Darwin, Charles Robert; Echinodermata; HMS *Challenger*; Murray, John; Thomson, Charles Wyville

Agassiz, Jean Louis Rodolphe

1807–1873

Naturalist and Founder of Museum of Comparative Zoology at Harvard College

Louis Agassiz was an established geologist, paleontologist, and ichthyologist in his native Switzerland before moving to the United States in 1847 to assume a professorship at Harvard College. In 1859, he founded the Museum of Comparative Zoology at Harvard, which became a leading training center and research facility for American zoologists.

Jean Louis Rodolphe Agassiz was born in Môtier-en-Vully, Switzerland, on 28 May 1807. He became interested in natural history and earned his Ph.D. from Munich and Erlangen Universities in 1829, publishing a monograph on the fishes of Brazil (*Selecta genera et species piscium quas in itinere per Brasiliam 1817–1820*) that same year. He studied under the famous French comparative anatomist Georges Cuvier (1769–1832), whose philosophy of nature and ideas about zoological classification greatly influenced him. In 1832, Agassiz became a professor at the College of Neuchâtel, but immigrated to the United States in 1847 after the death of his first wife, Cécile (née Braun, with whom he had three children). He accepted a professorship at the Lawrence Scientific School of Harvard College, in Cambridge, Massachusetts. He was remarried, to Elizabeth Cary, and was associated with Harvard until his death.

Agassiz's place within the history of science has been notoriously difficult to assess. He never wavered from an idealist Christian interpretation of nature in which biological species were seen as fixed, unchangeable entities within a divine plan, each occupying a preordained geographic zone. Based on this approach, thorough empirical scientific investigations could reveal this divine scheme. Agassiz opposed the idea of evolution in the face of widespread scientific support for it after 1859, and his views about fixed biological types, when extended to humans, led him to support racist ideas about nonwhite peoples. Yet he was a gifted practical scientist and administrator—two generations of American scientific naturalists were trained under Agassiz through his Harvard department

Louis Agassiz. (From the collections of the Library of Congress)

and the Museum of Comparative Zoology that he founded. Thus, from an institutional point of view, he had a profound impact on the development of scientific practice in the mid- to late-nineteenth-century United States.

Agassiz's career in Europe was marked by several important studies. For his five-volume *Recherches sur les poissons fossiles* (Researches on the fossil fishes; 1833–44), a landmark work of paleoichthyology, Agassiz examined some 1700 ancient species using the detailed empirical techniques of comparative anatomy and descriptive precision that would make him famous. He also produced a four-volume study of living and fossil echinoderms (1838–42). Between 1835 and 1845, Agassiz undertook a series of geological investigations of glacial formations throughout Europe. He formalized the concept of the geologically recent "Ice Age" into a general theory of geology. Ironically, Agassiz's ideas about glaciation served later evolutionists well in providing a satisfactory explanation for the geographic distribution of certain alpine species, although Agassiz himself saw the Ice Age as something more akin to the biblical flood.

After arriving at Harvard, Agassiz wasted little time establishing himself as an important figure within American scientific circles. He set about creating a tightly knit network of scientific practitioners, beginning with his rigorously trained Harvard students. Agassiz garnered popular acclaim as well, and his public lectures were lauded by the Boston literati. He became associated with the leading scientists of the day, such as Joseph Henry (1797–1878), director of the Smithsonian Institution, and Alexander Bache (1806–67), director of the U.S. Coast Survey. Agassiz was a leading member of the American Association for the Advancement of Science and a principal founder of the U.S. National Academy of Science in 1863.

In the late 1840s, Agassiz convinced Bache of the importance of marine zoological investigations and built the foundation for a long and fruitful collaboration with the Coast Survey. This situation was further enhanced by the arrival of engineer and naturalist Louis François de Pourtalès (1823/4–80) at the survey around the same time. Pourtalès was a former student of Agassiz's in Switzerland and somewhat of a specialist in the study of corals and echinoderms. Agassiz, who had become fully interested in studying starfish, sea urchins, sea anemones, and jellyfish, accompanied a Coast Survey excursion into Massachusetts Bay in 1847 to dredge for specimens, followed in 1851 by a two-month project examining keys and reefs off Florida. Similar excursions followed. After 1859, Agassiz served as an official scientific adviser to the Coast Survey.

In the 1850s, Agassiz began a multivolume *Contributions to the Natural History of the United States,* which he intended as an elaborate introduction to the specialized form of zoology that he envisioned. In the first volume (1857), his "Essay on Classification" appeared. It was later published in book form. In this essay, Agassiz most clearly articulated his philosophical beliefs about nature and his scientific views about zoological classification. Despite its inherent creationism, the essay outlined an approach to the study of zoology that synthesized morphology, embryology, paleontology, and geographic distribution. Agassiz outlined a rigorous program of empirical science to describe taxonomic relationships between groups of organisms.

In 1859, Agassiz's plans for a research facility at Harvard came to fruition with the opening of the Museum of Comparative Zoology (MCZ). His department moved into the new building, which possessed an immense collection (with many marine specimens gathered during Coast Survey excursions). Most important, Agassiz's research center attracted students who wished to become professional zoologists and who learned through practice. Between 1859 and 1864 alone, many of the foremost American naturalists would be trained at the MCZ, including Agassiz's son Alexander (1835–1910), who became director after his father's death. The *Bulletin of the Museum of Comparative Zoology,* not surprisingly, became a leading vehicle for the publication of zoological research.

During the 1860s, marine biologists in both Europe and America were becoming more interested in the possibility of life in the sea at depths previously thought devoid of life. Sounding surveys, many for cable telegraph companies looking to find ideal transoceanic routes for laying cable, had begun developing better sounding and dredging equipment. Agassiz's friend Pourtalès was involved in such work for the Coast Survey. In 1867–69, Pourtalès led a number of excursions off the east coast of Florida to test some new gear, successfully recovering sea urchins, sponges, and corals from depths of 850 fathoms. Agassiz himself participated in some of this work aboard the survey vessel *Bibb*. In 1871, he conducted further deep-sea research aboard the Coast Survey ship *Hassler* on its circumnavigation of South America.

In 1873, Agassiz established the Anderson School of Natural History on Penikese Island, Massachusetts. Intended as a combination summer school and marine biological station, the venture lasted two short seasons only, although Agassiz did not live to witness the failure. He died on 14 December 1873.

Agassiz's impact on the development of oceanography occurred largely through his Harvard department and the Museum of Comparative Zoology. Under his direction, zoology, especially of marine organisms, achieved new levels of disciplinary and institutional self-identity in the United States. Agassiz also established a lasting relationship with the U.S. Coast Survey that further enhanced marine biology at the MCZ.

J. Conor Burns

BIOGRAPHY
- Jean Louis Rodolphe Agassiz.
- Born on 27 May 1807 in Môtier-en-Vully, Switzerland.
- Earned his Ph.D. from Munich and Erlangen Universities, 1829.
- Became a professor at the College of Neuchâtel in 1832.
- Moved to the United States to become a professor at Lawrence Scientific School, Harvard College, 1847.
- In 1859, he founded the Museum of Comparative Zoology at Harvard, and in 1863, he helped establish the National Academy of Sciences.
- Died 14 December 1873.

SELECTED WRITINGS

Agassiz, Louis. *Selecta genera et species piscium quas in itinere per Brasiliam, 1817–1820*. Munich: Typis C. Wolfe, 1829.

———. *Recherches sur les poissons fossiles*. Neuchâtel, Switzerland: Petitpierre, 1833–44.

———. *Études sur les glaciers*. Neuchâtel, Switzerland: Jent et Gassmann, 1840.

———. "Of the Natural Provinces of the Animal World and Their Relation to the Different Types of Man." In Josiah Nott and George Gliddon, *Types of Mankind*. Philadelphia: Lippincott, 1854.

———. *Contributions to the Natural History of the United States,* 4 vols. Boston: Little, Brown/London: Trübner, 1857–62.

———. *An Essay on Classification*. London: Longman, Brown, Green, Longmans, and Roberts, 1859; reprint, Edward Lurie, ed., Cambridge, Mass.: Belknap Press of Harvard University Press, 1962.

FURTHER READING

Deacon, Margaret. *Scientists and the Sea, 1650–1900: A Study of Marine Science*. London and New York: Academic Press, 1971; 2nd ed., Aldershot, England and Brookfield, Vt.: Ashgate, 1997.

Schlee, Susan. *The Edge of an Unfamiliar World: A History of Oceanography*. New York: Dutton, 1973; London: Hale, 1975.

Winsor, Mary P. *Reading the Shape of Nature: Comparative Zoology at the Agassiz Museum*. Chicago: University of Chicago Press, 1991.

RELATED ARTICLES
Agassiz, Alexander Emmanuel Rodolphe; Echinodermata

Agnatha

The Latin name *agnatha* means "without jaws," a reference to the circular, rasping mouths seen in this small but biologically important group, also known as the *jawless fishes*. There are two extant types of jawless fishes: hagfishes and lampreys. Both are slimy, eel-shaped animals that have circular mouths and tiny, pin-sharp teeth on the tongue (hagfishes) or oral disks (lampreys) to rasp away at flesh. Unlike other fishes, agnathans lack scales, paired fins, or true gill arches. Like sharks and rays, their skeletons are made of cartilage instead of bone.

Agnathans are sometimes described as living fossils because they are similar to fossils of the earliest known vertebrates. Today there are about 80 to 90 species, but 500 million years ago there were many more. One of these prehistoric species was the ancestor of jawed fishes, and hence of all other vertebrates, including ourselves.

Taxonomic Classification

The classification of agnathans, and hence the classification of the entire vertebrate group, is fraught with controversy. According to many ichthyologists, hagfishes (class Myxini) and lampreys (class Cephalaspidomorphi) together make up the superclass Agnatha, one of the two major groups in the subphylum Vertebrata. This superclass also contains the extinct class Pteraspidomorphi. All other vertebrates, including jawed fishes, amphibians, reptiles, birds, and mammals, are placed in the superclass Gnathostomata (jawed vertebrates). This arrangement implies that hagfishes and lampreys are close relatives that both descended from early jawless vertebrates. However, careful study has revealed many striking differences between hagfishes and lampreys, suggesting that their superficial similarity is a consequence of convergent evolution rather than common ancestry. Most important, hagfishes lack any sign of a true backbone, a defining feature of vertebrates. This

absence can be interpreted in two ways: hagfishes might be vertebrates that lost their backbone during evolution, or perhaps they are more primitive creatures whose ancestors never possessed a backbone. Evidence suggests that the latter interpretation is correct. As a result, some scientists do not recognize hagfishes as vertebrates at all, and instead place them in the subphylum Myxini, a sister group to the subphylum Vertebrata within the phylum Chordata.

Hagfishes

Hagfishes are exclusively marine and most live in temperate waters at depths of more than 25 meters (82 feet). There are six recognized genera and 43 species of hagfishes. Hagfishes typically burrow in mud or sand on the seafloor, where they feed primarily on polychaete worms and fish corpses. Fishermen regard them with disgust because they produce copious amounts of sticky slime when caught and are often found burrowing into the

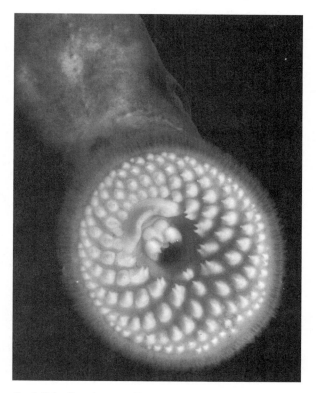

Oral disk of sea lamprey Petromyzon marinus. *(©Heather Angel)*

bodies of other fishes, sometimes damaging a catch. The ability to secrete slime is an important defense mechanism for hagfishes, but the sticky slime can impede movement and obstruct the gills. To rid themselves of excess slime, hagfishes can tie themselves in a knot, sloughing off slime as they pull themselves through the knot and enabling them to swim freely again.

Hagfishes have eel-like bodies and grow up to 110 centimeters (43 inches) in length. They have few conspicuous external features, apart from a tail fin and a cluster of slender tactile organs, called *barbels*, around the mouth. These are used for finding food in the muddy seafloor. A series of slime pores and gill openings run along either side of the body, and two shallow pits on the upperside of the head bear small, inconspicuous eyes. The "teeth" of hagfish, which consist of tiny spikes of keratin, are located only on the tongue. By manipulating the tongue or pressing it against a hard plate in the mouth, hagfish can bite chunks of flesh from dead or dying fish. The internal anatomy of hagfishes reveals important differences from other fishes, including an unusual circulatory system with four hearts and a rudimentary kidney.

Whereas female lampreys produce tiny eggs by the thousand, hagfishes lay a maximum of 30 large, leathery eggs, each about 2 to 3 centimeters (about 0.79 to 1.18 inches) wide. Tiny hooks on the eggs serve to hold them together and anchor them to the seafloor. The embryos develop in a different way from those of lampreys, and the young hatch as miniature adults, unlike the anatomically distinct larval lampreys.

Lampreys

Of the 41 recognized species of lampreys, 32 are almost always confined to fresh water, while the remaining nine species are *anadromous*; they migrate to fresh water to breed. Eighteen species are parasitic. Parasitic species attach themselves by the mouth to larger fishes and use their rasping teeth to bore through the flesh. They then suck out the victim's blood and body fluids.

Like hagfishes, lampreys have eel-like bodies and can grow up to 90 centimeters (35 inches) long, although nonparasitic and freshwater species seldom exceed 30 centimeters (12 inches). Unlike hagfishes, lampreys have dorsal fins, well-developed eyes with extrinsic muscles, a lateral line organ for sensing vibrations in water, and no barbels. The mouth consists of a flat round structure called the *oral disk*, with a small opening in the center. The surface of the oral disk is covered with small keratin "teeth" that are used to cling to the side of larger fish and bore through their flesh.

Lampreys spawn in freshwater rivers and streams. Males construct nests by removing large stones from the riverbed to make a shallow depression, and females deposit thousands of tiny eggs into these depressions, where the eggs stick to particles of gravel. The larvae that hatch out are very different from adult lampreys. Called *ammocoetes*, they have highly reduced fins and eyes, and lack oral disks. Ammocoetes are filter feeders. They bury themselves in muddy river bottoms and strain microorganisms from the water by pumping water through their gills. Food particles adhere to a layer of sticky mucus that covers the gill slits and lines a specially enlarged throat cavity, and the mucus is then swallowed.

Lampreys spend three to seven years of their life as ammocoetes, during which time they grow to a maximum length of about 10 centimeters (4 inches). Eventually they leave their burrows, and many species migrate to the ocean or a lake and undergo metamorphosis into the adult form. Parasitic adult lampreys then use their well-developed sense of sight to locate the large fishes upon which they prey, and grow much more quickly on this highly nutritious diet. Nonparasitic lampreys do not feed as adults. After hatching they stay near their spawning grounds and undergo short adult lives. These lampreys are thought to be nonmigratory "satellite" species that evolved from parasitic ancestors.

Uses

The unpleasant slime produced by hagfish makes them unsuitable as food, but their scaleless skin has long been used to make leather goods such as wallets. In contrast, lampreys are edible and are sometimes served as gourmet food. King Henry I of England is alleged to have died after consuming a massive plate of the fish. Lampreys have also found use in biological research, thanks to their unusually large nerves.

Ben Morgan

FURTHER READING

Bardack, D. "First Fossil Hagfish (Myxinoidea): A Record from the Pennsylvanian of Illinois." *Science,* Vol. 254 (1 November 1998), pp. 701–703.

Carroll, R. L. *Vertebrate Paleontology and Evolution.* New York: W. H. Freeman, 1988.

Forey, Peter, and Philippe Janvier. "Agnathans and the Origin of Jawed Vertebrates." *Nature,* Vol. 361 (14 January 1993), pp. 129–134.

Helfman, Gene S., Bruce B. Collette, and Douglas E. Facey. *The Diversity of Fishes.* Malden, Mass.: Blackwell Science, 1997.

Jensen, D. "The Hagfish." *Scientific American,* Vol. 214, No. 2 (1966), pp. 82–90.

Moyle, Peter B., and Joseph J. Cech. *Fishes: An Introduction to Ichthyology.* Englewood Cliffs, N.J.: Prentice Hall, 1982; 4th ed., Upper Saddle River, N.J.: Prentice Hall, 2000.

Nelson, Joseph S. *Fishes of the World.* New York: Wiley, 1976; 3rd ed., 1994.

Norman, Gilbert F. *Biology of Hagfish and Lamprey.* Washington, D.C.: ABBE Publishers Association, 1996.

RELATED ARTICLES

Cephalospidomorphi; Chordata; Gnathostomata; Myxini; Parasitism; Pteraspidomorphi

Agulhas Current

The Agulhas Current is a warm surface ocean current that flows in an approximately southwesterly direction in the Indian Ocean, parallel to the eastern coast of Africa. It carries warm water into southern latitudes. Depending on the season, the temperature of its water ranges from 14 to 26°C (57 to 79°F).

The Agulhas Current begins at about the Tropic of Capricorn and forms part of the gyre that includes the South Equatorial Current. South of Madagascar, the Agulhas Current is joined by water from the Mozambique Current, a continuation of the Somalia Current that passes through the Mozambique Channel, between the eastern coast of Africa and Madagascar. At about latitude 40°S, to the south of the southernmost tip of Africa, the Agulhas Current meets the cold water of the Benguela Current. Most of the water of the Agulhas Current turns to the east and flows toward Australia, but some of its water flows around the Cape of Good Hope and into the South Atlantic.

A typical western boundary current, the Agulhas Current is narrow, swift, and meandering. It is 100 kilometers (62 miles) wide and flows at an average 0.7 to 2.2 km (0.43 to 1.4 miles) per hour and at more than 9 km (5.6 miles) per hour off the southeastern coast of South Africa. Its speed varies with the seasons, owing to seasonal variation in the speed of the South Equatorial Current, but it is the second fastest of all ocean currents (after the Gulf Stream). For centuries, the strength of the Agulhas Current posed a

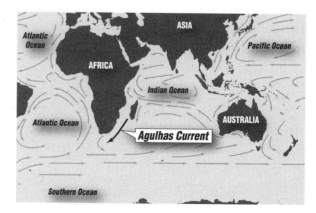

Agulhas Current.

serious hazard to shipping. Navigation is especially difficult where the Agulhas and Benguela Currents meet.

Michael Allaby

FURTHER READING
Kendrew, W. G. *The Climates of the Continents.* Oxford: Clarendon Press, 1922; 5th ed., Oxford: Oxford University Press, 1961.
King, Cuchlaine A. M. *Introduction to Physical and Biological Oceanography.* London: Edward Arnold/ New York: Crane Russak, 1975.
Njoku, E. G., and O. B. Brown. "Sea Surface Temperature." In R. J. Gurney, J. L. Foster, and C. L. Parkinson, eds., *Atlas of Satellite Observations Related to Global Change.* Cambridge and New York: Cambridge University Press, 1993.

RELATED ARTICLES
Benguela Current; Boundary Current; Equatorial Currents, North and South

Ahermatypic Coral

Ahermatypic corals are types of corals that do not form coral reefs. There are many different types of ahermatypic coral, all of which belong to the cnidarian class Anthozoa, along with reef-building (hermatypic) corals and sea anemones. Most ahermatypic corals lack the symbiotic algae found in hermatypic species.

Corals have simple bodies, called *polyps*, that resemble their close relatives the sea anemones. Unlike sea anemones, however, corals usually live in colonies made up of many individual polyps connected together. The main part of a polyp is a small, cylindrical mass of soft tissue that contains a central cavity divided into pockets by septa and also contains the reproductive organs. The top of the polyp bears a ring of stinging tentacles that catches planktonic organisms, which are transferred to a central mouth at the center of the oral disk that bears the tentacles. Coral polyps lack circulatory or respiratory organs and have no

brains. However, they have a simple nerve network and muscle fibers that enable them to move their tentacles and withdraw their bodies quickly when they sense danger.

Hermatypic corals are restricted to shallow tropical waters because the symbiotic algae that live within them need light. However, ahermatypic species can inhabit a more diverse range of habitats, including caves, deep waters, and temperate oceans. Ivory tree coral (*Oculina varicosa*), for instance, flourishes in deep water off the coast of Florida, and ahermatypic forms of scleractinian (true or stony) corals are common in cold temperate waters. Ahermatypic corals also grow on tropical coral reefs, where they are commonly found in deep or shaded parts of the reef. Because they have no symbiotic algae to supplement their food supply, they grow best where plankton is abundant.

Ben Morgan

FURTHER READING
Brusca, Richard C., and Gary J. Brusca. *Invertebrates.* Sunderland, Mass.: Sinauer, 1990.
Pechenik, Jan A. *Biology of the Invertebrates.* Boston: Prindle, Weber and Schmidt, 1985; 4th ed., Boston: McGraw-Hill, 2000.

RELATED ARTICLES
Cnidaria; Coral; Hermatypic Coral

Air–Sea Interaction

The physical and chemical properties of the ocean and the atmosphere are influenced by their mutual exchange. These two fluids interact in many ways. Energy is transferred from the atmosphere to the ocean primarily in the form of momentum from winds, which produces surface waves and currents in the upper ocean. Heat is also transferred back and forth between the ocean and the atmosphere. Air–sea temperature differences on a global basis are slightly negative, indicating overall that the transfer of heat is from the ocean to the atmosphere. When evaporation takes place, latent heat is released into the atmosphere from the ocean, as well as moisture. Conversely, precipitation from the atmosphere returns fresh water to the ocean. The exchange of heat and momentum between the ocean and the atmosphere does not, however, occur on similar time scales. Energy from the atmosphere, primarily due to surface winds, affects the upper layers of the ocean almost immediately. Primarily in the form of heat from the ocean, energy affects the atmospheric circulation on much longer time scales, ranging from weeks to months.

On smaller scales near the ocean surface, bubbles and spray are important vehicles for exchanging energy and matter between the ocean and the atmosphere. Bubbles serve as an important mechanism for gases to pass into and out of the ocean. Spray from breaking waves transfers moisture and salt directly into the atmosphere. Salt particles in the lower atmosphere in turn serve as nuclei for water droplets to collect on, leading to raindrops and thus the return of fresh water to the ocean. In addition to generating surface waves, surface winds carry dust particles from various manufactured (e.g., industrial) and natural (e.g, volcanic ash plus desert sands) sources that settle to the sea surface, where they enter the ocean and are eventually deposited on the seafloor. Through the exchange of gases, the atmosphere also transfers various pollutants into the ocean. In this regard, the atmosphere is often regarded as an important pathway for the movement of chemicals into the marine environment. Recent studies have indicated that as much as 25 percent of the pollutants that enter the Chesapeake Bay, for example, originate in the atmosphere.

Measurements of the various quantities that determine how much energy and matter is transferred back and forth between the ocean and the atmosphere are very difficult to calculate. This difficulty stems from the fact that the ocean surface is in a constant state of motion. Thus it is not surprising that these measurements are expensive to make and usually have a high degree of uncertainty associated with them.

Air–sea interactions are important on much larger scales as well. The El Niño phenomenon is the result of air–sea interactions on a global scale. Several times each decade, warm waters appear off the coast of Peru and across the tropical Pacific that are related to the weakening of the winds near the equator. Higher sea surface temperatures across the central Pacific in turn alter the atmospheric circulation. Rainfall occurs at locations that are normally dry, and droughts occur in places that usually receive ample precipitation. Although El Niño episodes begin in the tropical Pacific, they ultimately affect the entire planet because of their impact on the atmospheric circulation. However, El Niños vary greatly in their intensity and their duration, and our ability to predict the onset of these global events has so far been only partially successful.

Laurence C. Breaker

FURTHER READING
Kennish, M. J. *Practical Handbook of Marine Science.* Boca Raton, Fla.: CRC Press, 1989; 3rd ed., 2001.
Perry, A. H., and J. M. Walker. *The Ocean–Atmosphere System.* New York: Longman, 1977.
Wells, Neil. *The Atmosphere and Ocean: A Physical Introduction.* London and Philadelphia: Taylor and Francis, 1986; 2nd ed., Chichester, England, and New York: Wiley, 1997.

RELATED ARTICLES
El Niño; Energy from the Sea; Latent Heat, Fusion and Evaporation

Alaska Current

The Alaska Current is a surface ocean current that flows in an anticlockwise gyre in the Gulf of Alaska and North Pacific. It breaks away from the North Pacific Current at about 47°N 160°W, a position

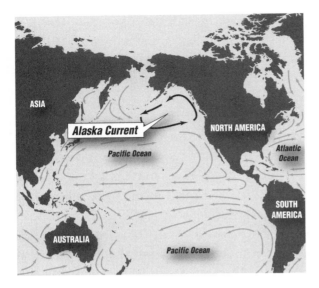

Alaska Current.

south of the tip of the Alaska Peninsula, and flows in a northeasterly direction until it is deflected by the North American landmass. This causes it to turn to the west and flow past Kodiak Island and parallel to and to the south of the Aleutian Islands.

Water from rivers that discharge into the Gulf of Alaska becomes incorporated in the Alaska Current. This reduces the salinity of the current to below 32.6 practical salinity units (psu). A relatively new theory states that the low salinities in the Gulf of Alaska are also caused by the low evaporation rate compared to salty waters in the North Atlantic, which are carried there by the Gulf Stream. Although the northward-flowing Alaska Current carries relatively warm water from the south, these temperatures [4°C (39°F)] are cool compared to the North Atlantic. Its average speed is about 1 kilometer (0.6 miles) per hour. The current is stronger in winter than in summer. In winter, low atmospheric pressure (the Aleutian low) remains stationary to the south of Alaska, bringing easterly winds that drive the current. In summer, high pressure predominates, producing westerly winds that retard the current.

The part of the Alaska Current that flows past the Aleutians is often called the Aleutian or Sub-Arctic Current, or the Alaskan Stream. It is

deeper and more regular than the Alaska Current flowing through the Gulf of Alaska, and faster. At a depth of 5 meters (16 feet) its speed sometimes reaches 3 kilometers (1.9 miles) per hour. These are characteristics associated with a western boundary current, while the shallow, more meandering Alaska Current is more typical of an eastern boundary current. The distinction justifies the use of separate names for the two currents. The Aleutian Current moves in a southwesterly direction, to the north of the North Pacific Current and parallel to it, carrying warm water into the North Pacific. As it approaches Asia, the current gathers warm water from the Kuroshio and cold water from the Oyashio. Finally, it turns to the southwest and rejoins the North Pacific Current.

Michael Allaby

FURTHER READING

King, Cuchlaine A. M. *Introduction to Physical and Biological Oceanography.* London: Edward Arnold/New York: Crane, Russak, 1975.
Knauss, John A. *Introduction to Physical Oceanography.* Englewood Cliffs, N.J.: Prentice Hall, 1978; 2nd ed. rev., Upper Saddle River, N.J.: Prentice Hall, 2000.

RELATED ARTICLES

Boundary Current; Gulf Stream; Kuroshio; Oyashio; Salinity

Albert I, Prince of Monaco
1848–1922
Pioneer Oceanographer and Research Patron

This French-born sailor, scientist, and philosopher—and sovereign governor of the principality of Monaco—founded two leading institutions of oceanography: the Oceanographic Museum of Monaco and the Oceanographic Institute of Paris. His research cruises, almost every summer between 1884 and 1915, advanced biological and physical oceanography.

Albert I of Monaco was born in Paris, France, into Monaco's royal family, son of Charles III of Monaco (Honoré Grimaldi) and Antoinette Ghislaine, countess of Mérode. By his teenage years, Albert was passionate about adopting "the career of a navigator," a vocation that his father encouraged. In 1866, Prince Charles entrusted the 18-year-old Albert to the Spanish navy, where he became a midshipman, learned to command a ship, and rose to the rank of sublieutenant. In 1868, Albert joined the French navy, and in 1870 he fought against Germany (then Prussia) as a lieutenant-commander in the Franco-Prussian War.

After the war, in 1873, Albert bought his first seagoing vessel, a 200-ton schooner, the *Pleiad*, which he renamed *Hirondelle* (Swallow). Between 1873 and 1884, Albert made regular summer cruises in the Mediterranean and North Atlantic. In 1884, he collected surface plankton in the Baltic Sea, and for cruises in 1885 he had the *Hirondelle* fitted with the latest scientific equipment. Between 1885 and 1915, Albert took part in 28 oceanographic expeditions, including four (1885–91) in the *Hirondelle I*, six (1892–97) in the steam-powered 600-ton schooner *Princess Alice I*, 12 (1898–1910) in the 1400-ton *Princess Alice II*, and finally, five (1911–15) in the 1650-ton *Hirondelle II*.

In 1885, Albert published his findings on the flow of the Gulf Stream. By the late 1880s, he had demonstrated the existence of the North Equatorial Current in the North Atlantic using the message-in-a-bottle technique, with hundreds of bottles and barrels dropped into the eastern Atlantic from the *Hirondelle*. Many of the floats were recovered weeks and months later at points south and west of the drop-off. This proved the existence of a North Atlantic gyre, for which the Gulf Stream is the western component. Albert's work studying the drift currents of the North Atlantic, together with the mapping of water temperatures and the movements of isothermal bodies of water, was to span three decades.

Scientists on board Albert's cruises made discoveries that sometimes had far-reaching effects. Albert conducted experiments using the venom of a cnidarian, the Portuguese man-of-war, *Physalia physalia*, which he injected into experimental animals to observe its effects. Physiologist Charles Richet (1850–1935), on one trip, injected cnidarian toxin into a dog as a vaccination to confer immunity against the venom. When the vaccination was repeated a few days later, the dog fell into shock and promptly died. This began an investigation that led Richet to discover and describe anaphylaxis (anaphylactic shock), a development for which he received the Nobel Prize for physiology or medicine in 1913.

In 1889, Albert's father died. Albert took on responsibilities as sovereign, steering political,

Caricature of Albert I, Prince of Monaco. (Hulton/Archive)

social, and economic reforms in the principality while continuing to pursue his passion for oceanography. During his almost-annual expeditions into the North Atlantic and Mediterranean, he invited colleagues from France and other nations, and with the support of specialist assistants, these teams investigated a wide range of physical and biological oceanographic phenomena. One focus was the invention and refinement of sampling methods. For example, the *nasse triédique* was a baited trap suspended in midwater, or on or close to the seafloor, at a predetermined depth. This captured creatures that had hitherto evaded the traditional nets and trawls in use. Specimens were preserved for examination and the reports of each cruise were published in full, providing a model that other scientific patrons, such as King Carlos of Portugal (1863–1908), were to adopt on research cruises.

In 1906, Albert established the Oceanographic Institute of Paris. It promoted research and teaching and held regular conferences on marine science. In 1910, Albert's Oceanographic Museum of Monaco, spectacularly sited on a rock overlooking the Mediterranean Sea, was inaugurated to house the growing collections from his oceanographic expeditions. In 1919, in Madrid, Spain, the prince launched the International Commission for the Scientific Exploration of the Mediterranean. Albert also founded research publications. For example, his *Bulletin du Musée Océanographique* (1904) became the *Bulletin de l'Institut Océanographique* (1906) and then the *Annales de l'Institut Océanographique* (1910).

By the beginning of the twentieth century, technologically advanced nations were beginning to acknowledge the need for marine research to underpin their economic and political aspirations. The benefits of international cooperation were being recognized, too. Representatives attending the 1899 International Geographical Congress in Berlin agreed on the necessity to compile all available depth-sounding data into a general bathymetric chart of the oceans. Prince Albert took on this work, in 1905 publishing the world's first bathymetric chart of all oceans, a summation of all previous work. After Albert's death in 1922, the International Hydrographic Bureau, which had been set up in Monaco, continued this work.

Some of Albert's ideas, accepted today, were far in advance of his time: for example, his warnings that parts of the Mediterranean and North Atlantic were being overfished, that airplanes could be used to spot schools of fish, and that marine sanctuaries should be created to protect wildlife.

In 1971, Prince Rainier III of Monaco created the Albert I of Monaco Prize for Oceanography. Its aim—reflecting the aspirations of Albert himself—was to "stimulate research by giving its highest official recognition and its esteem for a work accomplished, for dangers undergone and for discoveries made in the sea and under the sea where 'the unknown is still immense.'" Albert's patronage of research, together with his practical involvement and his commitment to scientific rigor and international cooperation, were major contributions to the development of oceanography in the late nineteenth and early twentieth centuries.

Trevor Day

BIOGRAPHY

- Prince Albert I of Monaco.
- Born on 13 November 1848 in Paris, France.
- Joined the Spanish navy in 1866 and the French navy in 1868, rising to the rank of lieutenant-commander.
- Sponsored and led oceanographic cruises in the Mediterranean Sea and Atlantic Ocean between 1884 and 1915.
- Founded the Oceanographic Institute of Paris in 1906 and the Oceanographic Museum of Monaco in 1910.
- Became the first president of the International Commission for Scientific Exploration of the Mediterranean Sea in 1910.
- Died 26 June 1922 in Paris.

SELECTED WRITINGS

Albert I of Monaco, Prince. "Some Results of My Researches on Oceanography." *Nature,* Vol. 85 (30 June 1898), pp. 7–11.

———. *La Carrière d'un Navigateur,* rev. ed. Monaco: Monaco Press, 1966.

FURTHER READING

Buchanan, J. Y. "The Oceanographical Museum at Monaco." *Nature,* Vol. 85 (3 November 1910), pp. 7–11.

Deacon, Margaret. *Scientists and the Sea, 1650–1900: A Study of Marine Science.* London and New York: Academic Press, 1971; 2nd ed., Aldershot, England, and Brookfield, Vt.: Ashgate, 1997.

McConnell, Anita. *No Sea Too Deep: The History of Oceanographic Instruments.* Bristol, England: Adam Hilger, 1982.

Sears, M., and D. Merriman, eds. *Oceanography: The Past.* New York: Springer-Verlag, 1980.

RELATED ARTICLES

Equatorial Currents, North and South; Gulf Stream; Mediterranean Sea; Temperature, Distribution of

Aleutian Arc

The Aleutian Arc is the curved configuration of mountain ranges and flanking submerged margins that forms the northern rim of the Pacific Ocean Basin. It extends from near Cook Inlet in southern Alaska on the east to the Kamchatka Peninsula (Russia), more than 3000 kilometers (1860 miles) to the west. The Aleutian Arc is located where two lithospheric plates (Pacific and North American) collide along a convergent plate boundary. It is marked by abundant earthquakes, some with magnitudes as large as 8 or 9 on the Richter scale. About 60 major volcanic centers of Quaternary age (1.65 million years ago to present) stretch from Hayes volcano, about 130 kilometers (81 miles) west of Anchorage, nearly 2500 kilometers (1550 miles) westward to Buildir volcano in the western Aleutian Islands. Thirty-seven have been active during the past 200 years.

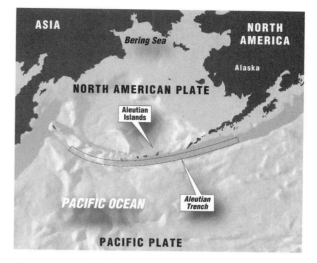

Components of the Aleutian Arc.

The arc's geologic history involves the consumption of thousands of cubic kilometers of the Kula and Pacific Plates. Over its life span of approximately 55 million years, processes associated with the Aleutian Arc have built an entire mountain range: Volcanoes have erupted, earthquakes have moved faults that both tear apart and build the arc, mountains have appeared and been eroded, and glaciers have waxed and waned.

The Aleutian Arc is a volcanic arc consisting of two very different segments that meet near Unimak Pass: the Alaska Peninsula segment to the east and the Aleutian Ridge segment to the west. The Alaska Peninsula segment is composed of the Alaska Peninsula, its adjacent islands, including Kodiak Island, and their continental and insular margins. It is a continental arc similar to the Cascades and Andes. The Aleutian Ridge segment is a massive, mostly submerged mountain range that includes both the islands and the submerged pedestal from which they protrude. This segment is an island arc with a width ranging from about 150 to 300 kilometers (90 to 190 miles). Relief of the Aleutian Ridge measured from the floor of the trench at about 7200 meters (23,600 feet) below sea level to the top of the highest volcanic peak at 2857 meters (9373 feet) is approximately 10,060 meters

(33,000 feet), making it one of the highest mountain ranges in the world.

There are no pre-Eocene (older than 56.5 million years) rocks on the Aleutian Ridge segment, whereas extensive outcrops of Mesozoic (248 to 65 million years old) rocks underlie Cenozoic (65 million years old to present) rocks on the Alaska Peninsula. Since the late Eocene (about 42 million years ago), the two segments have evolved similarly, although many of the processes were not quite synchronous.

The North American and Pacific Plates converge along the inner wall of the Aleutian Trench at about 7 to 8 centimeters (2.75 to 3.15 inches) per year. Convergence is nearly at right angles along the Alaska Peninsula, but because of the arcuate shape of the Aleutian Ridge, the angle of convergence lessens to the west. Along the central Aleutian Ridge near the island of Adak, for example, convergence is about 30° from normal to the magmatic (volcanic) axis. Motion between plates is nearly parallel along the far western Aleutian and Komandorsky Islands.

Morphology of the Aleutian Arc is that of a classic convergent margin boundary. From the deep ocean floor of the Pacific Plate to the deep Aleutian Basin region of the Bering Sea, the main parts of the arc are: trench, accretionary prism, fore-arc terrace and basin, magmatic axis, and back-arc basin.

Trench

The Aleutian Trench is nearly filled with sediment from the erosion of Alaska. Sediments from streams and glaciers are funneled into the trench through submarine canyons and then flow down the axis of the trench from east to west by turbidity currents. During times of lowered sea levels, which occurred several times during the past 2.5 million years, erosion was particularly intense and sediments poured into the trench in volumes that far exceed those of the present. Trench fill is several kilometers thick, particularly near Cook Inlet,

but even along the central part of the Aleutian Ridge near Amlia Island, sediment thicknesses of between 3 and 4 kilometers (1.9 to 2.5 miles) have been measured. In the far west near Attu Island, sediment thickness is about 1 kilometer (0.6 mile). Trench floor width averages about 20 kilometers (12 miles). Trench depths range from about 4500 meters (14,760 feet) off Kodiak Island in the east to more than 7200 meters (23,600 feet) in the central and western parts of the Aleutian Arc. The trench fill overlies crust of the oceanic (Pacific) plate. Oldest sediments in the trench fill are estimated to be 0.5 million years old.

Accretionary Prism

The accretionary prism is well developed all along the Alaska Peninsula and along most of the Aleutian Ridge. However, in the western part, beginning at about Kiska Island, the prism thins greatly because of the curvature of the arc (angle of convergence) and a decrease in the amount of available sediment. Most trench sediments are swallowed by the subduction zone. Seismic reflection data show that the lower parts of the trench fill and underlying ocean crust descend into the subduction zone under a nearly horizontal fault surface called a *décollement*. The upper layers of the trench fill, above the décollement, are bulldozed into the accretionary prism as fault-bounded sediment packages. The accretionary prism ranges in thickness from 0 to about 5 kilometers (0 to 3 miles) along the Aleutian Arc.

Fore-Arc Terrace and Basin

A very distinct terrace in the fore-arc region is as many as 60 kilometers (37 miles) wide. This terrace is best developed in the central part of the Aleutian Ridge near Amlia Island, where its surface lies about 4500 meters (14,750 feet) below sea level. The terrace is underlain by a sediment-filled basin, called a fore-arc basin, that contains up to 3 kilometers (1.9 miles) of sediment and sedimentary rocks overlying an older igneous rock basement that makes up the arc's framework. A high ridge on the seaward side of the terrace, called the *outer high,* separates the accretionary prism from the fore-arc basin.

Magmatic Axis

The present magmatic axis marks the location where volcanoes grow. Andesite and basalt, plus their sedimentary detritus, make up the major rock types found along the surface of the magmatic axis. Beneath the volcanoes, magma chambers crystallize to form plutons, which are coarse-grained igneous rocks such as diorite and gabbro. Many of the older plutons have been lifted to the surface and are now exposed. The magmatic axis has not remained in the same place throughout the arc's development but has moved north and south. It forms over the zone of melting that lies above the subduction zone, so that changes in the zone of melting cause a shift in the magmatic axis. The crust of the Aleutian Arc is generally between 20 and 24 kilometers (12.4 to 14.9 miles) thick and is made up mostly of rocks that formed previously along the magmatic axis. Summit basins such as the Amlia and Buildir Basins have formed near the magmatic axis as the arc is pulled apart by strike-slip faults.

Back-Arc Basin

A wide continental shelf lies north of the Alaska Peninsula segment, whereas a back-arc basin lies north of the Aleutian Ridge. This back-arc basin, mostly the Aleutian Basin, is floored by part of the Kula Plate that was trapped behind the Aleutian Arc when it fired up about 55 million years ago. The average depth of the basin floor is about 3600 meters (11,800 feet). Detritus eroded from Alaska and Siberia has added about 3 to 4 kilometers (1.9 to 2.5 miles) of sediment to the Aleutian Basin since it was trapped behind the Aleutian Ridge.

Tracy L. Vallier

FURTHER READING

Lonsdale, Peter. "Paleogene History of the Kula Plate: Offshore Evidence and Onshore Implications." *Geological Society of America Bulletin,* Vol. 100 (1987), pp. 733–754.

Ryan, Holl, and David W. Scholl. "The Evolution of Forearc Structures Along an Oblique Convergent Margin, Central Aleutian Arc." *Tectonics,* Vol. 8 (1989), pp. 497–516.

Scholl, David W., Tracy L. Vallier, and Andrew J. Stevenson. "Geologic Evolution and Petroleum Potential of the Aleutian Ridge." In David W. Scholl, Arthur Grantz, and John G. Vedder, eds., *Geology and Resource Potential of the Continental Margin of Western North America and Adjacent Ocean Basins; Beaufort Sea to Baja California.* Earth Science Series No. 6. Houston, Texas: Circum-Pacific Council for Energy and Mineral Resources, 1987; pp. 123–156.

Vallier, Tracy L., David W. Scholl, Michael A. Fisher, Terry R. Bruns, Frederick H. Wilson, Roland von Huene, and Andrew J. Stevenson. "Geologic Framework of the Aleutian Arc, Alaska." In George Plafker and Henry C. Berg, eds., *Geology of Alaska.* The Geology of North America Series, No. G-1. Boulder, Colo.: Geological Society of America, 1994; pp. 367–388.

RELATED ARTICLES

Accretionary Prism; Aleutian Islands; Bering Sea; Convergent Plate Boundary; Island Arc; Kula Plate; Pacific Plate; Plate Tectonics; Subduction Zone; Trench; Turbidity Current

Aleutian Islands

The Aleutian Islands comprise the longest archipelago in the world, measuring about 1770 kilometers (1100 miles) in an arcuate (curved) island chain that extends from the tip of the Alaska Peninsula at Unimak Pass (54°51' N latitude; 163°22' W longitude) to the west side of Attu Island (52°55' N latitude; 172°42' E longitude). The entire chain lies between 52 and 55°N latitudes and 163°W and 172°E longitudes. There are 124 islands with a total area of about 17,840 square kilometers (6890 square miles).

Fifty-seven volcanoes dot the islands, 46 of which are active. Twenty-six volcanoes have erupted since 1760.

The islands cap a mostly submerged mountain range, the Aleutian Ridge. The Aleutian Ridge is the oceanic segment of the Aleutian Arc and connects on the east to the Alaska Peninsula. The Aleutian Arc is located where two lithospheric plates converge. About 55 million years ago, the volcanic arc began forming where the denser Kula Plate was subducted beneath the more buoyant North American Plate. If the ocean water were removed, the Aleutian Ridge would be one of the longest and highest mountain ranges in the world. Its highest peak rises 2857 meters (9373 feet) above sea level, and the floor of the Aleutian Trench, the lowest point, is 7200 meters (23,622 feet) below sea level.

The climate of the Aleutian Islands is oceanic with heavy rainfall and fairly uniform but cool temperatures. The islands are shrouded perpetually by fog, mist, and rain. Sudden violent storms pose a threat to ships and people. The islands are treeless except where humans have succeeded in growing small conifers in sheltered valleys. In contrast to mainland Alaska, bears, wolves, wolverines, ground squirrels, weasels, and mosquitoes are absent. The Aleutian Islands boast the world's largest number of sea mammal species (23, counting the now extinct Steller's sea cow), 13 of which are cetaceans. At least 5 million seabirds flock to the islands to nest each summer.

The Aleutian Islands were purchased from Russia by the United States in 1867 as part of Alaska. Native Aleut Indians have occupied the islands for thousands of years, probably since the last sea-level low stand. In fact, the Aleutian Islands, rather than the Bering land bridge, may have served as stepping-stones for human migration to North America from Asia. At the advent of the Caucasian invasion from Russia (Vitus Bering recorded seeing the Aleutian Islands in 1741), the Aleut population was estimated to be between 16,000 and 25,000. This number had fallen to 2950 in 1885, and the population is now about 4000.

Japan invaded the Aleutian Islands in June 1942. The islands of Kiska and Attu were occupied by Japanese troops, and Dutch Harbor on Unalaska Island was bombed. On 11 May 1943, the United States invaded Attu Island, where 2351 Japanese and about 500 Americans were killed. Five thousand Japanese troops on Kiska Island escaped in ships before U.S. forces attacked on 15 August 1943.

The Aleutian Islands have been studied by scientists primarily since the end of World War II, beginning in the late 1940s. Oceanographic research was emphasized in the 1970s and 1980s, and volcanoes became the focus for research in the 1990s. Many scientific problems remain to be solved, such as the sources of large earthquakes, geologic history of volcanic eruptions, and maintenance of fisheries. However, research is languishing at the beginning of the new century because of the high cost of working in this challenging environment and the lack of national interest.

Tracy L. Vallier

Further Reading

Morgan, Lael, ed. *The Aleutians,* Vol. 7, No. 3. Anchorage, Alaska: Alaska Geographic Society, 1980.

Plafker, George, and Henry C. Berg, eds. *The Geology of Alaska.* Boulder, Colo.: Geological Society of America, 1994.

Vallier, Tracy L., David W. Scholl, Michael A. Fisher, Terry R. Bruns, Frederic H. Wilson, Roland von Huene, and Andrew J. Stevenson. "Geologic Framework of the Aleutian Arc, Alaska." In George Plafker and Henry C. Berg, eds., *The Geology of Alaska.* The Geology of North America Series, No. G-1. Boulder, Colo.: Geological Society of America, 1994; pp. 367–388.

Related Articles

Aleutian Arc; Bering Sea; Island Arc; Kula Plate; Pacific Ocean; Pacific Plate; Plate Tectonics

Algae

Algae are *marine protists* that are found from polar to tropical waters. They are most abundant at midlatitudes, can be planktonic or grow attached to a hard surface, and absorb gases and nutrients from the water. They are *photosynthetic*, which means that they use sunlight to make their own food and are found wherever light is present. Algae do not have stems, leaves, fruit, true roots, flowers, or seeds.

Some algae have a simple one-celled body called a *thallus*, comprised of a holdfast, stipe, and blade. The shape of the body or thallus may be dependent on the environmental pressures surrounding the algae. The thallus can be in the form of a solid mass, a flat sheet, a branched structure, a long filament, or can be encrusting. The *holdfast* attaches the algae to the substrate but does not take in water or nutrients. The *stipe*, which in some algae can grow to 35 meters (115 feet) in length, resembles a flexible stem and serves to connect the holdfast to the *blade*. Sexual reproduction and photosynthesis occur within the blade. Many algae have gas bladders that help keep them upright in the water.

There are three divisions of macroscopic algae: Chlorophyta (green algae), Ochrophyta (brown algae), and Rhodophyta (red algae). The *green algae*, such as the sea lettuce *Ulva*, are generally found in shallow waters and contain chlorophyll to absorb light. *Brown algae* live in moderate depths and contain chlorophyll plus a brown pigment. Brown algae include various kelp and rockweed and produce *algin*, a substance used in the food industry. The *red algae* can live in the deepest parts of the photic (light) zone and can absorb blue-green light. They are the most numerous and widespread of the large marine algae. Red algae include the *coralline algae*, which are important reef builders because of the calcium carbonate they incorporate into their cell walls. Red algae are also harvested for agar and *carrageenan*, a substance

found in certain foods. Algae play an important role in the marine environment, as providers of food and shelter for other organisms.

Erin O'Donnell

FURTHER READING
Duxbury, Alison B., and Alyn C. Duxbury. *Fundamentals of Oceanography.* Dubuque, Iowa: Brown, 1993; 2nd ed., 1996.
Nybakken, James W. *Marine Biology: An Ecological Approach,* 5th ed. San Francisco: Benjamin Cummings, 2001.
Solomon, Eldra P., Linda R. Berg, Diana W. Martin, and Claude Ville. *Biology.* Philadelphia: Saunders, 1985; 5th ed., Fort Worth, Texas: Saunders, 1999.

RELATED ARTICLES
Chlorophyta; Coralline Algae; Ochrophyta; Rhodophyta

Algal Ridge

Coral reefs are divided into a variety of zones, ranging from the outer reef, which withstands the force of incoming waves, to the inner reef, which is quieter and more secluded. Located in the outer reef, the *algal ridge* is a discrete coral reef zone that results from a combination of physical and biological factors.

Incoming waves crash on the seaward (or windward) side of the outer reef, which rises from the ocean depth to just at or below the surface. Corals located in deeper portions of the outer reef (called the *fore reef*) are massive and round, whereas in the shallower, buttress zones they are sturdy and branching. The highest point of this rising structure is called the *reef crest,* beyond which the reef levels off to the *reef flat.*

The algal ridge is located within the reef crest region and sits at a higher elevation than the reef flat, taking the full force of breaking waves and remaining awash from surf and surge movements. Reaching to within 0.3 meter (1 foot) of the surface, the algal ridge is dominated by calcareous red, or crustose coralline, algae (these are algae that, like reef corals, secrete and deposit calcium carbonate). By laying down a continuous mass of calcium carbonate in their tissues as they grow, these algae create a barrier that is partly responsible (along with other outer reef structures) for the prevention of waves striking adjacent coastlines and resulting in coastal erosion. The major genera of algae responsible for the formation of algal ridges are *Lithothamnion*, *Porolithon*, and *Hydrolithon*. In fact, another name for the algal ridge is *lithothamnion ridge*. Fauna is depauperate on the algal ridge and consists of species that can avoid being damaged or removed by the incoming waves and surf, such as snails, limpets, and sea urchins.

Algal ridges are best developed in coral reefs exposed to strong and persistent wave action, where there is little to no seasonal change in wind direction. In such reefs, algal ridges not only form carbonate constructions that act as buffers but also function as reef builders, cementing the reef constructions in the most stressed zones. Moreover, they compose a major portion of the total algal biomass in these zones, especially in reefs where algal ridges are prominent.

Manoj Shivlani

FURTHER READING
Adey, W. "Algal Ridges of the Caribbean Sea and West Indies." *Phycologia*, Vol. 17 (1978), pp. 361–367.
Nybakken, James W. *Marine Biology: An Ecological Approach*, 5th ed. San Francisco: Benjamin Cummings, 2001.
Sorokin, Y. I. *Coral Reef Ecology*. Berlin and New York: Springer-Verlag, 1993.
Steneck, R., and W. Adey. "The Role of Environment in Control of Morphology in *Lithophyllum congestum*, a Caribbean Algal Ridge Builder." *Botanica Marina*, Vol. 19 (1976), pp. 197–215.
Voss, G. L. *Coral Reefs of Florida*. Sarasota, Fla.: Pineapple Press, 1988.

RELATED ARTICLES
Algae; Coral; Coralline Algae; Coral Reef; Lithothamnion Ridge; Rhodophyta

Algin

Algin or alginic acid is a naturally occurring complex organic compound, a chain-forming polysaccharide composed of a polymer made up of blocks of mannuronic acid and guluronic acid. The various salts of alginic acid are called *alginates*. Because of its strong binding and gelling properties, alginic acid has many uses in the food, drug, cosmetics, and textile industries. Alginic acid occurs in varying amounts in all 1500 species of the brown seaweeds, yet most of the algin produced commercially is isolated from a few species. Brown seaweeds are common in cold waters along continental coasts; in many species, gas-filled bladders (pneumatocysts) keep photosynthetic parts of the seaweed floating on or near the surface of the water.

Alginic acid was first isolated about 1880 in the United Kingdom, a discovery that signaled the beginning of a new era in the use of seaweeds. Algin is found in cell walls and intercellular mucilage and plays an important structural role in the living algae. When the algae is harvested and the alginic acid and alginates extracted, the resulting compounds are used for their stabilizing, thickening, suspending, and film- and gel-forming abilities. Compared to the structural polysaccharides of higher plants, such as celluloses, hemicelluloses, and pectins, alginic acid is unique because it has a strong affinity for water. The hydrophilic (water-loving) nature of algin is what makes it so useful in so many industries.

Alginates are present in most species of brown algae, but they occur in exploitable quantities (30 to 45 percent dry weight) only in the larger kelps and wracks (Laminariales and Fucales). The algae, attached to rocks in intertidal and subtidal areas, is harvested by mechanical harvesters, trawls, grapnel, or by hand. On the west coast of North America, the giant kelp, *Macrocystis pyrifera*, and to a lesser extent,

Nereocystis and *Pelagophycus*, are used; the kelp is harvested from large beds off the coasts of California and Mexico. Some 120,000 tons wet weight of giant kelp are gathered each year using ships called *kelp cutters* that cut and collect the upper parts of the algae. *Macrocystis* is the largest seaweed in the world; the largest attached plant recorded was 65 meters (213 feet) long and the plants are capable of growing at up to 50 centimeters (20 inches) per day. On the east coast, rockweed, *Laminaria*, and *Ascophyllum* are harvested in smaller amounts.

Worldwide, about 22,500 tonnes (25,000 tons) of alginic acid per annum are extracted from seaweed. The main producers are the United States, Scotland, Norway, and China, with smaller amounts being produced in Canada, Japan, Chile, France, and Spain. *Ascophyllum nodosum* and *Laminaria hyperborea* are used in Norway and Scotland. Canada harvests *Ascophyllum* and *Laminaria*, and Japan produces alginates from a variety of Laminariales. A relatively recent addition to the alginate manufacturers is China, which produced about 9000 tonnes (10,000 tons) of alginates in 1994.

Quality and quantity of alginic acid differ according to plant and season. For example, the alginate from *Laminaria hyperborea* forms rigid, brittle gels that can tend to lose water. Alginate from *Macrocystis pyrifera* or *Ascophyllum nodosum* forms elastic gels that can be formed and deformed and still hold onto water. An important quality of algin is its ability to form edible gels by reacting with calcium salts; the rate of gel formation as well as the quality and texture of the gel is controlled by the calcium source. Commercially available alginates dissolve in hot or cold water to produce solutions with a wide range of viscosities or thickness.

Extraction methods of alginic acid vary, and many methods are patented and guarded carefully by industry leaders. An early way to obtain alginic acid was to grind up fresh seaweed and add dilute hydrochloric acid to remove soluble mineral salts. The alginic okacid was then extracted by a solution of sodium carbonate or soda ash, filtration, and precipitation by more acid. The crude pulp was shredded again and washed with treated water, with the fibrous material dried and sold as crude sodium alginate. Purer product was made by further filtration and precipitation and the addition of bleach and additional dilute hydrochloric acid. The alginic acid can be filtered and stored or converted into a salt by treatment with carbonate, oxide, or hydroxide.

Algin's gel forming, thickening/water holding, emulsifying, stabilization/binding, and film-forming properties have many uses, particularly in the food, industrial, and pharmaceutical fields. Algin is used in molding materials; cosmetics; soups; dental and food technology; bakery and candy products; dairy products; the pharmaceutical industry; and in fish, meat, sausage, and beverage processing. Algin is also used in a wide range of industrial products, including dyes, paints, and other coatings; paper and cardboard production; filters and adsorbents; textile production; pesticides, polishes, and lubricants; fire retardants and extinguishers; enameling and ceramics; and other applications.

Julia Copple Davenport

FURTHER READING
Chapman, V. J. *Seaweeds and Their Uses.* London: Methuen, 1950; 3rd ed., London: Chapman and Hall/ New York: Chapman and Hall in association with Methuen, 1980.
Graham, L. E., and L. W. Wilcox. *Algae.* Upper Saddle River, N.J.: Prentice Hall, 2000.
Lobban, C. S., and M. J. Wynne. *The Biology of Seaweeds.* Berkeley: University of California Press, 1981.
Prescott, G. W. *The Algae: A Review.* Boston: Houghton Mifflin, 1968.

RELATED ARTICLES
Kelp Forest; Ochrophyta; Pneumatocyst

Alpha Ridge

Located in the Canadian Basin of the Arctic Ocean, Alpha Ridge is an ocean plateau that extends toward Siberia from the northern Canadian margin. Originating near northwestern Ellesmere Island (84°N, 90°W), the ridge meets Mendeleev Ridge, which extends from the Siberian margin, at Cooperation Trough (84°N, 170°W). Together, the Alpha and Mendeleev Ridges form a composite ridge roughly parallel to Lomonosov Ridge, which is located near the North Pole. The ridge separates the Amundsen Abyssal Plain (also known as Siberia Abyssal Plain) on its north side from the Canada Abyssal Plain to its south. Approximately 900 kilometers (560 miles) in length by 280 to 390 kilometers (174 to 242 miles) in width, the Alpha Ridge consists of ridges and troughs oriented roughly parallel to its axis. Summit depths reach 1100 to 2000 meters (3600 to 6600 feet).

Alpha Ridge was first recognized as a distinct feature from echo soundings made by U.S. scientists operating from ice station Alpha during the International Geophysical Year (1957–58). Like other geologic features of the Arctic Basin, Alpha Ridge is poorly mapped, owing to its remoteness and Arctic Ocean ice cover, which make geophysical surveying difficult. As a consequence, the tectonic history of Alpha Ridge is uncertain, making it perhaps the largest ocean feature whose origin is unknown. Scientists have suggested that it formed during the Late Cretaceous (approximately 97 million to 65 million years ago) as a rifted continental fragment, a subsided piece of continental crust, an island arc complex, or a hotspot volcanic track. The latter is perhaps the most accepted explanation.

William W. Sager

FURTHER READING

"Arctic Ocean Floor" (chart). Washington, D.C.: National Geographic Society, 1971.

Perry, R. K., and H. S. Fleming. "Bathymetry of the Arctic Ocean" (chart). In A. Grantz, L. Johnson, and J. F. Sweeney, eds., *The Arctic Ocean Region: Decade of North American Geology*, Vol. L. Boulder, Colo.: Geological Society of America, 1990.

Wheeler, J. R., and J. F. Sweeney. "Ridges and Basins in the Central Arctic Ocean." In A. Grantz, L. Johnson, and J. F. Sweeney, eds., *The Arctic Ocean Region: Decade of North American Geology*, Vol. L. Boulder, Colo.: Geological Society of America, 1990; pp. 305–336.

RELATED ARTICLES

Arctic Ocean; Continental Margin; Hotspot, Lomonosov Ridge; Ocean Plateau; Volcanic Ridge

Alvin

Alvin, a deep-sea submersible operated by Woods Hole Oceanographic Institution (WHOI), is—by many criteria—the most successful piloted submersible in oceanographic history. The original *Alvin* was completed in 1964 to meet the request by WHOI researchers for a highly maneuverable, deep-diving vehicle. "Alvin" is a contraction of Allyn Vine (1914–94), the key WHOI scientist behind the submersible's creation. The submersible began life based on a steel personnel sphere 1.9 meters (6.2 feet) in diameter with a 1829-meter (6000-foot) depth capability. The three-person crew could look out through viewing ports, operate cameras, take samples, and maneuver the craft with thrusters mounted on the assembly that enclosed the sphere.

In 1966, *Alvin* located and helped recover a hydrogen bomb lost in the Mediterranean off Palomares, Spain. In 1968, during a launch, *Alvin* accidentally sank in 1524 meters (5000 feet) of water. It was recovered 10 months later, repaired, and became operational again in 1971. In 1973, *Alvin*'s original steel hull was replaced with a titanium hull, doubling its operating depth to 3658 meters (12,000 feet), close to the average depth of the world's oceans. During the submersible's remarkable career, *Alvin* crews have discovered the hydrothermal vent communities on the Galápagos Rift (1977) and explored the wreck of the RMS *Titanic* (1986).

Deep-sea submersible Alvin. *(© Woods Hole Oceanographic Institution)*

Alvin is refurbished and updated every three years. None of the original *Alvin* remains; all parts have been replaced and upgraded at least once, and in most cases, many times. In 1994, *Alvin*'s depth rating was increased to 4500 meters (14,764 feet). *Alvin* is currently used mainly for geophysical, biological, and geochemical investigations. Dives—usually with one pilot and two scientific observers—typically last 6 to 10 hours. *Alvin* can be customized for various operating configurations. As of December 2000, *Alvin*—in its various incarnations—had completed more than 3500 dives.

Trevor Day

FURTHER READING

Ballard, Robert D., and Will Hively. *The Eternal Darkness: A Personal History of Deep-Sea Exploration.* Princeton, N.J.: Princeton University Press, 2000.

Kaharal, Victoria A. *Water Baby: The Story of Alvin.* New York: Oxford University Press, 1990.

USEFUL WEB SITES

"Deep Submergence Vehicle ALVIN." <http://www.whoi.edu/marops/>.

"Voyage to the Deep." <http://www.ocean.udel.edu/deepsea/home/home.html>.

RELATED ARTICLES

Bathyscaphe; Deep-Sea Exploration; Deep-Sea Vent Water, Chemistry of; Galapágos Spreading Center; Hydrothermal Vent; Submersible

Amazon Fan

The Amazon Fan is a large fan-shaped deposit of sediment that lies seaward of the mouth of the Amazon River in the western Atlantic Ocean near the equator; it is one of the largest modern deep-sea fans in the world. The fan extends 700 kilometers (435 miles) beyond the continental shelf break and spreads out radially. The fan becomes wider as it progresses seaward over the outer part of the continental margin and grades into the Demerara Abyssal Plain. The Amazon Fan covers a seafloor area of about 330,000 square kilometers (127,000 square miles). The sediments of the Amazon Fan are more than 5 kilometers (3 miles) thick in places.

The Amazon River is the world's largest river; it discharges about 20 percent of all fresh water that reaches the oceans. The Amazon River and its tributaries drain this large volume of water from northern South America. As the rivers flow through the continent, they pick up huge quantities of land-derived (or terrigenous) sediment and transport it off the continent and into the Atlantic Ocean, often in turbidity currents. When the suspended sediment settles, it is deposited onto the seafloor.

The Amazon Fan began to develop in the early Miocene (about 23 million years ago) after the Andes Mountains were formed. Rates of sediment deposition and where sediments are deposited have varied considerably over time. For example, in the twenty-first century, sediments are being deposited on the shelf. When sea level was lower 18,000 years ago, sediments traveled farther seaward and were deposited on the fan. At times in the past, sedimentation rates have been as high as 20 to 25 meters (66 to 82 feet) per 1000 years in some locations on the fan. Since the fan first began forming millions of years ago, the Amazon River has deposited vast amounts of sediment in layers that when studied sequentially, reveal information about Earth's history. Scientists studied sediment cores taken from the Amazon Fan as part of the Ocean Drilling Program to understand such things as climate change, fan growth, glaciation, sea-level fluctuation, and variations in Earth's magnetic field.

Lynn L. Lauerman

FURTHER READING
ODP Leg 155 Scientific Party. "Drilling the Fantastic Amazon Fan." *Geotimes*, January 1995.
Rimington, Nicola, Adrian Cramp, and Andrew Morton. "Amazon Fan Sands: Implications for Provenance." *Marine and Petroleum Geology*, Vol. 17 (2000), pp. 267–284.

RELATED ARTICLES
Abyssal Plain; Atlantic Ocean; Continental Shelf; Deep-Sea Stratigraphy; Ocean Drilling Program; Submarine Fan; Turbidity Current

Amundsen, Roald
1872–1928
Norwegian Polar Explorer

Although Roald Engebreth Gravning Amundsen is most famous for his bold exploits as an explorer and adventurer, he will also be remembered for his significant contributions to the scientific study of some of the most remote and inaccessible places on Earth.

As a young boy growing up in a family of merchant sea captains and prosperous shipowners, Roald Amundsen dreamed of exploring the little-known lands and waters of the north polar basin. Born on 16 July 1872 in Borge, southeast of Oslo, Norway, he set his sights early in his youth on being the first person to reach the North Pole. Although he was eventually beaten to that goal in 1909 by an American, Robert Peary (1856–1920), Amundsen nevertheless managed to achieve a number of polar firsts. He was the first person to navigate a vessel through Canada's Northwest Passage, the first to lead a successful expedition across Antarctica to the South Pole, and probably the first to fly over the North Pole in an airplane.

Aside from an early foray into the study of medicine, Amundsen carefully planned from his youth for a life of polar exploration. He tried to inure his body to conditions of harsh cold by sleeping with the windows open, even in the winter, and he devoured the existing literature on polar exploration to familiarize himself with the successes and failures of those who went before him. Amundsen also realized that if he were ever to succeed at probing the treacherous and unfamiliar Arctic seas, he would have to become an accomplished sailor. His first major test as a sailor came as first mate aboard Adrien de Gerlache's 1899 *Belgica* expedition to Antarctica. After spending the winter in frozen isolation, and after the *Belgica*'s captain and most of its crew fell ill of scurvy, Amundsen took command and eventually sailed the ship to safety.

In 1903, Amundsen led his own Arctic expedition to navigate a northwest passage through the Arctic islands of Canada's far north. In June, Amundsen and his crew of six set out from Oslo in a 48-tonne, 22-meter (47-ton, 72-foot) sloop called the *Gjøa*. The arduous trek took three years to complete, as the expedition waited while the icy seas thawed enough to allow for navigation. Toward the end of the summer, the group found a natural harbor on King William Island. There they established an outpost and began studies to establish the position of the North Magnetic Pole. By August 1905, Amundsen's team had completed their scientific studies and cleared the icy waters of the passage. The *Gjøa* had navigated the northwest passage successfully, the first time the feat had ever been recorded.

Soon after his return to Norway, Amundsen began the long process of preparing for his next expedition, to explore the north polar basin further and to drift across the North Pole in a ship frozen into the Arctic sea ice. His countryman and fellow adventurer and scientist, Fridtjof Nansen (1861–1930), had made just such an attempt some years earlier in his ship, the *Fram*, and although he had been unsuccessful, Nansen willingly allowed Amundsen to borrow the still-seaworthy vessel to try his hand at the task. But the plan was altered quickly and boldly when news of Peary's accomplishment reached Amundsen. His new idea was to sail instead for Antarctica and then head overland to reach the South Pole. The Englishman Robert Falcon Scott (1868–1912) and his team had already set out with the same goal in mind, and Amundsen intended to beat them. When the expedition left Norway in August 1910, only Amundsen and a few of the ship's crew knew their true destination.

The expedition sailed to the Madeira Islands, supposedly for the purpose of oceanographic research, and then south to the Bay of Whales on the Ross Sea coast of Antarctica, where the *Fram* dropped anchor in January 1911. Not only was

the base he set up there 100 kilometers (62 miles) closer to the pole than Scott's base at Cape Evans, but it was also rich in animal life and was an ideal location at which to investigate south polar weather. Amundsen prepared carefully for the coming journey, making a preliminary trip to deposit food supplies along the first part of his route to the pole and back. To transport his supplies, he used sled dogs, which would prove to be key to his success.

On 20 October 1911, after months of preparation, Amundsen and four companions set off with four light sledges, each pulled by 13 dogs. Although the first stages of the journey were relatively easy, the Axel Heiberg Glacier posed a formidable barrier to the last leg of the journey across the polar plateau. However, on 14

Roald Amundsen. (From the collections of the Library of Congress)

December 1911, Amundsen and his men finally reached the South Pole and raised the Norwegian flag in triumph. The explorers finished recording scientific data at the pole before beginning the return journey on 17 December, and on 25 January 1912, they safely reached their base at the Bay of Whales after a round-trip journey of nearly 3000 kilometers (1870 miles). In the meantime, Scott had reached the South Pole on 17 January, but neither he nor any of the men who accompanied him survived the return journey.

Amundsen's victory in the race for the South Pole only whetted his appetite for new goals. In June 1918, the *Maud* expedition, outfitted with apparatus for oceanographic, meteorological, and geomagnetic measurements, set out to drift around the Arctic Basin, but never went farther north over the pole. Although the *Maud* expedition had failed to attain its geographic goal, the geophysical data it compiled made it one of the most important research projects ever carried out in the Arctic.

Amundsen received much acclaim for his previous exploits; however, his next endeavor—to fly over the North Pole—generated little interest from investors. He did eventually win financing from an American, Lincoln Ellsworth (1880–1951), and after an unsuccessful initial attempt, on 11 May 1926, he left Spitsbergen with Ellsworth aboard the dirigible *Norge*, along with Umberto Nobile (1885–1978), an Italian aviator who had constructed and flew the airship, and a crew of 12. They reached the North Pole in only 16 hours, and on 14 May, landed in Alaska.

Two years later, Amundsen undertook one last adventure. In May 1928, Nobile's new airship, *Italia*, crashed in the Arctic. Amundsen volunteered to take part in a rescue attempt, and on 18 June he was one of six men who left Norway by plane in search of the downed aircraft. Although Nobile and his crew were eventually rescued on 22 June, Amundsen's plane was never heard from again.

Amundsen's expeditions helped chart the frigid waters around both the north and south polar regions, amassing much useful data on polar weather patterns and ocean currents. He also helped establish the position of the North Magnetic Pole, and the measurements his expeditions collected on terrestrial magnetism in general were so extensive that it took experts until 1929, a year after Amundsen's death, to analyze them completely.

As formidable as Amundsen's achievements were, both as sheer feats of discovery and as contributions to the study of polar oceanography, climate, and geomagnetism, he never stopped searching for new and more ambitious goals. He may have been the first person to stand at the South Pole, but Roald Amundsen would forever be looking north.

Kenneth Meiklejohn

BIOGRAPHY

- Roald Engebreth Gravning Amundsen.
- Born on 16 July 1872 in Borge, Norway.
- First mate on the *Belgica* expedition off the coast of Antarctica, 1896–99.
- Navigated the Canadian Northwest Passage and plotted the location of the North Magnetic Pole, 1903–06.
- He led the voyage of the *Fram* to Antarctica, 1909–12, and on 14 December 1911, became the first person to reach the South Pole.
- Led the *Maud* expedition to the Arctic, 1918–25.
- In 1926, he flew over the North Pole.
- Died in June 1928.

SELECTED WRITINGS

Amundsen, Roald. *The Northwest Passage: Being the Record of a Voyage of Exploration of the Ship* Gjöa, *1903–1907*. London: Constable, 1908.

———. *The South Pole: An Account of the Norwegian Antarctic Expedition in the* Fram, *1910–1912*. Translated from the Norwegian by A. G. Chater. London: Murray, 1912; New York: Barnes and Noble, 1976.

Amundsen, Roald, and Lincoln Ellsworth. *The First Flight across the Polar Sea*. London: Hutchinson, 1927.

FURTHER READING

Bramwell, Martyn. *Polar Exploration: Journeys to the Arctic and Antarctic.* New York: Dorling Kindersley, 1998.

Decleir, Hugo, ed. *Roald Amundsen's* Belgica *Diary: The First Scientific Expedition to the Antarctic.* Bluntisham, England: Bluntisham Books, 1999.

Huntford, Roland. *Scott and Amundsen.* London: Hodder and Stoughton, 1979.

RELATED ARTICLES
Fram; Nansen, Fridtjof

Amundsen Sea

The Amundsen Sea is a marginal West Antarctic sea between Thurston Island (72°04'S, 99°00'W) and Cape Dart (73°04'S, 126°12'W). Its northern limit (hence its size) has no natural (topographic or bathymetric) definition. The sea was explored and named in 1929 by Norwegian Nils Larsen after Roald Amundsen (1872–1928), a Norwegian explorer who was a mate aboard the *Belgica*, the first ship to winter in Antarctica (1898–99).

Until the 1990s, the sea remained poorly studied, and its coastline inaccessible, because of perennial sea ice, which grew older and thicker than elsewhere around Antarctica. Since 1988, the sea ice cover decreased, exposing much of the shelf and coastline. The southernmost Amundsen Sea was not explored until 1994, when research vessel *Nathaniel B. Palmer* reached the calving front of the Pine Island Glacier at 75°S, 102°W. The summertime surface temperature varies from near freezing [below -1.5°C (29°F)] up to 3°C (37°F) above freezing, whereas the surface salinity ranges from 33.2 to 33.9 practical salinity units (psu). The Antarctic Slope Front is observed along the outer shelf and north of the shelf break, manifested mainly beneath the surface mixed layer. The net flow south of the front is presumed to be westward; direct observations are very scant. The circulation is poorly known; a cyclonic (clockwise) gyre and associated upwelling were observed in Pine Island Bay, at the southern extreme of the sea. The Amundsen Sea shelf is deep [400 to 600 meters (about 1300 to 2000 feet)]. Therefore, the nearly undiluted, warm, and salty Circumpolar Deep Water (temperature > +1°C, salinity > 34.7 psu) floods the shelf and causes rapid basal melting [9 to 15 meters (about 30 to 50 feet) per year] of the floating portions of glaciers [e.g., the Pine Island Glacier, which drains 200,000 square kilometers (about 77,000 square miles) of the West Antarctic Ice Sheet]. This high melt rate could lead to a relatively rapid disintegration of the West Antarctic Ice Sheet.

Igor M. Belkin

FURTHER READING

Alley, R. B., and R. A. Bindschadler, eds. *The West Antarctic Ice Sheet: Behavior and Environment.* Washington, D.C.: American Geophysical Union, 2001.

Jacobs, S. S., and R. F. Weiss, eds. *Ocean, Ice, and Atmosphere: Interactions at the Antarctic Continental Margin.* Washington, D.C.: American Geophysical Union, 1998.

Jeffries, M. O., ed. *Antarctic Sea Ice: Physical Processes, Interactions and Variability.* Washington, D.C.: American Geophysical Union, 1998.

RELATED ARTICLES
Gyre; Salinity; Upwelling

Anchor Ice

Sea ice, ice that is formed by the freezing of seawater, is found in polar and subpolar areas of the ocean. *Anchor ice* is a type of sea ice that forms on the seafloor around any convenient nucleus (such as rocks, gravel, and slow-moving or sessile benthic animals) in the area below the permanent ice layer. Anchor ice has been best studied and described in McMurdo Sound, Antarctica, although researchers have also found anchor ice in the Arctic along the Bering Sea coast of Alaska.

Anchor ice plays an important role in shaping the benthic ecosystem at McMurdo Sound. Anchor ice forms along the seafloor as jagged platelike crystalline sheets, and as the sheets grow they entrain organisms and substrate. Eventually, sheets of anchor ice grow large and buoyant. When pieces break free, they float upward to the sea ice above, carrying benthic material with them. Anchor ice also acts as a physical disturbance that creates a distinct vertical zonation pattern in McMurdo Sound. In this area, anchor ice almost completely covers the seafloor shallower than 15 meters (49 feet). Few organisms live in this zone, where the ice scours the substrate and freezes animals caught during ice formation. However, mobile animals can enter this zone during ice-free periods. Between 15 and 33 meters (49 and 108 feet), anchor ice is present but does not cover the seafloor, and cnidarians and other sessile fauna are abundant. A diverse invertebrate fauna that is dominated by sponges inhabits the seafloor deeper than 33 meters (108 feet), where anchor ice does not form.

Lynn L. Lauerman

FURTHER READING
Nybakken, James W. *Marine Biology: An Ecological Approach*, 5th ed. San Francisco: Benjamin Cummings, 2001.
Untersteiner, Norbert, ed. *The Geophysics of Sea Ice*. New York: Plenum Press, 1986.

RELATED ARTICLES
Antarctica; Arctic Ocean; Benthos; Southern Ocean

Anchoveta

The anchoveta, or Peruvian anchovy (*Engraulis ringens*), is one of about 140 species of clupeomorph fishes belonging to the family Engraulidae. It grows to about 20 centimeters (approximately 8 inches) in length. Its snout is pointed and its body rounded. It is found in the eastern South Pacific Ocean, from about latitude 6°S, off northern Peru, to about 42.5°S, which is the latitude of Chiloé, Chile.

Anchoveta live in coastal waters. They are sometimes found up to 160 kilometers (approximately 100 miles) from land, but most occur no more than 80 kilometers (approximately 50 miles) from the shore. Anchoveta breed at all times of year, but with peak spawnings in winter and spring. This species forms huge schools that feed near the surface at night and descend up to 50 meters (approximately 164 feet) below the surface by day. They are filter feeders, feeding on plankton, especially diatoms, copepods, krill, and the eggs of other fishes. The plankton is sustained by nutrients brought close to the surface by upwelling in the Peru Current. Consequently, anchoveta are wholly dependent on this upwelling.

Commercially, anchoveta are the most heavily exploited fish in the history of the world. They are caught by purse seining when the fish are about five or six months old and about 8 centimeters (approximately 3 inches) long. Most of the catch is used to make fishmeal. In 1971 the catch, mainly by the Peruvian fleet, amounted to more than 13 million tonnes (14 million tons), but the stock was being overfished. When an El Niño suppressed cold upwelling in 1972, this, combined with overfishing, reduced the catch to about 2 million tonnes (2.2 million tons) in 1973. Following a partial recovery, the 1982–83 El Niño reduced the catch even more, to only 94,000 tonnes (103,400 tons) in 1984. Stocks recovered further during the 1990s, with a peak catch of 12.5 million tonnes (13.8 million tons) in 1995. The anchoveta fishery is now regulated by the Peruvian and Chilean governments. This helps to prevent overfishing, but the U.N. Food and Agriculture Organization nevertheless classifies the anchoveta as an overexploited, although recovering, species.

The size of the catch continues to plummet in years when there is a strong El Niño. In 1997, for example, the combined Peruvian and Chilean anchoveta catch amounted to 7.69 million tonnes (8.48 million tons). A very strong El Niño began in 1997 and continued through 1998, reducing the catch in that year to 1.73 million tonnes (1.90 million tons). The El Niño ended abruptly in 1998. Stocks recovered rapidly, and the 1999 catch was 8.72 million tonnes (9.61 million tons). Such varied and currently unpredictable fluctuations make the livelihoods of South American fishing communities highly precarious, but they are not threatened with economic extinction. Given the sensible management that has allowed stocks to recover thus far, it seems likely that the anchoveta fishery will continue, albeit with years of abundance alternating with years of hardship.

It is not only the South American fishing boats that depend on the anchoveta. Like any abundant species, anchoveta is a key resource for an entire ecosystem. Anchovetas are hunted by large fishes such as the black marlin (*Makaira indica*) and the spectacular swordfish (*Xiphius gladius*), and by a wide array of smaller, pelagic species, such as skipjack tuna (*Euthynnus pelamis*). South American sea lions (*Otaria flavescens*) and several species of seabirds also feed on anchovetas.

Fluctuations in the anchoveta population have widespread ramifications on the ecosystems in which they live. When the anchovetas are numerous, bigger fishes, sea lions, and seabirds thrive, and guano—a valuable fertilizer that has been mined since the late nineteenth century—is deposited. When the anchovies disappear, the predator populations decline and so less guano is produced.

Michael Allaby

FURTHER READING
Moyle, Peter B., and Joseph J. Cech. *Fishes: An Introduction to Ichthyology*, 4th ed. Upper Saddle River, N.J.: Prentice Hall, 2000.
Nybakken, James W. *Marine Biology: An Ecological Approach*, 5th ed. San Francisco: Benjamin Cummings, 2001.

USEFUL WEB SITES
FAO. *Fisheries Circular 920 FIRM/C920*. Rome: c. <http://www.fao.org/docrep/003/w4248e/w4248e30.htm>.

RELATED ARTICLES
Clupeomorpha; Fisheries; Peru Current; Teleostei; Upwelling

Andaman Sea

The Andaman Sea is a marginal sea in the northeast Indian Ocean, located between the Malay Peninsula, Sumatra, and Andaman and Nicobar Islands. It extends from 5 to 17°N and from 92 to 99°E. Its area is 798,000 square kilometers (308,000 square miles). The bottom relief features flat, broad shelves in the east and north that drop off abruptly, especially the eastern shelf, down to 2000 meters (6562 feet), toward several deep subbasins [4180 meters (13,714 feet), maximum depth]. This is the only semienclosed sea in the Indian Ocean that contains deep depressions where the sea is connected to the ocean by relatively shallow straits.

The Andaman Sea climate and oceanography are monsoon-driven. Tropical postmonsoon cyclones bring very heavy rains, especially on the west coast of the Malay Peninsula [up to 400 centimeters (157 inches) per year]. Two major rivers, the Irrawaddy and Salween, together discharge 544 billion tonnes (600 billion tons) per year to the Gulf of Martaban (with a sharp runoff peak during the summer monsoon, June to August, when 90 percent of the annual runoff takes place), bringing the surface salinity there down to 20 practical salinity units (psu), while the rest of the sea has a surface salinity of 32 to 34 psu. The surface temperature is more uniform spatially and throughout the year, ranging between 27 and 30°C (80.6 to 86°F). Both rivers also carry an enormous amount of sediments [Irrawaddy alone, 234 million tonnes (260 million tons per year)]. The surface circulation pattern reverses with monsoons: The main summertime counterclockwise gyre centered at 10°N, 95°W becomes counterclockwise in winter. The strong and persistent monsoon winds also cause coastal upwelling, especially west of the Malay Peninsula, thus creating rich fishery grounds. The mean current from the South China Sea through the shallow Malacca Strait is toward the northwest; its average speed is 50 centimeters per second (98 feet per minute). Tides are important: The tidal range off Myanmar is 2 to 2.5 meters (6.6 to 8.2 feet), reaching 6 meters (20 feet) in the Gulf of Martaban.

Igor M. Belkin

FURTHER READING:

Shetye, S., and A. D. Gouveia. "Coastal Circulation in the North Indian Ocean." In A. R. Robinson and K. H. Brink, eds., *The Sea*, Vol. 11. New York: Wiley, 1998; pp. 523–556.

Varkey, M. J., V. S. N. Murty, and A. Suryanarayana. "Physical Oceanography of the Bay of Bengal and Andaman Sea." *Oceanography and Marine Biology: Annual Review*, Vol. 34 (1996), pp. 1–70.

RELATED ARTICLES

Bay of Bengal; Indian Ocean; Monsoon; Ocean Current; Salinity; Tide; Upwelling

Annelida

The phylum Annelida comprises approximately 15,000 described species of bilaterally symmetrical, tubular segmented worms. Members of this diverse group, which includes marine worms, earthworms, and leeches, can be found in marine, freshwater, and terrestrial environments. *Annelida* means "ringed," and the most distinguishing annelid feature is segmentation, the repetition of body parts. In the general annelid body plan, the *coelom* (the fluid-filled, mesoderm-lined cavity between the body wall and digestive tract) is divided into segments by partitions called *septa*, and branches of the circulatory, excretory,

and nervous systems are found in each segment. The complete digestive tract (i.e., mouth and anus) and some of the nerves, however, run the length of the body.

Other annelid characteristics include a closed circulatory system and respiration through skin or gills. Externally, the segments of many annelids bear paired bundles of *setae* (bristles) that are used for traction during movement. The phylum is subdivided into three classes.

The class *Polychaeta* comprises mainly marine worms (e.g., sand worms, tube worms, and clam worms) that can be found from the intertidal zone to extreme depths. A few species inhabit brackish or fresh water, or are parasitic. Polychaetes represent the most successful annelid group. The class contains most of the living annelid species (approximately 10,000). The name of the class refers to the many setae that adorn the paired *parapodia* (fleshy paddle-shaped appendages) found on the segments. Parapodia can be used for locomotion and for gas exchange. Most polychaetes have a well-developed head bearing sensory organs (e.g., eyes, antennae, palps, and tentacles). Some species have a foregut modified into a jaw-bearing eversible pharynx. Polychaetes generally have separate sexes, simple reproductive structures, and a free-swimming trochophore larva (similar to that found in mollusks).

The class is extremely diverse and is divided into 25 orders and 87 families. The general polychaete body plan can be highly modified within different groups to match differing lifestyles. Polychaetes can be predators, detritivores, or suspension feeders. Some polychaetes are *errant* (free swimming) and others are sedentary. Some species are pelagic and swim in the water column, others roam the surface of the seabed, some live between sand grains, and others live in tubes. Most polychaetes are less than 10 centimeters (3.9 inches) long but range from less than 1 millimeter to 3 meters (0.04 to 118.1 inches) long.

Members of the class *Oligochaeta*, which includes the earthworms, exhibit external segmentation. Oligochaetes lack a well-developed head and parapodia, and they have few setae (*oligochaete* means "few bristles"); those setae that are present are used for locomotion. The digestive tract in oligochaetes is adapted to handle decaying organic material. Oligochaetes are *hermaphroditic* (individual worms have both male and female gonads) and exhibit cross fertilization. Fertilization of eggs and direct development occur within a cocoon secreted by the *clitellum* (the swollen ring of glandular epidermis visible on the external surface of the worm). Of the approximately 3100 species of oligochaetes, most are terrestrial or live in fresh water; only about 200 marine species are known. They range in length from 0.5 millimeters to more than 3 meters (0.02 to 118.1 inches). Oligochaetes probably evolved from ancestral annelids independent of the polychaetes.

The leeches, which comprise the class *Hirudinae*, probably evolved from the oligochaetes. Like oligochaetes, leeches are hermaphroditic and have a clitellum. They have a reduced coelom and lack appendages, setae, and septa. Leeches appear to be segmented externally because of wrinkles that allow the animal to expand when feeding, but true segmentation is found only internally. Leeches possess muscular anterior and posterior suckers. About three-fourths of the approximately 500 species of leeches are *ectoparasites* (they live on, but outside, the host's body) adapted for sucking blood and tissue fluids from their hosts. The remainder of leech species are free-living predators and scavengers. Leeches are most abundant in fresh water, but some species are found in the sea and in moist terrestrial environments. They range in length from 1 to 25 centimeters (0.4 to 9.8 inches).

Lynn L. Lauerman

Worm on a sea fan. (© Jeffrey L. Rotman/Corbis)

FURTHER READING

Barnes, Robert D. *Invertebrate Zoology*. Philadelphia: Saunders, 1963; 6th ed., by Edward Ruppert, Fort Worth, Texas: Saunders, 1994.

Brinkhurst, Ralph O. *British and Other Marine and Estuarine Oligochaetes: Keys and Notes for the Identification of the Species*. Cambridge: Cambridge University Press, 1982.

Fauchald, Kristian. *The Polychaete Worms: Definitions and Keys to the Orders, Families and Genera*. Los Angeles: Natural History Museum of Los Angeles County, in conjunction with the Allan Hancock Foundation, University of Southern California, 1977.

Mann, Kenneth H. *Leeches (Hirudinae): Their Structure, Physiology, Ecology, and Embryology*. New York: Pergamon Press, 1962.

RELATED ARTICLES
Polychaeta

Anoxia

Anoxia is a condition in which an entity (e.g., animal tissue, seawater, or sediment) is completely lacking in molecular oxygen. This occurs in the ocean when oxygen consumption exceeds supply. Oxygen is required to sustain respiration in most life forms, but it is not distributed uniformly in seawater or in sediments. Vertical profiles (samples done at different depths) often show oxygen depletion to near-zero levels in certain layers.

In the open ocean, oxygen levels can approach zero in the oxygen minimum zone at depths from 500 to 1000 meters (1640 to 3300 feet). This low-oxygen zone occurs because organisms consume available oxygen, which is not replenished. There are a few reports of true anoxia occurring in the oxygen minimum zone off the coast of Peru, but even in the large oxygen minimum zone off the coast of Central America, the oxygen concentration is not truly zero.

In some locales (usually enclosed basins with shallow sills), stratification of water masses due to physical properties of water can lead to anoxia. When dissolved oxygen is consumed completely, microbial processes reduce dissolved sulfate in sea salt to produce hydrogen sulfide. Thus, most anoxic waters smell of rotten eggs. For example, the Black Sea's deep water is anoxic, because a halocline (salinity gradient) prevents oxygen-rich surface water from mixing with deeper water, and no dissolved oxygen exists below about 100 meters (330 feet). In the Cariaco Trench off Venezuela, a sharp thermocline (temperature gradient) prevents mixing; the trench is anoxic below 350 meters (1148 feet). Other examples of anoxic basins include some Norwegian and Canadian fjords and deep basins within the Baltic Sea. Recently, anoxic bottom waters have been found in the Gulf of Mexico west of the Mississippi River Delta, and the Santa Barbara Basin off California is nearly anoxic.

Anoxia in sediments occurs when there is limited or no exchange of the interstitial water between sediment grains. Diffusion of oxygen from overlying waters is inadequate to support the chemical oxidation processes involving organic matter and chemically reduced minerals. In many locales, only the uppermost sediment layer receives oxygen from the overlying water, leaving deeper layers anoxic (also called *anaerobic*). Marine organisms that inhabit environments where anoxia occurs have developed morphological, physiological, and behavioral adaptations to obtain enough oxygen when it is in short supply or to withstand limited periods of anoxia. Some species of bacteria function in the complete absence of oxygen.

Lynn L. Lauerman

FURTHER READING

Millero, Frank J. *Chemical Oceanography*. Boca Raton, Fla.: CRC Press, 1992; 2nd ed., 1996.

Pickard, George L., and William J. Emery. *Descriptive Physical Oceanography: An Introduction*. Oxford and New York: Pergamon Press, 1964; 5th ed., 1990.

RELATED ARTICLES
Black Sea; Oxygen; Oxygen Minimum Zone

Anoxic Basin

Anoxia is defined as the condition where no dissolved oxygen is available. This condition results when the consumption rate of oxygen exceeds the oxygen supply. In the photic zone this typically occurs when the oxidation of organic matter by bacteria exceeds the oxygen supply from the atmosphere. Below the photic zone, oxygen supply is dependent on diffusion and advection. Anoxic basins are typically enclosed basins where physical barriers and density stratification limits the advection of oxygen-rich surface water to deep waters. Runoff waters polluted with nutrient-rich fertilizers can also cause anoxia. Some well-studied anoxic basins include the Black Sea, the Baltic Sea, the Framvaren Fjord, and the Cariaco Trench.

There are two major types of anoxic basins. The most common type of anoxic basin occurs due to a strong salinity gradient or halocline. This is usually the result of a net outflow of low-salinity water from an estuary. The halocline creates a density stratification that prevents the mixing of low-saline oxic waters with high-salinity deep waters. This type of anoxic basin includes the Black and Baltic Seas, as well as many fjords, such as the Framvaren Fjord in Norway. In fjord-type basins, a physical barrier (shallow sill) prevents salty oxygen-rich seawater from entering the basin and sinking to the bottom.

The other major type of anoxic basin occurs due to a strong temperature gradient or thermocline. The thermocline also creates a density gradient, thus preventing the mixing of oxygen-rich surface waters with oxygen-poor deep waters. An example of this type of basin is the Cariaco Trench off the coast of Venezuela. This deep trench is isohaline and isothermal below 350 meters (1148 feet) and permanently anoxic from this depth to the seafloor.

Pollution from nutrient-rich fertilizers can also lead to anoxic conditions. Runoff carries these nutrients to the ocean, where productivity is stimulated. In order to respire (decompose or degrade) increased levels of organic matter, bacteria use up all available oxygen and cause the basin to become anoxic. This has happened recently in the Baltic Sea and Chesapeake Bay.

The biogeochemical cycles of oxygen, carbon, nitrogen, phosphorus, and sulfur are linked because they are all involved in the photosynthesis and respiration of organic matter in fixed stoichiometric ratios. In the presence of oxygen, organic matter is decomposed, with oxygen acting as the electron receptor. This is called *aerobic respiration*. In the absence of oxygen, *anaerobic respiration* takes place. During anaerobic respiration, organic matter is decomposed, with nitrate ion (NO_3^-) acting as the electron receptor. After all the nitrate ion is used up, sulfate ion (SO_4^{2-}) acts as the electron receptor. A product of this decomposition reaction is hydrogen sulfide (H_2S). As a result of this reaction, the bottom waters of most anoxic basins contain highly elevated concentrations of hydrogen sulfide. This gas is toxic to marine life; as a consequence, deep waters in anoxic basins contain little or no marine life other than anaerobic bacteria.

Daniel Schuller

FURTHER READING
Millero, F. *Chemical Oceanography.* Boca Raton, Fla.: CRC Press, 1996; pp. 389–420.
Open University Course Team. *Seawater: Its Composition, Properties, and Behavior.* Oxford: Pergamon Press/Milton Keynes, England: Open University, 1989; 2nd ed., rev. by John Wright and Angela Colling, Oxford and New York: Pergamon Press, 1995.
Pinet, P. *Invitation to Oceanography.* Sudbury, Mass.: Jones and Bartlett, 1998; pp. 207–209, 298–300.
Thurman, H. V. *Introductory Oceanography.* Upper Saddle River, N.J.: Prentice Hall, 1997; pp. 321–324.

RELATED ARTICLES
Biogeochemical Cycle; Black Sea; Estuary; Fjord; Hydrogen Sulfide; Nitrogen Cycle; Nutrient; Oxygen; Phosphorus

Anoxic Sediment

Anoxic sediments are sediments deposited beneath bottom waters that were oxygen deficient at the time of deposition. Just how oxygen deficient those bottom waters were is difficult to determine, even in present-day settings. However, anoxic sediments do indicate that bottom waters probably contained insufficient dissolved oxygen to support most benthic (bottom-dwelling) life. The concentration of dissolved oxygen in water usually can be measured down to about 0.1 milliliter of oxygen per liter of water [mL/L; or about 0.1 part per million (ppm); or about 5 micromoles per kilogram of water]. The terms *oxic, suboxic,* and *anoxic* refer to environments in which the water contains greater than 0.5 mL/L, 0.1 to 0.5 mL/L, and less than 0.1 mL/L dissolved oxygen, respectively. These are operational definitions of these terms; there are no concrete rules about these definitions. The terms *aerobic* and *anaerobic* refer to chemical and biological processes that occur in the presence and absence of oxygen, respectively, or under oxic and anoxic conditions. Thus, aerobic respiration occurs by organisms living under oxic conditions, and anaerobic respiration occurs by organisms living under anoxic conditions. The term *hypoxic* has been borrowed from the biomedical field to describe oxygen-deficient (<2 ppm) conditions in bottom waters of the northern Gulf of Mexico. In theory, organisms that require aerobic respiration cannot exist under anoxic conditions. Bottom waters on the Peru margin are anoxic in that they contain no measurable dissolved oxygen; however, submersible dives into these waters revealed abundant benthic and nektic (swimming) organisms (e.g., crabs and fish) that require aerobic respiration. Bottom currents are very strong on the Peru margin, and apparently enough dissolved oxygen is being brought in by those currents for aerobic respiration, even though no dissolved oxygen can be measured.

The reason that bottom waters become oxygen deficient is because dissolved oxygen is consumed by biological respiration of organic matter faster than it is brought in by bottom currents. This is called the *biological oxygen demand* (BOD). The higher the BOD, the faster oxygen is consumed. Under oxygen-deficient conditions, bottom waters may contain measurable dissolved oxygen (suboxic), but the underlying pore waters in the sediments may be anoxic because of anaerobic microbial respiration in the sediments. If burrowing benthic organisms on and in the sediments are eliminated under anoxic or suboxic conditions, the seasonal rain of sediment particles may form fine seasonal laminations. In fact, the presence of laminated sediments in a sequence of sediments is probably the best indicator that those sediments were deposited under anoxic conditions. Laminated anoxic sediments are presently being deposited in many anoxic marine basins, such as the Cariaco Basin off Venezuela, the Black Sea, and in many fjords. These types of environments are thought by some to be the environments of deposition of most of the world's petroleum source rocks. There are also many geochemical indicators of anoxic sediments. For example, the element molybdenum is one of several trace elements that precipitate from seawater under anoxic conditions with hydrogen sulfide in the water. Sediments deposited under oxic conditions usually have molybdenum concentrations of below 1 ppm, whereas sediments deposited under anoxic conditions may have tens of ppm of molybdenum. Laminated sediments that were deposited in the anoxic Cariaco Basin and Black Sea contain up to 150 ppm molybdenum.

Walter E. Dean

FURTHER READING

Arthur, Michael A., and Walter E. Dean. "Organic-Matter Production and Preservation and Evolution of Anoxia in the Holocene Black Sea." *Paleoceanography*, Vol. 13 (1998), pp. 395–411.

Calvert, Stephen E., and Thomas F. Pedersen. "Geochemistry of Recent Oxic and Anoxic Marine Sediments: Implications for the Geological Record." *Marine Geology*, Vol. 113 (1993), pp. 67–88.

Crusius, John, Stephen Calvert, Thomas Pedersen, and D. Sage. "Rhenium and Molybdenum Enrichment in Sediments as Indicators of Oxic, Suboxic, and Sulfidic Conditions of Deposition." *Earth and Planetary Science Letters,* Vol. 145 (1996), pp. 65–78.

Dean, Walter E., James V. Gardner, and David Z. Piper. "Inorganic Geochemical Indicators of Glacial-Interglacial Changes in Productivity and Anoxia on the California Continental Margin." *Geochimica et Cosmochimica Acta,* Vol. 61 (1997), pp. 4507–4518.

RELATED ARTICLES

Anoxia; Benthos; Black Sea; Bottom Current; Deep-Sea Sediment; Gulf of Mexico; Petroleum

Antarctica

Antarctica is the continent at the South Pole. Its area [13.2 million square kilometers (about 5.1 million square miles)] is greater than that of the United States and Mexico combined. Sea ice that extends from its shores during the southern winter nearly doubles this area. Antarctica is surrounded by the Southern Ocean, generally considered to be the body of seawater that extends from Antarctica's shores to the Antarctic convergence zone between 50 and 55°S, where Southern Ocean water at deep and surface levels interacts with warm sub-Antarctic water at midlevels.

Antarctica is the coldest and windiest place on Earth. In winter, air temperatures inland typically range between −48 and −12°C (−54.4 and 10.4°F), and on the coast between −40 and −5°C (−40 and 23°F). Summer air temperatures peak at 9°C (48.2°F) inland and 10°C (50°F) in coastal areas. Surface seawater temperatures range between −2 and 1°C (28.4 and 33.8°F). About 99.5 percent of the landmass is permanently covered in snow or ice. The icecap itself averages about 2 kilometers (about 1.25 miles) thick and in places is 4 kilometers (about 2.5 miles) deep. Antarctica's continental shelf is depressed by the weight of snow and ice and is unusually deep at 370 to 490 meters (about 1200 to 1600 feet) below sea level.

Biological productivity on the Antarctic continent is low, whereas that in the nutrient-rich waters of the Southern Ocean is seasonally high. Traditionally, Antarctic marine food webs are depicted with large phytoplankton forms being grazed by krill and other large zooplankton, which in turn are consumed by fish, squid, seals, whales, and seabirds ranging from albatrosses to penguins. This depiction is overly simplistic, because much of the energy flow is undoubtedly channeled from smaller phytoplanktonic forms, via protozoa and bacteria in the microbial loop. Also, many researchers recognize three distinct Antarctic marine zones, each with distinctive physical and biological characteristics: the coastal zone overlying the continental shelf and rarely free of sea ice; the seasonal ice zone beyond the continental shelf, which is largely free of sea ice in the summer; and the open ocean zone, which is free of sea ice all year but contains icebergs.

Antarctica and the Southern Ocean have been subject to significant biological exploitation during their short history of human occupation [British explorer James Cook (1728–79) pioneered Southern Ocean waters on his 1772–75 expedition]. For example, Antarctic fur seal colonies were heavily depleted by hunting in the 1820s and again in the 1870s. The Southern Ocean's population of larger baleen whales declined steeply due to whaling from the early 1900s until 1979, when a moratorium on the catching of larger whale species was declared. In 1994, the International Whaling Commission instituted a whale sanctuary around Antarctica in which commercial whaling is banned for at least 10 years.

Antarctica's near-pristine environment is of special interest to scientists. In 1985, British scientists identified the ozone hole over Antarctica. Ice cores from the ice cap provide a record of Earth's

In a scene from The White Continent *(c. 1950), a film about life in the Antarctic, the* Norsel *icebreaker quickly becomes trapped by pack ice. (Hulton/Archive)*

climate and atmospheric composition extending back for more than 160,000 years. The reflection of solar radiation from the Antarctic landmass and the descent of cool Southern Ocean waters play a pivotal role in global air circulation and in the ocean's thermohaline circulation. Scientists look to Antarctica and the Southern Ocean for early signs of global warming.

The Antarctic Treaty (1959) seeks to keep the Antarctic continent demilitarized and preserved for scientific research with minimal negative environmental impact. In 1972, the deep-drilling vessel *Glomar Challenger* found natural gas deposits in the Ross Sea. Offshore oil deposits exist and deposits of iron ore and coal have been

found on Antarctica itself. An Environmental Protocol (1991) bans mining and drilling for 50 years. The protocol, supplemented by later annexes, seeks to impose stringent environmental controls on Antarctic expeditions and scientific stations. As of the late 1990s, 18 nations were operating a total of more than 40 permanent scientific stations on Antarctica and the sub-Antarctic islands.

Trevor Day

FURTHER READING
Anderson, John B. *Antarctic Marine Geology.* Cambridge and New York: Cambridge University Press, 1999.
Battaglia, B., J. Valencia, and D. W. H. Walton, eds. *Antarctic Communities: Species, Structure and*

Survival. Cambridge and New York: Cambridge University Press, 1997.

Heacox, Kim. *Antarctica: The Last Continent.* Washington, D.C.: National Geographic Society, 1999.

King, J. C., and J. Turner. *Antarctic Meteorology and Climatology.* Cambridge and New York: Cambridge University Press, 1997.

Swithinbank, Charles. *An Alien in Antarctica: Reflections upon Forty Years of Exploration and Research on the Frozen Continent.* Blacksburg, Va.: McDonald and Woodward, 1997.

RELATED ARTICLES

Antarctic Circumpolar Current; Antarctic Margin; Cook, James; Glacial Marine Processes; Ice Cap; Krill; Ozone Hole; Phytoplankton; Seal; Southern Ocean; Thermohaline Circulation; Whaling

Antarctic Circumpolar Current

The Antarctic Circumpolar Current (also known as the West-Wind Drift) is an ocean current that flows in the Southern Ocean, around the coast of Antarctica. Its existence was first reported in 1775 by the British scientist and explorer James Cook (1728–79), and it is the only ocean current that flows all the way around the world, linking the basins of the Indian, Pacific, and Atlantic Oceans. This is possible because in the Southern Ocean there is no large landmass to deflect it. The current therefore flows for a total of 24,000 kilometers (about 14,900 miles), at a speed of 3 to 9 centimeters per second (0.06 to 0.17 knot).

The current is driven by the prevailing winds, which blow from west to east. These westerlies occur between about latitudes 30°S and 50 to 60°S. The southern margin of the westerlies marks the location of the polar front, separating tropical air masses to the north from polar air masses to the south. To the south of both the polar front and the Antarctic Circumpolar Current, the winds blow from the east, carrying very cold air from over the polar ice cap. The easterly winds generate a surface current called the Antarctic Polar Current. This flows from east to west, close to the coast, and should not be confused with the Antarctic Circumpolar Current.

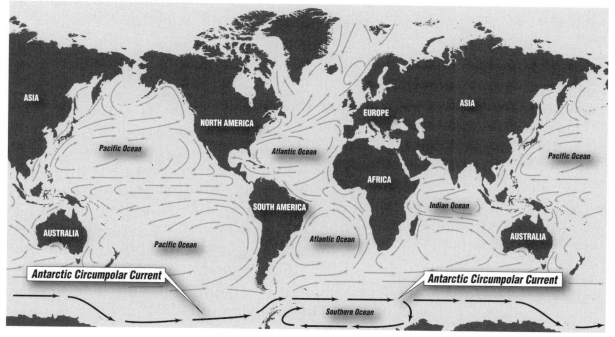

Antarctic Circumpolar Current.

The Antarctic Circumpolar Current is a strong current that extends from the ocean surface all the way to the seabed at a depth of 2000 to 4000 meters (6500 to 13,000 feet). It transports about 150 times more water than all the world's rivers combined. Scientists measuring the flow through Drake Passage, the stretch of water 800 kilometers (500 miles) wide between the southern tip of South America and the northern tip of the Antarctic Peninsula, found that 134 million cubic meters (4732 cubic feet) of water were passing every second. The water is cold, with an average temperature of −1 to 5°C (30 to 41°F), although there are pools of water 2 to 3°C (3.5 to 5.5°F) warmer than this. The water is also slightly less salty than water in the ocean to the north.

The Antarctic Circumpolar Current is by far the biggest of all ocean currents. It follows a wavy path, with eddies and meanders that can carry it far to the north. These disturbances affect the entire water column, all the way to the ocean floor. Sometimes the ends of meanders join, separating rings of water that drift away from the main current into warmer or cooler water, depending on whether they drift northward or southward. The arrival of water at a markedly different temperature strongly affects the weather conditions in the region it enters.

Michael Allaby

FURTHER READING

Knauss, John A. *Introduction to Physical Oceanography.* Englewood Cliffs, N.J.: Prentice Hall, 1978; 2nd ed. rev., Upper Saddle River, N.J.: Prentice Hall, 2000.
Marshall, Norman B. *Developments in Deep-Sea Biology.* Poole, England: Blandford Press, 1979.

RELATED ARTICLES

Antarctica; Bottom Water Formation; Cook, James; Ocean Current; Southern Ocean

Antarctic Margin

Antarctica is an ice-covered continent surrounded by the southern extensions of the Pacific, Indian, and Atlantic Oceans. The region where the continent declines to meet the ocean basin is known as the Antarctic Margin. Ice sheets terminate at the coast as ice cliffs or in the marine environment as ice shelves (floating glacial ice). In ice-free regions, soil development is minimal and vegetation is limited to a few varieties of lichens and mosses due to extreme cold and aridity. The margins are frequented by strong storms, and precipitation occurs almost exclusively in the form of snow. The average annual temperature is −15°C (5°F); therefore, no appreciable meltwater exists. Thus, Antarctica is the only continent with no rivers. Ice is discharged from the ice sheets primarily through wide ice streams, which deliver large icebergs directly to the marine environment.

During austral winters, sea ice extends from the coast to about 60°S, essentially doubling the size of the continent. As sea ice forms, salt is excluded, making the water more saline. These dense brines cascade off the shelf to form Antarctic Bottom Water (AABW), which spreads to the deeper parts of the world's oceans.

Tectonic Setting

Antarctica is composed of at least three tectonic elements: the Antarctic Peninsula, West Antarctica, and East Antarctica. The Antarctic Peninsula is a narrow volcanic arc more-or-less continuous with the South American Andes. The Antarctic Peninsula's Pacific Margin experienced a series of mid-ocean ridge/subduction trench collisions that proceeded successively from south to north. Basinward of the Shetland Islands on the northernmost tip of the Antarctic Peninsula, segments of a dormant Pacific spreading ridge and the Shetland Trench are topographically expressed. Bransfield Basin, a back-arc basin (an incipient ocean basin), separates the Shetland Islands from the Antarctic Peninsula mainland.

West Antarctica is essentially a large rift (attenuated continental crust). The average elevation of the West Antarctica Rift is below sea level. The

Pacific sector of West Antarctica is the Ross Sea and the Atlantic sector is the Weddell Sea. The uplifted shoulder of the West Antarctica Rift is the Transantarctic Mountains (TAM), which define the border with East Antarctica. On average, East Antarctica is above sea level but there are several deep basins (e.g., Wilkes Basin), and mountain belts in the interiors (e.g., Gamburtsev Subglacial Mountains) and coastal areas (e.g., the Yamato Mountains). On the Indian Ocean sector of East Antarctica, Prydz Bay is a failed rift related to separation of India and Antarctica.

Antarctic Cryosphere

Antarctica's current climate is a consequence of the continent's separation from South America, Africa, India, and Australia and its drift toward the South Pole. Drift started between 165 million and 149 million years (Ma) ago. Final separation of Antarctica from South America at the Drake Passage established a deep-marine circumpolar circulation. The resulting thermal isolation caused the growth of continental-scale ice sheets.

The Antarctic cryosphere contains three ice sheets that occupy the three main tectonic blocks. The large East Antarctic Ice Sheet (EAIS) is land-based, which means that it is grounded primarily above sea level. The relatively small West Antarctic Ice Sheet (WAIS) is marine-based, which means that it is grounded mainly below sea level. The Antarctic Peninsula Ice Cap (APIC) is a land-based system, far smaller than the EAIS and WAIS. The conventional wisdom concerning the evolution of the Antarctic Ice Sheets is that (1) the EAIS evolved first, attaining continental-scale proportions between 19 and 15 Ma, and has since been relatively stable; (2) the WAIS evolved between 6 and 5 Ma, and has since been inherently unstable, due to its capacity to respond to changes in sea level; and (3) the APIC evolved from an alpine system that probably has been particularly sensitive to climatic changes given its northern location.

Continental-Margin Geomorphology

The average width of the continental shelf is 100 kilometers (about 62 miles) except at the Ross and Weddell embayments, where the shelves are greater than 300 kilometers (about 186 miles) wide. Unlike low-latitude continental shelves, Antarctic shelves are severely overdeepened and fore-deepened. Topography on the inner shelf is deeply scoured, with depths exceeding 1000 meters (3280 feet). The most striking features on Antarctic shelves are the large glacially carved troughs and banks. Trough widths are several tens of kilometers, and depths exceed 200 meters (656 feet) below the elevation of the bank crest, thus greatly exceeding the dimensions of fluvial valleys.

The continental shelf break is at an average water depth of 500 meters (1640 feet). The uppermost slope generally is steep (10 to 15°) and dissected by gullies and canyons. Several large canyons extend beyond the base of the slope [between about 3000 and 4000 meters (about 9800 and 13,100 feet) water depth] across the low-gradient continental rise and abyssal plain [greater than 5000 meters (16,400 feet)]. There are several submarine banks that adjoin the shelf/slope (e.g., Iselin Bank in the Ross Sea), as well as isolated seamounts on the abyssal plains (e.g., Isla Orcas in the Weddell Sea).

Sedimentology

In the current interglacial, the primary agents of sediment transport are large ice streams. Transport of subglacially eroded terrigenous detritus to the margin occurs primarily via a conveyor-belt fashion within a meter-scale-thick layer of deforming fluidized sediment at the base of ice streams. At the grounding zone (zone where ice sheet is loosely coupled to the seafloor), the debouching of fluidized sediments creates sediment gravity flows that construct proglacial till-delta foresets (i.e., till deltas). In the outer shelf environments, diatomaceous glacial marine sediments drape the seafloor. Bioturbation, marine currents, and iceberg turbation rework and mix the sediments.

When ice sheets advance to the shelf edge, the zone of erosion and terrigenous sedimentation expands basinward. Sedimentologic studies indicate that subglacial and proglacial tills were deposited on the Antarctic shelves and slopes during the last glacial maximum (about 20,000 years ago). The sharp contact between the terrigenous sediments and the overlying diatomaceous drapes suggests that the transition from the glacial to the interglacial was relatively rapid and probably was related to sea-level rise associated with the melting of northern hemisphere ice sheets.

Stratigraphy

Because of hazards associated with icebergs, sea ice, and unpredictable weather, the Antarctic margins are neither well surveyed nor extensively drilled. Thus far, seismic stratigraphic studies show thick basinward-dipping sequences truncated by unconformities near the seafloor and at several subsurface levels. Thus far, the oldest strata sampled on the margin are about 40 Ma in age. The unconformities amalgamate on the overdeepened inner shelf where basement strata are exposed or below a veneer of recent sediment. On the outer shelf, unconformities exhibit topset geometry (horizontal to subhorizontal dip) and cross-cutting relationships that probably reflect multiple episodes of glacial advance across the margin. On the outer shelf/upper slope, unconformities truncate prograding sequences (basinward-dipping strata) interpreted as till deltas partially eroded as the ice sheet advanced to the shelf edge. The bulk prograding strata probably were deposited proglacially as mass flows. Prograding-slope sequences remain generally intact during successive glacial cycles. Stratified sediments draping the topset/foreset reflections are interpreted as diatom-rich pelagic sediments deposited during interglacials.

In the southeastern Weddell Sea, at least three large channel-levee complexes are buried below the toes of prograding-slope strata. The western levees are thickest, indicating that sedimentation was influenced by the Weddell Gyre deep-sea currents that flow from east to west. On the Weddell Sea abyssal plain and on the continental rise of Prydz Bay, Ross Sea, and the Antarctic Peninsula margins, drift and turbidite-fan sequences have been drilled. These turbidite sediments demonstrate that deep-sea fans can develop in the absence of fluvial systems on overdeepened shelves that could not have been emergent during the last glacial maximum.

Geopolitics and Economics

Several nations conduct scientific experiments in Antarctica, but there are no permanent inhabitants. Seven countries (Argentina, Australia, Chile, France, Great Britain, New Zealand, and Norway) claim territory in Antarctica, yet large sectors are unclaimed. The Antarctic Treaty is an international agreement that (1) freezes territorial claims, (2) permits scientific use of the continent, (3) promotes international cooperation for scientific purposes, (4) prohibits the use of Antarctica for military purposes, (5) places a moratorium on petroleum and mineral exploration until 2041, and (6) provides an inspection system to ensure that its provisions are not violated.

Thus far, wealth from Antarctica has been derived from the whale, seal fur, and shrimp (antarctic krill) industry. In 1973, gaseous hydrocarbons were detected in cores drilled in the Ross Sea by the *Glomar Challenger*. Given the remote location, harsh climate, and the likelihood that the moratorium will be extended, petroleum exploration on Antarctic margins is unlikely.

Philip J. Bart

FURTHER READING

Anderson, John B. *Antarctic Marine Geology.* Cambridge and New York: Cambridge University Press, 1999.
Bentley, Charles R. "Configuration and Structure of the Subglacial Crust." In Robert J. Tingey, ed., *The Geology of Antarctica.* Oxford: Clarendon Press/ New York: Oxford University Press, 1991.

Denton, George H., Michael L. Prentice, and Lloyd H. Burckle. "Cenozoic History of the Antarctic Ice Sheet." In Robert J. Tingey, ed., *The Geology of Antarctica.* Oxford: Clarendon Press/New York: Oxford University Press, 1991.

Dunbar, Robert B., John B. Anderson, Eugene W. Domack, and Stanley S. Jacob. "Oceanographic Influences on Sedimentation along the Antarctic Continental Shelf." In Stanley S. Jacobs, ed., *Oceanology of the Antarctic Continental Shelf.* Washington, D.C.: American Geophysical Union Antarctic Research Series, 1985.

RELATED ARTICLES

Antarctica; Bottom Water Formation; Continental Margin; Glacial Marine Processes; *Glomar Challenger;* Ross Sea; Weddell Sea

Anthozoa, see Sea Anemone

Anticyclonic Flow

Anticyclonic flow is the direction in which air flows around a center of high pressure, or anticy- clone. Viewed from a position directly above the North or South Pole, an anticyclonic flow moves in a direction opposite to that of Earth's rotation. It flows clockwise in the northern hemisphere and counterclockwise in the southern hemisphere. Air flows from an area of high atmospheric pressure (anticyclone) toward an area of low pressure (cyclone). Its speed is proportional to the pressure-gradient force (PGF), which is determined by the difference in pressure between the high and low.

As soon as the air begins to move, however, it is deflected by the Coriolis effect (CorF), due to Earth's rotation. The CorF acts at right angles to the PGF, deflecting air to the right in the northern hemisphere and to the left in the southern hemisphere. This deflection occurs regardless of the direction in which the air was originally moving. Air moving from east to west in the northern hemisphere, for example, turns to the north, then to the east, then to the south, and finally, resumes its original path but much farther to the south. When the PGF and CorF balance, the resultant force drives the airflow around the anticyclone on a path that is parallel to the isobars (lines joining points of equal

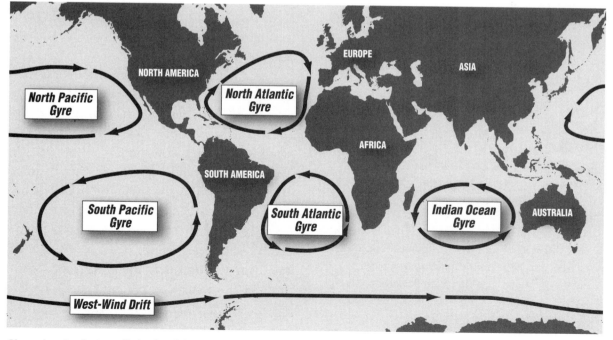

Six major circulation cells in the global ocean.

barometric pressure). This is an anticyclonic flow, and a wind that blows precisely parallel to the isobars is known as a *geostrophic wind.*

The geostrophic wind is found above about 500 meters (1640 feet). Below this height, friction slows the wind and alters the balance between the PGF and CorF. The magnitude of the CorF is proportional to the speed of the airflow. When friction reduces this speed, CorF weakens, but the PGF does not. Consequently, the air flows at an angle across the isobars. Because it then responds to the pressure gradient, the wind is known as a *gradient wind.* Over the sea, where friction is low, the wind crosses the isobars at between 10 and 20°, moving away from the high-pressure center. Over land the angle is up to 45°.

Ocean currents are also subject to the Coriolis effect. As warm currents flow away from the equator and cold currents flow away from the poles, they are deflected to the right in the northern hemisphere and to the left in the southern hemisphere. This deflection produces the oceanic gyres, which turn clockwise in the northern hemisphere and counterclockwise in the southern hemisphere. This is an anticyclonic circulation. Ocean currents are driven by the wind, so they respond only indirectly to the atmospheric pressure gradient force. Nevertheless, once the water is moving, it circulates anticyclonically.

Michael Allaby

FURTHER READING

King, Cuchlaine A. M. *Introduction to Physical and Biological Oceanography.* London: Edward Arnold/New York: Crane, Russak, 1975.

Knauss, John A. *Introduction to Physical Oceanography.* Englewood Cliffs, N.J.: Prentice Hall, 1978; 2nd ed. rev., Upper Saddle River, N.J.: Prentice Hall, 2000.

Nybakken, James W. *Marine Biology: An Ecological Approach,* 5th ed. San Francisco: Benjamin Cummings, 2001.

RELATED ARTICLES

Coriolis Effect; Cyclonic Flow; Pressure-Gradient Force

Aphotic Zone

The aphotic zone includes the depths at which sunlight is undetectable in water. Beneath the clearest oceanic waters the top of the zone is at about 1250 meters (4100 feet), but in turbid coastal waters it is much shallower, and in some estuaries it may be just 10 meters (33 feet). Because the average depth of the oceans is 3800 meters (about 12,500 feet), the aphotic zone is more voluminous than both the euphotic and dysphotic zones and is by far the largest habitat on the planet. The zone includes other bathymetric zones: the bathypelagic, abyssopelagic, hadalpelagic, bathyal, abyssal, and hadal.

Although water in a glass looks transparent, it both absorbs and scatters light. It is highly selective in the color of the light it absorbs. Only certain colors are absorbed by water; red light is absorbed most rapidly and blue-green light penetrates the deepest. Thus the deep ocean is dark, illuminated only by the dim flashes of light produced by animals (bioluminescence). In such a dark environment, communication by coded light signals produced by bioluminescence may be detected as far as 10 to 20 meters (33 to 66 feet) away. Longer distances can be achieved using sounds or chemicals.

The aphotic zone is remote from the main source of organic material—the photosynthetic activity of photosynthetic cells in the euphotic zone. There are other centers where chemosynthesis of organic matter occurs at the hydrothermal vents, based on the chemical energy provided by the oxidation of sulfide and methane fuels. However, this supplies only about 0.3 percent of the primary production in the oceans. Thus nearly all life in the aphotic zone is based on the organic matter that sinks down through the water column, and much of it is associated with marine snow, which consists of aggregations of small particles usually embedded on a matrix of mucus. It is also a cool zone; with a few exceptions, ocean waters deeper than about 1000 meters (3280 feet) range in temperature from 2 to 5°C (35.6 to 41°F). The combination of cool water temperatures and small, somewhat unpredictable organic inputs results in sparse life in the aphotic zone. Most of the inhabitants are sluggish and incapable of sustained swimming because active hunting and foraging are unlikely to win rewards before an animal runs out of reserves. Their physiological adaptations, such as reducing their metabolic needs and specialized enzyme structures, enable animals to exist in the aphotic zone but also restrict them to it.

Martin Angel

FURTHER READING

Childress, James J. "Are There Physiological and Biochemical Adaptations of Metabolism in Deep-Sea Animals?" *Trends in Ecology and Evolution*, Vol. 10 (1995), pp. 30-36.
Marshall, Norman B. *Developments in Deep-Sea Biology.* Poole, England: Blandford Press, 1979.
Ormond, Rupert F. G., John D. Gage, and Martin V. Angel. *Marine Biodiversity: Patterns and Processes.* Cambridge and New York: Cambridge University Press, 1997.
Randall, David J., and Anthony P. Farrell. *Deep-sea Fishes.* San Diego: Academic Press, 1997.

RELATED ARTICLES

Abyssopelagic Zone; Bathyal Zone; Bathypelagic Zone; Bioluminescence; Chemosynthesis; Dysphotic Zone; Euphotic Zone; Hadal Zone; Hadalpelagic Zone; Hydrothermal Vent; Water Column

Aplacophora

Aplacophora is a class of mollusks related to snails, clams, octopus, squid, and chitons. Few people know that the mollusks include a group called Aplacophora; most of them are very small, less than 5 millimeters (0.19 inch), living far beyond the shoreline, where mollusk collecting has been a common activity for centuries. Most aplacophorans belong to the deep-sea benthic fauna (deep-sea animals living on the bottom) at depths greater than 200 meters (660 feet) to hadal depths of 9000 meters (29,520 feet), where they are common, found wherever deep-sea collections have been made. There are about 350 known species. They are worm-shaped and, unlike most other mollusks, they have no shell; rather, they are covered with a shining coat of innumerable small needles or scales of calcium carbonate. They have a radula like other mollusks. One group of aplacophorans (Chaetodermomorpha or Caudoveata) are dioecious (with both males and females); they burrow in soft sediment, feeding on small organisms, mainly shelled single-celled Foraminifera. The other group (Neomeniomorpha or Solenogastres) are hermaphroditic. They have a narrow ridgelike foot upon which they creep, feeding on soft corals and other Cnidaria. The larvae are short-lived and nonfeeding and develop within a cellular covering that is absorbed at metamorphosis.

Aplacophorans are important in understanding both the ecology of the deep sea and the evolution of mollusks. An aplacophoran species can be numerically dominant in some localities, and some have very broad distributions, for instance from north to south on both the east and west sides of the Atlantic Ocean. Thus, aplacophorans can help in understanding the biogeography of the deep sea, that is, the dynamics of where animals of the deep-sea fauna occur. Aplacophorans are also considered to be an offshoot of the earliest primitive mollusk. Although there is no known fossil that is considered the ancestor of all living mollusks, the aplacophorans seem to have a primitive anatomy and so can give insight into what the ancestral mollusk might have been.

Amélie H. Scheltema

FURTHER READING

Barnes, Robert. *Invertebrate Zoology.* Philadelphia: W. B. Saunders, 1963; 6th ed., by Edward Ruppert, Fort Worth, Texas: Saunders College Publishing, 1994.

APLACOPHORA

Gage, John D., and Paul A. Tyler. *Deep-Sea Biology: A Natural History of the Deep-Sea Floor.* Cambridge and New York: Cambridge University Press, 1991.

Pechenik, Jan A. *Biology of the Invertebrates.* Boston: Prindle, Weber and Schmidt, 1985; 4th ed., Boston: McGraw-Hill, 2000.

Salvini-Plawen, L. V. "Early Evolution and the Primitive Groups." In E. R. Trueman and M. R. Clarke, eds., *The Mollusca*, Vol. 10, *Evolution.* Orlando, Fla.: Academic Press, 1985.

Scheltema, A. H. "Class Aplacophora." In P. L. Beesley, G. J. B. Ross, and A. Wells, eds., *Fauna of Australia.* Vol. 5, Part A, *Mollusca: The Southern Synthesis.* Melbourne, Australia: CSIRO, 1998.

Scheltema, A. H., and M. Jebb. "Natural History of a Solenogaster Mollusc from Papua New Guinea, *Epimenia australis* (Thiele) (Aplacophora, Neomeniomomorpha)." *Journal of Natural History,* Vol. 28 (1994), pp. 1297–1318.

RELATED ARTICLES
Cnidaria; Foraminifera; Mollusca

Arabian Sea

The Arabian Sea lies in the northwestern part of the Indian Ocean and covers a total area of approximately 3,862,000 square kilometers (1,491,000 square miles). It is bounded on the east by India, to the north by Pakistan and Iran, and to the west by the Arabian Peninsula and the Horn of Africa. The southern boundary runs from the Indian coast near Goa, south along the western side of the Laccadive Islands to the equator, where it trends southwest to the coast of Africa near Mombasa at approximately 5°S latitude.

The Arabian Sea has two major bathymetric (seafloor topography) basins, the Somali and Arabian Basins, which are divided by the Carlsberg Ridge, an extension of the Mid-Indian Ridge. Submarine plateaus border the two basins. The Seychelles Mauritius Ridge bounds the Somali Basin in the southwest, and the Chagos–Laccadive Ridge bounds the Arabian Basin on the east. The average depth of the sea is 2734 meters

(8970 feet), and the deepest point, Wheatley Deep at 5803 meters (19,034 feet), is located in the Somali Basin.

Special bathymetric and structural features of the Arabian Sea include a deep submarine canyon and its submarine alluvial fan that lie off the mouth of the Indus River; the Owens Fracture Zone, which displaces the Carlsberg Ridge; deep ocean ridges; and abyssal plains in both the Arabian and Somali Basins. Islands in the Arabian Sea include those of the Lakshadweep and Maldive chains plus Socotra and the Kuria Muria Islands.

Terrigenous sediments cover the continental slopes down to about 2744 meters (9003 feet). Below this, sediments consist of calcareous ooze (*Globigerina* shells, a genus of protozoans belonging to the Foraminiferida order), whereas basins below 3963 meters (13,000 feet) lie below the carbonate compensation depth and are covered by red clay. Sediments near the coast of Cape al-Hadd consist of greenish mud contaminated by naturally occurring hydrogen sulfide. At times, the area is called the *fish cemetery,* due to the lack of oxygen and consequent relative increase of hydrogen sulfide.

The Arabian Sea has a monsoon climate with monsoon winds greatly affecting the surface temperatures. During Northeast Monsoon winds, minimum temperatures of 24 to 25°C (75 to 77°F) occur in the central Arabian Sea, whereas temperatures exceeding 28°C (82°F) occur during Southeast Monsoon winds. During the rainy season (April to November), a salinity of 35 practical salinity units (psu) has been recorded, while during the dry season (November to March), a salinity of more than 36 psu has been recorded. High evaporation rates, in addition to highly saline waters from the Red Sea and the Gulf of Oman, contribute to the high salinity of the Arabian Sea.

Water circulation of the Arabian Sea reverses direction as a result of the seasonal changes in the monsoon winds. Significant currents include the complex Somali Current, the Southwest Monsoon Current, the Northeast Monsoon Drift, and the North Equatorial Current. In summer, upwellings develop along most of the coastline, with the most intense off Arabia.

Deanna Madison

FURTHER READING

Haq, Bilal U., and John D. Milliman, eds. *Marine Geology and Oceanography of Arabian Sea and Coastal Pakistan.* New York: Van Nostrand Reinhold Company/Scientific and Academic Editions, 1984.

Heirtzler, James R., et al. *Indian Ocean Geology and Biostratigraphy.* Washington, D.C.: American Geophysical Union, 1977.

Kennett, James. *Marine Geology.* Englewood Cliffs, N.J.: Prentice Hall, 1982.

RELATED ARTICLES
Mid-Ocean Ridge; Monsoon; Ocean Current; Ocean Plateau; Oxygen; Red Sea; Salinity; Submarine Canyon; Submarine Fan; Upwelling

Arctic Ocean

With a total area of approximately 14,000,000 square kilometers (5,400,000 square miles), the world's smallest ocean, the Arctic, is less than one-tenth the size of the world's largest ocean, the Pacific Ocean. Despite its small size, the Arctic Ocean is of great military and economic importance and its many resources include commercially exploitable reserves of fish and oil. Humankind's influence is far-reaching, however, and environmental problems such as ozone depletion, global warming, and pollution now threaten even the remotest areas of the Arctic Ocean.

General Characteristics

Located entirely within the Arctic Circle and centered roughly on the North Pole, the Arctic Ocean is a virtually landlocked body of water bordered by the continents of Asia, Europe, and North America. The Arctic is not just the smallest ocean, but also the shallowest: With an average depth of about 1300 meters (4260 feet), it is about one-fourth as deep as the other oceans and its maximum known depth, north of the Chukchi Sea (between Alaska and Siberia), is 5441 meters (17,851 feet). This is largely because about one-third of the ocean is underlain by continental shelf, much wider in the Arctic region than in the other ocean basins [it extends nearly 1200 kilometers (746 miles) from Siberia, for example].

The Arctic Ocean is divided by three ridges separated by abyssal plains: the major Lomonosov Ridge [some 3000 meters (9843 feet) high and running 1700 kilometers (1056 miles) from the New Siberia Islands to Greenland], and two smaller ridges, Alpha Ridge and the Arctic extension of a mid-ocean ridge (the Nansen Cordillera). The islands of the Arctic region—including Svalbard (Spitsbergen), Novaya Zemlya, the New Siberian Islands, numerous islands off North America (including Baffin Island, Ellesmere Island, and Victoria Island), and Greenland—divide it into seven seas: the Beaufort Sea (off the coast of Alaska and Canada), the Greenland Sea (between Greenland and Svalbard), the Norwegian Sea (between Norway and Greenland), the Barents Sea (northwest of Russia), the Kara Sea (east of Novaya Zemlya), the Laptev Sea (west of the New Siberian Islands), and the Chukchi Sea (between Alaska and Siberia).

Water enters the Arctic Ocean through two main sources. About 71 percent [61,000 cubic kilometers (14,600 cubic miles)] enters from the Atlantic Ocean via the North Atlantic current, which flows into the Barents Sea between Greenland and Norway. About 23 percent [20,000 cubic kilometers (4800 cubic miles)] enters from the Pacific Ocean through the Bering Strait between Alaska and Siberia and the rest enters through rivers and precipitation. Roughly two-thirds of the water leaving the Arctic Ocean exits via the east coast of Greenland, and the other third leaves between Labrador and the west coast of Greenland. These currents merge and provide one of the two main sources of deep water for the deep-ocean (thermohaline) circulation.

Resources

Unlike most other regions on Earth, the economy of the Arctic is still largely dependent on the exploitation of immediately local resources. With summer ocean temperatures often reaching a high of just 0°C (32°F), winter temperatures plunging as low as -51°C (-60°F), continuous darkness in winter, and ice [0.6 to 4 meters (2 to 13 feet thick)] covering the ocean year round above 75°N, it might

Arctic Ocean.

be supposed that the region would support little marine life. However, well-adapted mammals such as polar bears and seals, and birds such as gulls and guillemots, can be found at latitudes as extreme as 88°N. Commercially exploitable quantities of fish such as cod and halibut are found only in the warmer waters of the Barents and Kara Seas. Seals and whales, once hunted almost to extinction, are now more effectively protected through trade restrictions and bans on commercial fishing. Bowhead whales (*Balaena mysticetus*) remain the staple diet of the indigenous Inuit people of the Arctic region.

The Arctic is of intense commercial interest, notably for the extraction of oil and natural gas (particularly off the coast of Alaska) and minerals such as tin, polymetallic nodules, and aggregates (sand and gravel). Alaska now provides one-fourth of all U.S. oil, and petroleum corporations expect to invest some U.S.$5.2 billion between 1997 and 2002. Asian reserves are thought to be extensive but have not yet been explored thoroughly.

Exploration

Exploration of the Arctic Ocean dates back to the ancient Greeks and continues today. The first person to explore the region was probably Greek explorer Pytheas (ca. 400 B.C.). In fact, the name *arctic* comes from the Greek word *arktos* (bear); the constellation of the Great Bear was used by explorers to navigate in this region. Later explorations were made by the Vikings (ca. A.D. 800) and by European sailors from around 1500 onward.

Formal oceanographic study of the Arctic Ocean began with the infamous voyage of Fridtjof Nansen (1861–1930) in 1893. When his boat, the *Fram*, became locked in polar ice and was carried in the drift from the New Siberian Islands to Spitsbergen, he proved that the Arctic Ocean was a frozen body of water and not a continent. His bathymetric measurements noted water depths of 3350 to 3963 meters (about 11,000 to 13,000 feet),

which effectively confirmed the existence of an ocean basin and thus of an "Arctic Ocean."

The development of air flight during the twentieth century provided a new means of exploring the Arctic. Pioneering polar flights by explorers such as Roald Amundsen (1872–1928) paved the way for fast modern-day commercial flights across the Arctic Circle. From the 1930s onward, scientists from the Soviet Union and the United States used floating ice stations, icebreaking ships, and aircraft to study the Arctic. Although the surface of the Arctic Ocean has now been completely mapped, seafloor regions are less well charted. Indeed, one recent venture, the SCICEX (Science Ice Expeditions) program, more than doubled available data on the Arctic region by using the nuclear submarine USS *Hawkbill* to map the seafloor and simultaneously collect data on temperature, salinity, current flow, and other measures.

Future Challenges

Ironically, one of the most remote and inhospitable areas of the planet is also prone to some of its greatest environmental threats. The Barents Sea is of strategic military importance, as it marks the shortest route between Russia and the United States; the world's smallest ocean has the dubious distinction of having the world's largest concentration of nuclear submarines.

The influx of water from the Pacific and Atlantic Oceans, rivers, and precipitation makes the Arctic Ocean susceptible to pollution from almost anywhere on the planet. Traces of polychlorinated biphenyl (PCB) chemicals, pesticides, and toxic heavy metals, thought to have originated in Europe, North America, and Asia, have been found in the body tissues of the Inuit people and the wider ecosystem. Significant threats come from chemical factories in Russia. Over a period of 27 years, for example, the Usolye and Sayansk chemical plants have released more than 500 tonnes (550 tons) of mercury into the Angara

River, which flows via the Yenisey River to the Kara Sea, and poses a major threat to the Arctic ecosystem. Pollution from outside the Arctic affects the region in other, more dramatic ways. The Arctic ozone hole, caused largely by chemicals such as chlorofluorocarbons used in refrigerators, may have drastic long-term effects on marine life both in the Arctic region and globally.

One of the greatest concerns about the Arctic region is the observation that the entire ocean is warming. Ironically, a region once dominated by ice to such an extent that it was considered a continent is now witnessing temperature rises so dramatic that it may lose its ice entirely by the end of this century. In December 1999, University of Washington researchers reported that Arctic ice had lost some 40 percent of its volume in less than 30 years. In August 2000, oceanographer James McCarthy (1914–) reported a 1.6-kilometer (1-mile) wide area of open ocean very near the pole itself. Whether the ice loss is caused by a long-term climate change or by a short-term natural climatic fluctuation [e.g., the North Pole is believed to have been as warm as 14°C (57°F) within a small interval of time in the Late Cretaceous Period (about 90 million years ago)] is not yet known.

Important initiatives such as the Arctic Environmental Protection Strategy (AEPS) of 1991 aim to secure the long-term future of the region by stressing the need to protect entire ecosystems and involving indigenous people in "sustainable development." However, long-range pollution, ozone depletion, and global warming confirm that global threats also require global action if regions such as the Arctic are not to be transformed drastically by human activities.

Chris Woodford

FURTHER READING
Alexander, Bryan, and Cherry Alexander. *The Vanishing Arctic.* London: Blandford Press, 1996; New York: Facts On File, 1997.
Hodges, Glenn. "The New Cold War." *National Geographic,* March 2000, p. 30.
Kerr, Richard. "Will the Arctic Ocean Lose All Its Ice?" *Science,* Vol. 286, No. 5446 (3 December 1999), p. 1828.
Lee, Douglas. "Oil in the Wilderness: An Arctic Dilemma." *National Geographic,* March 1982, p. 858.
Lopez, Barry. *Arctic Dreams: Imagination and Desire in a Northern Landscape.* New York: Scribner's, 1986.
Miller, Pamela. *The Reach of Oil in the Arctic: Alaska USA.* Washington, D.C.: Greenpeace USA, 1997.
Monastersky, R. "Icy Signs of Warming Emerge in Arctic." *Science News,* Vol. 153, No. 8 (21 February 1998), p. 116.
Raliff, Janet. "Cetacean Seniors: Whales That Give New Meaning to Longevity." *Science News,* Vol. 158, No. 16 (14 October 2000), p. 254.
Rey, L., and B. Stonehouse, eds. *The Arctic Ocean: The Hydrographic Environment and the Fate of Pollutants.* London: Macmillan/New York: Wiley, 1982.
Tarduno, J. A., et al. "Evidence for Extreme Climatic Warmth from Late Cretaceous Arctic Vertebrates." *Science,* Vol. 282, No. 5397 (18 December 1998), p. 2241.

RELATED ARTICLES
Amundsen, Roald; Beaufort Sea; Bering Strait; Chukchi Sea; Continental Shelf; Deep-Ocean Circulation; Hydrosphere; Nansen, Fridtjof; Ocean Current; Petroleum; Seals; Thermohaline Circulation

Arthropoda

The phylum Arthropoda, meaning "jointed legs," contains over 900,000 species and includes spiders, mites, ticks, centipedes, millipedes, and crustaceans. Containing over 80 percent of Earth's species, arthropods have existed since Precambrian times, over 600 million years. The predominant arthropod fossil is of the now extinct trilobite. From fossil records, it is estimated that over 2000 species of trilobites once existed from the Cambrian to Permian periods.

The dominant marine subphylum of arthropods is Crustacea, which includes crabs, shrimps, lobsters, and barnacles. Other marine arthropod classes are Pycnogonida, the sea spiders, and Merostomata, the horseshoe crabs. Crustaceans also include the copepods, euphausiids, and many other smaller groups that make up the majority of zooplankton, which are tiny floating organisms within the *water column*, the vertical column of water extending from the surface of the ocean to the floor. A few insects also exist in the marine environment.

General Characteristics

Arthropods have an *exoskeleton* (an outer skeleton) composed of chitin, which is a rigid carbohydrate that covers the body with plates. They also have a segmented body with jointed appendages, a complete gut with a one-way digestive system, and a ventral nerve cord. Without the jointed appendages, arthropods would not be able to move, because the exoskeleton is quite rigid and inflexible. Arthropods also possess well-developed brains and sensory organs. A variety of lifestyles are represented within the arthropods, ranging from the sessile barnacles, which filter feed, to the highly mobile crabs and lobsters, which actively pursue prey and use their strong claws to kill.

Arthropods also have an open circulatory system with a dorsal heart comprised of one or more chambers. No capillaries are present. Openings in the heart, called *ostia*, allow blood to enter from the surrounding sinus, known as the *hemocoel*. The blood is pumped by the heart through the arteries into the sinuses surrounding the tissues and organs and is then pumped back to the heart. The blood may contain hemocyanin, a copper-containing pigment, which functions to transport oxygen from the gills to the tissues and cells.

Growth is achieved by *molting*, which is a process that occurs throughout the life cycle of the arthropod. The chitinous exoskeleton of arthropods does not allow growth, so they must shed or molt their exoskeletons. After molting, the arthropod goes through a growth spurt and is vulnerable for a period of time until the new skeleton hardens. Many animals will hide during this period to avoid predators, but some, like the mantis shrimp, *Gonodactylus bredini*, have developed other strategies to deter predators. Mantis

shrimp have strong forelimbs that they use to crush other organisms. When they are threatened they extend their forelimbs outward, which is thought to be an indicator of the size and strength of the shrimp. When the shrimp molts every two months, however, it is left vulnerable for approximately three days. The shrimp will continue to use this threat display, usually against smaller intruders, even though it is not powerful enough to defeat the other organism. One other benefit of molting is to rid the animal of any organisms that have attached to the exoskeleton, such as bryozoans or slipper shells.

Crustaceans

The five classes of crustaceans are Remipedia (the remipedes), Cephalocarida (the cephalocarids), Branchiopoda (including fairy shrimps, brine shrimps, and cladocerans), Maxillopoda (including mussel or seed shrimps, copepods, fish lice, and barnacles), and Malacostraca (including crabs, shrimps, and lobsters). Many of the crustaceans possess a body made up of two major parts: the abdomen and the cephalothorax, which consists of the head and the thorax. Crustaceans either have a cephalic shield that covers the head, or a carapace, which is the hard structure covering the bodies of most crabs. Specialized appendages act as feeding appendages, walking legs, gills, and swimming legs. Crustaceans have two pairs of antennae that function as sensory organs for taste and touch. The head contains antennal glands that remove wastes from the body. Their mouthparts are made up of two pairs of maxillae used for holding and managing food, and one pair of mandibles, used for chewing and biting food. Gas exchange is achieved by absorbing oxygen from the water by the gills. Many can also detect gravity forces with structures called *statocysts*.

Sexes are generally separate, with males transferring sperm to females using specialized appendages. Females generally carry the fertilized eggs on their bodies until they hatch. Crustaceans may hatch into nauplius larvae, which undergo several *metamorphoses*, or changes, before resembling the adult. They may have a mixed development where there are marked differences between each stage, or they may hatch directly into a miniature version of the adult.

Movement generally occurs by moving the limbs with internal muscles, although some crustaceans move by other means, and others, like the barnacles, do not move at all once the larval stages are complete. Barnacles are sessile animals attached to hard substrates or other animals, such as whales and turtles. They are housed in a cone-shaped shell and represent a problem for boat owners, because many will attach themselves to boat bottoms and must be scraped off regularly. Some crustaceans, such as the copepods and euphausiids (krill), drift with the ocean currents. They are an important part of the food chain and are eaten by fish and other organisms. Euphausiids are the primary food consumed by baleen whales.

Some planktonic crustaceans also exhibit *vertical migration*, which is characterized as movement up and down the water column in response to an external stimulus, such as the presence or absence of light. Typically, such organisms will migrate to feed near the surface at night, probably to reduce the risk of predation and to avoid high light intensity.

The order Decapoda contains well-known crustaceans: lobsters, crabs, and shrimps. *Decapod* means 10 legs and refers to the five pairs of walking legs that these organisms possess. Great diversity exists within the more than 10,000 species of this order. Lobsters exhibit a high degree of specialization, with 19 pairs of different appendages. Their antennae are highly sensitive to chemical detection and touch. They possess balance organs and some have large pinching claws known as *chelipeds*. The tail is composed of two pairs of uropods and a telson, which together with the flexing of the abdomen allow the lobster to swim backward, a useful trait when faced with predators. Crabs are less elongated than lobsters and shrimp, and have the abdomen permanently flexed under the cephalothorax. Most are scavengers, feeding on the bottom of ocean floors. Shrimp closely resemble lobster, having the same tail structure and a well-developed abdomen. All are high in commercial value and are harvested for food.

Other Arthropods

Little information is available on sea spiders. About 1000 species exist and all are marine. They are found in both shallow and deep waters and have coloration matching their environment. All are *benthic*, or bottom-dwelling, animals and feed on invertebrates such as bryozoans and hydroids.

The horseshoe crabs are considered to be living fossils. Their ancestors date as far back as the Devonian period, over 350 million years ago. They are found as deep as 22.5 meters (74 feet) but enter the intertidal zone to breed. Horseshoe crabs are benthic feeders.

The few species of insects that can be considered marine generally inhabit tidal pools, salt marshes, and estuaries, except for the water striders of the genus *Halobates*, which inhabit the surface of the open ocean.

Erin O'Donnell

FURTHER READING
Barnes, Robert. *Invertebrate Zoology.* Philadelphia: Saunders, 1963; 6th ed., by Edward Ruppert, Fort Worth, Texas: Saunders, 1994.
Brusca, Richard C., and Gary J. Brusca. *Invertebrates.* Sunderland, Mass.: Sinauer, 1990.
Buchsbaum, Ralph. *Animals Without Backbones.* Chicago and London: University of Chicago Press, 1938; 3rd ed., 1987.
Krebs, J. R. and N. B. Davies. *An Introduction to Behavioural Ecology.* Sunderland, Mass.: Sinauer, 1981; 3rd ed., Oxford and Cambridge, Mass.: Blackwell Scientific, 1993.
Lerman, Matthew. *Marine Biology: Environment, Diversity, and Ecology.* Menlo Park, Calif.: Benjamin Cummings, 1986.

Manton, S. M. *The Arthropoda.* Oxford: Clarendon Press, 1977.

RELATED ARTICLES
Crab; Crustacea; Horseshoe Crab; Insecta; Lobster; Remipedia; Shrimp

Artificial Reef

When a ship sinks in the ocean, it may be quickly colonized by a variety of organisms. The ship provides a habitat that may not have formed otherwise and becomes an artificial reef. Building artificial reefs is one way to provide habitat for organisms. Artificial reefs are constructed from materials such as cinder blocks, old ships, and oil rigs. Materials used to create these ecosystems are environmentally safe and are prepared by removing all toxic and hazardous substances. These artificial reefs have proven successful in supporting marine life.

Researchers examine the habitat in the area where they plan to add an artificial reef to determine the impact of the object on the ecosystem. Artificial reefs are successful because they provide the hard substrate, or surface, that is otherwise absent. Artificial reefs allow organisms that inhabit hard substrates to flourish in an otherwise sedimentary ocean floor, and within a short time the entire hard substrate community can be present in a once barren area.

Erin O'Donnell

FURTHER READING
Nybakken, James W. *Marine Biology: An Ecological Approach,* 5th ed. San Francisco: Benjamin Cummings, 2001.
Seaman, William, ed. *Artificial Reef Evaluation with Application to Natural Marine Habitats.* Boca Raton, Fla.: CRC Press, 2000.

USEFUL WEB SITES
Reef Ball Foundation.
    <http://www.reefball.com>.

South Carolina Department of Natural Resources.
    <http://www.dnr.state.sc.us/marine/pub/seascience/artreef.html>.

RELATED ARTICLES
Reef

Asexual

Asexual organisms have the ability to reproduce without involving union with another individual. This type of sexual lifestyle is common among the lower invertebrates and in colonial animals. There are several types of asexual reproduction, and unless a mutation occurs, the offspring will be genetically identical to the parent. In the single-celled protists, *fission*—through which the organism simply divides in half to create another individual—is common. Another type of asexual reproduction is *fragmentation*, which occurs when the organism's body breaks into two or more pieces that then regenerate or grow into complete organisms. This is common in flatworms and ribbon worms. Budding, which occurs in bryozoans, sponges, and cnidarians, is characterized by the production of a new body from certain body cells. Bryozoans live in a colony made up of many individuals and can easily add an individual by budding and thereby increase the colony size.

Sea anemones can reproduce by *pedal laceration*. As the animal crawls along the substrate, small pieces of the basal disk are torn off. Each piece can then regenerate into a clone of the original animal. *Parthenogenesis*, which means "virgin development," occurs when an animal develops from an unfertilized egg. Some crustaceans reproduce in this manner.

Asexual reproduction allows organisms to produce many young without another individual, but the disadvantage is that there is no genetic variation, as the offspring are only clones of the adult.

Erin O'Donnell

FURTHER READING

Nybakken, James W. *Marine Biology: An Ecological Approach,* 5th ed. San Francisco: Benjamin Cummings, 2001.

Solomon, Eldra P., Linda R. Berg, Diana W. Martin, and Claude Ville. *Biology.* Philadelphia: Saunders, 1985; 5th ed., Fort Worth, Texas: Saunders, 1999.

RELATED ARTICLES

Bryozoa; Cnideria; Crustacea

Asteroidea

The asteroids (sea stars or starfish) belong in the phylum Echinodermata. Most asteroids have five arms attached to a central disk, although some species have more than 20 arms, and all can regenerate arms that are lost. Sea stars are often brightly colored and are common bottom dwellers in intertidal and subtidal environments around the world. They can also be found at great depths. Asteroids range in size from less than 2 centimeters (0.8 inch) to greater than 1 meter (3.3 feet) in diameter. The approximately 1500 living asteroid species are divided into five orders: Platyasterida, Paxillosida, Valvatida, Spinulosida, and Forcipulatida.

Like all echinoderms, adult asteroids exhibit pentaradial symmetry. Their body is arranged in five parts around a central axis, but their larvae are bilaterally symmetrical. Sea stars are exclusively marine, lack excretory organs, have a well-developed coelom (body cavity), a diffuse nervous system, a water vascular system, and a tough calcareous endoskeleton that is covered by a thin ciliated epidermis.

The external surface of asteroids makes it clear why these animals are called *echinoderms*, which means "spiny skinned." Numerous blunt spines, dermal papillae or skin gills, and pedicellariae, tiny jawlike structures that help keep the animal's surface clean, cover the aboral or dorsal surface of many sea stars. Spines and pedicellariae also adorn the oral or ventral surface. Ambulacral grooves are also found on the oral surface and radiate out from the centrally located mouth to the tips of the arms. Tube feet, which are used for locomotion and feeding, lie within the grooves. The tube feet in some asteroid species bear suckers.

Internally, the stomach occupies most of the disk. The stomach is divided into two sections: the cardiac stomach, which in many species can be everted during feeding, and the pyloric stomach. Pyloric ducts connect the pyloric stomach to the pyloric ceca (digestive glands) found in each arm. Gonads lie on either side of each arm underneath the pyloric cecum. Most seastar species have separate sexes, although a few are hermaphroditic (have both male and female gonads). Some sea star species can reproduce asexually by breaking into two halves, a process called *fissiparity*. Most species, however, reproduce sexually by releasing sperm and eggs into the seawater, where they are fertilized. Fertilized eggs undergo typical deuterostome development with radial indeterminate cleavage. Embryos of most sea star species go through bipinnaria and brachiolaria larval stages. Some species, however, brood their eggs and the embryos undergo direct development.

Asteroids exhibit the prototypical echinoderm water-vascular system. The madreporite, which is a hard circular structure that protects the external opening of the water vascular system, sits on the aboral surface. The madreporite brings water from the outside into the sea star's body via the stone canal, which leads to the ring canal in the disk. The ring canal distributes water to the radial canals, which, like spokes on a wheel, run along the ambulacral grooves in the arms. Each radial canal, in turn, supplies water to the ampullae of the tube feet. The ampullae resemble pipette bulbs and serve as a fluid reservoir to activate the tube feet. Contraction of ampullae hydraulically extends the tube feet, whereas contraction of small muscles at the tip causes the tube feet to act as suction cups.

Ecologically, sea stars can play a key role in communities in which they live. A few sea star species are specialists and a few are suspension feeders, but most of these slow-moving animals are opportunistic predators and/or scavengers. Most sea stars will eat any dead matter they find, but they also prey on invertebrates, such as crustaceans, mollusks, annelids, and other echinoderms. In some communities, predation by sea stars controls predation or competition by other invertebrates and thereby helps maintain diversity. The tropical species *Acanthaster planci*, the crown-of-thorns sea star, which feeds on coral polyps, has played a major role in destroying coral reefs in the Indo-West Pacific.

Lynn L. Lauerman

FURTHER READING

Brusca, Richard C., and Gary J. Brusca. *Invertebrates.* Sunderland, Mass.: Sinauer, 1990.

Hendler, Gordon, John E. Miller, David L. Pawson, and Porter M. Kier. *Sea Stars, Sea Urchins, and Allies: Echinoderms of Florida and the Caribbean.* Washington, D.C.: Smithsonian Institution Press, 1995.

Lawrence, John. *A Functional Biology of Echinoderms.* Baltimore: Johns Hopkins University Press, 1987.

Morris, Robert H., Donald P. Abbott, and Eugene Haderlie. *Intertidal Invertebrates of California.* Stanford, Calif.: Stanford University Press, 1980.

Romashko, Sandra. *The Shell Book: The Complete Guide to Collecting and Identifying with a Special Section on Starfish and Other Sea Creatures.* Miami: Windward, 1974; 6th ed., 1992.

RELATED ARTICLES

Concentricycloidea; Crinoidea; Echinodermata; Echinoidea; Holothuroidea; Ophiuroidea

Atlantic Ocean

The Atlantic is the second largest of the world's major oceans. Its area is 82.36×10^6 square kilometers (31.8 million square miles). To the east and west it is bounded by the continents of Europe, Africa, and the Americas, and to the north by the shallow ridges between Greenland and Scotland. Its southern boundary is the Antarctic Convergence, a dynamic hydrographic boundary that varies in its location. It is a relatively young ocean. The North Atlantic began to open up at the beginning of the Jurassic Period about 200 million years ago, whereas the South Atlantic split started much later, about 100 million years ago.

Structural Features

The Atlantic Ocean has an average depth of 3600 meters (11,800 feet) and its volume is about 323 $\times 10^6$ cubic kilometers (77.5 million cubic miles). Its maximum depth of 8381 meters (27,497 feet) is in the Puerto Rico Trench. Its margins are tectonically passive, so deep trenches do not line the continental margins (in contrast to the Pacific's Ring of Fire). Down its center is the Mid-Atlantic Ridge, a chain of underwater mountains with an axial rift valley. Within this rift are aligned the spreading centers at which new ocean crust is continually forming. The annual rate at which the Atlantic continues to open up is slow, only about 2 millimeters (0.08 inch). Also in the rift are hydrothermal vents, from which hot sulfide-rich water is discharged. The immediate environs of the vents are inhabited by specialized faunas that exploit the ability of some bacteria to synthesize organic matter chemically, by oxidizing sulfides and methane. The islands of Iceland and the Azores archipelago are situated on the Mid-Atlantic Ridge and are volcanically active. In Iceland one can walk along the rift where it has been uplifted above sea level. At irregular intervals there are major transform faults at which the sections of the ridge have slipped sideways, sometimes by several hundreds of kilometers. Some of these faults, such as the Romanche and Charlie Gibbs Fracture Zones, provide deepwater connections through the ridge and are important in the deep circulation.

On either side of the ridge are extensive areas of abyssal plain. These vast expanses of flat, almost featureless seafloor are carpeted by pelagic sediments laid down over millions of years and interleaved by turbidite deposits. These turbidites originated from flows of debris from the

Atlantic Ocean.

continental margins that occurred primarily when sea levels were changing rapidly. In the South Atlantic, the deep trough flanking the Mid-Atlantic Ridge is blocked on the eastern side by the Walvis Ridge off southwestern Africa, but the trough on the western side is only partially blocked by a line of seamounts off Brazil.

Circulation

The general circulation pattern of the Atlantic Ocean is strongly influenced by the effects of Earth's rotation. There are major current gyres in the subtropics of both the North and South Atlantic. The gyre in the North Atlantic circulates clockwise, whereas the gyre in the South Atlantic circulates counterclockwise. There are narrow, fast-flowing boundary currents flowing poleward along the coasts of the Americas: the Gulf Stream and the Brazil Current. The return flows on the eastern sides are more diffuse and sluggish. In deep water there is a northward flow from the Southern Ocean though the western trough, some of which leaks through the fracture zones in the ridge into the eastern trough.

The Atlantic is the only ocean that has a deep-water connection with the Arctic Ocean. At the surface, warm Atlantic water flows into the Norwegian Sea, feeding the Spitsbergen Current and keeping the climate of northern Europe mild and the seas ice-free. These surface inflows are balanced by cold inflows spilling over the ridges between Iceland, the Faroes, and Scotland, and the East Greenland Current, which carries icebergs spawned from the Greenland glaciers (one of which sank the *Titanic*) southward toward Nova Scotia. These cold waters mix with ambient water and form a water mass known as North Atlantic Deep Water, which then spreads throughout all the other oceans, so whatever happens in the North Atlantic is likely to be transmitted rapidly through the global ocean.

The exact patterns of these circulation features have recently been found to undergo long-term cycles. The best indicator of these cycles found so far is the North Atlantic Oscillation (NAO), an index based on the ratio between low and high atmospheric pressure in Iceland and the Azores, respectively. This index shows oscillations with a variety of periodicities, notably 24 and 70 years. As more long-term data are gathered, many characteristics of the ecosystems are being found to undergo cyclic variations that are correlated with these NAO cycles, such as the abundances of copepods. Distinguishing between the effects of these long-term cycles and any changes induced by human activity is proving to be very difficult.

The South Atlantic receives surface inputs from the Indian Ocean in the form of large eddies that pass around the Cape of Good Hope (35°S), which introduce three times the volume of water coming around Cape Horn (55°S). Outflows from the Mediterranean and Caribbean also influence the internal environs of the Atlantic.

The currents along the equator are complex and vary seasonally. At the surface there is a strong eastward flow, but there is a strong undercurrent in the other direction. During the northern spring, some of the flow of this undercurrent diverts northward along the coast of South America and enters the Caribbean. These complex flows result in a doming of cold water off Angola in the south and Senegal in the north. El Niño–like events also occur here, but because the Atlantic is much narrower than the Pacific, the planetary wave, which transmits the effect along the equator, takes only three to four months to cross from west to east.

Along the coasts of northwestern and southwestern Africa, trade winds blow alongshore toward the equator. As a result of Coriolis forces, they push the surface waters offshore, which are replaced by cooler water that upwells from beneath the thermocline offshore. These upwelling waters are rich in nutrients and thus stimulate considerable phytoplankton growth, so these regions tend to be centers for major fisheries.

The North Atlantic plays a key and dynamic role in the global circulation of water, described as the "Ocean Conveyor." All the water in the Atlantic is exchanged about every 250 years, so its waters are considered to be "young." Thus there is not much time for plant nutrients (nitrates, phosphates, and silicate) to accumulate in the deep water, and consequently, the Atlantic tends not to be as productive as other oceans. Therefore, the upwelling area off northwestern Africa is only about half as productive as the comparable area off Oregon and California. However, winds blow dust from the African deserts over the Atlantic that is rich enough in iron to supply all phytoplankton requirements, so, contrary to regions of the Pacific and Southern Oceans, no iron limitation is occurring.

Biogeography

The patterns of biological processes and the distributions of species show five basic latitudinal zones: one tropical/subtropical zone, temperate zones north and south, and subpolar/polar zones north and south. In the high-latitude zones, productivity reaches a single maximum in summertime (boreal or austral), whereas in the temperate zones primary production peaks twice, with the highest in the spring and the lowest in the fall. At lower latitudes the production cycle fluctuates much less but shows a slight peak in the winter.

As a rule, the highest numbers of species of animals and plants inhabit low latitudes and the number declines toward the poles. However, superimposed on these basic patterns are the effects of the large-scale circulation patterns, especially in the highly oligotrophic centers of the major current gyres. These patterns are also disturbed by the effects of "mesoscale" eddies. These can persist for over a year and can carry communities and environmental conditions far beyond their normal limits. The most notable examples are cold-core Gulf Stream rings that carry coldwater species and patches of high productivity far into the otherwise oligotrophic waters of the Sargasso Sea. In the south, the eddies from the Indian Ocean also introduce exotic species and conditions.

The distributions of the species between oceans show imprints of events in the geological past. Five million years ago there was a shallow seaway across the Isthmus of Panama, so the shallow-living tropical species living on either side of the Isthmus are quite closely related. However, those species living at depths of 500 to 2000 meters (1640 to 6560 feet) are different, having been isolated ever since the Atlantic formed. Those living even deeper at abyssopelagic depths tend to be cosmopolitan; the implication is that there are no barriers to their spread at these depths, and their life cycles are typically so long that the deep water may be circulating rapidly enough for gene flow to inhibit speciation. This generalization does not apply to species inhabiting hydrothermal vents; the Atlantic vent communities are very different from those in the Pacific.

Martin Angel

FURTHER READING

Aiken, J., and A. J. Bale, eds. "The Atlantic Meridional Transect." *Progress in Oceanography,* Vol. 45 (2000), pp. 251–465.

Angel, Martin. "Pelagic Biodiversity." In Rupert F. G. Ormond, John D. Gage, and Martin V. Angel, eds. *Marine Biodiversity: Patterns and Processes.* Cambridge and New York: Cambridge University Press, 1997; pp. 35–68.

Belkin, I. M., S. Levitus, J. Antonov, and S. A. Malmberg. "Great Salinity Anomalies in the North Atlantic." *Progress in Oceanography,* Vol. 41 (1998), pp. 1–68.

Boltovskoy, Demetrio. "General Biological Features of the South Atlantic." In D. Boltovskoy, ed., *South Atlantic Zooplankton,* Vol. 1. Leiden, the Netherlands: Backhuys, 1999; pp. 1–42.

Fromentin, J. M., and B. Planque. "An Environment in the Eastern North Atlantic. II. Influence of the North Atlantic Oscillation on *Calanus finmarchicus* and *C. helgolandicus.*" *Marine Ecology Progress Series,* Vol. 134 (1996), pp. 111–118.

Fukumori, I., F. Martel, and C. Wunsch. "The Hydrography of the North Atlantic in the Early 1980s: An Atlas." *Progress in Oceanography,* Vol. 27 (1991), pp. 1–110.

Zenk, Walter, Ray G. Peterson, and Johann R. E. Lutjeharms. "New Views of the Atlantic: A Tribute to Gerold Siedler." *Deep-Sea Research II,* Vol. 46 (1999), pp. 1–527.

RELATED ARTICLES

Brazil Current; Continental Margin; Coriolis Effect; El Niño; Fracture Zone; Gulf Stream; Gyre; Mid-Atlantic Ridge; North Atlantic Drift; Norwegian Sea; Oceanic Crust; Southern Ocean

Atlantic Ocean Plates

The Atlantic Ocean basin contains a patchwork of plates, with parts of five major and two minor plates. To picture the plates, it helps to imagine a book lying open on a tabletop. At the center, corresponding to the book's spine, is the Mid-Atlantic Ridge, separating the eastern plates from the western plates. Both pages are torn near the middle, dividing the pages into top and bottom parts. On the right side are the Eurasian and African Plates at the top and bottom, respectively. On the left side are the North American and South American Plates. The Antarctic Plate, which floors the south end of the Atlantic basin, represents the tabletop. Missing in this analogy are the two small plates, Caribbean and Scotia Sea, torn bits of the left page.

The most striking feature of the Atlantic Ocean Plates is their symmetry, virtually a mirror around the Mid-Atlantic Ridge in the center. This symmetry reflects the formation of the ocean basin, explained in more detail below, with the continents on either side drifting away from the center. As a consequence, the major Atlantic plates all contain both continental and oceanic crust, and the continents form a "ring" around the oceanic crust at the center.

Plate Boundaries

MID-ATLANTIC RIDGE

A tour of Atlantic plate boundaries should start with the Mid-Atlantic Ridge, arguably one of Earth's longest and best-known mountain ranges. This ridge is the divergent plate boundary at which new ocean lithosphere forms as the plates on either side drift away from it. Indeed, it is the magnetic anomalies formed at the ridge crest and preserved in the ocean crust that provide most of our knowledge of the opening of the Atlantic Ocean. These anomalies show the extent and age of the ocean crust on either side of the basin in past times. Using these anomalies, scientists have determined the age of the ocean crust and found that it increases with distance from the Mid-Atlantic Ridge, from zero at the ridge crest to about 140 to 180 million years at the continental margins.

Current spreading (separation) rates across the Mid-Atlantic Ridge range from a slow 1.8 centimeters (0.7 inch) per year at Iceland (and slower at points north) to a moderate 4.1 centimeters (1.6 inches) per year along the southern part of the ridge. Because of the slow spreading at the Mid-Atlantic Ridge, this mountain range is characterized by rough topography and a well-developed axial rift valley. The ridge is also divided into numerous short segments, typically only a few tens of kilometers long, offset by deep transform faults that give rise to rough fracture zones crossing the basin nearly perpendicular to the ridge.

At its southern terminus, the Mid-Atlantic Ridge ends at the Bouvet Triple Junction (at 55°S latitude), where the South American, African, and Antarctic Plates meet. At the triple junction, the Mid-Atlantic Ridge connects to spreading ridges separating the South American and Antarctic Plates (the South Sandwich Rift) and the Antarctic and African Plates (the Southwest Indian Ridge). At its northern end, the Mid-Atlantic Ridge fades away. As it enters the Arctic Ocean (and disappears off Mercator projection), its name changes to the Nansen–Gakkel Ridge and its spreading slows to the point that the plate boundary becomes diffuse and difficult to trace near the northern coast of Siberia. Because this part of the North America–Eurasia plate boundary rests beneath the Arctic ice cap, it is poorly mapped.

EURASIAN–AFRICAN PLATE BOUNDARY

Relative motion between the Eurasian and African Plates is slow and mainly strike-slip (transform) in nature. This motion is taken up along the Azores–Gibraltar Fracture Zone, which meets the Mid-Atlantic Ridge at approximately 27°N, southwest of the Azores Islands. This confluence forms the Azores Triple Junction, where the Eurasian, African, and North American Plates meet. At its eastern end, the Azores–Gibraltar Fracture Zone connects with a complex series of plate boundaries in the Mediterranean Sea through the Strait of Gibraltar. Near the Atlantic entrance to the strait, in the Tagus Abyssal Plain, the fracture zone probably changes into a series of transforms and short subduction zone segments.

NORTH AMERICAN–SOUTH AMERICAN PLATE BOUNDARIES

Across the basin, in the western Atlantic, relative motion between North and South America is also slow. Much of the boundary between these two major plates is taken up by the Caribbean Plate and its complex boundaries. The Caribbean Plate is probably a Cretaceous-age (142 million to 64 million years ago) piece of what was once the Farallon Plate, from the Pacific Ocean, that became trapped between the two major plates. Subduction zones on the west and east sides of the Caribbean Plate wedge it between Pacific and Atlantic basins. On its west side, the Cocos Plate slides beneath the Caribbean Plate on the eastern boundary of the Pacific Ocean. On its east side, the North American and South American Plates

subduct beneath the Caribbean Plate at the Lesser Antilles Trench and island arc. Relative plate motion on the north and south sides of the Caribbean Plate is mainly slow strike-slip. Much of the northern plate boundary is a transform fault along the Cayman Ridge. This fault stretches from the Honduras–Belize border in Central America, through the Caribbean islands between Cuba and Hispaniola, to connect with the trenches east of the Caribbean near Puerto Rico. At the middle of this transform, a short spreading ridge segment, approximately 150 kilometers (93 miles) in length, forms ocean crust in the Cayman Trough. South of the Caribbean Plate, the plate boundary is also complex but mainly transforms along the northern margin of South America. The plate boundary connection between the Lesser Antilles Arc and the Mid-Atlantic Ridge is unclear because the relative motion between North and South America is small at this location, so no clearly discernible plate boundary morphology has been formed. Some scientists believe the boundary must be a transform fault, perhaps along one of the Mid-Atlantic Ridge fracture zones where the distance between the arc and spreading ridge is least. Others think the motion between the two major plates is taken up by diffuse deformation rather than a discrete plate boundary.

AFRICAN–ANTARCTIC PLATE BOUNDARY

From the Bouvet Triple Junction in the South Atlantic, two plate boundaries stretch east and west, separating the Antarctic Plate from Africa and South America. To the east, the Southwest Indian Ridge is a spreading ridge located approximately midway between Africa and Antarctica. This ridge has unusually rough topography because the spreading rate is low, about 1.7 centimeters (0.7 inch) per year, and because the ridge is made up of numerous short spreading segments separated by transform faults. Eastward past the south tip of Africa, the ridge continues into the Indian Ocean, where it is one of the major spreading ridge systems.

SOUTH AMERICAN–ANTARCTIC PLATE BOUNDARIES
The South Sandwich Rift is the mid-ocean ridge that stretches westward from the Bouvet Triple Junction. It separates the South American and Antarctic Plates and connects with the southern part of the Scotia Trench near the tip of the Antarctic Peninsula. Between the Antarctic Peninsula and the south tip of South America sits another small plate, the Scotia Sea Plate. Similar in size and shape to the Caribbean Plate farther north, the Scotia Sea Plate appears to be bounded on the north and south by transform faults that accommodate strike-slip relative motion between this small plate and the larger ones surrounding it. Because of its remote location, the boundaries surrounding this small plate are poorly mapped. The plate appears to be growing eastward with spreading in the back-arc basin behind the Scotia Island Arc. On the east and west, trenches and subduction zones bound the Scotia Sea Plate. The east side is a major trench and island arc system, whereas the west side is more complex. At the western entrance to the Drake Passage, the Antarctic plate boundary shifts from convergent to transform as it passes from the tip of South America to the tip of the Antarctic Peninsula. The result of these plate boundaries is similar to those around the Caribbean Plate—the Scotia Sea Plate is wedged between the major plates and acts as a "bearing," accommodating motion between them.

Tectonic History of the Atlantic Ocean

During the Permian Period, approximately 250 million years ago, there was no Atlantic Ocean. Instead, the continents were mostly gathered together into the supercontinent, Pangea. For reasons that are still not fully understood, the huge continental aggregate began to split into the continents that we recognize today, with North and South America drifting west relative to Eurasia and Africa. The split probably began about 200 million years ago, during the Triassic Period, with initial rifting in the Gulf of Mexico, Caribbean, and central Atlantic. By the Jurassic Period, about 165 million years ago, oceanic crust was forming between North America and Africa. At this time, the Gulf of Mexico had probably opened to much of its current width, but the South Atlantic and far North Atlantic remained firmly closed. At about 125 million years ago, during the Early Cretaceous Period, the South Atlantic began to form, with the southernmost part of the ocean opening first and the split traveling north. By this time, the central Atlantic was already more than 2000 kilometers (1240 miles) wide and 4000 meters (13,120 feet) deep. During the middle and Late Cretaceous Period (95 million to 80 million years ago) the northern Atlantic began to open, with Greenland and North America separating from Europe. By the end of the Cretaceous Period, at 65 million years ago, the Atlantic was a wide, deep-ocean basin from its southern end up to northern Greenland.

Since 65 million years ago (during the Tertiary Period), the final elements of the Atlantic basin came together in their present configuration. The basin continued to widen with the Mid-Atlantic Ridge near its center. During the early Tertiary, a spreading ridge jump transferred the Iberian Peninsula from the African Plate to the Eurasian Plate. Another jump shifted the Mid-Atlantic Ridge out of the Labrador Sea (on the west side of Greenland) to its present location. In the late Tertiary, Africa and Europe converged, nearly closing off the Mediterranean Sea from the Atlantic Ocean at the Strait of Gibraltar. In the western Atlantic, the Isthmus of Panama arose between North and South America to block communication between the Pacific and Atlantic Oceans. The closure of these equatorial pathways to ocean circulation isolated the Atlantic basin and may have been a major factor in causing the cooling of the global climate since the Cretaceous and early Tertiary Periods. By middle to late Miocene time (10 million to 5 million years ago), the present circulation pattern of Atlantic currents had been established.

Atlantic Basin Morphology

The shape of the Atlantic Ocean basin is a direct product of its plate boundary configurations and tectonic history. Ocean crust is shallowest when it first forms, at the mid-ocean ridge, and it subsides and cools with increasing age. Because the basin has opened continually, with the Mid-Atlantic Ridge at its center, the Atlantic is shallowest along the central ridge and becomes deeper east and west toward its margins. The spine of the Mid-Atlantic Ridge is cut by dozens of transform faults, which cause the ridge to have a segmented appearance and give rise to fracture zones that stretch east and west from the ridge toward the margins. Additionally, as a result of its history of opening, most of the Atlantic-bordering continental margins are passive, wide, and mantled with thick sedimentary wedges. Offshore of the major river mouths, sediments have buried the rough ocean crust to form flat abyssal plains. Exceptions to this characteristic are the trenches around the Lesser Antilles and Scotia subduction zones at the leading edges of the Caribbean and Scotia Sea Plates.

Many of the major islands and bathymetric highs arose from excessive volcanic activity related to mantle plumes. The island of Iceland, which sits astride the northern Mid-Atlantic Ridge between Greenland and Britain, is the product of an active mantle plume (hotspot). The buoyant hot mantle related to that plume elevates much of the northern Mid-Atlantic Ridge. Farther south, other islands and ridges, such as the Azores and Canary Islands in the northern and central Atlantic and the Walvis and Rio Grande Ridges in the southern Atlantic Ocean, are also thought to be products of mantle plumes.

Some other islands, part of the continental margins, such as the British Isles and the Falkland Islands, are continental fragments resulting from nonuniform rifting of the continents early in the formation of the Atlantic.

William W. Sager

FURTHER READING

DeMets, Charles, Richard Gordon, Donald Argus, and Seth Stein. "Current Plate Motions." *Geophysical Journal International,* Vol. 101 (1990), pp. 425–478.

Kearey, P., and F. J. Vine. *Global Tectonics.* Oxford and Boston: Blackwell Scientific, 1990; 2nd ed., Oxford and Cambridge, Mass.: Blackwell Science, 1996.

Kennett, James. *Marine Geology.* Englewood Cliffs, N.J.: Prentice Hall, 1982.

Klitgord, Kim D., and Hans Schouten. "Plate Kinematics of the Central Atlantic." In *The Geology of North America,* Vol. M: *The Western North Atlantic Region.* Boulder, Colo.: Geological Society of America, 1986.

Moores, Eldridge M., and Robert J. Twiss. *Tectonics.* New York: W. H. Freeman, 1995.

Nicolas, Adolphe. *The Mid-oceanic Ridges: Mountains below Sea Level.* Translated by Thomas Reimer. Berlin and New York: Springer-Verlag, 1995.

Rosencranz, Eric. "Structure and Tectonics of the Yucatan Basin, Caribbean Sea, as Determined from Seismic Reflection Studies." *Tectonics,* Vol. 9 (October 1990), pp. 1037–1059.

Segar, Douglas A. *Introduction to Ocean Sciences.* Belmont, Calif.: Wadsworth, 1998.

Seibold, Eugen, and Wolfgang H. Berger. *The Sea Floor: An Introduction to Marine Geology.* Berlin and New York: Springer-Verlag, 1982; 3rd. rev. and updated ed., 1996.

Strahler, Arthur N. *Plate Tectonics.* Cambridge, Mass.: Geo Books, 1998.

Sykes, Lynn R., William R. McCann, and Alan L. Kafka. "Motion of Caribbean Plate during the Last 7 Million Years and Implications for Earlier Cenozoic Movements." *Journal of Geophysical Research,* 10 December 1982, pp. 10,656–10,676.

Taylor, Brian, and Garry D. Karner. "On the Evolution of Marginal Basins." *Reviews of Geophysics and Space Physics,* Vol. 21 (November 1983), pp. 1727–1741.

Thurman, Harold V. *Introductory Oceanography.* Columbus, Ohio: Charles E. Merrill, 1975; 9th ed., with Elizabeth A. Burton, Upper Saddle River, N.J.: Prentice Hall, 2001.

Atlantic Ocean Stratigraphy

As is the case of any rifted basin, the stratigraphy of the Atlantic Ocean is strongly determined by the timing and nature of its rifting, combined with the changes in the circulation patterns and climate that have affected the area since that time. In such a large and north/south-oriented basin, there are major variations related to latitude, most notably in the abundance of glacial sediments in the northeast Atlantic since the onset of northern hemispheric glaciation 2.5 million years ago and the thick accumulations of biogenic sediments in the equatorial regions associated with the equatorial convergence zone that supports upwelling of nutrient-rich waters. Sedimentation at any given point on the Atlantic margins has also been affected by the influx of material from the adjacent continent, especially in the form of the large submarine fans that concentrate sandy material into large lobes that are fed by the major rivers that drain into the Atlantic. Of special importance are the Laurentian, Hudson, Niger, Amazon, Congo, and Orange Fans.

Rift–Drift Stratigraphy

Despite the lateral variability, there is a common stratigraphy recognized in the central Atlantic and linked to its initial rifting in the Late Jurassic (about 160 million to 145 million years ago). The oldest sediments recognized are continental rift deposits, typically quartz-rich river and alluvial fan sandstones and siltstones. These are highly laterally variable in thickness, being ponded in tilted fault blocks. Their development is naturally controlled by the style of extension, so that in nonvolcanic parts of the Atlantic margin, such as

Iberia off Spain and Portugal, there is a wide expanse of such sediment, whereas in volcanic margins, such as the U.S. east coast or eastern Greenland, the margin is narrow and syn-rift deposits are limited to narrow basins, occasionally cropping out on shore today (e.g., in New Jersey). These mostly subaerial sediments are succeeded by shallow marine sediments, usually in the form of platform and slope carbonates. A well-developed reef limestone structure allows the high-energy edge of the shelf to be easily traced in deep seismic profiles. During the earliest phases of opening, the Atlantic Basin was repeatedly isolated from the global ocean and allowed to desiccate, laying down thick sequences of salt in localized basins along both west and east margins. This salt has subsequently been reactivated and has flowed to produce diapirs that penetrate much younger sequences. Another consequence of the restricted circulation in the early Atlantic was a tendency for parts of the ocean to stagnate, allowing organic-rich black shales to accumulate as a result of the anoxic conditions on the seafloor. There are well-developed unconformity surfaces at the base of the rift sediments and also between the rift-related salts and early postrift carbonate rocks, the latter break being known as the *break-up conformity,* dated as Early Jurassic (about 206 million to 180 million years ago) in offshore eastern North America and as Aptian–Albian [Early Cretaceous (about 120 million to 100 million years ago)] in the southern Central Atlantic.

Post–Rift Sedimentation

The Atlantic margins show a general tendency for younger and younger sediments to onlap farther onto the continent with time, with the oldest syn-rift sediment typically located offshore near the rift axis. This is because after rifting the deformed crust cools, becomes stiffer, and tends to warp over increasingly broad wavelengths under the weight of sediment deposited along the edges.

The progressive rifting of the ocean from south to north during the Cretaceous Period gradually opened up the basin to more open pelagic conditions. The major lateral offsets of the Atlantic Basin along the fracture zones of the central Atlantic (e.g., Romanche, Vema) acted to prevent a through-going circulation pattern from establishing itself quickly after rifting in the equatorial Atlantic began 120 million years ago during the Aptian Stage. Planktonic foraminifers show that an open, deep marine connection was not available between the Tethys and the South Atlantic until the Turonian Stage (approximately 90 million years ago). Dominantly carbonate sedimentation in the Cretaceous was interrupted along the southeastern North American margin by slumping that has recently been tied to the meteorite impact event at the Cretaceous–Tertiary boundary. This event generated tsunami (seismic sea) waves that redeposited large volumes of sediment offshore.

Final rifting of the northeast Atlantic was delayed until the Paleocene (approximately 63 million years ago), when the initiation of the deep-seated Iceland Plume allowed spreading to migrate north of the Charlie Gibbs Fracture Zone into a region that had been extended many times over the Mesozoic (about 248 million to 65 million years ago) but where extension had always failed to progress to seafloor spreading. From the early Eocene a general cooling of the middle and deep water resulted in widespread sedimentation of siliceous biogenic sediment throughout the Atlantic Basin. These sediments continued to accumulate until the end of the early Miocene (approximately 16 million years ago), when calcareous ooze sedimentation became more prominent.

Start of Deepwater Flow

Opening of the northeast Atlantic was to have a major effect on the stratigraphy of the entire basin because it was through this passageway that cold, deepwater flow was initiated from sources in the Arctic Ocean. As the northeast Atlantic Ocean opened, the flow was initially blocked by the Greenland–Scotland volcanic ridge. However, as this subsided, deepwater flow began. A major erosion event dated at the Eocene–Oligocene boundary (35 million years ago) is known from the deep basins of the North Atlantic. There is no evidence to suggest a major sea-level fall at that time and its presence may be related to the deep erosive currents from the Arctic at that time. It is, however, clear that sea-level variation does play an important role is controlling the Atlantic stratigraphy. A mid-Oligocene (29 million years ago) erosion event is recognized throughout the Central and North Atlantic in the form of major channeling and erosion. This surface has been attributed to a fall in global sea level, enhancing continental erosion and maximizing redeposition onto the continental rise. Erosion offshore from west Africa related to this event removed up to 500 meters (1640 feet) of sediment at the shelf edge.

After the Eocene-Oligocene, deepwater current activity weakened but remained important, especially in the construction of the large sediment drift deposits of the North Atlantic, which were best developed offshore of eastern North America, southeastern Brazil, and between the British Isles and Greenland. These features are not deposited by turbidity currents but are instead contourites, representing an accumulation of sediment deposited from Arctic overflow water and from the western boundary currents that hug the topography of the continental margin. The drifts comprise a mixture of clastic sediments, mostly finer sands and silts, together with pelagic biogenic sediments. Although they may be thin, the large drifts are sometimes kilometers thick. Their geometry is typically elongated parallel to the current flow.

Plio-Pleistocene glaciation (2.5 million to 0.1 million years ago) has had a major impact on the stratigraphy of the Atlantic margins. Glaciation caused large sea-level falls, exposing wide areas of the continental shelves. In this setting, rivers cut canyons across the shelf, which were subsequently filled as sea level rose again in the Holocene (since 10,000 years ago). Sedimentation did, however, continue on the continental slope and rise. The glaciation was accompanied by increased desertification of the Sahara region, and a large volume of wind-blown dust from this region continues to accumulate in the adjacent North Atlantic Basin. In regions covered directly by the glaciers, erosion of the landward portions of the margin stratigraphy was locally intense. Farther offshore, large deltas of coarse, boulder-sized till were constructed, allowing the shelf edge to prograde seaward. The modern shelf break on the Greenland and Canadian margins is to a large extent defined by Pleistocene (1.64 million to 0.1 million years) glacial deltas. Deglaciation seems to have been a trigger to large-scale (tens of kilometers) slides on the continental margins. In the Norwegian Sea the giant Storegga Slide is believed to have been caused by the dissociation of frozen gas hydrate deposits within slope sediments, as a result of the changing water depth. A potentially catastrophic loss of hydrates destablized the slope, allowing emplacement of this semicoherent body far offshore into deep water. Similar large slides are known from the Virginia–Carolina coast.

Peter Clift

FURTHER READING
Doust, H., and E. Omatsola. "Niger Delta." In J. D. Edwards and P. A. Santogrossi, eds., *Divergent/Passive Margin Basins*. Tulsa, Okla.: American Association of Petroleum Geologists, 1989; pp. 201–238.

Emery, K. O., and Elazar Uchupi. *The Geology of the Atlantic Ocean*. New York: Springer-Verlag, 1984; p. 1050.

Hsü, K. J., and H. J. Weissert. *South Atlantic Paleoceanography*. Cambridge and New York: Cambridge University Press, 1985; p. 350.

Kidd, R. B., and P. R. Hill. "Sedimentation on Mid-ocean Sediment Drifts." In C. P. Summerhayes and N. J. Shackleton, eds., *North Atlantic Palaeoceanography*.

Oxford: Blackwell Scientific for the Geological Society of London, 1986; pp. 87–102.

Poag, C. W., and P. C. de Graciansky. *Geologic Evolution of Atlantic Continental Rises*. New York: Van Nostrand Reinhold, 1992.

RELATED ARTICLES
Deep-Sea Sediment; Diapir; Divergent Plate Boundary; Eustatic Sea Level; Glacial Marine Processes; Mid-Ocean Ridge; Submarine Canyon; Submarine Fan; Unconformity

Atmospheric Dust

Prevailing atmospheric winds provide an important pathway for the transport of continental materials to the oceans. Atmospheric dust is formed when winds pick up particles and transport them until they fall out of the atmosphere. Fallout is caused either by a weakening of the air currents or by adsorption to rain droplets and subsequent washout. Particles that fall out on the sea surface are eventually transferred to the seafloor by pelagic sedimentation. Some elements carried to the ocean via atmospheric dust play significant roles in chemical and biological processes.

Atmospheric dust contains a variety of particles from both natural and human-made sources. Natural sources include eroded crustal material, sea salts, volcanic and forest fire ash, and materials from outer space (micrometeorites). Anthropogenic processes that release particulates to the atmosphere include fossil-fuel burning, mining and ore processing, waste incineration, the production of chemicals, and farming practices (slash-and-burn agriculture).

The largest source of atmospheric dust is crustal material from Earth mobilized by wind erosion. Hence the primary regions of atmospheric dust formation are the windy, arid and semi-arid regions of the world: North Africa, eastern Asia, and the Middle East. Atmospheric dust from these regions has a major impact on the clay mineral and trace metal flux to the Atlantic, the

North Pacific, and in the north Indian Ocean. This is reflected in both pelagic sediments and the suspended particle distributions of these waters. For example, trade winds that blow across the Sahara Desert are responsible for the high concentrations of aluminum-rich clay minerals in subtropical Atlantic Ocean sediments. Moreover, atmospheric dust is an important transport mechanism for trace metals in mid-ocean gyre surface waters, due to their isolation from riverine input. In fact, atmospheric dust is the largest oceanic source for the metals arsenic (As) and lead (Pb).

Atmospheric dust also plays an important role in biological processes. Iron (Fe) is an essential element for life in the ocean because it is used for chlorophyll synthesis and various nitrogen processes. In fact, it has been discovered that lack of iron limits phytoplankton productivity in otherwise nutrient-rich areas. The present-day flux of iron via atmospheric dust to mid-ocean regions is estimated at 0.2 to 0.8 micromoles of iron per square meter (μmol Fe/m^2) per day (0.02 to 0.07 μmol Fe/ft^2 per day) in the North Atlantic and 0.08 to 0.16 μmol Fe/m^2 per day (0.007 to 0.016 μmol Fe/ft^2 per day) in the North Pacific. During windy arid times in the past, such as the last glacial period (ice age), iron-rich atmospheric dust loads were 10 to 50 times greater. Moreover, scientists have found that ice cores show a strong correlation between iron concentrations and low-atmospheric carbon dioxide (CO_2) concentrations. Because phytoplankton use atmospheric carbon dioxide during photosynthesis, it has been postulated that increased iron-stimulated productivity may have contributed substantially to the draw-down of atmospheric CO_2 levels during the last glacial period. Current oceanic iron-fertilization studies validate this hypothesis.

Atmospheric dust data are limited by sampling problems due to the vastness and remoteness of the regions wherein dust travels as well as spatial and temporal variability in dust formation and deposition. However, although difficult to measure, there is evidence that the magnitude of particle flux via atmospheric dust has a significant impact on oceanic chemical and biological processes, in both the present and the geologic past.

Daniel Schuller

FURTHER READING

Chester, R. *Marine Geochemistry*. Cambridge, Mass.: Blackwell Scientific, 1990; 2nd ed. Malden, Mass.: Blackwell Science, 2000.

Libes, S. M. *Introduction to Marine Biogeochemistry*. New York: Wiley, 1992.

Martin, J. H. "Glacial–Interglacial CO_2 Change: The Iron Hypothesis." *Paleoceanography*, Vol. 5 (1990).

Prospero, J. M. "Atmospheric Transport." In V. Ittekkot, P. Schafer, S. Honjo, and P. J. Depetris, eds., *Particle Flux in the Ocean*. New York: Wiley, 1996.

RELATED ARTICLES

Carbon Dioxide; Iron; Nitrogen; Nutrient; Photosynthesis; Photosynthesis and Iron Limitation; Primary Productivity; Trace Element; Trade Winds; Windblown Dust, Transport and Disposition of

Authigenic Sediment

Authigenic refers to mineral or rock constituents that are formed in place either on or directly under the floor of the ocean. These sediment particles are formed from submarine eruptions, hydrothermal eruptions, deposition from seawater, or metamorphism. Authigenic sediments record changes in the physical and chemical conditions that occurred both during and after deposition. By understanding the conditions that form authigenic sediments, oceanographers can interpret ancient paleoenvironments.

Authigenic sediments have diverse origins and usually are slow to precipitate from seawater. Authigenic sediment may be transported long distances, up to 1000 kilometers (621 miles) away from their sources. The five major groups of authigenic sediments are metal-rich sediments and iron oxides, manganese nodules, phosphorites, zeolites, and barites.

Metal-rich sediments and iron oxide deposits are commonly associated with active spreading ridges and are enriched in iron, manganese, copper, chrome, and lead. There are three types of deposits related to hydrothermal activity at spreading centers: iron-manganese–rich sediments, manganese-rich sediment, and iron-sulfide-manganese–depleted sediment. In general, the iron-manganese sediments are associated with fast-spreading ridges. Slow-spreading ridges have manganese–rich sediments, and iron-sulfide-manganese–depleted sediments are associated with spreading ridges of intermediate rates. These groups of authigenic sediment all result from the interaction of seawater as it percolates down through the oceanic crust and mixes with the magma-generated solutions that move upward through the crust during volcanic and plutonic activities.

First reported by the *Challenger* expedition in 1873, manganese nodules, containing manganese, nickel, copper, cobalt, iron, and other elements, represent a significant potential source of metals. Nodules are concentrically zoned. They remain unaltered at depth and thus are not formed or affected by the leaching and/or upward migration of buried nodules. There are four main explanations for their formation: hydrogenous origin, hydrothermal origin, weathering of submarine volcanic rocks and debris, and diagenitic origin through the remobilization of manganese in the sediment column and reprecipitation at the sediment–water interface. The rounded shape of nodules is caused by benthonic organisms that nudge or roll the nodules.

Phosphorites are sedimentary rocks that consist of phosphate. Phosphorite deposits are found in two major settings: Their continental shelf and upper slope deposits are as many as 30 centimeters (11.8 inches) and occur as slabs or nodules, whereas in some deepwater localities, thick deposits 100 meters (328 feet) thick or more are associated with organic-rich shale, chert, and dolomite. Phosphorus is a required nutrient for organisms in seawater, and phosphorite deposits are associated with areas of upwelling. Phosphorite is formed by the progressive replacement of carbonate by phosphorus in biogenic sediments in oxygen-depleted water. The Agulhas Bank of South Africa has one of the largest deposits linked to ancient upwelling.

Zeolites are colorless-to-white hydroaluminosilicates with compositions similar to those of the feldspars. Zeolites are found in sediments that accumulated slowly. The most common zeolites are phillipsite and clinoptilolite. Phillipsite may comprise as much as 50 percent of the carbonate-free sediment in areas where the rate of sedimentation is slow. In the Pacific Ocean, it is associated with oxides of iron and manganese, clays, palagonite (an altered volcanic glass), and volcanic debris. Phillipsite is thought to form predominantly from the alteration of palagonite. Clinoptilolite occurs in all oceans but is most common in the Atlantic Ocean. It forms mostly by alteration of rhyolite, glass, opaline silica, and other silicic volcanic material.

Barite occurs in sediment and fecal pellets as crystalline and microcrystalline phases. An association exists between barite and organic production. Barite is formed by biogenic activity along submarine volcanic sites and at spreading ridges (white smokers) by seawater percolating downward and mixing with ascending magma.

David L. White

FURTHER READING
Hatch, F. H., and R. H. Rastall. *The Petrology of the Sedimentary Rocks.* London: Allen, 1913; 7th ed., by J. T. Greensmith, London and Boston: Unwin Hyman, 1989.

Kennett, James. *Marine Geology.* Englewood Cliffs, N.J.: Prentice Hall, 1982.

Thurman, Harold V. *Essentials of Oceanography.* Columbus, Ohio: Charles E. Merrill, 1983; 6th ed., with Alan P. Trujillo, Upper Saddle River, N.J.: Prentice Hall, 1999.

Autonomous Underwater Vehicle

Most studies of the deep ocean make use of submersibles and remotely operated vehicles (ROVs). However, submersibles are expensive, and relatively few of them are available. ROVs require an operator constantly on hand to control and guide their movements, either in a nearby submersible or in a support ship on the surface. Autonomous underwater vehicles (AUVs) offer an alternative to ROVs. As their name suggests, they are able to operate independently, carrying out preprogrammed instructions and even reacting to unexpected problems. They are the first true robot explorers of the oceans.

AUV Features

Autonomous underwater vehicles have to carry all the equipment they need to survive and carry out their operations underwater for an extended period of time. The design of AUVs varies widely depending on their purpose; the ring-shaped robots designed to crawl along underwater pipelines searching for leaks or signs of corrosion are technically autonomous, but the term AUV is usually applied to sophisticated free-floating robot submarines.

Because free-floating AUVs have to move around underwater for long periods of time, they are usually given fishlike, streamlined designs to increase their engine efficiency and reduce the chance of becoming snagged on unexpected obstacles. These conditions are not so important for typical ROVs because ROVs spend only a short period of time underwater and are usually tethered to their control ship, or at least have an operator nearby.

An AUV's outer shell is usually made from carbon or glass fiber, which is lightweight and shock resistant. Inside, the various elements of the AUV are mounted on a strong metal frame (usually of aluminum). Another important requirement of a free-floating AUV is that it must have neutral buoyancy—when completely submerged, it should hang in the water without rising or sinking, and the weights of the various components must be balanced carefully. If necessary, additional weights, or lightweight foam blocks, can be added to the vehicle so that it ends up with the same density as the seawater it displaces. AUVs usually include a heavy weight that can be dropped automatically to abort the mission and send the vehicle rising rapidly to the surface.

AUVs usually move through the water using electric propellers or screws that are powered by onboard batteries. In addition to one or two large rear-mounted screws that push the vehicle along, other small propellers mounted around the vehicle can act as thrusters to move it in one direction or another. Some AUVs use control surfaces, similar to the aerofoils on an aircraft, instead of thrusters. These surfaces adjust their angles to change the drag on the vehicle, as it moves forward, and alter its direction. Sometimes a pressurized casing protects the vehicle's batteries, but the interior of the AUV is not generally pressurized, and all the instruments must be thoroughly protected against the water and low temperatures.

Within the AUV are a series of sensors that measure important data such as pressure, depth, speed, and direction, and feed data back to the mission controller, a sophisticated computer that makes decisions for the vehicle. The controller makes its decisions according to a preprogrammed script held in its memory. Usually, the script is highly detailed and aims to take account of every situation the vehicle might encounter, but recently some researchers have experimented with giving AUVs artificial intelligence. Although this makes the mission controller more complex, it allows the mission script to be simplified. The controller is given a basic set of rules and decides its own actions by assessing situations according to the rules. Although the rest of the vehicle is basically hardware, mission control relies on software and is probably the major area of research and improvement in AUVs today. The lack of suitable computer technology is the major reason why AUVs have become a reality only in the past decade or so.

As well as the AUVs' control systems, the interior has to contain many other instruments for navigation and tracking. Vehicles are typically fitted with acoustic devices that allow them to be tracked while underwater, global positioning system (GPS) or other satellite navigation systems that can identify their location when they surface, and radio beacons to call for retrieval once the mission is complete. The front of the AUV usually holds instruments specific to its mission and range, from sonar and cameras to temperature sensors, magnetometers, and mine neutralizers.

Applications of AUVs

Autonomous underwater vehicles have a potentially huge range of uses. At present one of the major barriers to a better understanding of the oceans is that scientists only have "snapshots" of conditions in small areas at particular times. As AUVs get smaller and cheaper, large numbers of them could be used to monitor the sea constantly. These AUV fleets could have a major influence on knowledge and future exploitation of the oceans, but several barriers remain to be overcome.

One of these problems is the establishment of accurate navigation systems for AUVs. At present, AUVs travel only over small distances, so most make use of dead reckoning, a calculation of their current position based on the speed and direction of their movement from a known starting position. However, if AUVs are to be released to roam for long distances across the seas, the errors involved in dead reckoning will multiply. Beneath the sea, AUVs are unable to use satellite

navigation, but other options include navigation via a network of underwater sonar beacons or by following a prepared map of the seafloor. Both of these solutions have their own problems, though, but some scientists think that map navigation could be coupled with other methods to produce an accurate system.

Another major problem for long-term AUV missions is communication. Traditionally, underwater communications are carried out through sound. An AUV can communicate with its base by a series of acoustic "pings," but over long distances and in turbulent waters, this information can easily be distorted. To solve this problem, scientists have developed a networking technology that borrows its principle from cellular phones. In an acoustic local area network (ALAN), signals are sent and received through a network of beacons, so whichever beacon is closest to the AUV receives the original signal and sends it back to base via a chain of other beacons.

At present, many AUVs are purely experimental vessels, but several have already found important applications. These include minesweeping and neutralization, acting as dummy targets in military submarine trials, and location of wreckage after air crashes. Most current AUVs, however, are used for oceanography and marine biology. Equipped with temperature and chemical sensors, cameras, and sonar, AUVs are able to monitor the conditions on ocean floors continuously, swim among shoals of fish, or investigate undersea communities without disrupting them.

In the future AUVs could have a much broader range of uses. These might include surveying and exploitation of mineral resources, as well as servicing of undersea machinery and pipelines associated with oil drilling and other mining operations. AUVs might also be used in the fishing industry either to locate and monitor fish stocks (and therefore help preserve a breeding population) or, like undersea robot sheepdogs, to herd fish in shoals from place to place. Other applications could include monitoring and cleanup of marine pollution and collecting data to aid weather and ocean current forecasting.

Giles Sparrow

FURTHER READING
Society for Underwater Technology. *Diverless and Deepwater Technology*. London and Boston: Graham and Trotman, 1989.
————. *Advances in Underwater Inspection and Maintenance*. London and Boston: Graham and Trotman, 1990.

USEFUL WEB SITES
Autonomous Undersea Systems Institute.
    <http://www.ausi.org>.
Franck Goddio Society.
    <http://www.underwaterdiscovery.org>.
Woods Hole Oceanographic Institute.
    <http://www.whoi.edu>.

RELATED ARTICLES
Bouyancy; Deep-Sea Exploration; Global Positioning System; Sonar; Submersible; Underwater Communication

Autotrophic

An autotrophic organism, or autotroph, is one that synthesizes its food from simple chemical compounds it obtains from its surroundings. The word is derived from Greek and means self (*autos*) nourishment (*trophe*). Autotrophy is based on chemical reactions that require a source of energy. In the pelagic zone, the necessary energy is supplied by sunlight, and the sequence of reactions that employs it constitutes the process of *photosynthesis*. Below the pelagic zone, where light levels are insufficient for photosynthesis, energy is supplied by chemical reactions. The process is called *chemosynthesis* and the organisms are said to be *chemoautotrophic*. Chemoautotrophic organisms also inhabit such environments as seabed sediments and estuarine muds.

Chemoautotrophs use carbon dioxide as a source of carbon for the synthesis of carbohydrates and obtain energy by oxidizing reduced substances such as hydrogen sulfide, iron (Fe^{2+} and Fe^{3+}), ammonia, and methane. Suitable compounds are abundant in the vicinity of hydrothermal vents and chemoautotrophs are common in vent communities. All of these organisms are prokaryotes. Some are bacteria, classified in the domain and kingdom Bacteria. Others belong to the domain Archaea and include members of the kingdoms Crenarchaeota and Euryarchaeota. The Crenarchaeota are extreme thermophiles (heat-loving organisms) that thrive in the hot conditions close to deep-sea vents. The Euryarchaeota, or methanogens, use methane as an energy source and are found in any anaerobic environment.

Photosynthesizing autotrophs are found near the sea surface. They include algae, which are protistans, and cyanobacteria, which are prokaryotes. Some single-celled algae drift in the plankton. Ecologically, they are the most significant primary producers of the marine ecosystem, occupying the position that is held by green plants on land. Seaweeds are multicelled protistans. They are also autotrophs and are found in shallow water and on seashores.

Michael Allaby

FURTHER READING
Nybakken, James W. *Marine Biology: An Ecological Approach*, 5th ed. San Francisco: Benjamin Cummings, 2001.
Rothschild, Lynn J., and Rocco L. Mancinelli. "Life in Extreme Environments." *Nature*, Vol. 409 (2001), pp. 1092–1101.

RELATED ARTICLES
Chemoautotrophic Bacteria; Chemosynthesis; Pelagic; Photosynthesis

Auxiliary General Oceanographic Research Vessel

Auxiliary General Oceanographic Research (AGOR) vessels are a series of U.S. oceanographic research vessels built according to the Naval Ship Engineering Center's AGOR hull design. Presently, 25 vessels have been built in the series.

The AGOR program was conceived in the 1960s as part of the U.S. Office of Naval Research's Tenoc (10-year plan for oceanography). Initially, all the ships were built to the same basic design, but this design has been steadily modified over the years to accommodate the suggestions of oceanographers, as well as to house the advanced equipment, submersibles, and ROVs (remotely operated vehicles) that may be used during some oceanographic missions.

Five AGOR ships are currently in service. The oldest are the research vessels (R/Vs) *Melville* and *Knorr*, built in the late 1960s but upgraded in 1992, while the others, R/Vs *Thomas G. Thompson*, *Roger Revelle*, and *Atlantis*, were all built in the 1990s. Each ship is about 84 meters (275 feet) long, with a beam about 15 meters (50 feet) long. All are fitted with heavy lifting equipment, winches, and workshops for servicing submersibles and other equipment.

Although all the AGOR ships are owned by the U.S. Navy, they are distributed around the country and leased to various oceanographic establishments; *Knorr* and *Atlantis* are based at the Woods Hole Oceanographic Institute in Massachusetts, *Melville* and *Revelle* at the Scripps Institution of Oceanography in California, and *Thompson* at the University of Washington.

Giles Sparrow

FURTHER READING

Pittenger, Richard F. "Replacing the Fleet." *Oceanus*, Vol. 40, No. 1 (Spring/Summer 1997).
"Seapower/Oceanography." *Sea Power*, January 1999, p. 282.

RELATED ARTICLES

Oceanographic Research Vessel

B

Backwash, see Littoral Zone Processes

Bacteria

Bacteria, the most abundant organisms on Earth, exist in every type of known habitat and play important ecological roles as primary producers, decomposers, and parasites. As well as being found in biologically rich surface waters and muddy seafloors, bacteria have colonized such inhospitable habitats as scalding deep-sea vents, extreme ocean depths, and deep sediment layers. Scientists classify bacteria into two kingdoms, Archeabacteria and Eubacteria.

Bacteria are single-celled organisms, but their cells are very different from those of plants, animals, or other single-celled organisms. Bacteria are prokaryotic cells. Unlike the eukaryotic cells of all other organisms, prokaryotic cells lack complex internal structures such as a nucleus, and their DNA exists as a simple circular molecule rather than as a tightly packed chromosome. Prokaryotic cells are almost 10 times smaller than eukaryotic cells, which enables bacteria to multiply rapidly into incredible numbers; for instance, the bacteria in the human mouth can outnumber all the people who have ever lived.

Because of their long evolutionary history, bacteria have developed an astounding diversity of lifestyles. Some are photosynthetic; like plants, they use the energy in sunlight to convert carbon dioxide from the atmosphere into energy-rich carbohydrate molecules. These photosynthetic bacteria include the cyanobacteria, which use the same green pigment (chlorophyll) that plants and green algae use to trap sunlight. Cyanobacteria exist as nanoplankton in surface ocean waters.

Many bacteria are decomposers. They feed on dead organic matter, such as decomposing bodies on the seafloor, and release nutrients back into the seawater as a result. Near the top of the sediment layer, where oxygen is abundant, most bacteria are aerobic; they use oxygen from seawater to break down organic molecules by aerobic respiration, the same chemical process that animals use to obtain energy from food. Below the surface, where oxygen levels fall, anaerobic bacteria predominate. These bacteria obtain energy by a form of respiration that does not require oxygen. The chemical by-products released by such reactions turn the sediment black. The bacteria in sea sediment provide food for microorganisms and other detritivores, forming an important part of the benthic food chain.

Bacteria have evolved a variety of ways of obtaining energy in the absence of oxygen or light. Many exploit sulfur-based chemicals. A spectacular example occurs in the inky blackness of the bathyal zone, where thermophilic (heat-loving) bacteria live on sulfur released by scalding volcanic vents. These bacteria provide the basis of a food chain that does not depend on sunlight or plants at all. The diverse community of animals that flourish around such vents includes giant tubeworms, clams, and blind white crabs.

Methanogenic (methane-producing) bacteria also live in the ocean depths. They are strict anaerobes that obtain energy by using hydrogen to convert carbon dioxide into methane. Methanogenic bacteria also live in the stomachs of cattle, where their action helps break down indigestible cellulose from grass. The belching of cows releases so much methane into the atmosphere that some scientists think the gas may be contributing to the greenhouse effect and global warming.

Nitrifying bacteria obtain energy by converting ammonia to nitrites or by converting nitrites into nitrates. In doing so, they play a vital role in the nitrogen cycle by releasing soluble nitrates into seawater as a waste product. Photosynthetic microorganisms and algae depend on these nitrates to manufacture organic compounds, and all organisms further up the food chain depend on organic compounds for food.

Ben Morgan

FURTHER READING
Nybakken, James W. *Marine Biology: An Ecological Approach,* 5th ed. San Francisco: Benjamin Cummings, 2001.
Postlethwait, John. *The Nature of Life.* New York: McGraw-Hill, 1989; 3rd ed., 1995.
Purves, William, et al. *Life: The Science of Biology.* Sunderland, Mass.: Sinauer; Boston: Grant Press, 1983; 5th ed., Sunderland, Mass.: Sinauer, 1998.

RELATED ARTICLES
Carbon Cycle; Cyanobacteria; Microbenthos; Nanoplankton; Nitrogen Cycle; Photosynthesis; Primary Productivity

Bacterioplankton,
see Bacteria

Baleen

Mysticete whales do not have teeth as adults but instead, a series of fringed plates, called *baleen,* that hang down from the upper jaw. Baleen resembles hair—hence these whales were named the mustached whales (from the Latin *mystax,* moustache, and *ceti,* whale). Baleen is composed of a compound similar to human fingernails and begins growing as soon as the whales are born. Each baleen plate is triangular in shape, with a smooth edge on the outside, the upper edge embedded in the gum, and the inner edge frayed. The series of fringed baleen creates a mesh inside the mouth of mysticete whales that effectively acts as a sieve to remove prey from the water. Right whales (family Balaenidae) have numerous (220 to 360 plates), long [up to 3 to 4 meters (10 to 13 feet)], thin baleen with thin fringes, which allows them to capture large quantities of small zooplankton (mostly copepods) as they swim slowly, mouth agape, through swarms of plankton at the ocean's surface. Rorqual whales (family Balaenopteridae) have 230 to 400 baleen plates of moderate length [0.3 to 1 meter (1 to 3 feet)] and many colors (black, gray, yellowish white, depending on the species) that they use while actively capturing krill and fishes. Gray whales (family Eschrichtiidae) have 130 to 180 yellowish-white baleen plates about 0.3 meter (1 foot) in length, with the fringes thicker than those of other baleen whales because their baleen can be abraded as they sieve crustaceans from the bottom sediments. Baleen continues to grow during a whale's life but is eroded at the ends during feeding. Baleen functions much like the gillrakers of fishes, such as basking sharks, that also filter prey from the water.

Jim Harvey

FURTHER READING
Berta, A., and J. L. Sumich. *Marine Mammals: Evolutionary Biology.* San Diego, Calif.: Academic Press, 1999.

Haley, Delphine, ed. *Marine Mammals of Eastern North Pacific and Arctic Waters,* 2nd rev. ed. Seattle, Wash.: Pacific Search Press, 1986.

Leatherwood, Stephen, and Randall R. Reeves. *The Sierra Club Handbook of Whales and Dolphins.* San Francicso: Sierra Club Books, 1983.

Slijper, E. J. *Whales.* Translated by A. J. Pomerans. New York: Basic Books, 1962.

RELATED ARTICLES
Cetacea; Mysticeti; Zooplankton

Baltic Sea

The Baltic Sea is a Y-shaped, semienclosed sea that lies between the Scandinavian countries and the northern European countries of Denmark, Germany, Poland, Estonia, Lithuania, Latvia, and Russia. Its longest margin lies approximately along 54°N from 10 to 27°E and is about 1600 kilometers (1000 miles) long. The other arm, the Gulf of Bothnia, stretches almost due north to 65°N. The Baltic's average width is only 190 kilometers (120 miles). It has a very restricted opening into the North Atlantic through an archipelago of islands off the northeastern coast of Denmark and through a gulf called the Skaggerak. Its total area of about 420,000 square kilometers (162,000 square miles) is only a quarter of its total catchment area. It is quite shallow—less than 100 meters (330 feet)—apart from three small deep areas. Thus it is like a very big estuary, and its surface salinities are only about 10 practical salinity units (psu) and rise to 15 psu in the deeps. During the last glaciation (20,000 years ago) it was a freshwater lake, and it became marine only about 4500 B.C. The water at the far ends of the big gulfs is barely saline, so in the cold winter much of the surface ices up. The tides are weak, but wind-generated seiches (tidelike oscillations of the water) cause sea levels to seesaw.

The input of pollutants from the big rivers that flow through some of Europe's most heavily industrialized areas cause major problems, and eutrophication has resulted from runoff of agricultural fertilizers rich in nitrates and discharges from sewage treatment plants rich in phosphates from detergents. Periodically, the deep water lacks oxygen completely. Historically the Baltic Sea was of considerable political importance in northern Europe; it provided the trade routes for the Hanseatic League and also a passageway for Soviet vessels during the Cold War.

Martin Angel

FURTHER READING

Leithe-Eriksen, Rune, ed. *The Seas of Europe Series: The Baltic.* London: Collins and Brown, 1992.

Ozsoy, Ermin, and Alexander Mikaelyan, eds. *Sensitivity to Change: Black Sea, Baltic Sea and North Sea.* NATO ASI Series, Partnership Subseries 2, *Environment;* Vol. 27. Dordrecht, the Netherlands, and Boston: Kluwer Academic, 1997.

USEFUL WEB SITES
"Baltic Sea Region: GIS, Maps, and Statistical Database." UNEP, (1 Sept. 2000). <http://www.grida.no/baltic>.

RELATED ARTICLES
Anoxia; Pollution, Ocean; Salinity; Seiche

Bar

Bar, a mariner's term, is a generic expression for a wide range of offshore ridges, mounds, and banks of unconsolidated material such as gravel and sand that are submerged at high tide. Bars are built by the action of waves and currents in shallow nearshore regions and are commonly located off gently sloping beaches that have an abundance of sand and other unconsolidated materials. A typical bar slopes gently toward the sea, has a rounded crest, and slopes more steeply toward the shoreline. Bars form slightly seaward of the waves' plunge point and are transient features, migrating toward, and then retreating from, the shoreline as wave height decreases and increases, respectively. For example, as wave height increases, an older bar is cut away, and a new bar forms seaward. In higher latitudes, the sizes and continuities of longshore bars depend on the seasons. Winter brings more storms and higher waves, thereby forming more bars and steeper beach faces; summer waves have less height and the beach foreshore has a much gentler gradient, with fewer and smaller bars or none at all.

Types of Bars

A longshore bar, the most common type, is an elongate sand or gravel ridge that forms parallel to the shoreline and generally at a distance of 3 meters to hundreds of meters (tens to hundreds of feet). Longshore bars are submerged features, at least at high tide, and are separated from the beach by a trough. They are easily recognized because waves break over them before reaching the beach face along the shoreline.

Other types of bars include a bay bar and bar-built estuary. The bay bar forms when currents from river runoff or tidal currents are too weak to keep the mouth of a bay open. An earlier formed spit (linear ridge of sediment attached to land at one end) extends across the bay and connects with the mainland or with another spit. This formation across the opening cuts the bay off from the open ocean. A bar-built estuary is shallow and is separated from the open ocean by sandbars deposited parallel to the coast by wave action. Lagoons that separate the barrier islands from the mainland are called *estuaries*. Examples of bar-built estuaries are the Laguna Madre on the Texas coast and Chincoteague Bay in Maryland. The Laguna Madre lagoon, between Corpus Christi and the mouth of the Rio Grande, formed as sea level approached its current level. The lagoon is protected from the open sea by Padre Island (a barrier island).

Bars can be obstacles to the safe navigation of ships and boats. For example, migrating bars of the Columbia River in Oregon and San Francisco Bay in California constantly remind captains about the complex interplay between waves and tidal currents. There is a danger of running ships aground; smaller boats can be overturned by waves that break across those bars.

All bars are barriers of some kind. The term *barrier* is often equated with *bar*, and some scientists argue that a bar is an intermediate phase in the development of a barrier. In general, a bar is a submerged feature at high tide, whereas a barrier is emergent at high tide. Barriers can be islands, reefs, and human-made features.

Barrier Islands

Some large elongate longshore bars build above the high-tide level and become islands. These are barrier islands and they are found adjacent to much of the world's coastline. In the United States, they are particularly well developed along the east and Gulf coasts, and examples include the North Carolina Outer Banks and Padre Island off the coast of Texas.

A geomorphic profile of a barrier island shows that from the ocean to the land, the island is composed of a beach, dunes, a barrier flat, a salt marsh, a lagoon, and land. The ocean beach is the normal beach that widens in the summer and erodes during the winter. Dunes are produced by sand blown inland by wind and are stabilized by vegetation. The plants are salt-spray resistant and are able to withstand burial by sand. The dune environment provides the primary protection for lagoons from flooding during storms. Within the dune field, there are numerous passes for the water to migrate. Barrier flats are flat areas created by sand deposited behind dunes during storms. The flats are quickly colonized by grasses, and if storm frequency decreases, can undergo a rapid ecological succession to thickets, woodlands, and forests. Salt marshes lie behind the barrier flat and consist of a low and a high salt marsh. The low marsh extends from mean sea level to high neap tide line, and the high marsh extends to the highest spring tide line. As overwash deposits enter the lagoon, parts exposed by the tide are filled and new marsh develops. Artificial dune enhancement, inlet filling, and other activities that prevent overwash and flooding will restrict new marsh development. Barrier islands slowly migrate landward, as shown by successive shorelines caused by rising sea level. As the barrier island migrates inland, it is being eroded at -0.4 to -1.5 meters (-1.3 to -4.9 feet) per year in all U.S. regions except the Maine–New York coastal region.

The origin of these barrier islands is complex, but most seem to have begun 18,000 years ago with the simultaneous glacial retreat and rise in seawater. Size of islands is variable, but they may exceed 100 kilometers (62 miles) in length and have widths of up to several kilometers. Barrier evolution is not well understood, and many details are specific to the features at the site of formation. Evolution of barriers is closely related to three critical factors: sand supply, sea-level fluctuations, and the intensity of waves and currents. If there is an uninterrupted sediment supply, a stable sea level, and low- to moderate-subsidence rate, the barrier will prograde seaward. However, if there is a reduction in the sediment supply, a rise in the sea level, and/or a high subsidence rate, there will be landward migration of the barriers. Present-day barriers began 5000 to 6000 years ago. During a sea-level rise, large amounts of sand are moved as the shore zones migrate landward. At about 4000 to 6000 years ago, the sea level stabilized, and barriers began to evolve into their present form.

Engineering Barriers

Engineering barriers include all edifices that are human-made, including groins, jetties, seawalls, breakwaters, and dams. The intent of these structures is to trap sand from upstream and to keep the harbor entrance open. Although these do trap the material on the upstream side, erosion is enhanced on the downstream side. The erosion causes costly additional artificial structures to be built or the mechanical transportation and deposition of sediment to eroded beach area. Dams along rivers trap sand. This blockage results in the loss of beaches downstream and the increased, artificial erosion cycle that develops when the floodgates open.

Mary White

FURTHER READING

Bird, E. C. F. *Coastal Landforms: An Introduction to Coastal Geomorphology with Australian Examples.* Canberra, Australia: Australian National University, 1965.

Bloom, Arthur L. *Geomorphology: A Systematic Analysis of Late Cenozoic Landforms.* Englewood Cliffs, N.J.: Prentice Hall, 1978; 3rd ed., Upper Saddle River, N.J., 1998.

Condie, Kent C. *Plate Tectonics and Crustal Evolution.* New York: Pergamon Press, 1976; 4th ed., Oxford and Boston: Butterworth-Heinemann, 1997.

Hatch, F. H., and R. H. Rastall. *The Petrology of the Sedimentary Rocks.* London: G. Allen, 1913; 7th ed. by J. T. Greensmigh, London and Boston: Unwin Hyman, 1989.

Kennett, James. *Marine Geology.* Englewood Cliffs, N.J.: Prentice Hall, 1982.

King, Cuchlaine A. *Beaches and Coasts.* London: Edward Arnold, 1959; 2nd ed., New York: St. Martin's Press, 1972.

Shepard, Francis P. *Submarine Geology.* New York, Harper, 1948; 3rd ed., New York: Harper and Row, 1973.

Thurman, Harold V. *Essentials of Oceanography.* Columbus, Ohio: Charles E. Merrill, 1983; 6th ed., Upper Saddle River, N.J.: Prentice Hall, 1999.

RELATED ARTICLES
Barrier Island; Coastal Morphology; Coral Reef; Delta; Estuary; Hurricane; Lagoon; Sea Level; Surf Zone

Barents Sea

The Barents Sea is a shelf sea in the European sector of the Arctic Ocean. It includes a large area of the wide continental margin, which is bounded by the islands of Spitsbergen and Franz Joseph to the north, Novaya Zemlya to the east, and Scandinavia and Russia to the south. It stretches from 68 to 80°N latitude and 15 to 55°E longitude. It receives a flow of relatively warm Atlantic Ocean water from the west around the North Cape of Norway. This inflow keeps the sea unexpectedly free of pack ice for much of the year, but a few icebergs occur that have been spawned from the glaciers on the islands to the north. Along its southern margin is the broad inlet of the White Sea, and to the east it links with the Kara Sea around the long curving island of Novaya Zemlya. Its total area is about 1,405,000 square kilometers (542,000 square miles). Its average depth is 229 meters (751 feet); a trough to the south of Spitsbergen is about 560 meters (1800 feet) deep. Its climate is subarctic because of the warm inflow of water from the Atlantic. Surface salinities are about 34 practical salinity units (psu), but in spring and early summer after the ice melts, cold ice meltwater with a low salinity overlies the warmer, more saline oceanic water. This stratifies the water, which favors vigorous growth of phytoplankton during the summer when there is continuous daylight.

The sea is a major fishing area for herring, cod, and salmon; over 1 million tonnes (1.1 million tons) were caught in 1967, but since then catches have declined by about 30 percent. There are

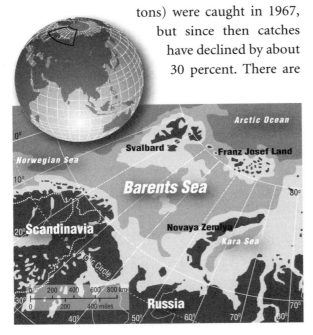

Barents Sea.

large populations of harp and ring seals, and in summer, whales. Polar bears are also abundant. However, the Barents Sea has recently become contaminated with radioactivity leaking into the sea from the decaying Soviet nuclear fleet and a sunken submarine. It also receives a considerable aerial input of pollutants from the major industrial centers in northern Europe.

Martin Angel

FURTHER READING
AMAP. *Arctic Pollution Issues: A State of the Arctic Report.* Oslo: Arctic Monitoring and Assessment Programme, 1997.
Herman, Yvonne, ed. *The Arctic Seas: Climatology, Oceanography, Geology and Biology.* New York: Van Nostrand Reinhold, 1989.

RELATED ARTICLES
Arctic Ocean; Continental Margin; Hydrosphere; Kara Sea; Radioactive Contamination; Salinity

Barnacle

The 1000 or so species that belong to the subclass Cirripedia are called *barnacles.* Barnacles are small shelled animals that are frequently seen clinging to rocks along the shoreline, often in great numbers. They look like tiny mollusks, but in fact they are crustaceans, relatives of crabs and lobsters. The subclass Cirripedia includes a number of parasitic species that live in or on the bodies of other sea animals.

There are four orders in the subclass Cirripedia: Thoracica (goose and acorn barnacles), Acrothoracica (burrowing barnacles in calcium carbonate substrates), Ascothoracica (parasitic cirripedes in anemones and echinoderms), and Rhizocephala (fungus-like parasitic cirripedes in decapod crustaceans).

Barnacles have become so well adapted to their specialized lifestyle that they look very different from other crustaceans. Unlike crabs and lobsters, most barnacles lack abdominal segments and appendages, and their heads and antennae are highly reduced. Most spend their adult lives permanently fixed, head down, to a solid object, such as a rock, a ship's hull, the skin of a whale, or the shell of a turtle. Rock-encrusting species, known as *acorn barnacles*, are the most familiar. They live completely enclosed in conical shells cemented to the rock. At high tide, special plates in the lid of the shell open up, allowing the barnacle to extend modified feathery limbs, or *cirri*, into the water. The cirri are used to filter tiny organisms from the plankton. *Goose barnacles*, which live on various hard substrates, have conspicuous stalks below their shells, and *burrowing barnacles* (order Acrothoracica) have dispensed with shells altogether, instead burrowing into the shells of mollusks and corals.

Cirripedes of the orders Rhizocephala and Ascothoracica are parasites. Rhizocephalans grow like fungi through the bodies of crabs and lobsters. Ascothoracicans embed themselves in the bodies of other invertebrates, such as echinoderms and cnidarians, or feed on them with piercing mouthparts.

Barnacles reproduce sexually and many are hermaphrodites (able to produce both male and female sex cells). The eggs mature inside the parent's body and give rise to free-swimming larvae called *nauplii*, similar to the larvae of other crustaceans. These grow through a number of distinct stages before metamorphosing into adult barnacles and settling on a rock or other object.

Ben Morgan

FURTHER READING

Brusca, Richard C., and Gary J. Brusca. *Invertebrates*. Sunderland, Mass.: Sinauer, 1990.

Fish, J. *A Student's Guide to the Seashore.* London and Boston: Unwin Hyman, 1989; 2nd ed., Cambridge and New York: Cambridge University Press, 1996.

Pechenik, Jan A. *Biology of the Invertebrates*. Boston: Prindle, Weber and Schmidt, 1985; 4th ed., Boston: McGraw-Hill, 2000.

RELATED ARTICLES
Crustacean; Filter Feeder; Maxillopoda; Parasitism

Barrier Island

Barrier islands are long, narrow islands that run parallel to the shoreline. Created by the accumulation of sand and gravel in shallow coastal zones, barrier islands often form a chain of islands running parallel to the mainland. Individual islands are separated from one another by tidal inlets, which allow the passage of water between the island and the mainland as the tides sweep in and out of the lagoon. Whereas the ocean side of a barrier island typically consists of beaches and sand dunes, the more sheltered mainland side can harbor maritime forests and salt marshes. One of the largest chains of barrier islands runs along the east coast of the United States, from New Jersey to the Gulf of Mexico.

Although all barrier islands are formed by the accumulation of sand and sediments, the origin of the debris and the mode of deposition can vary. Some island chains are built up from sediments that have been deposited by longshore currents. The origin of the sediments is often a combination of river sediments and sediments eroded off the shore by waves. It is speculated that many of today's barrier islands were formed when the sea level rose after the last Ice Age. Ancient beaches may have been flooded, leaving only the highest sand crests untouched. Additional sediments were deposited on these new islands by the rising water, which carried extraordinarily large accumulations of sand and sediments. These deposits were eventually shaped into long, thin islands by waves and currents.

Barrier islands are subjected continuously to wind and waves, which periodically flood the land and erode the beaches. Storms and hurricanes frequently form new inlets, block existing inlets, or otherwise change the shape of the

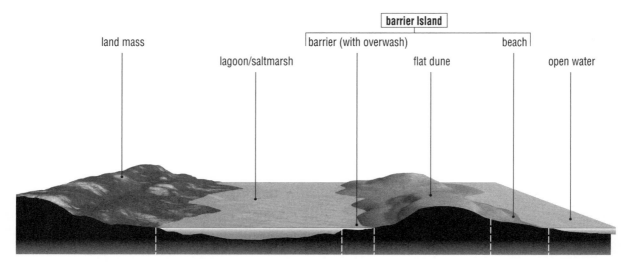

Elongated longshore bars develop into barrier islands with a profile like the one above.

island. Often, the action of the waves results in a slow migration of the island toward the mainland or in the direction of the longshore current. To maintain, as much as possible, the natural and human-made features on the island, islanders must come up with effective erosion control measures, such as jetties and regular dredging operations. Communities on the mainland benefit from the existence of these islands because of the barrier they provide to storm surges.

Sonya Wainwright

FURTHER READING

Stowe, Keith. *Essentials of Ocean Science.* New York: Wiley, 1987; 2nd ed., published under the title *Exploring Ocean Science,* New York: Wiley, 1996.

Thurman, Harold V. *Essentials of Oceanography.* Columbus, Ohio: Charles E. Merrill, 1983; 6th ed., with Alan P. Trujillo, Upper Saddle River, N.J.: Prentice Hall, 1999.

RELATED ARTICLES

Bar; Beach; Coastal Erosion; Coastal Morphology; Eustatic Sea Level; Littoral Zone Processes; Seacoast Classification

Barrier Reef

A barrier reef is a curved or linear coral reef formed some distance from and roughly parallel to a landmass and separated from it by a lagoon. The world's two largest and best-known barrier reefs are the Great Barrier Reef in Australia and an unnamed barrier reef off the coast of Belize. Barrier reefs are important for ecological and heritage reasons, but frequently also underpin the economy of islands or nearby coastal regions through tourism and marine produce (such as fish and pearls). Although barrier reefs (similar to other types of coral reefs) have come under increasing threat, growing environmental awareness and increasing interest in ecotourism may help to preserve their extraordinary biodiversity in the future.

Formation

Like any coral reef, a barrier reef is a dense framework of calcium carbonate built by organisms called *coral polyps* that have in their tissues symbiotic algae called *zooxanthellae*, which enhance the coral's ability to lay down calcium carbonate. The distinction between a fringing reef and a barrier reef is necessarily somewhat arbitrary, but the dimensions of the lagoon formed between the landmass and the coral reef are sometimes used to differentiate fringing from barrier reefs: the lagoon of a fringing reef is shallow [typically, less than 5 meters (16 feet) deep] and narrow [typically, closer than 500 meters (1640 feet) to the landmass], whereas the lagoon of a barrier reef exceeds these dimensions [typically, some miles wide and perhaps 20 to 80 meters (65 to 260 feet) deep]. The lagoon of the Great Barrier Reef varies between 16 and 160 kilometers (10 and 100 miles) wide and approximately 18 to 45 meters (60 to 150 feet) deep along its length. The width of a lagoon depends not just on the pattern of growth of the coral reef but also on the topography of the seafloor.

Structure

Although barrier reefs are usually referred to as a single entity, they usually have a number of components. The reef itself consists of a *fore reef* (the outer edge that meets the sea) and a *back reef* (the inner edge that meets the lagoon). The top of a fore reef usually consists of a steep wall of coral (perhaps angled at up to 60°); underneath, this slopes down more gently as a reef slope. Because of the action of breaking waves, the fore reef consists of a very dense mass of coral. It is supported by buttresslike arrangements of coral known as *spurs and grooves*, growing at right angles to the main reef, which provide considerable strength and resistance to the waves. By contrast, the sheltered waters inside the lagoon cause much less diverse coral formations to grow on the back reef. Finally, small islands of sand and deposits of shells, coral, or algae, known as *coral cays*, may form on top of the reef. At their largest, cays are a few feet high and a few acres across and may be either vegetated or unvegetated. Unvegetated sand cays can evolve into vegetated cays when accumulated sediment is colonized by grasses, shrubs, and trees such as palms or mangroves.

Examples

The Great Barrier Reef off the coast of Queensland, in northeastern Australia, is the world's largest and best-known barrier reef. Clearly visible from space, the reef is some 2300 kilometers (1430 miles) long and lies from 23 kilometers (14 miles) in the north to as much as 270 kilometers (168 miles) offshore in the south, and encompasses an area of 350,000 square kilometers (135,000 square miles). The name "Great Barrier Reef" is somewhat misleading, for it is a complex assemblage of approximately 3400 separate reefs and associated components, including barrier reefs, fringing reefs, patch reefs, ribbon reefs, lagoons, and both vegetated and unvegetated coral cays. Protected as a World Heritage Site by the United Nations Educational, Scientific, and Cultural Organization (UNESCO) since 1981, the reef has nevertheless faced a number of human and natural threats in recent decades, including ever-increasing tourism (the reef is visited by 1.5 to 2 million people each year), commercial fishing, oil and mineral exploration, and highly damaging outbreaks of the crown-of-thorns starfish (*Acanthaster planci*); in the future, these threats will be joined by other pressing problems, including coral bleaching and other uncertain impacts of climatic change.

The second largest barrier reef in the world (and the largest in the northern hemisphere), located in Belize, has been protected as a UNESCO World Heritage Site since 1996. The reef consists of seven major areas, including numerous reefs, three atolls, hundreds of cays, lagoons, mangrove swamps, and estuaries. Built from many different species of corals, the Belize reef is also home to numerous threatened species, including turtles, manatees, and the American marine crocodile. The conditions that make possible growth of the coral reef (and therefore its remarkable biodiversity) include relatively shallow water, low nutrient concentration and sedimentation rate, and the correct balance of temperature, salinity, and oxygen content to support coral growth. Unfortunately, like the Great Barrier Reef and many reefs elsewhere, the Belize reef has suffered the pressure of increasing visitors, although in the conservation of its rainforests and its oceanic biodiversity, Belize has long been a pioneer of sustainable tourism.

Other important barrier reefs include the 600-kilometer (373-mile) barrier reef off the island of La Grande Terre in New Caledonia in the South Pacific; the Great Sunda Reef, which rises from the continental shelf to the southeast of Kalimantan; the Great Sea Reef off the west coast of Fiji; and numerous barrier reefs associated with the islands of French Polynesia.

Chris Woodford

FURTHER READING

Bird, Eric. *An Introduction to Coastal Geomorphology,* 3rd ed. Oxford and New York: Blackwell, 1984.

———. *Submerging Coasts: The Effects of Rising Sea Level on Coastal Environments.* Chichester, England, and New York: Wiley, 1993.

Cannon, Lester, and Mark Goyen. *Exploring Australia's Great Barrier Reef: A World Heritage Site.* Surrey Hills, Australia: Watermark Press, 1989.

Connell, D. W. "The Great Barrier Reef Conservation Issue: A Case History." *Biological Conservation,* Vol. 3, No. 4 (1971), p. 249.

Hopley, D. "Continental Shelf Reef Systems." In R. W. G. Carter and C. D. Woodroffe, eds., *Coastal Evolution.* Cambridge and New York: Cambridge University Press, 1994.

RELATED ARTICLES
Barrier Island; Coral; Coral Atoll; Coral Reef; Fringing Reef; Great Barrier Reef; Lagoon; Patch Reef; Reef

Bathyal Zone

The bathyal zone refers to the benthic ecological zone that extends from the shelf break [usually at about 200 meters (656 feet)] down the continental slope and onto the base of the continental rise at 4000 meters (13,120 feet). About 11 percent of the total area of the ocean is bathyal. The continental slope is usually covered with sediments that either come from land or are pelagic in origin and underlain by continental rocks. The zone is often a linear strip bordering the margins of the continents across which there are strong lateral gradients as a result of the increasing depth. However, these gradients are often obscured by the nature of the sediments, which range from soft muds to sands and gravels, and where the currents are so strong they can strip off the sediment to uncover bare rock. Geological features such as canyons and sediment slides traverse the zone and disrupt its along-slope continuity. Hydrographic features that have a substantial impact on the bathyal communities can also occur.

Off the eastern U.S. seaboard there is a sharp boundary between the Gulf Stream and its countercurrent, which is marked by a change in the water temperatures and the benthic communities. In the tropical eastern Pacific and in the Western Indian Ocean there is an oxygen minimum zone that results in a sharp faunal boundary. Generally, the size of the standing crop of the benthic community is related to the productivity of the overlying water, but where the currents are strong or there is considerable eddy activity, the quantities of detrital organic matter reaching the seabed are altered. Where the seabed is muddy, deposit feeders such as holothurians abound. Once the currents have become strong enough to strip off the sediment, the basement rock is exposed. Suspension feeders such as sponge gorgonians can gain a hold and use the current to intercept passively suspended particles. Seeps can also occur where either methane or salty water leaks from the seabed and provides enriched environments inhabited by chemosynthetic communities.

Martin Angel

FURTHER READING

Gage, John D., and Paul A. Tyler. *Deep-Sea Biology: A Natural History of Organisms at the Deep-Sea Floor.* Cambridge and New York: Cambridge University Press, 1991.

Smith, Craig R., Lauren S. Mullineaux, and Lisa A. Levin, eds. "Deep-Sea Biodiversity: A Compilation of

Recent Advances in Honor of Robert R. Hessler." *Deep-Sea Research II,* Vol. 45 (1998), pp. 1–567.

RELATED ARTICLES
Benthic Boundary Layer; Continental Slope; Gulf Stream; Oxygen Minimum Zone

Bathymetry

Bathymetry is the measurement of ocean depths. It is also used as a term to describe the gross morphology of the seabed. Bathymetric measurements were first made by sounding, which is the lowering of a weight on the end of a rope until it hits the bottom. This slow, laborious, and imprecise method was replaced by echo sounding, which measures how long it takes for the echo of a transmitted high-frequency sound to return to a ship. Sound travels at about 1500 meters (4920 feet) per second, so if the echo returns after 2 seconds, the depth is about 1500 meters (the pulse taking 1 second to reach the bottom and the echo taking 1 second to return). The uncertainty of echo sounding arises because the velocity of sound in water varies according to the density of the water (i.e., with its temperature, salinity, and hydrostatic pressure). Therefore, the depth can be measured precisely only if the detailed physical structure of the water column is known. More recent technical developments have been based on oblique sonars, which transmit the sound pulses both vertically and obliquely. These provide an echogram of the seabed, which gives a sound picture of the bottom structure that can be several kilometers wide in deep water. Surprisingly, oblique radar on satellites is also proving to be extremely useful for the detection of shallow banks and shoals. The flow of tidal currents over the banks results in characteristic fine waves (capillary waves) forming on the sea surface, which the radars detect.

The depth of the ocean is highly variable. About 5 percent of Earth's surface is covered with

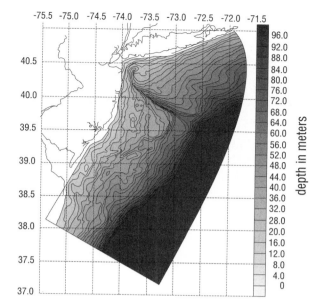

Bathymetry chart of area off the New Jersey coast. Lattitude is shown on left and longitude on top. (Adapted from Coastal Ocean Observation Lab, Rutgers University.)

shelf seas up to 200 meters (650 feet) deep. Continental slopes and rises with depths of 200 to 3000 meters (650 to 9800 feet) occupy about 11 percent, abyssal depths of 3000 to 6000 meters (9800 to 20,000 feet) occupy about 51 percent, and hadal depths in trenches greater than 6000 meters (20,000 feet) occupy about 2 percent. (The remaining 31 percent of Earth's surface is land.) There are abyssal plains where the bottom is monotonously flat, but there are also extensive underwater mountain ranges and volcanoes. The gross bathymetry of the oceans changes over millions of years as a result of the tectonic processes of seafloor spreading and continental drift. New seafloor is formed episodically in the rift valleys that lie along the axes of the mid-ocean ridges, thrusting the older crust sideways. There are two types of continental margins: passive margins where the spreading crust pushes the continental landmasses aside (continental drift) and active margins where the crust buckles down and slides (subducts) beneath the margins. Deep trenches form along the active margins where the greatest ocean depths occur.

Ocean crust that is newly formed at the mid-ocean ridges is extremely hot. As it cools, it shrinks, so the depth of the crustal rocks underlying the oceans increases as it spreads away from the ridge. Therefore, the older the crust, the deeper it gets. But as it gets older, it is covered with an increasing thickness of sediment. In the Pacific, for instance, the sediments are derived purely from the material produced by biological processes at the surface, because the deep trenches that flank the continental margins trap rock and debris that slide off the slopes after earthquakes. In the Atlantic, however, the margins are passive; these large debris flows are unimpeded and generate so much momentum that they can flow far out across the abyssal plains. Initially, they erode channels and canyons in the seabed, but as they eventually slow, they deposit vast quantities of turbidite deposits over the abyssal plains. Geologists have recently discovered another way that rock, sand, and gravel have become deposited on the ocean bed in the Atlantic. About every 5000 to 10,000 years, vast groups of icebergs have been released from the Arctic. As they have melted, they have dropped sand, gravel, and rocks onto the seabed that have formed thick layers on the bottom at temperate latitudes.

Bathymetry can also show where there are hotspots in the magma underlying the seafloor. The Hawaiian Islands are part of a 2000-kilometer (1240-mile)-long chain of volcanic islands and seamounts that developed as the spreading floor of the Pacific moved over a stationary hotspot.

Martin Angel

FURTHER READING
Erickson, Jon. *Marine Geology: Undersea Landforms and Life Forms.* New York: Facts On File, 1996.
Gross, M. Grant. *Oceanography: A View of the Earth.* Englewood Cliffs, N.J.: Prentice Hall, 1972; 7th ed., Upper Saddle River, N.J.: Prentice Hall, 1996.
Kennett, James. *Marine Geology.* Englewood Cliffs, N.J.: Prentice Hall, 1982.
Seibold, Eugen, and Wolfgang H. Berger. *The Sea Floor: An Introduction to Marine Geology.* Berlin and New York: Springer-Verlag, 1982; 3rd rev. and updated ed., 1996.

RELATED ARTICLES
Abyssal Plain; Continental Margin; Continental Slope; Mid-Ocean Ridge; Sonar

Bathypelagic Zone

The bathypelagic zone is an ecological depth zone in the open ocean that ranges from about 1000 to perhaps 4000 meters (3280 to 13,120 feet) and is situated between the mesopelagic and the abyssopelagic zones. Its precise depth limits vary because of lack of information about the area and differences among scientists. It is the upper zone of the deep ocean habitat that is permanently dark except for occasional flashes of bioluminescence, which is light produced by animals.

Bathypelagic water temperatures are usually quite cool (<5°C or 41°F); the only exceptions are parts of the northeastern Atlantic, where the Mediterranean outflow keeps temperatures above 8°C (46.4°F). In most oceans, there is a minimum in the dissolved oxygen concentrations associated with the permanent thermocline, but in the Eastern Tropical Pacific and Arabian Sea where oxygen concentrations in the overlying mesopelagic zone are exceptionally low, the levels begin to increase at the top of the zone.

The zone is usually recognized by changes in the species' composition, by the size spectrum of the pelagic communities, and by the dominant morphological adaptations. Although the larval stages of some bathypelagic species are spent near the surface, once they have metamorphosed into adults they become permanent bathypelagic residents and are restricted to the zone. The majority of bathypelagic species do not undertake vertical migrations, although one species of lantern fish and two species of prawns have been found to migrate daily between bathypelagic daytime depths and the euphotic zone.

Martin Angel

FURTHER READING

Childress, James J. "Are There Physiological and Biochemical Adaptations of Metabolism in Deep-Sea Animals?" *Trends in Ecology and Evolution* Vol. 10 (1995), pp. 30–36.

Cowles, David L., and James J. Childress. "Aerobic Metabolism of the Anglerfish Melanocoetus johnsoni, a Deep Pelagic Sit-and-Wait Predator." *Deep-Sea Research I,* Vol. 42 (1995), pp. 1631–1638.

Marshall, Norman B. *Developments in Deep-Sea Biology.* Poole, England: Blandford Press, 1979.

Nybakken, James W. *Marine Biology: An Ecological Approach,* 5th ed. San Francisco: Benjamin Cummings, 2001.

Randall, David J., and Anthony P. Farrell. *Deep-Sea Fishes.* San Diego: Academic Press, 1997.

RELATED ARTICLES

Abyssopelagic Zone; Bioluminescence; Euphotic Zone; Mesopelagic Zone; Pelagic; Vertical Migration

Bathyscaphe

The bathyscaphe, literally "depth ship," is a deep-diving vehicle comprising a gasoline-filled underwater "balloon" or "float" under which is slung a spherical cabin for two or three crew members. Belgian physicist Auguste Piccard (1884–1962) designed the first bathyscaphe, later working with the assistance of his son, Jacques Piccard (1922–). Auguste Piccard planned the bathyscaphe to be a substantial improvement on its inspiration, the *bathysphere,* a spherical diving chamber lowered from a ship. The bathysphere, invented and used by engineer Otis Barton (1899–) and zoologist William Beebe (1877–1962) between 1930 and 1934, made a record-breaking descent to 923 meters (3028 feet) in 1934. Barton and Beebe were the first to see live deep-sea creatures *in situ.*

The bathysphere was lowered from a mother ship by cable. Any movement of the mother ship

was transmitted to the bathysphere, with the danger of whiplash causing the cable to snap. The weight of the cable limited the depth of descent; if too long, the cable would pull apart under its own weight. The Piccards' bathyscaphe, being independent of the mother ship, did not suffer from the bathysphere's limitations. To descend, the bathyscaphe's ballast tanks were flooded with water. To ascend, ballast of steel shot or pellets was jettisoned. The ballast could be released incrementally by cutting the power to an electromagnetic device or dumped entirely if the power failed. The bathyscaphe's cabin housed a viewport at front and back. Thrusters provided limited maneuverability. Except in slow-moving deep water, the bathyscaphe was at the mercy of ocean currents.

The first bathyscaphe, launched in 1948, was sponsored by the Belgian government's *Fonds National pour la Recherche Scientific* (FNRS). Named FNRS-2, the bathyscaphe was damaged during unpiloted trials. The Piccards continued work with the FNRS and French navy until 1952 and then left the program to build their own bathyscaphe under Italian sponsorship. Named *Trieste* after the city in which it was built, the new bathyscaphe entered service in August 1953, and a month later the Piccards dived to a depth of 3150 meters (10,335 feet) in the Tyrrhenian Sea of the Mediterranean, a record-breaking descent at the time.

Meanwhile, the more conventional bathyscaphe design, the FNRS-3, was being developed by the French navy. Launched in June 1953, it proved to be a very serviceable craft. In February 1954, a French naval team descended in it to a depth of 4175 meters (13,698 feet) in the Atlantic Ocean, a new diving record. In the late 1950s, the French navy team continued work with FNRS-3, as well as with a bathyscaphe of novel design called *Archimede.*

In 1957, the U.S. Navy's Office of Naval Research (ONR) sponsored a series of *Trieste* dives in the Mediterranean. In 1958, the ONR purchased *Trieste* and it was transported to San Diego, California. In 1959, a heavily modified version of the *Trieste*—with a larger pontoon, greater ballast, and stronger cabin—was developed with the specific goal of diving to the deepest part of the world's ocean system. On January 23, 1960, Jacques Piccard and Lieutenant Don Walsh (USN) (1931–) descended to 10,912 meters (35,800 feet) in the Challenger Deep of the Marianas Trench. This depth record has yet to be equaled.

In April 1963, the *Trieste* was used to inspect the wreck of the U.S. submarine *Thresher*, sunk in about 2500 meters (8200 feet) of water. After this final mission, the *Trieste* was retired. In the following year, *Trieste*'s successor, *Trieste II*, returned to the wreck of the *Thresher*. At the end of the 1960s, it was employed to examine the wreck of the U.S. submarine *Scorpion* lost in the eastern Atlantic at 3500 meters (11,500 feet). The U.S. Navy operated various versions of *Trieste* until 1984. Only the Japanese remotely operated vehicle (ROV) *Kaiko* has approached the depth reached by *Trieste*, coming to within 0.6 meter (2 feet) of the depth record in 1995.

Trevor Day

FURTHER READING
Ballard, Robert D., and Will Hively. *The Eternal Darkness: A Personal History of Deep-Sea Exploration.* Princeton, N.J.: Princeton University Press, 2000.
Piccard, Jacques. *The Sun Beneath the Sea.* Translated from the French by Denver Lindley. New York: Scribner's, 1971.
Piccard, Jacques, and Robert S. Dietz. *Seven Miles Down.* New York: Putnam, 1961.
Walsh, Don. "The Exploration of Inner Space." In S. Fred Singer, ed., *The Ocean in Human Affairs.* New York: Paragon House, 1990; pp. 187–214.

RELATED ARTICLES
Alvin; Deep-Sea Exploration; Piccard, Auguste; Submersible; *Trieste*

Bathythermograph

The bathythermograph (BT) is a torpedo-shaped instrument used to record temperature changes of seawater with depth while a ship is under way, without interfering with normal ship routine. The BT is lowered into the sea and raised by means of wire rope and a "BT" winch. The thermal element of the BT consists of about 15 meters (49 feet) of copper tubing filled with xylene. The changing temperature in the water causes the xylene to expand and contract, causing pressure changes in the copper tubing. A stylus etches these expansions and contractions with changing temperature on a metal-coated glass slide. To measure depth, a copper aneroid capsule in the BT compresses as a result of changing pressure with depth as the BT sinks. The stylus etches the depth and temperature on a glass slide. The temperature range of a BT is between 0 and 32°C (32 to 90°F), with a depth range up to about 300 meters (984 feet). The BT data are recorded on a standard bathythermograph log. This has provided a standard message format for radio transmission of synoptic BT data for automatic data processing. BT measurements have traditionally been recorded on research vessels on a volunteer basis. Although the BT is a very reliable instrument requiring little maintenance, the expendable bathythermograph (XBT), which can measure temperature to greater depths than the BT, is in wider use today.

Philip Rabinowitz

FURTHER READING
Gross G. M. *Oceanography: A View of the Earth.* Englewood Cliffs, N.J.: Prentice Hall, 1972; 7th ed., 1995.
U.S. Naval Oceanographic Office. *Instruction Manual for Obtaining Oceanographic Data*, 3rd ed. Washington, D.C.: U.S. Government Printing Office, 1968.

RELATED ARTICLES
Expendable Bathythermograph; Temperature, Distribution of

Bay

Bays are coastal landforms that characterize much of the world's shoreline. They are similar in appearance to lagoons and estuaries. Geologists and geographers usually define a bay as either (1) an indentation or recess in the shoreline between promontories, such as capes and headlands, or (2) a more extensive embayment, smaller than a gulf but larger than a cove, that reaches inland as an arm of the sea. In contrast to lagoons, which are fronted by barrier islands, many bays have a broad opening to the sea.

Even casual reference to a world atlas will reveal that bays occur at all latitudes and can have water depths that range from a few meters (about 10 feet) to hundreds of meters (about 1000 feet). Some bays form the lower courses of, and are fed by, tributary rivers and thus become estuaries where fresh and salt waters mix (e.g., Chesapeake Bay). Others result from past tectonic or regional geologic processes (e.g., San Francisco Bay), including scour by glaciation (e.g., Bristol Bay, Alaska). Still others are the result of flooding of low-lying coastal topography during the most recent period of sea-level rise (e.g., Kyeonggi Bay, Korea).

Bays are ecologically important because they create sheltered habitat and, when fed by rivers, experience a range of water salinities. In temperate and tropical latitudes, their shorelines are characterized by beaches, wetlands, and mudflats; at higher latitudes, rugged and dissected highlands typically form the shorelines. Bays are ephemeral features geologically because they can form only during periods of rising sea level, are sensitive to sea-level fluctuations, and tend to fill with sediments.

John T. Wells

FURTHER READING
Eisma, D., and D. W. Park. "North and South Korea." In Eric Bird and Maurice Schwartz, eds., *The World's Coastline.* New York: Van Nostrand Reinhold, 1985.

Stumpf, Richard. "Sediment Transport in Chesapeake Bay during Floods: Analysis Using Satellite and Surface Observations." *Journal of Coastal Research,* Vol. 4 (1988), pp. 1–16.

RELATED ARTICLES
Coastal Morphology; Estuarine Circulation; Estuarine Sedimentation; Estuary; Lagoon; Shoreline Morphology

Bay of Bengal

The Bay of Bengal is a large extension of the Indian Ocean that curves northward. The bay is bordered on three sides by land: on the west by the Indian peninsula, on the north by Bangladesh, and on the east by Burma, Thailand, and the northern part of Malaysia. The southern border of the bay is an imaginary line drawn west-to-east roughly from the southern end of Sri Lanka to the northern end of the Indonesian island of Sumatra. The bay contains the Andaman and Nicobar islands, which mark the western boundary of the Andaman Sea, a part of the bay that lies between the islands, and Burma, Thailand, and Malaysia to the east. The Bay of Bengal lies between 80 and 98°E longitude and 5 and 22°N latitude.

Although it covers some 2,173,000 square kilometers (839,000 square miles), the Bay of Bengal is relatively shallow, averaging some 2600 meters (8500 feet) in depth. It is fed by several major Asian rivers, including the Ganges, Irrawaddy, Brahmaputra, Mahanadi, Godavari, Krishna, and Cauvery. As a result, the floor of the Bay of Bengal is cut by river canyons, and large areas of the bay's floor are covered with sediment from the rivers, thereby forming the Bengal submarine fan. Because of the fresh water coming into the Bay of Bengal from the rivers, the salinity of its waters varies greatly from shore to mid-bay.

The weather on the Bay of Bengal is dominated by monsoons, seasonal winds triggered by differences in temperature between the water and the surrounding land. From late May to early October, the summer monsoon blows from the southwest, bringing rain to Burma, Bangladesh, and northern India; in November and December the winter monsoon blows from the northeast, bringing rain to the lower eastern coast of India.

During the weeks preceding the onset of the monsoon rains and following their completion, tropical hurricanes, or cyclones, tend to form. These powerful storms frequently cause death and destruction to both bay fishermen and people who live in the coastal regions surrounding the bay. Despite the cyclones, the bay is of great economic importance to the people who live around it. Some 6 million tons of fish are taken from the Bay of Bengal every year. The wetlands and mangrove swamps found where the rivers

feed into the bay provide habitats for a variety of fish as well as prawns, a valuable export. In the southern, more saline parts of the bay, commercial tuna fishing is pursued. Natural gas deposits have also been found and drilled under the bay in recent years.

Mary Sisson

FURTHER READING

Subrahmanyam, Sanjay. *Improvising Empire: Portuguese Trade and Settlement in the Bay of Bengal, 1500–1700.* Delhi, India, and New York: Oxford University Press, 1990.

Villiers, Alan. *Monsoon Seas: The Story of the Indian Ocean.* New York: McGraw-Hill, 1952.

RELATED ARTICLES

Indian Ocean; Mangrove Forest; Monsoon; Submarine Fan

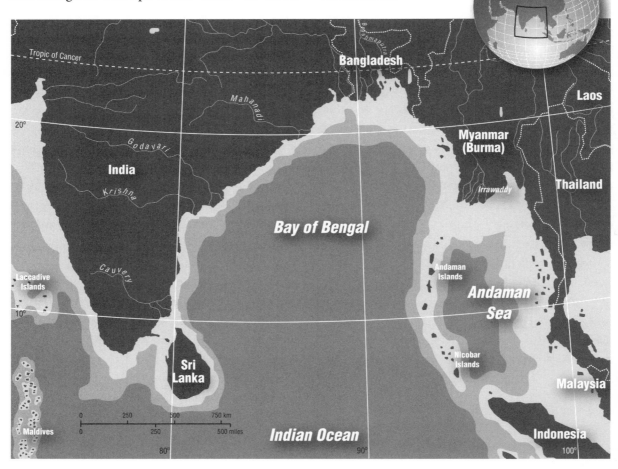

Bay of Bengal.

Beach

A beach is the unconsolidated sediment that extends from the zone of wave influence at low tide to a physical change on the shore, such as a berm or dune. A beach generally has a concave profile and consists of a *beach face,* which is the section exposed to the action of wave upwash; a *beach crest,* marking the landward limit of normal wave activity; and a *berm,* a landward-sloping bench or narrow terrace on the backshore part of a beach.

A beach is a transient, dynamic environment; waves transfer their energy to the land, sediment is moved landward and then seaward, erosion and deposition occur simultaneously, and the shape of the beach is constantly in change due to storm-generated waves. The beach sediment moves both parallel to the beach and perpendicular to the shoreline. If waves break perpendicular to the shoreline, *swash* (water moving up the beach to the berm) deposits sediment on the beach. *Backwash* (water that drains away from the shore to the sea) carries sediment back to the ocean. The dominant process of these two will determine if the sediment is deposited or eroded and thus if the beach is aggrading or degrading. Seasons affect a beach. In summer, the waves are small with little energy and are dominated by swash; sediment is carried shoreward, and the beach is in a building mode. In winter, storms generated at sea develop larger waves with more energy and are dominated by backwash; sediment is carried seaward, and the beach is in an eroding mode.

When waves approach the beach at an angle other than perpendicular, the wave is bent or refracted. This refraction causes the water to move parallel to the shoreline, creating a current called the *longshore current.* The longshore current erodes and carries sediment away from the beach. The sediment is later deposited in an area of lower energy. Swash and backwash combine with longshore current to move sediment along the beach. Grains are carried up the beach by the swash and

are returned down the beach by backwash, where they are captured and transported by the longshore current. The movement of the sand grains forms a zigzag pattern referred to as *littoral drift.*

The composition of beach materials depends on the composition of the material available locally. The beach may be composed of shell fragments if they were originally deposited in coastal waters and are moved landward. If basaltic volcanoes dominate the coast, such as along island arcs, the sands will be dark and composed of iron and magnesium-rich minerals. Grain size depends on the source. Coarse material is associated with a source from a beach cliff or other area of high energy, whereas fine material is associated with deposition from a river that flows through a lowland area. Regardless of composition or grain size, the beach material is constantly modified and moved by action of the waves.

Sediment is generally supplied to a beach by rivers. Longshore currents then erode and move the sand parallel to the coast. Sand then either creates barriers along the coast or is deposited into submarine canyons that exist offshore, a depositional process called *sediment compartmentalization.* Large amounts of sediment are lost to submarine canyons and they provide an important role in distributing sand to the deep sea. As long as this cycle remains uninterrupted, the beach will continue to exist in a state of more or less equilibrium. Once artificial barriers are erected to trap sand, the balance of the beach is altered. Engineering structures such as jetties, breakwaters, groins, and dams interrupt the longshore drift. Sand is deposited behind the structures, and the beach is eroded in front of the structure. Remediation often includes costly artificial beach replenishment.

David L. White

FURTHER READING
Kennett, James. *Marine Geology.* Englewood Cliffs, N.J.: Prentice Hall, 1982.
King, Cuchlaine A. *Beaches and Coasts.* London: Edward Arnold, 1960; 2nd ed., New York: St. Martin's Press, 1972.

Montgomery, Carla W. *Physical Geology,* 3rd ed.
    Dubuque, Iowa: Wm. C. Brown, 1993.
Thurman, Harold V. *Essentials of Oceanography.*
    Columbus, Ohio: Charles E. Merrill, 1983; 6th ed.,
    with Alan P. Trujillo, Upper Saddle River, N.J.:
    Prentice Hall, 1999.

RELATED ARTICLES
Bar; Coastal Erosion; Coastal Morphology; Longshore
Current; Shoreline Morphology

Beaufort Sea

The Beaufort Sea is an arm of the Arctic Ocean,
located in a region that is bounded approximately
by 70 to 75°N latitude and 125 to 155°W longitude. It extends along the northern coastlines of
Alaska and Canada from Point Barrow to the western edge of the Canadian Archipelago and is
flanked by the Chukchi Sea on the west and
Amundsen Gulf and Parry Strait on the east. Other
seas and gulfs dot the
Canadian archipelago,
including the Prince
Gustav Adolph and

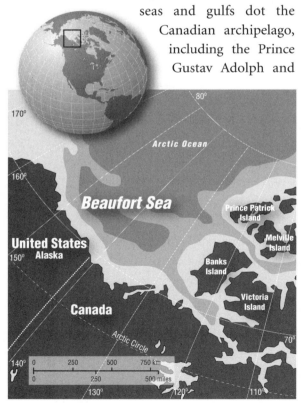

Beaufort Sea.

Sverdrup Seas. Beaufort Sea covers an area of
about 450,000 square kilometers (170,000 square
miles). The average depth is 1000 meters [m; 3300
feet (ft)] and the maximum depth is 4682 m
(15,361 ft). Beaufort Sea was named for Sir Francis
Beaufort (1774–1857), a British naval officer who
encouraged its exploration in the early nineteenth
century. Commercial whaling was an important
industry until the early twentieth century.

Mackenzie River enters the Beaufort Sea near
the town of Inuvik, Canada. It is the largest river
to enter the Arctic Ocean and delivers abundant
sediments. Coastal regions are mostly flat, wet,
and barely above sea level, with rare cliffs that
reach heights of 425 m (1398 ft). Beaufort Sea has
a relatively shallow continental shelf that is less
than 50 m (165 ft) deep. It extends up to 30 kilometers (19 miles) from shore. The continental
slope descends steeply to the Canada Basin. Shelf
sediments (mostly mud and sand) are ice rich
and consist of permafrost in the upper few
meters. Most shelf sediments were deposited during the last two glacial epochs.

The sea is entirely covered by pack ice from late
October or early November to June. The pack ice
is more than 5 m (16 ft) thick in many areas.
Some of the ice islands (icebergs) and ice ridges
have drafts of up to 50 m (165 ft). In fact, the
seafloor of the continental shelf has been scoured
by ice keels that gouge furrows in the sediment as
deep as 4 m (13 ft).

The surface layer of water, which extends to
250 m (820 ft) below sea level, is a mixture of
continental runoff, seasonal ice melt, and intrusion of water from the Bering Sea, Chukchi Sea,
and Mackenzie River. Oceanographic conditions
are greatly influenced by the circulation of the
Arctic Ocean. At the shelf margin, currents flow
westward and drag the pack ice with them.

The Beaufort Sea region has been a critical
hunting and fishing ground for many communities of aboriginal people for at least 5000 years.
The Alaskan coast is populated by the Inupiat,

who live mostly in the villages of Barrow, Kaktovik, and Nuiqsut. The Canadian coast is populated by the Inuvialuit. There are more than 40 marine fish species in the region. Wildlife consists of musk ox, caribou, reindeer, seabirds, polar bears, and seals. In the summer, Beluga whales and about 75 percent of the world's population of bowhead whales converge on the area.

Large economic oil and gas reservoirs of several geologic ages occur under Prudhoe Bay, an arm of the Beaufort Sea. Some of these reservoirs are known to extend farther offshore beneath the continental shelf. Beginning in 1977, oil from wells in and near Prudhoe Bay was sent to the port of Valdez in southern Alaska via the Trans-Alaska Pipeline. These wells are still in operation today. Chances for more commercial discoveries are considered good because of the favorable strata and structures beneath the Beaufort Sea. However, petroleum exploration and development in this region are hindered by the severe Arctic climate, polar ice cap, winter darkness, remoteness from support facilities and supplies, and a land claim settlement in 1984 between the Canadian government and the Inuvialuit.

Susan Morrell

FURTHER READING
Barnes, Peter W., Donald M. Schell, and Erk Reimnitz. *The Alaskan Beaufort Sea: Ecosystems and Environment.* Orlando, Fla.: Academic Press, 1984.
Dinter, David A. "Quaternary Sedimentation of the Alaska Beaufort Sea Shelf: Influence of Regional Tectonics, Fluctuating Sea Levels, and Glacial Sediment Sources." *Tectonophysics,* Vol. 114, pp. 133–161.
Grantz, Arthur, Steven D. May, and David Dinter. "Regional Geology and Petroleum Potential of the United States Beaufort and the northeasternmost Chukchi Seas." In David W. Scholl, Arthur Grantz, and John G. Vedder, eds., *Geology and Resource Potential of the Continental Margin of Western North America and Adjacent Ocean Basins: Beaufort Sea to Baja California.* Houston, Texas: Circum-Pacific Council for Energy and Mineral Resources, 1987; pp. 17–35.

RELATED ARTICLES
Arctic Ocean; Bering Sea; Chukchi Sea; Continental Shelf; Pack Ice; Petroleum

Bellingshausen Sea

The Bellingshausen Sea is an Antarctic body of water located between Thurston Island (about 100°W longitude) on the west and Alexander Island and the Antarctic Peninsula (about 75°W longitude) on the east. The northern boundary with the Pacific Ocean is the Antarctic Circle. It was named after a Russian admiral, Fabian Gottlieb von Bellingshausen (1778–1852), who discovered it in 1819. He sighted what he named Alexander I Land, the first land ever seen within the Antarctic Circle. However, due to poor viewing conditions and extensive ice coverage, he was not aware that he had discovered the massive Alexander Island instead of the continent.

Ocean currents flow in a northeasterly direction from the Bellingshausen Sea toward the coast and then turn to flow back to the southwest. The Bellingshausen Sea embayment is covered with ice year round. Therefore, many icebergs originate in the Bellingshausen Sea; more are encountered south of Palmer Archipelago than farther north in the area of the South Shetland Islands. The area between Adelaide Island and Charco Island is closely packed with ice, which indicates that the surface water is piled up near the coast, as expected by the dominant easterly currents and winds.

Two distinct water masses occur in the Bellingshausen Sea. Antarctic upper water occurs above 200 meters (656 feet), and Antarctic deep water extends from there to the bottom. A steep salinity gradient (33.76 to 34.59 practical salinity units) exists in the transition water that separates the upper and bottom waters. Minimum temperatures of the subsurface layer are colder than −1.5°C (29°F).

Bathymetry (seafloor topography) features include an abyssal plain, deep submarine canyons, and seamounts. Sediments in the Bellingshausen Sea consist primarily of glacial marine sediment that contains abundant dropstones. Compared to other Antarctic bodies of water, the abundance of phytoplankton in the Bellingshausen Sea is greater than that in the Drake Passage, Weddell Sea, or Bransfield Strait.

Deanna Madison

FURTHER READING

Craddock, Campbell, ed. *Antarctic Geoscience.* Symposium on Antarctic Geology and Geophysics, Madison, Wisconsin, 22–27 August 1977, International Union of Geological Sciences. Madison: University of Wisconsin Press, 1982.

Kennett, James P. *Marine Geology.* Englewood Cliffs, N.J.: Prentice Hall, 1982.

RELATED ARTICLES

Abyssal Plain; Bottom Water Formation; Ocean Current; Salinity; Seamounts; Water Mass

Benguela Current

Benguela is a town on the coast of Angola, on the western side of Africa at about 12°S latitude, and is the capital of a province of the same name. The town gives its name to an ocean current that flows parallel to the coast, toward the equator. The Benguela Current, which flows past Benguela, is the eastern boundary current in the South Atlantic. It forms part of the gyre in that ocean, breaking away from the Antarctic Circumpolar Current, then flowing northward along the west coast of southern Africa until it meets and joins the South Atlantic Equatorial Current. The current is broad and moves fairly slowly, at about 25 centimeters (0.82 foot) per second.

The water it carries originates in three other ocean currents. Most is subantarctic water fed into the current from the Antarctic Circumpolar Current. There is an additional contribution

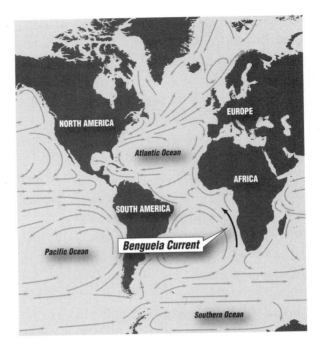

Benguela Current.

from water that flows around the Cape of Good Hope, out of eddies in the Agulhas Current, on the eastern side of southern Africa. Water also enters after crossing the South Atlantic from eddies in the Brazil Current, which flows southward along the eastern coast of South America. Water from the Agulhas Current is warm and relatively salty, because of the high rate of evaporation over the Indian Ocean. Water from the Brazil Current, entering farther north, is also warm. The cool, dense water from the Antarctic Circumpolar Current forms a stable layer beneath the warmer water from the Agulhas Current. This layer of cool water is an important spawning area for commercially valuable fish, including sardines and anchovies.

The Benguela Current is a typical eastern boundary current, with many upwelling areas of cold water that are rich in nutrients. The upwelling areas are most marked near Cape Fria, Namibia, at about 18°S and to the south of 31°S latitude during the summer, from September through March. Winds along the African coast are often from the south or southwest, and it is the wind that drives the current. Because of the rotation of Earth (the Coriolis effect) the current is deflected to the left in the southern hemisphere. As the surface water drifts away from the coast, cold water from a deeper level rises to the surface to take its place. Nutrients brought close to the surface by the upwelling areas are augmented by nutrients from the Agulhas Current, which carries water that has been thoroughly mixed by the severe winter storms that often occur in the southern Indian Ocean.

The nutrient-rich upwelling areas sustain large stocks of fish, and for many years the Benguela Current was second only to the Peru Current in the value of its fisheries. Sardines, known as *pilchards* in South Africa (*Sardinops ocellatus*), and anchovies (*Engraulis capensis*) are the most abundant species, although the sardine stocks collapsed through overfishing in the late 1960s, and in recent years there has been a reduction in anchovy spawning, possibly associated with a rise in the sea temperature. These and other species have been fished since the seventeenth century. The fish also feed seabirds, whose droppings are a source of guano, used as fertilizer. The guano harvest decreased greatly following failure of the sardine fishery.

Michael Allaby

FURTHER READING
Knauss, John A. *Introduction to Physical Oceanography.* Englewood Cliffs, N.J.: Prentice Hall, 1978; 2nd ed. rev., Upper Saddle River, N.J.: Prentice Hall, 2000.

USEFUL WEB SITES
Garzoli, Silvia, Arnold Gordon, and Christopher Duncan Rae. "Benguela Current Sources and Transports." U.S. World Ocean Circulation Experiment 1995 Report. <http://www-ocean.tamu.edu/WOCE95/Results/4garzoli_etal.html>.

RELATED ARTICLES
Agulhas Current; Antarctic Circumpolar Current; Brazil Current; Coriolis Effect; Eastern Boundary Current; Gyre

Benthic Boundary Layer

The benthic boundary layer (BBL) is the layer of water that directly overlies the seabed and is homogenously mixed as a result of the turbulent motions of the water generated by the friction between the water and the seabed. The layer is usually a few tens of meters (up to 300 feet) thick and is uniform in temperature and salinity. It is much cloudier than the overlying water. The turbidity, assessed optically by instruments called *nephelometers* that measure the degree to which light is scattered, can increase over tenfold in the boundary layer, so it is also referred to as the *nepheloid layer*. The load of suspended material ranges from 0.2 to 5 grams per liter, the highest values occurring when benthic storms occur.

Benthic Storms

Currents in the deep ocean are generally slow, about 1 to 3 centimeters per second (0.2 to 0.7 mile per hour). There are tidal oscillations in the deep ocean, so the currents fluctuate twice a day (i.e., *semidiurnally*). However, intermittently the flows increase considerably and start to resuspend unconsolidated sediments and generate ripple marks once they exceed 30 centimeters per second (0.67 mile per hour). Such events, known as *benthic storms*, are often associated with the passage of mesoscale eddies. These eddies are 20 to 200 kilometers (12.5 to 125 miles) in diameter, contain vast amounts of kinetic energy, and can persist for up to two years. Some stretch all the way from the surface to the bottom of the ocean. Mesoscale eddies can be encountered anywhere, but in some areas they are extremely common, such as off the eastern seaboard of the United States, where each year six or seven are formed as meanders that separate from the Gulf Stream. These storms may persist for several days, eroding away the surface sediment and redepositing it, along with its microfauna, elsewhere.

Turbidity Flows

Intermittently, sediments slip from the steeply sloping continental margins. These catastrophic events are often triggered by earthquakes and result in slumps that are like underwater landslides. As it slides down slope, sediment is entrained into the water, making it very heavy, so that the momentum of the flow can carry it far out over the abyssal plain as turbidity currents. The volumes of sediment involved can be enormous; one slump in the Norwegian Sea has been estimated to have carried 5000 cubic kilometers (1200 cubic miles) of sediment into deep water. However, in the Pacific Ocean the deep trenches that line the continental margins trap these flows, so BBLs in the Pacific tend to be quieter than those in the Atlantic Ocean.

Less catastrophic turbidity flows can also be generated during winter at high latitudes. The waters above the continental shelf cool faster than the water farther offshore and thereby become heavier, causing the density structure to become unstable. The cooler heavier water suddenly cascades downslope, often channeled down through canyons, and deposits fans of sediment at the ends of the canyons. Similar flows result from the large-scale circulation of the deep ocean; for example, cold dense water spills out of the Norwegian Sea through troughs in the sills between Great Britain and Iceland. These and other currents near the bottom are influenced by the Coriolis effect that results from Earth's planetary rotation. Thus, in the northern hemisphere currents turn to the right (clockwise) and often follow the contours of the slope. These contour-hugging currents, or *contourites*, both erode and deposit mud banks. They create different bed forms depending on their speeds. The fastest currents strip away all sediment, exposing the underlying bedrock. Moderate currents generate sand waves and ripple marks and form scour marks around rocks and manganese nodules. Slower currents form scour moats and streamers around and in the wake of the mounds and tubes created by the infaunal animals, such as polychaete and echiuran worms.

Physics of Water Flow

There is friction between water flows and the seabed. When the flows are slow and the bottom is smooth, a thin layer develops in which the water flow is viscous or laminar, described as the viscous sublayer. Immediately adjacent to the seabed there is no flow, but within less than 1 millimeter (0.04 inch) the flow increases smoothly and neither swirls nor eddies. About 10 centimeters (4 inches) above the seabed, the flow becomes turbulent and then increases logarithmically to at least 10 meters (33 feet) above the bottom. As the current speed increases, the viscous sublayer is disrupted and disappears. Any object that sticks up by more than a third of the sublayer develops a wake that disrupts it. The dividing line between hydrodynamic smoothness and roughness is determined by the ratio between inertial and viscous forces, characterized by the Reynolds number. The mounds and pits created by the benthic organisms, and even the organisms themselves if, like sponges, they stick up from the bottom, may increase the roughness of the seabed, increase the local turbulence, and modify the sedimentation of particles onto the seabed. Once the viscous sublayer is eroded, turbulent mixing not only begins to erode the surface sediments but also prevents sedimentation from taking place.

Biology of the BBL

The seawater–sediment interface is a major ecological feature. The characteristics of the BBL are very important to the species that inhabit the sediment interface. Sediment feeders need a depositional environment in which sinking particles are not kept in suspension and can be deposited on the bottom. Their feeding strategies involve the creation of mounds and hollows, which favor sedimentation into the hollows. Conversely, suspension feeders thrive better when the sedimenting particles are kept in suspension and are often more abundant where the currents are stronger. They have bodies that are structured to extend up through the viscous sublayer into the more turbulent layer above. Most collect their food passively by deploying nets and fans to intercept the particles being wafted past by the currents. Suspension feeders tend to thrive better where there are hard substrates to which they can attach themselves and over which the water flows tend to be more turbulent. However, if the currents become too strong, they may be damaged or even dislodged.

There is also an important guild of scavenging species, including large sharks and amphipod crustaceans, that feed on large carcasses of whales and large fish that sink onto the seabed. They have efficient ways of locating potential food. Series of pictures taken with time-lapse cameras baited with food and deployed at abyssal depths have shown just how quickly they can home in on the baits and consume them. At depths of 4000 meters (13,100 feet) a dolphin carcass lasts only a few days, and all the flesh on a gray whale carcass is consumed within a month. The suggestion is that by swimming up and down through the BBL, a scavenger can scan the water, "sniffing" out chemicals diffusing from any carcass.

The pelagic inhabitants of the BBL are described as being *benthopelagic*. There are many species that are endemic (unique) to this layer at depths deeper than about 2500 meters (8200 feet), but they remain almost totally unknown.

Chemical Fluxes Across the Water–Sediment Interface

Chemical substances are constantly moving from the water into the sediment and from the sediment into the water. These fluxes tend to modify the chemical characteristics of the water in the BBL. Oxygen is drawn into the sediment as it is used by the oxidation of any organic material in the sediments. Carbon dioxide tends to be released because calcium carbonate is rapidly dissolved at depths deeper than the carbonate compensation depth. Metallic ions are mobile in oxidized sediments and tend to be deposited at the redox boundary within the sediments, creating a flux across the interface. There are fine scale changes in the chemical environments around the burrows, mounds, and tubes of animals inhabiting the seabed.

Calcium Carbonate Compensation Depth

Calcium carbonate occurs in two mineralogical states, aragonite and calcite. The shells of pteropod mollusks are aragonite, whereas the carbonate tests of foraminifers are calcite. Both forms slowly dissolve in deep water, and most of the dissolution occurs at the surface of the seabed, with the aragonite dissolving at shallower depths. As a result, the carbonate content of pelagic sediments declines with depth, and the depths at which the content falls to less than 20 percent are described as the carbonate compensation depths (CCD). In the North Atlantic the CCD occurs only where depths exceed 5500 meters (18,000 feet), but in the North Pacific and Southern Ocean it is shallower than 3500 meters (11,500 feet) in places.

Martin Angel

FURTHER READING

Aller, J. Y. "Quantifying Sediment Disturbances by Bottom Currents and Its Effect on Benthic Communities in a Deep-Sea Western Boundary Zone." *Deep-Sea Research,* Vol. 36A (1989), pp. 901–934.

Angel, M. V. "Life in the Benthic Boundary Layer: Connections to the Mid-water and Sea Floor." *Philosophical Transactions of the Royal Society of London,* Series A, Vol. 331 (1990), pp. 15–28.

Gage, John D., and Paul A. Tyler. *Deep-Sea Biology: A Natural History of the Deep-Sea Floor.* Cambridge and New York: Cambridge University Press, 1991.

Richards, K. J. "Modeling the Benthic Boundary Layer." *Journal of Physical Oceanography,* Vol. 12 (1982), pp. 428–439.

Smith, C. R., and A. R. Baco. "Phylogenetic and Functional Affinities Between Whale Fall, Seep and

Vent Chemoautotrophic Communities." *Cahiers de Biologie Marine,* Vol. 39 (1998), pp. 345–346.

Thurston, M. H., B. J. Bett, and A. L. Rice. "Abyssal Megafaunal Necrophages: Latitudinal Differences in the Eastern North Atlantic Ocean." *Internationale Revue der Gesamten Hydrobiologie,* Vol. 80 (1995), pp. 267–286.

Van Weering, T. C. E., I. N. McCave, and I. R. Hall, eds. "Special Issue: Ocean Margin Exchange (OMEX I) Benthic Processes Study." *Progress in Oceanography,* Vol. 42 (1998), pp. 1–257.

RELATED ARTICLES

Abyssal Plain; Calcium Carbonate Compensation Depth; Continental Margin; Coriolis Effect; Gulf Stream; Turbidity Current

Benthos

The term *benthos* refers to the sea bottom and the organisms that live there. The benthos ranges from the land's edges to the deepest trenches of the oceans, and the seafloor in between can be divided into a number of depth zones. *Estuaries* are shallow areas where seawater and fresh water from land mix. The *intertidal* or *littoral zone* is the area between the highest high and lowest low tides. Ecologists often subdivide the intertidal zone into the *upper supralittoral* or *splash zone*; the *midlittoral,* which lies between mean high and low tide and is covered by water at least once a day; and the *infralittoral,* which is exposed to air only occasionally at very low tides.

The *subtidal zone,* which is sometimes called the *sublittoral zone,* extends from the low water mark to 200 meters (0.1 mile) depth. This region of the seafloor encompasses the *continental shelf,* which is the undersea extension of the continent, and comprises about 7–8 percent of the benthos. The *bathyal zone* includes the seafloor between 200 and 4000 meters (0.1 to 2.5 miles). It includes the *shelf break,* the steeply descending *continental slope,* and the more gradually descending *continental rise.* About 40 percent of

the seafloor is bathyal. The majority of the *benthos* (about 52 percent) is in the *abyssal zone,* which comprises the seafloor at depths of 4000 to 6000 meters (2.5 to 3.7 miles). The *hadal zone,* which comprises the world's undersea trenches, encompasses about 2 percent of the seafloor and extends from 6000 to 11,000 meters (3.7 to 6.8 miles). The benthos encompasses numerous types of substrate. Hard substrate of varying types can be found in the intertidal and subtidal zones and in deeper water on canyon walls and on mid-ocean ridges. Soft substrate is, however, by far the most abundant habitat for benthic organisms in most benthic zones.

The benthos includes a tremendous diversity of organisms: the eubacteria and archaebacteria, many algae divisions, many protist phyla, most invertebrate phyla, and all of the chordate subphyla have benthic representatives. Benthic animals can be *epibenthic* (live on top of the substrate) or *infaunal* (live in or burrow through sediment). They generally are categorized based on size. *Megafauna* are those organisms visible to the naked eye, *macrofauna* are larger than 500 micrometers (μm; 300 μm in the deep sea), *meiofauna* are larger than 63 μm (42 μm in the deep sea), and *microfauna* are smaller than 53 μm. Macrofaunal species comprise 98 percent of benthic animal biomass; the microfauna represent 99.9 percent of the total number of benthic organisms.

Methods for sampling the benthos vary depending on the zone to be studied. The intertidal is the easiest zone to study because it borders land. Collecting data about substrate type and collecting samples of plants and animals also are relatively easy in much of the subtidal zone because it is within human reach via scuba diving. Studying the benthos in the deeper zones of the oceans requires oceanographic research vessels and sophisticated equipment. For mapping topography of the seafloor, oceanographers use technologies such as multifrequency sonar and sidescan sonar. Coring and drilling devices dropped over the side of a ship are used to collect samples of the seafloor. Researchers use time-lapse, still, and video cameras to study abundance, dispersion, and behavior of benthic animals. Collecting animals requires towed nets, remote-operated vehicles (ROVs), or submersibles.

Lynn L. Lauerman

FURTHER READING
Coull, Bruce C., ed. *Ecology of Marine Benthos.* Columbia: University of South Carolina Press, 1977.
Gage, John D., and Paul A. Tyler. *Deep-Sea Biology: A Natural History of Organisms at the Deep-Sea Floor.* Cambridge and New York: Cambridge University Press, 1991.
Hedgpeth, J., ed. "Classification of Marine Environments and Concepts of Marine Ecology." In *The Treatise on Marine Ecology and Paleoecology,* Vol. 1, *Ecology.* Memoir 67 of the Geological Society of America. New York: Geological Society of America, 1957.
Holme, N. A., and A. D. McIntyre, eds. *Methods for the Study of Marine Benthos.* Oxford: Blackwell Scientific, 1971; 2nd ed., Boston: Blackwell Scientific, 1984.
Nybakken, James W. *Marine Biology: An Ecological Approach,* 5th ed. San Francisco: Benjamin Cummings, 2001.

RELATED ARTICLES
Continental Shelf; Continental Slope; Deep Sea; Hadal Zone; Intertidal

Bering Sea

The Bering Sea is a semienclosed subarctic body of water that comprises the northernmost reaches of the Pacific Ocean. Geographically, the sea is located between 52 and 66° N and 162°E and 157°W. Bounded by Alaska, the Bering Strait, and northeastern Siberia to the north and by the Alaska Peninsula and the Aleutian Islands to the south, the Bering Sea spans 2,274,000 square kilometers (878,000 square miles) and has some of the most productive waters on Earth.

The Bering Sea exchanges water with the Arctic Ocean and the Pacific Ocean. The Alaskan Stream, the Aleutian North Slope Current, the Bering Slope Current, the Anadyr Current, and the Kamchatka Current flow through the sea and influence its overall circulation patterns. It contains two distinct bathymetric (depth) regions: An extremely wide and relatively shallow [less than 150 meters (492 feet) deep] continental shelf [500 kilometers (311 miles) wide in the southeast to 800 kilometers (497 miles) wide in the north] lies to the northeast, and a deeper [3700 to 4000 meters (12,139 to 13,123 feet)] plain lies to the southwest. The shelf is smooth and featureless, except for the many islands and seven of the world's largest submarine canyons. Eight major sedimentary basins can be found in the Bering Sea: Aleutian Basin, Komandorsky (Commander) Basin, Bowers Basin, Anadyr Basin, Chirikov Basin, Norton Basin, Briston Basin, and Beringian Shelf.

Ice cover also affects physical and biological processes in the Bering Sea; the ice edge retreats into the Chukchi and Beaufort Seas during the summer but can extend more than 1700 kilometers (1056 miles) over the shelf during the winter.

Bathymetry, ice cover, temperature, circulation, water mixing, timing of the spring phytoplankton bloom, and other factors make the Bering Sea an extremely complex ecosystem. In studying the Bering Sea, researchers have subdivided the area into smaller distinct ecosystems, such as the eastern Bering Sea, the Aleutian Islands, the Gulf of Alaska, the Aleutian Basin, and the western Bering Sea. Others recognize seven physically and biologically distinct habitats in the southeastern Bering Sea alone. Biological and physical characteristics differ among regions, and these differences affect growth and survival of marine organisms.

The Bering Sea is one of the richest and most productive marine ecosystems on Earth. It supports over 450 species of fish and shellfish, 50 species of seabirds, 25 species of marine mammals, and the world's largest eelgrass beds. The ecosystem, which had long supported the indigenous peoples of the region, became a mecca for large-scale commercial fishing for shellfish and fish in the early 1950s. Currently, about 25 species of fish, crustaceans, and mollusks are commercially important. Over 2000 fishing boats from the United States, Canada, Russia, Japan, Norway, China, Taiwan, Poland, and the Koreas reap an annual seafood harvest worth over $1 billion. Fifty-six percent of the total U.S. annual seafood harvest comes from the Bering Sea.

Since the 1950s, researchers have documented dramatic changes in the Bering Sea ecosystem, such as declines in marine mammal and seabird populations and declines and increases in fish and shellfish populations. Determining what drives huge interannual variations in physical and biological parameters, however, is a difficult task. The intensity of fishing efforts as well as natural climate-driven changes in the area have led to concerns about whether the richness and productivity of the sea can be sustained. Some researchers fear that overfishing will lead to collapse of fisheries, as has happened in so many other locations in the world; in some areas of the Bering Sea, certain fish stocks already are depleted.

Lynn L. Lauerman

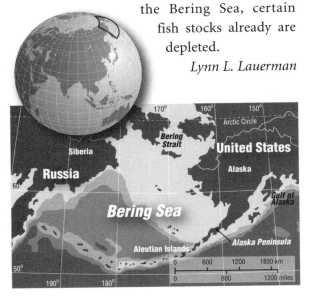

Bering Sea and Bering Strait.

FURTHER READING

National Research Council. *The Bering Sea Ecosystem.* Washington, D.C.: National Academy Press, 1996.

Wilimovsky, Norman J., Lewis S. Incze, and S. J. Westrheim, eds. *Species Synopses: Life Histories of Selected Fish and Shellfish of the Northeast Pacific and Bering Sea.* Seattle: University of Washington Press, 1988.

USEFUL WEB SITES

"Bering Sea and North Pacific Ocean Theme Page." <http://www.pmel.noaa.gov/bering>.

RELATED ARTICLES

Aleutian Islands; Arctic Ocean; Bathymetry; Beaufort Sea; Bering Strait; Chukchi Sea; Pacific Ocean; Phytoplankton

Bering Strait

Bering Strait is a narrow body of water that separates the continents of North America and Asia and links the Arctic Ocean with the Bering Sea. It is located at about 66°N latitude and between 168 and 170°W longitude. The narrowest part is between Cape Prince of Wales in Alaska and Cape Dezhnez in Siberian Russia, where the distance is approximately 88 kilometers (55 miles). The strait has a maximum depth of 52 meters (171 feet). Bering Strait was first discovered and explored by a Russian navigator, Semyon Ivanov Dezhnyov (1605–73), in 1648. It was not named, however, until 1728, when a Danish captain named Vitus Bering (1681–1741) sailed into the strait.

The U.S.–Russia boundary extends north–south through the strait. The Diomede Islands stand about midway between Cape Prince of Wales and Cape Dezhnez. The larger, Big Diomede (Ratmanov) Island belongs to Russia. About 5 kilometers (3 miles) to the east and across the International Date Line lies Little Diomede, which belongs to the United States. Fairway Rock lies in U.S. waters just south of Little Diomede Island. These islands have a combined area of about 16 square kilometers (6 square miles).

The Bering Strait region is uniformly shallow. This prevents significant water transport between the Pacific and Arctic Oceans. The winters are cold and severe. From October to June the Bering Strait is covered with pack ice, averaging 1.5 meters (5 feet) thick. In summer only drift ice remains. The shallow seafloor was mostly exposed during times of maximum continental glaciations and lowest sea levels. A land bridge formed over which humans and other animals migrated from Asia to North America. The Diomede Islands are populated by Eskimos, who subsist mostly on sea mammals and fish that occupy the region.

Susan Morrell

FURTHER READING

Coachman, Lawrence K., Knut Aagard, and R. B. Tripp. *Bering Strait: The Regional Physical Oceanography.* Seattle: University of Washington Press, 1975.

Hopkins, David M., ed. *The Bering Land Bridge.* Stanford, Calif.: Stanford University Press, 1967.

Hunt, William R. *Arctic Passage: The Turbulent History of the Land and People of the Bering Sea, 1697–1975.* New York: Scribner's, 1975.

RELATED ARTICLES

Arctic Ocean; Bering Sea; Chukchi Sea; Pack Ice

Bermuda Triangle

The Bermuda Triangle, sometimes called the *Devil's Triangle,* is an imaginary area of approximately 1,295,000 square kilometers (500,000 square miles) in the Atlantic Ocean. Although the U.S. Board of Geographic Names does not officially recognize the Bermuda Triangle, it is generally said to encompass a triangular region marked by apexes in Bermuda; Miami, Florida; and San Juan, Puerto Rico.

Since the mid-nineteenth century, interest in the Bermuda Triangle has been related to a high incidence of unexplained disappearances of ships, small boats, and aircraft. Many of these disappearances have been documented in high-profile magazines, science fiction stories, and popular books, giving the area a mysterious and supernatural reputation. Various theories proposing to explain the disappearances have been offered throughout the years. The most practical of these cite environmental causes and human error. Strengthening this line of reasoning are the area's unique environmental features. The Bermuda Triangle is one of the two places on earth from which a magnetic compass points toward true north rather than magnetic north. Another characteristic of the area is the swift-flowing, turbulent Gulf Stream. This, coupled with the unpredictable Caribbean–Atlantic weather pattern, gives rise to sudden storms and water spouts.

Although new reports of supernatural events continue to add to the legend surrounding the Bermuda Triangle, only a minuscule percent of the area's large number of visitors have ever experienced anything out of the ordinary.

Roger McHaney

FURTHER READING

Berlitz, Charles. *The Bermuda Triangle.* Garden City, N.Y.: Doubleday, 1974.

Taylor, Albert. "Bermuda Triangle Revisited." *Air Progress,* Vol. 47 (January 1985), pp. 20–21.

RELATED ARTICLES

Atlantic Ocean; Gulf Stream

Biodiversity

Biodiversity is a general term used to describe the rich variety of life on Earth. This variety is estimated at various levels of organization: (1) the genetic variation that occurs within an individual species; (2) the diversity of species or other taxonomic groups that occur within a locality, a region, or globally; and (3) the diversity of ecosystems

Coral reef in Manado, Indonesia, a prime example of a highly diverse ecosystem. (© Jeff Collett/Natural Visions)

within a locality, a region, or globally. Most estimates of biodiversity refer to level 2 or 3.

Terrestrial Versus Marine Biodiversity

When higher taxonomic levels (phyla and classes) are considered, biodiversity is greater in the sea than on land or in fresh water. Currently, of the 80 or so eukaryote phyla generally recognized, about 60 contain marine representatives, whereas terrestrial or freshwater representatives are found in about 40 each. Among the animal phyla commonly recognized, 33 of 34 have marine representatives and 14 of these phyla are exclusively marine. The current explanation for the preponderance of marine phyla is that more than three-fourths of Earth's living history took place in the sea prior to invasion of the land and fresh water. Most of the major body patterns and levels of organization we know today were established in the marine environment. Only a subset of these organisms then proceeded to invade freshwater and terrestrial habitats.

However, species diversity on land does appear to be much higher than that in the sea. More than 1.5 million terrestrial species have been described compared to some 250,000 marine ones. Part of this difference can be explained by the greater difficulty in sampling the marine environment compared to investigations on land. Since the 1980s, detailed investigations of microscopic benthic fauna (bottom-living animals) and the very smallest plankton (picoplankton) have revealed unexpectedly high levels of diversity. Nevertheless, even if adjustments are made for such new discoveries, it seems likely that there are at least double the number of species on land than there are in the oceans. Among arthropods (phylum Arthropoda), the largest predominantly marine subphylum, the Crustacea (crustaceans) has fewer than 45,000 marine representatives. In contrast, the largest predominantly terrestrial subphylum, Uniramia (mandibulate arthropods), contains about 1 million terrestrial species described so far.

Significance of Biodiversity

Why is biodiversity important? There are several arguments—practical and philosophical—as to why people should be concerned about biodiversity loss. A moral argument contends that people do not have the right to endanger species and destroy habitats simply to fuel the pursuit of economic riches. This argument applies whether people regard themselves as guardians of nature or simply cohabitants of the planet. Adopting a more human-centered view, reducing biodiversity diminishes people's enjoyment of nature and depletes the legacy left to their children. For example, if certain coral reefs are destroyed, future generations will be denied the opportunity to experience them.

On a practical level, the untapped variety of marine animals, plants, and microbes represent a store of biochemical riches. Several dozen useful substances, ranging from anticancer drugs to "natural" insecticides, have been harnessed from marine organisms since the 1980s. Many thousands more await discovery. If species are lost, what other invaluable substances might be lost as well?

The ecosystem services argument contends that biodiversity is important in maintaining the health of the environment. An ecosystem comprising a diverse community of organisms may perform services such as water purification and oxygen replenishment. A salt marsh, for example, can remove heavy metals from polluted groundwater. Phytoplankton in the open ocean are net removers of atmospheric carbon dioxide and are producers of oxygen.

Evidence is gradually accumulating that an ecosystem's ability to recover from environmental degradation may be greater if its biological community is diverse. If so, the very survival of Earth's biosphere might depend on maintaining a diverse global community of organisms.

Current Impacts on Marine Biodiversity

The U.S. Committee on Biological Diversity in Marine Ecosystems, reporting in 1995, recognized five activities as the most important agents of change—current and potential—affecting marine biodiversity at all levels: (1) fisheries operations, (2) chemical pollution (and eutrophication), (3) alteration of physical habitat, (4) invasions of exotic species, and (5) global climate change. These factors interact in complex ways, making the management of marine resources a formidable but urgent challenge.

Biodiversity Loss

Many stocks of commercially exploited marine species are monitored; unexploited populations only rarely so. One species of limpet, formerly common along the North Atlantic coast of the United States, has disappeared since the 1930s. Its absence was not formally documented until the 1980s, despite its disappearance taking place in the vicinity of the prestigious laboratories of New England where thousands of marine biologists are trained. What other species may have disappeared in localities where marine biologists are less diligent?

Commercially exploited populations can be driven close to extinction by overhunting or overfishing. This has happened in the case of some whales, reptiles, fish, crustaceans, and mollusks. For example, the Northern right whale, *Eubalaena glacialis,* after being hunted intensively during the nineteenth century, received legal protection in 1935. Since then, its numbers have failed to recover. Today, probably less than 1000 survive, and in their biggest stronghold, the northwestern Atlantic, their numbers seem to be declining, endangered by a combination of factors: inbreeding, collisions with ships, entanglement in fishing nets, and possibly pollution. In their case, and in the case of some other marine mammals and the rarer marine turtles, it will be decades before it is known whether their numbers are too depleted for reproduction and natural selection to reverse the losses. In some cases, pollution, habitat loss, or compensatory changes in the biological community may be preventing their recovery.

As for ecosystems, those most at threat are associated with the continental shelf, where human exploitation, pollution, and land-based activities have the greatest influence. Current estimates suggest that about 50 percent of the world's mangrove swamps have been lost in the last few centuries. In 1997, a global survey called Reef Check, carried out by 750 volunteer divers and 100 marine biologists, concluded that 90 percent of those coral reefs examined showed visible signs of damage from human activities.

Maintaining Marine Biodiversity

If marine biodiversity is important, how can it be conserved? Baseline data are needed, documenting the existing variety and composition of biological communities, to determine whether biodiversity is being compromised, and if so, how. To do this, more marine scientists need to be trained and recruited to undertake field studies, and more biologists encouraged to become specialists in taxonomy.

Protecting marine biodiversity must take into account that events in a particular locality may affect the survival of marine organisms hundreds or thousands of kilometers away. Spawning grounds may be very localized and widely separated from adult feeding grounds. The larval stages of some species disperse long distances. Also, human activities have effects at a distance. For example, inland deforestation may increase runoff and discharge sediment that could smother a coral reef many kilometers away. Where the activities of several countries affect a single body of water, the need for international cooperation is clear.

The establishment of marine protected areas (MPAs) within regional management schemes is a move in the right direction. Between the 1950s and the mid-1990s about 1300 MPAs were established. However, they vary greatly in size and in the degree of protection they confer on constituent ecosystems. Many MPAs are too small [areas less than 1000 hectares (2500 acres)] to incorporate the feeding, breeding, and nursery areas of some constituent species. Many MPAs are not incorporated into regional management schemes. Even where they are, regional schemes such as the Mediterranean Action Plan (MAP) and the Caribbean Environment Program (CEP) have a less than enviable record of success in implementing their objectives.

International treaties provide a means of limiting those human activities that might threaten the maintenance of biodiversity. Dozens of treaties, such as the 1973 Convention on International Trade in Endangered Species (CITES) and the 1978 International Convention on the Prevention of Pollution from Ships (MARPOL), concern the marine environment directly.

Biodiversity came to the fore at the United Nations Conference on Environment and Development in Rio de Janeiro in 1992. The conference resulted in the signing of the International Convention on Biodiversity (ICB) and the adoption of Agenda 21, which established guidelines under which the convention operates. The ICB, as a legal instrument, seeks to protect threatened genetic resources, species, and ecosystems. Annual meetings of the convention provide an international forum for discussion of biodiversity-related issues. In 1995, the meeting focused on marine biodiversity.

Trevor Day

FURTHER READING

Angel, Martin V. "Ocean Diversity." In C. P. Summerhayes and S. A. Thorpe, eds. *Oceanography: An Illustrated Guide.* London: Manson Publishing, 1996.

De Fontaubert, A. Charlotte, David R. Downes, and Tundi S. Agardy. *Biodiversity in the Seas: Implementing the Convention on Biological Diversity in Marine and Coastal Habitats.* Gland, Switzerland: International Union for Conservation of Nature (IUCN), 1996.

Earle, Sylvia, and Boyce Thorne-Miller. *The Living Ocean: Understanding and Protecting Marine Biodiversity.* Washington, D.C.: Island Press, 1991; 2nd ed., 1999.

Groombridge, B., and M. D. Jenkins. *Global Biodiversity: Earth's Living Resources in the 21st Century.* Cambridge, England: World Conservation Press, 2000.

Kelleher, Graeme. *Guidelines for Marine Protected Areas.* Gland, Switzerland, and Cambridge, England: International Union for Conservation of Nature (IUCN), 1999.

Margulis, Lynn. *Five Kingdoms: An Illustrated Guide to the Phyla of Life on Earth.* San Francisco: W. H. Freeman, 1982; 3rd ed., New York, 1998.

Ormond, Rupert F. G., John D. Gage, and Martin V. Angel. *Marine Biodiversity: Patterns and Processes.* Cambridge and New York: Cambridge University Press, 1997.

RELATED ARTICLES

Arthropoda; Benthic Boundary Layer; Continental Shelf; Coral Reef; Crustacea; Fisheries; Marine Sanctuary; Plankton; Pollution, Ocean

Biogeochemical Cycle

A biogeochemical cycle is a representation of the distribution of materials between reservoirs or compartments (such as surface water, deep water, biota, and sediments) and their conversion and transport by biological, geological, chemical, and physical processes. Commonly, the focus is on elements, such as carbon, nitrogen, and phosphorus, or compounds, for example, pollutants such as dichlorodiphenyltrichloroethane (DDT) and polychlorinated biphenyls (PCBs) that are of biological significance and are profoundly influenced by anthropogenic (human-caused) processes. A biogeochemical cycle gives, in shorthand, our current knowledge of the distribution of substances, and their movement between one region and another, with a broader perspective than that provided by a geochemical cycle. The biogeochemical approach is a further spur to interdisciplinary thinking and assists in environmental management.

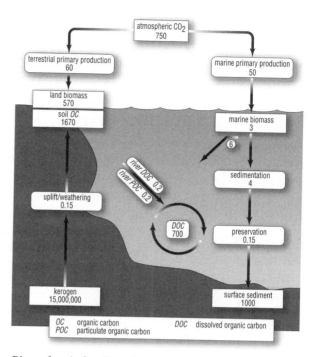

Biogeochemical cycling of organic carbon. [Adapted from S. Pantoja and S. Wakeham, "Marine Organic Geochemistry: A General Overview," in Chemical Processes in the Marine Environment (New York: Springer-Verlag, 2000.)]

Depicting a Biogeochemical Cycle

In depicting a biogeochemical cycle, the sphere under consideration (e.g., the global ocean system) is delineated. Usually, this is regarded as a closed system (with regard to mass conservation) and in a steady state, but it need not be. Partial systems of interest, such as a salt marsh, a seagrass bed, or a coral reef, could be considered, although in such cases, system boundaries need to be defined carefully, and unidirectional fluxes may be included as additions to the cycle itself. Within a biogeochemical cycle, compartments with relatively homogeneous content are defined, such as surface water, deep water, phytoplankton, zooplankton, surface sediment, and so on. Compartments are usually depicted by boxes and fluxes by arrows.

The conservation of mass is a prerequisite in establishing a biogeochemical model. If a steady state is assumed, fluxes to and from a compartment must balance. If observation shows that this is not the case, this is in itself a spur to further

research. It could indicate the omission of one or more important sources or sinks for which fluxes have not been incorporated, or it might confirm that there is a net change (depletion or buildup) of material over time.

Time scales for reactions within the system typically range over several orders of magnitude. They span biological and geochemical conversions at scales of much less than a year to geological processes, such as sediment diagenesis (geochemical reactions following recent burial) and movement of Earth's crust at time scales of hundreds to millions of years. The slow processes are usually regarded as constant or negligible, whereas fast processes are typically averaged over a year.

General Themes in Biogeochemical Cycles

In a marine biogeochemical cycle, inorganic substances are converted to organic substances and are incorporated in biological compartments through either photosynthesis (the use of light energy) by phytoplankton or attached plants or chemosynthesis (the use of energy from the oxidation of inorganic substances, or methane by bacteria). Once formed, this particulate organic matter (POM) is grazed by heterotrophic bacteria and protozoa and by zooplankton. They, in turn, are consumed by larger animals. When phytoplankton, attached plants, heterotrophic bacteria and protozoa, and animals die, or when they excrete waste, organic constituents are converted to inorganic substances by bacterial decomposition or other processes. In an inorganic form, they are once again available for uptake by phytoplankton and attached plants.

Inorganic substances commonly enter the ocean system as particles or dissolved ions weathered from continental rocks. However, some elements enter through hydrothermal vents at mid-ocean ridges or as in the case of nitrogen and carbon dioxide, they can enter from the atmosphere in gaseous form. Inorganic and organic substances exit the ocean system by incorporation in seafloor sediment and subsequent burial and compaction. This applies to both particulate material and dissolved substances, which can adhere to sinking detritus and mineral grains or may precipitate out of solution.

Over millions of years, buried sediment is compacted to form sedimentary rock. Sediment and sedimentary rock are eventually subducted at ocean trenches, or are scraped off a descending lithospheric plate and are raised to form islands, or are deposited on continental margins or landmasses. By weathering, erosion, and transport, their constituent inorganic substances enter the ocean system, thus completing the cycle. Alternatively, much of the subducted material will be ejected back onto Earth's surface as ash or lava from volcanic activity. This may enter the ocean system directly or may accumulate on land, where it is subject to weathering, erosion, and transport before reentering the ocean.

Three cycles are considered here, with an emphasis on biological processes in the marine environment. The carbon cycle is central to biological processes. Nitrogen and phosphorus cycles are of particular interest because some of their chemical constituents are nutrients and can limit marine primary productivity. The pools and fluxes of all three are strongly influenced by human activities.

CARBON CYCLE

Carbon is an essential component of all organic compounds and is fundamental to carbon-based life forms. In the ocean there is no scarcity of dissolved carbon dioxide (as carbonic acid, carbonate, and bicarbonate) to supply photosynthesizers with their carbon source. Carbon that is being actively cycled is dominated by dissolved inorganic carbon, predominantly bicarbonate dissolved in seawater [an estimated 39,000 gigatonnes (43,000 gigatons)]. Net marine photosynthesis, which is dominated by the smallest phytoplankton, is estimated to be 50 gigatonnes (55 gigatons) per year, about 45 percent of net global photosynthesis. The reservoir of marine biomass is comparatively small, at about 3 gigatonnes (3.3 gigatons), and most organic carbon is rapidly recycled in surface waters. The dominant organic carbon reservoir is dissolved organic carbon (DOC) at an estimated 700 gigatonnes (770 gigatons), most of it in the deep ocean. Carbon dioxide fixed in photosynthesis is incorporated in phytoplankton and attached marine plants and is consumed by heterotrophic bacteria and protozoa as well as animals. Through grazing, excretion, and cell rupture, an estimated 6 gigatonnes (6.6 gigatons) per year of particulate organic carbon (POC) is converted to DOC in the seawater pool. Although about half of the POC is grazed by zooplankton, the other half is probably processed via bacteria and protozoa in the microbial loop. Much of the fixed carbon dioxide, an estimated 40 gigatonnes (44 gigatons) per year, is later released as carbon dioxide by respiration of bacteria, protozoa, phytoplankton, or animals in the upper ocean. It reenters biota via photosynthesis. Less than 10 percent of annual primary production, about 4 gigatonnes (4.4 gigatons) per year, sinks as POC out of the upper ocean.

POC is efficiently decomposed as it descends through the water column and settles on the seafloor. Only about 0.15 gigatonne of organic carbon per year (0.3 percent of primary production) is buried in ocean sediments, contributing to the 1000 gigatonnes (1100 gigatons) of organic carbon in this pool. A small fraction of this (perhaps 0.05 percent of sedimentary organic carbon) will be converted to kerogen (fossilized insoluble organic material), which forms petroleum, coal, and natural gas deposits. At geological time scales, most carbon on Earth [an estimated 60 million gigatonnes (66 million gigatons)] is sequestered in sedimentary rocks, predominantly as inorganic carbonates from the chalky exoskeletons of marine phytoplankton.

The removal of atmospheric carbon dioxide by marine phytoplankton and the descent of POC through the water column is termed the *biological pump*. The burning of fossil fuels is increasing atmospheric carbon dioxide levels by an estimated 0.5 percent per year, and atmospheric methane levels have increased by at least 65 percent since preindustrial times. These greenhouse gases contribute significantly to enhanced global warming. Ways and means of mitigating their climatic influence are urgently sought, and a detailed understanding of the global carbon cycle will assist in making predictions about probable effects and may suggest remedial measures.

NITROGEN CYCLE

The element nitrogen is a component of amino acids, which form the building blocks of proteins and of purine or pyrimidine bases in nucleic acids and in important coenzymes such as ATP and NADP. The atmospheric abundance of nitrogen as diatomic nitrogen gas (N_2) is very high [4 million gigatonnes (4.4 million gigatons)] compared to nitrogen's abundance in oceanic water,

mainly as dissolved nitrogen [20,000 gigatonnes (22,000 gigatons)] and nitrate (NO_3^-) [570 gigatonnes (630 gigatons)]. Comparatively little nitrogen gas is "fixed" directly into organic nitrogen. The phytoplankton responsible, nitrogen-fixing cyanobacteria, can be a significant channel of nitrates in some nutrient-poor waters, such as those where coral reefs occur.

Phytoplankton and attached marine plants utilize nitrogen in one of three major forms: ammonium (NH_4^+), nitrite (NO_2^-), and nitrate (NO_3^-). Ammonium ions are made available by the bacterial decomposition of organic matter, by excretion from marine organisms, or by the bacterial conversion of urea and uric acid, excretory products of certain marine animals. Specialized bacteria oxidize ammonium ions to nitrites and others oxidize nitrites to nitrates. The processes that convert particulate organic nitrogen to forms that can be utilized by photosynthesizers are comparatively slow processes, and much of the conversion occurs below the photic zone. As a result, nitrogen in surface waters can become depleted and nitrogen is commonly a limiting factor to primary productivity in open-ocean surface waters. The relative availability of ammonium, nitrite, and nitrate ions changes seasonally and at different levels in the water column, and phytoplankton commonly are able to utilize nitrogen in each of these forms. In temperate waters, inorganic nitrogen is often a limiting factor in productivity during the summer because of the existence of a strong thermocline that effectively partitions the water column. In spring and fall, phytoplankton can utilize nitrogen compounds raised to surface waters by mixing.

Inorganic nitrogen, and to a lesser extent organic nitrogen, is added to the oceans by river flow and by weathering and erosion from the land, in addition to small amounts adhering to wind-blown dust particles and dissolved in rainwater. An equivalent amount is lost from the oceans by burying as seafloor sediment and by the conversion of nitrate to nitrogen gas by denitrifying bacteria. The nitrogen gas is lost to the atmosphere.

Locally, the balance between nitrogen addition and loss may be markedly perturbed by the presence of agricultural fertilizers in runoff and the discharge of sewage into the sea. This can lead to eutrophication—overgrowth of phytoplankton as a result of nutrient overabundance, with the potential to deplete waters of oxygen. However, denitrifying bacteria remove almost all land-derived nitrogen before it reaches the open ocean.

PHOSPHORUS CYCLE

Phosphorus is a vital constituent of biochemical components such as DNA, RNA, and coenzymes such as ATP and NADP. However, phytoplankton typically require only one phosphorus atom for every 12 to 20 nitrogen atoms. Phosphorus is found in organic tissue as phosphate (PO_4^{3-}) and is liberated in this or similar forms (HPO_4^{2-}, $H_2PO_4^-$, and triphosphate, $P_3O_{10}^{5-}$) that are soluble in seawater to varying degrees.

Unlike nitrogen or carbon (in the form of carbon dioxide), phosphorus is not present in the atmosphere as a gas, nor is it dissolved in water in this form. Phosphate is liberated fairly rapidly by bacterial decomposition of organic phosphorus compounds liberated from dead organisms or their parts. More than this, some zooplankton absorb, assimilate, and then excrete more than 50 percent of the phosphate they consume, as well as some of the ingested phosphate being eliminated in their fecal pellets and then made available by rapid bacterial decomposition. Unlike nitrogen, phosphate is commonly recycled within the photic zone. As a result, phosphorus is rarely a limiting factor in phytoplankton productivity. The Mediterranean Sea and parts of the western North Atlantic are exceptions to this general rule.

Where phosphates and nitrates enter the sea in large quantities in sewage, eutrophication may occur, leading to phytoplankton blooms that deoxygenate the water. Phosphate is leached by rain from phosphate-bearing rocks, and it is also a major constituent of natural and artificial agricultural fertilizers and so finds its way into the sea via runoff. Phosphate leaves the ocean system in both organic and inorganic forms buried in the sediment.

Limitations and Benefits of the Biogeochemical Approach

Biogeochemical cycles are, by necessity, simplifications of the real world. In compiling them, scientists are selective in what they include. For example, a time scale is chosen, such as processes occurring over the course of a year, which means that very short or very long time scales are excluded. Only a few compartments are delineated, and variation within a compartment may be considerable, even when their component materials appear to be well mixed. This can lead to misleading assumptions. For example, the turnover time of some forms of POC in surface waters, such as the smallest phytoplankton, may be days, whereas in larger phytoplankton, the turnover time may be weeks. The longer-term average may give little information about the short-term effect, say, of a sewage pollution incident that increases nutrient levels locally and alters phytoplankton composition.

A biogeochemical cycle typically depicts current relationships and can be extrapolated backward or forward in time only with caution. For example, atmospheric carbon dioxide concentrations are increasing, and the compartmentalization and flux of carbon species are based on observations within a few decades of modern science. Making assumptions about how a biogeochemical system will respond in the future, or has responded in the past, is fraught with difficulty. Paul G. Falkowski and 16 coauthors, in an article on the global carbon cycle appearing in the journal *Science* (2000), noted at least 11 hypotheses proposed to explain glacial–interglacial changes in atmospheric carbon dioxide levels.

The relative sizes of compartments reflect the preferences of their investigators. For marine scientists, the land may be perceived as a passive "sink" compartment; for terrestrial ecologists, the oceans may be so treated. Biogeochemical cycles, with their focus on the pooling and flux of materials, rarely consider aspects such as biodiversity, although they may highlight ecosystem services, such as salt marshes removing heavy metals from polluted groundwater.

Despite its limitations, the biogeochemical cycle approach is invaluable in the service of scientists and laypersons alike. Qantifying pools and fluxes and ranking processes by their importance enhances our understanding of ecosystem functioning. Such understanding contributes to environmental management and risk assessment and, assuming that policymakers listen and facilitate action, makes environmental problems more likely to be avoided or their effects mitigated.

The visual depiction of a biogeochemical cycle greatly aids in communicating complex and wide-ranging interactions in an accessible manner for public as well as scientific audiences. The structure and dynamics of a system are depicted together. For researchers, missing information is apparent immediately. This provides a focus for investigation. Individual fluxes that are missing can be calculated provided that all the other fluxes to and from the compartment are known.

Ultimately, biochemical cycles do not exist in isolation—they are coupled. For example, the ocean's biological pump could, theoretically, be made more efficient to extract more of the carbon dioxide produced by human activities. One approach being considered is to seed the ocean with iron in regions, such as the Southern Ocean, where iron seems to be a limiting factor of marine photosynthesis. Such manipulation has a number of effects, not least on nutrients, such as phosphate and nitrate, within other biogeochemical cycles. Modeling coupled biogeochemical cycles is currently a major challenge to marine scientists seeking to unravel the myriad influences on climatic change.

Trevor Day

FURTHER READING

Falkowski, Paul G., Richard T. Barber, and Victor Smetacek. "Biogeochemical Controls and Feedbacks on Ocean Primary Production." *Science*, Vol. 281 (10 July 1998), pp. 200–206.

Falkowski, P. G., et al. "The Global Carbon Cycle: A Test of Our Knowledge of Earth as a System." *Science*, Vol. 290 (13 October 2000), pp. 291–296.

Libes, Susan M. *Marine Biogeochemistry.* New York: Wiley, 1992.

Millero, Frank J. *Chemical Oceanography.* Boca Raton, Fla.: CRC Press, 1992; 2nd ed., 1996.

Schlesinger, William H. *Biogeochemistry: Analysis of Global Change,* 2nd ed. San Diego: Academic Press, 1997.

Summerhayes, C. P., and S. A. Thorpe, eds. *Oceanography: An Illustrated Guide.* New York: Wiley, 1996.

RELATED ARTICLES

Carbon Cycle; Climate Change; Dissolved Organic Matter; Hydrologic Cycle; Nitrogen Cycle; Ocean, Water Budget of; Particulate Organic Carbon; Photosynthesis and Iron Limitation

Biological Conditioning

Biological conditioning is the secretion into seawater of small quantities of organic compounds by the organisms living in the water. These organic compounds or metabolites often have an effect on other organisms in the water column, either enhancing or inhibiting them. It is also possible that these organic compounds could affect the organisms that produced them in either a negative or a positive way.

The organic compounds that are secreted include a number of classes of organic compounds. One such class is those that are toxic to other organisms. The most dramatic examples of toxins are those that are released by any of several species of the photosynthetic dinoflagellates. Whenever these organisms undergo a population explosion, even though each flagellate secretes only a minute amount of the toxin, the massive numbers of the dinoflagellates cause the toxins to reach concentrations in the water column that kill many other organisms. These are the red tides.

Another class of organic compounds is vitamins. Certain species of phytoplankton have requirements for vitamins and may be unable to thrive unless the vitamin is in the water. If the required vitamin is produced only by another phytoplankton species, there may well be a succession of species in the water column, with the vitamin-producing species present first, followed by the vitamin-requiring species.

Other potential biological conditioning compounds may include amino acids, carbohydrates, and lipids, but currently there is little evidence as to their role in the oceans.

James W. Nybakken

FURTHER READING
Nybakken, James W. *Marine Biology: An Ecological Approach,* 5th ed. San Francisco: Benjamin Cummings, 2001.

RELATED ARTICLES
Dinoflagellate; Photosynthesis; Phytoplankton; Red Tide

Biological Magnification

Biological magnification, or biomagnification, is the process whereby a bioaccumulated chemical increases in concentration in the tissues of organisms at successively higher levels of a food chain. Bioaccumulation is defined variously by different investigators, but here it is taken to mean that an organism concentrates a chemical in its tissues because the chemical is not metabolized and therefore builds up in the tissues. In a food chain, if the members of each trophic level do not metabolize the chemical, the chemical is progressively concentrated from one trophic level to the next. Top predators, including humans, are at

greatest risk of acquiring and bioaccumulating the largest concentration of the substance. If the bioaccumulating substance is toxic, top predators are at greatest risk of biological damage. The effects of biological magnification of toxic substances have been documented for both organic and inorganic substances.

The most serious of the documented cases of biomagnification affecting humans occurred in Minamata Bay, Japan, in the 1960s and early 1970s. Beginning in 1952, trace amounts of mercury were discharged into Minamata Bay by a manufacturing plant. The mercury was bioaccumulated by marine fauna, and a high proportion bioconverted to a more toxic form, methyl mercury. Investigations showed local plankton containing 5 parts per million (ppm) of mercury dry weight, intertidal bivalves 10 to 39 ppm, and fish 10 to 55 ppm. Fish and shellfish made up a high proportion of the diet of local fishermen and their families. About 800 cases of acute mercury poisoning (called *Minamata disease*) were reported among local people, with over 100 dying of the disease by 1974. Biological magnification of DDT and other organochlorines has been implicated in several well-documented episodes of seabird and marine mammal mortality.

Trevor Day

FURTHER READING
Beyer, W. Nelson, Gary H. Heinz, and Amy W. Redmon-Norwood, eds. *Environmental Contaminants in Wildlife.* Boca Raton, Fla.: Lewis Publishers, 1996.

Clark, R. B., Chris Frid, and Martin Attrill. *Marine Pollution.* Oxford: Clarendon Press/New York: Oxford University Press, 1986; 4th ed., Oxford and New York: Oxford University Press, 1997.

Mishima, Akio. *Bitter Sea: The Human Cost of Minamata Disease.* Translated by Richard L. Gage and Susan B. Murata. Tokyo: Kosei Publishing/Boston: Charles E. Tuttle, 1992.

RELATED ARTICLES
DDT; Food Chain; Food Web; Minamata Disease; Pollution, Ocean

Bioluminescence

Bioluminescence is the ability of organisms to produce light. It is a capability shared across the full spectrum of marine organisms, from bacteria to phytoplankton, especially dinoflagellates, cnidarians, crustaceans, and fish. The light is produced chemically when the enzyme luciferase catalyzes the oxidation of a protein luciferin. Although many species have the ability to synthesize their own luciferin/luciferase system, some fish, such as the ceratioid anglerfish, culture the luminescent *Photobacterium*. The midshipman fish, *Porichthys*, which has a magnificent series of ventral photophores, obtains its luciferin from the animals it eats; without the right kind of food, its lights go out. The bioluminescence is usually of low intensity, around 10^{-6} milliwatts per square centimeter, which is equivalent to the intensity of daylight at a depth of 800 meters (2625 feet) and blue in color ($\lambda = 450$ to 490 nanometers).

In the twilight and dark environments of the deep sea, light seems to be used for many of the same functions for which color is used by terrestrial animals. The simplest use is the release of a luminescent secretion of clouds into the water to deter and distract attackers. These distraction displays are a common feature in many pelagic species, including decapod shrimps such as *Acanthephyra*. Squid have a variety of strategies. Some simply squirt out a general "smoke screen" secretion and make their escape, whereas others take refuge within the cloud. Another ploy is to produce a coherent glowing decoy that mimics the squid's size and shape. The amphipod *Scina* demonstrates another type of deterrent display. It has light organs in the very tips of its long antennae and tail processes. When threatened it splays them wide and flashes furiously, appearing to be several times bigger. The deep-sea medusa *Atolla* produces elaborate pulsing displays of light that demonstrate how sophisticatedly simple neural

Liocranchia, *a squid with bioluminescent eyes. (© Peter Herring/Natural Visions)*

networks can function. Its display could be a warning similar to that of the gaudy colors of an arrow poison frog.

Light is also used for communication between species. Myctophid fishes (lanternfish) have species-specific arrangements of light organs, or photophores, along their flanks that are probably used to identify an individual's species to others. They also have light organs arranged along their bellies, surprisingly used as camouflage with a type of cryptic coloration. In the twilight zone they inhabit, organisms are vulnerable to visually hunting predators approaching from directly underneath because then they are silhouetted against the brighter light coming from the surface. Therefore, the ventral light organs breakup their outline, making them harder to see. Male lanternfish also have special light organs on their tails, which distinguishes them from females.

There are many fish that have luminous lures to attract their prey. Others have large light cheek organs with large greenish-blue reflectors that are probably used as flashlamps to illuminate their prey as they attack. One of the cheek organs of the fish *Malacosteus* has a red reflector, and, exceptionally, the light it emits is red (λ = ca. 700 nanometers). The visual pigment in the eyes of these fish is also exceptional in that it is sensitive to red light. The interpretation is that these fish hunt the scarlet prawns that inhabit depths of 1000 meters (3280 feet). The fish can see the prawns illuminated by its red headlamps, but the prawns are not able to see the fish's light.

Over tropical reefs in the Caribbean, tiny ostracods behave like fireflies, producing light displays at night while they dance in the water to attract mates and to defend patches of seabed. But there are many examples of bioluminescence for which we have no obvious or feasible explanation. One example is the brilliant displays produced by sea pens such as *Renilla*; they have no eyes and so must be oblivious to their own flashes and are not signaling to other sea pens. A speculative explanation is that by illuminating their attackers, the attackers become clearly visible to their predators.

Martin Angel

FURTHER READING

Hastings, James W., and James G. Morin. "Bioluminescence." In C. L. Prosser, ed., *Neural and Integrative Animal Physiology*. New York: Wiley-Liss, 1991; pp. 131–170.

Herring, Peter J. "Light, Colour and Vision in the Ocean." In Colin P. Summerhayes and Steve A.Thorpe, eds., *Oceanography: An Illustrated Guide*. London: Manson Publishing, 1996; pp. 212-227.

USEFUL WEB SITES

Marine bioluminescence Web page. <http://lifesci.ucsb.edu/~biolum>.

RELATED ARTICLES

Pelagic; Photophore

Biosphere

Biosphere describes the total living space of Earth, including the oceans that are a major part of the biosphere. Because some forms of life occur everywhere in the ocean, it is the most voluminous habitat on the planet. It covers 71 percent of Earth's surface to an average depth of 3800 meters [m; 12,500 feet (ft)]. Thus the oceans have an estimated volume of 1.368×10^9 cubic kilometers (32.8×10^8 cubic miles) and are equivalent to about 0.24 percent of Earth's total mass. About 5 percent of Earth's surface is covered by shallow shelf seas 0 to 200 m (0 to 650 ft) deep, which border the continental landmasses.

Most shelf seas are bounded offshore by a shelf break in which the slope of the seabed becomes abruptly steeper and forms the continental slope and rise, which extend down to depths of around 3000 m (9850 ft). The slopes account for a further 13 percent of the Earth's area. Beyond the slopes, abyssal depths of 3000 to 6000 m (9850 to 19,700 ft) extend over about 51 percent of Earth's surface. The deepest, or hadal depths, cover less than 2 percent of Earth's surface and include many ocean trenches where depths are greater than 6000 m (19,700 ft). The volume of habitat available to life in the oceans is about 168 times that of terrestrial habitats. Seawater scatters and absorbs light, so even below the clearest of oceanic water, sunlight ceases to be detectable below depths of 1000 to 1250 m (3280 to 4100 ft).

The photosynthetic activity of phytoplankton in approximately the upper 100 m (330 ft) supports nearly all life in the oceans. The majority of this, which is the most extensive biome on Earth, is dark and illuminated only by occasional flashes of bioluminescence (light produced by the organisms). It is a cool environment; water temperatures below 1000 m (3280 ft) mostly range between –0.9 and 5° C (30 and 41° F). It is a dynamic environment; Earth's oceans are completely stirred every 1500 years. Compared with evolutionary time scales, this stirring is very rapid and may help to explain why the global inventory of marine species appears to be only about one-tenth that of terrestrial ecosystems.

Martin Angel

FURTHER READING
Angel, Martin V. "What Is the Deep Sea?" In David J. Randall and Anthony P. Farrell, eds., *Deep-Sea Fishes*. San Diego: Academic Press, 1997.
Cohen, J. E. "Marine and Continental Food Webs: Three Paradoxes?" *Philosophical Transactions of the Royal Society of London* B, Vol. 343 (1994), pp. 57–69.
Independent World Commission on the Oceans. *The Ocean Our Future*. Cambridge: Cambridge University Press, 1998.

RELATED ARTICLES
Bioluminescence; Continental Slope; Hadal Zone; Photosynthesis; Phytoplankton; Trench

Bioturbation

Bioturbation is the mixing of sediments by animals. The animals responsible for bioturbation are called *bioturbators*. This mixing buries materials deposited from the water column, such as pollutants, nutrients, and naval mines. It also exposes previously buried materials to the water column, enhancing processes such as the flux of dissolved nutrients to the overlying water column.

Both sedimentary particles and the associated fluids can be mixed, although usually by different mechanisms and for different reasons. Particle burial usually results from animals feeding on nutritious materials, but because nutritious organic particles are very small and intermixed with the nutritionally poor minerals, the resulting mixing affects all the sedimentary particles to some extent. Defecation often occurs in a different place than feeding, causing the particles to be moved about. Particle bioturbation also results when animals move sediment to build burrows. Although particle bioturbation is usually studied

in the vertical direction—mixing particles from above with those from below—even greater mixing occurs in the horizontal direction, leading to processes such as changes in topography of the sediment–water interface. Fluid bioturbation usually results from irrigation of burrows. Because most sediments are devoid of oxygen, animals must draw oxygen-containing water from above the sediments for their respiration. This irrigation can cause other biological and chemical changes in the sediment, such as altered bacterial communities and oxidation of sulfide minerals.

Animals usually live close to the sediment–water interface to maximize their intake of food and water, and therefore bioturbation intensity is most intense close to this interface. Very little biological mixing is found below a depth of 10 to 20 centimeters (4 to 8 inches), except in certain areas. For example, deeply burrowing shrimp can reach up to 2 meters (6 feet) deep in the sediment.

Lawrence M. Mayer

FURTHER READING
Jumars, Peter A. *Concepts in Biological Oceanography*. New York: Oxford University Press, 1993.
Matisoff, G. "Effects of Bioturbation on Solute and Particle Transport in Sediments." In Herbert E. Allen, ed., *Metal Contaminated Aquatic Sediments*. Chelsea, Mich.: Ann Arbor Press, 1995.

RELATED ARTICLES
Deposit Feeder; Nutrient

Bivalvia

The Bivalvia is a large and significant class in the phylum Mollusca, comprising over 10,000 species, including clams, oysters, mussels, and scallops. A two-part shell that covers a soft body completely allows quick recognition of most species in this group. Bivalves are found in all world oceans, exploiting habitats from the high intertidal splash zone down to the deep-sea basins. For millennia, humans have exploited bivalves for food and for ornamentation. More recently, bivalves have been used as natural monitors of environmental health.

A hard, two-part, hinged calcareous shell easily separates most bivalves from their molluscan relatives, such as gastropods, chitons, and octopus. Inside the shell are paired gills (ctenidia) that are specialized for straining food from the water. The digestive and reproductive systems are located between the paired gills. In many species there is a muscular "foot" that is used for digging the shelled animal into sediments. Bivalves have no head, although some species do have eyes along the edge of their body (mantle).

Most bivalves have separate sexes (dioecious) and reproduce by broadcast spawning. Broadcast spawners discharge eggs and sperm into the water, with fertilization occurring in the open ocean. In most marine bivalve species, the fertilized egg develops into a planktonic trochophore and then a veliger larva before metamorphosing into the benthic adult. Several species of bivalves begin life as one sex and then change to the opposite sex (sequential hermaphrodites), and others are equipped with both male and female reproductive organs at the same time (simultaneous hermaphrodites).

Bivalves have successfully invaded almost all marine environments. Most species of bivalves live on or in offshore sediments of sand, silt, or mud. Mussels are a dominant component of many intertidal reefs, being well adapted to tolerate pounding waves and exposure to sun and wind. Oysters and their kin are capable of cementing their shells directly to rocks. Piddocks and other boring clams create burrows in soft rocks by using portions of their rasplike shell to drill a hole. A few species of bivalves live near hot, sulfurous hydrothermal vents or cold seeps. These deepwater dwellers have special bacteria (endosymbionts) in their gills that provide nutrition for the bivalve.

Three primary feeding modes have evolved in bivalves. Primitive groups feed on bottom deposits of organic material using specialized flaplike palps that are located next to the mouth. Suspension or filter feeding is used by most species. These bivalves have specialized gills (ctenidia) that not only allow the animal to derive oxygen from the water but also strain food particles. Filter feeders primarily strain microscopic plankton from the water. A few advanced bivalves in the group Septibranchia are carnivorous. Septibranchs lay buried in the sediments awaiting small crustaceans and worms that are quickly sucked directly into the stomach of these predators.

Hundreds of species prey on bivalves. Marine mammals such as walrus and sea otters include clams as a primary food item. Bottom fish continually search the ocean floor for tasty bivalve treats. Even invertebrates such as octopus and mantis shrimp count on a large supply of bivalves for food. Many species of bivalves have adapted to this intense predatory pressure by a variety of mechanisms, including burrowing deep into sediments or developing sharp spines on their shell.

Humans currently harvest nearly 10 million metric tons of bivalve mollusks each year, the equivalent weight of 2 million African elephants. Scallops, oysters, and mussels are particularly prized in the culinary world for their unique texture and flavor. In addition to harvesting bivalves in the wild, there is a large aquaculture industry for oysters and mussels. Pearl oysters are grown in many tropical oceans of the world, which yield an average of 7 million kilograms (15.4 million pounds) of pearls and mother-of-pearl shell products each year.

Several species of bivalves, in particular mussels and oysters, have been used for several decades as monitors of environmental health and water quality. As bivalves filter the water for food, they also filter a variety of toxins and heavy metals out of the water. Many of these toxins are stored in the tissues of the bivalve. These bivalves are frequently analyzed for heavy metals and carcinogens and indicate the overall water quality of the region in which they were collected.

Paul Valentich Scott

FURTHER READING

Coan, Eugene V., Paul Valentich Scott, and Frank R. Bernard. *Bivalve Seashells of Western North America.* Santa Barbara, Calif.: Santa Barbara Museum of Natural History, 2000.

Harbo, Rick M. *Shells and Shellfish of the Pacific Northwest: A Field Guide.* Madeira Park, Canada: Harbour, 1997.

Solem, G. Allan. *The Shell Makers: Introducing Mollusks.* New York: Wiley, 1974.

Yonge, C. M., and T. E. Thompson. *Living Marine Molluscs.* London: Collins, 1976.

RELATED ARTICLES
Benthos; Gastropoda; Mollusca

Black Sea

The Black Sea is enclosed in a deep oval basin in central Europe between 41 and 46°N latitude and 28 and 41°E longitude. Its dimensions, about 1180 kilometers (733 miles) by 260 kilometers (162 miles), give it an area of about 420,300 square kilometers (162,280 square miles). Its maximum depth is 2212 meters (7257 feet), and its volume is about 547,000 cubic kilometers (131,000 cubic miles).

The Black Sea is bordered by Turkey, Bulgaria, Romania, Ukraine, Russia, Moldova, and Georgia. It connects with the Aegean Sea (eastern Mediterranean) via the narrow seaway of the Bosporus, to the Sea of Marmara, and thence through the Dardenelles. To the east of the Crimean Peninsula it connects with the Sea of Azov. It receives the outflows of several major central European rivers: the Danube, Don, Dnepr, and Dnestr. Their freshwater outflows keep its salinity at about 22 practical salinity units (psu), about half that of normal ocean water, despite the inflows of high-salinity water (38 psu) from the

Mediterranean through the Bosporus. The river discharges also contain large quantities of dissolved organic matter, fertilizers, and pollutants from the heartland of central Europe. The deep waters of the Black Sea completely lack oxygen (anoxic) and contain large concentrations of dissolved hydrogen sulfide. So any iron object lowered below the thermocline at 155 meters (509 feet) becomes blackened with sulfide deposits, hence the sea's name. There are no tides, but strong winds can cause seiches (tidelike oscillations of the water) with amplitudes of nearly 30 centimeters (1 foot). There is a general anticlockwise circulation of currents in the sea.

Many species of fish migrate from the rivers to spawn in the Black Sea, including the sturgeon, but the numbers have been dwindling. Some reasons for this decrease include the building of major dams on rivers, an increase in pollutants, and recently, the introduction in ships' ballast waters of an exotic species of ctenophore, *Mnemiopsis*, which outcompetes the fish larvae for zooplankton.

Martin Angel

FURTHER READING

Besiktope, Sükrü T., Ümit Unluata, and Alexandru S. Bolega, eds. *Environmental Degradation of the Black Sea: Challenges and Remedies.* NATO Science Series, Vol. 56, *Environmental Security.* Dordrecht, the Netherlands, and Boston: Kluwer Academic, 1999.

GESAMP. "Opportunistic Settlers and the Problem of the Ctenophore *Mnemiopsis leidyi* Invasion in the Black Sea." *GESAMP Reports and Studies,* Vol. 58 (1997).

Murray, John, ed. "Black Sea Oceanography." *Deep-Sea Research,* Vol. 2A (Supplement) (1991), pp. S655–S1266.

RELATED ARTICLES
Anoxia; Anoxic Basin; Bosporus; Mediterranean Sea; Oxygen; Pollution,Ocean; Salinity; Seiche

Black Smoker, see Hydrothermal Vent

Blake Plateau

The Blake Plateau is an underwater platform of 130,000 square kilometers (50,000 square miles) that lies off the coast of the southeastern United States. The plateau is about 300 kilometers (185 miles) wide and lies between 74 and 81°W longitude and 28 and 34°N latitude. The plateau is between 700 and 1000 meters (2300 and 3300 feet) below sea level. It is bounded on the east by the steep Blake Escarpment, which drops quickly down to 5000 meters (16,400 feet) below sea level, and on the west by the Florida–Hatteras slope.

Oceanographers believe that the Blake Plateau was created some 170 million years ago, when what is now Africa began to separate from what is now North America. The separation stretched and thinned the continental crust where the Blake Plateau now lies, creating a wide, shallow seabed where coral flourished and built substantial reefs. About 65 million years ago, rising sea levels wiped out the reef-building coral and eventually triggered the Gulf Stream, a powerful current that flows over the Blake Plateau. The Gulf Stream has shifted course considerably over the years, leaving patterns of erosion on the plateau that scientists have studied closely.

Petroleum has been found and recovered beneath the Blake Plateau; in addition, it is covered with nodules of manganese. The coal-black nodules, which range from the size of golf balls to the size of potatoes, cover hundreds of square kilometers of the plateau. The Blake nodules are light compared to manganese nodules found elsewhere on the ocean floor, and because the Blake nodules rest on a comparatively high plateau, they are closer to the surface than other such nodules. In addition, the Blake nodules are completely unattached to the sea bottom, raising the prospect that they could be mined relatively easily.

Mary Sisson

FURTHER READING

Dillion, William P., and Peter Popenoe. "The Blake Plateau Basin and Carolina Trough." In R. E. Sheridan and J. A. Grow, eds., *The Atlantic Continental Margin, U.S.* Boulder, Colo.: Geological Society of America, 1988.

Emery, K. O., and Elazar Uchupi. *The Geology of the Atlantic Ocean.* New York: Springer-Verlag, 1984.

Sheridan, Robert E., and Paul Enos. "Stratigraphic Evolution of the Blake Plateau After a Decade of Scientific Drilling." In Manik Talwai, et al., eds., *Deep Drilling Results in the Atlantic Ocean: Continental Margins and Paleoenvironment.* Washington, D.C.: American Geophysical Union, 1979.

RELATED ARTICLES

Atlantic Ocean; Coral Reef; Deep-Sea Mining; Gulf Stream; Ocean Current; Ocean Plateau; Petroleum; Plate Tectonics

Blubber

Because marine mammals are homeothermic (i.e., they maintain their internal body temperature within certain levels often regardless of the external temperature), they usually must insulate themselves from colder oceanic water. Water is an excellent conductor of heat; therefore, ocean water would tend to cool a mammal rapidly if there were not some type of insulation. Although hair does provide a small amount of insulation, the thick layer of fat cells and fibrous tissue known as blubber generally minimizes heat loss in water. The thickness of the subcutaneous blubber layer can be less than 2 centimeters (.8 inch) in some seals and dolphins to 0.5 meter (20 inches) thick in Arctic whales, such as right whales. Blubber is also used by marine mammals as a means of storing energy. After many months of feeding, marine mammals can store substantial amounts of energy as fat, which they may use during periods of fasting. For instance, baleen whales that make long-distance migrations to their breeding areas may lose 20 percent of their body weight during the journey, much of the energy coming from the energy reserves in the blubber. Many pinnipeds also fast during the reproductive periods. The energy stored in their blubber allows male sea lions to remain on land for months defending their territories. Generally the thickness of the blubber does not change too much during fasting, but the amount of fat in the blubber declines during fasting. This characteristic allows the use of fat for energy but does not compromise the ability of the blubber to act as insulation. Blubber is certainly a benefit to marine mammals as insulation and energy storage, but it also fills in areas around the neck to provide a more streamlined marine mammal. The presence of blubber in marine mammals also has proved detrimental because whales and seals were hunted for the large amount of oil that could be rendered from their blubber.

Jim Harvey

FURTHER READING

Berta, A., and J. L. Sumich. *Marine Mammals: Evolutionary Biology.* San Diego: Academic Press, 1999.

Haley, Delphine, ed. *Marine Mammals of Eastern North Pacific and Arctic Waters,* 2nd rev. ed. Seattle: Pacific Search Press, 1986.

Leatherwood, Stephen, and Randall R. Reeves. *The Sierra Club Handbook of Whales and Dolphins.* San Francicso: Sierra Club Books, 1983.

Slijper, E. J. *Whales.* Translated by A. J. Pomerans. New York: Basic Books, 1962.

RELATED ARTICLES

Cetacea; Pinnipedia

Bosporus

A narrow strait connecting the Black Sea with the Sea of Marmara and ultimately the Mediterranean Sea, the Bosporus has long been recognized for its military and strategic importance. The Bosporus, located near Istanbul, Turkey, divides the continents of Europe and Asia while connecting the busy ports of the Black Sea with the world's oceans. The straight is only 30 kilometers (19 miles) long.

At its widest point, it is 3.7 kilometers (2.3 miles) wide, and at its narrowest—a spot pinched on both sides by centuries-old fortresses—it is only 750 meters (2460 feet) across. Located at 41°N latitude and 29°E longitude, the Bosporus varies from 37 to 124 meters (121 to 407 feet) deep at midstream. Water flows through the strait both ways; a higher current flows from the Black Sea to the Sea of Marmara, while a deeper current flows the opposite direction. Migratory fish use the strait to enter and exit the Black Sea, making the Bosporus a fertile fishing ground.

These days, the primary use of the Bosporus is for shipping. Some 45 million tonnes (50 million tons) of cargo pass through the straits every year. Oil shipping has become especially common through the Bosporus, thanks to a boom in oil production in the Caspian Sea region that is likely to increase. The large number of cargo ships going through the Bosporus, combined with the narrowness of the strait and its tricky currents, has resulted in many accidents and oil spills. The government of Turkey has attempted to restrict the number and types of ships that can pass through the Bosporus, but the government has been blocked by a 1936 international

Bosporus.

treaty requiring vessels to be allowed to pass freely through the strait in times of peace.

Mary Sisson

FURTHER READING

Freely, John. *The Bosphorus.* Mercan and Istanbul, Turkey: Redhouse Press, 1993.

Macfie, A. L. *The Straits Question: 1908–1936.* Thassaloniki, Greece: Institute for Balkan Studies, 1993.

Shotwell, James Thomson, and Francis Deák. *Turkey at the Straits: A Short History.* New York: Macmillan, 1940; reprint, Freeport, N.Y.: Books for Libraries Press, 1971.

RELATED ARTICLES

Black Sea; Caspian Sea; Fisheries; Mediterranean Sea; Petroleum

Bottom Current

Conditions at the bottom of the ocean are very different than conditions at the surface. For example, the surface of the ocean is nearly flat but the bottom of the ocean contains canyons, hills, and mountain ranges. Winds act on surface waters and cause surface currents but do not affect abyssal waters. The deep ocean circulation is important because it transports bottom waters away from their source region, replenishing bottom waters throughout the world's oceans. Bottom currents are also important in coastal areas, where they can play an important role in moving sediments and plankton.

Abyssal Circulation

The waters at the bottom of the ocean are heavier (colder) than those that lie above. They are moved along the bottom of the ocean by bottom currents. Abyssal currents are deep enough that they are not affected by the wind but are caused by differences of density between adjacent water parcels. This is similar to pouring syrup into a cup of water. The heavier syrup will flow to the bottom of the cup, pushing aside the water and displacing it upward from the bottom of the cup.

Bottom currents move bottom waters northward from their formation region around Antarctica (mostly in the Weddell Sea). These waters are cooled near the surface by the atmosphere and thence sink to the ocean bottom. They are called *Antarctic Bottom Waters.* The rate at which they are formed is 7×10^6 cubic meters (9×10^6 cubic yards) per second. They are transported eastward around Antarctica by the Circumpolar Current but slowly fill the bottom of the Atlantic, Indian, and Pacific Oceans.

Abyssal currents are usually very weak, less than 1 centimeter (less than 0.4 inch) per second, although they may be considerably stronger near ocean boundaries. In regions where the ocean bottom is flat, bottom currents are highly variable in direction. They are strongest along western boundaries (due to Earth's rotation), and when they flow over steep topography they are constrained by the topography to flow parallel to isobaths. Topography also plays an important role in determining the path followed by bottom waters.

In the Atlantic Ocean, bottom waters are carried north from the Circumpolar Current to about 40°N. The principal path of the current is along the western boundary of the South and North Atlantic Oceans. In the eastern South Atlantic, the bottom current fills the Cape Basin, flowing northward along the eastern boundary of the Mid-Atlantic Ridge, but is blocked at 35°S by Walvis Ridge. The eastern basins of the Atlantic Ocean are filled by bottom waters that move through the Mid-Atlantic Ridge at the equator in the Romanche Fracture Zone. Bottom currents then spread Antarctic Bottom Waters north and south along the eastern side of the Mid-Atlantic Ridge, filling the remaining basins in the eastern North Atlantic. North of 40°N, Atlantic bottom waters consist of North Atlantic Deep Waters, which originate as intermediate depth waters in the Norwegian Sea. The Norwegian Sea waters enter the North Atlantic over the Iceland–Faroe Ridge and through the Denmark Straits.

Bottom currents fill the Indian Ocean with Antarctic Bottom Water in a manner similar to the Atlantic. Although there are strong bottom currents in the Mozambique Basin, flow is blocked by the Mozambique Strait. So bottom currents along the eastern boundary of the Southwest Indian Ocean Ridge fill the Southwest Indian Basin and then flow through gaps in the ridge into the Madagascar Basin. They then continue north into the Somali and Arabian Basin to 15°N along the western boundary of the Indian Ocean. The eastern basins are filled by flow into the South Australian Basin via flow through the Australian Antarctic Discordance at 124°E. The bottom currents then flow north into the Perth, Wharton, and North Australia Basins as a western boundary current along the Ninetyeast Ridge. Bottom currents fill the Central Indian Ocean Basin through gaps in the Ninetyeast Ridge near 10 and 5°S.

The bottom waters of the Pacific Ocean are renewed more slowly than in the Atlantic and Indian Oceans. Waters that reach the northern hemisphere are carried by bottom currents to the east of New Zealand into the Southwest Pacific Basin and then through the Samoa Passage into the Melanesian and Northwest Pacific Basins. The Northeast Pacific Basin is then filled by very slow eastward flow. Two basins in the South Pacific—the Tasman Sea in the west and the Chile Basin in the east—are filled directly from the Circumpolar Current but are blocked to the north.

Coastal Regions

In coastal regions, bottom currents are important because they transport sediment and plankton and can cause erosion around the foundations of off-shore structures. In many cases, the direction of these motions can be quite different from that of the surface waters. The best example of this occurs in stratified estuaries where surface currents transport

fresh waters toward the sea and bottom currents transport seawater toward the head of the estuary.

Benthic Boundary Layers

A benthic boundary layer exists at the bottom of the sea within which the horizontal velocity decreases from a value representative of the bottom current, u, to zero at the bottom. This change in velocity with depth is called *velocity shear* and is caused by the stress, τ_b, due to the friction between the bottom current and the bottom. The bottom stress is usually modeled by a quadratic rule, for example $\tau_b = \rho B_D u^2$, where ρ is water density and B_D is the drag coefficient. The drag coefficient depends on the roughness of the boundary and has a typical magnitude of 10^{-3} to 10^{-2}. If the bottom stress becomes too large, a portion of the bottom sediments will resuspend and move with the fluid. This produces a distinctive wavelike pattern on the ocean floor. As the current speed (and bottom stress) increases, patterns of ripples and dunes are found.

In addition to the benthic boundary layer described above, a benthic Ekman layer is set up if the water currents are steady and there is sufficient depth of water. This layer can be thought of as an upside-down version of the Ekman layer created at the surface of the ocean by wind stress. In the northern hemisphere, the bethnic Ekman layer has currents that decrease and rotate to the left as the bottom is approached.

Turbidity Currents

Turbidity currents are caused when sediments are stirred into the water. The sediment will cause the water to become heavier and hence flow down-slope. Coarse sediments such as sand and gravel can also be moved by these flows. The first evidence of these currents came from geological observations of sand and gravel layers in the deep ocean, far from where wave action might have carried them. Observations of powerful bottom currents also occurred south of the Grand Banks after an earthquake in 1929; submarine cables located downslope from the earthquake epicenter broke sequentially with increasing depth. More recently, turbidity currents have been observed in submarine canyons. Turbidity currents not only transport large volumes of sediment across the continental shelf and slope, but over millennia can also create features in the ocean bottom through erosion.

Curtis A. Collins

FURTHER READING

Knauss, John A. *Introduction to Physical Oceanography.* Englewood Cliffs, N.J.: Prentice Hall, 1978; 2nd ed. rev., Upper Saddle River, N.J.: Prentice Hall, 2000.

Neumann, Gerhard. *Ocean Currents.* Amsterdam and New York: Elsevier, 1968.

Warren, Bruce. "Deep Circulation of the World Ocean." In *Evolution of Physical Oceanography.* Cambridge, Mass.: MIT Press, 1981; pp. 6-41.

RELATED ARTICLES

Antarctic Circumpolar Current; Benthic Boundary Layer; Bottom Water Formation; Ekman Layer; Mid-Atlantic Ridge; Ocean Current; Turbidity Current

Bottom Water Formation

The densest waters of the world's oceans, which occupy the greatest depths, are known as bottom waters. Bottom waters are formed primarily in the high latitudes, where the combination of low temperatures, evaporation, and ice formation produces cold salty water that is denser than the surrounding water. Bottom water formation is an integral part of the cycle of sinking and rising water masses known as *thermohaline circulation.* This circulation is important for transporting heat from one region to another, especially from low to high latitudes, and thus has a major impact on climate. In addition to its importance for climate, the sinking of newly formed bottom water allows organisms to colonize the deep ocean because it carries dissolved oxygen that was absorbed at the

sea surface. Without this major source of oxygen, many parts of the deep ocean would become anoxic. In today's ocean, bottom waters are formed only at a few locations: in isolated locations around Antarctica and in the North Atlantic.

With an average temperature of −0.4°C (31.3°F) and an average salinity of 34.6 practical salinity units (34.6 pounds of salt in every 1000 pounds of water), bottom water around Antarctica is the densest of the large water masses in today's ocean. It is formed primarily in the Weddell Sea, a sheltered basin on the coast of Antarctica. The large peninsula on the western perimeter of the basin forms a barrier between the Weddell Sea and the Antarctic Circumpolar Current, the current that circulates around Antarctica and distributes water to all the major ocean basins. The partially secluded location of the bay, in addition to the exceptionally low atmospheric temperatures at the Weddell Sea, allow very cold salty water to accumulate in the basin. Some Antarctic Bottom Water also forms in the Ross Sea, a similar embayment, located in the Pacific sector of the Antarctic coastline.

To sink to the bottom of the sea, a water mass must first increase its density by lowering its temperature and increasing its salinity. Due to the frigid winter temperatures around Antarctica, incoming water is quickly chilled to near-freezing temperatures, especially near the surface, where seawater is in contact with atmospheric temperatures that range from -20 to -30°C (-4 to -22°F) in winter. Cooling alone, however, would not increase the density sufficiently. The most important step in achieving the necessary density appears to be the increase in salinity that is caused by sea ice formation. Once surface water in the bay has reached the freezing point of seawater [-1.9°C (28.6°F)], it begins to form ice on the sea surface. During the freezing process, most of the sea salt is released back into the water because sea ice incorporates only a small portion of the salt. The formation of sea ice thus leads to the concentration of salt in the unfrozen water, increasing its salinity and therefore its density. The rate of sea ice formation is especially high near the coastline because cold winds from the continent blow the ice out to sea, making room for more sea ice.

Some researchers believe that large ice shelves in the Weddell and Ross Seas play an additional role in the formation of Antarctic Bottom Water. These thick sheets of ice are the floating extensions of glaciers that drain into the sea from Antarctica. Almost half of the water on the continental shelf of Antarctica is underneath ice shelves, some of which are 2 kilometers (1.2 miles) thick. The water pressure at the base of the ice shelves is considerably higher than at the surface. As a result, the freezing point of the water is lowered from −1.9°C (28.6°F) to as low as −3.4°C (25.9°F), allowing water in contact with the ice sheets to cool to temperatures lower than normally achievable at the surface. This extra cooling at depth lowers the water temperature in parts of the Weddell Sea to below −3°C (26.6°F), a few degrees lower than that of any other water mass.

The salinity and temperature changes of the coastal water eventually make the water so dense that it flows down the continental shelf and onward to the open ocean around Antarctica. On the way, it mixes partly with overlying water so that the water that actually fills the deepest portions of the South Pacific, Atlantic, and Indian Oceans is a mixture of the Antarctic shelf water with other water masses. It is this mixture that is generally known as Antarctic Bottom Water.

Bottom water formation in the northern hemisphere takes place in the Greenland and Norwegian Seas, where chilly winter temperatures cool the warm surface water that flows northward from the tropics. Due to a high degree of evaporation, Atlantic surface waters are generally saltier than surface waters in the other major oceans, so that water reaching the Greenland and Norwegian Seas is also unusually salty. Cooling of the saline surface water produces very dense water that sinks to the seafloor, where it is contained by several large underwater ridges that stretch out between Greenland and the British Isles. This cold dense water eventually overflows across several relatively low sills and becomes the densest component of the deep waters formed in the North Atlantic. Bottom water formed in the Greenland and Norwegian Seas is known by many names, such as North Atlantic Bottom Water, Nordic Sea Overflow Water, and Greenland–Iceland–Norwegian Sea overflow water.

Sonya Wainwright

FURTHER READING
Pinet, Paul R. *Invitation to Oceanography.* Minneapolis/St. Paul, Minn.: West Publishing, 1996; 2nd ed., Sudbury, Mass.: Jones and Bartlett, 1998.
Talley, Lynne. "North Atlantic Circulation and Variability, Reviewed for the CNLS Conference." *Physica D*, Vol. 98 (1996), pp. 625–646.
Thurman, Harold. *Introductory Oceanography,* 5th ed. Columbus, Ohio: Merrill Publishing, 1988; 9th ed., Upper Saddle River, N.J.: Prentice Hall, 2001.

RELATED ARTICLES
Antarctic Circumpolar Current; Norwegian Sea; Ocean Basin; Ross Sea; Salinity; Thermohaline Circulation; Water Mass; Weddell Sea

Boundary Current

A boundary current is an ocean current that flows in an approximately northerly or southerly direction (poleward or equatorward) close to the eastern or western margin of the ocean. They form part of the current systems called *gyres*, which transport warm water away from the equator and cold water away from polar regions in each of the oceans.

On either side of the equator the trade winds, blowing from the northeast in the northern hemisphere and southeast in the southern hemisphere, drive surface ocean currents from east to west. These are the Equatorial Currents. As they approach the continents bordering the oceans, they are deflected away from the equator. The track of the current that crosses the North Atlantic curves to the right as it enters the Caribbean. The current that crosses the North Pacific turns north as it approaches the Philippines. There is a similar pattern in the southern hemisphere, where the Equatorial Currents turn to the left and head south as they approach the continents. The currents continue to flow away from the equator (poleward) on paths that are parallel to the continental coasts. They are then called *boundary currents.*

As they move farther from the equator, the currents enter a different system of prevailing winds. These are from the west, and they drive the currents across the oceans. On the opposite side of the ocean, the currents are deflected once again by a continent. This time they turn toward the equator and continue by flowing back toward the equator (equatorward) parallel to the coast. They have then become boundary currents again. Thus there are two types of boundary currents. Those that flow poleward occur on the western margins of the oceans, so are called *western boundary currents.* Those on the eastern margins of the oceans, called *eastern boundary currents,* flow equatorward.

The system of western boundary currents in the North Atlantic begins with the Antilles Current, flowing past the Great Antilles in the Caribbean, continues as the Florida Current, and then becomes the Gulf Stream, which forms in the Gulf of Mexico. In the South Atlantic, the Brazil Current is the boundary current that flows along the South American coast. The western boundary current in the North Pacific is the Kuroshio, which flows past the coast of Kyūshū, the most southerly of the main islands of Japan. The East Australia Current is the western boundary current in the South Pacific, and the Agulhas Current, flowing past the coast of Africa and between Africa and Madagascar, is the western boundary current in the Indian Ocean. The corresponding eastern

boundary currents are the Canaries Current in the North Atlantic, the Benguela Current in the South Atlantic, the California Current in the North Pacific, the Peru Current in the South Pacific, and the West Australia Current in the Indian Ocean. Other, smaller currents feed into the main boundary currents. These include, for example, the Alaska (or Aleutian) Current and Oyashio in the North Pacific and the Labrador Current in the North Atlantic.

Because they carry water away from the equator, western boundary currents are warm. They tend to be deep, narrow, and fast-moving. This narrowing and acceleration of currents on the western sides of oceans is called *western intensification.* It is caused by the fact that the magnitude of the Coriolis effect increases with latitude (it is zero at the equator and reaches a maximum at the poles). The deflection due to the Coriolis effect increases with distance from the equator in the poleward flow and decreases with distance from the pole in equatorward flow. It is this change, combined with the prevailing winds, that makes western boundary currents narrower, deeper, and faster than eastern boundary currents. The Gulf Stream transports about 55×10^6 cubic meters (1940×10^6 cubic feet) per second; the Kuroshio, 65×10^6 cubic meters (2300 million cubic feet) per second; and the Brazil, 10×10^6 cubic meters (350 cubic feet) per second.

Eastern boundary currents carry cold water. They tend to be shallow, broad, and slow-moving. The Canaries Current, corresponding to the Gulf Stream, carries 16×10^6 cubic meters (565×10^6 cubic feet) per second.

Michael Allaby

FURTHER READING

Emiliani, Cesare. *Planet Earth: Cosmology, Geology, and the Evolution of Life and Environment.* Cambridge and New York: Cambridge University Press, 1992.

Knauss, John A. *Introduction to Physical Oceanography.* Englewood Cliffs, N.J.: Prentice Hall, 1978; 2nd ed. rev., Upper Saddle River, N.J.: Prentice Hall, 2000.

Bowers Ridge

Bowers Ridge is a large ocean plateau in the Bering Sea that extends northward from, and nearly perpendicular to, its structural connection with the Aleutian Ridge. It curves sharply westward in an arcuate (curved) shape and subsequently forms a series of subsurface ridges that merge with Shirshov Ridge, an ocean plateau that extends south from Cape Olyutorsky in Russia. Bowers Ridge is located between 174°E and 178°W longitude and 52 and 55°N latitude. The shallowest part of Bowers Ridge is about 200 meters (650 feet) deep and the ridge rises more than 3.5 kilometers (2.2 miles) above the surrounding Bering Sea floor. The crust is between 21 and 29 kilometers (13 and 18 miles) thick, similar in thickness to the crust beneath the Aleutian Islands.

Bowers Basin bounds Bowers Ridge on the south and the Aleutian Basin bounds it on the north. Bowers Basin may have formed during a short phase of back-arc spreading in the Early Tertiary (about 40 million years ago). The Aleutian Basin is probably floored by an Early Cretaceous (about 130 to 110 million years old) fragment of the Kula Plate that was trapped behind the Aleutian island arc when it began forming about 55 million years ago.

A trench filled with as much as 10 kilometers (6.2 miles) of sediment borders the north edge of Bowers Ridge. Apparently, south-directed subduction of Aleutian Basin crust occurred beneath Bowers Ridge during its formation. Geomorphology, magnetic signature, dredged rocks, and structural setting suggest that Bowers Ridge is a subsided island arc.

Tracy L. Vallier

FURTHER READING

Cooper, Alan K., Michael S. Marlow, and David W. Scholl. "Geologic Framework of the Bering Sea Crust." In David W. Scholl, Arthur Grantz, and John G. Vedder, eds., *Geology and Resource Potential of the Continental Margin of Western North America and Adjacent Ocean Basin: Beaufort Sea to Baja California.* Houston, Texas: Circum-Pacific Council for Energy and Mineral Resources; Tulsa, Okla.: AAPG Bookstore, 1987.

Marlow, Michael S., and Alan K. Cooper. "Wandering Terranes in Southern Alaska: The Aleutian Microplate and Implications for the Bering Sea." *Journal of Geophysical Research*, Vol. 88 (1983) pp. 3439–3446.

Scholl, David W., Tracy L. Vallier, and Andrew J. Stevenson. "Geologic Evolution and Petroleum Geology of the Aleutian Ridge." In David W. Scholl, Arthur Grantz, and John G. Vedder, eds., *Geology and Resource Potential of the Continental Margin of Western North America and Adjacent Ocean Basins: Beaufort Sea to Baja California.* Houston, Texas: Circum-Pacific Council for Energy and Mineral Resources; Tulsa, Okla.: AAPG Bookstore, 1987.

Box Corer

Used primarily on scientific oceanographic cruises, box corers are instruments designed to collect quantitative sediment samples from the seafloor. Although there are many sizes and shapes, most box corers consist of a steel box surrounded by a larger steel frame. The box, which is typically about 50 by 50 by 50 centimeters (20 by 20 by 20 inches), is lowered onto the ocean floor by a cable, where, under the force of gravity, it sinks into the sediments. Inside the box are several cylindrical tubes, open at the bottom, which collect the sediments to be studied. The penetration depth is usually less than 50 centimeters (20 inches) but can be increased to about 100 centimeters (40 inches) when lead weights are attached to the top of the box. The large steel frame ensures that the box is in the vertical position when it penetrates the sediments. Once the box has come to a standstill, a trigger mechanism releases trapdoors, which close and seal all the sediments inside the box. After the box has been hoisted up to the ship, the sample cylinders are removed and stored for future laboratory analysis.

The box corer is the preferred sampling tool when the material to be collected consists of unconsolidated sediment and the recovery of undisturbed sediment samples is a priority. Unlike other coring tools such as high-powered drills, box corers are designed to minimize agitation of the sediment, allowing the preservation of fine depositional layers. Box corers are used exclusively for soft sediments and can recover only the top 1 meter (3 feet) of the sediment layer.

Sonya Wainwright

FURTHER READING

Nybakken, James W. *Marine Biology: An Ecological Approach,* 5th ed. San Francisco: Benjamin Cummings, 2001.

RELATED ARTICLES

Deep-Sea Exploration; Deep-Sea Sediment; Grab Sampler

Brachiopoda

The brachiopods, or lamp shells, belong to the phylum Brachiopoda. The name is derived from the Greek *brachium,* "arm," and *poda,* "feet." Brachiopods have existed for at least 600 million years; the greatest number of brachiopods lived during the Paleozoic Era. From fossil records, it is estimated that more than 12,000 species once existed. Today, only about 335 species exist. Brachiopods are commonly found on the continental shelf but are present at almost all ocean depths and average in size from 4 to 6 centimeters (approximately 1.6 to 2.4 inches) across the largest area of the shell.

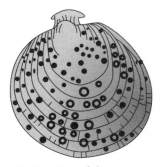

Gwynia capsula *(Brachiopoda).*

Brachiopods are similar to clams, in that both animals have bodies enclosed by two shells (valves). Shells are positioned dorsally and ventrally (top and bottom) in brachiopods and right to left in clams. Brachiopods are divided into two classes: Articulata is a class comprised of species possessing shells that hinge by means of a tooth-and-socket joint; Inarticulata is a class that contains species with unhinged shells held together by muscle.

Brachiopods have separate sexes and their fertilization occurs externally. They begin life as free-swimming larvae until the production of the shell causes the animals to become too heavy to float. The animals then sink and attach to the substrate, where they continue life as sedentary animals. Brachiopods are stationary, bottom-dwelling marine animals that attach to a surface either by a pedicle, a stalklike appendage, or by cementing the ventral valve to the substrate. Only one genus, *Lingula,* anchors into the sand instead of attaching to the substrate.

Brachiopods feed using the lophophore, a structure resembling an arm covered by tentacles, and the structure from which the group name, *lophophorates,* is derived. Water containing small food particles is moved through the mantle cavity between the shell valves by beating of cilia located on the lophophore. Food particles are trapped on the lophophore tentacles and directed to a food groove at the base of the lophophore, in which they move by ciliary action to the centrally located mouth.

Erin O'Donnell

FURTHER READING

Barnes, Robert. *Invertebrate Zoology.* Philadelphia: Saunders, 1963; 6th ed., by Edward Ruppert, Fort Worth, Texas: Saunders, 1994.

Brusca, Richard C., and Gary J. Brusca. *Invertebrates.* Sunderland, Mass.: Sinauer, 1990.

Buchsbaum, Ralph. *Animals Without Backbones.* Chicago: University of Chicago Press, 1938; 3rd ed., 1987.

Fretter, V., and A. Graham. *A Functional Anatomy of Invertebrates.* New York: Academic Press, 1976.

RELATED ARTICLES

Benthos

Branchiopoda

Some of the most primitive forms of crustaceans are found in the class Branchiopoda. The class contains about 900 living species, including brine shrimp, fairy shrimp, and water fleas, and is divided into four to eight orders. In addition, Branchiopoda has an extensive fossil record, dating back at least 400 million years.

Because Branchiopoda encompasses such a wide variety of species, generalizations about the class are difficult to make. The typical branchiopod has compound eyes, a segmented body, and four or more paddlelike trunk limbs. Most species of branchiopods use their trunk limbs to swim and to feed, but some use specialized antennae for swimming. Branchiopods range in size from .25 millimeters to 10 centimeters (.01 to 4.0 inches).

Most branchiopods are found in fresh water, but brine shrimp thrive in salty inland water and are commonly used as food for aquarium fishes. Some branchiopods are predators, but most live by gathering food particles, algae, and smaller organisms from the water using the fine hair on their limbs as filters. Branchiopods are an important food source for fish.

Some species of branchiopods live in shallow puddles and ponds that can dry up during the summer or freeze during the winter. These species produce extremely hardy eggs that can survive drought or cold and will hatch only when conditions are favorable. Most branchiopods

Magnified ventral view of a swimming male brine shrimp, member of the Branchiopoda class. Actual size ranges to 15 mm (0.6 in). (© Frank Lane Picture Agency/Corbis)

have separate sexes, but some species are hermaphroditic, with the same individual having both male and female reproductive organs. In some species the eggs do not have to be fertilized in order to mature.

Mary Sisson

FURTHER READING

Brusca, Richard C., and Gary J. Brusca. *Invertebrates.* Sunderland, Mass.: Sinauer, 1990.

Covich, Alan P., and James H. Thorp, eds. *Ecology and Classification of North American Freshwater Invertebrates.* San Diego, Calif.: Academic Press, 1991.

Maitland, Peter. *Biology of Fresh Water.* New York: Wiley, 1978; 2nd ed., New York: Chapman and Hall, 1990.

Pennak, Robert. *Fresh-Water Invertebrates of the United States.* New York: Ronald Press, 1953; 3rd ed., subtitled *Protozoa to Mollusca,* New York: Wiley, 1990.

RELATED ARTICLES
Crustacea

Brazil Current

The Brazil Current is a surface ocean current that flows southward in the South Atlantic, parallel to the coast of South America. The current begins at about latitude 5°S, level with Cape de Saõ Roque, where it breaks away from the South Equatorial Current. It then flows southward to between latitude 30 and 40°S, approximately at the same latitude as Montevideo and Buenos Aires, where it meets the Falkland Current flowing northward and is deflected. The Brazil Current then flows in an easterly direction and joins the Antarctic Circumpolar Current. The Brazil Current forms the western side of the South Atlantic Gyre and is therefore a western boundary current.

Although the Brazil Current flows approximately parallel to the coast, there are large meanders and eddies, especially between 22 and 30°S latitude, and in the latitude of Cape Frio (23°S) it flows from east to west rather than from north to south. These changes in the direction of the Brazil Current are believed to be due to interactions with the Antarctic Intermediate Water beneath the surface current.

The current is shallow. Nowhere is it more than 100 to 200 meters (330 to 660 feet) deep. It is also slow, moving at a speed of 2 to 4 kilometers per hour (1.2 to 2.5 miles per hour) and transporting about 10 million cubic meters (353 million cubic feet) of water per second. It carries warm, saline water away from the equator. The temperature of water carried by the current is between 19 and 27°C (66 to 81°F) and its salinity is 36 to 37 practical salinity units (psu), compared with the average salinity of seawater, which is 35 psu.

The waters of the Brazil Current are exploited commercially. Crustaceans, snapper, tuna, and shark are caught in the northern section. The phytoplankton is more productive in the southern section, supporting fisheries for groupers, croaker (fish of the family Sciaenidae), and bonito.

Michael Allaby

FURTHER READING

King, Cuchlaine A. M. I*ntroduction to Physical and Biological Oceanography.* London: Edward Arnold; New York: Crane, Russak, 1975.

Njoku, E. G., and O. B. Brown. "Sea Surface Temperature." In R. J. Gurney, J. L. Foster, and C. L. Parkinson, eds., *Atlas of Satellite Observations Related to Global Change.* Cambridge: Cambridge University Press, 1993; pp. 242–243.

RELATED ARTICLES
Antarctic Circumpolar Current; Equatorial Currents, North and South; Salinity

Brittlestar

Brittlestars belong to the phylum Echinodermata, which means "spiny skinned," and the class Ophiuroidea, which means "snakelike." The approximately 2000 species are closely related to sea stars and exist in all oceans and all depths, from the intertidal zone to the abyss. Existing mostly in tropical areas, their bodies are up to 2.54 centimeters (1 inch) in diameter and about 20 centimeters (8 inches) in length. Brittlestars are radially symmetrical, so they can be divided in half in more than one way to produce a mirror image. (Humans are bilaterally symmetrical and can be divided in only one way to produce a mirror image.) Brittlestars are composed of a flattened central disk and five arms set off distinctly from the disk. The arms are used for feeding, digging, and as sensory organs. Brittlestars have tube feet, like their relatives the sea stars, but do not have suckers. Like all echinoderms, they possess a water vascular system, which is an internal hydraulic system consisting of internal water-filled canals and external tube feet. They occur in a variety of colors.

The name *brittlestar* refers to the ability of these organisms to *autonomize*, or break off, their arms, which is a useful skill when trying to escape predators. If they are seized, they can release the arm and escape. The animals then regenerate the missing arm. Brittlestars' endoskeletons, or internal skeletons, are made of calcium carbonate. Most brittlestars are benthic dwellers and feed in a variety of ways. Some filter feed by moving their arms in the water, collecting plankton on their tube feet and mucus strands underneath their arms. The mucus and plankton "balls" are then moved toward the centrally located mouth and jaws by the tube feet. Predatory brittlestars use their arms to envelop prey and pull them into the mouth. Others feed by scavenging or deposit feeding. They have a simple gut, consisting of a mouth leading into a large stomach. Food and waste pass through the mouth, as there is no anal opening. Ten openings, called *bursal slits*, lie at the bases of the arms in the disk and lead into bursal sacs that allow exchange of gases between body fluids and water. Movement is achieved by using one arm in front as a guide, two arms at the side to "row," and two arms trailing behind the animal.

Some species reproduce asexually by dividing in half; others have separate sexes. In sexual reproduction the gonads are attached to the bursal walls and gametes are released to the outside via the bursal slits. Some species exhibit sexual dimorphism, the male being much smaller than the female. In these species, the male is actually carried around by the female, a strategy that probably increases reproductive success, as the male and female do not have to expend energy searching for a suitable mate. Some species are hermaphroditic, having both male and female organs. *Ophiothrix lineata* has a commensal relationship with the large sponge *Callyspongia vaginalis*, the brittlestar keeping the sponge clean by eating particles on it, and the sponge offering food and protection to the brittlestar.

Erin O'Donnell

FURTHER READING
Brusca, Richard C., and Gary J. Brusca. *Invertebrates.* Sunderland, Mass.: Sinauer, 1990.
Buchsbaum, Ralph. *Animals Without Backbones.* Chicago: University of Chicago Press, 1938; 3rd ed., with Mildred Buchsbaum, John Pearse, and Vicki Pearse, 1987.
Hyman, L. H. *The Invertebrates: Echinodermata*, Vol. 4. New York and London: McGraw-Hill, 1955.

RELATED ARTICLES
Echinodermata; Ophiuroidea

Broken Ridge, see Kerguelen Plateau and Broken Ridge

Bromine

Bromine is an element of relatively high concentration in seawater, averaging 65 parts per million (milligrams per kilogram) by weight.

Because this element is much more abundant in the oceans than on land, it was first discovered early in the nineteenth century from evaporated seawater. The high concentration of bromine enables profitable removal of the element at an industrial scale. In seawater bromine is found primarily in the chemical form of bromide ion (Br^-). In this form it shows little chemical reactivity, which allows it to accumulate to high concentrations. The bromide ion is colorless and odorless, in contrast to the elemental form of bromine (Br_2), whose smell provided its name (which means "stench" in Greek).

Many marine organisms have evolved abilities to use bromine in biochemical compounds, for various purposes. For example, some plants, such as red macroalgae, and invertebrate animals, such as worms in sediments, create toxic organic molecules that contain bromine atoms. These compounds may be used to control bacteria or discourage predators and may become valuable natural products for medical purposes. Another compound containing bromine, methyl bromide, is both produced by marine plants and consumed by marine bacteria; researchers actively study it because in the atmosphere it is capable of destroying ozone. Toxic bromine-containing compounds can be created if seawater is treated by chlorination. Although the atmosphere is important in short-term bromine cycling, over geological time scales most bromine is lost from the ocean via evaporative salt formation or burial of bromine-containing organic matter.

Lawrence M. Mayer

Further Reading

Goldschmidt, Victor. *Geochemistry*. Oxford: Clarendon Press, 1958.
Horne, Ralph. *Marine Chemistry*. New York: Wiley-Interscience, 1969.

Related Articles

Seawater, Composition of

Brown Algae, see Ochrophyta

Bryozoa

Bryozoans are a phylum of colonial animals that are found in all ocean habitats, from the intertidal zone to abyssal depths. Although a few species occur in brackish or fresh water, there are about 6000 living marine species, with many more known as fossils, dating back to the Paleozoic Era (600 million to 200 million years ago).

Individual members of a bryozoan colony are usually less than 1 millimeter (0.04 inch) in length, although they can collectively form patches up to 1 meter (39 inches) in size. Members of the colony, known as *zooids*, are designed for specific functions, including feeding, reproduction, and defense. A feeding zooid extends a crown of ciliated tentacles that direct food into its mouth by generating water currents. Bryozoa reproduce in a variety of ways, with most being hermaphroditic (with both sexes in the same colony). Colonies also grow asexually by budding from a single, sexually produced larva. Bryozoa larvae can be planktonic and in some cases will swim and feed for a substantial time

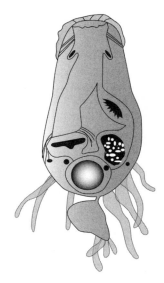

Monobryozoon ambulans *(Bryozoa)*.

before settlement. Other larval types do not feed and swim only long enough to find a suitable surface for growth. Bryozoans can either grow as crusts on rock surfaces, shells, and algae, or occur as treelike or foliate forms rising from an attached point. Colonies can be mistaken for sponges, corals, tunicates, and even algae. After barnacles, bryozoans are the most common fouling organism, found on ship hulls and water intakes. Because of the small size of the individual zooids, one must study Bryozoa with a dissecting microscope to fully appreciate their great diversity in shape and form. Recent studies have isolated a number of bioactive compounds from bryozoan tissues, some of which are of great medical interest. Based on their anatomy, the Bryozoa are related to two other small phyla, the Brachiopoda and Phoronida.

Henry W. Chaney

FURTHER READING

McKinney, Frank K., and Jeremy B. C. Jackson. *Bryozoan Evolution.* Boston: Unwin and Hyman, 1989; University of Chicago Press ed., Chicago: University of Chicago Press, 1991.

Ryland, John S. *Bryozoans.* London: Hutchinson, 1970.

Soule, John S., Dorothy F. Soule, and Donald P. Abbott. "Bryozoa and Entoprocta: The Moss Animals." In Robert H. Morris, Donald P. Abbott, and Eugene C. Haderlie, eds., *Intertidal Invertebrates of California.* Stanford, Calif.: Stanford University Press, 1980.

RELATED ARTICLES
Brachiopoda; Phoronida

Buoyancy

Buoyancy is the upward force experienced by any body or parcel of water that is less dense (lighter) than its ambient surroundings. Neutral buoyancy occurs when the two densities are the same. The density of seawater is determined by its temperature, salinity, and the hydrostatic pressure and is also increased by any material suspended in it. Seawater becomes buoyant when it is warmed or mixed with fresh water (as a result of rainfall, ice melting, or river outflow). Water is slightly compressible, so deep down in a body of water the hydrostatic pressure produced by the water's weight compresses it and increases its density. If water rises, it expands and cools; therefore, subtle changes in the density of seawater when it sinks or upwells become significant when considering how the global (thermohaline) circulation of oceans redistributes thermal energy and chemical properties.

Most body tissues, especially skeletal structures containing calcium carbonate, are heavier than seawater. If pelagic organisms can reduce their density so that their buoyancy is neutral, they save energy because they no longer have to expend it to maintain their depth. It also improves their maneuverability. Animals achieve neutral buoyancy in various ways. The most efficient is to have a gas-filled organ, but this becomes less efficient and more demanding energetically as depth increases. Other methods are either to increase the lipid content of their body or to replace sodium ions in their blood with lighter ammonium ions, or sulfate ions with chloride ions.

Martin Angel

FURTHER READING

Denton, Eric J., and Norman B. Marshall. "The Buoyancy of Bathypelagic Fishes Without a Gas-Filled Swimbladder." *Journal of the Marine Biological Association of the United Kingdom,* Vol. 37 (1958), pp. 753–767.

Marshall, Norman B. *Developments in Deep-Sea Biology.* Poole, England: Blandford Press, 1979.

Nybakken, James W. *Marine Biology: An Ecological Approach,* 5th ed. San Francisco: Benjamin Cummings, 2001.

Sanders, N. K., and J. J. Childress. "Ion Replacement as a Buoyancy Mechanism in a Pelagic Deep-Sea Crustacean." *Journal of Experimental Biology,* Vol. 138 (1988), pp. 333–348.

Thurman, Harold V. *Essentials of Oceanography.* Columbus, Ohio: Charles E. Merrill, 1983; 6th ed.,

with Alan P. Trujillo, Upper Saddle River, N.J.:
Prentice Hall, 1999.

RELATED ARTICLES
Salinity; Thermocline; Thermohaline Circulation;
Upwelling

Bycatch

Bycatch is the unintentional capture and death of small fish, marine mammals, and seabirds as a result of fishing practices. Along with deliberate overfishing, bycatch is one of the biggest threats to ocean life today.

Globally, the bycatch problem is enormous. Most fishing practices are designed to catch one or two salable and profitable species. Any unwanted catch is simply thrown back overboard, alive or dead. On average, this amounts to 25 percent of the catch, or around 24.5 million tonnes (27 million tons) of material every year, but in some fisheries the bycatch outweighs the salable harvest manyfold.

Bycatch can include dolphins and other mammals caught in nets and killed when they cannot reach the surface to breathe, fish that are cut by sharp nets, and seabirds that are caught when they try to take the bait from hooks in longline fisheries. As well as killing these animals, bycatch disrupts the food chain by removing food sources essential to other sea creatures. Bycatch also includes the small and unprofitable juveniles of various commercially fished species, which therefore cannot live to grow and reproduce themselves, further threatening the stocks of some species.

There are a variety of solutions to the problems of bycatch, but the additional expense involved can make alternative fishing methods unattractive unless legislation enforces them. For example, traps are more efficient than nets for catching shrimp and allow unwanted animals to be released alive. Similarly, tuna can be caught with traditional fishing lines and rods, and sonar buoys can be attached to purse seine nets to warn away dolphins.

Ultimately, bycatch will be reduced only by economic pressure—dolphin-friendly tuna and other products caught by safe fishing methods are now widely available, but slightly more expensive. Consumer pressure is already leading to a decrease in bycatch, and hopefully, this trend will continue in the future.

Giles Sparrow

FURTHER READING
Solving Bycatch: Considerations for Today and Tomorrow.
Fairbanks, Alaska: University of Alaska Sea Grant
College Program, 1996.
Symposium on the Consequences and Management of
Fisheries Bycatch. *Fisheries Bycatch: Consequences and
Management.* Fairbanks: University of Alaska Sea
Grant College Program, 1997.

RELATED ARTICLES
Driftnet; Fisheries; Food Chain; Purse Seine

C

Calcium

Calcium is an important alkaline earth element found in the ocean. It is used biologically and can be found in deep-sea sediments. Moreover, reactions involving calcium help transport carbon dioxide to deep waters and change the alkalinity of seawater. Calcium is also found in minerals that make up oceanic crust.

Calcium is the fifth most abundant element in seawater, present at 412 parts calcium per million parts seawater. The total amount of dissolved calcium in all the world's oceans is approximately 4.9×10^{14} tonnes (5.45×10^{14} tons). It is one of the six conservative salts that make up 99 percent of seawater salinity. (The other salts are, in order of decreasing concentration, chlorine, sodium, magnesium, sulfur, and potassium.) Calcium is always found in nearly the same concentration ratio with respect to these salts by the principle of constant proportions.

Rivers transport calcium from the terrestrial biosphere to the oceanic hydrosphere through erosional processes. An important reaction in the weathering of sedimentary rock is

$$CaCO_{3\,(\text{solid, in sedimentary rock})} + CO_{2\,(\text{rainwater})} + H_2O_{(\text{rainwater})} \leftrightarrow Ca^{2+}_{(\text{aqueous})} + 2HCO_3^{-}_{(\text{aqueous})}$$

Dissolved calcium in the ocean exists as Ca^{2+} ion (from the reaction above) and is incorporated by many marine plants and animals that make hard skeletons of calcium carbonate ($CaCO_3$).

The biological utilization of calcium is a major component in its global cycle. Calcium is present in the marine environment at such high concentrations that the amount used by organisms in relation to the total abundance is very small. Dissolved calcium is sometimes referred to as a *biointermediate constituent* of seawater because in areas of very high productivity it shows some depletion; however, organisms never exhaust the supply of calcium. Some of the calcium carbonate hard parts formed by marine organisms such as foraminifera redissolve when the organisms die and sink from the surface to deep waters. This releases calcium and carbonate ions back into the water via the following reaction

$$CaCO_{3\,(\text{solid})} \leftrightarrow Ca^{2+}_{(\text{aqueous})} + CO_3^{2-}_{(\text{aqueous})}$$

The double arrow indicates that the reaction can proceed in either direction. The formation of solid calcium carbonate by organisms in surface waters and the dissolution of sinking calcium carbonate in deep waters is very important in transferring carbon dioxide (CO_2) to the abyss. Carbon dioxide exists in the ocean partially as bicarbonate ion ($[H]CO_3^{[1-]\,2-}$). Therefore, the formation of solid calcium carbonate and its subsequent sinking transfers carbon dioxide to depth. The dissolution of calcium carbonate at depth increases the alkalinity of deep waters by releasing basic carbonate ions. The depth at which the rate of dissolution of solid calcium carbonate is increased dramatically is referred to as the *lysocline*.

In some areas of the world, sinking solid calcium carbonate is preserved and thus comprises a major portion of pelagic sediments. The depth where solid calcium carbonate forms a significant portion of the sediment's composition is known as the *calcium carbonate compensation depth*. The lysocline and calcium carbonate compensation depth often occur at the same depth. Calcium also exists in minerals such as anhydrite ($CaSO_4$), calcium-rich plagioclase feldspar ($CaAl_2Si_2O_8$), and pyroxine ($CaSi_2O_6$), which make up basalt or oceanic crust.

Daniel Schuller

FURTHER READING

Millero, Frank J. *Chemical Oceanography.* Boca Raton, Fla.: CRC Press, 1992; 2nd ed., 1996.
Open University Course Team. *Ocean Chemistry and Deep-Sea Sediments.* Oxford and New York: Pergamon Press, in association with Open University, Milton Keynes, England, 1989.
———. *Seawater: Its Composition, Properties and Behavior.* Oxford and New York: Pergamon Press, in association with Open University, Milton Keynes, England, 1989; 2nd ed., 1995.
———. *The Ocean Basins: Their Structure and Evolution.* Oxford and New York: Pergamon Press, in association with Open University, Milton Keynes, England, 1989; 2nd ed., Oxford: Butterworth-Heinemann in association with Open University, 1998.

RELATED ARTICLES

Acidity and Alkalinity; Calcium Carbonate Compensation Depth; Carbon Dioxide; Constant Proportions, Principle of; Foraminifera; Oceanic Crust; Salinity

Calcium Carbonate Compensation Depth

Calcium carbonate ($CaCO_3$), the material of which seashells are made, is one of the major constituents of sediments in the deep sea. In the open ocean, microscopic shells of $CaCO_3$ are secreted by plankton and sink to the seafloor. The solubility of $CaCO_3$ increases with pressure, so that the seafloor resembles snow-capped mountains, with white $CaCO_3$ accumulating on topographic highs but no $CaCO_3$ preservation in the deepest abyss. The transition between high-$CaCO_3$ and low-$CaCO_3$ sediments in the ocean is called the *carbonate compensation depth* (CCD). Chemically, $CaCO_3$ interacts with hydrogen ions in seawater, and on time scales of thousands of years and longer, the $CaCO_3$ cycle in the ocean interacts with the CO_2 of the atmosphere. For example, the depth of the CCD varied synchronously with glacial–interglacial climate cycles throughout the past several million years. The CCD is also projected to rise in the coming millennium in response to rising CO_2 concentration in the atmosphere.

Several minerals form with the chemical composition of calcium carbonate; the dominant ones in the ocean are calcite and aragonite. Aragonite is more soluble than calcite and tends to be found in shallow-water sediments associated with coral reefs and tropical carbonate banks such as in the Bahamas. Calcite is the dominant form in sediments of the deep sea because of its greater stability at high pressure. Calcite in the open ocean is produced primarily by planktonic algae called *coccolithophorids*, of which a species called *Emiliania huxlii* is dominant today. Because algae are plants that rely on the energy of sunlight to photosynthesize, coccolithophorids grow and produce their calcite shell plates, called *coccoliths*, only in the sunlit top 100 meters (328 feet) or so of the ocean. Calcite is also produced by a family of protista called *foraminifera*, which may live throughout the water column or in sediments at the bottom. Shells of foraminifera preserved in deep-sea sediments are used by climate scientists and oceanographers as clues to the chemistry and temperature of the ocean at times in the past.

The rate at which $CaCO_3$ dissolves in sediments depends on pressure, seawater pH, and on chemical reactions that may occur within the sediment. The dominant control is pressure. When $CaCO_3$

dissolves in water to release Ca^{2+} and CO_3^{2-}, there is a net decrease in volume. An increase in pressure forces $CaCO_3$ into the more compact dissolved state, and for this reason, the solubility of $CaCO_3$ is greater in deeper waters than in shallow waters. Both calcite and aragonite are stable in most surface waters of the ocean and reach the stability boundary at some depth beneath the surface. This depth is called the *saturation horizon*. Because calcite is more stable than aragonite, the saturation horizon for calcite is deeper than that for aragonite [typically, 3 to 4 kilometers (1.9 to 2.5 miles) for calcite and 1 kilometer (0.6 miles) for aragonite]. The saturation state of $CaCO_3$ is determined by multiplying the concentrations of Ca^{2+} and CO_3^{2-} as $\Omega = [Ca^{2+}][CO_3^{2-}]$, where Ω is called the *solubility product*. The solubility product is compared with a *solubility constant*, written as K_{sp}, a number that decreases as the pressure increases. Above the saturation horizon, the solubility product $[Ca^{2+}][CO_3^{2-}] > K_{sp}$, and the mineral is said to be *supersaturated* and will have no tendency to dissolve; below the saturation horizon, the solubility product is $< K_{sp}$ and the mineral is undersaturated. The more undersaturated the solution gets, the faster the mineral dissolves.

The distribution of $CaCO_3$ on the seafloor also depends on biological processes within the ocean and the patterns of deep-ocean circulation, as these affect the concentration of CO_3^{2-}. (Ca^{2+} is more concentrated than CO_3^{2-} in seawater and less variable.) Dissolved CO_3^{2-} reacts with dissolved CO_2 in a chemical equilibrium $CO_3^{2-} + CO_2 + H_2O \leftrightarrow 2HCO_3^-$. An increase in dissolved CO_2 is generally associated with a decrease in CO_3^{2-} or vice versa; one goes up, the other goes down. This relationship between CO_2 and CO_3^{2-} couples the organic carbon cycle, driven by the production and degradation of soft body tissues of plankton, with the inorganic carbon cycle, that is, $CaCO_3$. The concentration of CO_2 in deep ocean water is higher than it is at the sea surface because of the degradation of organic matter that sinks down from above (dead

phytoplankton, zooplankton fecal pellets, etc.). Biological degradation of organic carbon, called *respiration*, can be written as $CH_2O + O_2 \leftrightarrow CO_2 + H_2O$, where CH_2O is a simplified formula for organic matter. As waters age in the deep sea, their oxygen levels go down, CO_2 concentrations rise, CO_3^{2-} decreases, and the waters get more corrosive to $CaCO_3$. For this reason, the CCD in the Pacific Ocean is shallower than it is in the Atlantic Ocean. Deep waters in the Pacific have been isolated for longer from contact with the atmosphere and have a lower CO_3^{2-} concentration.

A third factor that plays a part in the distribution of $CaCO_3$ on the seafloor is organic carbon that degrades within the sediment. Organic carbon and $CaCO_3$ rain to the sediment surface and are mixed down into the sediment by the stirring action of benthic animals. Within the sediment, the degradation of organic carbon depletes CO_3^{2-} in the pore fluid between the solid grains, causing $CaCO_3$ to dissolve. Of the calcite that rains to the seafloor at or above the saturation horizon, perhaps 20 to 40 percent dissolves, driven by benthic respiration reactions.

The "snow-capped peaks" distribution of $CaCO_3$ on the seafloor has been known for decades. It was described by Gustaf Arrhenius from the Swedish Deep Sea Expedition in 1947–48. Equatorial Pacific sediment cores from that expedition also revealed systematic rising and falling of the CCD, which were later verified to be correlated with advances and retreats of the great ice sheets: the glacial–interglacial cycles. More recently, measurements of the concentration of CO_2 in bubbles of ancient air trapped in polar ice caps have shown that the concentration of CO_2, a greenhouse gas, fluctuated in synchrony with the glacial cycles. CO_2 is a greenhouse gas implicated in global warming today and must certainly have contributed to the climate changes associated with glacial cycles. The correlation of CCD with CO_2 and ice sheets documents linkages among $CaCO_3$, the ocean carbon cycle, and the climate of Earth.

One pattern of CCD variation over the glacial cycles is a shift in $CaCO_3$ deposition from Atlantic to Pacific during glacial time. Today, salty water cools in the North Atlantic and becomes dense enough to sink, filling the deep Atlantic with water of chemical properties resembling surface waters, including a high concentration of CO_3^{2-}. This process is called *deepwater formation* or *deepsea ventilation*. Because of ventilation, the CO_3^{2-} concentration, the saturation horizon, and the CCD today are deeper in the Atlantic than in the deep ocean on average. During glacial time, ice cover in the North Atlantic and its marginal seas pushed the sites of open-water contact with the atmosphere toward the south, with the end result that the rate of deepwater formation decreased. Its density also decreased relative to the density of the deep ocean, so that what ventilation there was did not penetrate as deeply into the deep Atlantic. This decrease in deep ventilation depleted the concentration of CO_3^{2-} in the deep ocean, and as a result, the CCD in the Atlantic became shallower.

The opposite pattern is seen in the Pacific and Indian Oceans, with deeper CCD during glacial times. This is because, on time frames longer than 10,000 years or so, if less $CaCO_3$ is buried in the Atlantic, more must be buried elsewhere, everything else remaining equal. The ocean manages to achieve this stability using a trick called *calcium carbonate compensation*. On time scales of thousands of years and longer, this mechanism controls the pH (acidity) of the ocean and influences the concentration of CO_2 in the atmosphere. The mechanism works by balancing the budget for input and removal of dissolved $CaCO_3$ to the ocean. Dissolved $CaCO_3$ comes in to the ocean via rivers from dissolution of rocks on land, a process called *chemical weathering*. In the ocean, solid $CaCO_3$ is produced from dissolved Ca^{2+} and CO_3^{2-} by corals and plankton as described above. Finally, solid $CaCO_3$ is removed from the ocean by burial in sediments. Over long enough periods of time, calcium carbonate compensation acts to balance the books for $CaCO_3$ in the ocean, so that influx from weathering balances burial in sediments.

How Calcium Carbonate Compensation Works

The rate of solid $CaCO_3$ production in the ocean exceeds the supply of dissolved $CaCO_3$ from rivers by a factor of 10 or so. Therefore, for the output to balance the input, most of the $CaCO_3$ produced must redissolve rather than be buried in sediments. The factor that determines what fraction of the $CaCO_3$ production dissolves is the depth of the saturation horizon, which divides the ocean into $CaCO_3$-preserving sediments above and $CaCO_3$-dissolving sediments below. The saturation horizon determines the area of the seafloor that is covered with high-$CaCO_3$ sediments, where $CaCO_3$ can accumulate. The depth of the saturation horizon, in turn, is controlled by the concentration of CO_3^{2-} in the deep ocean. If CO_3^{2-} is high, calcite can tolerate a greater pressure before it begins to dissolve.

The concentration of CO_3^{2-} acts like a thermostat in the ocean, adjusting itself to balance the budget for $CaCO_3$. If, for example, more dissolved $CaCO_3$ enters the ocean from rivers than leaves by burial in sediments, the concentration of CO_3^{2-}, the dissolved form of $CaCO_3$, will increase. This drives the saturation horizon to deeper levels, enabling a greater fraction of the $CaCO_3$ produced by plankton in the ocean to be buried. In this way the global concentration of CO_3^{2-} responds to changes in deep-water circulation or chemistry, the weathering rate, or changes in the planktonic $CaCO_3$ production rate, to ensure that over long time frames $CaCO_3$ burial in sediments equals the input (weathering) rate. If a change in deep-sea ventilation in the Atlantic decreases its $CaCO_3$ burial, calcium carbonate compensation ensures that the Pacific and Indian Oceans bury more to compensate.

Another pattern is observed at the transitions between glacial and interglacial stages, known as dissolution and preservation "spikes." At the end of a glacial stage, the CCD in the Pacific and Indian Oceans apparently moves deeper for a few thousand years. This is accompanied by preservation of shells of open-ocean organisms called *pteropods*, made of aragonite. The saturation state of bottom water must have increased considerably for the soluble mineral aragonite to survive dissolution as it sat on the seafloor. During transitions from interglacial to glacial stages, there appears to be a dissolution spike of calcium carbonate, where the concentration of $CaCO_3$ decreases in deep-sea sediment cores.

These transition spikes are probably linked with shifts in the distribution of carbon between ocean, atmosphere, and terrestrial biosphere reservoirs. Recall that in the chemistry of seawater as described above, the concentration of CO_3^{2-} is coupled to the concentration of CO_2. Therefore, the calcium carbonate compensation mechanism, by regulating the CO_3^{2-} concentration of the ocean, also affects the ocean concentration of CO_2. An increase in weathering, for example, would require an increase in CO_3^{2-} to drive an increase in $CaCO_3$ burial in the steady state. Because CO_3^{2-} and CO_2 are inversely related, an increase in CO_3^{2-} will decrease the concentration of CO_2. This in turn would decrease the CO_2 concentration of the atmosphere.

The same processes can be invoked in the reverse direction by changing the CO_2 concentration of the atmosphere and watching the response of the ocean $CaCO_3$ cycle. During the last four glacial intervals, CO_2 was approximately one-third lower than it was during the preanthropogenic interglacial intervals as recently as the year 1750 (before the increase in CO_2 from human activity). No one knows why atmospheric CO_2 underwent these cycles, but they represent a major shift in carbon from the atmosphere to someplace, presumably the ocean. In addition, carbon isotopes preserved in deep-sea foraminiferal shells tell us that the amount of carbon in the terrestrial biosphere decreased as well during glacial time, another major carbon shift. In the ocean, sea level dropped as water froze into continental ice sheets, exposing the continental shelves that are a major depocenter for $CaCO_3$ today. These rearrangements in the carbon cycle must have driven the ocean budget for $CaCO_3$ out of balance, generating excess dissolution (at the beginnings of glacial stages) or preservation (at the ends). The calcium carbonate compensation mechanism presumably acted to restore $CaCO_3$ burial toward balance with the weathering flux, limiting the perturbation to a duration of 5000 to 10,000 years (a geologist's "spike").

An analogous process is beginning today and will continue for thousands of years, in response to the release of CO_2 from human activity (combustion of fossil fuel and conversion of forested land to agriculture). The increasing CO_2 concentration in the atmosphere drives excess CO_2 to dissolve in surface waters of the ocean. Mixing and overturning in high latitudes carries this excess CO_2 into the deep ocean. The increase in CO_2 decreases CO_3^{2-}, provoking a dissolution response from the $CaCO_3$ on the seafloor. Eventually, most of the anthropogenic CO_2 emission will end up as dissolved HCO_3^- in seawater. From a human point of view, this process is of little relevance; fossil-fuel neutralization by the ocean $CaCO_3$ cycle will take thousands of years, and the effect on atmospheric CO_2 in the coming decades is projected to be small.

David Archer

FURTHER READING

Archer, D., H. Kheshgi, and E. Maier-Riemer. "Multiple Timescales for Neutralization of Fossil Fuel CO_2." *Geophysical Research Letters*, Vol. 24 (1997), pp. 405–408.

Arrhenius, G. "Sediment Cores from the East Pacific: Properties of the Sediments." In H. Pettersson, Nils Jerlov, and Börje Kullenberg, eds., *Reports of the Swedish Deep Sea Expedition, 1947–1948.* 10 vols. Stockholm: Elanders, 1975; pp. 1951–1957.

Berner, Robert A. *Early Diagenesis: A Theoretical Approach.* Princeton, N.J.: Princeton University Press, 1980.

Broecker, W. S., and T. H. Peng. *Tracers in the Sea.* Palisades, N.Y.: Lamont-Doherty Geological Observatory, Columbia University, 1982.

———. "The Role of $CaCO_3$ Compensation in the Glacial to Interglacial Atmospheric CO_2 Change." *Global Biogeochemical Cycles*, Vol. 1 (1987), pp. 15–29.

Broecker, W. S., and T. Takahashi. "Neutralization of Fossil Fuel CO_2 by Marine Calcium Carbonate." In N. R. Andersen and A. Malahoff, eds., *The Fate of Fossil Fuel CO_2 in the Oceans.* New York: Plenum Press, 1977.

Farrell, J. W., and W. L. Prell. "Climate Change and $CaCO_3$ Preservation: An 800,000 Year Bathymetric Reconstruction from the Central Equatorial Pacific Ocean." *Paleoceanography*, Vol. 4 (1989), pp. 447–466.

Stumm, W., and J. J. Morgan. *Aquatic Chemistry: An Introduction Emphasizing Chemical Equilibria in Natural Waters.* New York: Wiley, 1970; 3rd ed., 1996.

RELATED ARTICLES

Calcium; Carbonate Platform; Carbon Cycle; Carbon Isotope; Deep-Sea Sediment; Oxygen

California Current

The California Current is the eastern boundary current that flows southward along the eastern margin of the North Pacific Ocean parallel to the western coast of North America. It begins in the latitude of Oregon and ends at about the Tropic of Cancer (23.5°N), which is the latitude of the southern tip of Baja California. The California Current curves to the west and joins the North Equatorial Current flowing from east to west across the tropical North Pacific. The California Current carries cold water toward the equator. It also receives water and nutrients from rivers flowing into the ocean.

Like most eastern boundary currents, the California Current is broad, diffuse, and slow-moving. It transports about 10 million cubic meters (353 million cubic feet) of water per second. It meanders and generates eddies, some of which are still strong as much as 500 kilometers (310 miles) from the shore. When its meanders and eddies are included, the California Current in fact comprises a system of currents that extends for 1000 kilometers (620 miles) from the U.S. coastline.

Near the edge of the continental shelf, an undercurrent flows continuously toward the North Pole at an average depth of 200 meters (660 feet) beneath the California Current, at a speed of about 15 centimeters per second (0.33 mile per hour). A narrow northward-flowing current found in winter is called the Davidson Current. It results from a change in wind direction and is related to the surfacing of the deep countercurrent.

Although major ocean currents are conventionally described in terms that make them appear permanent and stable, in fact they are subject to change. They are driven by winds, and therefore climatic shifts that alter the speed and/or direction of the prevailing winds will affect them. The California Current is affected by El Niño Southern Oscillation (ENSO) events. These have been recorded throughout the 500 years during which climate observations have been written down in North America.

Although the overall movement of water is from north to south, there are many large eddies, so there are many places within the current system where water is not flowing southward. In the many places

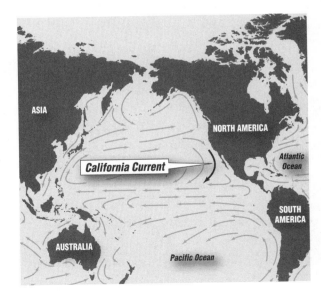

California Current.

where eddies carry water away from the coast, upwelling brings cold water close to the surface.

The upwelling water is rich in nutrients that have drifted down from the upper layer of the ocean. These add to those contributed by rivers, and together they sustain a large and diverse population of plankton and vertebrate animals. These include sea lions, harbor seals, porpoises, and sea otters, as well as commercially important fishes such as sockeye salmon (*Oncorhynchus nerka*).

Michael Allaby

FURTHER READING

Knauss, John A. *Introduction to Physical Oceanography.* Englewood Cliffs, N.J.: Prentice Hall, 1978; 2nd ed. rev., Upper Saddle River, N.J.: Prentice Hall, 2000.

Miller, A. J., et al. "Observing and Modeling the California Current System." *EOS Transactions, American Geophysical Union,* Vol. 80 (1999), pp. 533–539.

RELATED ARTICLES

Boundary Current; Eastern Boundary Current; Gyre; Upwelling

Canary Current

The Canary (or Canaries) Current is an ocean current that flows toward the equator on the eastern side of the North Atlantic Ocean. As an eastern boundary current, it forms part of the North Atlantic gyre, beginning where it breaks away from the Gulf Stream at approximately 42°N latitude. It turns to the south off the coast of Africa and joins the North Equatorial Current at about 15°N, at the latitude of Senegal.

The Canary Current is more than 1000 kilometers (about 620 miles) wide and moves slowly, at an average 2 kilometers (about 1.2 miles) per hour, with variable speed. It is strongest near the coast and accelerates as it passes between the Canary Islands, which lie off the coast of North Africa, and it is stronger in winter than in summer. There are eddies in the current, the largest being off Cape Bojador (27°N) on the Moroccan

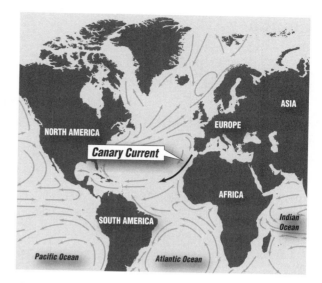

Canary Current.

coast and Cape Blanco (21°N) on the Mauritanian coast. The current accelerates at these eddies.

The Canary Current carries cool water. This reduces mean temperatures in the Canary Islands, giving them a more pleasant climate. It is also responsible for frequent sea fogs off the northwestern coast of Spain and Portugal, as warm, moist air moving eastward is chilled by contact with the cool sea surface. The low temperature of the current is caused by the upwelling of cold water due to offshore winds that blow from the subtropical high-pressure region over Africa. The upwelling brings nutrients close to the surface. These sustain an extensive planktonic population, which in turn supports valuable fisheries. The most commercially important fishes include horse mackerel, chub mackerel, sardines (pilchards), and octopus.

Michael Allaby

FURTHER READING

Kendrew, W. G. *The Climates of the Continents,* 5th ed. Oxford: Clarendon Press, 1961.

Sellers, William D. *Physical Climatology.* Chicago: University of Chicago Press, 1965.

RELATED ARTICLES

Boundary Current; Eastern Boundary Current; Equatorial Currents, North and South; Gulf Stream; Upwelling

Capillary Waves

Capillary waves, also called *ripples*, are the smallest wind-generated surface waves. They have a maximum wavelength (distance between one wave crest and the next) of only 1.73 centimeters (0.68 inch) and a period (the time taken for a wave to travel one wavelength) of less than 1 second. Capillary wave heights are less than 2 millimeters (0.1 inch). Surface waves of longer wavelength are called *gravity waves*. Capillary waves form when small gusts of wind act on the water surface for short periods of time. They feature a rounded crest and a V-shaped trough.

Capillary waves gain their name from capillarity, a property of surface tension. In capillary waves, their small size means that surface tension (forces acting on the water surface resulting from the mutual attraction of water molecules) is the principal force that restores that wave to equilibrium and moves it forward. The comparatively small energy content of capillary waves means that water's viscosity (internal friction) is significant in dissipating the wave energy. Capillary waves disappear rapidly when the wind ceases, which means that capillary waves detected by satellite microwave technology can be used to infer the strength of low-speed surface winds. Capillary waves are also of significance because they increase wave surface roughness, thereby aiding the conversion of wind energy to wave energy when a wind-driven gravity wave is building.

Trevor Day

FURTHER READING
Open University Course Team. *Waves, Tides and Shallow Water Processes.* Oxford and New York: Pergamon Press, in association with the Open University, Milton Keynes, England, 1989; 2nd ed., Boston: Butterworth-Heinemann, in association with the Open University, 1999.
Smail, J. "The Topsy-Turvy World of Capillary Waves." *Sea Frontiers*, Vol. 32, No. 5 (1986), pp. 331–337.

Young, Ian R., and Greg J. Holland. *Atlas of the Oceans: Wind and Wave Climate.* Oxford and Tarrytown, N.Y.: Pergamon Press, 1996.

RELATED ARTICLES
Gravity Wave; Wave; Wave Energy; Wave, Fully Developed Sea

Carbonate Platform

Carbonate platforms, sometimes called *carbonate shelves*, develop in shallow waters off the coast of continents. The platforms are broad, shallow shelves that extend seaward from the continent. The presence of platforms in the geologic record indicates a warm, marine environment with little terrigenous sediment input.

Carbonate platforms develop by direct precipitation of carbonate mud and by the accumulation of shells and skeletal fragments of carbonate-secreting organisms. Reef communities are common; most carbonates today are of biogenic origin. Carbonate precipitation is a function of oceanographic conditions, climate, and the rate of terrigenous input. Carbonate buildup occurs on both active and passive continental margins. Any features such as submarine canyons that disrupt the continental shelf also disrupt deposition of the carbonate platform. Carbonate platforms form in warm climates. Warm water temperatures, like those found near the equator, enhance carbonate deposition. Although water temperature is important, the critical factor for platform formation is the amount of terrigenous detritus deposited in the platform area.

Terrigenous sediment dominates throughout the shallow parts of the oceans, and carbonate deposition occurs only where the terrigenous input is minimal. Because terrigenous sedimentation is highest along the nearshore areas, carbonate content increases seaward and reaches maximum content on the outer shelf. The distribution of carbonate platforms reflects the decrease in continental-derived sediment rather than an increase in the carbonate precipitation rate. Along the east coast of the United States, the change in terrigenous sediment occurs at Cape Hatteras. North of Cape Hatteras, terrigenous sediment predominates, whereas south of this area, carbonate content increases to the Florida Keys.

Modification of sedimentation and carbonate character occurred during the Quaternary Period (1.64 million years ago to present), when sea level fluctuated. Modern shelf deposits reflect a mixture of present-day sediment and Pleistocene (1.64 to 0.01 million years ago) relict material. Areas of active carbonate precipitation and reef building are the Bahama Banks, Florida Keys, Australia's Great Barrier Reef, Persian Gulf, and Red Sea.

David L. White

FURTHER READING
Kennett, James. *Marine Geology.* Englewood Cliffs, N.J.: Prentice Hall, 1982.
Montgomery, Carla W. *Physical Geology,* 3rd ed. Dubuque, Iowa: Wm. C. Brown, 1993.
Thurman, Harold V. *Essentials of Oceanography.* Columbus, Ohio: Charles E. Merrill, 1983; 6th ed., with Alan P. Trujillo, Upper Saddle River, N.J.: Prentice Hall, 1999.

RELATED ARTICLES
Continental Shelf; Detritus; Great Barrier Reef; Red Sea; Reef; Submarine Canyon

Carbon Cycle

The element carbon is essential to life on Earth as the key chemical ingredient of all the organic molecules that make up living organisms. Indeed, *organic chemistry* is the chemistry of carbon compounds. Carbon passes from one living organism to another and between living organisms and the atmosphere, fresh water, and oceans, and back to living organisms. This flow constitutes the biological carbon cycle.

Carbon is also cycled by nonbiological processes. Carbon dioxide (CO_2) is released into the atmosphere by volcanic eruptions. Some of the atmospheric CO_2 dissolves in rainwater and falls on land as carbonic acid (H_2CO_3). Carbonic acid reacts with calcium carbonate ($CaCO_3$) in carbonate rocks to yield soluble calcium (Ca^{2+}) and bicarbonate (HCO_3^-) ions. These are carried to the sea by rivers and groundwater.

Atmospheric carbon dioxide (CO_2) also enters seawater by diffusing across the water surface. The solubility of CO_2 in seawater varies inversely with the water temperature. At average sea-level atmospheric pressure, water can hold 3.35 grams per liter (0.45 ounces per gallon) at 0°C (32°F), but only 1.45 grams per liter (0.19 ounces per gallon) at 25°C (77°F). Some carbon remains in the seawater as dissolved CO_2 and a small amount as H_2CO_3, but about 99 percent of the carbon forms bicarbonate and carbonate (CO_3^{2-}) ions. Salts such as chlorine (Cl^-) supply negative ions. Metals such as calcium (Ca^{2+}), potassium (K^+), and magnesium (Mg^{2+}) contribute positive ions. If the concentration of positive ions increases, a higher proportion of the dissolved carbon will be as carbonate. As the concentration of dissolved carbon increases or that of the positive ions decreases, a greater proportion of dissolved carbon will be in the form of bicarbonate. As the relative proportions of positive and negative ions change, so does the proportion of dissolved carbon present as carbonate or bicarbonate. In this way, the presence of bicarbonate and carbonate ions helps maintain a constant seawater alkalinity (pH). Balances are maintained between the concentrations of atmospheric and dissolved carbon dioxide and between bicarbonate and carbonate ions in water.

Ocean currents transport carbon. The net carbon transport poleward exceeds the equatorward transport, because as water cools during its poleward migration, its capacity for CO_2 increases. The resulting imbalance is corrected by *downwelling,* a process that transfers cold surface waters to the deep ocean. The amount of carbon transferred to the deep ocean by downwelling is determined by the amount present in surface waters, and this in turn is determined by the atmospheric CO_2 concentration. Carbon is returned to surface waters by *upwelling*.

Atmospheric carbon dioxide is absorbed by green plants and certain bacteria (photosynthetic organisms). Using sunlight as a source of energy, these organisms synthesize simple carbohydrates. This is the way that carbon enters the biological carbon cycle. Nonphotosynthetic organisms are directly or indirectly dependent for their dietary carbon compounds on the photosynthetic organisms. Marine plants, comprising the phytoplankton, also photosynthesize carbohydrate, using dissolved carbon dioxide as a source of carbon, and like terrestrial plants, form the base of food webs that sustain all marine animals.

Metabolic wastes from living organisms, together with the remains of dead organisms, sustain another group of organisms. These decompose the material on which they feed, progressively breaking down large organic molecules into smaller, simpler molecules.

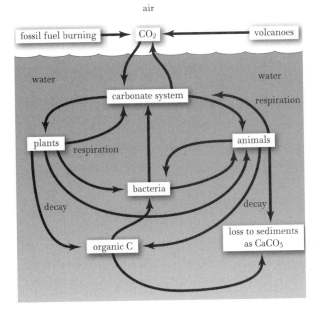

Carbon cycle in bodies of water.

Decomposition involves the oxidation of carbon to CO_2. In seawater, this joins the dissolved CO_2 and is known as dissolved organic carbon (DOC). Some of it is taken up by living organisms and remains in the biological carbon cycle and some is converted to carbonate or bicarbonate and joins the nonbiological cycle.

This almost balances the cycle, but not quite. Many aquatic organisms use carbonate ions to grow shells made from calcium carbonate ($CaCO_3$). When these organisms die, some of their shells fall to the sea or lake floor, where they accumulate as sediment. As they sink, the shells enter water where the CO_2 concentration steadily increases and the temperature decreases. Calcium carbonate dissolves at lower temperatures and higher CO_2 concentrations. At the calcium carbonate compensation depth, at approximately 4500 meters (14,760 feet), the rate at which $CaCO_3$ dissolves is equal to the rate at which it enters from above. Consequently, sediments rich in carbonate are not found below 6000 meters (19,700 feet).

Some of the accumulated sediment is slowly converted to carbonate sedimentary rock, such as chalk and limestone, removing carbon from the cycle. A proportion of this "buried" carbon is subducted into Earth's mantle at destructive plate margins and eventually returned to the cycle by volcanic eruptions. The remainder remains buried until movements of Earth's crust raise the rocks above the surface, where they are exposed to weathering processes that slowly return the carbon dioxide to the air.

Carbon is also buried when plant and animal remains accumulate in anaerobic environments, where their decomposition is arrested for lack of oxygen. These remains are slowly transformed into coal, natural gas, and oil, the *fossil fuels*. Burning the fuels completes the oxidation of their carbon, returning it to the air as carbon dioxide.

Michael Allaby

FURTHER READING

Allaby, Michael. *Basics of Environmental Science.* London and New York: Routledge, 1996; 2nd ed., 2000.

Campbell, Neil A. *Biology.* Menlo Park, Calif.: Benjamin Cummings, 1987; 5th ed., 1999.

Emiliani, Cesare. *Planet Earth: Cosmology, Geology, and the Evolution of Life and Environment.* Cambridge and New York: Cambridge University Press, 1992.

Nybakken, James W. *Marine Biology: An Ecological Approach,* 5th ed. San Francisco: Benjamin Cummings, 2001.

RELATED ARTICLES

Calcium Carbonate Compensation Depth; Carbon Dioxide; Climate Change; Dissolved Organic Matter; Photosynthesis; Phytoplankton; Salinity; Seawater Buffer; Seawater, pH of

Carbon Dioxide

Carbon dioxide is one of the two common oxides of carbon. It is a gas that consitutes 0.03 percent of our atmosphere by volume. In the atmosphere it acts as a *greenhouse* gas, allowing in short-wavelength radiant energy from the Sun but absorbing the longer-wavelength energy that gets reflected from land and sea. Hence the more carbon dioxide there is in the atmosphere, the warmer the mean temperature of Earth's atmosphere tends to become. Analysis of past atmospheres, such as by analyzing the gas bubbles trapped deep in the ice of the Greenland ice cap, shows that during past geological eras the atmospheric content was considerably higher than at present. Even so, drastic cuts (>50 percent) in emissions are required if disastrous climate changes are to be avoided.

At normal atmospheric pressure, carbon dioxide has a freezing point of −78.5°C (less than −109.3°F), freezing directly into a solid known as *dry ice.* At high pressures it will form a liquid and it has a triple point at −56.6°C (less than −69.9°F) and 5.11 atmospheres of pressure between being a solid, a liquid, or a gas. So if carbon dioxide gas is lowered into the ocean, it liquefies at depths of around 3000 meters (about 9850 feet). Liquid carbon dioxide forms complexes with water known as *clathrates,* which reduce its tendency to dissolve. Otherwise, it is highly soluble in water; up to 90 cubic centimeters (5.5 cubic inches) of it can dissolve in a liter of water at normal atmospheric pressure and temperature. But like all gases, as pressure increases and temperature cools, more of it will dissolve, and vice versa. Once dissolved, it associates with the water to form bicarbonate (about 93 percent) and carbonate ions (about 6 percent) and carbonic acid (about 1 percent), in proportions subject to various dynamic chemical equilibria:

$$CO_2 + H_2O \leftrightarrow H_2CO_3$$
forming carbonic acid

$$H_2CO_3 \leftrightarrow H^+ + HCO_3^-$$
carbonic acid dissociated into bicarbonate ion

$$HCO_3^- \leftrightarrow H^+ + CO_3^{2-}$$
bicarbonate ion dissociated into carbonate ion

Since bicarbonate ions can act as either hydrogen ion acceptors or donors, they are effective at buffering the acidity (pH) of seawater (i.e., keeping the pH relatively constant). Thus the pH of seawater normally varies between only 7.8 and 8.4 (a pH of 7.0 is neutral).

Carbon dioxide plays a key role in many biological processes. It is produced as a by-product of oxidative metabolism of organic matter by all aerobic organisms, both plants and animals. Photosynthetic plants use it directly (or indirectly as bicarbonate ions) in the synthesis of carbohydrates, exploiting the radiant energy in sunlight. Many aquatic animals and plants synthesize carbonates to form internal or external skeletal structures. However, because the solubility of carbon dioxide increases with pressure, synthesizing calcium or magnesium carbonate becomes increasingly hard work with depth.

The partial pressure of carbon dioxide dissolved in the waters of the upper ocean is constantly adjusting to be in equilibrium with the partial pressure of the gas in the atmosphere. Where the surface ocean is cold, more carbon dioxide dissolves in it, and if this water then sinks into the deep ocean through the formation of bottom waters, it effectively removes carbon dioxide from the atmosphere. This is a process called the *solubility pump*. When the rate of photosynthesis is high, particularly during spring blooms, the phytoplankton uses up a large proportion of the carbon dioxide in the surface water, so that the ocean tends to dissolve more. Any organic or inorganic carbon that sinks into the deep ocean is exporting carbon dioxide, a process known as the *biological pump*. In the deep water, the oxidation of exported organic matter in respiration and the dissolution of carbonate skeletons release carbon dioxide back into solution, boosting the carbon dioxide content of the deep ocean. When deep ocean water upwells back to the surface, its content of dissolved carbon dioxide is at a higher partial pressure than the atmosphere, so that it vents it back into the atmosphere. Therefore, the ocean at high latitudes is drawing down the carbon dioxide content of the atmosphere, but at low latitudes it is boosting it. Thus, understanding the carbon cycle in the oceans is a difficult but important component of elucidating rates of global warming resulting from burning fossil fuels and felling forests.

Martin Angel

FURTHER READING

Bates, N. R., T. Takahashi, D. W. Chipman, and A. H. Knap. "Variability of pCO₂ on Diel to Seasonal Timescales in the Sargasso Sea near Bermuda." *Journal of Geophysical Research*, Vol. 103 (1998), pp. 15567–15585.

Houghton, J. T., et al. *Climate Change 1995: The Science of Climate Change.* Cambridge: Cambridge University Press, 1996.

Millero, Frank J. *Chemical Oceanography.* Boca Raton, Fla.: CRC Press, 1992; 2nd ed., 1996.

Siegenthaler, U., and J. L. Sarmiento. "Atmospheric Carbon Dioxide and the Sea." *Nature*, Vol. 365 (1993), pp. 119–125.

Watson, A. J. "Are Upwelling Zones Sources or Sinks of CO₂?" In C. P. Summerhayes et al., eds., *Upwelling in the Oceans: Modern Processes and Ancient Records.* New York: Wiley, 1995.

Wigley, T. M. L., and D. S. Schimel, eds. *The Carbon Cycle.* Cambridge and New York: Cambridge University Press, 2000.

RELATED ARTICLES
Bottom Water Formation; Carbon Cycle; Seawater, pH of

Carbon Isotope

Naturally occurring carbon consists of the stable isotopes ^{12}C and ^{13}C. These isotopes represent 98.89 and 1.11 percent, respectively, of total carbon abundance. Scientists apply the differences between the $^{13}C/^{12}C$ ratios to determine the source of the carbon in inorganic and organic carbon, in igneous melts, in metamorphic rocks, and in gold-bearing fluids; to study fluid and wall rock interaction; and as a geothermometer.

The various isotopes of carbon are preferentially assimilated (fractionated) during physical and chemical processes. The isotopes are measured and are reported as parts per mil (‰). These values are then compared to a standard according to the equation

$$\delta^{13}C‰ = \frac{^{13}C/^{12}C \text{ (sample)} - ^{13}C/^{12}C \text{ (standard)}}{-[^{13}C/^{12}C \text{ (standard)}]}$$

Originally, the standard for carbon was a Cretaceous (144 to 65 million years ago) belmenite known as PDB found in South Carolina. The PDB standard was chosen because its isotopic values of carbon were close to that of average limestone. PDB has been consumed, and the standards are now a carbonatite [National Bureau of Standards (NBS) –18] and a marine limestone (NBS –19).

Organic carbon is light and depleted in $\delta^{13}C$ and enriched in $\delta^{12}C$. This fractionation is due to the conversion of inorganic carbon into organic carbon. The $\delta^{13}C$ range for biologic material is from −20 to −30‰; the average terrestrial biomass is −26‰. Methane is the most depleted of all carbon compounds at −80‰, resulting from anaerobic formation and/or the thermal alteration of petroleum.

Carbon occurs as oxides (CO_2, bicarbonate, and carbonates), reduced forms (methane and organic carbon), and in elemental forms (diamond and graphite). The $\delta^{13}C$ values for different materials show the range of fractionation and how carbon may be used to determine source area.

- Meteorites (carbonaceous chondrites) have a $\delta^{13}C$ value of −25 to 0‰.
- Mantle material (carbonatite, kimberlite, and diamond) have $\delta^{13}C$ values that range from −3 to −8, with an average value of −6‰.
- MORB averages −6.6‰.
- Seawater, by definition, has a $\delta^{13}C$ value of 0‰.
- Marine carbonate has a narrow range between −1 and −2‰.
- Marine bicarbonate varies from −2 to 1‰.

Values for ancient seawater are not constant, which indicates that changes have occurred during the evolution of the planet. Permian (290 to 248 million years ago) seawater had a $\delta^{13}C$ value of 6‰ and Cretaceous seawater had a $C\delta^{13}$ value of 4.8‰. The most striking change was Proterozoic (2450 to 570 million years ago) seawater with a $\delta^{13}C$ of 13‰. This may represent the global onset at about 2.0 billion years ago of increased photosynthesizing bacteria. A very distinct isotopic shift in the $\delta^{13}C$ values (a decrease of 0.7‰) occurred in the late Miocene Epoch (about 10 million to 5 million years ago) with simultaneous global cooling. The isotopic shift represents a widespread ocean circulation and upwelling pattern heralding the change from the old ocean to the modern ocean.

Carbon isotope fractionation is temperature dependent and is applied as a geothermometer in metamorphic rocks. Carbon isotopes are most accurate at temperatures below 600°C (1112°F). Two systems presently in use are the calcite–graphite system and the carbon dioxide–graphite CO_2–graphite system. When carbon and oxygen isotopes are combined, an accurate temperature history can be determined.

The radioactive isotope that forms in the atmosphere by neutron interaction and represents a negligible percent of the total carbon is ^{14}C. It has a very short half-life of 5730 years, mixes readily with other carbon, and is assimilated by living tissue. These characteristics make ^{14}C applicable to date materials younger than about 40,000 years. In oceanography, ^{14}C is used to determine the residence time of dissolved carbon compounds and to monitor and quantify primary organic production.

David L. White

FURTHER READING

Gross, M. Grant. *Oceanography: A View of the Earth*, 3rd ed. Englewood Cliffs, N.J.: Prentice Hall, 1982.

Kennett, James. *Marine Geology*. Englewood Cliffs, N.J.: Prentice Hall, 1982.

Rollinson, Hugh. *Using Geochemical Data: Evaluation, Presentation, Interpretation*. Harlow, England: Longman Scientific and Technical/New York: Wiley, 1993.

RELATED ARTICLES
Organic Geochemistry; Petroleum; Radiometric Dating

Caribbean Sea

The Caribbean Sea is the second-largest sea in the world. It forms the southernmost part of the Intra-Americas Seas (IAS) region, a complex regime that includes the Gulf of Mexico, the Straits of Florida, and adjacent waters. The Caribbean Sea comprises 2,512,950 square kilometers (970,250 square miles) between 22 and 8°N latitude and 88 and 60°W longitude. A string of islands from the Greater Antilles to the Lesser Antilles (including Cuba, Hispaniola, Puerto Rico, the Virgin Islands, and the Windward and Leeward Islands, for example) partially separates the tropical Caribbean Sea to the north and east from the Atlantic Ocean. The Yucatán Peninsula of Mexico and Central American countries border the Caribbean Sea to the west, and the northern coast of South America forms its southern boundary.

The Caribbean Sea is unique among the world's seas, but it is often called the American Mediterranean Sea. It includes four deep ocean basins: Yucatán Basin, Cayman Basin, Colombia Basin, and Venezuela Basin. The average depth is greater than 1800 meters (5900 feet); waters around the islands bordering the Caribbean to the east are shallower. The deepest area recorded to date, 7535 meters (24,721 feet), is the Cayman Trench between Jamaica and the Cayman Islands.

The bottom of the Caribbean Basin is characterized by old oceanic crust (formed more than 65 million years ago). It is relatively thick [about 10 kilometers (6 miles)] because of the many volcanic eruptions that took place during its development. It formed in the eastern Pacific and migrated northeast to its present position. The Isthmus of Panama closed off the Caribbean from the Pacific starting about 9 million years ago; the land bridge was complete by 2.5 million years ago. The eastern boundary of the Caribbean is a convergent plate boundary: The South American Plate is subducting under the Caribbean Plate, which is why there are many active volcanoes in this region.

Caribbean Sea.

Surface water circulation in the Caribbean is highly variable and influenced by trade winds and strong tidal currents. Water currents generally enter the region from a myriad of passages on its southeast edge, move westward, then northward through the Caribbean region. The main current is the Caribbean Current, which flows westward off the northern coast of South America (near the Antilles) and then northward along the eastern coast of Central America (where it is known as the Cariaco Current). It then becomes the Yucatán Current, which flows through the Yucatán Channel (the fastest section of the current) and then becomes the Loop Current that enters the Gulf of Mexico. The complex current system exits toward the Atlantic via the Straits of Florida as the Florida Current and has often been called the birthplace of the Gulf Stream. Various eddies that spin both clockwise and counterclockwise often characterize flow patterns throughout the Caribbean. Deepwater circulation is not well understood.

Most of the water in the Caribbean is clear, warm, and less salty than the Atlantic. The average salinity is 36 practical salinity units (psu). The salinity is lower in some areas, especially near the Orinoco, Amazon, and Magdalena estuaries on the northern coast of South America, where river water dilutes the saltwater. Surface temperature is 25 to 28°C (77 to 82.4°F).

The Caribbean region, often called a tropical paradise, supports many coastal marine ecosystems, including fisheries that are valuable to the economy. The most productive region lies off the northern coast of South America, where nutrients from rivers and upwelling along the coast support fisheries. Examples of well-known marine fauna and flora include the spiny lobster, coral reef fishes, endangered sea turtles, conch, mangroves, and seagrasses. Recent studies have indicated that the complex Caribbean Sea ecosystem suffers from overfishing, damage from storms and tourism activities, and increased land development and population.

The diverse Caribbean region, broken into a myriad of 38 independent states, associated states, and colonies, has a history rich with tales of Spanish, British, French, Dutch, American, Danish, and Swedish settlers. The region is subject to intense tropical storms and hurricanes in summer and early fall, as well as volcanic activity and earthquakes. Tourism is the region's main economy.

Kristen M. Kusek

FURTHER READING

Pickard, George L. *Descriptive Physical Oceanography.* Oxford and New York: Pergamon Press, 1964; 5th enl. ed., Oxford and Boston: Butterworth-Heinemann, 1995.

Snyderman, Marty, and Clay Wiseman. *Guide to Marine Life: Caribbean, Bahamas and Florida.* New York: AquaQuest Publications, 1996.

RELATED ARTICLES

Atlantic Ocean; Convergent Plate Boundary; Gulf of Mexico; Gulf Stream; Ocean Current; Plate Tectonics; Salinity

Carnivora

Although the term *carnivore* means simply "flesh eater," the mammalian order Carnivora refers specifically to 10 families of predominantly flesh-eating mammals, most of which feed through hunting (although one species, the giant panda, is a herbivore, and many are omnivorous). The Carnivora are represented at sea mainly by the suborder Pinnipedia: seals, sea lions, and walruses. Other seagoing carnivores include the sea otter and the polar bear.

Carnivores range in size from the tiny least weasel (*Mustela nivalis*), which weighs a mere 30 to 70 grams (1 to 2.5 ounces), to the gigantic elephant seal (*Mirounga leonina*), which can reach 3600 kilograms (4 tons) in weight. All members of the order are equipped with effective killing weapons, notably their long and sharp canine teeth, which in the walrus can grow into dramatic tusks. To aid the hunt, carnivores generally have a good sense of smell as well as sharp vision and hearing, and many use sensitive whiskers to feel their way in the dark or underwater. Carnivores also have larger brains than other mammals of the same size and are more intelligent, reflecting their ability to outsmart their ever-wary prey.

The most numerous of the marine carnivores are the pinnipeds, which scientists divide into three families: Otariidae (fur seals and sea lions), Phocidae (true seals and elephant seals), and Odobenidae (walruses). All are superbly adapted to life in the water, with streamlined bodies, limbs modified into flippers, short but dense fur, and a thick layer of insulating blubber under the skin. True seals and sea lions differ in the way that they swim and walk. True seals are more streamlined and use their powerful hind flippers for propulsion and their small front flippers for steering. Although swift and acrobatic underwater, they are unable to walk on land and must shuffle along the ground on the belly. Sea lions use their strong front flippers for propulsion and steer with their hind flippers; on land they can support their weight with the front flippers and "walk" on all fours.

Seals and sea lions mainly eat fish and cephalopods (octopus, squid, and cuttlefish), which they outmaneuver underwater. In contrast, walruses grub around on the seafloor for clams, using their sensitive whiskers to locate the food in the muddy water. Pinnipeds usually breed in the spring, on land or on ice. Many species gather in large colonial breeding sites called *rookeries*, where males may battle with each other for possession of harems of fertile females. In some species, such as elephant seals, the males are much larger than females and engage in bloody fights over mates.

Sea otters (*Enhydra lutris*) are members of the family Mustelidae, which also includes weasels, mink, wolverines, and badgers. Sea otters are animals that live in kelp beds of the north Pacific and are one of the few mammal species that has acquired a knack for using tools. After finding a clam or mussel on the seafloor, a sea otter will float on the surface on its back, place the catch carefully on its stomach, and use a flat stone to smash the prey open. The common or Eurasian otter (*Lutra lutra*) inhabits rivers as well as coastal habitats and is found in North America as well as in Europe and Asia.

Polar bears (*Ursus maritimus*) are equally at home exploring pack ice in the Arctic or swimming through freezing waters, or under the ice, and they are sometimes seen miles out to sea. Their main prey are seals, but they also eat fish, seaweed, birds, and caribou, and will scavenge at whale carcasses when the opportunity arises.

Ben Morgan

FURTHER READING

Bonner, Nigel W. *Seals and Sea Lions of the World.* New York: Facts On File, 1994.

Macdonald, David. *The Encyclopaedia of Mammals.* London: Unwin Hyman, 1989.

Miller, David. *Seals and Sea Lions.* Stillwater, Minn.: Voyageur Press, 1998.

Riedman, Marianne. *The Pinnipeds: Seals, Sea Lions, and Walruses.* Berkeley: University of California Press, 1990.

RELATED ARTICLES

Pinnipedia; Seal; Sea Lion; Walrus

Carrageenan

Carrageenan is the term for a family of polysaccharides extracted from several species of red seaweed, most commonly from the species *Chondrus crispus*, also known as *Irish moss*. Valued for its ability to form a large variety of gels when added to water, carrageenan enhances the quality of many processed foods and improves the texture of cosmetics and medicines. The three main types of carrageenans—kappa (κ), iota (ι), and lambda (λ)—each have unique properties. κ-carrageenan makes rigid gels, ι-carrageenan produces more pliable gels, and λ-carrageenan does not gel in water but interacts with proteins to stabilize dairy products.

The addition of carrageenan to commercial food products such as sauces, salad dressings, and dips adds viscosity, or in the case of ice cream, creates a smoother texture by preventing the formation of ice crystals. Most of the carrageenan used in the food industry makes its way into dairy or meat products. In dairy products it stabilizes emulsions, which keeps the products from separating, melting, or precipitating. In meat products, including pet food, it enhances juiciness by increasing the water-holding capacity of the meat. The most common application for carrageenan in the cosmetics industry is in toothpaste, where it improves texture and forms an emulsion.

Researchers are currently investigating the potential use of carrageenan in newly developed contraceptives that may be able to prevent an unwanted pregnancy and simultaneously protect against human immunodeficiency virus (HIV) and other sexually transmitted diseases. Scientists have found that carrageenan helps these products bind the surface of the HIV virus, making it harder for it to adhere to cells and infect them.

The industrial production of carrageenan began in the 1940s, when the spread of convenience foods created a growing need for food additives that would ensure the quality of taste and texture that people had come to expect. In 1961 it was approved by the U.S. Food and Drug Administration for use as an emulsifier, stabilizer, and thickener in food. In recent years the demand for carrageenan has continued to rise steadily by about 5 percent per year, reaching a worldwide demand of 20,000 tonnes per year.

Sonya Wainwright

FURTHER READING
Levring, Tore, Heinz Hoppe, and Otto Schmidt. *Marine Algae: A Survey of Research and Utilization.* Hamburg, Germany: Cram, De Gruyter and Co., 1969.

Trainor, Francis Rice. *Introductory Phycology.* New York: Wiley, 1978.

USEFUL WEB SITES
"An Introduction to Carrageenan." <http://www.philexport.org/members/siap/intro.htm>.

RELATED ARTICLES
Algae; Algin; Irish Moss

Carson, Rachel Louise
1907–1964
American Marine Biologist and Naturalist

Rachael Carson was an aquatic biologist, marine zoologist, naturalist, and best-selling author. She is best known for her book *Silent Spring*, first published in 1962 and republished many times since. The book helped alert the public and government to the dangers arising from the overuse of synthetic pesticides, especially DDT (dichloro-diphenyltrichloroethane). In the United States, the message of *Silent Spring* contributed to the formation of a public environmental awareness that made ecological issues part of mainstream political discussion.

Silent Spring was the culmination of a lifetime dedicated to aquatic and marine research and to writing about nature and conservation. Rachel Louise Carson was born 27 May 1907 in Spring Dale, Pennsylvania. Starting her undergraduate studies at the Pennsylvania College for Women in 1925, Carson studied English before changing her major to biology. She graduated magna cum laude in 1929 and went on to a summer research fellowship at the Marine Biological Laboratory in Woods Hole, Massachusetts. In the autumn of the same year, she began graduate studies at Johns Hopkins University, which she completed with a master of arts degree in marine zoology in 1932. Carson taught at the University of Maryland, College Park, and Johns Hopkins University. She joined the U.S. Bureau of Fisheries in 1936 as a junior aquatic

Rachel Carson. (© Bettmann/Corbis)

biologist. (The Bureau of Fisheries became the Fish and Wildlife Service in 1940.) While working at the Bureau of Fisheries, Carson began publishing articles on nature and conservation in the *Baltimore Sun*. In 1948 she was named editor-in-chief of the Fish and Wildlife Information Division. She resigned from government service in 1952 to pursue an already successful writing career.

An article in the *Atlantic Monthly* in 1937 was the basis for her first book, *Under the Sea Wind* (1941). Her second book, *The Sea around Us* (1951), won a National Book Award and became a national best-seller. A third book, *The Edge of the Sea* (1955), also enjoyed considerable popularity. Carson started writing her most famous book, *Silent Spring,* in 1958, although it had been conceived as early as 1947. *Silent Spring* appeared as a serial in the *New Yorker* in June and July of 1962, before being published as a book in September of that year.

All three of Carson's books on the ocean examined the relationship between life and the sea.

The narrative of each work explores similar ideas and themes: the life cycle of sea-dwelling creatures, the relationship between the ocean's physical environment and ocean life, and the interrelationships between life on land and life in the sea. In *Under the Sea Wind*, Carson examines the relationship between the life cycle of birds and fish and ocean winds and currents. Similarly, the *Sea around Us* looks at the cyclic relationship between land and sea, especially the ocean processes that create and erode land and influence world climate patterns. *The Edge of the Sea* offers an account of life at the edge of the ocean and the means by which creatures survive in the harsh environment created where land meets ocean tides, surf, and currents.

The title of *Silent Spring* is taken from the grim fable that opens the book. The fable describes a town that, because of the indiscriminate spraying of pesticides, is confronted with a barren spring, devoid of singing birds, hatchlings, fish, and insects. After that ominous forecast, the book provides a scientific account in lay language of the growing body of scientific evidence that pointed to the ill effects of the overuse of pesticides. Carson criticizes the wide use of DDT and other chlorinated organic insecticides, including aldrin, dieldrin, chlordane, and heptachlor, as well as the broad use of organic phosphate insecticides, such as parathion and malathion. Not only do many pesticides persist in the environment without completely degrading for up to 20 years, but they also accumulate in the fat tissues of birds, fish, and land animals. This means that grazing and foraging animals absorb and retain pesticide residues by eating plant matter, while animals higher in the food chain absorb and retain pesticide residues by eating their prey. A buildup of pesticide residue in an animal can result in a number of toxic effects that may lead to organ damage, causing birth defects, sterility, or death. Carson's most contentious claim was that DDT and other insecticides posed similar threats to humans. To prevent all these problems, she strongly advocated a more judicious use of pesticides and alternative methods of pest control.

Silent Spring is sometimes credited with creating a public outcry that resulted in federal and state governments placing restrictions on the use of DDT and other pesticides between 1962 and 1970. This is true only in part. The ill effects of DDT and other pesticides had been well documented in scientific literature before 1962, and this had already generated some public attention. In addition, the then recent identification of thalidomide as a cause of severe birth defects in infants had already made the U.S. public sensitive to the unanticipated dangers of human-made chemicals.

However, *Silent Spring* did help to give expression to growing public concern about human-made chemicals. In response, professional associations representing chemists and the companies manufacturing pesticides, including the Manufacturing Chemists Association, the National Agricultural Chemicals Association, the Velsicol Chemical Corporation, and the Monsanto Chemical Company, questioned the book's scientific claims and Carson's scientific credibility. President John F. Kennedy responded by requesting that the Science Advisory Committee investigate the extent and implications of pesticide use in the United States. The committee's report, released on 15 May 1963, vindicated Carson's research in *Silent Spring* and recommended new policies governing the adoption and use of agricultural pesticides.

The ongoing popularity of Carson's writing may be attributed to her elegant literary style, which readers find compelling, as well as her scientific accuracy, which detractors found impossible to fault. By virtue of being enormously popular, Carson's books helped promote public understanding of principles of natural conservation, as well as public awareness of the deleterious effects of human activities on the natural environment.

Jay Foster

BIOGRAPHY

- Rachel Louise Carson.
- Born on 27 May 1907 in Spring Dale, Pennsylvania.
- Daughter of Robert Warden Carson and Maria Frazier McLean.
- Early education at Springdale Grammar School, Springdale High School, and Parnassus High School.
- Graduated from high school in 1925, and in the same year entered Pennsylvania College for Women (now Chatham College) on scholarship.
- Began studies in English but two years later changed her major to biology.
- Received her bachelor of arts degree, magna cum laude, in biology in 1929.
- Held a summer fellowship at the Marine Biological Laboratory in Woods Hole, Massachusetts.
- Began graduate studies in marine zoology at Johns Hopkins University in 1929, for which she received a master of arts degree in 1932.
- Worked as an aquatic biologist with the U.S. Bureau of Fisheries (later the U.S. Fish and Wildlife Service) from 1936 to 1952.
- The last three years of service were as the editor-in-chief of the Information Division's publications.
- Received the Distinguished Service Award of the Department of the Interior after retirement from the service.
- For literary and scientific work, received a National Audubon Society Medal, an American Geographical Society Medal, and was elected to the American Academy of Arts and Letters.
- Died 14 April 1964 in Silver Spring, Maryland. Posthumously awarded the President's Medal of Freedom.

SELECTED WRITINGS

Carson, Rachel. *Under the Sea Wind*. New York: Dutton, 1941.

———. *The Sea around Us*. New York: Oxford University Press, 1951; rev. ed., 1961.

———. *The Edge of the Sea*. New York: Houghton Mifflin, 1955.

———. *Silent Spring*. Boston: Houghton Mifflin, 1962.

FURTHER READING

Brooks, Paul. *The House of Life: Rachel Carson at Work*. Boston: Houghton Mifflin, 1972.

Gartner, Carol B. *Rachel Carson*. New York: Frederick Ungar, 1983.

Hynes, H. Patricia. *The Recurring Silent Spring.* New York: Pergamon Press, 1989.

McCay, Mary A. *Rachel Carson.* New York: Twayne/ Toronto: Maxwell Macmillan Canada, 1993.

Waddell, Craig, ed. *And No Birds Sing: Rhetorical Analyses of Rachel Carson's* Silent Spring. Carbondale: Southern Illinois University Press, 2000.

RELATED ARTICLES
DDT; Food Chain; Pollution, Ocean

Cascadia

The name *Cascadia* has been used by Earth scientists to describe both the Cascade Mountains and mountain building and volcanic events that occurred during the past 35 to 40 million years in the Pacific Northwest (Cascadia orogeny). *Cascadia* was also the name given to a mythical offshore landmass that supposedly lay in the northeastern Pacific Ocean immediately beyond the present edge of the continent. *Cascadia* now refers to a large region in the northwestern United States and southwestern Canada that is affected by the Cascadia subduction zone. The Cascadia subduction zone is a tectonically dynamic region that spawns menacing geologic hazards in the Pacific Northwest. Large-magnitude earthquakes, volcanic eruptions, landslides on steep sides of volcanoes, and tsunamis all threaten the well-being of millions of people.

Cascadia incorporates three ocean plates (Gorda, Juan de Fuca, and Explorer Plates), part of the continental North American Plate, a subduction zone (the Cascadia subduction zone), a volcanic arc (Cascade volcanoes), and some accreted terranes (e.g., the Olympic Mountains of western Washington). Cascadia has distinct boundaries on the seafloor, but the continental boundaries are not as well defined. Cascadia is bounded on the south by the Mendocino Fracture Zone and a northeast projection from its intersection with the California coastline to a point just east of Mt. Lassen in California. On the west, Cascadia is bounded from south to north by the Gorda Ridge, Blanco Fracture Zone, Juan de Fuca Ridge, and Explorer Ridge. Cascadia's northern boundary is the eastward onshore extension of Explorer Ridge, thence down the eastern side of the Cascade Mountains at about 120°W longitude.

The three small plates being subducted within the Cascadia subduction zone are remnants of a much larger plate, the Farallon Plate, which has been essentially swallowed beneath North America. The Gorda Plate on the south is separated from the Juan de Fuca Plate by the Blanco Fracture Zone, and the Juan de Fuca Plate, the largest of the three, is separated from the Explorer Plate by the Nootka fault zone. The Explorer Ridge is offset several times by small transform faults and then collides with the Queen Charlotte strike-slip fault along the continental margin at about 50°N latitude.

Cascadia is drawing the attention of scientists because of potential geologic hazards. In 1700, the Cascadia subduction zone experienced a large earthquake, perhaps as large as a magnitude 9.0 according to tsunami records in Japan and geologic data from along the Oregon and Washington coasts. No earthquakes of that magnitude have occurred since then, nor have earthquakes occurred along the subducting slab in the last 60 or so years since seismographs have been used to measure them. The subduction zone is locked and another large earthquake is expected. Scientists just do not know when it will occur.

Volcanoes pose a threat in Cascadia. Mt. Baker, Mt. Rainier, Mt. St. Helens, Mt. Hood, and Mt. Lassen have all erupted since records began early in the nineteenth century. The eruption of Mt. St. Helens in 1980 was a wake-up call for preparation. More than 60 people lost their lives and property damage totaled many millions of dollars. Potential landslides on all volcanoes pose a great danger to the populace, particularly around Mt. Rainier, where housing developments and commercial properties are sited on ancient landslides and debris flows that cascaded off Mt. Rainier in the past. For those living along the coast, tsunamis also pose a threat after large-magnitude earthquakes.

Tracy L. Vallier

FURTHER READING

Hyndman, Roy D. "Giant Earthquakes of the Pacific Northwest." *Scientific American*, December 1995.

McCaffrey, Robert, and Chris Goldfinger. "Forearc Deformation and Great Subduction Earthquakes: Implications for Cascadia Offshore Earthquake Potential." *Science*, Vol. 267 (1995), pp. 856–858.

McKee, Bates. *Cascadia: The Geologic Evolution of the Pacific Northwest.* New York: McGraw-Hill, 1972.

Orr, Elizabeth L., and William N. Orr. *Geology of the Pacific Northwest.* New York: McGraw-Hill, 1996.

RELATED ARTICLES

Explorer Plate; Farallon Plate; Gorda Plate; Juan de Fuca Plate; Juan de Fuca Ridge; Pacific Ocean; Subduction Zone; Terrane

Cascadia Deep-Sea Channel

Cascadia deep-sea channel is located off the coast of Oregon and Washington. This submarine drainage network is one of the ocean's more unusual products of sedimentation by turbidity currents.

The architecture of Cascadia channel is similar to that of an underwater river, meandering across the abyssal floor for a total distance of nearly 2000 kilometers (1240 miles). The flat channel bottom (thalweg) is from 600 to 3500 meters (1970 to 11,500 feet) across; constructional levees rise 40 to 300 meters (130 to 985 feet) above the thalweg. Deep-sea terrigenous sediments originate mostly from the Columbia River and the Strait of Juan de Fuca. At first, turbidity currents funnel through Willapa, Grays, Quinault, and Juan de Fuca submarine canyons. These canyons incise the Cascadia accretionary prism (North America Plate) and merge downslope into a coalescing network of tributary channels. The main channel hooks south across the Juan de Fuca Plate to its confluence with Vancouver valley before running into the Blanco Fracture Zone. At that point, Cascadia channel makes an abrupt right-hand turn of nearly 120° and flows west onto Tuffs Abyssal Plain (Pacific Plate). The complete transport path therefore crosses three lithospheric plates.

Cascadia channel was more active during the last glacial period, when sea level was approximately 130 meters (425 feet) below what we see today. A unique layer of sediment, the Mazama ash bed, provides a marker horizon for stratigraphic correlation. Gigantic volumes of volcanic ash were swept into the ocean after the violent explosion of what we now call Crater Lake, located in Oregon. Scientists believe that large earthquakes triggered 13 turbidity currents since the eruption, which occurred about 7000 years ago. Thus, investigations of sediments in Cascadia deep-sea channel help seismologists shed light on the potential for destructive earthquakes in the Pacific Northwest.

Michael B. Underwood

FURTHER READING

Adams, John. "Great Earthquakes Recorded by Turbidites Off the Oregon–Washington Coast." In Albert M. Rogers, Timothy J. Walsh, William J. Kockelman, and George R. Priest, eds., *Assessing Earthquake Hazards and Reducing Risk in the Pacific Northwest.* USGS Professional Paper, No. 1560. Washington D.C.: U.S. Geological Survey, 1996; pp. 147–158.

Griggs, G. B., A. G. Carey, and L. D. Kulm. "Deep-Sea Sedimentation and Sediment–Fauna Interaction in Cascadia Channel and on Cascadia Abyssal Plain." *Deep-Sea Research*, Vol. 16 (1969), pp. 157–170.

Griggs, G. B., and L. D. Kulm. "Sedimentation in Cascadia Deep-Sea Channel." *Geological Society of America Bulletin*, Vol. 81 (1970), pp. 1361–1384.

Hampton, M. A., H. A. Karl, and N. H. Kenyon. "Sea-Floor Drainage Features of Cascadia Basin and the Adjacent Continental Slope, Northeast Pacific Ocean." *Marine Geology*, Vol. 87 (1989), pp. 249–272.

RELATED ARTICLES

Accretionary Prism; Cascadia; Deep-Sea Channel; Deep-Sea Sediment; Submarine Canyon; Turbidity Current

Caspian Sea

The Caspian Sea is the world's largest inland sea. It covers about 386,400 square kilometers (149,200 square miles). The sea is about 1200 kilometers (750 miles) from north to south, but from east to west it is much narrower, averaging only about 320 kilometers (200 miles) across. The Caspian Sea is located between 37 and 48° N latitude and 47 and 55°E longitude. Several former republics of the Soviet Union surround the Caspian. On the west lie Russia and Azerbaijan (the nation's capital, Baku, is located on the Caspian coast), to the north and east is Kazakstan, and to the east lies Turkmenistan. The sea is bordered on the south by Iran, the only country bordering the Caspian Sea that was never part of the Soviet Union.

The Caspian Sea is essentially an enormous lake—water that flows into the sea does not flow out into the ocean, although until about 18,000 years ago the Caspian Sea was a much larger body of water that connected to the ocean via the Black Sea to the west. Most of the water in the Caspian Sea comes from the Volga, Ural, and Terek Rivers, all of which flow into the sea from the north. As a result, the sea's water is almost fresh in the north but becomes quite saline to the south, and the sea contains both freshwater and saltwater fish.

The surface of the Caspian Sea is about 27 meters (89 feet) below sea level. The water level has fluctuated greatly over the centuries, depending mainly on the flow of the Volga. Water from the Volga has often been diverted for use in agriculture and industry upstream; that diversion, combined with warm weather, contributed to a 3-meter (9.8-foot) drop in the level of the Caspian Sea from 1929 to 1977. The drop left coastal fishing villages far from water and decimated the sea's sturgeon population, the source of Russia's famed caviar. In an attempt to boost the sea level, Soviet engineers in 1980 dammed off the Kara-Bogaz-Gol Gulf, formerly a large bay located in what is now Turkmenistan. Those efforts, combined with rainier and cooler weather, resulted in the Caspian regaining some 2 meters (6.5 feet) in its water level.

The Caspian Sea is of particular interest in modern times because it lies atop potentially huge oil and natural gas reserves. The region has always been oil-rich—Italian explorer Marco Polo reported in the thirteenth century that residents of Baku dug onshore oil wells by hand and used the liquid as fuel and for ointments. But the collapse of the Soviet Union in the early 1990s opened the area to Western oil firms and has set off an intense and ongoing round of international jockeying for access to the undersea riches.

Mary Sisson

FURTHER READING

Amirahmadi, Hooshang, ed. *The Caspian Region at a Crossroads: Challenges of a New Frontier of Energy and Development.* New York: St. Martin's Press, 2000.

Croissant, Michael P., and Bülent Aras, eds. *Oil and Geopolitics in the Caspian Sea Region.* Westport, Conn.: Praeger, 1999.

Cullen, Robert. "The Rise and Fall of the Caspian Sea." *National Geographic*, Vol. 195, No. 5 (1999), pp. 2–35.

Rodionov, Sergei N. *Global and Regional Climate Interaction: The Caspian Sea Experience.* Boston: Kluwer Academic, 1994.

RELATED ARTICLES

Black Sea; Petroleum

Central Rift Valley, see Mid-Ocean Ridge

Cephalaspidomorphi

The Cephalaspidomorphi (from the Greek *kephale*, head; *aspidos*, shield; and *morphe*, form) is regarded, as in Joseph S. Nelson's *Fishes of the World* (1994), as a class within the superclass

Agnatha (agnathans or jawless fishes). It comprises the extinct orders Anaspidiformes, Galeaspidiformes, and Cephalaspidiformes, and the extant order Petromyzontiformes (including the 41 described species of living lampreys). The extinct orders date between the Silurian and Devonian Periods (439 to 362.5 million years ago), with most fossils from freshwater deposits. Galeaspidiforms and cephalaspidiforms feature a bony shield covering the head region, hence the name given to the class as a whole.

Lampreys are superficially similar to hagfishes (superclass Agnatha, class Myxini). Both are slimy, eel-like, and are without jaws, scales, and paired fins. However, the two groups differ anatomically and physiologically; for example, lampreys have vertebrae, hagfishes do not. Due to these structural differences, the taxonomic relationships between these groups have recently come under increased scrutiny, and recent work has suggested that the lampreys are more closely related to jawed fishes than to hagfishes.

In adult lampreys, the single nostril is used solely for smell and has no connection with the gills. Respiratory water enters and exits through seven pairs of gill openings. Adult lampreys have two eyes, with a third light-sensitive organ, the pineal eye, situated between them. The adult lamprey's head is armed with a ventral sucker (oral disk) bearing numerous teeth, which it uses to attach to the surface of its host or prey.

Most lamprey species are parasitic or predatory as adults, with many predatory species believed to be derived from parasitic ones. A lamprey uses its toothed tongue to rasp at the flesh of its host—commonly a teleost fish—to draw blood and break down tissues that the lamprey consumes. Lampreys release anticoagulants to maintain the flow of blood. After release, the victim may die from fluid loss or wound infection. In some species, adults are nonpredaceous: They have a degenerate alimentary canal and do not feed at all. They live for a few months before spawning and dying.

Lampreys have a scattered distribution in temperate and subtropical regions, with most species (subfamily Petromyzontinae) found in the northern hemisphere and only four species in the southern (subfamilies Geotriinae and Mordaciinae). Lampreys are absent from tropical and high polar regions. Some lampreys are anadramous (spawning in fresh water and maturing in the sea), while others, such as the three species of *Icthyomyzon* found in the United States, spend their entire lives in fresh water. Both modes of life sometimes occur within the same species. In the United States, the marine lamprey, *Petromyzon marinus*, exists in both anadramous and land-locked forms.

Lampreys spawn in the gravel-bottomed shallows of streams and rivers. A male constructs an oval nest depression. At spawning, the female attaches her oral disk to the upstream side of the nest. The male attaches his oral disk to the side of her head, and wraps around her body. As she lays eggs, the male fertilizes them. The sticky eggs adhere to pebbles in the nest and soon become covered in loose sand and debris. Typically, the adults die after spawning.

The number of eggs released by a female ranges from 1000 to 200,000 or more, depending on the species. The eggs hatch into small larvae, called *ammocoetes*, which stay in the nest until they reach about 1 centimeter (0.4 inch) long. Older ammocoetes burrow in the substrate during the day and emerge at night to feed on algae, detritus, and microbes filtered from the water. The larval phase is extended, from 3 to 17 years, depending on species and situation. The larvae metamorphose into adults over a few months.

The inadvertent introduction of sea lampreys, *Petromyzon marinus*, into the North American Great Lakes led to the catastrophic collapse of some local fisheries between the 1920s and 1950s. Poisoning of the ammocoete larvae, and more recently, release of sterile adults in spawning areas, were introduced as control measures, and restocking programs have helped to reestablish traditional fish stocks.

Trevor Day

FURTHER READING
Hardisty, M. W. *Biology of Cyclostomes.* London: Chapman and Hall, 1979.
Long, J. A. *The Rise of Fishes: 500 Million Years of Evolution.* Baltimore: Johns Hopkins University Press, 1995.
Moyle, Peter B., and Joseph J. Cech. *Fishes: An Introduction to Ichthyology,* 4th ed. Upper Saddle River, N.J.: Prentice Hall, 1999.
Nelson, Joseph S. *Fishes of the World.* Upper Saddle River, N.J.: Prentice Hall, 1982; 4th ed., 2000.
Paxton, John R., and William N. Eschmeyer, eds. *Encyclopedia of Fishes,* 2nd ed. San Diego: Academic Press, 1998.

RELATED ARTICLES
Agnatha; Gnathostomata; Myxini; Parasitism; Pteraspidomorphi

Cephalocarida

The class Cephalocarida (subphylum Crustacea) includes only four genera and nine species of tiny marine benthic crustaceans ranging in size from 2.0 to 3.7 millimeters (0.08 to 0.15 inch) in length. They are considered to be among the more primitive of the Crustacea and are characterized by having a body with a head followed by a thorax of eight segments and an abdomen of 11 segments terminating in an anal segment that bears caudal rami. The head is covered by a head shield. Seven of the eight thoracic segments support flattened, biramous appendages that are used both in locomotion and in feeding on bottom detritus. The eighth segment may or may not have appendages. The abdomen lacks appendages. There is a lack of knowledge of the internal anatomy, and mating has never been observed. However, the animals are known to be hermaphroditic and some brood their eggs. The developmental sequence is known for two of the

species, and in both cases they go through a series of larval and juvenile stages before becoming adults. The life span is unknown.

James W. Nybakken

FURTHER READING
Brusca, Richard C., and Gary J. Brusca. *Invertebrates.* Sunderland, Mass.: Sinauer Associates, 1990.
Schram, F. R. *Crustacea.* New York: Oxford University Press, 1986.

RELATED ARTICLES
Crustacea

Cephalopoda

Squids, octopuses, cuttlefish, and nautiluses make up the class Cephalopoda, one of seven subdivisions of the phylum Mollusca. Although close cousins of the slow-moving slugs and snails, the cephalopods are highly mobile predators, with streamlined bodies capable of sudden movement and a head surrounded by long, muscular arms and tentacles for seizing prey. As well as being among the fastest swimmers of the invertebrate world, they include the largest invertebrates. The giant squid (*Architeuthis* sp.) can reach an incredible 18 meters (59 feet) in length and has eyes larger than a car's headlights. The giant squid has never been seen alive in its natural habitat. Cephalopods are also thought to be the most intelligent invertebrates, with a highly developed brain and nervous system.

Many octopuses hide in crevices during the day and can squeeze their long and flexible bodies through surprisingly tiny holes to escape from danger. When they emerge to feed they use their huge eyes and superb vision to locate prey. Octopuses and squids are highly effective hunters. Like all cephalopods, they move by jet propulsion, squirting a powerful jet of water out of a muscular structure called a *siphon*, which can be directed either forward or backward, thus jetting the animal through the water. The tentacles are covered with suckers to hold on to slippery victims, and serve as touch and taste sensors that indicate whether food is edible. Cephalopods have a sharp parrotlike beak for tearing prey apart, and they have little trouble dismembering even well-protected animals such as crabs. Like other mollusks, they have a toothed structure in the mouth called the *radula* that scrapes food into the mouth.

Because cephalopods have such a good sense of vision, they use visual signals to communicate. Male squids, for instance, can change their color and body patterns rapidly to attract females or to display aggression to rival males. Some cephalopods also change color to startle attackers or to blend into their surroundings. These spectacular color changes are made possible by hundreds of tiny pockets of pigment, called *chromatophores*, embedded in the skin. Each chromatophore sac is connected to a set of muscles that can open or close the sac to make the pigment visible. Some species, such as the fire squid (*Lycoteuthis* sp.), are bioluminescent, producing flashes of light to communicate in darkness.

The 650 or so species of cephalopods are split into two subclasses: Coleoidea (squids, octopuses, and cuttlefish) and Nautiloidea (nautiluses). Members of the Coleoidea can be recognized by their number of arms and tentacles and the presence or lack of an internal shell. Octopuses have eight arms, no tentacles, and no internal shell; squids have a small internal shell, eight arms, and two tentacles; and cuttlefish have eight arms, two tentacles, and a large internal shell containing air spaces for buoyancy. Cuttlefish are also shorter than octopuses or squids and cannot swim as quickly. Octopuses usually live near the coast in rocky habitats or coral reefs; squids inhabit the open ocean, sometimes at great depth; and cuttlefish live mainly on the continental shelf.

The four to six species of nautiluses have an external, plano spiral-shaped shell for protection. As they grow they add new chambers to the shell, and the inner chambers contain air for buoyancy. Nautiluses live in deep water of the continental shelf near the bottom and are thought to be close relatives of ammonites, prehistoric cephalopods whose distinctive spiral shells are among the most common fossils dating from the age of the dinosaurs.

Ben Morgan

FURTHER READING
Banister, Keith, and Andrew Campbell. *The Encyclopaedia of Underwater Life*. London: Allen and Unwin, 1985.
Barnes, Robert. *Invertebrate Zoology*. Philadelphia: Saunders, 1963; 6th ed., by Edward Ruppert, Fort Worth, Texas: Saunders, 1994.
Brusca, Richard C., and Gary J. Brusca. *Invertebrates*. Sunderland, Mass.: Sinauer, 1990.
Pechenik, Jan A. *Biology of the Invertebrates*. Boston: Prindle, Weber and Schmidt, 1985; 4th ed., Boston: McGraw-Hill, 2000.

RELATED ARTICLES
Bioluminescence; Crustacea; Mollusca; Nautilus

Cetacea

The order Cetacea includes the toothed whales (suborder Odontoceti) and the baleen whales (suborder Mysticeti), both marine mammals that are highly evolved for aquatic life. The cetaceans are streamlined, similar to fishes, which reduces hydrodynamic drag. The cetaceans have gone through an evolutionary reconfiguring of the skull called *telescoping*, where the premaxillary and maxillary bones of the snout have become elongated, effectively moving the air passage, or blowhole(s), to the top of the head. This enables them to come to the surface in a more horizontal position as they breathe; therefore, they simply roll along at the surface with the top of the head and back barely breaking the water's surface. They have become streamlined by internalizing most of the reproductive organs, having smooth skin with no hair or limited amounts, only paddlelike front limbs, and no hind limbs. Two innominate bones, which support the reproductive organs internally, are all that remain of the pelvic region after a 50-million-year evolution from their ancestral land carnivores. Most cetaceans have a dorsal fin that helps stabilize the animal as it swims and powerful, horizontally flattened flukes that propel them. The flukes move up and down by large muscles that attach to the top and bottom of the caudal peduncle (tail stock).

Cetaceans give birth to only one calf after about one year of gestation. The mothers nurse the calf by forcibly ejecting the milk using muscles around the mammary glands. The calf is usually weaned in six to eight months, growing rapidly on the high fat content of the milk. For instance, a blue whale calf can gain 90 kilograms (200 pounds) of mass per day, and in eight months grow from a birth length of 7 meters (23 feet) to 15 meters (49 feet).

The large baleen whales, which feed on krill, copepods, and fishes, may migrate great distances between the feeding and calving/breeding areas. Many of the smaller toothed whales, which eat fishes and squids, may also migrate, but shorter distances than the baleen whales. Many cetacean populations are in poor shape because of overharvesting in the past or from disturbance or pollution associated with their habitat. Baleen and sperm whales (the largest toothed whale) were hunted throughout the world's oceans, in many cases bringing the populations to critically low levels. Although now protected in certain areas, many populations still have not recovered.

Jim Harvey

FURTHER READING

Berta, A., and J. L. Sumich. *Marine Mammals: Evolutionary Biology.* San Diego: Academic Press, 1999.

Haley, Delphine, ed. *Marine Mammals of Eastern North Pacific and Arctic Waters,* 2nd rev. ed. Seattle, Wash.: Pacific Search Press, 1986.

Leatherwood, Stephen, and Randall R. Reeves. *The Sierra Club Handbook of Whales and Dolphins.* San Francicso: Sierra Club Books, 1983.

Pryor, K., and K. S. Norris, eds. *Dolphin Societies: Discoveries and Puzzles.* Berkeley: University of California Press, 1991.

Slijper, E. J. *Whales.* Translated by A. J. Pomerans. New York: Basic Books, 1962.

RELATED ARTICLES
Blubber; Echolocation; Mysticeti; Odontoceti

Chaetognatha

The phylum Chaetognatha contains about 50 species of creatures that are more commonly known as arrow worms. Although Chaetognatha is categorized in the animal kingdom, their development in the evolutionary line is unclear. But they are believed to have some relation to echinoderms and chordates. Chaetognaths have transparent to

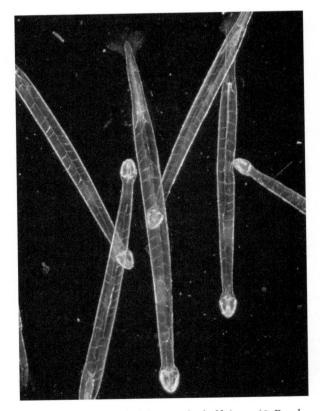

Arrow worms magnified three and a half times. (© Frank Lane Picture Agency/Corbis)

opaque elongated, laterally flattened bodies and can range in size from 3 to 100 millimeters (0.1 to 4 inches) long. They are exclusively marine creatures, live throughout the water column, and constitute an important part of plankton.

All chaetognaths are ravenous predators, consuming primarily small crustaceans, other chaetognaths, and small fishes. They detect prey using vibration receptors and swim in quick motions by contracting the longitudinal muscles in their lengthy bodies. (Chaetognaths also have fins, which they use to keep themselves from sinking while at rest.) They grab their prey with hooklike spines held in special sacs in their heads, then hold their prey with their spines while secreting a toxin that serves to immobilize the prey. The prey is ingested whole and chaetognaths are such voracious feeders that they sometimes wipe out plankton populations by consuming all the available food.

Chaetognaths are also hermaphroditic, and each individual chaetognath produces both sperm and eggs. Some chaetognath species cross-fertilize, but others self-fertilize. The fertilized eggs are discharged into the water by some species, while in others the fertilized eggs are carried by the adult until maturity.

Mary Sisson

FURTHER READING

Bone, Q., H. Kapps, and A. C. Pierrot-Bults. *The Biology of Chaetognaths.* Oxford and New York: Oxford University Press, 1991.
Guglielmo, L., and A. Ianora. *Atlas of Marine Zooplankton, Straits of Magellan: Amphipods, Euphausiids, Mysids, Ostracods, and Chaetognaths.* Berlin and New York: Springer-Verlag, 1995.

RELATED ARTICLES

Chordata; Echinodermata; Plankton

Chalk

Chalk is a special variety of pelagic rock that is intermediate between carbonate ooze and limestone and is a product of diagenesis (dissolution, reprecipitation, recrystallization, and compaction). The change occurs with increasing depth below the seafloor and time. Chalk is soft, generally white, earthy, and often porous and friable. Chalk usually forms in a marine environment and is composed of tests, or outer shells of floating, calcareous microorganisms. Coccolithophores (coccoliths) and other calcareous nannoplankton are the most prominent microorganisms found in chalk, but the remains of other pelagic organisms, much as foraminifera, and even some bottom dwellers, as well as nodules of chert and pyrite, may also be present.

Microorganisims die and settle through the water column. Their tests accumulate on the seafloor to form carbonate ooze. Beneath the seafloor, the volume of the ooze decreases due to dewatering, packing changes, and decreased porosity. The transformation of carbonate ooze to chalk generally occurs at a subbottom depth of about 100 meters (330 feet), whereas the transformation to limestone occurs at about 1 kilometer (3300 feet). Porosity of carbonate ooze is about 70 percent and reduces to about 10 percent for limestone. A volume reduction of about 30 percent accompanies the change from ooze to chalk to limestone. Reprecipitation of secondary calcite overgrowths begins when a grain-supporting framework has been established allowing calcite to precipitate along and around the microorganism. Recrystallization begins inside the microorganism's chambers, forming euhedral calcite crystals; the pore spaces are filled and the particles are bonded together by the calcite.

Chalk tends to form moderate to thick, well-bedded deposits in the pelagic realm that are particularly extensive in the late Cretaceous (about 90 to 65 million years ago) period. The best examples of Cretaceous chalk beds on land are in Normandy, France, and the white cliffs of Dover along the southeast coast of England. There are two depositional environments for chalk deposits in Normandy, France. One is a prolonged phase of quiet, low-energy deposition with some bioturbation that is associated with the flint and chert nodules. The other is a higher-energy environment suggested by the cross bedding, slump features, graded beds, and turbidity currents, indicating that bottom currents were active at the time of deposition and lithification. The depth range of the deposits that resulted in chalk formation in Normandy is between 100 meters and 600 meters (330 and 2000 feet) based on the flora and fauna associated with chalk. In present-day oceans, chalk forms from calcareous ooze that was deposited above the calcium carbonate compensation depth (CCD), the depth at which carbonate sediment disappears, which can reach depths of nearly 4000 meters (13,000 feet).

Chalk is formed primarily of coccolith material and is classified as a biomicrite. Coccoliths may form up to 80 percent of some chalk beds. The preservation of the coccolith plates is good, but they may easily be damaged by degradation and compaction during lithification and break into smaller fragments. Calcite overgrowths and recrystallization during diagenesis often obscure the plates. Dissolution of the plates occurs during transport to the bottom of the sea. Below 4 kilometers (2.5 miles), plates are dissolved completely, as the water is undersaturated in calcium carbonate.

Chalk is white if it contains more than 90 percent calcite. The most common impurities associated with chalk are the clays smectite and illite. Authigenic pyrite is sometimes present, as is hematite, which gives some chalk deposits a distinctive red color. Radiolaria, diatoms, and other siliceous organisms are incorporated in the bottom sediment and may be the source for silica nodules.

Mary White

FURTHER READING
Blatt, Harvey, Gerard Middleton, and Raymond Murray. *Origin of Sedimentary Rocks.* Englewood Cliffs, N.J.: Prentice Hall, 1972; 2nd ed., 1980.

Hatch, F. H., and R. H. Rastall. *The Petrology of the Sedimentary Rocks.* London: G. Allen, 1913; 7th ed., by J. T. Greensmith, London and Boston: Unwin Hyman, 1989.
Hutchinson, Charles S. *Economic Deposits and Their Tectonic Setting.* New York: Wiley, 1983.
Kennett, James P. *Marine Geology.* Englewood Cliffs, N.J.: Prentice Hall, 1982.
Williams, Howel, Francis J. Turner, and Charles M. Gilbert. *Petrography: An Introduction to the Study of Rocks in Thin Section.* San Francisco: W. H. Freeman, 1954; 2nd ed., 1982.

RELATED ARTICLES
Bioturbation; Calcium Carbonate Compensation Depth; Deep-Sea Sediment; Foraminifera; Pelagic; Plankton

Chelicerata

The best-known members of the subphylum Chelicerata (or Cheliceriformes) are spiders, scorpions, ticks, and mites. Most members of this large and successful group of arthropods live on land. However, two groups—horseshoe crabs and sea spiders—are exclusively marine.

Like other arthropods, chelicerates have segmented bodies covered by a jointed, external skeleton. But unlike most arthropods, they do not have a clearly separate head. Instead, the head and thorax form a combined structure called the *cephalothorax* (or *prosoma*). The rear part of the body is the *abdomen* (or *opisthosoma*). The cephalothorax typically bears two pairs of appendages flanking the mouth and four pairs of legs, but there are no antennae. The first pair of appendages next to the mouth are pincerlike structures called *chelicerae*. These are usually specialized for feeding, but their precise role varies among chelicerates. For example, spiders use their chelicerae as fangs to inject venom, while horseshoe crabs have grasping chelicerae to seize prey, and scorpions have small, grinding chelicerae for chewing.

Behind the chelicerae is the second pair of appendages, called *pedipalps*. These too serve a diverse range of functions, usually with a sensory role. They are often used as feelers for tasting and handling food. Adult male spiders have highly modified pedipalps that are used to transfer sperm to females. The large claws of scorpions are also modified pedipalps.

The subphylum Chelicerata is usually split into three classes: Arachnida (spiders, scorpions, ticks, and mites), Merostomata (horseshoe crabs and their prehistoric relatives), and Pycnogonida (sea spiders). However, some scientists do not consider sea spiders to be chelicerates and thus follow an alternative classification. According to the alternative system, the subphylum is known as Cheliceriformes and is split into just two classes: Pycnogonida (sea spiders) and Chelicerata (chelicerates).

The vast majority of arachnids live on land. However, some mites have adapted to aquatic habitats, including the sea. These tiny creatures can be found on sand, in seaweed, and on the seafloor up to great depths. Many are free living, but others are parasites of crustaceans, mollusks, and fish. Parasitic mites frequently have chelicerae modified to form a piercing *stylet*, which is used to suck blood from the host.

Members of the class Merostomata were most diverse and numerous hundreds of millions of years ago. Among the fossil species were spectacular "sea scorpions" that grew up to 3 meters (10 feet) long. Today, only five species remain, known as *horseshoe crabs* (although they are not crabs). The body of a horseshoe crab is covered by a rounded, flattened shell called a *carapace*, with a long tail spike, or *telson*, at the rear. Horseshoe crabs crawl along the seafloor in shallow waters in search of worms, mollusks, and other invertebrates, which they seize with their chelicerae and break up with spiny projections at the base of the legs. One of the best-known species is *Limulus polyphemus*, the common horseshoe crab, which is found on the Atlantic and Gulf coasts of North America.

Sea spiders are not true spiders, although their eight slender legs make them look similar to terrestrial spiders. Most are less than 1 centimeter (0.4 inch) long, but some deep-sea species have leg spans up to 70 centimeters (28 inches) across. The central part of the body is very thin and narrow. As a result, the intestine and internal reproductive organs extend into the legs. The legs are attached to lateral extensions of the central trunk, and the abdomen is greatly reduced. Sea spiders have a special extension of the body called a *proboscis*, which bears the terminal mouth and is used for sucking up food. Most are predators that use the proboscis to pierce the bodies of invertebrate prey and suck out their body fluids. However, some use their chelicerae to clip flesh off hydroids and pass it into the mouth, and others graze algae. There are around 1000 species of sea spiders. They are found from shallow waters to depths of 7 kilometers (4.3 miles).

Underside of a female horseshoe crab. (© Frank Lane Picture Agency/Corbis)

The sexes are separate in most chelicerates and reproduction often involves complex mating behavior. The female's eggs are usually fertilized either internally or as they are laid; free spawning never occurs. The eggs may be abandoned after laying or the female may brood them. In sea spiders the eggs are brooded by the male on special male appendages called *ovigers*. In many chelicerates the newly hatched young look like miniature adults, but there are exceptions. Some spiders hatch as six-legged "larvae" that become eight-legged only after molting. Horseshoe crabs hatch as euproöps larvae, which superficially resemble a trilobite. Some sea spiders produce unique protonymphon larvae, which live in close association with cnidarians, mollusks, or echinoderms. Little is known about this relationship, but it is probably either parasitic or commensal.

Ben Morgan

FURTHER READING

Brusca, Richard C., and Gary J. Brusca. *Invertebrates.* Sunderland, Mass.: Sinauer, 1990.

Nybakken, James W. *Marine Biology: An Ecological Approach,* 5th ed. San Francisco: Benjamin Cummings, 2001.

Pechenik, Jan A. *Biology of the Invertebrates.* Boston: Prindle, Weber and Schmidt, 1985; 4th ed., Boston: McGraw-Hill, 2000.

RELATED ARTICLES

Arthropoda; Horseshoe Crab; Pycnogonida

Chemical Tracer

Chemical tracers are substances whose movement through ocean water is tracked to provide information about various physical, chemical, and biological processes. For example, following the flow of radioactive chemicals present in the effluent from nuclear plants at Sellafield in England and Cap-de-la-Hague in France has provided a great deal of information about ocean circulation in the North Sea and the Norwegian–Greenland Seas.

A wide variety of chemicals have been used as tracers. A good tracer is a substance that is *conserved* (changed in concentration only by mixing), easily measured with high precision, present only in the water mass under study (and not in nearby masses), and nonpolluting. Naturally present in seawater, oxygen and salt make the simplest tracers, but because oxygen is removed from the water (e.g., by marine creatures), it is less than perfect. More precise studies use unusual tracer chemicals that enter the oceans in a variety of ways. Radioactive isotopes (unstable, radioactive forms of elements) such as cesium-137, strontium-90, and plutonium-239 or 240 have been introduced into the oceans by nuclear testing, nuclear power plant discharges, and accidents such as the nuclear explosion at Chernobyl in the Ukraine (former Soviet Union) in 1986. Other radioactive tracers, including carbon-14, tritium, and aluminum-26, are formed when cosmic rays strike Earth from space. Chlorofluorocarbons (CFCs), the chemicals implicated in the depletion of Earth's ozone layer, have been introduced into the atmosphere in large quantities, for example, through aerosol propellants and industrial processes. They make excellent tracers because they can be measured very sensitively and followed easily. Other tracers include silicates, phosphates, and sulfur hexafluoride (SF_6).

Tracers can be used in a variety of ways. It is relatively easy to measure the salinity (saltiness) and oxygen content of water in one place and use these tracers to track the same water as it moves elsewhere (e.g., from the surface of the ocean to the depths). Another method involves injecting a tracer such as sulfur hexafluoride into the ocean in one place and following its progress over weeks or months to provide information about current patterns.

Radioactive tracers and CFCs are known as *transient tracers* because their concentration in the atmosphere is constantly varying. Because atmospheric concentrations of CFCs, such as the refrigerant gas Freon (CFC-11), have varied in an observable way over recent decades, it is possible to measure their concentration in different areas of the oceans and calculate when those water masses were last at the ocean surface. This technique has recently been used in studies showing how global warming affects the deep ocean circulation. Radioactive tracers (sometimes known as radionuclides) can also be used to work out the timescales of ocean processes using a process similar to radiocarbon dating, the technique by which archaeologists date ancient organic matter.

Chemical tracers have greatly advanced our understanding of ocean processes. Notable experiments have included the early 1970s Geochemical Ocean Sections (GEOSECS) program, which pioneered the large-scale use of multiple tracers, and the 1980s Transient Tracers in the Ocean (TTO) study, which investigated ocean mixing through the movement of radioactive tracers introduced by nuclear bomb tests in the late 1950s and early 1960s. More recent studies, such as the World Ocean Circulation Experiments (WOCE), an ongoing global survey of the world's oceans, and the Joint Global Ocean Flux Study (JGOFS), an investigation of how biologically active elements such as carbon are exchanged between the atmosphere and the oceans, have also made extensive use of tracer studies.

Chris Woodford

FURTHER READING

Albarède, Francis. "Isotopic Tracers of Past Ocean Circulation: Turning Lead to Gold." *Science*, 15 August 1997, p. 908.

Broecker, Wallace S. "Chaotic Climate." *Scientific American*, November 1995, p. 44.

Von Blanckenburg, Friedhelm. "Tracing Past Ocean Circulation?" *Science*, 3 December 1999, p. 1862.

Woods, J. D. "The World Ocean Circulation Experiment." *Nature*, 11 April 1985, p. 501.

RELATED ARTICLES

Deep-Ocean Circulation; Pollution, Ocean; Radiometric Dating

Chemoautotrophic Bacteria

The term *chemoautotrophic* refers to organisms that use reduced inorganic compounds, primarily hydrogen sulfide, as an energy source to make organic matter from carbon dioxide rather than using light (as in photosynthesis) or consuming other organisms (heterotrophs). Bacteria are simple microorganisms that often act as decomposers, breaking down organic compounds into nutrients that can be used by other organisms. Bacteria may also be chemoautotrophic, serving as a primary source of energy in many unique assemblages and environments.

Some bacteria found near hydrothermal vents are chemoautotrophic and may serve as the base of a food chain, nourishing complex and diverse assemblages of animals. Hydrothermal vents, which release hot water [up to 350°C (662°F)] and reduced sulfur compounds, are located at tectonically active regions throughout the world. The vents located on the deep-sea floor [1500 to 3200 meters (4920 to 10,500 feet) deep] often contain a biomass so much greater than that of the surrounding areas that they are referred to as "oases" in otherwise barren "deserts."

Heterotrophic animals around hydrothermal vents can consume the chemoautotrophic bacteria directly by grazing or filter feeding. Some invertebrates around the vents, such as the vestimeniferan worm *Riftia pachyptila* and the clam *Calyptogena magnifica*, display a mutualistic symbiosis with chemoautotrophic bacteria. The animal host benefits because it receives energy in the form of organic compounds from the bacteria. The bacteria are protected, growing in cell "factories" in the gills of the clams, and in the transformed gut, or trophosome, of the vestimeniferan worm, where they are provided with the reduced compounds and oxygen they require. Symbiotic associations between chemoautotrophic bacteria and marine invertebrates are believed to occur in over 100 species from five different phyla.

Chemoautotrophic bacteria are also found around hot springs, shallow-water hydrothermal vents, and near recently discovered areas called *cold seeps*, which ooze reducing chemicals such as sulfides, methane, or other hydrocarbons at ambient seafloor temperatures. These cold seeps are not associated with heat-inducing tectonic activity; they release hydrocarbon-rich fluids pressurized by sediment squeezing, gas production, or hydrostatic processes. Massive carbonate structures are often produced by the hydrocarbon-consuming bacteria that generate high levels of alkalinity and dissolved inorganic carbon in pore fluids, resulting in supersaturation and subsequent deposition of carbonates. These cemented carbonate deposits stand out in sharp contrast to the flat, desolate surroundings and provide hard surfaces for diverse organisms to settle on and attach to.

Like the filamentous species of the genus *Beggiatoa*, chemoautotrophic bacteria are found in sulfur springs, organic-rich freshwater sediments, coastal marine sediments, salt marshes, and deep-sea hydrothermal vents. However, communities based on chemoautotrophic bacteria are not found only in marine and freshwater habitats. A limestone cave in Romania has been discovered where microbial mats containing chemoautotrophic bacteria grow in air pockets within thermal [21°C (69.8°F)] waters rich in hydrogen sulfide. These bacterial mats serve as the base of a food web supporting 48 species of cave-adapted terrestrial and aquatic invertebrates. Clearly, chemoautotrophic bacteria play an essential role in a diverse array of environments, providing a primary source of energy where photosynthesis is either absent or limited.

Matt Forrest

FURTHER READING

Cavanaugh, Colleen M. "Microbial Symbiosis: Patterns of Diversity in the Marine Environment." *American Zoologist*, Vol. 34 (1994), pp. 79–89.

Nybakken, James W. *Marine Biology: An Ecological Approach*, 5th ed. San Francisco: Benjamin Cummings, 2001.

Sarbu, S. M., T. C. Kane, and B. K. Kinkle. "A Chemoautotrophic Based Cave Ecosystem." *Science*, Vol. 272 (28 June 1996), pp. 1955–1957.

Southward, A. J. "Animal Communities Fueled by Chemosynthesis: Life at Hydrothermal Vents, Cold Seeps and in Reducing Sediments." *Journal of Zoology*, Vol. 217 (1989), pp. 705–709.

RELATED ARTICLES

Cold Seep; Food Chain; Heterotrophic; Hydrothermal Vent; Photosynthesis

Chemosynthesis

Chemosynthesis is a process by which organic materials are produced from carbon dioxide and water using the energy stored in the bonds of reduced compounds such as hydrogen sulfide and/or methane. Typically, most organisms derive their energy either directly or indirectly from photosynthesis. However, chemosynthetic bacteria that thrive in benthic sediments are able to utilize the energy found in methane and various reduced metallic compounds to affect the production of organic compounds from carbon dioxide and water. Some groups of these bacteria are well suited to conditions that are thought to have existed on Earth billions of years ago, leading some scientists to theorize that they are representative of ancient life forms.

Chemosynthetic bacteria are the primary producers of the food web in hydrothermal vent and cold seep ecosystems. Scientists in the research submersible *Alvin* first discovered hydrothermal vents near the Galápagos Islands in 1977. In terms of oceanic production, hydrothermal vents tend to support a high biomass of living organisms that are entirely dependent on the chemosynthetic bacteria. Associated fauna such as giant vestimentiferan tube worms, bristle worms, yellow mussels, clams, and many gastropod mollusks are among the animals found in these unique ecosystems. Levels of organic carbon 500 times the expected are associated with hydrothermal vents at 2500 meters (8200 feet) in depth near the Galápagos Islands.

Anne Beesley

FURTHER READING
Barnes, R. S. K., and R. N. Hughes. *An Introduction to Marine Ecology*. Oxford and Boston: Blackwell Scientific, 1982; 3rd ed., Oxford and Malden, Mass.: Blackwell Science, 1999.
Dawes, Clinton. *Marine Botany*. New York: Wiley, 1981; 2nd ed., 1998.
Gage, John D., and Paul A. Tyler. *Deep Sea Biology: A Natural History of Organisms at the Deep Sea Floor.* Cambridge and New York: Cambridge University Press, 1991.
Nybakken, James W. *Marine Biology: An Ecological Approach,* 5th ed. San Francisco: Benjamin Cummings, 2001.

RELATED ARTICLES
Benthos; Cold Seep; Hydrothermal Vent; Photosynthesis

Chitin

Chitin is a tough and flexible carbohydrate that forms a major component of the body exoskeleton of arthropods, such as crabs, lobsters, and insects. It is also found in bacteria, in the cell walls of fungi, and in hard body parts of a wide range of invertebrates.

Chitin is similar to the carbohydrate cellulose, which makes up plant cell walls. Like cellulose, it is fibrous and difficult to digest. Cellulose molecules are built up from the sugar glucose, but chitin molecules are made from glucosamine, a sugar derived from glucose. Glucosamine is an amino sugar; its molecules contain the element nitrogen, which is normally found in proteins rather than carbohydrates. The glucosamine units join end to end to form long chains, giving chitin great strength.

Invertebrates use chitin primarily for protection and support. It is tough and flexible. The soft bodies of caterpillars are protected by a chitin-rich cuticle, but other arthropods require additional protection. The cuticles of adult insects and crustaceans are made rigid by a protein called *sclerotin*, which lies on top of the chitin layer. Crabs and lobsters gain further protection from calcium-containing minerals such as aragonite and calcite, which are incorporated into their shells (carapaces). Altogether, only about 25 percent of a crab or lobster's shell is chitin.

People have discovered a range of uses for chitin from marine crustaceans. Because it is strong and fibrous but breaks down slowly, it is an ideal material for making biodegradable sutures (surgical stitches). It is also used for thickening food and strengthening paper and has a range of uses in the chemical industry.

Ben Morgan

FURTHER READING
Brusca, Richard C., and Gary J. Brusca. *Invertebrates.* Sunderland, Mass.: Sinauer, 1990.
Pechenik, Jan A. *Biology of the Invertebrates.* Boston: Prindle, Weber and Schmidt, 1985; 4th ed., Boston: McGraw-Hill, 2000.

RELATED ARTICLES
Arthropoda; Crustacean

Chiton, see Polyplacophora

Chlorinity

The term *chlorinity* refers to the chlorine concentration of seawater. Until about 1960 oceanographers determined chlorine concentrations by chemical methods and multiplied the chlorinity by a factor of 1.80655 to determine salinity. Chlorine (Cl) is the most abundant element making up the dissolved salts in seawater. The component is one of five nonmetallic elements grouped together in the periodic table because of similar properties. Chlorine (fluorine, bromine, iodine, and astatine) are halogens, or salt-formers; compounds containing halogens are called salts.

Dissolved inorganic salts comprise 3.5 percent of an average volume of seawater. The chloride (Cl^-) constitutes 55.04 percent by weight of the solid matter dissolved in seawater. When seawater is evaporated, due to dryness, the most abundant precipitated salt is NaCl, common table salt. Sodium ions (Na^+) are the second most abundant ion found in seawater. Evaporation is still used to extract table salt from seawater.

The concentration ratios of the 11 major ions dissolved in seawater are almost constant, and this relationship (the *law of constant proportions*) means that total salt concentration, or *salinity*, can be calculated by measuring the concentration of a single ion such as chlorine. For example, a typical seawater sample has a salinity of 35 practical salinity units (psu), which means that it has 35 grams (0.08 pound) of dissolved salts in 1000 grams (2.2 pounds) of water and a chlorinity of 19.37 grams (0.04 pound). Nowadays, oceanographers measure electrical conductivity (the ability of ions to carry a charge through a solution) to determine salinity.

Lynn L. Lauerman

FURTHER READING
Millero, Frank J. *Chemical Oceanography.* Boca Raton, Fla.: CRC Press, 1996.
Nybakken, James W. *Marine Biology: An Ecological Approach,* 5th ed. San Francisco: Benjamin Cummings, 2001.

RELATED ARTICLES
Salinity; Sea Salt

Chlorofluorocarbon

Chlorofluorocarbons (CFCs), also known as *Freons*, are commonly used as refrigerants in households and the food-processing, storage, and transport industry. CFCs are very similar to hydrocarbons, except hydrogen molecules are substituted with one or more chloride and/or fluoride atoms. CFCs are used as water mass tracers to determine age and movement of water. They can be added to a mass of water in the upper ocean and detected as the mass of water circulates through the water column.

The use of CFCs developed in the 1930s as an alternative to more toxic refrigerants such as methyl chloride, anhydrous ammonia, and sulfur dioxide. In response to a 1929 refrigeration leak in Cleveland, Ohio, General Motors directed a team of chemists, including Thomas Midgley, Albert Henne, and Robert McNary, to develop a nontoxic refrigerant that would be safe for consumer and industrial use. The researchers discovered the value of CFCs for their nonflammable and nontoxic properties. The introduction of CFC-based refrigeration led to an increased standard of living for consumers and an expanded availability of foods throughout the country.

CFCs have been used as water mass tracers to identify water masses that contribute to deep-ocean water formation. Tracer ratios (pairs of two different CFCs) help determine the age of the young component in a water-mass mixture. CFCs from the atmosphere have been identified in North Atlantic Deep Water (NADW), indicating mixing rates and the age of deepwater masses. Historical use of CFCs in industry has altered the natural concentrations of atmospheric and marine CFCs, which limits their application.

In 1973, the Rowland–Molina theory was introduced by chemists F. Sherwood Rowland and Mario Molina, who theorized that the release of CFCs into the atmosphere was resulting in the depletion of Earth's protective layer of atmospheric ozone (O_3). Research has indicated that CFCs are highly inert in the lower atmosphere, known as the *troposphere.* However, in the presence of high-energy ultraviolet light in the upper atmosphere, or *stratosphere*, CFCs react with ozone, creating chloric oxide (ClO) and atmospheric oxygen (O_2). In addition, ClO reacts with another pollutant, nitric oxide (NO), to yield chloride and nitrous oxide

(NO_2). The chloride atom degrades ozone to O_2 and monatomic oxygen (O), resulting in a chain reaction of ozone destruction.

In September 1987, the Montreal Protocol was signed by 59 of 93 attending nations to impart the first global restrictions on the manufacture of CFCs. In 1992, the U.S. Environmental Protection Agency (EPA) initiated a ban on CFCs. Recently, claims refuting the role that CFCs play in stratospheric ozone depletion have surfaced. Pending research indicates that CFCs contribute a fraction of the atmospheric chlorine as compared to seawater evaporation, ocean biota, volcanic offgasing, and other natural factors, and that the absence of alternative refrigerants further minimizes the role that CFCs may play in ozone depletion.

Alison Kelley

FURTHER READING

Maduro, Rogelio A., and Ralf Schauerhammer. *The Holes in the Ozone Scare: Scientific Evidence That the Sky Isn't Falling.* Washington, D.C.: 21st Century Science Associates, 1992.

Manahan, Stanley E. *Environmental Chemistry.* Boston: Willard Grant Press, 1972; 7th ed., Boca Raton, Fla.: Lewis Publishers, 2000.

RELATED ARTICLES
Water Mass

Chlorophyll

Chlorophyll is a pigment found in photosynthetic organisms. Located in protists and plants, but not in bacteria, the structures containing chlorophyll are called *chloroplasts* and are essential to *photosynthesis*, the process by which an organism converts light energy into chemical energy. Pigments in general reflect only specific wavelengths of visible light, and chlorophyll absorbs red and blue light while reflecting green light, giving it a green appearance. The structure that enables it to absorb light energy is a porphyrin ring that contains carbon and nitrogen atoms, surrounded by a

magnesium atom. The ring is surrounded by electrons that are able to move around freely. Because the electrons can migrate, the ring can transfer energized electrons to other molecules, allowing it to absorb sunlight and transfer energy.

Different types of chlorophyll exist. The main types found in the green algae are chlorophyll *a* and chlorophyll *b*. Chlorophyll *a* enables light energy to be transformed into chemical energy and is present in all algae. Chlorophyll *b* is an accessory pigment and aids in the photosynthetic process. There are, however, other forms of chlorophyll that, along with other accessory pigments, enable algae to absorb other wavelengths of visible light.

Organisms that contain chlorophyll are the primary producers of the marine environment. They include the eukaryotic red, green, and brown algae, diatoms, many dinoflagellates, and other single-celled and colonial algae. Photosynthetic bacteria such as the cyanobacteria are among the prokaryotic primary producers.

Erin O'Donnell

FURTHER READING

Bold, Harold C., and Michael J. Wynne. *Introduction to the Algae: Structure and Reproduction.* Englewood Cliffs, N.J.: Prentice Hall, 1978; 2nd ed., 1985.

Duxbury, Alison B., and Alyn C. Duxbury. *Fundamentals of Oceanography.* Dubuque, Iowa: Brown, 1993; 2nd ed., 1996.

Raven, Peter H., Ray F. Evert, and Susan E. Eichhorn. *Biology of Plants.* New York: Worth, 1970; 6th ed., New York: W. H. Freeman, 1999.

Solomon, Eldra P., Linda R. Berg, Diana W. Martin, and Claude Ville. *Biology.* Philadelphia: Saunders, 1985; 5th ed., Fort Worth, Texas, 1999.

RELATED ARTICLES
Algae; Chlorophyta; Photosynthesis; Rhodophyta

Chlorophyta

The green algae, members of the phylum *Chlorophyta*, have been studied extensively because of the many similarities between some of the greens and members of the plant kingdom. In general, chlorophytes have a bright, grass green color. Some may appear pale green, due to deposits of calcium carbonate on their cell surfaces; others look orange to red because of carotenoid pigments that hide the chlorophylls *a* and *b* found in almost all the species. A few species are colorless, but their cell structure and molecular sequences place them firmly in this phylum.

Nearly all green algae have flagellated cells at some point in their life cycles. These flagella usually occur in pairs or multiples of two. They are equal in length and smooth. The membranes within the chloroplasts show the same arrangement of stacks as is seen in plant cells. The food storage product, starch, is stored inside the chloroplast, an arrangement unique to the green algae and plants.

The cell walls of some greens contain cellulose, as do plants. Several green algae growing in tropical ocean waters have calcified cell walls. Fossils of these cell walls that are 600 million years old have been found. Even older fossils of the filamentous *Cladophora* have been discovered in Precambrian rocks 700 million to 800 million years old.

Although all the green algae appear to have a common ancestor, they have radiated into a large number of shapes and habitats. Within the phylum it is possible to find single flagellated cells, single nonflagellated cells, colonies both motile and nonmotile, filaments, sheets of cells, and large cells with many nuclei.

At present the phylum is divided into five major groups. Only two of these contain marine forms, the prasinophyceans and the Ulvophyceae. Among the former group are species commonly believed to be modern descendants of the earliest green algae. Most of them are single-celled flagellates. Others are nonmotile, almost spherical single cells. The presence of one or more layers of tiny scales outside the plasma membrane characterizes most of the species of prasinophyceans. Unusual acids in these scales are also found in the

cell walls of higher plants, suggesting an ancestral relationship. The patterns of cell division found in this group have some characteristics similar to those of the Ulvophyceae, such as the presence of the nuclear envelope in the earlier stages of mitosis. However, the persistence of microtubules used to move the chromosomes through the process in prasinophyceans is more typical of higher plants. The relationship between the Ulvophyceae and the prasinophyceans is evidenced by small, diamond-shaped scales found on the reproductive cells of some ulvophyceans.

The Ulvophyceae make up a large taxon both in size of individuals and number of genera and species. Organisms in this group may be filamentous, grow as bladelike sheets, or have large multinucleate cells. They include genera such as *Ulva*, for which the taxon is named, which is eaten by a variety of organisms, including humans. Fouling algae such as *Enteromorpha* attach to hulls of boats and ships and must be scraped off. Emerging pests such as *Codium* can overgrow in areas where fish farms add excess nutrients to ocean waters.

One of the more unusual features of members of the Ulvophyceae is their type of cell division, called *closed mitosis*. Here the nuclear envelope remains intact throughout the process. By the last stage in the process the nucleus appears dumbbell-shaped, with a cluster of chromosomes at each end. (The higher plants and the group of green algae most closely related to them have open mitosis in which the nuclear envelope disappears early in mitosis.)

The most striking members of the Ulvophyceae are the multinucleate genera. They are made up of a single cell, yet some can be 1 meter or more long. Others take the shape of branched feathers or whisk brooms. Still others look like small parasols emerging from the sandy ocean floor. Because of the unusual shape of the latter, they have been used widely for laboratory studies of cell and developmental biology.

Bette H. Nybakken

FURTHER READING

Bold, H. C., and M. J. Wynne. *Introduction to the Algae*, 2nd ed. Englewood Cliffs, N.J.: Prentice Hall, 1985.

Graham, Linda E. *The Origin of Land Plants*. New York: Wiley, 1993.

Graham, L. E., and L. W. Wilcox. *Algae*. Upper Saddle River, N.J.: Prentice Hall, 2000.

Pickett-Heaps, Jeremy D. *Green Algae*. Sunderland, Mass.: Sinauer, 1975.

Raven, Peter H., Ray F. Evert, and Susan E. Eichhorn. *Biology of Plants*, 6th ed. New York: W. H. Freeman, 1999.

RELATED ARTICLES

Algae; Ochrophyta; Phytoplankton; Rhodophyta

Chondrichthyes

All jawed fishes can be broadly divided into two taxonomic groups, the cartilaginous fishes (class Chondrichthyes) and the bony fishes, often termed the "Osteichthyes" [comprising the classes Acanthodii (an extinct group called "spiny sharks"), Sarcopterygii (lobe-finned fishes), and Actinopterygii (ray-finned fishes)]. There are about 950 recognized species of cartilaginous fishes, including sharks (about 400 species), rays and skates (about 490 species), and chimeras (about 58 species). The Chondrichthyes have a longer evolutionary history than the extant bony fishes, arising during the Silurian Period (over 400 million years ago) and becoming well established in the world's oceans by the Devonian Period (408.5 to 362.5 million years ago).

Most ichthyologists recognize two subclasses of chondrichthyan fishes, Holocephali (chimeras) and Elasmobranchii (sharks, skates, and rays), although interrelationships within these subclasses are less certain. These groups are linked mainly on the basis of the presence of shared characteristics, including cartilaginous skeletons, toothlike placoid scales, internal fertilization, and the presence of copulatory organs ("claspers") in males, fin rays stiffened by horny rays called ceratotrichia, no gas bladder, and a spiral valve intestine. Anatomical differences between holocephalans and elasmobranchs are many and include, respectively, the presence of a fleshy operculumlike gill covering rather than gill slits, an upper jaw fused to the cranium (autostylic suspension) rather than a protrusible jaw connected to the cranium by ligaments (hyostylic suspension), tooth plates that continue to grow during development rather than being continuously replaced, separate urogenital openings rather than a single opening or cloaca, and differences in the position and structure of the gill chamber.

The cartilaginous skeleton in chondrichthyans is often calcified but rarely, if ever, ossified, although bone has been reported in the small-spotted cat shark (*Scyliorhinus canicula*). The skin of most chondrichthyans is covered with hard teethlike scales (placoid scales, or denticles), giving it a rough, sandpaperlike texture. However, chimeras have smooth, naked skin with minute denticles, when present, confined to the midback. Unlike most bony fishes, cartilaginous fishes lack a swim bladder and have adapted to the problem of buoyancy control by storing lightweight lipids in their livers and, in some species, by generating lift with their fins.

Little is known about the biology and life history of the holocephalans, which live in cold waters in the depths of the Atlantic, Pacific, and Indian Oceans. These fishes typically have a large head, huge iridescent eyes, a copulatory organ (tentaculum) located on the head in males in addition to claspers, and a tapered body ending in a thin tail (hence the common name "ratfish"). The teeth are fused into distinctive toothplates that are used for crushing hard-shelled prey, and a venomous spine precedes the first dorsal fin. Most species live near the seafloor, where they hunt bottom-dwelling invertebrates such as mollusks and crustaceans. Swimming in chimeras is facilitated through movements of the pectoral fins.

Most sharks are highly evolved predators, using a range of senses to locate prey. Olfactory senses can detect chemical cues and can be used to recognize distant prey items. Vision is important at close range, particularly to distinguish moving objects. *Lateral line organs* on the body surface serve as distance touch receptors, responding to vibrations in the water. Sharks (and other elasmobranchs) also possess electrosensitive cells called *ampullae of Lorenzini* that can detect electrical stimuli, helping them locate prey and navigate in dark or murky water. Although most sharks are apex predators, the two largest species of sharks, the whale shark (*Rhincodon typus*) and the basking shark (*Cetorhinus maximus*), feed by straining plankton from the water. Sharks swim by flexing a powerful, muscular tail, and typically have torpedo-shaped bodies adapted for speed.

Rays and skates have flat bodies adapted to life on the seafloor, although a few species live near the surface. Unlike most fishes, they swim by beating large, winglike pectoral fins rather than by flexing the tail. The eyes are located on the top of the body, ideally placed to watch for predators and prey while hiding or resting on the seafloor. The mouth is typically located on the underside of the body, except in the mobulid rays. Many skates and rays feed at night and use electoreception and/or olfactory senses rather than vision to locate prey. Skates and rays often remain buried in the benthos during the day to avoid predation. Some are ambush predators, waiting for prey to come into striking range before attacking.

Ben Morgan

FURTHER READING
Hamlett, W. C., ed. *Sharks, Skates, and Rays: The Biology of Elasmobranch Fishes.* Baltimore: Johns Hopkins University Press, 1999.

Moyle, Peter B., and Joseph J. Cech. *Fishes: An Introduction to Ichthyology,* 4th ed. Upper Saddle River, N.J.: Prentice Hall, 2000.

Nelson, Joseph S. *Fishes of the World,* 3rd ed. New York: Wiley, 1994.

Paxton, John R., and William N. Eschmeyer, eds. *Encyclopedia of Fishes,* 2nd ed. San Diego: Academic Press, 1994.

Stevens, John D. *Sharks,* 2nd ed. New York: Checkmark Books, 1999.

Taylor, Leighton, ed. *Sharks and Rays.* Alexandria, Va.: Time-Life Books, 1997.

RELATED ARTICLES
Acanthodii; Actinopterygii; Elasmobranchii; Holocephali; Lateral Line; Osteichthyes; Ray; Sarcopterygii; Shark; Skate

Chondrostei

The Chondrostei comprise one of two subclasses of ray-finned fishes in the Actinopterygii class (the other being the Neopterygii). Actinopterygian fishes with the most ancestral characteristics are placed in the Chondrostei, the name reflecting the largely cartilaginous skeletons of modern forms: the bichirs (order Polypteriformes) and the sturgeons and paddlefishes (order Acipenseriformes). Chondrosteans share some ancestral characteristics, such as spiracles, heterocercal (upper lobe longer than lower lobe) or abbreviated heterocercal tails, scales joined by a peg-and-socket arrangement and covered with ganoine (ganoid scales), secondarily derived cartilaginous skeletons, and more fin rays than fin supports in the dorsal and anal fins. However, there is great structural diversity within this taxon and strong evidence that the Chondrostei may not be derived from a common ancestor (monophyletic) but rather serve as a "catch-all" category of primitive bony fishes. In total, there are three extant families of chondrosteans, eight genera, and 36 species.

Early chondrosteans probably dated back to the late Silurian Period (about 420 million years ago), but complete fossil records do not appear until the middle to late Devonian Period, about 380 million years ago. Among bony fishes, only the acanthodians are of greater antiquity. Most of the early chondrosteans are placed in the extinct order Paleonisciformes, a group of small [5 to 25 centimeters (approximately 2 to 10 inches)] fishes, which flourished throughout the late Paleozoic Era (about 300 to 248.2 million years ago). The success and dominance of this group over other jawed fishes of the time (e.g., acanthodians, placoderms) is believed to be due to changes in jaw and fin structure, which led to more diverse feeding habits and increased mobility. In addition to the Paleonisciformes, there are approximately eight extinct orders of chondrosteans in addition to the two extant orders. The extant orders are highly derived, relict species that bear little resemblance to extinct forms. Sturgeons (family Acipenseridae) are large, freshwater, and anadromous, long-lived fishes of North America, Europe, and Asia. They are prized for their eggs (caviar) and have been heavily overfished as a result. Two species of paddlefishes (family Polyodontidae) occur in large rivers of North America and China. Paddlefishes have a long snout that may be used to detect weak electric fields, such as those given off by potential prey. There is some difficulty in placing the freshwater bichirs and reedfishes of Africa (family Polypteridae) into the Chondrostei. Their pectoral and dorsal fins are unlike those of any other fishes, they have a lung attached to the ventral part of the esophagus, and there are several other differences in skeletal and soft anatomy that foster the belief that they should be placed in their own subgroup. In accordance, polypterids are often placed into the taxa Brachiopterygii or Cladistia.

Joseph J. Bizzarro

FURTHER READING
Bond, Carl E. *Biology of Fishes.* Philadelphia: W. B. Saunders, 1979; 2nd ed., Fort Worth, Texas: Saunders College Publishing, 1996.
Carroll, R. L. *Vertebrate Paleontology and Evolution.* New York: W. H. Freeman, 1988.
Helfman, Gene S., Bruce B. Collette, and Douglas E. Facey. *The Diversity of Fishes.* Malden, Mass.: Blackwell Science, 1997.
McCune, A. R., and B. Schaffer. "Triassic and Jurassic Fishes: Patterns and Diversity." In Kevin Padian, ed., *The Beginning of the Age of Dinosaurs: Faunal Change Across the Triassic–Jurassic Boundary.* Cambridge and New York: Cambridge University Press, 1986; pp. 171–181.
Moyle, Peter B., and Joseph J. Cech. *Fishes: An Introduction to Ichthyology.* Englewood Cliffs, N.J.: Prentice Hall, 1982; 4th ed., Upper Saddle River, N.J.: Prentice Hall, 2000.
Nelson, Joseph S. *Fishes of the World,* 3rd ed. New York: Wiley, 1994.

RELATED ARTICLES
Acanthodii; Actinopterygii; Fins; Neopterygii; Placodermi; Sarcopterygii

Chordata

Chordata is one of the 34 major divisions, or phyla, into which the animal kingdom is divided. Members of this phylum include the best known animals, such as fish, amphibians, reptiles, birds, and mammals.

Biologists once divided the animal kingdom into vertebrates (animals with backbones, such as mammals) and invertebrates (animals without backbones, such as worms). These terms are still used, but they no longer play a fundamental role in classification because they provide an unbalanced view of the animal kingdom. Instead, the kingdom is now divided into four phyla that reflect major branches in the animals' early evolutionary tree. The vertebrates all belong to one of these branches, along with a number of closely related invertebrates.

There are about 50,000 species in the phylum Chordata, 47,000 of which are vertebrates. All members of the phylum are characterized by three distinct features. One feature is the appearance of a stiffened rod of tissue (a *notochord*) along the back of the embryo; in vertebrates this develops into the backbone. A second universal feature is the possession of a nerve cord along the back, which in vertebrates becomes the brain and spinal cord. Finally, all chordates, at some stage in their life cycle, possess gill slits in the throat, a vestige of their marine origin. In fish these develop into gills, but in land vertebrates they appear only in the embryo.

Chordates are described as bilaterally symmetrical, which means that they have a distinct front and rear and symmetrical left and right sides (unlike starfish or sea anemones, which are radially symmetrical). All members of the phylum have a mouth, a digestive tract, and an anus, and most possess a tail. Although a few species can reproduce asexually, all are capable of sexual reproduction, and there are usually separate male and female sexes.

The phylum Chordata is split into three subphyla: Tunicata (or Urochordata), Cephalochordata (or Acrania), and Vertebrata (or Craniata). *Tunicates* (subphylum Tunicata) are small marine animals that generally live attached to the seafloor. Also known as *sea squirts*, they feed by filtering water through their gill slits and bag-shaped bodies. As adults they appear to be unlikely relatives of vertebrates, but their free-swimming larvae look like tadpoles and possess the distinctive chordate notochord. The larvae also have a spinal nerve cord, but this disappears when they metamorphose into adults. In one class of tunicates, the Larvacea, the tadpolelike form persists in the adult.

Cephalochordates (subphylum Cephalochordata), or *lancelets*, are primitive fishlike animals that lack scales or brains. They retain a notochord as adults, have well-developed muscles, and swim by undulating the body. Cephalochordates wriggle into the sand on the seafloor until they are half buried, with their head exposed to the water. Like tunicates, they feed on small particles of food filtered out of the water.

The *vertebrates* (subphylum Vertebrata) are distinguished from the rest of the chordates by the possession of a brain, which is protected by a skull. Vertebrata is divided into two superclasses: Agnatha (jawless fish) and Gnathostomata (all

other vertebrates, including jawed fish, amphibians, reptiles, birds, and mammals).

Ben Morgan

FURTHER READING
Brusca, Richard C., and Gary J. Brusca. *Invertebrates.* Sunderland, Mass.: Sinauer, 1990.
Margulis, Lynn. *Five Kingdoms: An Illustrated Guide to the Phyla of Life on Earth.* San Francisco: W. H. Freeman, 1982; 3rd ed., New York, 1998.
Postlethwait, John. *The Nature of Life.* New York: McGraw-Hill, 1989; 3rd ed., 1995.
Purves, William, et al. *Life: The Science of Biology.* Sunderland, Mass.: Sinauer/Boston: Grant Press, 1983; 5th ed., Sunderland, Mass.: Sinauer, 1998.

RELATED ARTICLES
Agnatha; Larvacean; Tunicate

Chronometer

A chronometer is a mechanical clock or watch engineered to high precision and designed to keep accurate time over weeks or months at sea. Before the arrival of radio and satellite communications, marine chronometers were vital tools of navigation, and they are still kept aboard many ships.

The first chronometer was built by English clockmaker John Harrison (1693–1776) in the mid-eighteenth century as a solution to the problem of finding longitude. At the time navigators knew how to find their latitude easily when away from port, using the elevation of the Sun at midday or the pole star at night to calculate how close to the pole they were. But longitude cannot be calculated in this way. The determination of longitude, which is a measure of an east-west position, depends on the time when the Sun reaches its highest point in the sky (i.e., the noon altitude of the Sun). The Sun reaches its highest point in the sky (local noon) 4 minutes earlier for each degree of longitude a ship moves east around Earth. Without an accurate clock set to the time of the home port, it is impossible to measure this

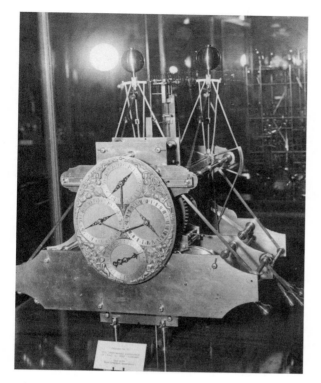

First marine timekeeper, built in 1735 by English clockmaker John Harrison. (Hulton/Archive)

time difference. The problem with most clocks of Harrison's time was that they were very sensitive to temperature changes and the pitching and rolling of a ship would interfere with the steady movement of the pendulum. Harrison solved these problems in 1735 with a huge [34-kilogram (75-pound)], elaborate mechanism, and then created something more like the modern chronometer in 1759.

A modern chronometer usually consists of a well-made watch mounted in a casing with bearings that allow it to remain level even as the ship rolls around. The chronometer also uses a special spring design, which unwinds steadily to provide a driving force for the watch and a unique type of escapement to control and limit the spring's unwinding. Other common features of chronometers are compensators, which counteract the tendency of some watch components to expand or shrink when heated or cooled, and winding mechanisms, which keep

the chronometer running as it is wound. Mechanical chronometers are now obsolete and have been replaced by cheap electric watches.

Giles Sparrow

FURTHER READING

Sobel, Dava. *Longitude.* New York: Walker, 1995.
Whitney, Marvin E. *The Ship's Chronometer.* Cincinnati, Ohio: American Watchmakers Institute Press, 1985.

RELATED ARTICLES
Navigation

Chukchi Sea

The Chukchi Sea is a large sea in the southern Arctic Ocean, flanked on the east by Point Barrow, Alaska, and Beaufort Sea; on the west by Wrangel Island, Russia, and East Siberian Sea; and on the south by the Seward Peninsula of Alaska, Bering Strait, and Siberia. The north boundary is the base of the continental slope. It is roughly incorporated within 66 to 72.5°N latitude and 158 to 178°W longitude.

Chukchi Sea has a maximum area of approximately 375,000 square kilometers (145,000 square miles), which is about the size of the state of Montana in the United States. Most of the sea is floored by a shallow continental shelf, which is less than 60 meters (200 feet) deep. Greatest depths, however, are at the base of the continental slope in the Canada Basin, where the seafloor is more than 3000 meters (9800 feet) below sea level.

Surface currents flow from east to west, influenced by the Coriolis effect, which drives winds and currents in a clockwise direction. Pack ice covers the Chukchi Sea from late October to June, and part of the area is ice-free for short periods in the late summer only in favorable years.

The Chukchi Sea continental margin is underlain by rocks that are Mississippian (about 363 to 323 million years old). In the southern part of Chukchi Sea, the continental shelf seafloor is underlain by a thick, sediment-filled trough called Hope Basin, which has 5.8 kilometers (3.6 miles) of sediments younger than about 50 million years. There is some petroleum potential in rocks of several ages that underlie shallow parts of the Chukchi Sea, but exploration and exploitation are hindered by the severe Arctic climate, polar ice pack, absence of harbors, and long winter darkness.

Further Reading

Grantz, Arthur, and Steven D. May. "Regional Geology and Petroleum Potential of the United States Chukchi Shelf North of Point Hope." In David W. Scholl, Arthur Grantz, and John G. Vedder, eds., *Geology and Resource Potential of the Continental Margin of Western North America and Adjacent Ocean Basins: Beaufort Sea to Baja California.* Houston, Texas: Circum-Pacific Council for Energy and Mineral Resources, 1987, pp. 37–58.

Related Articles

Arctic Ocean; Beaufort Sea; Bering Strait; Continental Slope; Coriolis Effect

Ciguatera

Ciguatera is a serious, occasionally fatal disease of humans that follows the eating of certain fish that live in the vicinity of coral reefs between latitudes 35°N and S. The illness was first described in the sixteenth century by Spanish explorers in Cuba. They attributed it to a small snail they called *cigua*, hence the name for the disease. The ship's surgeon on HMS *Bounty* (of *Mutiny on the Bounty* fame) died from ciguatera. In most cases, however, the illness disappears on its own after a few days, although neurological symptoms sometimes persist much longer and may recur years later, usually following a change in dietary habits or the consumption of alcohol. When death occurs, it is due to heart and respiratory failure.

The immediate cause of the illness is a group of poisons that are known collectively as *ciguatoxin*. Ciguatoxin is present in the fish and is not destroyed by cooking, drying, salting, or freezing. The first symptoms usually appear within two to five hours after ingesting the poison. These begin with numbness and tingling around the mouth, sometimes spreading to the fingers and toes, followed by nausea, abdominal cramps, vomiting, and diarrhea. The victim also suffers headache, aching muscles and joints, dizziness, and weakness that may amount to prostration. The heartbeat may become irregular and blood pressure may fall. Hot objects can feel cold and cold objects hot: This is one of the very few unambiguous clinical signs of ciguatoxin poisoning. Another is that all the symptoms intensify following the consumption of an alcoholic drink.

There is no reliable diagnostic test, although there are reliable tests to identify fish containing the poison. These are likely to be used only after an outbreak of poisoning has been recognized, however. Identifying ciguatera relies entirely on observing the symptoms and learning what the victim ate in the hours preceding their onset.

For many years the disease seemed very mysterious, as the symptoms are not consistent. Although there is a complete list of all likely symptoms, a victim may suffer from just some of them, the symptoms of one victim often differ from those of another, and the symptoms can be explained by illnesses other than ciguatera. Nor is it possible to link the symptoms to the consumption of any particular fish species. Almost any of the larger fish can cause ciguatera, but the same species varies in toxicity from time to time and from place to place, and there is no evident pattern in the distribution of the poison. The fish most often responsible include barracuda, amberjack, blackjack, grouper, mackerel, hogfish, and red snapper. The fish themselves are immune to the poison. Ciguatera affects only humans.

It was not until 1977 that the source of ciguatoxin was finally identified as the dinoflagellate *Gambierdiscus toxicus*. *G. toxicus* is ordinarily uncommon on healthy reefs with an abundance of living coral, but it can appear where surfaces of dead coral have been covered by mats of algae. The dinoflagellate inhabits the surface of the algae and is ingested by herbivorous fish that feed on it. Carnivorous fish that feed on the herbivores then ingest the toxin, which can accumulate in their tissues. This explains the erratic occurrence of ciguatoxin poisoning. The chemical composition and structure of ciguatoxin is now known, as is its effect on the body.

The frequency of ciguatera is not known, but because of the difficulty of diagnosis, it is likely that the incidence is underreported. There was an outbreak in Puerto Rico in 1981 that affected 49 people, of whom two died, and there was a further outbreak in Palm Beach County, Florida, in 1988, affecting more than 100 people.

Michael Allaby

USEFUL WEB SITES

Blythe, Donna G., Donald P. de Silva, and Susanne Cramer-Castro. "Ciguatera." *Miami Medicine*, August 1992.
<http://www.rehablink.com/ciguatera/poison.htm>.
"Ciguatera."
<http://hgic.clemson.edu/factsheets/HGIC3661.htm>.
Hawaii Department of Health. "Ciguatera Fish Poisoning." Undated.
<http://www.hawaii.gov/health/resource/comm_dis/cddcigua.htm>.
Marine Biotoxins Program: "Ciguatoxin and Maitotoxin."
<http://www.chbr.noaa.gov/CoastalResearch/CTXMTXinfo.htm>.
U.S. Food and Drug Administration, Center for Food Safety and Applied Nutrition. "Ciguatera." *Bad Bug Book: Foodborne Pathogenic Microorganisms and Natural Toxins Handbook*, 1992.
<http://vm.cfsan.fda.gov/~mow/chap36.html%20>.

RELATED ARTICLES
Dinoflagellate

Clay Mineral

The term *clay* has two meanings, one referring to the size of individual particles and one pertaining to the crystal structure of those particles. Geologists generally consider sedimentary particles with a diameter smaller than 0.002 millimeters (0.0008 inch) to be clay, but these small particles can actually consist of quartz, calcite, or any other mineral that occurs in the ocean. *Clay minerals*, on the other hand, are distinguished by their unique sheetlike crystal structure that gives them special properties, such as electrically charged surfaces and magnetic behavior. Chemically, they are hydrous aluminum silicates, and they have a wide range of possible compositions.

Origin of Clays

Marine clay minerals are formed in one of two ways: Either they wash in as detritus from the continents, or they form *authigenically*, precipitating in place. Detrital clays are originally formed by weathering of continental rocks. They are delivered to the world ocean primarily by river discharge, but significant amounts of clay minerals are also transported by wind to be deposited in the ocean very far from their source. In the sea far from land, such as in the central Pacific, wind-blown clay can be very significant because no continental sources are nearby. The vast majority of clays in the ocean were brought in from the continents, but some can form from seawater or by alteration of preexisting clay or volcanic ash. Although chemical reactions can alter clays somewhat, the mineral composition of seafloor environments is generally a direct reflection of the dominant soil environments on nearby continents. This realization by marine geologists during the 1960s and 1970s contradicted previous conclusions that the clay minerals found in marine sediments are largely the product of chemical reactions with seawater.

Mineral Structure

Clay minerals are composed of two different types of sheets, tetrahedral and octahedral. *Tetrahedral* refers to a sheet of four-sided structures made by silica and alumina, whereas *octahedral* refers to a sheet of eight-sided structures generally made by alumina, iron, or magnesium. Clay minerals with one of each of these sheets comprising a layer are known as *1:1 clays,* while those that have one octahedral sheet sandwiched between two tetrahedral sheets are known as *2:1 clays.* The structure of these sheets is important in determining the physical and chemical behavior of clay minerals. For example, one type of 2:1 clay, called *smectite,* can hold water, positively charged ions, or organic molecules between its layers, making them expandable and giving them shrink-and-swell properties.

Mineral Types

Ocean clays are dominated mostly by four types: chlorite, illite, kaolinite, and smectite. In practice, most marine sediment has at least some of each type. The relative proportion of each depends on the rock type and climate of nearby continents. For example, tropical soils that are heavily weathered typically yield high amounts of kaolinite, such as off the coasts of tropical Africa and Australia. In contrast, chlorite and illite are produced by weakly developed soils in higher latitudes or in mountain ranges, and they dominate the far northern and southern oceans. Smectites are usually produced by the chemical alteration of volcanic ashes, and they are most common in the volcanically active Pacific.

X-ray Diffraction Analysis

In the laboratory, three types of analysis are commonly made on clays. The first of these is the determination of mineralogy—that is, which of

Clay minerals, which consist of strongly bound sheets of silica tetrahedrons and alumina octahedrons. (Institut Laue-Langevin, France. Image maintained at <http://www.ill.fr/dif/3D-crystals/layers>)

the crystal structures discussed above are found in a particular sample of clays. This is routinely accomplished by an analytical procedure known as *x-ray diffraction* (XRD). In this procedure, a sample of clay is placed on a glass slide and allowed to dry after removal of the coarser material by gravity settling or centrifugation. It is then exposed to x-rays, which diffract at certain angles from the sample. The x-rays are received by an x-ray detector, and the angles are read by a measuring device called a *goniometer.* The different clay minerals have particular angles at which x-rays will diffract through the sample, and this property can be used to identify them. Many additional types of treatments are used to identify clay minerals more specifically, such as heating samples and then reexposing them to x-rays, since some clays will change with heating. The science of clay mineralogy by XRD is in many ways an art, and one that has been developed over many years to deal with the complexity of natural clays. In practice, most clay-rich sediments contain a mixture of the major clay types, and the laboratory analyst must use x-ray or other techniques to determine how much of each type is present in a sample.

Grain Size Analysis

The second common type of analysis carried out on clays is the determination of grain size distribution. The goal of this analysis is to quantify the amount of coarse, medium, and fine clay present in a sediment sample. This can be a useful property to know, because clays of varying sizes can be transported by marine currents differently, and because certain clays may trap fluids or gases beneath the seafloor more effectively than others. Grain size distribution analysis is done routinely by using the *Stokes settling velocity,* which states that particles of a certain size will settle in water at a certain rate. In the lab, one can employ devices that use x-rays, lasers, or infrared beams to measure the amount of clay sample suspended in a small chamber. As the coarser clays settle out, the device will "see" fewer and fewer grains, and the size distribution of the sample can be estimated. A *Coulter counter,* which uses electrical conductivity to count and size individual particles, may also be used. A similar analysis can be done with settling columns, where the analyst will suspend a sample in some liquid and take samples out of the column. As more and more of the clay settles out, the samples taken out of the column will have less and less clay. These samples are then dried and weighed, giving the distribution of grain sizes in the original sample.

Geochemical Analysis

The third common laboratory analysis involving clays is geochemical analysis. These are analyses carried out to determine the chemical composition or behavior of clays. Geochemical analyses may be carried out using many different types of instruments, such as electron microscopes, emission spectrometers, mass spectrometers, and others. Other experiments may be carried out on clays to determine properties of clay samples such as cation exchange capacity, which is the ability of a clay to release positively charged ions from its interlayer sites and gain others from surrounding water. The geochemical properties of clays are important because they can affect the chemistry of surrounding water.

Importance of Clays

Understanding clays and clay minerals has become an important part of marine geology in recent years. The link between continental soils, climate, and clays in adjacent ocean basins makes them a useful indicator of climates over geological time. By looking at changes in clay mineral composition in sedimentary layers from deep-sea cores, past changes in climate can be reconstructed. Clays can also play an important role in the formation and trapping of oil, because fluids do not easily flow through their pore spaces. It is also clear that chemical reactions involving clay minerals can occur on the seafloor in evaporative settings such as the Red Sea, and also in the weathering of submarine volcanic rocks such as basalt at mid-ocean ridges. Clays are some of the most abundant materials in the oceans, and they play an important role in determining the composition and chemistry of seafloor environments.

Daniel M. Deocampo

FURTHER READING
Hathaway, John C. "Clay Minerals." In Roger G. Burns et al., eds., *Marine Minerals.* Washington, D.C.: Mineralogical Society of America, 1979.
Kennett, James. *Marine Geology.* Englewood Cliffs, N.J.: Prentice Hall, 1982.
Millot, Georges. *Geology of Clays: Weathering, Sedimentology, Geochemistry.* Translated by W. R. Farrand and Hélène Paquet. New York: Springer-Verlag, 1970.
Moore, Duane M., and, Robert C. Reynolds, Jr. *X-Ray Diffraction and the Identification and Analysis of Clay Minerals.* Oxford and New York: Oxford University Press, 1989; 2nd ed., 1997.

Velde, B. *Introduction to Clay Minerals: Chemistry, Origins, Uses and Environmental Significance.* London and New York: Chapman and Hall, 1992.

RELATED ARTICLES
Authigenic Sediment; Deep-Sea Sediment; Turbidite; Windblown Dust, Transport and Deposition of

Cleaning Behavior

Cleaning behavior is a phenomenon that is common among marine animals. Close interactions between two species—where one apparently "cleans" the other—are well documented. Such a cleaning symbiosis typically involves two parties: a cleaner of one species and a client or host—usually a larger individual—of another species.

Isabelle M. Côté in a 2000 review describes two categories of cleaning symbiosis. The first, termed *incidental cleaning,* is the cleaner's removal from the client's body surface of debris, attached invertebrates, and epiphytic algae. This behavior is essentially similar to a fish grazing on any suitable substrate and is not associated with special "cleaning" behaviors on the part of cleaner or client. Herbivorous reef fishes grazing on the shell of a sea turtle is an example.

The second category of cleaning symbioses, however, involves specific behavioral and morphological adaptations that appear to facilitate cleaning. For example, wrasses of the genus *Labroides* establish cleaning stations on coral reefs. A wrasse typically performs a zigzag "dance" that attracts a client. A client, in turn, hovers with its fins spread, mouth open, and gill covers flared, apparently inviting attention from the cleaner fish. The black surgeonfish, *Acanthurus achilles,* turns bright blue prior to being approached by the cleaner wrasse, *Labroides dimidiatus.* The cleaner moves in and removes ectoparasites, bacteria, diseased or injured tissue, or other attached material from the skin, mouth, or gills of the client.

Côté reported that 107 species of teleost fish and 24 decapod crustaceans, such as the Pederson cleaning shrimp, *Periclimenes pedersoni,* are known to be cleaners of the second category. More than three-fourths of cleaners are facultative (they rely on cleaning for only part of their diet); the remainder are obligatory cleaners (dependent on cleaning for virtually all their food). Most cleaning symbioses have been described in tropical waters, but cleaning symbioses undoubtedly occur in temperate regions.

Since the late 1950s, a central question has been whether cleaning symbioses are truly of benefit to both parties. The answer is much less settled than appears at first sight. Early studies, such as those of C. Limbaugh reporting in *Scientific American* in 1961, claimed that the presence of cleaner fishes on coral reefs was necessary for the health of the local fish community. However, many studies since have failed to confirm this.

Although cleaner fish undoubtedly consume ectoparasites, it has proved difficult to demonstrate experimentally that parasite removal has had a demonstrable effect on the parasite load of the client in the short to long term. Researchers such as G. S. Losey have even suggested that cleaner fish capitalize on the client's appetite for tactile stimulation and that cleaners are effectively "behavioral parasites" rather than being of demonstrable benefit to the client. However, one study by Alexandra Grutter (1963–), reported in *Nature* in 1999, did clearly show that cleaner wrasses, *Labroides dimidiatus,* reduced the parasitic isopod load on client fish.

In the calculation of costs and benefits to cleaner and client, there are many factors to consider. Cleaners benefit from having food items brought easily to them. Clients may benefit from having parasites removed and from having wounds cleaned. However, clients may be at risk from the cleaners themselves or their mimics. Cleaners may damage clients by consuming scales and mucus. The cleaner wrasse, *Labroides dimidiatus*, is mimicked in appearance and behavior by at least one species of blenny that bites chunks out of the unsuspecting client. The coevolution of specific ritualized behaviors, and the existence of cleaner mimics, suggests that some cleaning symbioses have a long evolutionary history.

Trevor Day

FURTHER READING
Côté, Isabelle M. "Evolution and Ecology of Cleaning Symbioses in the Sea." *Oceanography and Marine Biology: An Annual Review,* Vol. 38 (2000), pp. 311–355.
Grutter, A. S. "Cleaner Fish Really Do Clean." *Nature,* Vol. 398 (1999), pp. 672–673.
Limbaugh, C. "Cleaning Symbiosis." *Scientific American,* Vol. 205, No. 2 (1961), pp. 42–49.
Nybakken, James W. *Marine Biology: An Ecological Approach,* 5th ed. San Francisco: Benjamin Cummings, 2001.
Rohde, Klaus. *Ecology of Marine Parasites.* St. Lucia and New York: University of Queensland Press, 1982; 2nd ed., Wallingford, England: CAB International, 1993.

RELATED ARTICLES
Commensalism; Crustacea; Parasitism; Symbiosis; Teleostei

Climate Change

Climate change is the progressive transformation of Earth's climate in response to human activities. Often referred to as a *global warming* because it involves a gradual heating up of Earth and its atmosphere, climate change has been a controversial issue since the first World Climate Conference in 1979 called for nations "to foresee and prevent potential man-made changes in climate." Although there is now broad scientific consensus that climate change is occurring, the likely effects on Earth's ecosystems and human society remain uncertain, and the world's political leaders remain divided on the question of what should be done to address the problem.

Causes

Exactly how Earth's climate responds to global warming is still not completely understood, but the basic scientific principle is a simple one. Some of the gases in Earth's atmosphere [known as *greenhouse gases*—chiefly carbon dioxide (CO_2) and methane] behave similar to the glass in a greenhouse. Incoming radiation from the Sun warms Earth, and because warm objects radiate heat, some of it is reemitted back toward space. But less radiation escapes than arrives, causing some heat to be trapped inside Earth's "greenhouse." Without this natural greenhouse effect, Earth would be about 20°C (36°F) cooler and a dramatically different planet. However, since the industrial revolution began in the eighteenth century, humankind has released large quantities of CO_2 into the atmosphere, mainly by burning fossil fuels such as coal and oil and by destroying forests. Between 1750 and the present day, the atmospheric concentration of CO_2 has increased by 31 percent, enhancing the natural greenhouse effect and causing Earth to warm by a small but significant amount [approximately 0.6°C (about 1°F) over the twentieth century]. The concern is that the concentration of CO_2 will continue to increase, causing a bigger temperature rise and drastic climate change.

Although disputed by a relatively small number of skeptical scientists, there is now broad scientific agreement about climate change. Established by the United Nations Environment Programme and the World Meteorological Organization in 1988, the Intergovernmental Panel on Climate Change (IPCC) published summaries of the current science and predicted future effects of climate change in 1990, 1995, and 2001. In January 2001, it reported that "the present CO_2 concentration has not been exceeded during the past 420,000 years and likely not during the past 20 million years. The current rate of increase is unprecedented during at least the past 20,000 years." This is neither a temporary nor a trivial change, for as the IPCC reported: "Human influences will continue to change atmospheric composition throughout the 21st century" and "Global average temperature and sea level are projected to rise" under all the computer modeling scenarios tested. Citing "new and stronger evidence" that recent climate change is anthropogenic (human-caused), the IPCC predicted that "anthropogenic climate change will persist for many centuries."

Effects

The effects of climate change are predicted to be widespread and dramatic—perhaps nowhere more so than in the oceans. According to the IPCC, the increase in atmospheric CO_2 will result in an average global surface temperature increase of 1.4 to 5.8°C (about 2.5 to 10.4°F) between 1990 and 2100 and a sea-level rise of 0.09 to 0.88 meter (0.30 to 2.89 feet) over the same period (partly because warming oceans will expand in volume and partly through melting ice caps and glaciers). The IPCC believes that there are "likely" to be substantial changes in weather patterns, including generally higher maximum temperatures and more hot days, more intense precipitation in the northern hemisphere, an increase in the variability of summer monsoons, an increase in tropical cyclones, and an increase in the frequency of El Niño events. Another significant oceanic change is a predicted weakening of the thermohaline circulation, causing a reduction in heat transport to high latitudes of the northern hemisphere. According to the IPCC, "Beyond 2100, the thermohaline circulation could completely, and possibly irreversibly, shut down in either hemisphere" if climate change is drastic enough. Many people believe global warming is already well under way; according to the World Meteorological Organization, the 1990s was the hottest decade of the millennium.

With around two-thirds of the world's people living within 60 kilometers (37 miles) of the coast, rising sea levels could prove to be one of the biggest environmental challenges of the twenty-first century. According to a 1992 report by the World Wildlife Fund, a sea-level rise of just 50 centimeters (1.6 feet), a little over half that predicted by the IPCC for the twenty-first century, would inundate 40,000 square kilometers (15,400 square miles) of China where over 30 million people now live. Other low-lying areas especially at risk include Bangladesh and the Nile delta region of Egypt. Measures to avert climate change have been passionately supported by the Alliance of Small Island States (AOSIS), a lobbying group representing low-lying island nations, some of which will disappear entirely if IPCC predictions come true. For example, according to a 1997 report by Environmental Defense, the island of Kiribati is expected to be completely inundated with a 80-centimeter (2.6-foot) sea-level rise around 2090 to 2100, and around 85 percent of Malé (the capital of the Maldives) will be underwater by the following decade.

The rich biodiversity of Earth's ecosystems is intimately related to climate across the planet; significant increases in temperature, precipitation, and weather patterns may prove catastrophic for some habitats and species. According to the Global Coral Reef Monitoring Network's (GCRMN) report *Status of Coral Reefs of the World 2000*, "Coral reefs may yet prove to be the first major marine ecosystem to show significant impacts from global climate change . . . [which poses] an equal or even greater threat to coral reefs than direct anthropogenic impacts." GCRMN predicts that without urgent action, 40 percent of the world's coral reefs will be lost by 2010 and 60 percent by 2030.

Habitats and species may survive climate change if they can migrate to higher (and cooler) latitudes or altitudes quickly enough. Shifts in some species are already evident, but whether this is definitely caused by global warming is not yet known. Thus, in Monterey Bay, California, studies have found that invertebrates such as limpets, sea stars, and snails significantly shifted their range northward between the 1930s and the 1990s. Also on the west coast of the United States, numbers of sooty shearwaters declined by about 90 percent between 1987 and 1994, apparently because of a significant warming of the California Current. But for polar ecosystems that response is impossible: There is simply nowhere for them to go. In the last 25 years or so, the numbers of Adelie penguins in Antarctica have declined by 33 percent due to significant losses of winter sea ice; in the Canadian Arctic, the population of Peary caribou declined by 95 percent between 1961 and 1997, due largely to increased snowfall thought to be connected to a warming world. As a result, climate change may have a dramatic impact on marine ecosystems. According to *Turning Up the Heat,* a report published in 2000 by the World Wildlife Fund: "Global climate change is an additional stress on already stressed species and ecosystems, and may be the 'straw that breaks the camel's back' for many types of marine life."

Responses

Efforts to curb global warming have centered on the UN Framework Convention on Climate Change (UNFCCC), which was signed by 154 nations at the Earth Summit in Rio de Janeiro in 1992 and came into effect the following year. Its objective is to achieve "stabilization of greenhouse gas concentrations in the atmosphere at a level that would prevent dangerous anthropogenic interference with the climate system . . . within a time-frame sufficient to allow ecosystems to adapt naturally to climate change . . ." Quite how this should be achieved, however, remains a matter of international controversy. In Kyoto, Japan, in 1997, developed nations agreed to cut their emissions of greenhouse gases, but developing nations were exempted from mandatory action. Mainly for this reason, the United States, the world's largest emitter of greenhouse

gases, repeatedly expressed its unhappiness with the so-called Kyoto Protocol and pulled out of the agreement entirely in 2001. Although the European Union and many other nations have vowed to meet their Kyoto obligations, it remains uncertain whether this action will be enough to make a significant difference to global warming. According to Jerry Mahlman, director of the Geophysical Fluid Dynamics Laboratory (GDFL) at Princeton: "It might take another 30 Kyotos over the next century" to achieve that aim. Whether the world's leaders will choose to risk drastic and irreversible climate change or commit to what some see as equally drastic economic changes remains to be seen.

Chris Woodford

FURTHER READING

Drake, Frances. *Global Warming: The Science of Climate Change.* London: Edward Arnold and New York: Oxford University Press, 2000.
Gelbspan, Ross. *The Heat Is On: The Climate Crisis, the Cover-up, the Prescription.* New York: Perseus Books, 1998.
Houghton, John. *Global Warming: The Complete Briefing.* New York and Cambridge: Cambridge University Press, 1997.
Karl, Thomas, and Kevin Trenberth. "The Human Impact on Climate." *Scientific American,* December 1999, p. 62.
Leggett, Jeremy. *The Carbon War.* New York and London: Penguin, 2000.
Malakoff, David. "Thirty Kyotos Needed to Control Warming." *Science,* Vol. 278 (19 Decmeber 1997), p. 2048.
McCarthy, James J., ed. *Climate Change 2001: Impacts, Adaptation, and Vulnerability.* Geneva: Intergovernmental Panel on Climate Change (IPCC), 2001.
Watson, R. T., ed. *Climate Change: The IPCC Working Group I Third Scientific Assessment Report.* Geneva: Intergovernmental Panel on Climate Change (IPCC), 2001.

RELATED ARTICLES
El Niño; La Niña; Sun, Radiant Energy of; Thermohaline Circulation

Clupeomorpha

The Clupeomorpha is a subdivision of bony fishes within the class Actinopterygii (ray-finned fishes). In *Fishes of the World* (1994), Joseph S. Nelson recognizes two clupeomorph orders: the extinct Ellimmichthyiformes (five species) and the extant Clupeiformes (anchovies, herrings, pilchards, sardines, shads, and sprats: five families, 83 genera, and about 357 species). Members of the Clupeiformes are called *clupeoids*, the herringlike fishes. They are streamlined, often silvery fish with moderately large scales and no fin spines. Most are small [15 centimeters (6 inches) long or less], but the wolf herrings (family Chirocentridae) may grow to 1 meter (about 3.3 feet).

Clupeoids are distinguished by a characteristic arrangement of bones that supports the rays of the tail (caudal) fin and a unique connection (the *recessus lateralis*) between the gas bladder and the utriculus of the ear. All but one species (*Denticeps clupeoides*) lack a lateral line. Many clupeoids feature modified scales (scutes) that are sharp-pointed at the posterior edge. Most clupeoids inhabit the shallow water and surface layers of temperate and tropical seas; only a few species live in fresh water. Most adult clupeoids are plankton feeders and use modified gill rakers to filter the water for zooplankton. A few clupeoids are toothed predators. For example, the saber-tooth thryssa, *Lycothrissa crocodilus*, of tropical America eats other fishes.

Clupeoids are egg layers and commonly produce prodigious numbers of pelagic eggs that are externally fertilized. North Atlantic herring, *Clupea harengus*, comprise many distinct stocks that gather in spawning aggregations in shallow water. The timing of spawning ranges from spring to fall, depending on stock, and is probably triggered by changes in light regime and sea surface temperature. Other clupeoids also undertake seasonal spawning migrations. In spring, the American shad, *Alosa sapidissima*, makes spawning runs from the sea into major river systems.

Clupeoids are immensely important as food for humans and as sources of fish oil, animal feed, and agricultural fertilizer. Throughout the twentieth century their dense schools were very heavily exploited by commercial net fisheries. In the 1990s, clupeoids accounted for about 30 to 35 percent by weight of the reported global marine fish catch, according to Food and Agriculture Organization (FAO) annual statistics. Fourteen species of clupeoid—eight anchovy (genus *Engraulis*) and six pilchard (*Sardina* or *Sardinops*) —accounted for the bulk of this catch. In 1970, the catch of Peruvian anchoveta, *Engraulis ringens*, exceeded 13 million tonnes (14 million tons) but declined in the early 1970s, probably as a result of overfishing and unfavorable environmental conditions (the 1972 El Niño facilitated this crash). Stocks have only partially recovered.

Trevor Day

FURTHER READING
Moyle, Peter B., and Joseph J. Cech. *Fishes: An Introduction to Ichthyology*, 4th ed. Upper Saddle River, N.J.: Prentice Hall, 1999.
Nelson, Joseph S. *Fishes of the World*. Upper Saddle River, N.J.: Prentice Hall, 1982; 4th ed., 2000.
Parfit, M. "Diminishing Returns: Exploiting the Ocean's Bounty." *National Geographic*, Vol. 188, No. 5 (November 1995), pp. 2–37.
Paxton, John R., and William N. Eschmeyer, eds. *Encyclopedia of Fishes*, 2nd ed. San Diego: Academic Press, 1998.

RELATED ARTICLES
Actinopterygii; Elopomorpha; Euteleostei; Fisheries; Osteoglossomorpha

Cnidaria

The phylum Cnidaria (sometimes called Coelenterata) encompasses over 9000 species of radially symmetrical animals that include marine forms such as corals, jellyfish, sea anemones, and sea fans, and freshwater forms such as hydra. Cnidarians range in size from almost microscopic individuals to coral colonies that extend for many meters to jellyfish that are more than 2 meters (6.6 feet) across and trail 30-meter (98.4-foot)-long tentacles.

The typical cnidarian body consists of an outer epidermis, an inner gastrodermis, and a jellylike layer of *mesoglea* sandwiched in between. Cnidarians possess a nerve net that represents the evolution of the first true nerve cells of the animal kingdom. Cnidarians usually have an oral opening (mouth) surrounded by tentacles that bear stinging cells called *cnidocytes* (from which the phylum gets its name). The stinging capsules, called *nematocysts*, are used for capturing prey and for defense. Cnidarians have an incomplete digestive system—the oral opening serves as both mouth and anus. The mouth leads to a blind gastrovascular cavity in which digestion takes place. Cnidarians typically alternate between a sessile columnar *polyp*, in which the mouth faces upward, and a motile bell-shaped *medusa*, in which the mouth faces downward. Polyps reproduce asexually to generate medusae. Medusae, in turn, reproduce sexually, which results in a *planula* larva that settles onto a substrate and develops into a polyp; then the cycle begins again. Many variations of this *alternation of generations* exist, however.

Cnidarians are divided into four classes:

The class Hydrozoa includes about 2700 species of animals, such as hydroids, hydrocorals, and siphonophores. Most hydrozoans have separate polyp and medusa stages and have separate sexes. Hydrozoans are mainly marine, but freshwater representatives exist. They can live individually or in colonies. Some species, such as the Portuguese man-of-war (*Physalia* sp.), form floating colonies of polyps and medusae in which individuals are specialized for feeding, defense, and reproduction.

The Scyphozoans are the true jellyfish, and the medusa stage dominates. The polyp stage in scyphozoans is either reduced or absent; when present, the polyp's only function is to produce new medusae by asexual budding. Jellyfish generally drift in ocean currents, but they also can swim by contracting the muscles of the bell. The approximately 200 species of scyphozoans, which range in size from 2 centimeters (0.8 inch) to 3 meters (9.8 feet) in diameter, are mainly marine organisms.

The class Anthozoa is a diverse group of about 6000 species. Anthozoans are exclusively marine. Members of this class lack the medusoid stage; the polyp reproduces both sexually and asexually. The gastrovascular cavity in anthozoans is divided into chambers by vertical partitions that serve to increase surface area available for digestion. Anthozoans can be solitary or colonial. Gorgonians, sea pens, sea pansies, soft corals, and a few other forms are grouped together in the subclass Octocorallia. They are composed of colonial polyps bearing eight pinnate tentacles. The subclass Hexacorallia includes the anemones and the reef-building corals. Black corals and tube anemones comprise the subclass Ceriantipatharia.

Sea wasps and box jellyfish belong to the class Cubozoa. These small medusae [15 to 25 centimeters (5.9 to 9.8 inches) tall] inhabit all tropical seas but are most abundant in the Indo-West Pacific. Cubozoan stings are extremely toxic and those of two genera, *Chironex* and *Chiropsalmus*, can be fatal to humans.

Lynn L. Lauerman

FURTHER RESEARCH
Brusca, Richard C., and Gary J. Brusca. *Invertebrates.* Sunderland, Mass.: Sinauer, 1990.
Faulkner, Douglas, and Richard Chesher. *Living Corals.* New York: C.N. Potter, 1979.
Friese, U. Erich. *Sea Anemones: . . . as a Hobby.* Neptune, N.J.: T. F. H. Publications, 1993.
Headstrom, Richard. *The Weird and the Beautiful: The Story of the Portuguese Man-of-War, the Sailors-by-*

the-Wind, and Their Exotic Relatives of the Deep. New York: Cornwall Books, 1984.

Muscatine, Leonard, and Howard M. Lenhoff, eds. *Coelenterate Biology: Reviews and New Perspectives.* New York: Academic Press, 1974.

Romashko, Sandra. *The Coral Book: A Guide to Collecting and Identifying the Corals of the World.* Miami: Windward, 1975.

RELATED ARTICLES

Gorgonian; Hermatypic Coral; Planula; Polyp; Zooxanthellae

Coastal Aquifer

Coastal aquifers are important water resources in many areas that border the oceans and seas. An aquifer is a permeable (fluid can flow through) layer of sediment, either a sand or gravel bed or a porous sandstone with little cementing material, that contains groundwater. It is capped by sediment or rock that is impermeable, or nearly so. In many coastal settings, aquifer systems are characterized by sequences of porous and permeable sediment and rock layers with varying hydraulic properties. Under natural undisturbed conditions, an equilibrium seaward hydraulic gradient exists within each aquifer, with excess fresh water discharging to the sea. The fresh water often flows out onto the ocean floor, either on the continental shelf and upper slope area or along the walls of a submarine canyon. Well-known examples of such systems are on the North Atlantic and Israel coastal plains, in the Monterey Bay region of California, and on the Llobregal delta in Spain.

A wedge-shaped body of denser, more saline seawater develops beneath the lighter and fresher water in coastal aquifers. Landward movement of seawater within coastal aquifers is referred to as seawater intrusion. Any change in the flow regime within the freshwater region induces movement of the freshwater-saltwater interface. The consequence of sustained heavy groundwater withdrawal in coastal areas is that wells near the shore eventually draw salty groundwater and must be abandoned. The seawater intrusion and well abandonment continues as long as pumpage is sustained or if there is a decrease in water recharge.

Seawater intrusion is an important element to consider in plans for the proper management of groundwater in coastal aquifers. Under predevelopment conditions, fresh water in aquifers adjacent to the coast has a seaward gradient, resulting in groundwater being discharged into the ocean. If this seaward gradient is reversed, the flow of fresh water into the ocean will cease. If the condition that caused the reversal continues, sea water will displace fresh water in the offshore part of the aquifer and move landward.

Seawater intrusion in the lower Salinas Valley of the Monterey Bay region has been evident since the 1940s. It began in the shallower 55-meter (180-foot) aquifer and later occurred in the 122-meter (400-foot) aquifer when deeper wells were drilled to avoid the 55-meter intrusion. Abundant irrigation wells and a growing urban population are placing more and more pressure on the region's freshwater resources.

Agricultural activity can be greatly curtailed and the quality of drinking water compromised if sea water is allowed to contaminate important aquifers. This negatively affects the economy of an area. There are several courses of action to either prevent or mitigate seawater intrusion into coastal aquifers:

1. *Reduce pumping.* Groundwater levels must be restored to sea level or above, and the seaward hydraulic gradient of fresh water reestablished and maintained.

2. *Use supplemental water.* Other sources of supplemental water are necessary, including reclaimed wastewater, groundwater from sites not affected by the intrusion, reservoir water from outside the region, and river water.

3. *Increase recharge.* This might be accomplished by slowing water flow in recharge areas such as

rivers and on alluvial fans at the base of mountains with the use of small coffer dams. In addition, partially cleaned and drinkable wastewater from sewage treatment plants can be pumped into the aquifer.

4. *Set water well standards.* Degraded water must be kept enclosed and not allowed to move from one aquifer to another. This can be accomplished through the proper construction and destruction of water wells.

Tracy L. Vallier

FURTHER READING

Frind, E. O. "Seawater Intrusion in Continuous Coastal Aquifer-Aquitard Systems." *Advancements in Water Resources,* Vol. 5 (1982), pp. 89–97.

Kazmann, Raphael G. *Modern Hydrology.* New York: Harper and Row, 1965.

Shepard, Francis P. *Submarine Geology.* New York: Harper and Row, 1948; 3rd ed., 1973.

Todd, D. K. *Ground Water Hydrology.* New York: Wiley, 1964.

RELATED ARTICLES

Coastal Morphology; Continental Margin; Delta; Salinity; Seacoast Classification

Coastal Erosion

Coastal erosion is the name given to various geological processes by which the sea washes away (erodes) features of the coastline, such as beaches and cliffs; it takes place in parallel with marine deposition, the process by which the coastline is built up elsewhere. On average, it has been estimated that about 14,000 waves strike each exposed piece of coastline every day. Given the force exerted by each wave [a typical wave may exert pressures of about 10,000 kilograms per square meter (2050 pounds per square foot)], erosion can systematically destroy not just soft areas such as sandy beaches, but even bedrock. With half of Earth's population and nine of its ten largest cities located near coastlines, and with significant sea-level rises predicted because of climate change, coastal erosion will become an increasingly important (and expensive) concern for safety and environmental policy in the future.

Processes of Coastal Erosion

Coastal erosion is caused by a variety of geological processes, and its effects are exacerbated by a number of human activities. The processes by which cliffs are eroded include the mechanical action of breaking waves (including the force of the waves, compressed air that opens up cracks, and the use of broken bits of cliff hurled back by the waves as a kind of abrasion tool), weathering (which includes the breakdown of rock surfaces by repeated wetting and drying), corrosion (in which seawater gradually dissolves the rock), and bioerosion (especially notable in the tropics, where organisms bore into or graze on rock and gradually break away its surface). Processes such as these lead to the familiar forms of coastal morphology, such as sea caves, arches, and stacks.

Beaches are eroded mainly by destructive wave action. Winter storms cause high winds, and high winds cause steep, energetic, and therefore destructive waves. These transport sand from the top of a beach (the berm or the dunes) to form offshore bars because the backwash (the movement of sediment as the wave retreats to sea) is strong. During winter, the bars are built at the expense of the berm; during spring and summer, the process is normally reversed, unless storm waves of considerable intensity have transported sediment deeper into the sea beyond the reach of normal waves. Erosion does not just move sand back and forth between the berm and the bars, however. Longshore currents systematically transport sand from one end of a beach to another and carry enormous quantities of sediment [e.g., an estimated 1.36 tonnes (1.5 million tons) of sand are carried past Oxnard on the California coast each year]. Other types of currents produce short-term changes in the appearance of a beach, such as ripple marks and cusps (circular swirl marks).

Although erosion is a dynamic natural process, its effects can be increased dramatically by human activities. Increased groundwater removal in coastal areas due to increased urbanization can accelerate the collapse of cliffs. Engineering works carried out to prevent coastal erosion in one place (see "Controlling Coastal Erosion" below) frequently increase the effects of erosion nearby. Dredged navigation channels and jetties near harbors substantially increase the erosion of beaches. The damming of rivers for hydroelectric power, flood control, or irrigation reduces the supply of sediment to beaches, whose resultant smaller volume makes them more vulnerable to erosion in the future.

Coastal Erosion at Work

Examples of coastal erosion are easy to find; according to some estimates, 80 to 90 percent of the U.S. coastline—including major cities such as New York, Miami, and New Orleans—is undergoing erosion. One of the most visible examples of erosion is the need to move or replace lighthouses at regular intervals. For instance, the Cape Cod Light in southern Massachusetts was replaced three times during the nineteenth century. Furthermore, Cape Cod's oldest lighthouse, the Highland Light, was built 150 meters (490 feet) from the ocean in 1797; today, it stands just 30 meters (98 feet) from the coast. The once-onshore lighthouse at Morris Island near Charleston, South Carolina, now stands on an island 500 meters (1640 feet) offshore. At Beachy Head on the south coast of England, a converted lighthouse was picked up with hydraulic rams and moved back 15 meters (50 feet) from the cliff edge in January 1999 after a major cliff rockfall.

Rates of erosion vary dramatically from place to place according to the type of bedrock, wave size, slope of the local seafloor, and degree of exposure to storm winds. Erosion in Florida is relatively low—0.1 meter (4 inches) per year—due largely to the resistant limestone bedrock found there. But around the Gulf coast, the coast of Louisiana experiences average erosion of 4.2 meters (13.8 feet) per year, partly because its bedrock is less resistant and partly because of other factors, such as rising sea level.

The process of coastal erosion is not always as gradual as these average figures imply. Indeed, those who build or buy property near the coast often gain a false sense of security through the relative stability of a coastal region, only to find their homes destroyed by a sudden violent storm. In one of the worst disasters in U.S. history, a hurricane struck in 1900 at Galveston, Texas, killing up to 8000 people and flooding the area by up to 5 meters (16 feet). A freak storm in Suffolk, England, in 1953 reduced parts of the coast there by some 27 meters (89 feet). Although violent storm waves are popularly associated with the worst examples of erosion, much smaller surf also can be immensely destructive. At Oceanside, California, swells of perhaps only 1 to 2 meters (3.3 to 6.6 feet) have regularly caused devastation by picking up cobbles from the beach and hurling them like artillery shells at beach houses. Seismic sea waves (tsunamis) can cause considerable coastal erosion where the coastlines are susceptible.

Controlling Coastal Erosion

With U.S. residents taking 2 billion trips to the beach and spending billions of dollars at coastal resorts each year, preserving beaches and other coastal features is not just a matter of protecting property but also an economic necessity. The two principal methods of controlling erosion are by building defenses that will prevent it from taking place and replacing the materials lost by erosive processes. Sea defenses (sometimes called *hard stabilization*) include groins (sturdy fences built perpendicular to beaches to prevent the longshore drift of sand), jetties and break-waters (often built from large boulders, called *riprap*, to protect harbor entrances or beaches by dissipating the energy in oncoming waves), and seawalls. But such measures are expensive and often controversial. The construction of jetties and breakwaters often disrupts the transport of sand to such a degree that it causes considerable erosion of sand in some places and considerable accumulation of sand in other places where it is not needed; this requires costly dredging to move the sand from one place to the other. Nevertheless, sea defenses are increasingly popular. About 80 percent of Georgia's coast and almost all of New Hampshire's are artificially engineered in this way.

Erosion of beaches may be controlled in other ways. One method favored by the U.S. Army Corps of Engineers (responsible for most coastal protection in the United States), *sand replenishment* (or *beach nourishment*), involves adding large quantities of sand to replace that lost from eroded areas. However, this method is environmentally controversial. For example, when clay-rich sand was imported into Miami Beach, Florida, from the Everglades at a cost of U.S.$64 million, the clay particles were subsequently washed offshore, where they damaged coral reefs. Even when successful, the effect is often short-lived and the process must be repeated again and again. A new beach constructed at Ocean City, New Jersey, at a cost of U.S.$5.2 million was removed by storms in just two months.

The cost of controlling erosion is increasing constantly. In 1996, the Army Corps spent U.S.$9 billion replenishing beaches just on the 200-kilometer (120-mile) New Jersey coastline. Critics argue that this is a futile attempt to resist natural forces, but tourism is worth U.S.$12 billion annually to New Jersey, and coastline property is valued at U.S.$34 billion. Every year, millions of dollars are spent on sand replacement projects in the United States and even more is spent on civil engineering works. Critics argue that this policy and federally subsidized flood insurance, in the form of the controversial National Flood Insurance Program (NFIP), have encouraged considerable coastal development in areas already prone to erosion, which has thus become a significant burden on the U.S. taxpayer. With sea levels predicted to rise through global warming, the problem of coastal erosion is certain to become even more pressing and expensive. According to one estimate, a 1-meter (3.3-foot) rise in sea level would require sea defenses costing the United States alone more than U.S.$500 billion per year.

Chris Woodford

FURTHER READING

Bascom, Willard. "Beaches." *Scientific American*, August 1960, p. 80.

Committee on Coastal Erosion Zone Management, Water Science and Technology Board, Marine Board, Commission on Engineering and Technical Systems, National Research Council. *Managing Coastal Erosion.* Washington, D.C.: National Academy of Sciences Press, 1990.

Committee on Engineering Implications of Changes in Relative Mean Sea Level [and] Marine Board, Commission on Engineering and Technical Systems, National Research Council. *Responding to Changes in Sea Level: Engineering Implications.* Washington, D.C.: National Academy of Sciences Press, 1987.

Dean, Cornelia. *Against the Tide: The Battle for America's Beaches.* New York: Columbia University Press, 1999.

Hansom, J. *Coasts.* Cambridge and New York: Cambridge University Press, 1988.

King, Cuchlaine A. *Beaches and Coasts.* London: Edward Arnold, 1960; 2nd ed., New York: St. Martin's Press, 1972.

Komar, Paul, ed. *Handbook of Coastal Processes and Erosion.* Boca Raton, Fla.: CRC Press, 1983.

Pilkey, Orrin, and Katharine Dixon. *The Corps and the Shore.* Washington, D.C.: Island Press, 1998.

Shepherd, Francis. *Geological Oceanography: Evolution of Coasts, Continental Margins, and the Deep-Sea Floor.* New York: Crane, Russak, 1977.

RELATED ARTICLES
Beach; Coastal Morphology; Littoral Zone Processes; Longshore Current; Seismic Sea Wave (Tsunami); Wave

Coastal Front

Fronts are boundaries that separate different air masses in the atmosphere or different water masses in the ocean. In the ocean, fronts are locations where physical, chemical, biological, and optical properties change abruptly. Oceanic fronts can occur anywhere where two water masses with different properties meet. However, there are preferred locations where most ocean fronts are found. These locations include the boundaries along the world's major current systems, such as the northern edge of the Gulf Stream, the subarctic and subtropical fronts that occur in both hemispheres that separate major water masses or current systems in each ocean, and in coastal areas where many different water masses meet and intermingle. Fronts are often observed at the ocean surface but usually extend far below the surface. Fronts are regions where waters come together or converge. Consequently, marine biota are drawn into frontal regions and tend to accumulate there.

In coastal waters, fronts are often referred to as *coastal fronts*. In coastal areas several different types of fronts occur. Coastal fronts that separate freshwater outflows from rivers and estuaries are called *plume fronts*. Fronts occur in regions of coastal upwelling where deep waters are lifted to the surface, forming boundaries that separate the upwelled waters near the coast from the waters farther offshore. Fronts also occur near the offshore boundary of the continental shelf and are called *shelf break fronts*. Finally, *shelf-sea* or *tidal fronts* occur in coastal areas where large changes in tidal mixing take place.

Laurence C. Breaker

FURTHER READING
Fedorov, K. N. *The Physical Nature and Structure of Oceanic Fronts*. Translated by Nadia Demidenko. Berlin and New York: Springer-Verlag, 1986.
Mann, K. H., and J. R. N. Lazier. *Dynamics of Marine Ecosystems*. Boston: Blackwell Scientific, 1991; 2nd ed., 1996.

RELATED ARTICLES
Front; Upwelling

Coastal Morphology

Coastal morphology, Earth's form at the coast, affects how human populations live at the coast. It determines how and where we can build homes and other structures along the coast, the types of recreational activities possible, the kinds and abundance of plants and animals at the coast, and how susceptible the coast is to a number of natural hazards. Understanding coastal morphology enables planners and managers to make better decisions in coastal areas. The world's coastlines are made up of a variety of complex landforms that developed by interaction of geologic and physical processes. Scientists have studied coastal morphology for centuries to try to understand why the morphology varies from place to place and how it might change in the future.

Forces Changing the Coast

The coast is dynamic and responds to many forces acting over a range of time (from seconds to millennia) and length (from meters to thousands of kilometers) scales. Two of the most important agents modifying the coast are sea- and land-level change. Worldwide, sea level was as much as 130 meters (425 feet) lower 18,000 years ago. At this lower sea level, areas now underwater were exposed to terrestrial processes such as river cutting and wind erosion. Many of the coastal landforms today are the result, at least in part, of this lower sea level. A good example of a coastal landform formed by a combination of erosion at lower sea level and the subsequent rise in sea level is an estuary. There were times in the past when sea level was higher than it is today. Higher sea levels leave their mark on the coast above the elevation of the present shoreline.

Changing land levels act in concert with changing sea level to create coastal landforms. Where there is either tectonic uplift (caused by pressures created when tectonic plates collide, such as earthquakes lifting the land) or isostatic uplift (caused by removing a load that was depressing Earth's crust, such as the melting of glaciers reducing the weight pushing on Earth's crust), coastal landforms are found at elevations higher than expected. A good example of this are elevated shorelines that were formed by wave action and are now found hundreds of feet above the present sea level.

At high latitudes glaciers can be a powerful force that molds the coast. Glacial processes create coastal landforms through both erosion and deposition (addition of sediment). For example, fjords are formed where a glacier excavates a valley that is later filled by a rising sea level. Furthermore, the tops of glacial moraines form islands off some coastlines where melting continental glaciers left sediment on the present-day continental shelves.

Extreme events may serve as important morphological agents. Hurricanes and tsunamis (often referred to incorrectly as tidal waves), although infrequent and restricted to certain parts of the world, can have large effects on coastal morphology because they can be such powerful events. Less powerful, more frequent forces may also alter the coast.

Coastal morphology is shaped by waves and currents. Areas where waves are large look different than those where waves are small, and the power of large waves creates dramatic landforms. Like waves, currents may either erode or build

the coast. Inlets, openings between bays or lagoons and the coast, often are formed and maintained by the erosive power of currents. Tidal currents, the flow of the water associated with tides, can be a dominant force forming coastal morphology. For example, where tides in bays are strong enough to move large quantities of sediment, they may control the location and type of landforms of the bay. The rise and fall of tides also sweep wave and current energy over a broad region. The range of tides is a key factor in beach morphology and other forms composed of loose sediment.

Much the world's coastlines are not composed of sediment but are rocky. On rocky coasts, geologic factors, such as rock strength and spatial variations in the strength, play a primary role in determining morphology. Coasts where the rock strength varies alongshore are irregular, with protruding

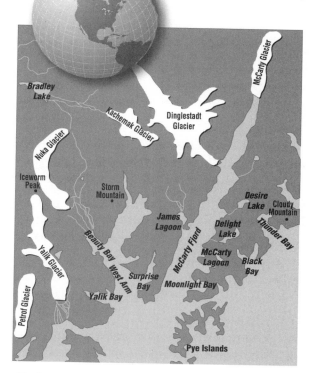

Glacier processes helped to form the complex coastal morphology of the Kenai Fjords on southern Alaska's Kenai Peninsula.

headlands consisting of strong rocks and embayments consisting of weak rocks. Another geologic phenomenon, volcanic eruptions, creates a distinctive coastal morphology. Lava flows entering the sea create benches and black sand beaches. Earthquakes affect morphology by changing the level of the land at the coast. For example, cliffs are prevalent on the west coast of the United States, where many earthquakes have acted to lift the coast.

Biological and climatic factors also mold the coast. In the tropics, corals build reefs that not only create buffers to wave energy but also supply beaches with sediment from their breakdown. Organisms in both tropic and temperate climates are agents of erosion. Different climates also create different coastal landforms through their influence on the rates and types of weathering of rocks. Climate also affects the rate of sediment delivery to the coast and thereby its morphology.

Classification of Coasts

Early studies of coastal morphology described primarily the types and locations of landforms. In the early twentieth century the first classification systems were developed in an attempt to understand why coasts in different areas of the world varied. The first classification scheme grouped coasts into four categories: (1) shorelines of submergence, (2) shorelines of emergence, (3) stable shorelines, and (4) composite shorelines. *Shorelines of submergence* are coasts that exhibit landforms developed by a large long-term rise in sea level, a good example being a coast with drowned river mouths. *Shorelines of emergence* are coasts formed as they are rising relative to sea level. This is caused by tectonic or isostatic uplift, by a falling sea level, or by a combination of the two. A *stable shoreline* is one where landforms do not change rapidly. *Composite shorelines* are a mixture of the other three types of coasts.

As more was learned about the processes that shape coasts, the classification of coasts matured

to reflect the increased knowledge. In the 1960s and 1970s, as the theory that Earth's crust is composed of distinct separate plates moving relative to each other (plate tectonics) became accepted, coastal geomorphologists (scientists who study coastal geomorphology) developed classification schemes tied to the location of the coast relative to plate boundaries. These classifications recognized that both terrestrial and marine processes form a coast and that some processes affect short stretches of coast (small scale) while others affect thousands of kilometers of coast (large scale).

Coastal landforms can be classified by their size. *First-order features* are associated with moving tectonic plates and long-term, large sea-level fluctuations. The dimensions of these features are on the order of 1000 kilometers (620 miles) along the coast, 100 kilometers (62 miles) in the onshore to offshore, and 10 kilometers (6.2 miles) in height. First-order features include mountain ranges, coastal plains, and the continental shelf. Coastal plains are broad, flat areas of coast. The continental shelf is a gently sloping region offshore from the present shoreline to the shoreline at the last-lower sea-level stand. *Second-order features* are associated primarily with processes of erosion and deposition that modify first-order features. The along-coast, onshore–offshore direction and height of these features is on the order of 100 kilometers (62 miles) by 10 kilometers (6.2 miles) by 1 kilometer (0.62 mile). These features include erosional landforms produced by glaciers and depositional landforms such as coastal sand dune fields. *Third-order features* are created by processes that change over short stretches of coast. These features are on the order of 10 kilometers (6.2 miles) along the coast, 1 kilometer (0.62 mile) in the onshore-offshore direction, and 0.1 kilometer (0.062 mile) in height. Beaches and other landforms created by wave action fall into this category. Classification schemes are still being refined as we gain more knowledge of the world's coastlines. The field of coastal morphology is growing rapidly, and there are hundreds of publications each year on this subject.

Common Coastal Landforms

Coastal landforms are created both by erosion of a coast and by accretion (addition) of new coast. Erosional forms include sea cliffs, sea caves, headlands, sea arches, sea stacks, and marine terraces. Accretional forms include deltas, spits, barrier islands, beach ridge plains, coastal sand dunes, and tidal salt marshes. Some coastal landforms are created by a combination of erosion and accretion. These include estuaries and coastal lagoons. Beaches, one of the most recognizable coastal landforms, can change from an erosional to accretional form during the course of a year or during a single storm.

Sea cliffs form where rocks or consolidated sediments are eroded by wave action. Cliffs may be either nearly vertical where cut into strong material or protrude at a lower angle when cut into weaker material or where there are seaward-dipping joints (planes of weakness) in the rock. Sea cliffs may be hundreds of feet high. The height of the cliff is usually more a function of the height of the material eroded than of its composition. The rate of retreat of a sea cliff depends on the composition and structure of the cliff and marine and terrestrial factors. Marine factors affecting the rate of retreat of sea cliffs include the wave energy eroding it, the width of the beach buffering the wave attack, and the tidal range bringing waves to the cliff's base. The primary terrestrial factor affecting retreat is the amount of groundwater in the cliff. Groundwater will weaken the cliff and either allow it to be eroded more easily by waves or induce landslides (another way that cliffs retreat). Sea cliffs composed of weak material, such as the chalk cliffs in Holderness, England, may retreat 1.5 meters (5 feet) or more a year. A variety of morphologic features form where a cliff's resistance to erosion varies either alongshore or with elevation in the cliff.

Sea caves form where an area of cliff is more easily eroded than the cliff on either side. Waves attack this less-resistant area and excavate a cavity. A cave is created as the cavity grows and where the overlying material is strong enough to form a ceiling. Sea caves can be extremely large. In some locations, they extend hundreds of feet inland.

Headlands, portions of coast that extend farther seaward than the adjacent areas, form in sections of coast that are resistant to erosion. Headland size ranges from small (tens of feet wide extending tens of feet into the sea) to very large (tens of miles wide extending miles into the sea).

When land between the point of a small, narrow, cliffed headland and the shore erodes, either a *sea arch* or a *sea stack* may be created. Sea arches, like sea caves, begin to form when a weak portion of the headland is eroded at the bottom and the top portion remains intact. To become a sea arch, the bottom part of the headland must be eroded completely, leaving only a hole. If both the bottom and top of the weak zone are eroded, the point of the headland is isolated from the shore, forming a sea stack.

Marine terraces are nearly flat areas above the present shoreline that may extend miles inland. They are formed when a rock seafloor that is planed off by wave action is lifted out of the water. On many coasts, uplift is produced by a series of earthquakes. The combination of fluctuating sea level and repeated earthquakes over a long period of time can form a staircase of marine terraces and sea cliffs along a coast. In some locations, there are more than a dozen marine terraces bordering the coast. The morphology of a terrace is an outer flatter portion with a gradient of 0.007 to 0.017 (a 7- to 17-foot rise in 1000 feet) and a steeper, slightly concave inshore portion with gradients of 0.02 to 0.04. In populated regions, houses are often built on marine terraces because their flatness makes construction easy.

Deltas are deposits of sediment brought to the coast by rivers. For more information on deltas, see the "Delta" article.

Spits are accretional bodies attached to the coast at one end and free at the other end. Spits may be composed of sand, gravel, or cobbles. Spits form when sediment is transported alongshore by waves approaching the shore obliquely. The dominant direction of longshore transport determines the direction that the spit grows. The free end of the spit usually curves back, forming a hook. This recurve is caused by waves that bend around the end, transporting sediment. Most spits are low lying, although sand dunes may form on them and raise their surface. They may be narrow (hundreds of feet wide) or wide (miles wide), depending on the supply of sediment, the wave climate, and the depth of water where they form. They can be many miles long. Spits may become detached from the coast and become *barrier islands*.

Beach ridges are small ridges (usually only several feet high) that form at the farthest inland point where storm waves deposit sand and other sediment. On a coast with a large sediment supply building the beach out or where sea level is falling, a series of beach ridges may form. This sequence of beach ridges with intervening beaches, called *beach ridge plains*, forms as younger beach ridges accrete seaward of the older ridges.

Another common accretional landform on the coast is the *sand dune*. Coastal sand dunes form where winds blow sand inland from the beach. Sand in dunes is usually finer than beach sand. Transverse dunes, a common form, are oriented perpendicular to the wind direction. They have a triangular profile with a more gentle stoss (the upwind side) slope on the windward side and a steeper (usually 32°) lee (the downwind side) slope. This asymmetry is created by sand grains traveling across the stoss side and avalanching down the lee side. Dunes move in the direction of the wind by this process, much like tank tread rolling forward. Dunes often form dune fields with several or many dunes. They may have either a straight or parabolic ridgeline. Coastal sand dunes can be more than 30 meters (100 feet) high.

Salt marshes are transitional ecosystems, located in areas of sedimentary deposits in the intertidal zone of estuaries, bays, and other low-energy coastal zones. A salt marsh forms when salt-tolerant plants first begin to grow on accreting sediment at or above the low-tide waterline.

Coastal Evolution

The morphology of the coast today is the result of forces that have been acting for many years. Sometimes the coast changes rapidly (e.g., a delta that erodes rapidly because it has lost its sediment supply), and sometimes it changes slowly (e.g., a rocky shoreline that is resistant to erosion). An interesting problem to think about is the effect of human activities on the coast. How will global warming and building structures (e.g., seawalls and dams) affect how the coast evolves?

Bruce E. Jaffe

FURTHER READING

Bird, Eric. *Coastal Geomorphology: An Introduction.* New York: Wiley, 2000.

Davis, John Lloyd. *Geographical Variation in Coastal Development*, 2nd ed. (Geomorphology Texts, Vol. 4, General Editor, K. M. Clayton). London: Longman Group, 1980.

Inman, Douglas, and C. E. Nordstrom. "On the Tectonic and Morphologic Classification of Coasts." *Journal of Geology*, Vol. 79 (1971), pp. 1–21.

Komar, Paul. *Beach Processes and Sedimentation*, 2nd ed. Upper Saddle River, N.J.: Prentice Hall, 1998.

Shepard, Francis. *Submarine Geology*, 3rd ed. New York: Harper and Row, 1973.

Short, Andrew, ed. *Handbook of Beach and Shoreface Morphodynamics.* New York: Wiley, 1999.

RELATED ARTICLES

Barrier Island; Beach; Coastal Erosion; Delta; Estuary; Eustatic Sea Level; Glacial Marine Processes; Lagoon; Littoral Zone Processes; Plate Tectonics; Salt Marsh; Tide; Wave

Coastal Zone Color Scanner

The Coastal Zone Color Scanner (CZCS) was a satellite remote sensing instrument flown aboard the U.S. satellite *Nimbus 7* between 1978 and 1986. The Nimbus series of satellites were designed to test experimental remote sensing instruments, and the CZCS proved highly successful.

Principle of Operation

As its name suggests, the CZCS was designed to observe coastal waters using a range of colors. By producing images in various wavelengths of light, the instrument could detect the absorption of particular wavelengths by the green pigment chlorophyll in plankton and other surface vegetation, as well as by mapping sediment particles suspended in the water and measuring changing surface temperatures.

The CZCS gathered light from a small spot on the ground below using a rapidly rotating flat mirror, angled at 45° so that it reflected light into the aperture of a Cassegrain (reflecting) telescope. The telescope collected and focused the light, producing an intensified beam that was then split in two by a glass wedge. Then one beam was directed to a cooled electronic detector that measured the level of infrared radiation at the spot being monitored, while the other was further split through a polychromator, which divided the light into five separate beams of particular colors and directed each beam onto a separate electronic detector to measure the intensity of its light.

The *Nimbus 7* satellite circled Earth at an altitude of 955 kilometers (593 miles) in an orbit that took it close to Earth's North and South Poles, so that as Earth rotated beneath it, the satellite would pass over most of the planet's surface within just a few days. The satellite's orbit also slowly changed so that it remained "Sun-synchronous"; in other words, it kept the same orientation in respect to the Sun, so the illumination of the surface below remained constant.

The collecting mirror rotated eight times each second, but was exposed to Earth's surface for only 27.5 microseconds in each rotation. The rest of the time, the mirror was directed toward either a calibrating light source (whose known properties allowed operators to adjust the instrument's sensitivity) or at deep space. The result was a series of scans providing electronic values for the intensity of the different wavelengths along a narrow strip of Earth's surface. Each strip was 1556 kilometers (967 miles) long, centered on the nadir (the point directly below the satellite) and only a few kilometers wide. The satellite's rapid movement along its orbit allowed the scan strips to be built up into maps of the ocean and coast below. At best, the CZCS could resolve details down to 800 meters (2625 feet) across.

Uses of Data

The CZCS detected radiation in six different channels. The infrared detector monitored radiation with wavelengths around 11.5 micrometers—much longer than visible light—while the visible light was split into bands focused on 443, 520, 550, 670, and 750 nanometers. Information from the infrared instrument was used to calculate the sea's surface temperature, while the 443- and 670-nanometer visible wavelengths corresponded to the strongest absorption of light by chlorophyll, the chemical that powers photosynthesis in plankton and vegetation. Images in these wavelengths therefore showed areas of high chlorophyll concentrations as dark. The 520- and 550-nanometer images were used to verify the chlorophyll maps produced by the instrument—550 nanometers was particularly important, since this is the wavelength of light most strongly reflected by chlorophyll. Genuine chlorophyll sources would show up brightly at this wavelength. The 750-nanometer wavelength similarly helped to distinguish surface vegetation from plankton actually in the water. Combined together, the images from all these wavelengths could be reconstructed into maps showing the wide variety of sea colors, or computer-analyzed and given false colors to highlight various features.

Giles Sparrow

FURTHER READING
Barale, Vittorio, and Peter M. Schlittenhardt, eds. *Ocean Colour: Theory and Applications in a Decade of CZCS Experience.* Dordrecht, the Netherlands, and Boston: Kluwer Academic Publishing, 1993.
Rees, Gareth. *The Remote Sensing Data Book.* Cambridge and New York: Cambridge University Press, 1999.

RELATED ARTICLES
Satellite Remote Sensing

Coccolithophore, see Haptophyta

Cocos Plate

The Cocos Plate is a small tectonic plate located east of Central America. It is roughly the shape of a triangle with vertices off the coasts of Panama (9°N, 83°W) and Mexico (20°N, 105°W), and on the East Pacific Rise (0°, 107°W) in the Pacific Ocean. The Cocos Plate is bounded by the Caribbean Plate to the east, the North American Plate to the north, the Pacific Plate to the west, and the Nazca Plate to the south. It is thought to be a remnant of an ancient lithospheric plate called the Farallon Plate. Along with the Nazca Plate, the Cocos Plate is floored entirely by basaltic ocean crust. The composition of the sediment blanket covering this crust consists of a thin layer of hydrothermal deposits, calcium carbonate ooze, and terrestrial sediments eroded from Central America. A small accretionary prism has evolved on the landward edge of the Middle America Trench. Several significant geologic features are associated with the Cocos Plate, including hydrothermal vents, earthquakes, and volcanoes.

Hydrothermal vent fields are characteristic of two of the Cocos Plate's boundaries. The first diffuse hydrothermal vents found in the ocean were located in 1977 at 2500 meters (8200 feet) depth at the Galápagos Spreading Center, the divergent plate boundary between the Nazca and Cocos Plates. These particular vents are warm water springs where water slowly emerges from the seafloor at temperatures 6 to 20°C (43 to 68°F) above the ambient bottom water [1 to 2°C (34 to 36°F)]. This amazing discovery led to further discoveries of hydrothermal vents along most spreading ridges of the world, including the East Pacific Rise, the spreading ridge that is the border between the Cocos and Pacific Plates. Studies of associated black smokers, chimneys, and chemosynthetic biological communities have increased our knowledge of the formation of mineral deposits and the origin of life.

The boundary between the Cocos and Caribbean Plates is a convergent plate boundary. The interaction between these plates causes widespread seismic and volcanic activity in Central America, which has important socioeconomic consequences. The Cocos Plate is moving northeast, away from the Pacific and Nazca Plates, at the geologically lightning-quick rate of approximately 100 millimeters (3.94 inches) per year. This causes the Cocos Plate to collide with the western edge of the Caribbean Plate, where it forms the Middle America Trench and attendant subduction zone. Here, the denser oceanic crust of the Cocos Plate is thrust, or subducted, under the less dense continental crust of the Caribbean Plate. As the Cocos Plate plunges beneath the Caribbean Plate, enormous pressures and temperatures cause earthquakes and volcanic eruptions. These earthquakes and volcanoes have proven to be very destructive for life and property in the Central American region.

Daniel Schuller

FURTHER READING
Brown, J., A. Colling, D. Park, J. Phillips, D. Rother, and J. Wright. In G. Bearman, ed., *Ocean Chemistry and*

Deep-Sea Sediments. Oxford: Pergamon Press, in association with the Open University, Milton Keynes, England, 1989.

Burke, K., C. Cooper, J. Dewey, P. Mann, and J. Pindell. "Caribbean Tectonics and Relative Plate Motions." In William E. Bonini, Robert B. Hargraves, and Reginald Shagam, eds., *The Caribbean–South American Plate Boundary and Regional Tectonics,* Vol. 162. Boulder, Colo.: Geological Society of America Memoir, 1984; pp. 31–63.

Mattson, P. "Caribbean Structural Breaks and Plate Movements." In William E. Bonini, Robert B. Hargraves, and Reginald Shagam, eds., *The Caribbean–South American Plate Boundary and Regional Tectonics,* Vol. 162. Boulder, Colo.: Geological Society of America Memoir, 1984; pp. 131–152.

Wright, John, and Dave Rothery, eds. *The Ocean Basins: Their Structure and Evolution.* Oxford and New York: Pergamon Press/Milton Keynes, England: Open University, 1989; 2nd ed., Oxford: Butterworth-Heinemann, in association with the Open University, 1998.

USEFUL WEB SITES

Rothman, Robert. "Plate Tectonics and the Formation of the Galápagos Islands." 2000. <http://www.rit.edu/~rhrsbi/GalapagosPages/Vulcanism2.html>.

RELATED ARTICLES

Accretionary Prism; Chemosynthesis; Convergent Plate Boundary; Divergent Plate Boundary; Galápagos Spreading Center; Hydrothermal Vent; Mid-Ocean Ridge; Nazca Plate; Pacific Plate; Plate Tectonics; Seafloor Spreading; Subduction Zone

Coelacanth

The coelacanth (*Latimeria chalumnae*) is the sole surviving species of the subclass Coelacanthimorpha and belongs to an ancient class of animals known as the Sarcopterygii (lobe-finned fishes). Along with the coelacanth, the extant sarcopterygians include the air-breathing lungfishes (infraclass Dipnoi) that live in Australia, Africa, and South America. Sarcopterygians are also linked to the tetrapod vertebrates (amphibians, reptiles, birds, and mammals), which are believed to have descended from a common ancestor within this group. Coelacanths were common before and during the Mesozoic Era (247.5 million to 65 million years ago) and were thought to have become extinct 60 to 70 million years ago, when they disappeared from the fossil record. However, in December 1938, fishermen caught a 1.5-meter (5-foot)-long specimen near the coast of South Africa. The discovery, akin to finding a living dinosaur, caused great excitement among scientists and made the species famous worldwide as a "living fossil."

Coelacanths are important to science because of their presumed taxonomic relationship to the tetrapods. Amphibians are thought to have descended from a now-extinct group of sarcopterygians, either within the subclass Coelacanthimorpha or Osteolepimorpha (the extinct rhipidistians). Scientists believe that the stout, lobe-shaped fins of ancestral sarcopterygians gradually evolved into limbs as they adapted to life on land. The coelacanth's DNA sequence indicates a close relationship to modern amphibians, and its hemoglobin (the oxygen-carrying pigment in blood) is similar to that of tadpoles. In addition, the bones of the paired fins articulate with the pectoral and pelvic girdles in a manner analogous to that of tetrapods. However, the coelacanth lacks lungs necessary for adaptation to life on land. Rhipidistians, however, had well-developed lungs. This characteristic, combined with strong fossil evidence, supports an alternative lineage from within the Osteolepimorpha. Scientific debate continues regarding this issue.

After the first coelacanth was caught, the hunt was on to obtain more specimens, and a reward was offered. But it was not until 1952 that the second coelacanth was found, this time in the Comoro Islands, northwest of Madagascar (where the fish is known to locals for its abrasive skin, which can be used like sandpaper). Since then over 200 coelacanths have been found around the

Comoros and in Indonesia, but few have been kept alive for long. Until recently, what little scientists know about these fish came from studies of their anatomy. However, submersible observations made during the last decade have greatly expanded our understanding of coelacanth biology.

The coelacanth lives near the seafloor at depths of 150 to 250 meters (490 to 820 feet), in association with rocky volcanic slopes, where it uses caves for refuge. Coelacanths feed at night on large bottom fishes, including small sharks, which they apparently detect through electroreception with an organ located in the snout (rostral organ). In addition to prey detection, it is theorized that this organ is used in navigation, and it has been demonstrated that coelacanths exhibit homing behavior, returning to the same cave to rest during the daytime. In contrast to original scientific opinion, coelacanths use their fins for stabilization as they drift in bottom currents, not for walking on the bottom. This species is rare throughout their range and may be limited in number by their specific habitat requirements.

Coelacanths are ovoviviparous, and females retain up to 20 eggs in the body cavity where the young hatch and develop during a gestation period of approximately 13 months. Although the age and growth characteristics of this species are still poorly known, coelacanths just under 2 meters (6.6 feet) have been aged at 11 years. Coelacanths exhibit a primitive osmoregulatory strategy and are nearly isosmotic with seawater, maintaining high concentrations of urea in the blood, much like sharks and rays. This characteristic, along with the presence of a spiral-valve intestine, has led some scientists to link the coelacanth more closely to the Chondrichthyes (cartilaginous fishes) than the bony fishes (Osteichthyes).

Ben Morgan

FURTHER READING

Bond, Carl E. *Biology of Fishes*. Philadelphia, Pa.: W. B. Saunders, 1979; 2nd ed., Fort Worth, Tex.: Saunders College Publishing, 1996.

Carroll, R. L. *Vertebrate Paleontology and Evolution*. New York: W. H. Freeman, 1988.

Clouthier, R., and P. E. Ahlberg. "Morphology, Characters, and the Interrelationships of the Basal Sarcopterygians." In M. L. J. Stiassny, L. R. Parenti, and G. D. Johnson, eds., *Interrelationships of Fishes*. San Diego: Academic Press, 1996; pp. 445–480

Glausiusz, Josie. "The Old Fish of the Sea." *Discover*, January 1999.

Gorr, T., and T. Kleinschmidt. "Evolutionary Relationships of the Coelacanth." *American Scientist*, Vol. 81 (1993), pp. 72-82.

Helfman, Gene S., Bruce B. Collette, and Douglas E. Facey. *The Diversity of Fishes*. Malden, Mass.: Blackwell Science, 1997.

Moyle, Peter B., and Joseph J. Cech. *Fishes: An Introduction to Ichthyology*. Englewood Cliffs, N.J.: Prentice Hall, 1982; 4th ed., Upper Saddle River, N.J.: Prentice Hall, 2000.

Thomson, Keith Stewart. *Living Fossil: The Story of the Coelacanth*. New York: W. W. Norton, 1991.

RELATED ARTICLES
Chondrichthyes; Dipnoi; Osmoregulator; Osteichthyes; Sarcopterygii

Coelenterata, see Cnidaria; Ctenophora

Cold Seep

Various types of fluids flow out of the seafloor into the ocean in several geologic settings. One way to classify these processes is by the temperature of the fluid. Hydrothermal circulation associated with volcanic activity at active plate boundaries (e.g., mid-ocean ridges) results in active venting of hot fluids. In contrast, more gentle seepage of much colder fluids ("cold seeps") is an increasingly recognized process on continental margins. Cold seeps are important because they (1) affect the recycling of carbon and other nutrients, (2) alter the topography of the seafloor, (3) result in the destruction and formation of minerals, (4) can support chemosynthetic communities (e.g., tube worms), and (5) affect the chemistry of the ocean.

Since their discovery in the early 1980s, cold seeps have been found at active and passive continental margins at water depths ranging from 400 to 6000 meters (1310 to 19,700 feet). Seepage is related to processes such as tectonically induced stresses, compaction, hydrocarbon escape, artesian flow (confined water under pressure that flows when tapped by a well), and mass wasting (e.g., slumping). Fluid compositions range from hypersaline to fresh and can be petroleum- and/or sulfide-rich. Cold seeps are not just a recent phenomenon. Using the modern deposits as analogs, ancient cold seep deposits are being recognized now as well.

Groundwater Cold Seeps

The discharge of groundwater into the ocean in the coastal zone and through the seafloor farther offshore is a common but not well quantified process. The amount of groundwater discharging directly into the coastal ocean may be significant. One study off South Carolina estimates that the volume of groundwater flowing into the coastal zone could be as high as 40 percent of river input into the oceans. Farther offshore, artesian flow has been noted on numerous continental shelves around the world, including offshore Florida, the Arabian Gulf, Adriatic Sea (Gulf of Kastela), and offshore Lebanon. In addition, fresh- to brackish-water plumes have been noted beneath the seafloor off the U.S. east coast, extending as far as 130 kilometers (81 miles) offshore. On some margins, such as the base of the west Florida escarpment, hypersaline, sulfide-rich groundwaters are seeping out of the margin into ocean waters. Because much groundwater flow and seepage may not be as easily recognized as the artesian flow systems, the magnitude of seepage into the ocean could be much higher than is currently estimated.

Hydrocarbon Cold Seeps

Hydrocarbons are generated by either the bacterial or thermal breakdown of organic matter in sediments. Thus, hydrocarbon seeps are likely to occur in any sedimentary basin, particularly where petroleum source rocks or reservoirs are present. Hydrocarbon seepage, ranging from bacterial-generated methane to thermogenic liquid petroleum, has been described at both active and passive continental margins. Examples include the northern Gulf of Mexico, North Sea, Monterey Bay, California, North Carolina continental slope, and the accretionary prisms of Barbados, Oregon–Washington, Nankai–Japan, and Peru, among others. Hydrocarbons must migrate to the seafloor from their site of formation, which is accomplished via a variety of mechanisms largely dependent on the geologic setting. In general, hydrocarbon-charged fluids escape directly into seawater by diffuse flow or by focused venting, often along faults and fractures.

Biological Communities

Dense benthic chemosynthetic communities have been found at numerous cold seep sites characterized by petroleum- or sulfide-rich fluids. Similar to organisms found at hydrothermal vent sites, these communities are believed to derive their energy from reduced carbon and/or sulfur compounds with assistance from symbiotic bacteria rather than by photosynthesis. Not surprisingly, cold-seep communities generally resemble hydrothermal vent organisms with tube worms, mussels, and clams as some of the common constituents. These chemosynthetic-dependent organisms attract other ocean life (e.g., fish and crabs), forming a dense biologic community in the deep sea. Thus far, a total of 211 species have been cataloged from cold-seep sites. However, a recent detailed survey noted only 13 common species between cold-seep and hydrothermal vent communities. These numbers should be judged as preliminary because much more thorough exploration of these environments remains to be conducted.

Other Consequences of Seepage

The migration of cold fluids to the seafloor is not a passive process. Both erosive and constructive products have been attributed to seepage. Probably the most common erosive feature associated with seeps is pockmarks, which are hollow depressions or craters on the surface of the seafloor. Pockmarks, with dimensions typically about 50 to 100 meters (165 to 330 feet) in diameter and 2 to 3 meters (6 to 10 feet) deep, form as a result of rapid fluid escape from the seafloor, causing displacement of fine-grained sediment. Seepage through steep-sided carbonate platforms such as the west Florida escarpment is believed to help shape its morphology by solution undercutting and steepening of the slope. Dissolution from seep fluids has also been attributed to playing a role in the formation of some submarine canyons in a process called *spring sapping*. In some regions, positive topographic features composed of mud, called *mud volcanoes* or *mud diapirs*, have been described associated with release of gas beneath the seafloor. Especially at methane-rich seeps, lithified sediments at the seafloor are common. In most cases, these are nodular masses, thin hard layers, or slabs cemented by various carbonate minerals such as calcite and dolomite. In general, carbonate minerals precipitate when methane is oxidized at or near the seafloor. Depending on the pressure and temperature conditions at the seafloor, natural gas hydrates have also been described associated with hydrocarbon seeps (e.g., Gulf of Mexico). Gas hydrates are icelike compounds composed of water and gas, often methane, which form under high-pressure and low-temperature conditions.

The Future

We are still a long way from completely understanding the operation of cold-seep systems and many of the ecologic aspects of the biologic communities that thrive at these sites. Therefore, future research will probably focus on continued basic cataloging of seep sites. The flux of chemicals from seep sites certainly affects global geochemical cycles, which can have important implications. For example, understanding the global carbon cycle, the sizes of the sources and sinks, and how carbon shifts or migrates from one to the other is critically important if we are to understand the effects of the increasing carbon dioxide content of the atmosphere from human input. However, the input of carbon from below the seafloor to the ocean and potentially to the atmosphere from cold seeps is only crudely known.

Mitchell J. Malone

FURTHER READING

Beauchamp, B., H. R. Krouse, J. C. Harrison, W. W. Nassihuk, and L. S. Eluik. "Cretaceous Cold-Seep Communities and Methane-Derived Carbonates in the Canadian Arctic." *Science*, Vol. 244 (1989), pp. 53–56.

Dando, P. R., and M. Hovland. "Environmental Effects of Submarine Natural Gas." *Continental Shelf Research*, Vol. 12 (1992), pp. 1197–1207.

Hovland, M., and A. G. Judd. *Seabed Pockmarks and Seepages: Impact on Geology, Biology, and the Marine Environment.* London and Boston: Graham and Trotman, 1988.

"Old Worms." *National Wildlife*, Vol. 38, No. 4 (June/July 2000), p. 10.

Pain, S. "Monster Journeys." *New Scientist*, Vol. 152, No. 2054 (2 November 1996), p. 14.

Paull, C. K., B. Hecker, R. Commeau, R. P. Freeman-Lynde, C. Neumann, S. Golubic, J. E. Hook, E. Sikes, and J. Curray. "Biological Communities at the Florida Escarpment Resemble Hydrothermal Vent Taxa." *Science*, Vol. 226 (1984), pp. 965–967.

Sibuet, M., and K. Olu. "Biogeography, Biodiversity, and Fluid Dependence of Deep-Sea Cold-Seep Communities at Active and Passive Margins." *Deep-Sea Research*, Part II, Vol. 45 (1998), pp. 517–567.

RELATED ARTICLES

Carbon Cycle; Chemosynthesis; Gas Hydrate; Hydrocarbon Seep; Hydrothermal Vent; Methane Seep; Symbiosis

Colligative Properties

Colligative properties are those properties of a solution that are affected by the number of solutes in a solvent, regardless of the chemical properties of the solutes. Colligative properties include vapor pressure, osmotic pressure, boiling and freezing points, temperature of maximum density, and heat capacity. For example, when you add antifreeze to the water in your car's radiator, you increase the number of solutes present in the original solution (the water), thereby lowering the freezing point and raising the boiling point. This same principle is present in some marine organisms, such as a group of Antarctic fish, the Notothenoids, that contain antifreeze compounds in their blood.

Imagine that the sea is a large bowl of alphabet soup, where the macaroni noodles represent elements and ions, collectively called *solutes*. For millions of years continental runoff containing the dissolved components of the crust have flowed into the sea, providing a fertile soup to nourish primordial life. Every element present on the planet is dissolved in the sea. However, in seawater the majority of solutes by mass are comprised of six ions (chlorine, sodium, calcium, potassium, magnesium, and sulfate) that are distributed in constant proportions in seawater. This phenomenon is known as *Marcet's principle,* or the *principle of constant proportions*. These proportions can be used to calculate salinity, from which inferences are possible regarding colligative properties.

Changes in salinity therefore affect colligative properties, since this would signify a change in the amount of solutes present. Such changes may occur, for example, when sea ice forms. The ice is almost pure water, leaving behind the solutes and contributing to a localized body of supersaline solution. The supersaline solution has a depressed freezing point, allowing it to remain a liquid at lower temperatures, which also allows for an increase in density. The shift in these colligative properties causes the heavier water to sink to the bottom, until it reaches a body of water of similar density. The sinking of cold seawater is what drives the thermohaline circulation of the oceans. Similar physical processes that change colligative properties include evaporation, precipitation, and mixing of water bodies.

Biological systems can affect colligative properties as well. Blooms of phytoplankton may deplete surface waters of nutrient type ions such as nitrate and phosphate. More important, the distribution of calcium, one of the six major ions, is controlled by biological processes. For instance, phytoplankton incorporate calcium carbonate into their tests or shells, depleting levels in the euphotic zone. The tests eventually sink and either are buried in shallower seas or are dissolved at greater depths. This yields a distribution of calcium carbonate that is vertically segregated if the rate of sinking is greater than the rate of input.

These examples demonstrate that both physical and biological systems are involved with the distribution of solutes and therefore colligative properties within the ocean. Colligative properties of seawater allow for gradients, whether density driven or pressure driven, that provide for stratification and ultimately thermohaline circulation throughout the world's oceans.

Judah Goldberg

FURTHER READING

Millero, Frank J. *Chemical Oceanography.* Boca Raton, Fla.: CRC Press, 1992; 2nd ed., 1996.

Open University Course Team. *Seawater: Its Composition, Properties, and Behavior.* Oxford: Pergamon Press/Milton Keynes, England: Open University, 1989; 2nd ed., rev. by John Wright and Angela Colling, Oxford and New York: Pergamon Press, 1995.

RELATED ARTICLES

Calcium; Constant Proportions, Principle of; Hydrosphere; Thermohaline Circulation

Commensalism

Symbiosis describes a permanent or long-lasting relationship between members of different species. Symbiosis is pervasive in the natural world, and many different types of association exist. Scientists subdivide symbioses into categories based on factors such as whether the association is harmful or beneficial, and whether one or both partners are affected.

Commensalism is a type of symbiosis in which one partner benefits and the other partner neither benefits nor is harmed. The word *commensal* was coined by Pierre-Joseph van Beneden (1809–94) in 1876 to describe an association between animals in which one shares food captured by the other; the partners were viewed as "messmates" eating from the same table. Commensalism has since taken on a broader meaning and includes many types of "taking without harming"; in addition to food, the association may provide shelter, protection, substrate, or transportation to one of the partners. Commensalism also includes *inquilism*, which is a relationship in which one animal lives in the tube or burrow of another, or in its digestive tract. It can be difficult to discern if a given relationship is truly commensal or if the host also receives some benefit from the association; the latter situation is called *mutualism.*

In a commensal relationship the organism receiving the benefit is called the *commensal* and the other partner is the *host.* Commensals that live on other animals are called *epizoites;* those that live inside their hosts are called *endozoites.* Commensals can be highly specific to a particular host or they may associate with many different host types. The relationship may be *facultative,* in which the commensal can also be free-living, or *obligate,* in which the commensal is highly adapted to living with its host and cannot live on its own.

Commensal relationships are extremely common in the marine environment. For example, ciliate protists often live in clam gills, on the external surfaces of crustaceans, and in the guts of sea urchins. Hydroids, the most common commensal cnidarian, live in association with other invertebrates, such as polychaete worms, clams, snails, gorgonians, sea pens, and tunicates. In some cases, the hydroid benefits nutritionally: Two-tentacled hydroids, which live on the rim of the tube built by their polychaete host, obtain food. Other hydroids live on hermit crab shells and snail shells, where they hitch a ride. Still others benefit from a substrate that allows them to inhabit an otherwise uninhabitable environment such as sand. Turbellarian flatworms often live in the digestive tracts of marine invertebrates and in the mantle cavities of mollusks; in both cases the commensal is protected from predators and may also obtain food. Entoprocts, which inhabit the respiratory currents of polychaete worms, also benefit from food and protection. Commensal bryozoans obtain transportation and a substrate

A remora is attached to the underside of a spotted eagle ray as it swims in the Indian Ocean off the coast of the Maldive Islands. (© Amos Nachoum/Corbis)

from their crustacean hosts. Annelids such as scale worms commonly live on other echinoderms, on mollusks, and in polychaete tubes; other commensal polychaetes inhabit the mantle cavities of chitons and limpets. Commensal crustaceans include some species of copepods, amphipods, and decapods. Pea crabs are common commensals that are often found in polychaete tubes or in the mantle cavities of bivalves. Most molluskan commensals are small bivalves that are associated with urchins, shrimps, and crabs. Fish commensals, which include pilot fishes and remoras, often receive protection from predators as well as food from their hosts. In addition to simple one-on-one relationships, an organism may host many different commensal animals. For example, on the Pacific coast of North America, an echiuran worm's U-shaped burrow hosts at least four different commensal species, including a fish, a scale worm, a clam, and a shrimp.

Lynn L. Lauerman

FURTHER READING

Ahmadjian, Vernon, and Surindar Paracer. *Symbiosis: An Introduction to Biological Associations.* Oxford: Oxford University Press, 2000.

Dales, R. P. "Commensalism." In J. E. Hedgpeth, ed., *The Treatise on Marine Ecology and Paleoecology,* Vol. I, *Ecology.* Geological Society of America Memoir, Vol. 67 (1957), pp. 391–412.

Henry, S. Mark, ed. *Symbiosis.* New York: Academic Press, 1966.

Nybakken, James W. *Marine Biology: An Ecological Approach,* 5th ed. San Francisco: Benjamin Cummings, 2001.

RELATED ARTICLES

Epizoic; Mutualism; Symbiosis

Compass

The compass is one of the earliest tools used in navigation. The exact origins of the tool are unknown, although it was used in Europe and China by the twelfth century. The first compasses were what are now called *magnetic compasses.* They took advantage of an observation that a needle-shaped magnet, or even just a magnetized metal needle, will point north when floated in water. By the thirteenth century, European navigators were mounting magnetized needles on pivots in bowls marked with the cardinal directions, a design that has barely changed over the centuries.

Magnetic compasses work because Earth is enveloped in a magnetic field that stretches from north to south. Earth's magnetic field exerts a force on all other magnets, pushing them into alignment with it. This force is fairly weak and works only on magnets that are in a relatively frictionless environment. The magnetic north pole is near, but does not line up exactly with, the geographic North Pole. As a result, magnetic compasses do not always point true north, a defect that Europeans began to recognize in the fifteenth century. Attempts to compensate for the variation between true north and magnetic north were made more difficult by the tendency of the magnetic poles to wander about slowly.

Improvements to the compass continued to be made. In the mid-eighteenth century a method of magnetizing steel was devised that caused the metal to retain its magnetic character for much longer than before. Throughout the nineteenth century the design of the compass was improved constantly to make the needle swing more freely; that way the needle would remain pointing north even if the vessel that the compass was on changed direction quickly.

The early twentieth century saw the development of the first nonmagnetic compass, which ultimately freed the compass from the magnetic north. The compass, called a *gyrocompass,* uses gyroscopes, wheels that spin around a single axis. With a gyrocompass, a series of gyroscopes are nestled within each other, attached in such a way that the axis of one gyroscope is perpendicular to the axis of the next gyroscope in. The outer gyroscopes absorb any motion, leaving the inner, marked gyroscope pointing solidly at true north, or any other direction that the maker of the compass desires.

Mary Sisson

FURTHER READING
Eyster, Bill. *Thataway: The Story of the Magnetic Compass.* South Brunswick, N.J.: A.S. Barnes, 1970.
Ferry, Ervin S. *Applied Gyrodynamics, for Students, Engineers and Users of Gyroscopic Apparatus.* New York: Wiley, 1933.
Hine, Alfred. *Magnetic Compasses and Magnetometers.* London: Adam Hilger, 1968.

RELATED ARTICLES
Navigation

Compensation Depth

The compensation depth is the depth in the ocean at which the rates of photosynthesis and cellular respiration for a phytoplankton cell are equal. Because photosynthesis depends on light, the compensation depth can also be defined in terms of *light intensity* (also called *compensation intensity*): It is the depth in the water column to which only 1 percent of the light that reaches the sea surface penetrates. The water column above the compensation depth is called the *euphotic zone.*

Because seawater absorbs light, light availability decreases with depth, and at some point it disappears altogether. At the compensation depth, there is only enough light for phytoplankton cells to fix energy at a rate that equals the rate of energy loss due to cellular metabolism. Thus, at the compensation depth, net energy production is zero. At shallower depths, the rate of photosynthesis exceeds that of respiration; at deeper depths more energy is used in respiration than is created by photosynthesis, and a net loss of energy occurs.

Compensation depth is rarely deeper than 200 meters (656 feet). It varies depending on factors

that alter light availability, such as time of year, time of day, geographical location, and water clarity. For example, the compensation depth tends to be deeper in clear, open ocean waters than in particle-laden coastal waters, and upwelling or springtime mixing events can change the compensation depth in a given locale.

Lynn L. Lauerman

FURTHER READING
Nybakken, James W. *Marine Biology: An Ecological Approach,* 5th ed. San Francisco: Benjamin Cummings, 2001.
Valiela, Ivan. *Marine Ecological Processes.* New York: Springer-Verlag, 1984; 2nd ed., 1995.

RELATED ARTICLES
Compensation Intensity; Critical Depth; Euphotic Zone; Phytoplankton

Compensation Intensity

The compensation intensity in the water column is a way of defining compensation depth in terms of light intensity: It is the intensity of light at which the processes of photosynthesis and respiration are equal. Compensation intensity can vary slightly for different species of phytoplankton, but in general it is defined as the depth in the water column to which 1 percent of the radiation received at the ocean surface penetrates. The water above this depth, which is the compensation depth, is defined as the *euphotic zone*, and it is where photosynthesis occurs in the oceans.

The compensation intensity represents the lower limit for photosynthesis and phytoplankton growth to occur. Light intensity in the water column varies depending on the quantity of dissolved and suspended material (including phytoplankton cells) in the water because these substances absorb and reflect light and reduce light penetration. The depth of the euphotic zone also varies with parameters such as time of day, season, and geographic location. Even in the clearest oceanic waters compensation intensity rarely is deeper than 200 meters (656 feet); in coastal waters during a spring bloom it may be as shallow as 10 meters (33 feet). Thus, primary production is limited to a very narrow zone.

Lynn L. Lauerman

FURTHER READING

Nybakken, James W. *Marine Biology: An Ecological Approach,* 5th ed. San Francisco: Benjamin Cummings, 2001.

Valiela, Ivan. *Marine Ecological Processes.* New York: Springer-Verlag, 1984; 2nd ed., 1995.

RELATED ARTICLES

Compensation Depth; Critical Depth; Euphotic Zone; Phytoplankton

Competitive Exclusion

In its simplest definition, *competitive exclusion* is an ecological principle that says that complete competitors cannot coexist. In ecology, *competition* refers to an interaction among organisms for a resource that is necessary to life but occurs in limited supply. Such competition among organisms of the same species is called *intraspecific competition*; among individuals of different species it is called *interspecific competition*. Although competition may be for a number of different resources, in the marine environment it is usually limited to a few factors, of which light, nutrients, food, and space are the most significant. Where a competitive interaction occurs, there are two possible outcomes: Either the two competitors manage to share the limited resource, in which case both competitors are hampered in their growth, development, or reproduction and the populations of both species are limited; or one manages to exclude the other. The latter condition is competitive exclusion.

Competitive exclusion usually occurs between two closely related species. For example, the shores of New England host two species of

barnacles, *Chthamalus stellatus* and *Semibalanus balanoides*. In the midintertidal zone both barnacles settle out, but *Chthamalus* later disappears from the midintertidal, due to competition from *Semibalanus*, which overgrows, uplifts, or crushes the smaller *Chthamalus* to take over the limited space. Competitive exclusion usually involves two closely related species, although this is not always the case. For example, in the intertidal zone of the Pacific Northwest in Washington state, space is the limited resource and therefore the one for which competition occurs. In this habitat the mussel *Mytilus californianus* is the dominant space competitor, and in the absence of predators it is able to competitively exclude many other intertidal invertebrates, such as barnacles, which are not closely related.

The competitive exclusion principle has a long and controversial history in ecology. It was first formally elucidated by Gauss in 1934, who wrote: "As a result of competition two similar species scarcely ever occupy similar niches, but displace each other in such a manner that each takes possession of certain peculiar kinds of food and modes of life in which it has an advantage over its competitor." In this case the term *niche* refers to the role of the organism in the community. Similar ideas about competitive exclusion, although not as well defined, occur in earlier biological writings.

The controversial aspect of the competitive exclusion principle pertains mainly to the various attempts among ecologists to verify this rule in field and laboratory studies. Most of these studies in natural communities have failed to detect ongoing competitive exclusion, usually because of slight differences among the potentially competing species, which suggested that they were not complete competitors in all aspects of their ecology. However, there are some good examples of ongoing competitive exclusion where there have been introductions of alien species into habitats where they did not occur naturally. For example, in San Francisco Bay the native mud snail *Cerithidea californica* has been outcompeted over much of its mudflat habitat by two introduced snails with similar ecological characteristics: *Batillaria attrementaria* and *Ilyanassa obsoleta.* Such studies suggest that competitive interaction may have occurred in the past in natural communities.

Another problem with the principle has to do with how complete the overlap for the competed resources must be before exclusion occurs. Where overlap is low, both species might continue to exist. Also, cases of nearly complete overlap of one resource may not lead to competitive exclusion if two or more resources are important to the competing species and there is little overlap in the second or other resources.

James W. Nybakken

FURTHER READING

Krebs, Charles J. *Ecology: The Experimental Analysis of Distribution and Abundance.* New York: Harper and Row, 1972; 5th ed., San Francisco: Benjamin Cummings, 2001.

Nybakken, James W. *Marine Biology: An Ecological Approach,* 5th ed. San Francisco: Benjamin Cummings, 2001.

RELATED ARTICLES
Competitive Interference; Ecology; Intertidal

Competitive Interference

Organisms that share a common need for a limiting resource are said to be in competition for that resource. Resources include such things as food, shelter, and mates. Competition is an ecologically important factor that can influence the evolution of species and the composition of plant and animal communities. Competition can occur simply by one organism using up, or *exploiting*, a resource so that it is unavailable to others. Alternatively, competition can occur by one organism actively interfering with another's access to a resource: *competitive interference.* Competitive interference can be within one species (*intraspecific*) or between different species (*interspecific*). The concept of a species's niche is important to understanding interspecific competition. A *niche* is the set of conditions/resources that a species needs to survive and reproduce (i.e., type of food, shelter, temperature range, etc.). The more the niches of two species overlap, the greater the potential for competition between the species.

Types of Competitive Interference

Competitive interference can involve direct physical contact or inhibition from a distance. Direct physical contact can take the form of actual combat or can simply be overgrowth/smothering. Many species have evolved behaviors or physical traits that equip them well for aggressive contests with competitors. Territorial fish, such as the male three-spot damselfish and the stickleback, are vigorously aggressive in defending territories from competitors since fish lacking a territory are unable to attract a mate. Some of these fish (e.g., damselfish) can injure competitors by biting or sharply flapping their tail. Many decapod crustaceans (e.g., crabs, lobsters) are also fiercely competitive, with numerous species possessing weapons (such as claws and spines) that make them formidable opponents in contests for resources.

Other marine organisms do not possess features that suit them well for combat but are able to inflict injury on competitors through other means. The barnacle, *Semibalanus balanoides*, is a good illustration of an animal that does not possess obvious weaponry, but is still a very strong competitor. *S. balanoides* and a smaller species of barnacle, *Chthamalus stellatus*, compete for space in the intertidal area of rocky shores. *S. balanoides* is located in the zone nearest the water, while *C. stellatus* is found higher up the beach. In a now classic series of experiments in Scotland, it was shown that larvae of *C. stellatus* settle in the lower intertidal zone but are undercut and popped off by *S. balanoides*. *C. stellatus* is able to colonize the upper beach only because *S. balanoides* cannot tolerate the drier conditions found there. Comparable cases of competition for space on rocky shores can be found among species as diverse as algae and ascidians (e.g., sea squirts). For instance, the encrusting red algae *Chondrus crispus* forms a solid turf on wave-exposed shores in Nova Scotia and is able to grow over and exclude the brown algae *Fucus evanescens*. Similarly, several species of sea squirts have been observed to overshadow and eventually smother preexisting bryozoans (colonial animals that sometimes resemble seaweed).

Rather than using physical force, other marine organisms use a form of *allelopathy* (i.e., water-borne chemicals to interfere with and discourage competitors from a distance). Bare zones are often observed around sponges and soft corals. These organisms produce toxins that can kill or injure other nonmobile, encrusting organisms that compete with them for space. For example, the liver sponge *Plakortis halichondroides* causes the stony coral *Agaricia lamarcki* to expel its symbiotic algae (i.e., to become "bleached"), which weakens the coral. Another documented case of allelopathy in competition for space is among the soft corals [Alcyonacea (e.g., *Sinularia flexibilis*)], which can cause the death of neighboring stony corals (e.g., *Acropora* species) without direct physical contact. Similarly, the sea anemone *Condylactus gigantea* uses chemical defenses to deter nearby filamentous algae from germinating.

Predicting the Outcome of Competitive Interactions

To predict the outcome of competitive interactions, mathematical models have been developed. The best known is the *Lotka–Volterra model,* named for the developers of the model. The model includes terms for the current number of individuals of each species, the carrying capacity

for each species (i.e., the highest number of individuals of each species that the environment can support, or "carry," in the absence of the competitor), and the degree of negative impact that each species has on the other (i.e., how "strong" a competitor each species is). When the terms of the model for a particular competitive interaction between two species are known from previous observation or sampling, the model can predict whether one species will competitively exclude the other from the local area or whether the species can coexist. The model makes the following general conclusions: (1) competitive exclusion will eventually occur if one species is a better competitor than the other; (2) coexistence can occur only if both species are weak competitors; and (3) the outcome of the interaction depends on starting numbers of each species when both are strong competitors. The model has been criticized for having some limitations, including the assumption that the environment is stable—that the amount of resources (carrying capacity) and the competitive ability of each species is unchanging.

In fact, although the Lotka–Volterra model offers a good start in making predictions, many habitats are not stable and coexistence of competitors occurs where the model predicts competitive exclusion. Resources can sometimes be found in unstable, ephemeral patches. Such patchiness of the environment can allow a weaker competitor to persist if that species tends to find the temporary resource patches before the stronger competitor. A case in point would be fish competing for food in patches of algae that form and then are quickly broken up by winds and waves. The introduction of a predator can also alter the balance of a competitive interaction. A predator that preferentially attacks a strong competitor can forestall competitive exclusion of weaker competitors. For example, when the predatory starfish, *Pisaster ochraceus*, is introduced onto rocky shorelines, it can prevent mussels (a strong competitor) from overgrowing weaker competitors (e.g., algae, sea urchins, limpets, barnacles). The starfish continually open up space before the mussels can completely exclude all competitors.

Effects on Competitive Interference on Competitors

Competitive interference can have negative effects on both the winners and losers in the interaction. Of course, injury or death is sometimes the price paid by the loser in fighting matches or in allelopathic interactions. Also, as competitors are forced to divert time and/or energy toward combat or other competition as well as toward the avoidance of competition, they have less left for growth and reproduction. In this way, both winners and losers suffer negative consequences of competition. For example, as competition for food among shorebirds increases, they spend more time in direct combat (flapping wings and pecking) and ultimately forage less successfully. Time and energy can also be drained by the use of bluffing ploys to forestall actual combat. In this way, the outcome of the competitive interaction may be decided by the intensity (fierceness) of threatening displays or other cues. These threat signals can take the form of visual, acoustic, or hydrodynamic cues. Illustrations of all three types can be found among crustaceans. Mantis shrimp and many crabs spread their chelae (front claws) in a characteristic visual threat display during competition for food, mates, or shelter sites. In doing so, the animals maximize their apparent size. True to their name, snapping shrimp use their large claws to send an acoustic signal (a snapping sound) when defending a shelter or territory against intruders. Finally, several crustaceans send hydrodynamic (and possibly chemical) signals by forcibly ejecting urine from their nephropores during provocation.

Because of the potential negative influence of competition on one or both species, species often make long-term adjustments to reduce the level of competition and to permit coexistence. One species may switch to resource types that are not usable and/or are not preferred by a competing species. Reduction in amount of niche overlap between competitors, known as *niche separation* or *habitat partitioning*, eases competition. Niche separation can be reversible over the shortterm (i.e., can expand niche if the competitor is removed) or can result in a permanent change that occurs over generations. The physical characteristics of competing species may also diverge with evolution in a process known as *character displacement*. For example, the bills of competing bird species may become increasingly differently shaped over many generations, so that ultimately the two species are not able to consume the same types of prey, and competition is reduced or eliminated.

Mary E. Clark

FURTHER READING

Fitzgerald, J. G. "The Reproductive Behavior of the Stickleback." *Scientific American,* April 1993, pp. 80–85.

Holden, C. "The Bluffing Shrimp." *Science,* Vol. 270 (1995), pp. 237–238.

Marshall, L. G. "The Terror Birds of South America." *Scientific American,* February 1994, pp. 90–95.

Nybakken, James W. *Marine Biology: An Ecological Approach,* 5th ed. San Francisco: Benjamin Cummings, 2001.

Smith, R. L. *Ecology and Field Biology,* 5th ed. New York: Harper Collins, 1996; 6th ed., San Francisco: Benjamin Cummings, 2001.

Weiner, J. *The Beak of the Finch: A Story of Evolution in Our Time.* New York: Knopf, 1994.

RELATED ARTICLES

Algae; Competitive Exclusion; Coral; Crustacea; Ecology; Exploitive Competition; Intertidal; Sea Anemone; Symbiosis

Concentricycloidea

Sea daisies (class Concentricycloidea) are tiny, flower-shaped animals found on rotting wood in deep ocean waters. They are related to sea stars (class Asteroidea) and make up one of the six classes into which scientists divide the echinoderms. Some experts think they are really a type of armless sea star, but most classify them as a distinct group.

Sea daisies were discovered in 1986 near the coast of New Zealand. The first species (*Xyloplax medusiformis*) was found on rotting wood at a depth of more than 1000 meters (3280 feet), and a second (*Xyloplax turnerae*) was discovered on wood placed deliberately in deep water near the Bahamas. Both have flat, circular bodies less than 1 centimeter (0.4 inch) wide. Around the edge of the body is a ring of spines, arranged like a daisy's petals.

Like most echinoderms, sea daisies are radially symmetrical, which means that their bodies have no front, back, left, or right. A rigid internal skeleton made of overlapping plates of calcium carbonate (chalk) protects the body, and the skin is stretched over this skeleton. Oxygen and nutrients are carried around the body by a network of fluid-filled tubes. This network, called the *water vascular system,* is one of the distinctive features of echinoderms. Like sea stars, sea daisies possess *tube feet* on their undersides, which are extensions of the water vascular system. These are used for moving on the seafloor and for gripping surfaces, and they also allow substances to pass in and out of the water vascular system. The tube feet of sea daisies are arranged in a single circle— a pattern seen in no other echinoderms.

Little is known about the natural history of sea daisies. The first species to be discovered has no mouth or intestine and is thought to feed on dissolved substances released by bacteria on rotting matter. The second species has a mouth and stomach like those of a sea star and perhaps feeds in a similar manner.

Ben Morgan

FURTHER READING

Brusca, Richard C., and Gary J. Brusca. *Invertebrates.* Sunderland, Mass.: Sinauer Associates, 1990.

Pechenik, Jan A. *Biology of the Invertebrates.* Boston: Prindle, Weber and Schmidt, 1985; 4th ed., Boston: McGraw-Hill, 2000.

RELATED ARTICLES

Asteroidea; Echinodermata

Congo Canyon

A 280-kilometer (175-mile)-long submarine canyon that cuts into the Angolan Plateau off the west coast of Africa, the Congo Canyon is the largest underwater canyon in the South Atlantic and the only true submarine canyon in the entire Atlantic Ocean that actively carries sediment to the ocean floor. The Congo Canyon actually begins some 25 kilometers (15.5 miles) to the east of the Atlantic Ocean, cutting into an estuary of the Congo River, Africa's largest river. At the mouth of the Congo River, the Congo Canyon is already some 450 meters (1480 feet) deep. It zigzags west across the 90-kilometer (56-mile)-wide Angolan Plateau, ending at the Congo Fan, an underwater fan valley some 2650 meters (8700 feet) deep where much of the sediment that flows through the Congo Canyon is deposited. The canyon is about 14 kilometers (9 miles) wide, and the V-shaped canyon is about 700 meters (2300 feet) deep from the top of its walls to the canyon floor. The canyon is located at 6° S latitude and between 9 and 12°E longitude.

The Congo Canyon was cut by the Congo River about one-and-a-half million years ago, when sea levels were lower than they are now. The canyon carries sediment from the Congo River out to the ocean. The Congo River carries a large amount of silt, and were it not for the Congo Canyon, the river's estuaries would fill up in a fairly short amount of time. Because of all the material passing through the Congo Canyon, its depth changes frequently, and underwater cables placed in the canyon are quickly broken by the fast-flowing debris. The canyon's bends do not appear to be a result of sediment action; however, the canyon is located atop a number of salt deposits that are slowly rising up through the seafloor.

Mary Sisson

FURTHER READING

Uchupi, Elazar. "Angola Basin: Geohistory and Construction of the Continental Rise." In C. Wylie Poag and Pierre Charles de Graciansky, eds., *Geological Evolution of Atlantic Continental Rises.* New York: Van Nostrand Reinhold, 1992.

Whitaker, J. H. McD., ed. *Submarine Canyons and Deep-Sea Fans: Modern and Ancient.* Stroudsburg, Penn.: Dowden, Hutchinson and Ross, 1976.

RELATED ARTICLES

Diapir; Submarine Canyon; Submarine Fan

Constant Proportions, Principle of

Oceanographers define *salinity* as the total mass of dissolved solids in 1 kilogram (2.2 pounds) of seawater, expressed as practical salinity units (psu). The average kilogram of seawater consists of 965 psu water and 35 psu dissolved solids, or salts. From place to place, however, this composition can vary by several psu. An important discovery in oceanography was that the ratio of major dissolved solids that make up seawater salt is remarkably constant worldwide. This principle of constant proportions or principle of constant composition was firmly established by English chemist William Dittmar (1833–92) in 1884 during the worldwide oceanographic cruise of the HMS *Challenger.*

Although almost every element can be found in the ocean, only six ions make up over 99 percent of ocean salt. In decreasing order of concentration, they are chloride (Cl^-), sodium (Na^+), magnesium (Mg^{2+}), sulfate (SO_4^{2-}), calcium (Ca^{2+}), and potassium (K^+). The ratio of these six salts with respect to each other does not vary from place to place. They are known as *conservative salts* because a plot of any one of them with respect to total salinity will always yield a straight line. Another way to understand this principle is to compare Red Sea seawater with equatorial Pacific seawater. Although Red Sea seawater is much more saline (approximately 40 psu total dissolved solids) than equatorial Pacific seawater (approximately 35 psu total dissolved solids), the ratio between the concentrations of the six conservative salts is identical for both waters. That is, $[Cl^-]$ / $[Na^+]$ / $[Mg^{2+}]$ / $[SO_4^{2-}]$ / $[Ca^{2+}]$ / $[K^+]$ for Red Sea seawater equals $[Cl^-]$ / $[Na^+]$ / $[Mg^{2+}]$ / $[SO_4^{2-}]$ / $[Ca^{2+}]$ / $[K^+]$ for equatorial Pacific seawater or any other ocean water.

The principle of constant proportions was a major breakthrough in oceanography. Previous to this discovery, the only way to determine salinity was to evaporate off water from a predetermined mass of seawater and compare the weight of the solid residue left behind (the salt) to the total mass of the original sample. This method is unreliable because it is impossible to ensure that the salt residue is completely dry—salt crystals hold on to variable amounts of water molecules. The discovery of the principle of constant proportions allowed for rapid, accurate determination of seawater salinity. All one had to do was measure the amount of a single major ion, because all the other major dissolved solids occur in fixed amounts relative to that ion. Oceanographers typically measured chloride [in parts per thousand (ppt)] for determining the salinity of seawater because it is the most abundant salt in seawater and it is relatively easy to measure its concentration. However, it is difficult to distinguish analytically between chloride and the other halogens (mainly bromide and iodide in trace concentrations), so oceanographers actually measured the chlorinity, or chloride plus halogens. Chlorinity can easily be converted to salinity by the formula salinity (psu) = 1.80655 × chlorinity (ppt).

Today, oceanographers rarely use chlorinity for the determination of salinity. Instead, oceanographers take advantage of the electrical conductivity of seawater to make determinations of salinity. The *salinometer* is a device that measures seawater salinity on the basis of electrical conductivity. The salinometer is much easier and more practical to use than the labor-intensive chemical determination of chlorinity; however, the principle of constant proportions still holds true.

Daniel Schuller

FURTHER READING
Open University Course Team. *Seawater: Its Composition, Properties, and Behavior.* Oxford: Pergamon Press/Milton Keynes, England: Open University, 1989; 2nd ed., rev. by John Wright and Angela Colling, Oxford and New York: Pergamon Press, 1995.
Pinet, Paul R. *Invitation to Oceanography.* Minneapolis/St. Paul, Minn.: West Publishing, 1996; 2nd ed., Sudbury, Mass.: Jones and Bartlett, 1998.
Thurman, Harold V. *Introductory Oceanography.* Columbus, Ohio: Charles E. Merrill, 1975; 9th ed., Upper Saddle River, N.J.: Prentice Hall, 2001.

RELATED ARTICLES
Calcium; Chlorinity; Salinity; Salinometer

Continental Borderland

A continental borderland is a continental margin that consists of a series of seafloor basins and ridges. It is essentially a very complex continental slope. Individual basins are much deeper than the continental shelf break. The best example of a continental borderland, and the region for which the name was proposed, is offshore southern California (United States) and Baja California Norte (Mexico) between about 34 and 29°N latitude and 121 and 115°W longitude. Other areas with irregular borderlandlike margins are in the South China Sea and the Coral Sea.

The California continental borderland measures about 1000 kilometers (620 miles) long by 150 kilometers (93 miles) wide. The eastern boundary is defined by the continental shelf break, and the western boundary lies at the base of Patton Escarpment at a depth of approximately 2925 meters (9600 feet). About 20 basins make up the borderland, some of which reach maximum depths of 2800 meters (9200 feet). The basins are separated by ridges that range in depth from 200 to 2000 meters (656 to 6560 feet). Terrigenous sediment floors the nearshore basins, whereas hemipelagic (mixed terrigenous and pelagic) sediment dominates the outer basins. Restricted circulation in bottom waters of the deeper basins allows the concentration of organic carbon in near-anoxic conditions.

Surface-water circulation is dominated by the south-flowing California Current. Upwelling occurs because of the Coriolis effect and the nearly constant winds that blow from the southeast.

The topography and geologic structures in the California continental borderland are related to the San Andreas fault system. The tectonic regime that ultimately formed the continental borderland began about 29 million years ago when the Pacific Plate collided with North America. Tectonic activity that formed the present basin-and-ridge topography occurred mostly in the last 10 million years.

Tracy L. Vallier

FURTHER READING
Emery, Kenneth O. *The Sea off Southern California.* New York: Wiley, 1960.
Kennett, James P. *Marine Geology.* Englewood Cliffs, N.J.: Prentice Hall, 1982.
Shepard, Francis P., and Kenneth O. Emery. *Submarine Topography off the California Coast: Canyons and Tectonic Interpretation.* New York: The Geological Society of America, 1941.
Vedder, John G. "Regional Geology and Petroleum Potential of the Southern California Borderland." In David W. Scholl, John G. Vedder, and Arthur Grantz, eds., *Geology and Resource Potential of the Continental Margin of Western North America and Adjacent Ocean Basins—Beaufort Sea to Baja, California.* Houston, Texas: Circum-Pacific Council for Energy and Mineral Resources, 1987.

RELATED ARTICLES
Anoxic Basin; Continental Margin; Continental Shelf; Continental Slope; Coriolis Effect; Patton Escarpment; Pelagic; Petroleum; Plate Tectonics

Continental Drift, see Seafloor
Spreading

Continental Margin

If you could remove the water from the ocean basins, perhaps the first thing you would notice is that Earth's surface appears at two distinctly different levels. The continents tower over the ocean basins, with the median elevation of the continents at 840 meters (2756 feet) above sea level and the median ocean depth 3800 meters (12,467 feet) below the sea. The dichotomy is a consequence of compositional differences between continental and oceanic crust, which result in a slight difference in density. The lighter, thicker continental crust is more buoyant than the thinner, denser oceanic crust, and as a result, it "floats" higher on the underlying plastic upper mantle. Where continent meets ocean, there is a declivity from the heights of the continent to the depths of the sea. This juncture is the continental margin.

Margin Types
Continental margin shape and structure are defined by the presence or absence of a plate boundary. In general, margins fall into two categories: those that do not contain a plate boundary (passive margins) and those that do (active margins). *Passive margins* are usually the trailing edges of continents that are drifting apart with the formation of an oceanic basin. Because it is still widening, with the Mid-Atlantic Ridge forming new crust at its center, the Atlantic Ocean is almost totally surrounded by passive margins. For this reason, passive margins are often called *Atlantic type*. They contain no plate boundary, and the tectonic motion of these margins is mainly slow subsidence as they cool after the rifting event that created them. As a result of the slow sinking, passive margins are characterized by low coastal plains, sediment-dominated estuaries formed mainly by river erosion, and a wide continental shelf. The eastern seaboard of North America is a classic example of this type of margin.

Active margins contain either a convergent or a conservative (transform) plate boundary, with the former being more prevalent. Such margins are being actively deformed, with the result that topography is often steep and the margin may be undergoing rapid subsidence or uplift. Coastal mountains are common and the coastline is often backed by a cliff, caused by wave erosion of the rising land. Coastal embayments are rarer than on passive margins and frequently are a result of faulting. River drainage is limited by nearby mountainous terrain, so the total load of sediments on an active margin is usually small. Because of the lesser amounts of sediment and because of tectonic uplift and subsidence, active margin continental shelves tend to be narrow, and margin slopes are slightly greater than their passive counterparts. The Pacific Ocean is characterized by active margins because it is largely circumscribed by convergent plate boundaries. Indeed, active margins are often called *Pacific type*. The west coast of South America, where the Nazca Plate dives beneath the continent, creating the Andes Mountains, is an archetypical active margin. Transform margins are less regular in form than convergent boundary margins, but the west coast of North America, where the San Andreas Fault system allows the Pacific Plate to slide past, is a good example.

Margin Structure
Continental margin structure is determined by the tectonic processes that create it. Most passive margins were formed by continental rifting. During rifting, the continental crust is fractured by faults as it is pulled apart. Often, the initial rifting is accompanied by heating and uplift from mantle upwelling. The faulting creates a thinner

crust at the edge of the continent, with a rough upper surface consisting of tilted fault blocks. Erosion of the uplifted rift margins tends to fill the troughs with coarse syn-rift sediments. As stretching continues, the continental crust thins until it is broken apart and mafic (rich in magnesium and iron) magmas intrude the gap to form oceanic crust. As a result of the stretching and erosion, the continental crust thins seaward to the junction with oceanic crust (see figure). This attenuated crust is termed *transitional.* Because it is thinner than the rest of the continent and because it becomes denser as it cools after rifting, the transitional continental crust subsides and collects a thick sedimentary wedge that buries the join between continent and ocean.

Active margins usually consist of an oceanic plate sliding beneath a continental plate. The contact of the two plates is an extensive thrust fault at the contact between the downgoing plate and the overriding plate. This fault breaches the seafloor at the axis of a deep-sea trench. Two factors arising from the plate collision characterize the continental margin. First, the subducting plate causes melting in the upper mantle, which

results in magma rising through the crust to form a line of volcanoes parallel to the trench. Because of this activity, much of the continental margin consists of volcanic rocks and volcanogenic sediments. Second, the collision causes compression, which deforms the rocks and sediments of the margin. Together, the volcanic heat and tectonic compression cause the margin rocks and sediments to be altered into metamorphic rocks. The sediment mantle on active margins tends to be thin because the source regions are small and the trench often consumes sediments that are deposited into it.

Margin Sediments

Approximately 75 percent of Earth's sediments reside in continental margins. This occurs because most sediments are derived from land and are delivered to the ocean by rivers. Flowing downslope, the sediments accumulate on the continental margin.

Most margin sediments are incorporated into passive margins, where sedimentary wedges are commonly 10 to 15 kilometers (6.2 to 9.3 miles) thick. As a passive margin slowly subsides beneath

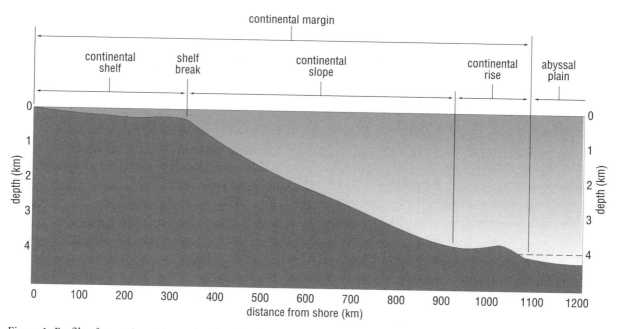

Figure 1: Profile of a continental margin, showing the shelf, slope, and rise.

the sea, subaerial syn-rift sediments are replaced by marine sediments. Often, a thick layer of salt and other evaporites is deposited atop the rift sediments because initial flooding of the basin is intermittent, allowing the basin to dry out. With continued basin opening and margin subsidence, a thick wedge of sediment accumulates, the type depending on region and sediment sources. In tropical seas bordered by land with few rivers, marginal sediments may be characterized by calcium carbonate, and reefs may grow in shallow water. A present-day example is the Yucatán margin in the southern Gulf of Mexico. On margins with many rivers, siliciclastic (noncarbonate) sediments dominate, as on the east coast of the United States. Where a major river enters the ocean, it may drop a huge pile of sediment on the margin, forming a deep-sea fan. Often, abundant organic matter from the land is incorporated into the margin sediments, and after burial it is transformed into hydrocarbons. This is why most of Earth's hydrocarbon reservoirs are on passive continental margins.

Active margins do not usually develop a thick "layercake" sediment pile like those of passive margins. Because rivers are short, sediments are derived from local sources. Moving downslope from the continent, the sediments may pond in small, local basins or arrive in the trench. The fate of sediments in the trench depends on the tightness of the contact between the subducting (descending) and overriding plates. Where the coupling is tight, most sediments are not carried down with the subducting plate but are incorporated into a complex, highly faulted wedge consisting of sediments scraped off the subducting plate and sediments derived from the margin. If the coupling is looser, many of the sediments are carried down the subduction zone by the descending plate. In such places, the subducting plate may rub off the base of the overriding plate (a process called *tectonic erosion*), causing rapid margin subsidence. Attesting to a lack of sediment

cover, dredges from the landward trench wall surface on such margins routinely recover old, lower crust rocks, presumably from the exposed core of the overriding plate crust.

Shelf, Slope, and Rise

Continental margins are often divided into three provinces—shelf, slope, and rise—based on water depth and slope angle. These provinces are usually developed best on passive margins (see figures), where sedimentation dominates over tectonics, but often, active margins can be similarly divided. The shelf is a broad, flat area closest to land. It is an underwater extension of the coastal plain with typical slope angles of less than 0.5°. At the outer edge of the shelf is an abrupt change to steeper slopes, called the *shelf break* or *slope break*, that defines the boundary with the slope province. The shelf break is typically around 130 meters (427 feet) deep but may be several times greater in polar regions, where icebergs scrape the shelf as they march to sea. Shelf width varies considerably, from a few kilometers to more than 400 kilometers (249 miles), with an average of 78 kilometers (48 miles). The continental slope stretches from the slope break downward to the continental rise with a typical slope of about 4 to 5°, with a few places having locally precipitous slopes of 35 to 90°. The lower boundary of the slope is usually indistinct but occurs where the steeper angle of the slope gives way to the reduced angle of the continental rise, usually at

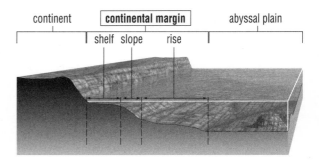

Figure 2: Cross section of a continental margin, showing the shelf, slope, and rise.

depths of 1500 to 3000 meters (4900 to 9800 feet). Continental rises are broad areas 100 to 1000 kilometers wide (62 to 621 miles) of low slope angle, typically less than 1°, at the base of the margin. Rises often grade seaward into flat abyssal plains on the deep seafloor.

The shelf, slope, and rise features of passive continental margins develop mainly from sedimentation and the effects of sea-level variations. During ice ages, sea level drops to near the shelf break, exposing the continental shelves. Erosion on the shelves causes them to be flattened, and sediments derived from the land are carried offshore. Indeed, the 130-meter (425-foot) average shelf break indicates the approximate depth of the sea-level fall during the last ice age. Sediments are deposited near the shelf break and cascade down the slope in turbidity currents, which are similar to underwater avalanches. At the rise, the slope flattens and the turbidity currents slow down, dropping their sediment load. Thus the continental rise consists of huge piles of sediment. Between ice ages, sea level is high, and sediments often are deposited on the shelf, only to be eroded during the next sea-level drop. As the cycle is repeated, more sediments accumulate on the continental margins, building them seaward.

William W. Sager

FURTHER READING
Boillot, Gilbert. *Geology of the Continental Margins.* Translated by A. Scarth. New York and London: Longman, 1981.
Dietz, Robert S. "Geosynclines, Mountains, and Continent-Building," In John Tuzo Wilson, ed., *Continents Adrift and Continents Aground.* San Francisco: W. H. Freeman, 1976.
Kennett, James. *Marine Geology.* Englewood Cliffs, N.J.: Prentice Hall, 1982.
Moores, Eldridge M., and Robert J. Twiss. *Tectonics.* New York: W. H. Freeman, 1995.
Seibold, Eugen, and Wolfgang H. Berger. *The Sea Floor: An Introduction to Marine Geology.* Berlin: Springer-Verlag, 1982; 3rd ed., 1996.
Strahler, Arthur N. *Plate Tectonics.* Cambridge, Mass.: Geo Books, 1998.
Thurman, Harold V. *Introductory Oceanography.* Columbus, Ohio: Charles E. Merrill, 1975; 9th ed., with Elizabeth A. Burton, Upper Saddle River, N.J.: Prentice Hall, 2001.

RELATED ARTICLES
Abyssal Plain; Coastal Morphology; Continental Borderland; Continental Shelf; Continental Slope; Convergent Plate Boundary; Isostasy; Turbidity Current

Continental Shelf

The continental shelf is the gently sloping part of the seafloor that extends from the shoreline toward the deep ocean. It is the submerged platform of the adjacent continent and forms the landward part of a broad province referred to as the *continental margin.* Continental shelves extend seaward from every continent, but their widths vary tremendously, ranging from only a few kilometers (approximately 2 miles) to greater than 500 kilometers (approximately 310 miles). Whereas seismically active continental margins, characterized by earthquakes and volcanoes, have narrow continental shelves, passive continental margins usually have wide continental shelves. However, since the average width is only about 80 kilometers (50 miles), continental shelves account for less than 10 percent of the total area of the ocean, yet they are of great importance as fishing grounds, sites for exploration of oil and gas, and as repositories for minerals and sand.

Between 15,000 and 20,000 years ago, when sea level was approximately 130 meters (425 feet) lower than it is today, continental shelves were terrestrial landforms. In most respects, they were an equivalent of the present-day coastal plain. Rising sea level from melting of glaciers, termed the *Holocene transgression,* flooded these former coastal plain surfaces, producing the continental shelves. Shallow marine seas that are nearly enclosed by continents form another type of flooded shelf area, referred to as *epicontinental seas*. Hudson Bay, the North Sea, and the Yellow Sea are examples of epicontinental seas that are similar in many ways to true continental shelves.

The shelf break or shelf edge is delineated by an abrupt increase in bottom slope. The shelf break is an important physiographic feature in the ocean because it marks the location of the shoreline prior to the Holocene transgression. Although the average slope across most shelf areas is less than one-half of a degree, continental shelves include many diverse morphologic features that are indicative of terrestrial processes: channels, canyons, depressions, sand ridges, moraines, wave-cut terraces, and old river deltas. Sediments from glaciers and remains of Pleistocene land animals (older than 10,000 years), such as mastodons and mammoths, provide additional evidence of a terrestrial origin for most of these features.

Shelf Sediments

The sediments that blanket continental shelves have been derived primarily from five sources: rivers, glaciers, marine organisms, seafloor erosion, and shoreline erosion. In certain areas of the world there have also been minor contributions from windblown silt, chemically precipitated minerals, and ash and debris from volcanoes. Approximately 70 percent of shelf sediments are classified as relict; that is, they are deposits from an earlier period when continental shelves were terrestrial environments. They are now out of equilibrium with their present depositional environment. Most relict sediments were deposited by rivers or ice sheets and thus contain a mixture of gravel, sand, and mud. Relict sediments can sometimes be differentiated from modern sands by their iron-stained and pitted surfaces, which reflect past terrestrial weathering processes.

Sedimentary characteristics on the shelf are controlled by climate and, to a lesser degree, ocean currents. For example, glacial sediments are restricted to higher latitudes where rock is broken down mainly by mechanical processes. These sediments have coarse grain sizes. Muddy sediments predominate in humid tropical and subtropical environments where rock is deeply weathered by chemical processes. These sediments are found seaward of large rivers and on shelves that are protected from wave action. Much of the sand that is carried by rivers is trapped in estuaries and never reaches the continental shelf. Calcium carbonate is sediment secreted by marine organisms that live at all latitudes. However, carbonate sediments are quickly diluted by sediments from other sources and are prevalent only in regions that have a negligible supply of land-derived sediments.

Sediments on the continental shelf form many types of morphologic features, referred to collectively as *bed forms*. Most are relict, but large bed forms in the shape of elongate sand ridges are thought to be a product of present-day tidal currents. Other features, referred to variously as *sand waves, sand ribbons,* and *sand patches,* may provide clues as to current speeds and direction of sediment movement. Not all features have positive relief; ancestral river channels, scour depressions, and furrows have negative relief and indicate past or present processes of sediment erosion.

Marine life on the bottom can be influenced by sediment type. Certain organisms are best suited to very specific sediment sizes. Coarse-grained sediments, which occur where the bottom is constantly shifting, are favorable for sedentary organisms such as sponges, which can withstand abrasion. Fine-grained sediments, which occur where the currents are weak, are especially favorable for organisms such as worms, which build burrows and feed on organic material that is trapped in the muddy sediment. As a result of their terrestrial origin, the mixture of sediment types on the continental shelf does not display a uniform spatial distribution, and bottom-dwelling organisms reflect this patchiness in their own faunal distributions.

Carbonate Shelves

Some continental shelves are dominated by sediments that have a biogenic origin. These shelves are composed mainly of calcium carbonate from organisms such as reef-building corals and occur where there is little input of land-derived sediment. Because the production of carbonate material and its preservation are tied to climate as well as oceanographic factors, carbonate shelves are most characteristic in shallow, tropical seas. The term *carbonate buildup* is used to describe significant accumulations of carbonate material on the shelf, and the term *reef* describes accumulations that grow upward and are maintained in the wave zone. The west coast of Florida and the Great Barrier Reef of Australia are examples of tropical to subtropical carbonate shelves. Despite the influence of climate, carbonate shelves can also occur in temperate latitudes where the carbonate material is provided by barnacles, mollusks, and other organisms that are less dependent on temperature than are corals.

Shelf Processes

Although most of the sedimentary features on continental shelves are thought to be relict, they are subject to constant reworking by marine processes. Tides, waves, wind-driven currents, and storm surge may cause sediment movement on continental shelves. Wider continental shelves generally have higher tide ranges and thus stronger tidal currents. Strong tidal currents can mobilize sands and even gravels. Because of a process called tidal resonance, some epicontinental seas, such as the Yellow Sea, have greatly increased tidal amplitudes and are dominated by tidal sand ridges. Along shelves with a low tide range, waves are usually the dominant process. The oscillatory motion imparted to the bottom by waves has little effect on the shelf during fair-weather conditions,

disturbing sediments to depths no greater than 10 to 20 meters (33 to 66 feet). However, large storms may suspend sediments as far offshore as the shelf break, attesting to the importance of large but infrequent events.

Winds are also important because they produce currents as they blow across the surface of the water. Wind-driven currents are especially important in causing upwelling and downwelling on continental shelves, processes by which bottom water rises to the surface and surface water sinks toward the bottom, respectively. Whereas upwelling brings nutrient-rich materials from the bottom, downwelling carries oxygen-rich waters to greater depths; these exchange processes are important in supplying the needs of marine organisms. Continental shelves will be of great interest in the future because of the political and economic implications of relatively dense, but diminishing populations of marine life.

John T. Wells

FURTHER READING

Bouma, A. H., H. L. Berryhill, R. L. Brenner, and H. J. Knebel. "Continental Shelf and Epicontinental Seaways." In Peter Scholle and Darwin Spearing, eds., *Sandstone Depositional Environments.* Tulsa, Okla.: American Association of Petroleum Geologists, 1982.

Kennett, James P. *Marine Geology.* Englewood Cliffs, N.J.: Prentice Hall, 1982.

Seibold, E., and W. H. Berger. *The Sea Floor: An Introduction to Marine Geology.* Berlin: Springer-Verlag, 1982; 3rd ed., 1993.

Swift, D. J. P. "Continental Shelf Sedimentation." In D. J. P. Swift and D. B. Duane, eds., *Marine Sediment Transport and Environmental Management.* New York: Wiley, 1976.

Symonds, Philip, Olav Eldholm, Jean Mascle, and Gregory Moore. "Characteristics of Continental Margins." In Peter Cook and Chris Carleton, eds., *Continental Shelf Limits.* Oxford: Oxford University Press, 2000.

RELATED ARTICLES

Continental Margin; Continental Slope; Delta; Geologic Time; Paleoceanography; Reef; Upwelling

Continental Slope

The continental slope is a transitional part of the continental margin. Specifically, it is a physiographic province of the ocean that extends from the edge of the continental shelf to the top of the continental rise. Unlike the continental shelf, which is simply a flooded extension of the adjacent continent, the continental slope is considerably steeper (gradients of 1 to 5 degrees), more variable, and was not exposed to terrestrial weathering processes during the last low stand of sea level, approximately 15,000 to 20,000 years ago. Continental slopes are relatively narrow, averaging only 20 to 100 kilometers (12 to 62 miles) wide, and are incised by several types of valleys that serve as conduits for transporting sediments. There is much evidence to suggest that, starting near the edge of the continental shelf, sediments are transported periodically down the continental slope under the force of gravity and are deposited as thick accumulations on the continental rise or beyond. Continental slopes are thus especially important because of their role in the transfer of sediment from the continents to the deep ocean.

Continental slopes are highly variable. Although the upper boundary at the shelf break is relatively easy to define, the lower boundary is not. It typically extends to water depths that generally range from 1500 to 3500 meters (4920 to 11,500 feet). The base of the slope is variable in depth and hard to define because it merges with sediments that have been deposited in the continental rise, or in some cases it extends into depressions, called *deep-sea trenches*, such as the Peru–Chile Trench, where depths exceed 8000 meters (26,200 feet). The surfaces of the continental slope can be outcroppings of rock, thick deposits of land-derived sediments, or even diapirs (extrusions) of shale that have been thrust upward. Although mud is the most common type of sediment, sand and gravel are also present. Continental slopes comprised of calcium carbonate are less common but can occur where there has been biogenic production of calcareous (shell) material and a low input of terrestrial sediment. Accumulations of terrestrial sediment are especially thick along continental slopes off large river mouths.

In areas where oxygen levels in the lower part of the water column are low (oxygen minimum layer), continental slope sediments can become enriched by organic matter. These anoxic sediments are not extensive in the oceans today but have been widespread in the past. Vertical expansion of the oxygen minimum layer in regions of upwelling can lead to large accumulations of organic carbon and sulfur in the form of pyrite. Organic-rich sediments formed under conditions of low oxygen are called *sapropels*.

Types of Continental Slopes

Several types of continental slopes can be identified on the basis of their tectonic and sedimentary history. Continental slopes along tectonically active margins, such as the Pacific margin, occur where the leading edge of a continent overrides oceanic lithosphere (the outermost, rigid unit of Earth), forcing sediments against the continental landmass. This type of margin is usually characterized by an accretionary wedge of highly deformed sediments. Continental slopes along passive margins, such as the Atlantic margin, occur in relatively quiet and stable tectonic settings. This type of margin is characterized by thick accumulations of relatively undisturbed sediment, derived from land and mixed with biogenic sediments.

Another type of continental slope occurs when deltas prograde or build out across the shelf edge, supplying the slope with huge masses of sediment that have been transported directly from rivers. These slopes are subsiding from the weight of overlying sediments, and the sedimentary units have a down-warped appearance. The slopes can be highly unstable due to rapid deposition of sediments that do not have time to dewater and solidify. Calcareous reefs and diapirs of shale or salt produce yet another type of continental slope, typified by the slope provinces in the Gulf of Mexico. Reefs and diapirs create structures on the bottom that act as dams, which through time trap sediments that smooth out their vertical relief. Regardless of origin, continental slopes usually do not have horizontal trends that mimic the irregularities of the shoreline but are straight or gently curved.

Although sea level has not been low enough to expose the surface of the continental slope, it has nevertheless played a role in altering the character of the slope. Changes in sea level influence the amount of sediment as well as the grain size of the sediment that is delivered directly to the slope. At high stands of sea level, only the fine-grained suspended sediments will be transported across the shelf to the continental slope. At lower stands of sea level, sediments are deposited closer to the edge of the continental shelf, and coarse sediments are more likely to be moved onto the continental slope. An additional influx of sediment onto the slope can create instabilities, such as slumps and slides, which are important in shaping the slope morphology.

Slump blocks can be enormous in size. One of the largest, located in the northwestern Atlantic, is approximately 400 meters (1300 feet) thick and 50 kilometers (30 miles) long. Other types of gravity-induced instabilities include rock falls and avalanches. The frequency of these mass movement processes is unknown. Sediment grain flows also occur on the continental slope. These processes are the result of interaction between individual sediment grains, the interstitial water that surrounds the grains, and turbulence.

Submarine Canyons and Turbidity Currents

Submarine canyons are steep V-shaped valleys that incise the continental slope. They are widespread on many slopes but absent on others. Their walls show evidence of scour and they are clearly conduits for funneling sediments across the continental slope. Indeed, canyons are similar to rivers in that they have natural levees, sinuous channels, and the ability to erode into the underlying sediments. Moreover, on narrow continental margins, such as along the California coast, submarine canyons can undergo headward erosion, intersecting the littoral zone where sediments are being transported along the coast in shallow water. These beach sediments can then move offshore to great water depths when they encounter the head of a submarine canyon.

Many submarine canyons line up remarkably well with the mouths of large rivers, most notably the Congo, Indus, Ganges, and Amazon. However, the origin of these canyons cannot be attributed directly to erosion by rivers since sea level, even at its previous low stand, would still have been well above the level of the canyons. It is likely, though, that canyons were more active at this time, owing to the proximity of the river-borne sediment. The connection to river mouths suggests erosion of canyons by *turbidity currents,* powerful downslope movements of dense mixtures of sediment and water. Turbidity currents can be triggered by earthquakes, storms, or simply by oversteepening from sediment buildup, for example, near the head of a canyon. The deposits from turbidity currents, called *turbidites,* typically consist of sand and interbedded finer-grained oceanic sediments; they may also contain gravel at the bases of their deposits. Turbidites are characterized by graded beds that display a characteristic succession of grain sizes and sedimentary structures, ranging from coarse sediments at the bottom to fine sediments at the top. Deposits from turbidity currents may also contain plant and animal debris derived from the shallow waters of the continental shelf. When turbidity currents reach the base of the continental slope they deposit their sedimentary loads, because of a decrease in gradient. Graded beds are thus the result of waning current strength during the period of deposition and are capped by long periods of slow deposition of pelagic (oceanic) mud. The deposits are often fan-shaped and may extend well out into the abyssal depths of the ocean.

Sediments that are deposited at the base of the continental slope can be modified subsequently by contour currents, deep currents that flow horizontally along the slope and rise. Contour currents have speeds of 10 to 20 centimeters per second (0.35 to 0.70 foot per second) and produce thin deposits called *contourites*. Because of the great water depths and variability of landforms, much remains to be learned about contourites, turbidity currents, and their role in the evolution of continental slopes.

John T. Wells

Further Reading

Bouma, Arnold. "Continental Slopes." In Larry Doyle and Orrin Pilkey, eds., *Geology of Continental Margins*. Tulsa, Okla.: Society of Economic Paleontologists and Mineralogists, 1979.

Cook, Harry, Michael Field, and James Gardner. "Characteristics of Sediments on Modern and Ancient Continental Slopes." In Peter Scholle and Darwin Spearing, eds., *Sandstone Depositional Environments*. Tulsa, Okla.: American Association of Petroleum Geologists, 1982.

Davis, Richard. *Depositional Systems*. Englewood Cliffs, N.J.: Prentice Hall, 1983; 2nd ed., 1992.

Seibold, E., and W. H. Berger. *The Sea Floor: An Introduction to Marine Geology*. Berlin: Springer-Verlag, 1982; 3rd ed., 1993.

Shepard, F. P., and R. F. Dill. *Submarine Canyons and Other Sea Valleys*. Chicago: Rand McNally, 1966.

Symonds, Philip, Olav Eldholm, Jean Mascle, and Gregory Moore. "Characteristics of Continental Margins." In Peter Cook and Chris Carleton, eds., *Continental Shelf Limits*. Oxford: Oxford University Press, 2000.

Related Articles

Continental Margin; Continental Shelf; Diapir; Reef; Submarine Canyon; Submarine Fan; Turbidite; Turbidity Current

Convergence

Convergence in the oceans occurs when waters move toward a common line or point. Convergences can occur over a large range of spatial scales, from microturbulence to large-scale convergences occurring over thousands of kilometers. Winds blowing over the sea surface drive the ocean gyres that form the large-scale surface circulation in the ocean basins. Ekman transport, a part of the Ekman theory of wind-driven currents, leads to convergence in the centers of these gyres. This surface convergence drives downwelling, where surface waters are forced downward into the interior of the oceans. These large-scale convergences and associated downwellings act to aerate the deep oceans and drive large-scale thermohaline circulation.

Convergences also occur in other parts of the oceans. One of the most robust convergences in the oceans is the Antarctic Convergence. This zone of convergence circles Earth in the Southern Ocean at a latitude of about 50°S south of the Atlantic and Indian Oceans and 60°S south of the Pacific Ocean. The cooler waters on the southern side of the convergence are moving slowly northward and beneath the warmer surface waters on the northern side of the Antarctic Convergence. Farther again to the north, the Subtropical Convergence delineates subtropical waters from the subantarctic waters that lie between the Antarctic and Subtropical Convergences. Both these convergences are permanent features of the Southern Ocean.

Transient and semipermanent convergences often occur in the coastal zone. These may be associated with recirculating flows consisting of individual eddies or groups of eddies. Eddies often form in coastal regions when current flows are disrupted by protruding features of the coast, for example coastal headlands. Small-scale convergences and divergences are also often associated with tidal fronts around the mouths of estuaries.

Persistent winds blowing over the sea surface can lead to the development of *Langmuir circulation*

Forces that produce convergence.

cells, which incorporate zones of convergence and divergence. These cells are in the form of horizontal corkscrew or helical motions that align themselves with the wind. These cells develop over the top few meters of the oceans and are separated by zones of convergence and divergence. The zones of convergence are distinguishable as lines of foam, seaweed, and other debris that accumulate in the convergence. These lines, often called *windrows,* are a convenient way to identify Langmuir circulation cells.

Mark T. Gibbs

FURTHER READING

Cushman-Roisin, Benoit. *Introduction to Geophysical Fluid Dynamics.* Englewood Cliffs, N.J.: Prentice Hall, 1994.

Pickard, George L. *Descriptive Physical Oceanography.* Oxford and New York: Pergamon Press, 1964; 5th ed., Oxford and Boston: Butterworth-Heinemann, 1995.

Pinet, Paul R. *Invitation to Oceanography.* Minneapolis/St. Paul, Minn.: West Publishing, 1996; 2nd ed., Sudbury, Mass.: Jones and Bartlett, 2000.

Pond, Stephen, and George Pickard. *Introductory Dynamical Oceanography.* Oxford: Pergamon Press, 1979; 2nd ed., Oxford: Butterworth-Heinemann, 2000.

Segar, Douglas A. *Introduction to Ocean Sciences.* Belmont, Calif.: Wadsworth, 1998.

RELATED ARTICLES

Divergence; Eddy; Langmuir Circulation; Ocean Current; Tide

Convergent Plate Boundary

Convergent plate boundaries, also referred to as *convergent margins,* are Earth's most dynamic regions where mountain ranges form and oceanic crust is recycled. Convergent plate boundaries also are known as *active, seismic, collision,* and *Pacific margins.* The major consequences of convergence are compression and melting, which produce earthquakes, mountain ranges, volcanoes, and subduction zones. A volcanic arc is a common result of plate convergence. Convergent plate boundaries have three major types of plate convergence: continental plate–continental plate convergence; continental plate–oceanic plate convergence; and oceanic plate–oceanic plate convergence.

The consequences of convergence depend primarily on the thickness and composition of the colliding plates. Continents have thick crusts and oceans have thin crusts. Some continental crusts reach thicknesses as great as 90 kilometers (56 miles) and the average thickness is about 36 kilometers (22 miles). Continents are bulky and buoyant, composed of less dense materials on average than oceanic crust. The ocean crust averages about 10 kilometers (6 miles) thick and has a larger relative amount of the more dense elements such as iron and magnesium in its rocks. When two continental plates collide, a mountain range is built and extensive uplift occurs. When a continental plate converges with an oceanic plate, the lighter and more buoyant continental plate overrides the oceanic plate and a subduction zone forms. When two oceanic plates converge, the older and therefore deeper plate descends beneath the younger and shallower plate, forming a subduction zone. The consequences of continental plate–oceanic plate and oceanic plate–oceanic plate collisions are shown in the figure.

Continental Plate–Continental Plate Convergence

The highest mountain range in the world, the Himalayas, formed where the Indian and Asian continental landmasses converged. India was attached to Antarctica until about 150 million years ago, when it broke off from the supercontinent, moving northward as a consequence of seafloor spreading. As the "continent" of India approached Asia, basins between the converging continents filled with sediments. Finally, continental margin met continental margin, subduction ceased, and the collision pushed up the margins of those colliding continents into the present-day Himalayas. Converging continents were common in the past and scars of their collisions appear as mountain ranges elsewhere: Europe colliding with North America formed the Appalachian Mountains about 350 million years ago; and Africa colliding with Europe produced the Alps before later tectonic activity opened the Mediterranean Sea.

Continental Plate–Oceanic Plate Convergence

A subduction zone generally forms where a continental plate collides with an oceanic plate. Parts of the continental crust and uppermost mantle above the subduction zone melt and volcanoes erupt on the surface; huge plutons called *batholiths* intrude the crust and crystallize to a granitic composition. A fore-arc region develops that is composed of preexisting continental crust and mantle, sediment-filled basins, and accreted oceanic materials. An outstanding example of continental plate–oceanic plate convergence is the dynamic region along the western coast of South America, where the Antarctic, Nazca, and Cocos Plates are grinding their way relentlessly toward the continent and

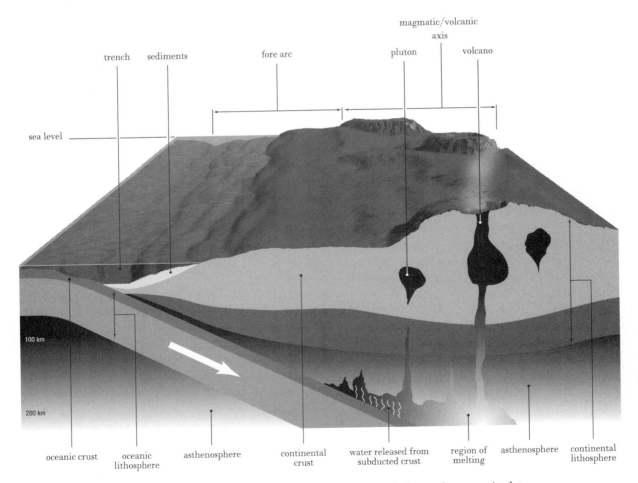

Cross section of a plate boundary formed at the convergence of a continental plate and an oceanic plate.

slowly diving beneath it. A high mountain range, the Andes, grew landward of the subduction zone as a result of the collision.

Oceanic Plate–Oceanic Plate Convergence

Where two oceanic plates collide, one slides under the other. The older and denser plate dives beneath the younger more buoyant plate along a subduction zone. An island arc is created. A trench forms, the fore-arc region encompasses a basin, volcanoes erupt along a volcanic or magmatic axis, and in some places a back-arc basin grows by seafloor spreading behind the magmatic axis. Part of the trench near the southern Mariana Islands, the Challenger Deep, is the deepest ocean floor in the world. Mount Everest would easily fit in that trench and its peak would still be 2 kilometers (1.25 miles) beneath the ocean surface. An accretionary prism blankets the inner walls of trenches if they are full of sediments. In places, however, the sediment fill is minimal and the accretionary prism is either thin or nonexistent. In these places, parts of the inner trench wall slide into the trench and are subsequently subducted. The Pacific Ocean basin is rimmed by island arcs that are forming because of oceanic plate–oceanic plate convergence. The major ones are the Aleutian, Kuril, Bonin, Mariana, Solomon, New Hebrides, and Tonga Island Arcs.

Earthquakes

An earthquake zone defines the downgoing oceanic plate (slab) as it dives beneath the overriding plate. This is the *Wadati–Benioff zone*, named after its discoverers. Compressional forces build up to such an extent during subduction that the downgoing plate finally ruptures, causing an earthquake. The largest earthquakes thus far recorded occur deep in these subduction zones; some have magnitudes of 9.0 or greater on the 10-point Richter magnitude scale. The

hypocenter or *focus* (the point at which the earthquake occurs within the crust or mantle) can be as deep as 670 kilometers (416 miles). *Epicenters* (points on Earth's surface directly above the hypocenter) occur within about 300 kilometers (186 miles) of the trench, depending mostly on the dip of the subduction zone. For example, earthquake epicenters will be closer to the trench if the dip is steep.

Magmatism

Volcanic and plutonic magmas (melted rocks that are lavas on Earth's surface) form above the downgoing plate in subduction zones where heat and pressure regimes are appropriate for melting to occur. Magmas change (through an igneous process called *differentiation*) and become more buoyant, move upward through the mantle and crust, form the roots of volcanoes, and pour out onto the surface as lava flows and pyroclastic materials. While magmas cool within Earth's crust and upper mantle, minerals grow through a process called *fractionation* and then settle out of the magmas by gravity, thereby changing the compositions of the remaining magmas. If mineral crystals (denser and richer in the elements iron and magnesium) are removed sequentially from a magma during fractionation and gravity settling, the remaining minerals that grow in the magma concentrate less dense elements such as potassium, silicon, and sodium, and different rocks form as a consequence. For example, basalt magmas differentiate by fractionation and gravity settling to form andesite and rhyolite rocks that are less dense and richer in lighter elements. Similarly, magmas that form plutons deep in the crust can fractionate from an original gabbro (plutonic equivalent of basalt) composition to granodiorite and granite, which are coarse-grained igneous rocks rich in the minerals quartz and feldspar. Andesite, granodiorite, and granite are volumetrically the prevalent rock products of subduction zone magmatism.

Sedimentation

Large piles of sediment are deposited along convergent plate boundaries, particularly if uplift of the resulting mountain ranges is rapid and rainfall is heavy. The Himalayas are an excellent example, but the absence of an adjacent deep-sea trench has led to the deposition of sediments on large submarine fans such as the Indus and Bengal fans off India. Elsewhere, both continental and intraoceanic volcanic arcs contribute a broad range of sedimentary products, some derived from eruptions of pyroclastic materials and others by erosion. These sediments fill trenches and fore-arc basins and contribute to the formation of accretionary prisms.

Other Factors

Convergent plate boundaries are more complex where colliding plates move at angles to one another. Even though a subduction zone and trench are present, parts of either or both plates may become tectonic slivers and fault-bounded fragments that move parallel and subparallel to the margins' boundaries for long distances without being subducted. Parts of the Aleutian Island Arc, for example, have been wrenched tectonically from the overriding plate and are moving westward to collide with the Kamchatka Peninsula of Russia. Many tectonic slivers and fragments of convergent plate boundaries, called *terranes*, make up large parts of the Pacific Northwest, southwestern Canada, and the Kamchatka Peninsula.

Tracy L. Vallier

FURTHER READING

Condie, Kent C. *Plate Tectonics and Crustal Evolution.* New York: Pergamon Press, 1976; 4th ed., Oxford and Boston: Butterworth-Heinemann, 1997.

Davidson, John P., Walter E. Reed, and Paul M. Davis. *Exploring Earth: An Introduction to Physical Geology.* Upper Saddle River, N.J.: Prentice Hall, 1997.

Garrison, Tom. *Oceanography: An Invitation to Marine Science.* Belmont, Calif.: Wadsworth, 1993; 3rd ed., 1998.

Gill, James B. *Orogenic Andesites and Plate Tectonics.* Berlin and New York: Springer-Verlag, 1981.

Kennett, James P. *Marine Geology.* Englewood Cliffs, N.J.: Prentice Hall, 1982.

Seibold, Eugen, and Wolfgang H. Berger. *The Sea Floor: An Introduction to Marine Geology.* Berlin and New York: Springer-Verlag, 1982; 3rd ed., 1996.

RELATED ARTICLES

Accretionary Prism; Aleutian Arc; India Plate; Island Arc; Oceanic Volcanic Rock; Pacific Plate; Plate Tectonics; Subduction Zone; Terrane; Tonga Island Arc; Trench

Cook, James

1728–1779

Maritime Explorer and British Naval Officer

During the late eighteenth century, English marine navigator James Cook helped to establish England as a European leader in scientific exploration, particularly of the largely uncharted regions of the South Pacific. He surveyed Newfoundland and commanded three major naval expeditions between 1763 and 1779, conclusively charting many islands in the South Pacific as well as New Zealand, the east coast of Australia, the west coast of North America, and coastlines in the Arctic and Antarctic.

James Cook was born in 1728 in Marton-in-Cleveland, Yorkshire, England. Between 1746 and 1755 he was apprenticed to a Whitby coal shipping merchant. During this time, Cook, who never had much formal education, learned the practical aspects of navigation. In his spare time, Cook studied geometry, trigonometry, and astronomy, and read navigation manuals. Restless, perhaps, with the repetitive coal traffic routes of the North Sea, Cook volunteered for the Royal Navy in 1755, where he was promoted rapidly to master of HMS *Pembroke*.

Soon enough, Cook saw plenty of military action against the French in Canada at the taking of Louisbourg and the capture of Quebec in 1758–59, decisive victories during the Seven

Years' War. In Canada, Cook learned land surveying from an army engineer, and for the next several years he was involved in charting Canadian territory between short visits to England. On one return visit in 1762 he married Elizabeth Batts after a six-week courtship; within four months he was off again, having been appointed surveyor of the notoriously difficult and dangerous coastline of Newfoundland, where he employed his knowledge of both marine and land surveying techniques. Over the next few years, Cook spent spring through fall there, producing one of the most accurate sea charts of his day. He also documented a solar eclipse from Newfoundland.

By 1766, Cook had established himself as a talented navigator, mapmaker, and amateur scientist, having caught the attention of the Royal Society of London, one of the oldest and most prestigious scientific organizations in the world. He also developed a reputation as a stern but equitable leader capable of inspiring the morale of his crew. Thus, when the Royal Society and the Admiralty decided to organize a major expedition to the South Pacific to measure the transit of Venus across the Sun's disk, he was chosen to lead it. This somewhat rare astronomical event was considered of paramount importance for refining knowledge about distances between Earth, Venus, and the Sun, as well as for verifying terrestrial longitudes. Taking measurements from locations around the globe would greatly reduce the margin of error, and this meant venturing into places generally unknown to western Europeans. The expedition was also to document and classify unknown flora and fauna. The expedition would also involve testing a number of dietary plans to determine the best means to counteract the effects of scurvy.

In May 1768, Cook was promoted to lieutenant by the Royal Navy and appointed commander of the *Endeavor*, a converted Whitby-built coal vessel, nearly 30 meters (98 feet) long and 368 tons.

The *Endeavor* was squat and slow by Royal Navy standards but eminently suited to hauling vast amounts of cargo and withstanding heavy weather. In other words, it was perfect for a long-term, coordinated scientific expedition the likes of which had not been seen before. On 26 August, the *Endeavor* departed with a total crew of 94, including botanist and Royal Society member Joseph Banks (1743–1820), whose team of eight would catalog many new botanical and zoological specimens. One of Banks's men had been a student of the famous Swedish naturalist and systematist Carl Linnaeus (1707–78). Charles Green (1735–71) was the Royal Society's choice for astronomer, accompanied by one assistant and numerous astronomical and navigational instruments. Many of these men, including Cook, also became amateur ethnographers as they encountered natives of the South Pacific islands, usually in order to trade shipboard items for food.

James Cook. (From the collections of the Library of Congress)

Cook's first expedition was a remarkable success, lasting nearly three full years. After rounding Tierra del Fuego, the *Endeavor* reached Tahiti by April 1769, established relations with the Tahitians, and observed the transit of Venus. For the next year and a half, Cook and his men explored the region, circumnavigating and charting Tahiti and New Zealand, eventually making their way up the east coast of New Holland (Australia). All the while, Banks's team collected and documented flora and fauna, finding a particularly rich diversity of new plant forms at a place they named Botany Bay (near present-day Sydney). Cook guided the ship through the perilous Great Barrier Reef and then to Batavia (on the island of present-day Java), a thriving Dutch port settlement where many of Cook's crew contracted malaria or dysentery and died, after remarkably having no such deaths by disease up to that point. Cook and the tired remnants of his crew, including Banks (who became rather famous afterward), returned to England in July 1771. Almost immediately, plans for a second voyage to depart a year later were under way.

Two new ships, the *Resolution* and the *Adventure*, both similar to the *Endeavor*, were outfitted for another long-term expedition that would completely circumnavigate the globe. Cook captained the *Resolution*, Tobias Furneaux (1735–81) the *Adventure*. Two astronomers (William Bayley and William Wales) and a naturalist (Johann Forster) went along, accompanied by a complement of assistants. Cook and the astronomers were to work on the vexing problem of determining longitude at sea by testing four new chronometers. One, designed by John Harrison (1693–1776), proved to be the first such device sufficiently accurate for the task, a major event in the history of navigation science. Previously, a cumbersome series of astronomical observations and mathematical calculations were required, which could be done accurately only under the most perfect of conditions.

Cook led the expedition around the Cape of Good Hope, Africa, before entering and further exploring the South Pacific. Numerous islands were discovered or definitively charted (including the Marquesas, Tonga, the New Hebrides, New Caledonia, and Easter Island), and many new botanical species and genera were identified. Cook's crew also encountered and documented many native peoples, including some they had met previously. Cook and Forster, in fact, were fascinated by the diversity of native customs throughout the islands, and they judged that two large cultural groups (Polynesians and Melanesians) had migrated and mingled throughout the region.

Cook's major cartographic accomplishments of his second voyage rested, first, in conclusively demonstrating that no major continent existed in the region of the southern hemisphere east of New Zealand. Such a landmass, often called *terra australis,* had long been theorized to exist in this vicinity to balance out the landmasses of the northern hemisphere. Second, Cook became the first European explorer to cross the Antarctic Circle, which the *Resolution* did several times, encountering strange masses of floating ice, dubbed *ice islands, pack ice,* or *table* (or *field*) *ice,* depending on size and consistency. Cook and Forster conducted a number of experiments to test the freezing point of salt water, previously believed an impossibility. Cook professed that if terra australis existed, it lay beneath the Antarctic ice, useless to anyone.

The *Resolution*, having become separated from the *Adventure* during the voyage and its crew depressed, eventually made its way back to England via Cape Horn in July 1775, more than three years after departing. In the summer of 1776, as America proclaimed independence from England, Cook embarked on his final voyage, in command of the *Resolution*. Accompanied by the *Discovery* (commanded by Charles Clerke), the goal of this voyage was to locate a northwest passage across the North American continent by working eastward from the North Pacific. After island hopping the South Pacific for over a year, Cook and crew turned northward, charting Christmas Island and Hawaii in the process and developed a relationship with the Hawaiian islanders. By August, Cook had charted his way up the northwest coast of North America, correcting many earlier cartographic errors, and into the Bering Strait, where the expedition was halted by ice. After having determined conclusively that the landmass west of the strait was Asia, Cook sailed the ships to Hawaii, hoping to winter there before making another attempt at the Bering Strait. Cook was unable to determine whether the landmass east of the strait was indeed part of the North American continent or a possible giant Alaskan island.

In Hawaii, however, relations with the natives became very strained after some tools and one of the *Discovery*'s boats were stolen from Cook's men. Details of this incident, not surprisingly, are vague. Violence frequently occurred during many of Cook's encounters with natives, but so, too, did acts of friendship and kindness. Cook was, in fact, renowned for being more balanced in his dealings with natives than many Europeans of his day. It has been suggested that Cook's health and mood had degenerated after contracting an intestinal illness during his second voyage. He may have grown weary of the sea during this third voyage, especially in the face of failing to find the northwest passage. Whatever the reasons, on 14 February 1779, Cook's handling of the theft escalated to a riot in which he and four of his marines were killed.

Cook's three voyages established a new precedent for long-term expedition science that would serve as a solid foundation for increasingly precise forms of oceanography in the centuries to come. He greatly refined and expanded geographic and hydrographic knowledge of the Pacific, and his expeditions furthered biological, astronomical, and navigational science as well. In his own day, he was highly praised for attention to shipboard hygiene, imposing systems of diet and cleanliness on his crews, thus diminishing the occurrence of disease on his ships at sea.

J. Conor Burns

BIOGRAPHY

- James Cook.
- Born on 27 October 1728 in Marton-in-Cleveland, Yorkshire, England.
- Apprenticed to a Whitby coal shipping merchant, 1746.
- Largely self-taught in scientific and navigational subjects.
- Volunteered for the Royal Navy in 1755, served in Canada in 1758–62 during the Seven Years' War.
- Appointed by the Admiralty to survey Newfoundland, carried out between 1763 and 1766.
- Commanded the first voyage aboard the *Endeavor* to observe the transit of Venus from South Pacific, 1768–71.
- Commanded a second voyage (1772–75) with *Resolution* and *Adventure* to explore South Pacific in more detail, crossing the Antarctic Circle and proving the utility of marine chronometer in the process.
- Commanded the third voyage (1776–80) to the Pacific with *Resolution* and *Discovery* to look for a northwest passage.
- Killed 14 February 1779 during a dispute with Hawaiian islanders.

SELECTED WRITINGS

Cook, James. *A Voyage Towards the South Pole, and Round the World. Performed in His Majesty's Ships the* Resolution *and* Adventure, *in the Years 1772, 1773, 1774, and 1775*, 2 vols. London: printed for W. Strahan and T. Cadell, 1777.

———. *The Journals of Captain James Cook on His Voyages of* Discovery. J. C. Beaglehole, ed., 3 vols. Cambridge: Published for the Hakluyt Society at the University Press, 1955–1974.

FURTHER READING

Hough, Richard. *Captain James Cook*. London: Hodder and Stoughton, 1994.

Withey, Lynne. *Voyages of* Discovery: *Captain Cook and the Exploration of the Pacific*. New York: Morrow, 1987.

RELATED ARTICLES

Bering Strait; Navigation

Copepod

Copepods comprise a large and diverse subclass of mainly aquatic crustaceans. They inhabit fresh water and moss or moist soil, but most species are marine; they can be found from the intertidal to the deepest trenches and from the polar seas to the hot water around hydrothermal vents. Copepods can be pelagic, benthic, symbiotic, and parasitic, and as a group they represent one of the most abundant organisms in the sea. Free-swimming species dominate the zooplankton assemblage throughout the world's oceans and are extremely important in marine food webs. Most copepods are transparent, but some species are bright red, orange, purple, blue, or black. The majority of species range in length from less than 1 millimeter (mm) (0.04 inch) to 10 mm (0.39 inch), but some free-living individuals can be longer than 1.5 centimeters (cm) (0.59 inch), and some parasitic species exceed 25 cm (9.84 inches) in length.

Like all crustaceans, copepods have mandibles for biting and grinding food and two pairs of antennae. Copepods lack compound eyes and usually lack appendages on the abdomen. They also lack a carapace but have a well-developed cephalic shield. Most are divided into three distinct body regions. Copepods have separate sexes, and sperm are transferred to the female as a package called a *spermatophore*. Females carry fertilized eggs in a sac attached to the body. Eggs hatch as the first of six nauplius larval stages and then pass through five copepodid stages before metamorphosing into adults.

Taxonomically, copepods belong in the phylum Arthropoda, subphylum Crustacea, class Maxillopoda, and subclass Copepoda. The approximately 9000 described species of copepods are divided into 10 orders. The most frequently encountered free-living forms are the calanoids and cyclopoids, both of which are mainly planktonic, and the harpacticoids,

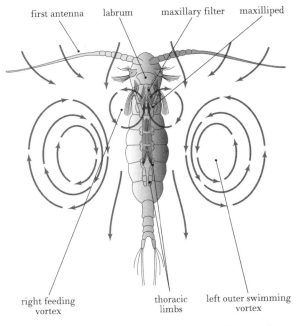

Feeding mechanism in a copepod. [Adapted from W. D. Russell-Hunter, Aquatic Productivity (New York: Macmillan, 1970.)]

which are mostly benthic. The platycopioids and gelyelloids are free-living, the misophrioids and mormonilloids are free-living and planktonic, the siphonostomatoids and poecilostomatoids are exclusively parasitic (on invertebrates and fishes), and the monstrilloids parasitize invertebrates as larvae but are planktonic as adults. Benthic harpacticoids generally are detritivores or they feed on the microorganisms living on sediment grains. Parasitic copepod species, which parasitize almost every phylum of animal in the water, can be external or internal and usually have a modified body form. Free-living holoplanktonic copepods exhibit a characteristic short, cylindrical body shape. Long antennae help copepods to maintain their position in the water column and prevent sinking. They are weak swimmers and exhibit a characteristic jerky motion.

Copepods are the most important and numerous members of the net zooplankton (organisms large enough to be caught in nets), of which they represent 70 to 90 percent of the biomass. They graze on phytoplankton by filtering cells out of the water with the appendages around the mouth or by catching them with appendages. Some species also prey on other zooplankton. In many pelagic areas of the ocean, only a few species are numerically dominant. For example, *Calanus finmarchicus* is the dominant copepod in the Atlantic. In the North Pacific, *Neocalanus plumchrus* and *Neocalanus cristatus* are the dominant copepods. Other common copepod genera include *Acartia*, *Pseudocalanus* and *Microcalanus*. Copepods are the major grazers of bloom-forming diatoms and dinoflagellates in the oceans; the life cycles of these grazers are synchronized with spring phytoplankton blooms, and these crustaceans can regulate phytoplankton population dynamics.

Ecologically, planktonic copepods are the main link between the larger phytoplankton and higher trophic levels. By grazing on phytoplankton and then getting eaten by larger animals, copepods transfer energy through the food chain to larger organisms (such as fishes and baleen whales). In addition, copepod fecal pellets sink out of the upper reaches of the water column and thereby transfer energy to deeper water.

Lynn L. Lauerman

FURTHER READING

Brusca, Richard C., and Gary J. Brusca. *Invertebrates.* Sunderland, Mass.: Sinauer, 1990.

Dussart, Bernard H., and D. Defaye. *Copepoda: Introduction to the Copepoda.* Amsterdam: SPB Academic, 1995.

Huys, Rony, and Geoffrey A. Boxshall. *Copepod Evolution.* London: Ray Society, 1991.

Nybakken, James. *Marine Biology: An Ecological Approach*, 5th ed. San Francisco: Benjamin Cummings, 2001.

Schram, Frederick R. *Crustacea.* New York: Oxford University Press, 1986.

USEFUL WEB SITES

Smithsonian Institution. "World of Copepoda." <http://www.nmnh.si.edu/iz/copepod>.

RELATED ARTICLES

Arthropoda; Benthos; Crustacea; Food Web; Grazing; Holoplankton; Maxillopoda; Meroplankton; Net Plankton; Parasitism; Pelagic; Symbiosis

Copepodid, see Copepod

Coral

Corals are marine animals that resemble tiny sea anemones. Most species live in colonies made up of hundreds of individual organisms, or polyps, that are joined together by extensions of their bodies and supported by an external skeleton. In shallow tropical waters the skeletons of corals build up to form coral reefs, which harbor an incredible diversity of marine life.

Scientists classify corals as members of the class Anthozoa, within the phylum Cnidaria. Other cnidarians include jellyfish, sea anemones, and hydroids. Like these close relatives, corals possess a simple anatomy. Their body shape is described as radially symmetrical, which means that it is arranged around a circular plan. At the top of a coral is a ring of tentacles, which is used to capture food. The bottom of the body sits in an externally secreted calcium carbonate cup. The tentacles surround a central mouth leading to an internal cavity where food is digested. Since the mouth is the body's only opening, it also serves as an anus. The body wall of a coral consists of only two layers of cells: an outer epidermis and an inner gastrodermis, between which is a jellylike filling called *mesoglea*. Muscle cells in the body wall and in the septa of the gastrovascular cavity enable corals to move their tentacles and withdraw from danger. A simple nerve net controls the muscle cells, but there is no brain.

Like other cnidarians, corals are predators. Their tentacles are armed with tiny stings that capture and paralyze planktonic prey. In clear waters, where plankton is less abundant, many

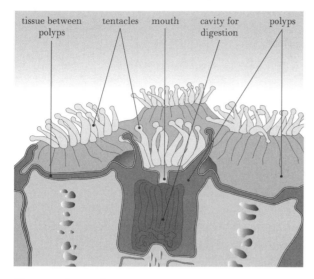

tissue between polyps   tentacles   mouth   cavity for digestion   polyps

Features of a coral.

corals contain single-celled algae called *zooxanthellae*, which live inside the polyps and give them a variety of colors. The relationship between the algae and the corals is mutually beneficial (symbiotic): The corals provide protection and waste products such as carbon dioxide, which is vital for photosynthesis, and the algae provide the coral with food molecules. In many of the world's coral reefs, corals have recently lost their symbiotic algae, causing a phenomenon known as *bleaching*. Bleached corals turn white and will die if the zooxanthellae are not reacquired within a certain time. The culprit is thought to be increased sea temperatures, which stress the corals, leading to expulsion of the algae.

Many cnidarians have a complex life cycle involving two different body forms: a free-swimming stage called a *medusa stage* (such as a jellyfish) and a *polyp stage,* in which they live anchored to the seafloor. Corals have eliminated the medusa stage from their life cycle and exist only as polyps. They reproduce sexually by producing sperm and egg cells, which fuse to form an embryo. The embryo grows into a free-swimming larva that eventually settles on the seafloor and turns into a new polyp. The polyp then reproduces asexually, dividing over and over into

hundreds of genetically identical polyps that together form a colony.

A coral colony is supported and protected by a skeleton made of calcium carbonate (chalk). The most familiar corals are the stony corals, which produce a hard external skeleton into which the polyps can withdraw for protection. Soft corals and horny coral produce internal skeletons, consisting of needlelike spikes called *spicules.* As the polyps continue to reproduce asexually, the colony expands and the skeleton grows larger. Some coral skeletons grow into spectacular fan shapes, others look like deer antlers or organ pipes, and some look like human brains.

Ben Morgan

FURTHER READING

Barnes, Robert. *Invertebrate Zoology.* Philadelphia, W. B. Saunders, 1963; 6th ed., by Edward Ruppert, Fort Worth, Texas: Saunders College Publishing, 1994.
Brusca, Richard C., and Gary J. Brusca. *Invertebrates.* Sunderland, Mass.: Sinauer, 1990.
Pechenik, Jan A. *Biology of the Invertebrates.* Boston: Prindle, Weber and Schmidt, 1985; 4th ed., Boston: McGraw-Hill, 2000.

RELATED ARTICLES

Biodiversity; Cnidaria; Filter Feeder; Polyp; Symbiosis; Zooxanthellae

Coral Atoll

A coral atoll is one of three main coral reef types (the other two are fringing reefs and barrier reefs) as first classified by naturalist Charles Darwin (1809–82) in 1842 in his work *The Structure and Distribution of Coral Reefs.* An atoll is an approximately horseshoe- or ring-shaped coral reef system enclosing a lagoon that is typically no more than 50 meters (165 feet) or so deep.

There are some 330 atolls, all but a handful of them in the Indo-Pacific. The largest atoll is probably Kwajalein Atoll in the Marshall Islands of the western Pacific. The 90 or so islets of this atoll surround a lagoon that is more than 70 kilometers (43 miles) long and 32 kilometers (20 miles) wide with a lagoon area of about 1720 square kilometers (664 square miles). The word *atoll* is derived from the Maldivian word for "place."

Atoll Formation

Naturalists and mariners have had a long-held fascination with coral atolls, knowing that the organisms that form them grow only in shallow water [up to about 100 meters (330 feet) deep], but the atolls themselves emerge from deep water, often more than 1 kilometer (0.6 mile) deep. During Darwin's famous voyage on HMS *Beagle* (1831–36) he visited Tahiti and viewed from a nearby hill the barrier reef that encircled the island of Moorea. Based on this and other observations, Darwin surmised that such an island, continuously subsiding beneath the waves, would eventually form a coral atoll enclosing a land-free lagoon.

Darwin's subsidence theory proposes that a coral atoll develops from coral growth on the rim of a volcanic island. Initially, the volcanic island is skirted by a growth of coral forming a fringing reef (little or no lagoon between the reef and the island). Then, as the island subsides over many thousands of years, a barrier reef (with a substantial lagoon between reef and island) is formed. Eventually, the island subsides entirely, leaving a ring of coral enclosing a lagoon containing no visible land.

Darwin's subsidence theory has largely been vindicated. In 1952, geological drilling on Eniwetok Atoll in the Marshall Islands confirmed the existence of volcanic rock at a depth of 1406 meters (4613 feet) below the modern reef top. The volcanic island has subsided, and over 49 million years reef-building corals had grown upward, one generation on top of the remains of the previous one, keeping pace with the rate of subsidence to consolidate a reef system that was many hundreds of meters thick. Similar results

have since been confirmed at many other Pacific atoll sites, although in most cases the coral platform is much less thick. Modern plate tectonics provides the explanation as to how emergent oceanic volcanoes subside as they move away from the hotspot that created them.

However, not all coral atolls are of volcanic origin. The Maldives and Laccadive Islands of the Indian Ocean, and those of the Queensland Plateau of the Pacific Ocean, have originated

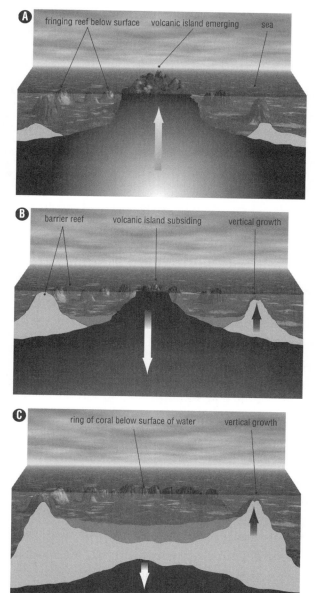

Creation of a coral atoll.

from continental crust fragments, rather than oceanic volcanoes. However, once established, the subsidence of these fragments (and/or a sea-level rise) has established atoll formations in a similar manner to those of oceanic origin. Maldivian atolls are unusual, in comparison to others, in having emergent structures in the lagoon. Air strips and tourist resorts are commonly built on such sites, within the comparative protection of the atoll ring.

Coral Growth

Coral atolls form where gradual island subsidence (and/or rising sea level) is coupled with environmental conditions that encourage reef-building (hermatypic) coral polyps to grow prolifically. To grow well, hermatypic corals must remain immersed in seawater for all or most of the time and receive strong sunlight as well as considerable water movement. Reef-building polyps grow and multiply best where the water is shallow [less than 50 meters (165 feet) deep], mean annual water temperatures lie in the range 23 to 25°C (73 to 77°F), the seawater is of near-normal salinity, and surface water has low turbidity. The algae (zooxanthellae) that grow symbiotically inside reef-building coral polyps require moderately high light levels and clear water for photosynthesis. The zooxanthellae, plus nitrogen-fixing cyanobacteria associated with coral reef sponges, give these ecosystems their enormously high productivity in what are otherwise nutrient-poor waters. Upward rates of growth of a coral reef vary from a few millimeters to 3 centimeters (1.2 inches) per year under favorable conditions.

Reef Islands

Coral islands develop from atolls in one of two ways: uplift or accretion. Crustal movements may uplift parts of the atoll system above sea level. This has happened in the case of the Aldabra Islands in the western Indian Ocean.

Aldabra's four islands constitute parts of an oval atoll—about 30 kilometers (19 miles) long and 13 kilometers (8 miles) wide—that encloses a large lagoon. The islands—typical for uplifted atolls—have a calcareous land surface pitted and sculpted by rain weathering.

Many of the coral islands in the central and southern Pacific and those of the Maldives in the Indian Ocean originated by accretion rather than uplift. Fragments of reef broken off by storms and powerful waves are typically deposited on the windward side of the atoll. This material is added to by finer reef detritus and other material brought in by persistent currents and smaller waves. Beaches form alongside the shoal and light material may become heaped into dunes by wind action. The new island, comprised almost entirely of loose calcium carbonate deposits, is readily weathered by rain, which dissolves the chalk and redeposits it around loose material, gradually consolidating a cementlike structure. Once colonized by animals and plants, biological detritus such as guano from bird feces helps soils to establish. Because of the remoteness of some of these islands, the diversity of the terrestrial flora and fauna that colonizes them is relatively low. If the islands are long-lived, adaptive radiation may give rise to unique forms.

Whether formed by accretion or uplift, atoll islands tend to be low-lying, often only 3 meters (10 feet) or less above extreme high tide, and are vulnerable to storm damage and changes in sea level. Nevertheless, such reef islands have been inhabited for many thousands of years by seafaring peoples such as the Maldivians in the Indian Ocean and the Polynesians and Micronesians in the south Pacific. The future of some low-lying islands is threatened by global warming and the sea-level rise predicted during the next 100 years.

Cross Section of a Coral Atoll

The zonation on a mature coral atoll is the most complex of any of the major reef types. In fact, a mature atoll commonly includes elements of the other types of reef. Once coral islands are established in the atoll ring, a barrier reef and a fringing reef may occur outside the islands. Even a simplified cross section through the atoll ring will thus reveal the following structure, from outside to inside: outer reef slope, surge channel, barrier reef, outer reef flat, outer lagoon, fringing reef, coral island, and an inner lagoon containing patch reefs (clumps of mixed coral in shallow water) and other formations such as microatolls (ring-shaped formations several meters across formed from single saucer-shaped coral colonies such as *Porites*).

Value of Coral Atolls

Aesthetically, coral reefs are arguably the most spectacular biological communities on the planet. Recent estimates by Allegra Small and colleagues at the Smithsonian Institution suggest that, in total, coral reefs have a species diversity similar to rainforests on land (in the range 1 to 3 million species), but they occupy a much smaller area (about 5 percent that of rainforests), so their species density may be the highest of any of Earth's biomes.

Coral reefs make a major contribution to the economies of many developing nations in tropical zones, including those small island nations that have relatively few land-based resources. Many tropical island communities in the Maldives, Seychelles, and French Polynesia gain most of their gross national product from tourism, with coral reefs as a major draw.

With the intense competition for space on a coral reef, and the need for sessile organisms to fend off a wide variety of predators, chemical defense has become a key survival strategy for many reef species. There is a wealth of biochemical potential in the organisms inhabiting coral reefs. Pharmacologists and chemists are in the process of testing a range of medicinal drugs of marine origin, which have anticancer,

antibacterial, and antiviral potential. Coral reefs are seen as a vast reservoir of potential medicines and useful structural materials. For example, a potent anticancer drug, dubbed Eleutherobin, was recently extracted from the rare Australian soft coral, *Eleutherobia*. The calcium carbonate skeletons of corals are now cut and shaped to provide microporous splints that encourage the healing of bone fractures.

Threats to Coral Atolls

On time scales of years, coral reefs appear to be highly fragile ecosystems, yet capable of rapid recovery. On longer time scales, the calcareous structure of a reef system seems to persist and grow (albeit intermittently) over millions of years, despite the rise and fall of sea levels and global climatic change.

Socioeconomic pressures encourage the short-term direct exploitation of reef resources. Some atolls are stripped of their diverse fish populations, partly for food, and partly to supply the aquarium trade for exotic fish. Some of the methods used, such as cyanide to stun fish or dynamiting to kill fish, are highly destructive to the reef structure. Shells and corals are still collected as tourist curios in some localities. Shoreline developments can have dire consequences. Coral atolls are highly susceptible to pollution from sewage discharges and from stormwater runoff that can carry with it all manner of pollutants, including oils, heavy metals, and suspended sediments that smother reefs. Atoll resorts are sometimes constructed from calcareous materials harvested from living reefs. Once built, the resorts impose many demands, ranging from alterations in sea current and sedimentation patterns to direct damage to the reef from boating and anchor damage and scuba and snorkeling activities. Alien species that compete with indigenous species are introduced by design or accident. Estimates made by the Global Coral Reef Monitoring Network in 2000 indicated that 11 percent of the world's coral reefs had been lost pre-1998 due to human impacts, with a further 16 percent destroyed in 1998 during the largest closely monitored El Niño event on record.

Currently, El Niño events, coupled with global warming, are believed to be the most serious short-term threats to coral atolls. In 1997–98, a sustained 1 to 2°C (1.8 to 3.6°F) temperature rise above normal maximums occurred in many tropical areas, coinciding with a strong El Niño. This produced the most extensive coral-bleaching event on record. Atolls in the Maldives and Seychelles were severely affected, with 70 to 99 percent coral mortality (as surface area) on many reefs.

Coral bleaching is the whitening of reef-building corals caused by the loss of their symbiotic algae, on which they depend for much of their nutrition. The widespread coral bleaching in 1997–98 was attributed to raised sea-surface temperatures aggravated by high levels of ultraviolet radiation, which affected the physiology of coral polyps, causing them to eject their zooxanthellae. If bleaching conditions are maintained for 10 weeks or more, this can lead to the death of polyps. A coral-bleaching event may halt the production of larvae, thus affecting coral recruitment for the following year or so.

Low-lying coral islands, such as those of the Maldives in the Indian Ocean and Kiribati and the Marshall Islands in the Pacific, are less than 3 meters (10 feet) above extreme high water levels. With the IPCC (1995) estimating a 50-centimeter (20-inch) mean global sea-level rise by 2100, the protection offered by coral reefs to wave energy and storm surges can be sustained only if corals grow upward at the same rate as sea levels rise. There are fears among some marine scientists that increased atmospheric carbon dioxide (CO_2) levels might raise CO_2 concentrations in the surface waters, increasing seawater's acidity and reducing rates of calcification (the

formation of calcium carbonate skeletons by corals). If coral growth is regularly impaired by bleaching events and anthropogenic (human-caused) factors, the seashore protection these corals offer may no longer be provided. In addition, climatic change appears to be making weather patterns less predictable and more extreme: Larger storms and changes in oceanic circulation patterns are likely.

Trevor Day

FURTHER READING

Adey, Walter H., Ted A. McConnaughey, Allegra M. Small, and Don M. Spoon. "Coral Reefs: Endangered, Biodiverse, Genetic Resources." In C. Sheppard, ed., *Seas at the Millennium: An Environmental Evaluation*, Vol. III, *Global Issues and Processes*. Oxford: Elsevier, 2000; pp. 33–42.

Birkeland, C., ed. *Life and Death of Coral Reefs.* New York: Chapman and Hall, 1997.

Dubinsky, Z., ed. *Coral Reefs: Ecosystems of the World 25.* Amsterdam and New York: Elsevier, 1990.

Gray, William. *Coral Reefs and Islands.* Newton Abbot, England: David and Charles, 1993.

Karlson, R. H. *Dynamics of Coral Communities.* Boston: Kluwer Academic, 1999.

Westmacott, S., K. Teleki, S. Wells, and J. M. West. *Management of Bleached and Severely Damaged Coral Reefs.* Gland, Switzerland, and Cambridge: International Union for the Conservation of Nature and Natural Resources, 2000.

Wood, Rachel. *Reef Evolution.* Oxford and New York: Oxford University Press, 1999.

USEFUL WEB SITES

"Coral Reef Degradation in the Indian Ocean (CORDIO)." <http://www.cordio.org>.

National Oceanic and Atmospheric Administration. "Coral Reef Online." <http://www.coralreef.noaa.gov>.

———. "Global Coral Reef Watch." <http://www.coral.aoml.noaa.gov/crw>.

RELATED ARTICLES

Barrier Reef; Climate Change; Coral; Coral Bleaching; Coral Reef; Darwin, Charles Robert; Fringing Reef; Plate Tectonics; Polyp; Reef

Coral Bleaching

Coral bleaching is the whitening of hermatypic corals that occurs when pigment-bearing zooxanthellae are expelled. Hermatypic corals are the reef-building corals (phylum Cnidaria, class Anthozoa, order Scleractinia) that inhabit tropical waters. They are distinguished from ahermatypic corals by the presence (usually) of dinoflagellate symbionts called *zooxanthellae* that live within their tissues. Hermatypic corals house and protect their symbionts and provide them with a constant supply of the nutrients needed for photosynthesis. Pigments in zooxanthellae give corals their bright colors and are also used for photosynthesis, which provides corals with as much as 90 to 95 percent of their nutrition.

Bleaching occurs when the symbiotic relationship between reef-building corals and their zooxanthellae breaks down. When hermatypic corals expel some or all of their zooxanthellae, the white calcareous skeleton produced by corals shines through their transparent tissues. Bleaching often results in a loss of 60 to 90 percent of the zooxanthellae within a coral, and the remaining zooxanthellae can lose 50 to 80 percent of their photosynthetic pigments. Corals can recover from bleaching and regain symbionts if exposure to stress is short, but if they are under stress and without zooxanthellae for prolonged periods of time, they will die.

Hermatypic corals thrive when their environment meets fairly strict requirements. They do best when the average annual seawater temperature is between 23 and 25°C (73 to 77°F) and when salinity is between 32 and 35 practical salinity units (psu). Most live in water shallower than 25 meters (82 feet); none live deeper than 50 to 70 meters (164 to 230 feet). Hermatypic corals cannot tolerate high levels of sediment in the water column, nor can they be exposed to air for very long. Scientists believe that bleaching results from physical and/or environmental stresses that alter the tolerable ranges of these parameters. Anthropogenic factors such as pollution, dilution, and excess sedimentation can put stress on coral reefs, as can natural disturbances such as storms, flooding, predation, pathogens, and El Niño–Southern Oscillation (ENSO) events, which are interannual climatic fluctuations that change water temperature.

The most common stress implicated in coral bleaching is increased temperature. Temperature increases of only 1 or 2°C above mean averages during summer months can cause bleaching. Bleaching most commonly occurs during summer months, when solar irradiance is at its peak and corals are exposed to excess levels of

Coral head showing the effects of bleaching, a result of rising seawater temperatures that killed 10 percent of the world's corals in 1998. The darker areas are the normal color due to the symbiotic algae that live inside the coral; the lighter areas are where algae has died off. (Associated Press, UCLA)

ultraviolet light. Both of these stresses may be affected by global climate change. Global warming and ENSO events can alter seawater temperatures, and depletion of the ozone layer increases the amount of ultraviolet radiation reaching Earth's surface.

Coral bleaching has been recognized for decades, but it has been occurring in increasing frequency and geographic extent since the late 1970s. Most of the world's coral reef areas, including reefs in the Caribbean, western Atlantic, eastern Pacific, central Pacific, western Pacific, Indian Ocean, Arabian Gulf, and Red Sea, have experienced coral bleaching and some coral mortality during the 1980s. The worst year on record for coral bleaching throughout the world was 1998; in some areas 90 percent of the corals were dead or dying because of bleaching. Most of these bleaching events coincided with large-scale ENSO events.

Coral reefs represent a unique and important ecosystem that covers about 1,554,000 square kilometers (600,000 square miles) of the shallow inshore waters of the tropics. Coral reefs are productive oases (gross primary production of 1500 to 5000 grams of carbon per square meter per year) in the midst of tropical waters characterized by low productivity (18 to 50 grams of carbon per square meter per year) and are home to an exceptionally high diversity of invertebrate, vertebrate, and plant species. They also protect coastal areas from storms. Increases in coral bleaching may result in mass mortality and extinction of coral species and in displacement or loss of many associated flora and fauna. Mass coral mortality may also negatively affect certain fisheries as well as diving tourism.

Lynn L. Lauerman

FURTHER READING
Glynn, P. W., et al. "Experimental Responses of Okinawan (Ryukyu Islands, Japan) Reef Corals to High Sea Temperature and UV Radiation." *Proceedings of the 7th International Coral Reef Symposium.* Mangilao: University of Guam Press, 1994; pp. 27–28.
Goreau, T. J. "Coral Bleaching in Jamaica." *Nature*, Vol. 343 (1990), p. 417.
Nybakken, James W. *Marine Biology: An Ecological Approach*, 5th ed. San Francisco: Benjamin Cummings, 2001.
Porter, J. W., and O. W. Meier. "Quantification of Loss and Change in Floridian Reef Coral Populations." *American Zoologist*, Vol. 32 (1992), pp. 625–640.
Veron, J. E. N. *Corals in Space and Time: The Biogeography and Evolution of the Scleractinia.* Ithaca, N.Y.: Comstock/Cornell, 1995.

RELATED ARTICLES
Coral Reef; Hermatypic Coral; Symbiosis

Coralline Algae

Coralline algae are red marine algae belonging to the division Rhodophyta. These organisms play an important role in the formation and maintenance of coral reefs and benthic communities. The algae absorb calcium carbonate from the water and incorporate it into hard supporting cell walls. Strong cell walls help to cement the reef together and allow the reef to withstand constant stress from the movement of waves, while remaining flexible enough to allow the cell walls to bend but not break. These extremely productive organisms contain red pigments, present in all red algae, which color the surface of the body and enable the algae to absorb light in deeper areas of the ocean. Coralline algae may be epiphytes, meaning that they grow on or attach to other plants but do not parasitize them. They also provide a surface upon which other organisms are able to grow.

Coralline algae may encrust rocks and other objects or form erect branches that attach to a firm substrate, or surface. Encrusting forms are known as *nongeniculate* coralline algae, while erect forms are known as *geniculate* coralline algae. There are some species that grow unattached.

Researchers suggest two theories as to how unattached forms develop. One is that the unattached forms are really broken-off pieces of another individual that proceed to grow on their own; the other is that the algae have grown around another object, such as a shell or rock. Coralline algae form algal ridges, which calcify much more quickly than any other areas on the reef. They also cover large areas of the ocean floor in colder waters. Coralline algae are one of the primary suppliers of calcium carbonate and sand within the reef system. The strong cell walls also benefit the algae by deterring predators, like grazing urchins. Coralline algae typically reproduce sexually, but may reproduce in other ways, including fragmentation, an asexual method of reproduction where an individual develops from a piece of another individual.

When coralline algae die, the color bleaches out of the cell walls, leaving a white skeleton. Most species of algae are too fragile to leave behind fossils. The sturdy skeleton of the coralline algae, however, has enabled researchers to study the fossil record of these organisms and discover species no longer present in the oceans. The fossil record indicates that coralline algae came into existence in either the late Jurassic or mid-Cretaceous periods (180 million to 100 million years ago). Live forms are difficult to study in the laboratory, due to their nutritional needs and problems associated with calcification.

Erin O'Donnell

FURTHER READING
Margulis, Lynn, John O. Corliss, Michael Melkonian, and David J. Chapman, eds. *Handbook of Protoctista.* Boston: Jones and Bartlett, 1990.
Nybakken, James W. *Marine Biology: An Ecological Approach,* 5th ed. San Francisco: Benjamin Cummings, 2001.
Woelkerling, William J. *The Coralline Red Algae.* Oxford and New York: Oxford University Press, 1988.

RELATED ARTICLES
Algae; Algal Ridge; Benthos; Coral Reef; Rhodophyta

Coral Reef

A reef is a wave-resistant structure of calcium carbonate formed from the closely packed shells or skeletons of numerous reef-building organisms. A coral reef is a calcareous structure established in tropical, shallow waters primarily by reef-building (hermatypic) corals, principally scleractinian or stony corals (phylum Cnidaria, class Anthozoa, order Scleractinia), but with additional calcium carbonate produced by various algae and other calcium carbonate-secreting invertebrate animals. A coral reef supports an astonishingly complex and diverse assemblage of marine plants and animals.

Like other forms of coral, scleractinian coral polyps use tentacles to capture plankton for food. However, the unique feature of the reef-building forms is the symbiotic algae (zooxanthellae) within their tissues. The algae photosynthesize and provide the polyps with energy-rich organic compounds from photosynthesis and supply the bulk of their carbon requirements. Zooxanthellae, in return, receive essential nutrients from the coral and are harbored within a comparatively safe and constant environment. The combination of algal photosynthesis and the polyp's physiological processes supports the formation of an extensive calcium carbonate exoskeleton. The skeletons of coral colonies form a complex three-dimensional framework. As the corals grow, their skeletons are attacked by a wide variety of reef-boring organisms, including sponges, clams, and worms. The sediment from these activities fills the cracks in the reef structure, and when the polyps die, the calcareous framework builds outward as new polyps establish on top. The activities of countless millions of colonies produce massive reef structures that reach hundreds of meters deep over millions of years. Many other organisms, ranging from coralline algae to sessile crustaceans and bivalve mollusks, play their part in consolidating the reef structure.

The Great Barrier Reef of eastern Australia, about 2000 kilometers (1245 miles) long, is a complex of more than 2500 reefs established over a period of time following sea-level rises during the current interglacial period. It is the largest biological construction in the ocean.

Distribution of Coral Reefs

Hermatypic corals require a fairly exacting range of conditions in order to establish reefs. First, the zooxanthellae require moderately strong sunlight for photosynthesis. Hermatypic corals grow in clear water up to depths of 100 meters (330 feet) or so, although in clear water coral diversity decreases steeply below about 40 meters (130 feet). Turbidity strongly limits coral growth. Thus, coral reefs establish in clear, nutrient-poor waters where suspended sediment is sparse and planktonic productivity is relatively low. Second, hermatypic corals require seawater of near-normal salinity. Although they can withstand slightly hypersaline conditions, they die quickly when seawater is diluted. Long stretches of coral along a coastline typically have breaks or gaps where freshwater runoff enters the sea. Third, coral polyps do not withstand desiccation well and need to be immersed in seawater for all or most of the time; they tend to be restricted to the lower intertidal and below. Fourth, coral reefs grow best where surface seawater temperatures are habitually within the range 18 to 30°C (64 to 86°F). Their global distribution is fairly well contained within the 20°C (68°F) surface-water winter isotherm. Coral reefs are extensive in the Indian Ocean and its marginal seas; in the west, central, and southern Pacific; and in the Caribbean area and off the coast of Florida. Where unsuitable temperature, or high sedimentation or nutrient levels prevail, hermatypic corals may still grow, but they do not establish reefs.

Types of Coral Reef

Three main types of coral reef were identified by naturalist Charles Darwin (1809–82) in his publication *The Structure and Distribution of Coral Reefs* (1842). This broad classification—fringing reef, barrier reef, and atoll—remains to this day. A fringing reef is parallel to, and continuous with, a shoreline, or lies very close to it. If there is a body of water (lagoon) between reef and land, it is narrow and shallow. A barrier reef also forms parallel to the shore but at a greater distance; the lagoon is deeper and may be tens of kilometers wide, as in the case of the Great Barrier Reef. An atoll is a horseshoe- or ring-shaped reef system surrounding a land-free lagoon and rising out of deep water far from land. In 1842, Darwin proposed his subsidence theory for atoll formation, whereby a coral atoll forms from fringing and barrier reefs when an oceanic volcanic island gradually subsides. His theory was validated in the 1950s, with evidence from geological drillings on Pacific atolls.

Almost all coral atolls are found in the Indian or Pacific oceans. They form where oceanic volcanic islands, or sometimes islands of continental origin such as the Maldives and Seychelles, subside, or are inundated by rising sea level. Initially, a newly emerged island develops a fringing reef. As the island gradually subsides, or is inundated, the reef, now some distance from the shore, continues to grow upward as a barrier reef. In time, the original island submerges entirely and the reef system becomes an atoll. Eventually, the atoll itself may disappear, if subsidence or inundation outpaces the rate of coral growth. In such a case, a seamount is formed. The sequence may be arrested or reversed at any stage if environmental conditions change to preclude coral growth, if subsidence halts, or if sea levels rise or fall abruptly with global climatic change. Alongside continents, fringing reefs and barrier reefs are stable endpoints in themselves and do not form part of a developmental sequence leading to atoll formation.

Coral Biogeography

In terms of the generic and species composition of scleractinian corals, the Atlantic and Indo-Pacific are effectively separate provinces. Eighty genera of hermatypic corals (more than 500 species) have been described for the Indo-Pacific, with only 36 genera (about 60 species) for the Caribbean. The Indo-Pacific is regarded as the original source of scleractinian corals, with the Caribbean center becoming separated from it much later (but at least 50 million years ago), following major climatic and geological events.

Coral Reef Morphology

The detailed morphology of a reef system is highly variable, and many subdivisions within the basic classification—fringing reef, barrier reef, and atoll—have been identified. However, the three reef types share common morphological features: a reef front, a reef flat, and a lagoon (inner) slope.

The seaward edge of the reef, called the *reef front,* often contains two major elements: an upper spur-and-groove zone and a lower fore-reef slope. The spur-and-groove formation consists of a series of bioconstructed ridges (spurs) arranged roughly perpendicular to the reef edge. Between these are sediment-filled pockets (grooves). The spur-and-groove arrangement disperses much more wave energy than would an uninterrupted wall of coral. The fore-reef slope varies from a gentle incline to a near-vertical slope. Zonation is apparent on the reef front, the fastest-growing part of the reef. On the reef crest, which is subject to intense battering by waves and periodic exposure to air, a ridge of encrusting calcareous algae is typically found.

In the zone below the reef crest are corals that are fairly resistant to wave stress and require more-or-less continuous immersion. In the Caribbean, elkhorn coral (*Acropora palmata*) commonly occupies this zone. In the Indo-Pacific, other species of *Acropora*, particularly encrusting or short, branching forms, often predominate. An intermediate zone, the mid-slope, extends from a few meters to depths of 10 to 40 meters (33 to 131 feet), depending on local conditions. Branching forms, such as *Acropora formosa* (Indo-Pacific) and *Acropora cervicornis* (Caribbean), occupy the mid-slope's upper part, with more massive forms, such as *Porites* (Indo-Pacific and Caribbean), on its lower area. Below, on the deep slope, reduced light intensity limits the diversity of scleractinian corals, which include some Agariciidae (e.g., *Pachyseris*), Pectiniidae (e.g., *Echinophyllia*), and Mussidae (e.g., *Cynarina*) in the Indo-Pacific, and *Agaricia* and *Helioseris* species in the Caribbean. Soft (alcyonacean) corals, horny (gorgonian) corals, and sponges are found higher up the slope, but they may be abundant in the lower zone, especially in the Caribbean. They gain their nutrient requirements by consuming plankton and drifting detrital material, although many coral reef sponges also harbor symbiotic cyanobacteria, from which they obtain organic compounds produced by photosynthesis.

Behind the reef crest is the more-or-less flat top of the reef, appropriately called the *reef flat, reef terrace,* or *back-reef.* Exposure to air limits the upward growth of the coral, hence the flattened top of the reef. The reef flat may be several meters wide or hundreds of meters across. Its character is very variable. It may contain channels several meters deep and be strewn with storm-deposited boulders or rubble toward its outer edge, with areas of sand or biodetritus toward its inner edge. Fine sediments may support dense beds of seagrasses. In those fringing reefs where a lagoon is entirely absent, the landward side of the reef flat may merge with a sandy or rocky shoreline, which may support mangroves. In barrier reefs and some fringing reefs, the reef flat descends into a lagoon.

The outer part of the reef flat usually has an abundant coral growth behind the algal ridge.

However, as the inner protected reef flat is approached, the coral growth and diversity decline and areas of debris and sediment are more common. In the Indo-Pacific, tall, branching *Acropora* species may dominate here, or where sediment has accumulated, massive corals such as *Symphyllia* and *Porites* may be found.

The *lagoon slope* (inner slope) of the reef is usually well protected from turbulence, and in this quiet water—as in some of the pools and channels of the reef flat—delicate branching corals can establish, such as the staghorn (*Acropora cervicornis*) in the Caribbean and *Seritapora* in the Indo-Pacific. The lagoon slope may be crowded with live coral, or, in contrast, may be rubble or muddy sand. In the lagoon itself, clumps of coral such as pinnacles and knolls, and more extensive areas of coral, called *patch reefs*, are commonly found. Here, as on the fore-reef slope, there may be a staggering variety of coral forms: branches, whorls, and columns, as well as compact and massive growths.

Coral Reef Biodiversity

Estimates from the late 1990s by Allegra Small and others at the Smithsonian Institution suggest that coral reefs, as a biome, harbor between 1 and 3 million species of organism, a biodiversity similar to that of rainforests on land. However, whereas in rainforests the bulk of species are accounted for by higher plants and arthropods, in coral reefs, the biodiversity is spread broadly across more than 25 phyla of protists, plants, and animals. Also, coral reefs cover an area less than 10 percent that of rainforests; species density is greater on coral reefs.

Like rainforests, coral reefs owe their enormous diversity, at least in part, to the multiplicity of habitats provided by complex three-dimensional structures. In the case of coral reefs, the reef is perforated by pits, chambers, and channels, at all scales of size, from microscopic to several meters across, and associated habitats such as seagrass beds, sandy sediments, rocks, and coral debris add to this spatial diversity.

The high productivity of coral reefs is largely accounted for by the close coupling between algal photosynthesis and the secondary production of hermatypic coral polyps. Values for gross primary productivity [1.5 to 5 kilograms per square meter (3.3 to 11 pounds per square yard) per year] are among the highest for any marine ecosystem. Nutrients can be recycled without leaving the coral platform. Suspension-feeding organisms, including the reef-building corals themselves, capitalize on the thin soup of plankton swept over the reef from adjacent open-water areas.

To casual observation, corals and fishes dominate the living biomass of the reef ecosystem. However, various algae, including encrusting coralline forms and green calcareous algae, contribute to the reef and provide food for a wide range of herbivorous fish and invertebrates. Almost every invertebrate phylum is richly represented in a coral reef ecosystem, and about 25 percent of all marine fish species are associated with coral reefs. The intense competition for food and space has produced, in response, a very wide range of survival strategies, notable of which is the production of toxins, either to combat predation or to prevent overgrowth by adjacent sessile colonial forms.

Coral reefs have great economic value, especially for small island states that have few land-based resources and depend on seafood for protein supplies and on tourism for income. Attention is now focusing on coral reefs as a biochemical repository of immense pharmaceutical potential. At least some of the toxins employed by reef species are likely to have antiviral, antibacterial, or anticancer properties.

Threats to Coral Reef Systems

Anthropogenic (human-caused) factors have had a profound negative impact on coral reefs in the last 30 years. In some cases, however, it has proved difficult to disentangle whether detrimental impacts are caused by human actions, natural events, or a combination of both. For example, the crown-of-thorns (*Acanthaster planci*), a coral-consuming sea star, has proliferated in the western Pacific since the early 1960s and "plagues" of sea stars have severely damaged 5 percent of coral reefs on the Great Barrier Reef and affected a further 12 percent. Patches of coral can recover if the sea star density is low, but where the density is high, large areas are stripped of live coral, causing invasion of new coral forms and major changes in species composition. Initially, researchers suspected a human influence was the cause. However, in 1989, an examination of fossils in the Great Barrier Reef showed that the sea star has periodically been very abundant during the last 80,000 years. The proliferation of the crown-of-thorns may be part of a natural cycle of abundance.

Estimates in the *Status of Coral Reefs of the World: 2000* report by the Global Coral Reef Monitoring Network (GCRMN) suggest that 27 percent of the world's coral reefs have been destroyed. Assuming a "business-as-usual" scenario, many of the 16 percent of reefs lost during the 1998 El Niño event are likely to recover. However, the report noted the threat of the loss of a further 32 percent of coral reefs by 2030. Historically, coral reefs have been shown to recover from occasional natural disruptions, such as hurricanes, predator plagues, and disease. However, persistent disturbances from human activities may be more damaging. Different influences may work together to undermine the health of coral populations, making them more susceptible to environmental stresses. A short list of such factors includes the following:

- Removal of preferred fish species, altering the balance of herbivorous and predatory fishes on coral reefs

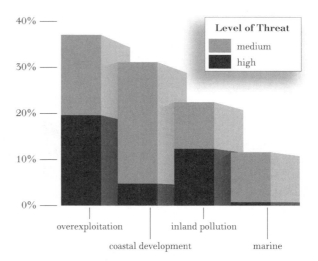

Types of threats to coral reefs. [Adapted from Dirk Bryant et al, Reefs at Risk (http://www.wpi.org/wri/reefsatrisk)]

- Fishing practices that directly damage the reef structure, such as using explosives, or using cyanide to stun fish for the aquarium trade
- Removal of live coral and shellfish for tourist curios
- Shoreline developments that alter drainage and coastal current patterns, increase turbidity, dilute seawater, and make aquatic pollution (ranging from sewage contamination and nutrient enrichment to the introduction of pesticides, heavy metals, and oil) more likely
- Direct damage to coral reefs from such tourist activities as boating, snorkeling, and scuba diving
- Introduction of alien species (e.g., in ballast water) that compete with indigenous ones
- Mining of the coral reef structure for use in building construction

Although much can be achieved by encouraging the conservation and sustainable use of coral reef ecosystems, El Niño events, in concert with global warming, are believed to be the most serious short-term threat to coral reefs. During the strong El Niño of 1997–98, surface temperatures of 1 to 2°C (1.8 to 3.6°F) above normal maximums were maintained for months on end in many tropical areas. This was enough to trigger

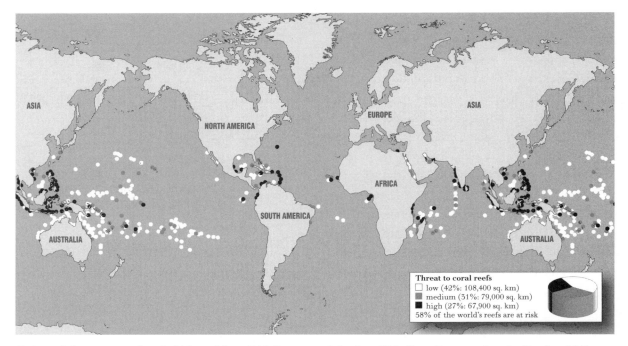

Estimated threats to coral reefs. [Adapted from Dirk Bryant et al, Reefs at Risk (http://www.wpi.org/wri/reefsatrisk)]

the most extensive coral-bleaching event on record, with incidences straight across the longitudinal and latitudinal range of coral reefs. On some Indo-Pacific reefs, 70 to 99 percent of the coral surface cover was killed.

Bleaching occurs when reef-building corals eject their symbiotic algae. Raised sea surface temperatures aggravated by high levels of ultraviolet radiation were cited as the main cause of the 1997–98 bleaching event. Bleaching conditions that last 10 weeks or more kill polyps and can drastically decrease coral recruitment. Coral polyps are less able to withstand a coral bleaching event if they are weakened by other factors. Similarly, bleached colonies are more susceptible to other negative impacts, such as disease, competition from overgrowing algae, or attacks from coral predators.

In the late 1990s, the Intergovernmental Panel on Climate Change (IPCC) estimated a rise of 1 to 2°C (1.8 to 3.6°F) in mean global sea-surface temperatures by the year 2100, based on global warming under enhanced greenhouse conditions. Coral bleaching is likely

to become a more frequent and widespread phenomenon in the coming decades. At the same time, climatic change is making weather patterns more extreme, with larger storms and unpredictable changes in oceanic circulation, both of which are likely to further disrupt coral reef ecosystems.

Trevor Day

FURTHER READING

Adey, Walter H., Ted A. McConnaughey, Allegra M. Small, and Don M. Spoon. "Coral Reefs: Endangered, Biodiverse, Genetic Resources." In C. Sheppard, ed., *Seas at the Millennium: An Environmental Evaluation*, Vol. III, *Global Issues and Processes*. Amsterdam and New York: Pergamon Press, 2000; pp. 33–42

Birkeland, C., ed. *Life and Death of Coral Reefs*. New York: Chapman and Hall, 1997.

Chadwick, Douglas H. "Kingdom of Coral: Australia's Great Barrier Reef." *National Geographic*, Vol. 199, No. 1 (2001), pp. 30–57.

Dubinsky, Z., ed. *Coral Reefs: Ecosystems of the World 25*. Amsterdam and New York: Elsevier, 1990.

Gray, William. *Coral Reefs and Islands*. Newton Abbot, England: David and Charles, 1993.

Kaplan, E. H. *A Field Guide to the Coral Reefs of the Caribbean and Florida.* Boston: Houghton Mifflin, 1982.

Karlson, R. H. *Dynamics of Coral Communities.* Boston: Kluwer Academic, 1999.

Mather, Patricia, and Isobel Bennett, eds. *A Coral Reef Handbook,* 3rd ed. Chipping Norton, Australia: Surrey Beatty, 1993.

Westmacott, S., K. Teleki, S. Wells, and J. M. West. *Management of Bleached and Severely Damaged Coral Reefs.* Gland, Switzerland, and Cambridge: International Union for the Conservation of Nature and Natural Resources, 2000.

Wood, Rachel. *Reef Evolution.* Oxford and New York: Oxford University Press, 1999.

USEFUL WEB SITES

National Oceanic and Atmospheric Administration. "United States Coral Reef Task Force." <http://coralreef.gov>.

———. "Coral Health and Monitoring Program." <http://www.coral.noaa.gov>.

RELATED ARTICLES

Barrier Reef; Climate Change; Coral; Coral Atoll; Coral Bleaching; Darwin, Charles Robert; Fringing Reef; Plate Tectonics; Polyp; Reef; Scleractinia

Coral Sea

The Coral Sea, in the southwestern Pacific Ocean, is bounded on the west by the coast of Queensland (Australia), on the north by New Guinea and the Solomon Islands, on the east by the New Hebrides Island Arc, and on the south by New Caledonia. The Coral Sea extends approximately from 10 to 20°S and from 145 to 165°E. It covers an area of 4,791,000 square kilometers (1,850,000 square miles). To the south it merges with the Tasman Sea. In May 1942 the Coral Sea was the scene of a critical Allied victory in World War II.

Bathymetry (seafloor topography) of the Coral Sea is marked by distinct structural boundaries, including features such as the continent of Australia, island arc ridges, submarine plateaus, three broad rises, three major basins, and several minor troughs and basins. Three of the world's greatest trenches exist near the eastern margin of the Coral Sea. New Hebrides Trench marks the deepest spot in the Coral Sea, 7661 meters (25,135 feet). Huge atolls and coral platforms break the surface abruptly from seafloors with intermediate depths of 1000 meters (3281 feet). Much of the Coral Sea basin is covered by pelagic red clay and globigerina ooze (remains of microscopic protistans predominantly from the genus *Globigerina*). Turbidite deposits of olive-colored silts occur a few inches below the red clay deposit in the abyssal plain of Papua New Guinea.

The Coral Sea was named for the Great Barrier Reef, a coral barrier reef that runs parallel to the Queensland coast of Australia for more than 2000 kilometers (1200 miles) and borders the western edge of the Coral Sea. Several major shipwrecks show that the reefs and shallow waters inhibit ocean shipping. The Australian tourist industry benefits from an estimated 1.6 million visitors to the Great Barrier Reef annually.

Water surface circulation changes during the year. The South Equatorial Current enters the Coral Sea between the Solomon Islands and New Hebrides from January to March under the influence of the monsoons. During the rest of the year, the Trade Wind Drift is dominant. These two currents supply the East Australian Current, which flows over the continental slope of eastern Australia.

The Coral Sea is an important nesting site for seabirds and turtles as well as a winter haven for the humpback whale. Seamounts make up a unique deep-sea environment that is characterized by a fauna ruled by suspension feeders such as corals. Recent studies report the discovery of more that 850 species from seamounts in the Tasman Sea and southeastern Coral Sea. Of these, about 30 percent are new to science.

Deanna Madison

CORAL SEA

FURTHER READING

Burns, R. E., J. E. Andrews, et al. *Initial Reports of the Deep Sea Drilling Project,* Vol. 21. Washington, D.C.: U.S. Government Printing Office, 1973.

McCormick, Herbe. "Above and Below the Clear Coral Sea." *Cruising World,* Vol. 24, No. 5 (May 1998), p. 34.

Richer de Forges, Bertrand, Anthony J. Koslow, and G. D. B. Poore. "Diversity and Endemism of the Benthic Seamount Fauna in the Southwest Pacific." *Nature,* Vol. 405, No. 6789 (22 June 2000), p. 944.

RELATED ARTICLES

Continental Slope; Coral Reef; Great Barrier Reef; Island Arc; New Hebrides Island Arc; Seamount; Solomon Sea; Trench; Turbidite

Coriolis, Gaspard-Gustave de

1792–1843

French Engineer and Physicist

Gaspard-Gustave de Coriolis is perhaps best known for describing what is now called the *Coriolis effect,* or sometimes the *Coriolis force,* an effect of motion on a rotating body that has become especially important to understanding the movements of terrestrial airmasses and ocean currents. He was also the first to derive formulas expressing kinetic energy and mechanical work, and gave those expressions their modern scientific meanings.

Coriolis, as he called himself, was born in Paris on 21 May 1792, the revolutionary year in which the French Republic was proclaimed. During the Revolution, his aristocratic family fled to Nancy, where Coriolis was brought up and attended school. In 1808, he placed second in his class in the entrance examination for France's training ground for civil servants, the École Polytechnique, and upon graduation he served for several years with the highway engineering corps of the École des Ponts et Chaussées in the Meurthe-et-Moselle district and in the Vosges Mountains. To support his family after the death of his industrialist father,

in 1816 Coriolis accepted a post as tutor of mathematical analysis and mechanics at the École Polytechnique on the recommendation of the noted mathematician Augustin-Louis Cauchy (1789–1857). Coriolis dedicated himself to the teaching of science and rose in the academic ranks to become professor of mechanics at the École Centrale des Artes et Manufactures in 1829. There he teamed up with physicist Claude Navier (1785–1836) teaching applied mechanics and eventually succeeded him upon his death in 1836 as the chair of applied mechanics at the École des Ponts et Chaussées and as a member of the Académie des Sciences. Coriolis continued teaching at the École Polytechnique until 1838, when he succeeded chemist Pierre Dulong (1785–1838) as director of studies. Coriolis was a very effective administrator and continued to serve in that role until his already poor health worsened in the spring of 1843. He died in Paris on 19 September 1843.

Coriolis studied mechanics and engineering mathematics, especially the principles of friction, hydraulics, and machine performance. After 10 years of systematic investigation, inspired in part by the work of engineer and physicist Lazare Carnot (1753–1823), Coriolis published his first major work, *Du calcul de l'effet des machines* (On the calculation of mechanical action), in 1829. Coriolis believed that a rational mechanics should be developed in order to arrive at general physical principles that could then be applied to an analysis of the operation of motors and other machinery. Part of his conception of mechanics involved the formulation of precise terms and definitions, and he proposed a number of changes to the standard terminology of his day. He succeeded in establishing the use of the word *work* as a technical term in mechanics, defining it as the displacement of force through a certain distance. He also applied the term *force vive* (kinetic energy), his second important innovation, to the principle of the transmission of work. As important to mechanics as these changes in viewpoint were, by developing their theoretical implications and by applying them to his investigation of the motions of moving parts in machines, Coriolis would eventually make a major contribution toward a comprehensive general theory of motion in rotating reference frames.

Coriolis's most notable contribution is his description of the Coriolis force or effect, which appears in his 1835 paper "Sur les équations du mouvement relatif des systèmes de corps" ("On the equations of relative motion of systems of bodies"). In that seminal work he showed that Newton's laws of motion could be used in a rotating frame of reference if an inertial force, acting on a body at right angles to its direction of motion, is included in the equations of motion. As an object moves through a rotating reference frame, the Coriolis effect predicts that it will follow a curved path rather than a straight line, an apparent deflection of the path of the object. Although the object does not actually deviate from its path, it appears to do so because of the rotation of the reference frame itself.

Coriolis thought that the effect he had discovered was the result of a complementary centrifugal force due to the rotation of the frame of reference, and he clearly regarded this force to be just as real as the usual centrifugal force. This way of thinking about the Coriolis effect has some advantages in explaining certain physical phenomena. Although Coriolis himself never extended his results to the earth sciences, the Coriolis effect has become especially significant in meteorology, physical geology, and oceanography. Earth is a rotating frame of reference, and motions over its surface are subject to the accelerations predicted by the Coriolis effect. Thus the Coriolis effect figures prominently in studies of the dynamics of the atmosphere, in which it helps to describe the movements of prevailing winds and the rotational motion of storms, as well as in studies of ocean currents and their movements.

The Coriolis effect is based on the principles of the conservation of angular momentum and the conservation of rotational kinetic energy. In the case of hurricanes and other large storm systems at middle latitudes, the Coriolis force can be said to cause the air to rotate around low-pressure centers in a cyclonic fashion. The term *cyclonic* implies not only that the fluid, whether air or water, rotates in the same direction as the underlying Earth, but also that the rotation of the fluid is caused by Earth's rotation. Thus, the air flowing around a hurricane spins counterclockwise in the northern hemisphere and clockwise in the southern hemisphere, as does Earth itself. If Earth did not rotate, the air would flow directly in toward a low-pressure center, but on a spinning Earth, the Coriolis force causes the air to deviate such that it travels around the low-pressure center. The central role

Gaspard-Gustave de Coriolis. (Institut de France, Académie des Sciences)

that Coriolis's work plays in helping to explain phenomena in the Earth sciences would please a man who so consistently sought to unite both theory and application.

Kenneth Meiklejohn

BIOGRAPHY

- Gaspard-Gustave de Coriolis.
- Born on 21 May 1792 in Paris, France.
- Attended the École Polytechnique and began teaching there in 1816.
- Became professor of mechanics at the École Centrale des Artes et Manufactures in 1829.
- In 1836, he succeeded Claude Navier as chair of applied mechanics at the École des Ponts et Chaussées and became a member of the Académie des Sciences.
- In 1838, he succeeded Pierre Dulong as director of studies at the École Polytechnique.
- Died in Paris on 19 September 1843.

SELECTED WRITINGS

Coriolis, G. *Du calcul de l'effet des machines, ou, Considerations sur l'emploi des moteurs et sur leur évaluation pour servir d'introduction a l'étude spéciale des machines.* Paris: Carilian-Goeury, 1829.

————. "Sur le principe des forces vives dans les mouvements relatifs des machines." *Journal de l'École Polytechnique,* Vol. 13 (1832), pp. 265–302.

————. "Sur les équations du mouvement relatif des systèmes de corps." *Journal de l'École Polytechnique,* Vol. 15 (1835), pp. 144–154.

————. *Théorie mathématique des effets du jeu de billard.* Paris: Carilian-Goeury, 1835.

FURTHER READING

Costabel, Pierre. "Coriolis." In C. C. Gillespie, ed., *Dictionary of Scientific Biography,* 17 vols. New York: Scribner's, 1971.

Grattan-Guiness, Ivor. *Companion Encyclopedia of the History and Philosophy of the Mathematical Sciences,* 2 vols. London and New York: Routledge, 1994.

————. "Work for the Workers: Advances in Engineering Mechanics and Instruction in France, 1800–1830." *Annals of Science,* Vol. 41, No. 1 (1984), pp. 1–33.

Stommel, Henry M., and Dennis W. Moore. *An Introduction to the Coriolis Force.* New York: Columbia University Press, 1989.

RELATED ARTICLES

Coriolis Effect; Cyclonic Flow; Earth, Rotation of

Coriolis Effect

The rotation of planets has a curious effect on the movement of air and water; over long distances they tend to curve. On Earth this effect takes place during the formation of hurricanes, tornados, and ocean gyres; on Jupiter it takes place in the rotating red spot. Features as diverse as Earth's trade wind system and ocean upwelling zones, the flight of missiles, orbiting satellites, and the trajectory of bombs are all influenced by the Coriolis effect, which was first explained in 1835 by French mathematics professor Gaspard-Gustave de Coriolis (1792–1843).

The Coriolis effect is also called the *Coriolis force,* since it is used in the equations governing fluid motion in the ocean. It results from Newton's first law of motion, which states the principle of inertia: An object in motion will continue its state of motion unless acted upon by a force. That is, an object moves in a straight line unless some force is applied. This principle can be explained by observing two people on a merry-go-round playing a game of catch. The pitcher throws a slow, straight ball to the catcher, who sees the ball's flight as a curve. A person viewing this action from a helicopter, however, would see the ball's flight as perfectly straight. Both views of this incident are valid. The people on the merry-go-round explain the curved trajectory using the Coriolis force, which acts at right angles to the motion.

On Earth, people at different latitudes move through space at different speeds. Due to Earth's rotation, a stationary object on the equator has an eastward velocity of about 1600 kilometers (990 miles) per hour. A person at Earth's poles has no such eastward velocity, although he or she rotates once each day. This eastward motion varies from

254

pole to equator, but of course, we are not aware of this. If a missile is fired southward from the pole, it will not have an initial eastward velocity. As the missile moves south, it appears to curve westward, which is toward the right when viewed in the direction of the movement. If the missile's flight takes a half hour, the total westward "deflection" is 7.5° longitude, since the rotational speed of Earth is 15° per hour. A missile fired northward from the equator tends to veer to the right as it moves to higher latitudes. We may say the missile "takes with it" its original eastward movement of 1600 kilometers (994 miles) per hour. When it reaches a higher latitude where Earth's eastward velocity is slower, the missile again appears to curve to the right.

Explaining that an object in motion in any direction in the northern hemisphere is deflected to the right of the motion is less intuitive than a north–south motion. In the southern hemisphere moving objects are deflected toward the left when we face in the direction of travel. The Coriolis force can then be summarized as follows: In the northern hemisphere an object in motion is deflected toward the right; in the southern hemisphere an object in motion is deflected toward the left; the magnitude of the Coriolis force is greatest at the poles; the magnitude is zero at the equator; and the magnitude is proportional to speed.

An example of the deflection that occurs in the Coriolis effect is the German "Big Bertha" cannon used in World War I. The cannon could hurl a projectile 100 kilometers (62 miles) in 3 minutes. To compensate for the Coriolis deflection, gunners aimed about 1000 meters (3281 feet) left of their target. At ocean current speeds, the Coriolis force is weak compared to gravity (about 1/100,000). This small force is effective when acting in a direction perpendicular to gravity, which is "sideways." In response to the Coriolis force, the sea surface tilts upward along the right-hand side of ocean currents in

the northern hemisphere. As a ship crosses the 100-kilometer (62-mile)-wide Gulf Stream between the U.S. coast and Bermuda, it moves about 1.5 meters (5 feet) uphill because of this tilt. Not only does the sea surface tilt up, but also its thermocline (the boundary layer between the warmer, upper ocean and the cooler depths) tilts downward. Oceanographers have measured the thermocline tilt with thermometers since 1900 and in so doing have mapped an ocean current's speed and direction. Currents computed this way are called *geostrophic* or "earth-turning" currents.

The flow of surface ocean currents in the Atlantic and Pacific Ocean basins conforms to the Coriolis effect. The North Atlantic Gyre and its counterpart, the South Atlantic Gyre, rotate clockwise and counterclockwise, respectively. Sea level at the center of these gyres is higher than at the edges, in keeping with the geostrophic nature of the ocean current system. Large northern hemisphere rivers tilt slightly upward along their right banks; deep inflow of waters to large estuaries also tilt upward on the right-hand side of channels.

The coastal and equatorial upwelling are effects of the Coriolis force. The wind blows from the north generally parallel to the coast in the northern hemisphere (i.e., the west coast of the United States). If it blows from the south in the southern hemisphere (i.e., Peru and Chile), the surface waters move offshore, perpendicular to the wind direction. The surface waters must be replaced from below [from about 200 meters (656 feet)]. In upwelling areas, surface temperatures are relatively cool and nutrient-rich compared with waters just offshore, because cooler, nutrient-rich waters are found beneath the surface. The deflection of currents to the right of the wind (NH) and to the left (SH) is a direct consequence of the Coriolis force. Such wind-generated currents are called *Ekman currents*. There is a similar upwelling situation along the equator where the Ekman currents are directed away from the equator both to the north and south of the equator.

One of the most remarkable effects of the Coriolis force and Ekman currents is that half of the world's fisheries catch comes from upwelling areas. Without the Earth rotation and the Coriolis force, this would not be the case. Winds are also affected by the Coriolis force. If Earth were not turning, air would flow directly from areas of high pressure to areas of low pressure. Because of the Coriolis force, winds in the northern hemisphere blow clockwise around areas of high pressure and counterclockwise around low-pressure storms. Northern hemisphere hurricanes (also called *typhoons* or *cyclones*) spiral counterclockwise around the low-pressure center of these great storms. The Coriolis force is responsible for the prevailing trade winds that generally blow from the northeast, north of the equator, and from the southeast, south of the equator. Without the Coriolis force, trade winds would blow directly from north to south.

Even if the Coriolis effect is called an *apparent force* or a *pseudoforce*, it is treated mathematically, as are other forces, such as gravity or pressure. The Coriolis force produces observable effects in the large-scale motion of winds and ocean currents.

William W. Broenkow

FURTHER READING
Baker, D., Jr. "Models of Ocean Circulation." *Scientific American*, Vol. 222, No. 1 (1970), p. 114.

Durran, D., and S. Domonkos. "An Apparatus for Demonstrating the Inertial Oscillation." *Bulletin of the American Meteorological Society,* Vol. 77 (1996), p. 557.

French, A. P. *Newtonian Mechanics.* New York: W. W. Norton, 1971.

Persson, A. "How Do We Understand the Coriolis Force?" *Bulletin of the American Meteorological Society,* Vol. 79 (1998), p. 1373.

Stommel, Henry, and Dennis Moore. *An Introduction to the Coriolis Force.* New York: Columbia University Press, 1989.

Thurman, Harold V., and Alan P. Trujillo. *Elements of Oceanography.* Upper Saddle River, N.J.: Prentice Hall, 1999.

USEFUL WEB SITES
"General Characteristics of the World's Oceans: Ocean Currents." <http:icp.giss.nasa.gov/research/oceans/oceanchars/currents.html>.

RELATED ARTICLES
Coriolis, Gaspard-Gustave de; Ekman Transport; Earth, Rotation of; Gyre; Thermocline; Upwelling

Cosmopolitan

In marine science, *cosmopolitan* is a term that refers to the geographical distribution of a given taxonomic group of organisms. Cosmopolitan means that the group is distributed throughout the world's oceans wherever the habitat is suitable. It is unlikely that any single marine species is found throughout the oceans of the planet, because of the large range of physical factors found in the oceans. However, higher taxonomic groupings may well be cosmopolitan in distribution. For example, members of the crustacean order Decapoda (crabs, lobsters, shrimp) can be found throughout the world's oceans in both the water column and in all benthic habitats. Similarly, the molluscan class Bivalvia (clams, mussels, oysters) is cosmopolitan in benthic habitats throughout the oceans. Taxonomic groups that have a cosmopolitan distribution generally have a structure and physiology that is adaptable to a wide range of environmental conditions.

James W. Nybakken

FURTHER READING
Nybakken, James W. *Marine Biology: An Ecological Approach,* 5th ed. San Francisco: Benjamin Cummings, 2001.

RELATED ARTICLES
Benthos; Bivalvia; Crustacea

Co-Tidal Chart

A co-tidal chart displays how the characteristics of a tide change from place to place. The tidal information on a co-tidal chart is presented as two intersecting sets of lines, one representing tidal amplitude (co-amplitude lines) and the other representing tidal phase (co-phase lines).

There are two types of co-tidal charts. The first type is used by navigators for predicting the tide height offshore. These charts show nonharmonic quantities representative of the whole tide (i.e., the sum of all harmonic constituents). They are intended for use in a semidiurnal tidal regime, but tides in a mixed, mainly semidiurnal regime have also been plotted. The co-amplitude lines, which are colored green, join places having the same *mean spring range,* usually measured in meters. The mean spring range is the difference between the levels of mean high water springs and mean low water springs. The level of *mean high water springs* is the average, during a year when the average maximum declination of the Moon is 23.5°, of the heights of two successive high waters at spring tides; the level of *mean low water springs* is defined similarly. The co-phase lines, in red, join places having the same *mean high water interval* (i.e., the average time lag of high water at the place after the transit of the Moon across the Greenwich meridian); this is measured in hours and minutes.

The second type of co-tidal chart concerns a single harmonic constituent. In this case, the co-amplitude lines join at places having the same amplitude for that constituent, and the co-phase lines join at places having the same equilibrium phase lag (i.e., the lag of the real tide behind the equilibrium tide). Thus the co-tidal chart shows the spatial variation of the harmonic constants for a given constituent. The amplitude is often measured in meters, and the equilibrium phase lag in degrees. Co-tidal charts for oceans are always of this type, so that to show the whole tide in an ocean, a set of such charts is required, one for each major harmonic constituent (see figure).

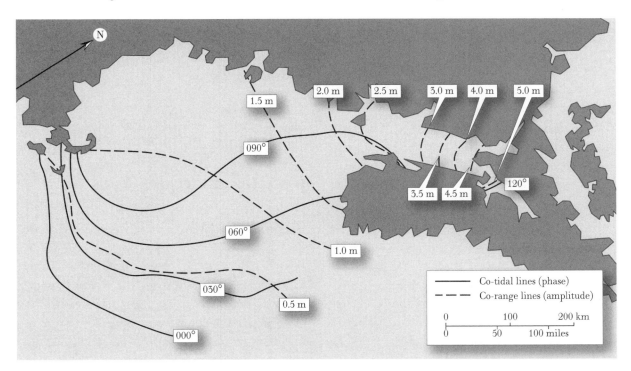

Sample of a co-tidal chart.

A co-tidal chart is constructed by interpolating between known values of amplitude and phase at places where the tide has been measured. Ideally, such interpolation should be carried out by applying the dynamic equations of tidal motion, taking into account the bathymetry (i.e., the depth of the sea). In deep water, the co-amplitude and the co-phase lines will intersect orthogonally; the deviation from orthogonality is a measure of the friction in the sea.

Ken George

FURTHER READING

Cartwright, David Edgar. *Tides: A Scientific History.* New York: Cambridge University Press, 1999.

Defant, Albert. *Physical Oceanography,* 2 vols. New York: Pergamon Press, 1961.

Doodson, Arthur T., and H. D. Warburg. *Admiralty Manual of Tides.* London: His Majesty's Stationery Office, 1941.

RELATED ARTICLES

Diurnal and Semidiurnal Tide; Sun and Moon, Tidal Effect of; Tide

Countershading

Many pelagic fishes that live near the surface are countershaded with dark backs and pale bellies. This is a form of camouflage or cryptic coloration. From above, the fish's dark back is nearly invisible against the darkness of the deep ocean. From the side, the fish's dark back is well illuminated, but the pale belly is in shadow, so that the fish appears uniformly colored and almost the same color as the water around it. In addition, in mackerel and herring the upper parts are vertically banded with dark-bluish vertical bars that help further to disrupt the fish's outline.

In many species silvering enhances the paleness of the underside. This silvering effect is the result of the skin containing layers of regularly sized and spaced platelets of a white pigment called *guanine*. This regular arrangement of platelets causes structural interference of the light, similar to how a thin film of oil reflects all the colors of the rainbow. But in this case it reflects white light. Countershading becomes ineffective from directly underneath. Sunlight shining through the surface of the water is refracted, creating a bright circular patch of light, called *Snell's circle*. Any fish swimming across Snell's circle cannot avoid being clearly silhouetted.

Deeper down at mesopelagic depths, fish such as myctophids (e.g., *Myctophum punctatum*) and hatchetfish (e.g., *Argyropelecus aculeatus*) have evolved, creating a solution to this silhouette problem. They have lines of light-emitting organs, or photophores, along their bellies that break up the outline of the fish's silhouette. Countershading is not restricted to fish and is also seen in many species that always live at the surface (neustonic), such as the nudibranch *Glaucus* and blue pontellid copepods.

Martin Angel

FURTHER READING

Herring, Peter J. "Light, Colour and Vision in the Ocean." In Colin P. Summerhayes and Steve A.Thorpe, eds., *Oceanography: An Illustrated Guide.* New York: Wiley, 1996.

RELATED ARTICLES

Copepod; Cryptic Coloration; Pelagic; Photophore

Cousteau, Jacques-Yves

1910–1997

Filmmaker and Joint Inventor of the Aqualung

French marine explorer and filmmaker Jacques Cousteau was the joint inventor of the aqualung (with engineer Émile Gagnan). Cousteau's films of his undersea explorations captured the public's imagination and made him famous worldwide.

Jacques-Yves Cousteau was born in 1910 in the market town of St. André-de-Cubzac in southwest

France. An adventurous child, he learned to swim at the unusually young age of 4, and by 13 had made his first film, using an early Pathé movie camera. In 1930 he entered the French naval academy at Brest, where he enrolled to become a pilot. His ambitions to fly were cut short in 1936 when he crashed his father's sports car and broke both arms just weeks before his pilot's exams. At first, doctors wanted to amputate one of Cousteau's arms, but he refused and eventually regained full use of both.

After leaving the Brest academy, Cousteau was stationed at a naval base in Toulon as an artillery instructor. He swam regularly in the Mediterranean to strengthen his arms and began to develop a passion for underwater exploration, using homemade goggles and experimental snorkels to further his exploits. After the surrender to Germany, he played an active role in the French Resistance as a spy; he was later awarded the Légion d'Honneur and Croix de Guerre for his work. Nevertheless, he still found time to pursue his interest in diving. He traveled to Paris to meet the French engineer Émile Gagnan, who had devised an ingenious valve that enabled wartime automobiles to run off bottled gas instead of gasoline. In 1943, Cousteau and Gagnan adapted the valve to take compressed air from a cylinder and deliver it to a diver's mouthpiece at the same pressure as that of the surrounding water. The result was the *aqualung*, or *scuba* ("self-contained underwater breathing apparatus"). Previous inventors had developed diving systems based on tanks of compressed air and breathing valves, but Cousteau and Gagnan's system was the first fully automatic device that delivered air on demand at ambient pressure. The aqualung revolutionized marine biology and exploration by making diving simple and safe, and it made scuba diving a popular pastime. Equipped with aqualungs, masks, and fins (flippers), divers had unprecedented freedom and mobility underwater.

Jacques Cousteau. (Associated Press, The Cousteau Society)

Patents on the invention made a fortune for both Gagnan and Cousteau.

The aqualungs that divers use today are similar to Gagnan and Cousteau's original design, but advances in technology have made modern aqualungs more efficient. In the original aqualung, a single device, the *regulator*, was used to supply the diver with air at ambient pressure. The regulator was attached to the diver's mouthpiece by two hoses (one for inhalation and another for exhalation), and thus was known as a *twin-hose, single-stage regulator*. In modern aqualungs there are two regulators: one attached to the top of the cylinder and another in the diver's mouthpiece. The first regulator reduces the air pressure to an intermediate level, and the second regulator converts this to ambient pressure. Called a *two-stage, single-hose regulator*, this aqualung makes breathing underwater much easier than with the aqualung developed by Cousteau and Gagnan. Another advance was

259

the invention of the *rebreather*, a device that recycles exhaled air and thus extends the life of the diver's air supply, allowing longer dive times. Exhaled air passes through a chamber where carbon dioxide is removed, before being mixed with the main air supply from the tank. Rebreathers are quieter than conventional aqualungs because fewer bubbles are released into the water. This feature is of particular benefit to biologists, as it allows them to get closer to marine animals without disturbing them.

Cousteau remained in the navy after World War II. With naval backing he set up an undersea research group to improve scuba technology and to develop new techniques of underwater photography. As well as clearing German mines from around French ports, Cousteau's divers recovered marble columns from a 2000-year-old archaeological site off the Tunisian coast. Cousteau himself was an avid diver and set a world record in 1947 by reaching a depth of 100 meters (328 feet). He avoided "the bends," a potentially fatal condition caused by sudden release of dissolved nitrogen in the blood as a diver ascends, by spending the minimum amount of time submerged.

In the 1950s, Cousteau set up the first of a series of nonprofit organizations to finance his continuing underwater explorations. His exploits began to make him well known, and his first book, *The Silent World* (1953), coauthored with fellow diver Frédéric Dumas, was an instant hit. With the help of U.S. journalist James Dugan, Cousteau turned his daily logs into a fast-paced and lively book aimed at a mass audience. It went on to sell more than 5 million copies in 22 languages. The story of Cousteau's underwater adventures, told from the moment of trying his first aqualung, captured the public's imagination. Vivid descriptions of encounters with octopuses, morays, mantas, and sharks helped to dispel some of the popular conceptions about "monsters" of the deep and inspired

many readers to develop an interest in marine life. In an age when people were becoming fascinated with the possibility of space exploration, Cousteau succeeded in making underwater exploration just as glamorous.

In 1956, a film was released that was to make Cousteau and his ship *Calypso*, a converted minesweeper, famous worldwide. Also called *The Silent World*, the film was compiled from footage taken during hundreds of dives during a trip through the Red Sea and the Indian Ocean. It opened with a spectacular scene of divers descending into dark waters, each carrying a flashlight that illuminated the stream of bubbles rising from his aqualung. "Divers are true spacemen," announced the dramatic narration. *The Silent World* stunned audiences with beautiful images of coral reefs and their colorful inhabitants, revealed in unprecedented clarity through Cousteau's pioneering photographic techniques. It also showed the violence of the undersea world. When a baby whale accidentally ran into *Calypso*'s propellers and was killed, one of the divers strapped its body to the ship's hull. Ready with the camera, Cousteau filmed as a crowd of some 30 sharks devoured the whale's body in a feeding frenzy, turning the sea pink with its blood.

Cousteau was a skillful self-publicist and lobbied to help ensure *The Silent World*'s success. He strategically docked *Calypso* near the French city of Cannes during the film's showing at the Cannes Film Festival and later spent several weeks in Los Angeles promoting the film prior to the Academy Awards. In 1957 it won the Palme d'Or in Cannes and an Academy Award for best documentary feature of the year.

In addition to his work on the aqualung, Cousteau also collaborated with Swiss scientist Auguste Piccard on design of the first *bathyscaphes*, small diving vessels, or submersibles, used to explore the ocean depths. The development of such craft enabled scientists to explore the mid-ocean ridge and led to the discovery of unique ecosystems around deep-sea vents.

In 1957, Cousteau became head of the Conshelf Saturation Dive Program, a research project in which volunteers dubbed "oceanauts" spent weeks at a time living in pressured containers on the ocean shelf. The project achieved little of scientific value, but the publicity it generated confirmed Cousteau's status as a world celebrity, and a film of the enterprise *World without Sun* won an Academy Award in 1964. However, some critics, while praising the film as visually impressive, complained that certain scenes appeared to have been faked, an accusation that lingered with several of Cousteau's later films. Cousteau himself came under attack at the time of the Conshelf project for his claims that human colonies would eventually immigrate permanently to the seafloor, and that surgical advances would soon enable "menfish" to breathe unaided in water, like fish.

After the Conshelf project Cousteau pursued a career as a television documentary filmmaker, stimulating enormous interest in marine life, arguably his greatest achievement after his work on the aqualung. His films and television programs won three Oscars, 10 Emmys, and many other awards.

Sadly, Cousteau's later years were clouded by personal losses and family quarrels. With his first wife, Simone, he had two sons: Philippe and Jean-Michel. Jean-Michel was the older son, but Cousteau fell out with him and saw Philippe as his successor. In 1979, Philippe died in a plane crash at sea, so Jean-Michel became heir apparent to the Cousteau empire. Over subsequent years, father and son argued constantly over how best to run Cousteau's diverse enterprises. Simone died in 1990 and Cousteau remarried. He had two more children, Diane and Pierre-Yves, with Francine Triplet, his second wife. He died in Paris in 1997.

Ben Morgan

BIOGRAPHY
- Jacques-Yves Cousteau.
- Born on 11 June 1910 in St. André-de-Cubzac, France.
- Educated at a variety of schools in France and the United States.
- Entered École Navale in Brest (national naval academy of France) in 1930; graduated 1936.
- Developed aqualung with engineer Émile Gagnan in 1943.
- Founded Undersea Research Group of French navy in 1945.
- Set a world record for free diving in 1947.
- Became Capitaine de Corvette in the French navy in 1948 and president of the French Oceanographic Campaigns in 1950.
- Published the best-selling book *The Silent World* in 1953.
- Released the feature film *The Silent World* in 1956.
- Appointed director of the Oceanographic Museum of Monaco in 1957. Appointed head of Conshelf Saturation Dive Program in 1957.
- Died 25 June 1997 in Paris.

SELECTED WRITINGS

Cousteau, Jacques. *World without Sun*. New York: Harper and Row, 1965.
———. *The Ocean World*. New York: Abrams, 1979.
Cousteau, Jacques, and Philippe Cousteau. *The Shark: Splendid Savage of the Sea*. Garden City, N.Y.: Doubleday, 1970.
Cousteau, Jacques, and Philippe Diolé. *Life and Death in a Coral Sea*. Translated by J. F. Bernard. Garden City, N.Y.: Doubleday, 1971.
———. *Octopus and Squid*. Translated by J. F. Bernard. Garden City, N.Y.: Doubleday, 1973.
Cousteau, Jacques, and Frédéric Dumas. *The Silent World*. London: Hamish Hamilton/New York: Harper, 1953.
Cousteau, Jacques, and Yves Paccalet. *Whales*. Translated by I. Mark Paris. New York: Abrams, 1988.

FURTHER READING

Madsen, Axel. *Cousteau: An Unauthorized Biography*. New York: Beaufort Books, 1986.
Munson, Richard. *Cousteau: The Captain and His World*. New York: Morrow, 1989.

RELATED ARTICLES
Bathyscaphe; Piccard, Auguste; Scuba

Crab

With their large pincers, eyes on stalks, and distinctive sidelong gait, crabs are among the most familiar marine invertebrates. They are also among the most successful and are found in every ocean as well as in coastal, estuarine, and even terrestrial habitats. Some species live in the inky black world of the ocean depths and have lost the power of sight. Others have made a successful transition to life on land, although they occasionally visit the sea and must return to water to breed. There are about 5900 species of crabs, ranging in size from under 1 centimeter (0.4 inch) wide to 4 meters (13 feet) across. All are classified as members of the crustacean order Decapoda. Crabs are distinguished from other decapods, such as lobsters and shrimps, by their shorter abdomens, which are often folded or flexed under the body, with the notable exception of hermit crabs. There are two major groups: the true crabs (infraorder Brachyura) and the hermit crabs and their relatives (infraorder Anomura).

The body plan of a crab is similar to that of a lobster and consists of three main parts: the head, thorax, and abdomen. Whereas an insect's head and thorax are connected by a flexible joint, those of a crab or lobster are fused to form a single structure called the *cephalothorax*, which is protected by a broad shell called a *carapace*. The head bears a pair of stalked eyes, two pairs of sensitive antennae (feelers), and smaller appendages used either for feeding or to circulate water through the gills. The thorax bears five pairs of legs; the front pair is modified to form large pincers and the rear pairs are used for walking or swimming. The abdomen of brachyuran crabs is very small and folds tightly under the cephalothorax for protection. However, hermit crabs have a large and soft abdomen that does not fold under the body, so for safety they live inside snail shells that they carry around as mobile homes.

Most crabs are scavengers, feeding on detritus and dead animals found on the seafloor, but some species are herbivores and others are predators. The impressive claws are used for feeding or self-defense, although male fiddler crabs use a greatly outsized claw to battle with rival males to attract females. Although crabs are protected by their tough outer carapace, many still fall victim to cephalopods (octopuses and squid) and other predators. To escape detection, decorator crabs cover their bodies with a living coat of seaweed and small marine animals such as sponges. Held in place by tiny hooks, the decorations grow into a tangled mass, completely hiding the crab's body. Other crabs hold stinging sea anemones in their claws to intimidate enemies and collect food, and hermit crabs often place anemones on their adopted shells for added protection.

Unlike many invertebrates, crabs exist as separate male and female sexes. After mating, the female carries her eggs in a mass attached to the abdomen until they are ready to hatch. Some crab species hatch from their eggs as miniature adults, but most start life as tiny larvae called *zoea*. These look very different from the parents and live among the plankton—the community of tiny floating organisms in the sea's surface waters. After molting several times, the zoea eventually change into megalopa larvae. These larvae have claws and legs like adult crabs, but their abdomens are stretched out like those of lobsters. Eventually, the megalopa larvae settle on the seabed and slowly take on the adult shape.

The horseshoe crabs are neither crabs nor crustaceans but relatives of scorpions and spiders (subphylum Chelicerata). Sometimes described as living fossils, they have changed little in hundreds of millions of years.

Ben Morgan

FURTHER READING

Brusca, Richard C., and Gary J. Brusca. *Invertebrates*. Sunderland, Mass.: Sinauer, 1990.

Fish, J. *A Student's Guide to the Seashore*. London and Boston: Unwin Hyman, 1989; 2nd ed., Cambridge and New York: Cambridge University Press, 1996.

Nybakken, James W. *Marine Biology: An Ecological Approach*, 5th ed. San Francisco: Benjamin Cummings, 2001.

Pechenik, Jan A. *Biology of the Invertebrates*. Boston: Prindle, Weber and Schmidt, 1985; 4th ed., Boston: McGraw-Hill, 2000.

RELATED ARTICLES
Crustacea; Horseshoe Crab; Malacostraca

Crinoidea

The Crinoidea is a class within the phylum Echinodermata. The crinoids go by the common names of feather stars and sea lilies, and are all exclusively marine. Crinoids consist of a stalk attached to the aboral surface, which is the surface opposite the mouth of a cup-shaped body (called the *calyx*) to which five or more feathery arms are attached (up to 200 arms in feather stars and a maximum of 40 arms in sea lilies). Crinoids come in a variety of designs; they can be drab or brightly colored, solid or striped.

Crinoids represent the oldest class of living echinoderms. Fossil records indicate that crinoids were much more abundant in the past than in modern times. Most of the 625 living crinoid species are feather stars. These free-moving forms have a very reduced stalk, they can grip the substrate with jointed appendages called *cirri*, and they can crawl or swim using their arms. Distribution of feather stars ranges from the intertidal zone to great depths, and many species are abundant on coral reefs (e.g., approximately 550 species are found in Indo-Pacific waters). Sea lilies are *sessile* (they stay attached to the substrate) and stalked; their stalks can be as long as 1 meter (3.3 feet). Sea lilies had their heyday during the Paleozoic Era (570 million to 250 million years ago), and only about 80 species are alive today, most living in water greater than 100 meters (328 feet) deep.

Like other echinoderms, crinoids are *deuterostome coelomates* (meaning that the body cavity is derived from larval pouches). Larvae are *bilaterally symmetrical*, but adults exhibit pentaradial symmetry (the body is arranged in five parts around a central oral-aboral axis). They have a water vascular system, a well-developed digestive tract, and no excretory system. All echinoderms also have an internal skeleton composed of calcareous ossicles (plates) that is covered by a thin epidermis. In crinoids, skeletal plates of the calyx are fused, but those of the arms are articulated and appear jointed. Crinoids can regenerate arms or parts of arms that are lost.

Unlike most echinoderms, crinoids lack a *madreporite* (the external opening to the water vascular system found in other echinoderm classes). Other features unique to crinoids include the structure of the arms and the location of the mouth, both of which are related to *suspension feeding* (where they catch particles of food suspended in the surrounding water). The feathery articulating arms of crinoids extend into the water column to catch food particles. Feathery extensions called *pinnules*, from which the name *feather star* is derived, adorn each side of each arm, and the arms and pinnules bear tube feet. The oral surfaces of arms and pinnules are also lined with open ciliated grooves called *ambulacral grooves*. When a crinoid feeds, the mucus-covered tube feet collect food particles and flick them into the ambulacral grooves; cilia then propel the food toward the mouth. In all other living echinoderm classes, the oral side of the body is positioned downward toward the substrate. In crinoids, however, the mouth faces upward, ready to ingest food collected by the arms. The anus in crinoids also is located on the oral surface.

The arms of crinoids also serve as the locus for reproduction. Crinoids do not have distinct gonads; rather, cells within the arms produce gametes. All crinoids have separate sexes. Some females shed eggs into the surrounding seawater to be fertilized; others brood their eggs in sacs in the wall of the arm or pinnule. Development of a free-swimming nonfeeding vitellaria larva follows fertilization. Ultimately, the larva settles and attaches to a substrate, where it metamorphoses into an adult. Feather stars pass through a stalked stage before becoming free-swimming adults.

Lynn L. Lauerman

FURTHER READING

Barnes, Robert. *Invertebrate Zoology.* Philadelphia: Saunders, 1963; 6th ed., by Edward Ruppert, Fort Worth, Texas: Saunders, 1994.

Brusca, Richard C., and Gary J. Brusca. *Invertebrates.* Sunderland, Mass.: Sinauer, 1990.

Hendler, Gordon, John E. Miller, David L. Pawson, and Porter M. Kier. *Sea Stars, Sea Urchins, and Allies: Echinoderms of Florida and the Caribbean.* Washington, D.C.: Smithsonian Institution Press, 1995.

Lawrence, John. *A Functional Biology of Echinoderms.* Baltimore: Johns Hopkins University Press, 1987.

RELATED ARTICLES

Echinodermata

Crinotoxin

A crinotoxin is a poisonous substance released by an animal into its environment. Most crinotoxins are produced by glands in an animal's skin and are released through pores. Biologists distinguish between crinotoxins and two other types of animal poisons: venoms and oral poisons. *Venoms* are poisonous substances that are injected into a victim via a special tooth, spine, or other sharp structure. *Oral poisons* are toxic substances within the body of an animal that act on predators that swallow the animal's flesh.

Many animals depend on poisons to defend themselves against predators. Crinotoxins work by coating the body surface of the animal. If a predator touches or bites the animal, the toxin quickly causes unpleasant symptoms. Land animals that produce crinotoxins include blister beetles (*Cantharis vesicatorea*), poison-arrow frogs, and certain millipedes. Handling such animals

can cause symptoms ranging from skin rashes and blisters to irregular heartbeat, paralysis, and even death. Such animals often have brightly colored skin to warn would-be attackers.

Marine animals that produce crinotoxins include certain sponges, flatworms, and fish. A sponge known as red moss (*Microciona prolifera*), found off the eastern coast of the United States, produces a crinotoxin that causes rashes, blisters, and skin swellings in people who touch the sponge. The European flatworm *Leptoplana tremellaris* has an even more potent crinotoxic defense. A poison produced in its skin causes heart attacks when injected into animals. Fortunately, this species has never been known to kill a human.

Crinotoxic fish include a lamprey species native to the Atlantic (*Petromyzon marinus*) and a tropical species called the soapfish (*Rypticus saponaceus*). Both produce a toxic slime. The lamprey's slime irritates the digestive tract of any animal that swallows it, causing diarrhea.

Ben Morgan

FURTHER READING

Paxton, John R., and William N. Eschmeyer, eds. *Encyclopedia of Fishes.* San Diego: Academic Press, 1994.

RELATED ARTICLES

Agnatha; Porifera

Critical Depth

Phytoplankton cells inhabiting the euphotic zone of the ocean undergo two competing processes. During photosynthesis, which depends on the availability of light, primary producers convert inorganic building blocks into energy-rich organic compounds; during cellular respiration, which occurs at all times, phytoplankton cells use energy. The critical depth, like the *compensation depth*, is depth at which these two processes are equal. The *compensation depth*, however, is specific to an individual phytoplankton cell and is defined as the depth at which rates of photosynthesis and respiration are equal. In contrast, *critical depth* represents a 24-hour integration of photosynthesis and respiration of all phytoplankton cells; it is the depth at which total photosynthesis and total respiration for the algal population in the water column are equal.

At the compensation depth, phytoplankton cells are exposed to about 1 percent of the light intensity received at the sea surface; at this light intensity (the compensation intensity) the rate of photosynthesis for a given phytoplankton cell exactly equals its rate of respiration, and net energy production is zero. The compensation depth defines the lower limit of the euphotic zone. The upper water column, however, can experience significant vertical mixing. Vertical mixing can affect the dynamics of the water column by carrying nutrients upward into the euphotic zone and by transporting phytoplankton cells out of the lit zone and below the compensation depth.

The concept of critical depth takes vertical mixing into account. It explains how net energy production can be positive or zero even when phytoplankton cells are mixed out of the euphotic zone: Phytoplankton cells can spend time below the compensation depth as long as they spend at least an equivalent amount of time above it. Thus, critical depth can also be defined as the deepest depth in the water column to which phytoplankton cells may be mixed and still spend enough time above the compensation depth so that the two competing processes are equal.

Because critical depth is an averaged value for a population and takes vertical mixing into account, it is always deeper than the compensation depth. For net production to occur in the water column, the depth of the mixed layer must be shallower than the critical depth. When the mixed layer extends deeper than the critical depth, total respiration exceeds total plant production and energy loss occurs.

The depth of the mixed layer, temperature, season, geographic location, light availability, and nutrient availability all are interrelated and together determine the productivity of ocean waters. Tropical seas, for example, have abundant light and deep compensation depths throughout the year, but they experience little to no mixing and are low in nutrients. Therefore, productivity is low but constant. Polar seas are not nutrient limited and may be well mixed, but overall productivity is low because phytoplankton receive sufficient light for photosynthesis for only a few months out of the year. Temperate seas exhibit the most seasonal variability in primary productivity. Summer months generally are characterized by low productivity because nutrient levels are low and thermal stratification prevents vertical mixing. Primary productivity is also low during the winter, when light is less available and when storms generate a mixed layer that exceeds the critical depth. The typical spring bloom that characterizes many temperate seas occurs when light intensity increases, wind strength decreases, thermal stratification begins, and vertical mixing is lessened so that the critical depth exceeds the depth of the mixed layer. A smaller peak in productivity also occurs in the fall.

Lynn L. Lauerman

FURTHER READING
Cushing, D. H. *Productivity of the Sea.* Oxford Biology Reader No. 78. London: Oxford University Press, 1975.
Lalli, Carol M., and Timothy R. Parsons. *Biological Oceanography: An Introduction.* Oxford and New York: Pergamon Press, 1993; 2nd ed., Oxford: Butterworth-Heinemann, 1997.
Nybakken, James W. *Marine Biology: An Ecological Approach,* 5th ed. San Francisco: Benjamin Cummings, 2001.
Parsons, Timothy R., Masayuki Takahashi, and Barry Hargrave. *Biological Oceanographic Processes.* New York: Pergamon, 1973; 3rd ed., 1984.
Valiela, Ivan. *Marine Ecological Processes.* New York: Springer-Verlag, 1984; 2nd ed., 1995.

RELATED ARTICLES
Compensation Depth; Euphotic Zone; Phytoplankton

Critical Tide Level

Critical tide levels are those points where there is a sharp change in exposure or immersion time over a very short vertical distance in the intertidal zone of a shore. Such critical tide levels usually occur on shores that are subject to a mixed tide regime where there are two high and two low tides per lunar cycle and the highs and lows are not equal in height. As a result of this phenomenon, an intertidal organism at one point on the shore that was within the tidal range of both of the two daily high tides may be covered by water every six hours, whereas if the organism were to move slightly higher out of the range of the lower of the two high tides, it would not be immersed in water for 12 hours. Such a dramatic change in exposure to air may exceed the tolerance limits of some intertidal organisms, thus limiting their distribution. Therefore, critical tide levels were offered as one of the early explanations for the striking zonation patterns of organisms observed on rocky intertidal shores around the world. Since its original promulgation in 1946, this hypothesis has been tested in various places around the world and it has been difficult to find good correlations, probably because a large number of other biological and physical factors are also acting to forge the zonation patterns.

James W. Nybakken

FURTHER READING
Doty, M. S. "Critical Tide Factors That Are Correlated with the Vertical Distribution of Marine Algae and Other Organisms along the Pacific Coast." *Ecology*, Vol. 27 (1946), pp. 315–328.
Nybakken, James W. *Marine Biology: An Ecological Approach*, 5th ed. San Francisco: Benjamin Cummings, 2001.

RELATED ARTICLES
Intertidal; Tide

Cromwell Current, see Equatorial Undercurrent

Crustacea

Crustacea is a diverse subphylum of the phylum Arthropoda (animals with jointed legs), including more than 40,000 species, the majority of which are marine. They are frequently the dominant group of marine invertebrates, particularly in the pelagic realm. Many are important species in marine ecosystems, and many are exploited commercially.

Crustaceans possess segmented bodies and external skeletons. There is a basic three-part body structure: a head, a thorax, and an abdomen. The head is composed of five segments, has two pairs of antennae, and typically has three pairs of mouthparts. Each thoracic segment carries a pair of appendages adapted for walking, swimming, or collecting food. In most groups there is a pair of limbs on each abdominal segment. These pairs of limbs are multifunctional, being used for swimming, respiration, or carrying eggs or larvae. Eyes, when present, are usually compound. The central nervous system is arranged with a ganglionic ring around the esophagus, which is linked to a ladderlike arrangement of a nerve cord connected to a pair of ganglia in each segment lying ventrally. However, this pattern can be greatly modified. In crabs, for instance, there is a single ganglionic mass posterior to the esophagus. Their feeding ranges from herbivory to carnivory and detritivory.

Crustaceans have a rigid external outer skeleton of chitin, a polysaccharide, which is often hardened and toughened either by tanning or by being invested with calcium carbonate. Since a crustacean is encased within a rigid external skeleton, to grow it must shed its old skeleton (*molt*) and inflate itself with water before producing a new skeleton, secrete a new flexible skeleton, and inflate itself with water before hardening the new skeleton. The limbs are jointed and are modified for walking, swimming, handling food, sieving particles from the water, and extracting oxygen from the water.

There are five classes: Remipedia, Cephalocarida, Branchiopoda, Maxillopoda, and Malacostraca.

Remipedia. There are a few cave-dwelling species known. These species are small, elongate, and blind. The head and first trunk segment are combined to form a cephalothorax, behind which is a trunk composed of 30 similar segments, each carrying a pair of leaflike lateral limbs.

Cephalocarida. This class includes a few species of blind animals that inhabit the spaces between sand grains. The first examples were discovered living in the sands of Long Island Sound as recently as 1955. Typically, they have 19 trunk segments; only the nine anterior segments carry limbs.

Branchiopoda. This class includes a wide variety of animals with limbs that are uniform and leaflike (foliaceous). Each of the various groups of branchiopod has a different number of trunk segments, which in some species carry limbs but in others, do not. Most branchiopods live in fresh water, but there are a few marine planktonic species, including *Podon* and *Evadne*. Most can reproduce *parthenogenetically*; their eggs do not require fertilization in order to hatch into viable young, so when conditions are right, their populations can increase very quickly. Sexual reproduction leads to the production of resting eggs, which can remain viable on the bottom for many months, and can survive being desiccated.

Maxillopoda. This grouping includes several subclasses, most of relatively small but ecologically important orders: the Ostracoda, Copepoda, and Cirripedia (barnacles). The bodies of the Ostracoda are totally enclosed in a bivalved carapace or shell, superficially resembling bivalved mollusks. The benthic ostracods have highly calcified shells, which are often highly sculptured and fossilize readily. Micropaleontologists find them extremely useful in identifying potential oil-bearing deposits. Planktonic ostracods are less

well known, despite often being second in abundance in the mesoplankton, after the Copepoda.

Copepoda are so important that they merit their own encyclopedic entry and so are not discussed further here. The Cirripedia or barnacles are probably familiar to anyone who has explored rocky shorelines, because they form an abrasive encrustment over weed-free surfaces of rock or boulders. Their larvae are planktonic and settle gregariously on any vacant surfaces. Once settled, they secrete a covering of hard calcareous plates and feed by combing suspended particles out of the water by kicking their feathery legs. Some species are stalked and are present low down the shore and in deep water. Goose barnacles settle on any floating objects in the open ocean, and together with other barnacles, were a major problem to wooden sailing ships, increasing their drag and slowing them down. Some species are external epizoites of whales and turtles, and some are internal parasites of crabs. The latter have larvae that are typical of barnacles, but they find a host and develop into networks of tissue that ramify through the host's internal tissues.

The Mystacocarida, a subclass not discovered until 1943, in Long Island Sound, are tiny animals inhabiting the spaces (interstices) between grains of sand on the seabed.

Malacostraca. This is a very diverse subclass of the larger, more charismatic, crustaceans, including crabs, shrimps and prawns, isopods, amphipods, and krill. Typically, the thorax consists of eight segments and the abdomen consists of six segments. The thorax is often covered by a carapace. The legs are typically Y-shaped, with the inner branch developed into a gill. It includes a number of important orders and superorders.

Leptostraca is a curious order, containing just seven known species. They are anomalous in having seven abdominal segments. One genus, *Nebaliopsis*, is an enigmatic bathypelagic species, and all the others are shore dwelling.

Stomatopoda, or mantis shrimps, have flattened and elongated bodies, elongated stalked eyes, abdominal gills, and massive clasping claws at the end of the second thoracic limbs. They are powerful predators, with most living in burrows. They range in size from just over an inch to over a foot in length.

Mysidacea are shrimplike animals that are usually distinguishable from other shrimps and krill by their balance organ (statocyst), located in the base of one of the tail appendages. Many are shallow-water species living by filter feeding close to the bottom. There are a few pelagic species. *Gnathophausia* species are bathypelagic and can reach lengths of nearly a foot and live for seven years. They brood the eggs and early larval stages.

Cumacea and *Tanaidacea* are mostly small benthic species that live buried within the sediment. They are occasionally caught in the water, either when the sediment is eroded by strong currents or when males leave the sediment in search of females.

Isopoda is the second largest order of crustaceans. Sowbugs are familiar terrestrial representatives of this group; the sea slater *Ligia* can occur abundantly on rocks at the top of the shore (supralittoral), usually emerging at night when the atmosphere is humid. There are many marine species, most of which are benthic. A few are pelagic and several are either external or internal parasites. Their bodies are typically flattened dorsoventrally and their abdominal limbs function as gills.

Amphipoda is another diverse order of crustaceans in the oceans. Their bodies are usually flattened from side to side (laterally), the exception being the whale lice, *Cyama*. Their eyes are placed inside the head on either side, but some deep-living species have lost them. In some of the planktonic species, the eyes have become extremely elaborate compound structures; in *Streetsia*, for example, they occupy most of the elongate anterior region of the head. Interesting

behavior is seen in *Phronima*; each female takes over a salp in which she sits swimming while her brood of offspring cling to the inner walls of the house, eating any food that is wafted in. *Alicella* species are the largest, attaining lengths of over 15 centimeters (6 inches). They live in deep water, where they scavenge on corpses that land on the bottom. There are also some very bizarre amphipods: *Caprella* is skeletal-like and adapted to clambering among seaweeds on the shore.

The larger species of malacostracans belong to a superorder known as the *Eucarida*. The order Euphausiacea includes the 87 known species of krill. These shrimplike animals are important species in many pelagic food webs, notably in the Southern Ocean. The inner branch of each thoracic limb is developed into a large external gill, whereas in the order Decapoda the gill branches of the thoracic legs are enclosed within a side chamber of the carapace. The decapods include shrimps, lobsters, and crabs, and contain some of the largest and most specialized species. Their first three thoracic limbs are developed into feeding appendages and the remaining five pairs are walking legs, often with one or more pairs being *chelate* (i.e., developed into a pair of claws, which in crabs and some lobsters are extremely large and powerful). In prawns the abdominal limbs are used for swimming and the thoracic legs are generally slender, with the first two or three pairs being chelate. The abdomen tends to bend forward, so that at any sign of danger, the shrimp snaps it closed and shoots backward. In true crabs the abdomen is tightly folded beneath the carapace, which encloses the rest of the body. The abdominal limbs are reduced and used only by females to carry their developing eggs. Many of the larger crabs are exploited commercially and command high prices, including stone crabs (*Cancer*) and the giant spider crab of Japan (*Macrocheir keampferi*), which is the largest living arthropod. The smallest crabs are parasitic and live on the gills of bivalve mollusks, in the tubes of other invertebrates, or entombed within living coral. The anomuran crabs have asymmetrical bodies and soft enlarged abdomens. They are adapted to occupying empty snail shells. Many anomura crabs, particularly in the family Lithodidae, have symmetrical bodies with the small abdomen reflexed beneath the thorax just as in brachyuran crabs. Anomurans are distinguished from brachyurans by having only three pairs of walking legs and antennae outside the eyes. The most extreme variant is the semiterrestrial robber crab (*Birgus*). It climbs palm trees and uses coconut shells to protect its abdomen. However, *Birgus* still has to return to the sea to spawn since its larvae, like those of most decapods, are planktonic. Fertilization is internal, and often the males can mate only with newly molted females whose carapaces are still pliable. The fertilized eggs are usually brooded until they hatch, and the developing planktonic larvae undergo a series of major larval forms before metamorphosing into the adult.

Martin Angel

FURTHER READING

Barnes, Richard, Peter Calow, Peter Olive, and David Golding. *The Invertebrates: A New Synthesis.* Oxford and Boston: Blackwell Scientific, 1988; 2nd ed., 1993.

Bliss, Dorothy E., ed. *The Biology of the Crustacea.* New York: Academic Press, 1982.

Schram, Frederick R., ed. *Crustacean Phylogeny—Crustacean Issues.* Rotterdam, the Netherlands: A.A. Balkema, 1983.

USEFUL WEB SITES

"Crustaceans." <http://nmnhwww.si.edu/gopher-menus/ Crustaceans.html>.

RELATED ARTICLES

Arthropoda; Branchiopoda; Cephalocarida; Chitin; Crab; Malacostraca; Maxillopoda; Pelagic; Remipedia

Crustal Plate, see Plate Tectonics

Cryptic Coloration

Many animals are camouflaged, or cryptically colored, as an adaption to reduce their visibility to both their predators and their prey. In well-lit habitats many predators hunt by sight, so the harder it is for any species to be seen, the more likely it is for them to survive. Similarly, predators that ambush their prey need to remain invisible, so stonefish and wobbegong sharks have color patterns similar to the seabed on which they patiently await the approach of their next victim.

On rocky shores herbivores such as prawns and shrimp are not only colored like the rocks and seaweeds among which they live but also have a chameleonlike ability to change their color as they move around. Many of the species that specialize in browsing on certain species of benthic algae or animals are colored and patterned like their food species. Cowries have mantle folds that cover their shells, which are colored like the sponges on which they feed. Similarly, some nudibranch mollusks have body colors and shapes that make them almost invisible when they are on the specific types of hydroid or sponges they feed on. In the Sargasso Sea, a bizarre assemblage of animals has adapted to living among the floating Sargassum weed. Not only are they the same color as the weed, but also their bodies are covered with warts and excrescences that make them look much like the weed.

In deep midwater, prawns that look bright scarlet in daylight are in fact cryptically colored. Their habitat lacks red light, so their functional color is black; their red pigmentation has an additional advantage in that it does not reflect the blue-green light of most bioluminescence. The cryptic coloration of mesopelagic fishes is just as extraordinary. They have highly silvered, mirrorlike sides that reflect light of exactly the same color and

Camouflaged false stonefish. (© Jeffrey L. Rotman/Corbis)

brightness as the background. At depths of 1000 meters (3280 feet), close to the limit of detectable daylight, the majority of the fish are totally black.

Martin Angel

FURTHER READING

Denton, Eric J. "On The Organization of Reflecting Surfaces in Some Marine Animals." *Philosophical Transactions of the Royal Society of London B,* Vol. 258 (1970), pp. 285–313.

Herring, Peter J. "Light, Colour and Vision in the Ocean." In Colin P. Summerhayes and Steve A. Thorpe, eds., *Oceanography: An Illustrated Guide.* New York: Wiley, 1996.

RELATED ARTICLES

Bioluminescence; Countershading

Cryptofauna

Although cryptofauna can refer to all organisms living in protected or concealed microhabitats, collectively called *infauna*, the term is most widely used and best understood in coral reef ecosystems. In coral reefs, where there is an abundance of protected and concealed habitats, *cryptofauna* refers to a group of organisms that bore into the reef substrate (*true borers*), and both sessile and motile encrusters that reside in bioeroded holes and crevices (*opportunists*). All types of cryptofauna are an integral part of coral reef ecosystems, and they play vital roles in the ecology of reefs.

In Greek, *crypto* means hidden or secret, and *fauna* refers to all wild organisms in a particular area. Thus, cryptofauna means the hidden or secret organisms, which accurately describes the behavioral ecology of the motile types; however, the boring and sessile cryptofauna are usually less hidden than their motile counterparts.

The motile cryptofauna are among the least visible of coral reef fauna, as most remain hidden under coral platforms or ledges or bore into the calcium carbonate skeleton itself; nevertheless, they are both diverse and abundant. As many as 800 different cryptofaunal species have been counted on some reefs, and there are nearly 500 individuals per 10 cubic meters (353 cubic feet) of reef substrate in the most densely populated coral reefs. A single reef species in Florida, *Oculina arbuscula*, provides shelter for over 300 species of cryptofauna. Polychaetes, mollusks, crustaceans, echinoderms, and fish dominate the motile cryptofauna. Although most of these groups are present on all parts of coral reefs, there is a strong spatial distribution on the dominance of groups from the outer reef to the reef flat. For instance, in studies conducted in French Polynesia, scientists found that polychaetes and crustaceans dominate the outer reef slope. In the shallower, calmer waters of the reef flat, mollusks and crustaceans dominate the cryptofauna.

The sessile cryptofauna is composed mainly of bryozoans, sponges, tunicates, and polychaete worms. Although their diversity and abundance still need to be studied carefully, recent research suggests that sessile cryptofauna are as ubiquitous as their motile counterparts. Sessile forms grow and proliferate very effectively, due to their ability to reproduce asexually and their domination of the undersides and edges of corals and coral platforms.

The boring cryptofauna consists of groups that actually bore into the calcium carbonate of coral reefs, and these include the sponges, bivalve mollusks, sipunculans, and polychaetes. By boring, they effectively create future habitats for their motile and sessile counterparts. Similar to other cryptofauna, the boring groups are very numerous on coral reefs. Scientists have identified as many as 220 species of boring crytofauna in single colonies of coral.

Cryptofauna play a number of important ecological roles on coral reefs. By boring into the calcium carbonate substrate and through coral grazing, cryptofauna serve as significant bio-eroders. Also via their boring activities, these organisms provide a variety of habitats for current and future residents in the tightly spaced three-dimensional reef environment. Due to their

diversity and abundance, cryptofauna also serve several roles in the reef food web. There are a variety of feeding strategies, including suspension feeders, deposit feeders, grazers, and predators, among others. These strategies assist in the recycling of organic matter on coral reefs, and the cryptofauna strengthen the trophic links between benthic and pelagic communities. Often described as the rainforests of the seas, coral reefs are greatly enriched by the presence of the marine equivalent of insects: the cryptofauna.

Manoj Shivlani

FURTHER READING
Hutching, P. A. "Non-colonial Cryptofauna." In D. R. Stoddart and R. E. Johannes, eds., *Coral Reefs: Research Methods*. Paris: UNESCO, 1978, pp. 251–263.
Nybakken, James W. *Marine Biology: An Ecological Approach*, 5th ed. San Francisco: Benjamin Cummings, 2001.
Reaka-Kudla, M. L., D. E. Wilson, and E. O. Wilson, eds. *Biodiversity II: Understanding and Protecting Our Biological Resources*. Washington, D.C.: John Henry Press, 1997.

RELATED ARTICLES
Bryozoa; Coral Reef; Crustacea; Echinodermata; Grazing; Infauna; Mollusca; Polychaeta; Sipuncula

CTD Profiler

A CTD profiler measures the conductivity, temperature, and depth (hence the acronym CTD) as it descends toward the seabed in order to build up an overall picture of ocean conditions. These three pieces of information can be combined to calculate the pressure and density of various regions of the ocean, and these data can be used to build models of large-scale ocean circulation.

Profiler Instruments
A CTD profiler must contain three separate sensors, one for conductivity, one for temperature, and one for pressure (to provide depth information).

1. *Conductivity*. Conductivity allows the density of seawater to be measured because it indicates the level of salinity and therefore the amount of dissolved salts within a given volume of water. Traditional conductivity sensors measured the resistance of seawater to a current flowing between two exposed electrodes, but this method is rarely used today because the electrodes tend to corrode rapidly and the sensor has to be exposed directly to the water. Instead, conductivity is measured by *induction*—as seawater passes by a sensor, it carries a minute electric current, which induces a similarly small current in a wire inside the instrument. The latest conductivity sensors are made of ceramic semiconductor materials and can be cast into open-bored cylinders so that the water causing the induction actually flows through the sensor.

2. *Temperature*. Temperature sensors are either resistance thermometers or thermistors. *Resistance thermometers* rely on large changes in the electrical resistance of a platinum wire caused by small changes in temperature; *thermistors* are made of semiconductors that allow more electricity to flow through them as the temperature increases. Platinum resistance thermometers are far more accurate than thermistors, but thermistors react to temperature changes more rapidly; often the two techniques of temperature measurement are used together.

3. *Depth*. Depth is calculated by changes in the water pressure acting on a *strain gauge*, a device that stretches or compresses a conducting wire, causing its electrical resistance to change. As with the temperature sensors, the changing resistance is measured using a resistance bridge, a sort of seesaw in which the balance of three other resistors is adjusted to match the resistance of the sensor.

Feedback and Data Collection

All three measurements feed back and affect each other; for example, temperature changes alter the properties of the conductivity sensor and the strain gauge. Sophisticated electronic circuitry is used to take these changes into account and produce the most accurate possible results, while the sensors are constantly calibrated against internal standards. CTD profiles rely on acquiring continuous data from a profiler as it moves along a horizontal or vertical track through the sea. Profilers can be attached to submersibles and ROVs (remotely operated vehicles), but may also be deployed independently. To prevent them from getting caught up in ocean currents, profilers are often dropped down vertical cables suspended between a mooring on the seabed and a buoyant float on or close to the surface. They can even be fitted with rollers that allow them to crawl up and down the cable according to instructions sent from an operator onboard the ship. The data collected are recorded either on magnetic tape or in solid-state memory inside the profiler, or they are transmitted back to the surface through acoustic signals.

Giles Sparrow

FURTHER READING
Grasshof, K., K. Kremling, and M. Ehrhardt, eds. *Methods of Seawater Analysis*, 3rd completely rev. and extended ed. Weinheim, Germany, and New York: Wiley-VCH Publishing, 1999.
Thurman, Harold V. *Essentials of Oceanography*. Columbus, Ohio: Charles E. Merrill, 1983; 6th ed., with Alan P. Trujillo, Upper Saddle River, N.J.: Prentice Hall, 1999.

RELATED ARTICLES
Ocean Circulation; Salinity; Submersible

Ctenophora

The Ctenophora, or comb jelly, are an enigmatic phylum of gelatinous organisms; all are marine but there are both benthic and pelagic species.

Perhaps the most familiar species is the sea gooseberry, *Pleurobrachia pileus*, which washes up on Atlantic beaches during the summer

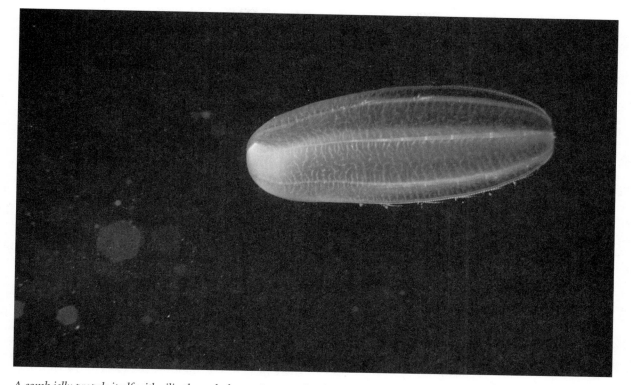

A comb jelly propels itself with cilia through the sea 5 meters (16 feet) under the sea ice, Antarctica. (© Rick Price/Corbis)

looking like blobs of jelly. Their basic body design is similar to that of cnidarians, with two layers of tissue separated by an infill of a watery gelatinous material. The basic body plan is radially symmetrical, modified in many species to be bilaterally symmetrical. There is a simple saclike gut with a mouth but no anus. One group of species (Tentaculata) has tentacles armed with adhesive cells or colloblasts, which trap its prey. These tentacles may be very short or trail 10 or 20 times the body length behind the swimming animal. The other group (Nuda) lack tentacles and capture their prey by enveloping them whole.

Most propel themselves through the water using the synchronized beating of the eight bands of ciliary plates that are arranged in radial rows (comb plates) over the surface of the body. Venus's girdle (*Cestum veneris*), which possesses a body that is compressed laterally into a band up to 1.5 meters (5 feet) long, swims by slow undulations of its body. Many of the species are so fragile that they disintegrate in nets and when

placed in preservative. Therefore, knowledge of the distributions, ecology, and morphology of many of the species has come from direct, in situ observations by divers, or from specimens collected using "slurp guns" on submersibles.

Despite their fragility, ctenophores are voracious carnivores that eat plankton and fish larvae. In some species the feeding is highly specialized; for example, larvaceans may be engulfed in their gelatinous houses. The larvacean soon abandons its house and is digested, while the house is discarded. Species of *Beroë* eat only other ctenophores, and so even when no other ctenophores occur in a plankton sample, the occurrence of *Beroë* indicates that other ctenophores were once present.

Ctenophores can have a major impact on the local ecology. For instance, the accidental introduction of *Mnemiopsis* into the Black Sea has radically altered the plankton communities and has destroyed local fisheries. Shallow-water ctenophores tend to be transparent, colored only by the iridescence of the four pairs of comb plates. Many of the deepwater species are tinged with red or purple.

Martin Angel

FURTHER READING

Barnes, Richard, Peter Calow, Peter Olive, and David Golding. *The Invertebrates: A New Synthesis.* Oxford and Boston: Blackwell Scientific, 1988; 2nd ed., 1993.

Harbison, G. R., and L. P. Madin. "Ctenophora." In Sybil Parker, ed., *Synopsis and Classification of Living Organisms.* New York: McGraw-Hill, 1982; pp. 705–715.

Mianzan, H. W. "Ctenophora." In Demetrio Boltovskoy, ed., *South Atlantic Zooplankton,* vol. 1. Leiden, the Netherlands: Backhuys, 1999; pp. 561–573.

RELATED ARTICLES

Cnidaria; Larvacean; Pelagic; Plankton

Current Meter

A current meter is used to measure and record the speed and direction of ocean currents. Current meters have a wide range of designs, depending on the measurement method being used and the conditions in which they will operate (i.e., time and space scales).

Methods of Current Measurement

Ocean currents may be calculated directly or indirectly. Direct methods involve placing instruments in the water that are affected directly by movement of the water around them, and either transmit this information to the surface or record it for later retrieval. Their major disadvantage is that unless a network of instruments is distributed throughout a wide area of ocean, direct measurements do not necessarily provide an accurate picture of large-scale current movements.

Indirect measurements, on the other hand, derive calculations of water movements from other information, such as water salinity and temperature, collected by a CTD profiler. Using these data to calculate water pressure in widely separated areas allows an overall pressure map of the sea to be drawn that shows changes in the pressure between different areas, and therefore the probable relative direction and strength of current flows. The disadvantage of indirect measurements is that they cannot provide information on absolute current strengths and provide only a large-scale picture of slowly changing major water movements. Neither technique is ideal for all purposes, so oceanographers tend to use a combination of the two.

Mechanical Measurements

Most methods for direct mechanical measurement of currents rely on the same basic principle as the first current meters. Water flows through an encased, freely spinning propeller, which is able to pivot so that it always faces into the current. The rate of spin and orientation of the propeller are converted into electrical signals and then stored on magnetic tape or transmitted acoustically back to a ship or undersea listening device (hydrophone).

The accuracy and data-collecting ability of current meters like this have improved rapidly since the 1980s through the introduction of electronic measuring devices. Modern vector-averaging current meters (VACMs) can measure the propeller's rate of rotation and orientation many times each turn. This allows scientists to see how currents change from moment to moment. Earlier electrical systems could record the propeller's average rotation only over several spins.

The placement of current meters is just as important as the actual design of the recording device. Different strategies for deployment are used depending on precisely what information is required. The simplest and most popular method is also the oldest, linking several (usually up to a dozen) separate instruments together on a cable with a heavy anchor at one end and an extremely buoyant float at the other. A chain of current meters can be paid out over the side of a survey ship, its position charted accurately, and then left to record the changing currents for weeks or months before retrieval. The buoyant float is very important because although it may not stretch all the way to the surface, it will keep the chain vertical and help prevent sideways drift in even the strongest currents. The current meters may also be fitted with other measuring instruments in order to record properties such as changing ocean temperatures and pressures. When the time comes for retrieval, an acoustic signal transmitted from the recovery ship to the anchor triggers a mechanism that releases the chain, allowing the float to rise to the surface.

Meters can make continuous measurements and return the data to a survey ship by cable or sonar, or record the current at set intervals ranging from a few seconds to an hour or more. These intermittent measurements may be taken instantaneously or be the result of averaging over long or short periods to compensate for small-scale effects such as individual waves. Whereas continuous meters are normally linked to, and draw power from, survey ships or submersibles (and so can make measurements only for a few hours or days at a time), longer-term measurements can be made with free-floating meters or instruments attached to the seafloor.

Currents move vertically as well as horizontally, but it was not until the 1960s that a suitable method of measuring these water flows was invented. A vertical current meter consists of a rotating cylinder with fins around its outside, which spins at varying speeds and in different directions depending on whether the water around it is moving up or down. To prevent this type of meter drifting vertically with the currents, it is important that it has neutral buoyancy.

Although permanently anchored floats are an important method of current measurement, they are not ideal for every situation. Sometimes oceanographers want to measure how the current changes with location in a large volume of water, producing a vertical or horizontal current profile rather than just spot measurements. For vertical current profiles, there are two main alternatives. One is to use a variation on the traditional current meter, which crawls up and down an anchored cable in response to commands from the surface or preset instructions. Submersibles and remote-operated vehicles (ROVs) may also be fitted with current meters so they can record horizontal or vertical profiles.

The other technique is the free-fall current profiler, a weighted device that is dropped into the sea and sinks rapidly, recording the strength and direction of the currents as it falls. A free-falling profiler will not drop vertically to the ocean floor—the currents will push it off course—so fitting it with a traditional current meter would be futile. Instead, oceanographers use the drift of the falling profiler itself as a measure of the currents around it. The profiler's position can be tracked with sonar in relation to fixed points on the seafloor—either natural acoustic sources or reflectors, or sonar beacons (transponders) already dropped into position. Another way of measuring its movement is to fit the device with electronics that can measure minute flows of electricity generated as the currents carry the profiler through Earth's magnetic field.

Other Methods

In recent years, electrical and mechanical current meters have been replaced for many uses (particularly in oceanography) by acoustic Doppler current profiling (ADCP) and Aanderaa current meters. An Aanderaa meter or other ADCP device produces regular pulses of sound with high frequencies at around 2 megahertz. As these sound waves propagate out through the water, they are scattered by plankton and other small particles. Some of the sound waves are reflected directly back, returning to the meter, where they are detected by a transducer that records their frequency and direction electronically. When the reflecting material is moving relative to the meter, the returning sound is Doppler shifted, to higher frequencies when the particles are moving toward the recorder and to lower frequencies when they are moving away. By combining two measurements at right angles with the measurements of an internal compass, the current meter can work out the speed and direction of the material's movement, and hence the current.

For long-term measurements of major ocean circulations, though, the simplest method is often just to release buoys that float on the surface or drift at a set depth. These probes can be carried by the currents for many years and may be tracked by various methods. Surface buoys can be fitted with transponders, which send out a signal to reveal their location when "interrogated" by a code broadcast by satellite. More sophisticated versions may collect a wide range of oceanographic data and regularly broadcast it to a dedicated satellite, which returns the information to a land-based receiving station.

Underwater drifters, known as *sofar floats*, must be tracked by sonar. They are fitted with a low-powered sonar beacon that broadcasts sound waves of extremely low frequency, around 250 hertz (cycles per second). These low-frequency, long-wavelength sounds can travel for thousands of kilometers through the water without losing their signal strength. When they are detected by networks of underwater hydrophones on the coast or moored in the deep sea, the time taken for the signal to travel from the drifter can be worked out and its present position calculated.

Giles Sparrow

FURTHER READING

IEEE Oceanic Engineering Society. *1999 IEEE 6th Working Conference on Current Measurement.* Piscataway, N.J.: IEEE, 1999

Thurman, Harold V. *Essentials of Oceanography.* Columbus, Ohio: Charles E. Merrill, 1983; 6th ed., with Alan P. Trujillo, Upper Saddle River, N.J.: Prentice Hall, 1999.

RELATED ARTICLES

Acoustic Doppler Current Profiler; CTD Profiler; Ocean Current; Sofar; Sonar

Cyanobacteria

Also called *blue-green algae,* cyanobacteria are photosynthetic bacteria (domain Bacteria, kingdom Monera) that live in the ocean surface and coastal waters. They form part of the phytoplankton, the microscopic photosynthetic organisms that provide the basis of the food chain for nearly all marine life. They are important as primary producers. Like plants and green algae, cyanobacteria use the green pigment chlorophyll to trap the Sun's energy and build energy-rich carbohydrate molecules from water and carbon dioxide. They also convert atmospheric nitrogen into nitrates, important nutrients that algae and plants require to manufacture complex organic molecules such as proteins, to supplement the meagre amount of nitrates present in seawater.

Like other bacteria, cyanobacteria have cells that are *prokaryotic*—they lack complex internal structures such as cell nuclei, and their DNA exists as a simple molecule rather than as a tightly packed chromosome. Their chlorophyll is located in special infoldings of the plasma membrane rather than in chloroplasts, where they are located in most plants. Some cyanobacteria are free floating, but many group together into colonial mats or filaments.

Cyanobacteria are more common in freshwater habitats than in the ocean, but they occasionally form toxic blooms in coastal water. In shallow tropical seas they sometimes grow in mats, building up slowly into solid pedestals called *stromatolites.* Evidence from fossil stromatolites indicates that cynobacteria existed on Earth more than 2.7 billion years ago, making these one of the oldest known groups of organisms on Earth. Scientists believe that ancient cyanobacteria played an important role in changing the composition of Earth's prehistoric atmosphere, increasing the oxygen level and making the planet more hospitable to life.

Striking similarities between cyanobacteria and the chloroplasts in plants suggest a close evolutionary relationship. According to the now widely accepted serial endosymbiotic theory, at least some of the chloroplasts are descendants of cyanobacteria that entered the cells of ancestral green algae in a symbiotic relationship. Over time, these symbiotic cyanobacteria lost the ability to live independently and became chloroplasts.

Cyanobacteria were once commonly known as blue-green algae because they release oxygen as they photosynthesise, unlike other photosynthetic groups of bacteria that do not. They are now recognized as bacteria since they are prokaryotic.

Ben Morgan

FURTHER READING
Postlethwait, John. *The Nature of Life.* New York: McGraw-Hill, 1989; 3rd ed., 1995.
Purves, William, et al. *Life: The Science of Biology.* Sunderland, Mass.: Sinauer/Boston: Grant Press, 1983; 5th ed., Sunderland, Mass.: Sinauer, 1998.

RELATED ARTICLES
Bacteria; Chlorophyll; Nanoplankton; Nutrient; Photosynthesis; Phytoplankton; Primary Productivity

Cyclonic Flow

Air tends to move from centers of high pressure toward centers of low pressure. It does not travel in a straight line, however. The rotation of Earth beneath the moving air causes it to follow an approximately circular path. *Cyclone* is the meteorological name for a center of low pressure, and *cyclonic* describes the direction in which air flows around a cyclone. This is anticlockwise in the northern hemisphere and clockwise in the southern hemisphere.

All centers of low pressure are called cyclones, but cyclones that form in temperate latitudes differ from those that form in the tropics. Temperate or extratropical cyclones are also called *depressions*. They are often produced by frontal systems that form between air masses.

Tropical cyclones are not associated with fronts, cover a much smaller area, and generate much more violent conditions. Air circulates cyclonically around both types of cyclone.

A gradient of pressure exists between two points where the atmospheric pressure is different. Air is driven down the gradient by a *pressure-gradient force* (PGF). The magnitude of the PGF is proportional to the steepness of the gradient. Because air moves into areas of low pressure, cyclonic flow involves the convergence of air.

The most extreme examples of cyclonic air flow are found in *tropical cyclones* (also known as *hurricanes* and *typhoons*) and tornadoes. Tropical cyclones are large weather systems, up to 900 kilometers (560 miles) in diameter. Wind speeds are strongest around the center, where they are never below 120 kilometers (75 miles) per hour and can exceed 240 kilometers (150 miles) per hour. Most tropical cyclones develop over a period of a week or two but seldom sustain their maximum power for longer than a few days. *Tornadoes* are an entirely different phenomenon, produced by intense storm clouds. They are seldom more than about 350 meters (1150 feet) in diameter and often much smaller, and most survive for no more than a few minutes. Winds around the central vortex can exceed 320 kilometers (200 miles) per hour.

Air and water that move over the surface of Earth are deflected by the *Coriolis effect* (CorF). The CorF deflects moving bodies to the right in the northern hemisphere and to the left in the southern hemisphere. The magnitude of the CorF is proportional to the speed of the moving air or water and increases with latitude, from zero at the equator to a maximum at the poles. CorF acts at right angles to the PGF. When the two balance, the air circulates around the cyclone, which then constitutes a cyclonic flow.

Cyclonic flow is associated with convergence, and convergence can produce cyclonic flows at sea, resulting in *whirlpools*. They occur in narrow straits where the water is deep and where a strong current generated by a rising tide meets the return current of the preceding ebb tide. This sets up a rotational flow whose direction is determined by the configuration of the coastlines and the topography of the seabed. These exert a stronger influence than the CorF.

A *vortex* can develop in a whirlpool where the water is very deep at the center of the flow. In this case the speed of the current accelerates toward the center, due to the conservation of angular momentum, then spirals rapidly downward into a depressed center. Small objects and even small boats can be drawn down into the central depression. A more common danger to small vessels arises from the big waves produced when a strong wind blows in the opposite direction to the current. There are many famous whirlpools. Charybdis, in the Strait of Messina between Italy and Sicily, is featured in the *Odyssey*. The Maelstrom, off northern Norway, is mentioned in

Norse and Viking mythology and is also well known, as is the Corryvreckan, in the Hebrides off the west coast of Scotland.

In the open ocean, convergence can produce large-scale eddies that flow cyclonically. These are also called whirlpools, but a whirlpool in the open ocean never develops into a vortex with a depressed center capable of engulfing ships.

Michael Allaby

FURTHER READING
Allaby, Michael. *Dangerous Weather: Hurricanes.* New York: Facts On File, 1997.
———. *Dangerous Weather: Tornadoes.* New York: Facts On File, 1997.
Knauss, John A. *Introduction to Physical Oceanography.* Englewood Cliffs, N.J.: Prentice Hall, 1978; 2nd ed. rev., Upper Saddle River, N.J.: Prentice Hall, 2000.

RELATED ARTICLES
Anticyclonic Flow; Convergence; Coriolis Effect; Pressure-Gradient Force; Vorticity

D

Darwin, Charles Robert

1809–1882

English Naturalist

Charles Robert Darwin is best known for his book, *On the Origin of Species by Means of Natural Selection, or the Preservation of Favoured Races in the Struggle for Life,* the first edition of which was published in 1859. In this book he proposed the theory of natural selection and thus became the father of the theory of evolution. His theories and writings have had implications far beyond the boundaries of science, as they implicitly challenge the fundamentalist religious views of creationists.

Following his father's career path, Darwin began medical training in Edinburgh, Scotland, but could not stomach the dissections and found the lectures intolerably dull. So while in Edinburgh he spent much time naturalizing, and collected marine specimens with the local fishermen. At the age of 16, his first scientific contribution was on marine biology. He described powers of movement in the ova of the seamat *Flustra* and found that the black globules on a seaweed, *Haminthalia,* were the eggcases of a marine leech and not the reproductive organs of the seaweed. These early discoveries were the first indications of Darwin's meticulous powers of observation and critical approach to conventional beliefs. After dropping out of medicine, he began religious studies at Cambridge University, where he came under the

influence of the Reverend John Heslow (1796–1861), who had just become the university's first professor of botany. Henslow recommended Darwin for the post of naturalist on the round-the-world surveying cruise of the HMS *Beagle* (1831–36) under the command of Captain Robert Fitzroy (1805–65). At age 22, Darwin sailed on the cruise that was to change the course of his life.

Henslow gave him Charles Lyell's new book, *Principles of Geology,* to take on the cruise,

Charles Darwin. (From the collections of the Library of Congress)

279

instructing him to read it but on no account to believe it. Lyell had expounded the concepts of geological stratigraphy, arguing that rock strata had been laid down sequentially, so that younger rocks overlie older rocks. These ideas were considered revolutionary at the time. During the cruise Darwin recognized evidence of glaciations, sea-level rise, and vulcanism, and found fossil beds of extinct mammals. In his excursions to the Andes he found fossils of marine animals high up in the mountains and soon became convinced that Earth had a geological past and had not been created instantaneously. The visit of the *Beagle* to the Galápagos Archipelago, where each island is inhabited by similar but distinct varieties of giant tortoise, marine and land iguanas, and a bewildering assortment of finches, traditionally is considered to have been the inspiration for Darwin's ideas. Each island race was so similar to species found on the other islands that it seemed hard to believe that they were unrelated, but the immutability of species was a central tenet of Christian fundamentalist beliefs.

On his return Darwin began to work on and write up his collections and notes. He clearly regarded himself more as a geologist, and in 1842, 1844, and 1846 he produced three books: one on coral reefs, one on volcanic islands, and one on geological observations on South America. In *The Structure and Distribution of Coral Reefs* (1842), he proposed a theory on the origins of atolls. According to Darwin, the corals start to grow around the fringes of volcanic islands. The increasing burden of coralline rock weighs down the volcanic rocks, and the top of the island is eroded by waves. As the foundation rock sinks, the corals keep growing, forming a ring of islands around a central lagoon. Based on Darwin's theory, atolls are formed of coralline rocks built up on a foundation of volcanic rocks. His theory was eventually vindicated in 1953, when deep boreholes were drilled into Eniwetok Atoll. Another product of his *Beagle* collections was a taxonomic treatise on barnacles published in 1851, which remains to this day an important source of information on these economically important crustaceans.

Persistent poor health prevented him from going to sea again. In 1839 he married a cousin, Emma Wedgewood, a member of the wealthy family famous for the manufacture of porcelain, which provided him with an independent income. He was able to continue to research how species can be changed by selection, both naturally and by selective breeding. He was strongly influenced by the writing of Thomas Malthus (1766–1834), who had shown mathematically that while populations can grow geometrically, food resources increase arithmetically. So the question became: Could competition for food resources be the driving force that naturally selects the more successful individuals, thereby changing species over time? As early as 1837, Darwin began to write in his notebooks about how species can change. He drafted an outline of his theory and left it with a note to his wife to publish it if he died suddenly, but fearful of the storm it would raise, he held back from publishing his ideas. Darwin had become a recluse, but he developed a circle of intimate friends who regularly visited him and discussed his ideas. Among these was Thomas Henry Huxley (1825–95). When Alfred Russell Wallace (1823–1913), a self-funded animal collector in Malaysia, sent Darwin a draft of a paper "On the Tendencies of Varieties to Depart Indefinitely from the Original Type," independently outlining the concept of natural selection, Huxley persuaded Darwin to present his theory in public. So Darwin, jointly with Wallace, presented his theory to the Linnean Society in London in 1858, and in the following year Darwin published his book *On the Origin of Species*. It was an exhaustive compendium of the evidence Darwin had amassed over the preceding 20 years. It was divided into three main sections, dealing with variation, the struggle for existence, and the survival of the fittest, and there were two chapters on geographical distribution. Reaction built up to a crescendo when in June 1860 there was a tempestuous and acrimonious debate at the British Association for the Advancement of Science at Oxford. Darwin retired to the quiet of the countryside, while his champions argued publicly for his theory. In the years that followed he continued to carry out his research, which resulted in the publication of a series of books dealing with fertilization in orchids, variation of species under domestication, the descent of man, insectivorous plants, cross- and self-pollination in plants, plant movements, and the importance of earthworms.

Darwin was primarily a superb observer of the natural world. His approach was multidisciplinary, merging aspects of biology, geology, and social science. He found it impossible not to question basic beliefs when observation revealed serious inconsistencies. It is hard to appreciate just how difficult and dangerous it was at the time to question the fundamental views that underpinned religious beliefs and social attitudes. Darwin's book on natural selection liberated scientific thinking from the constraints of religious ideas and opened up new avenues of inquiry and research into the natural world. It was in this new atmosphere of scientific excitement and liberation that the *Challenger* expedition, which initiated modern oceanography, was planned and funded. Several of Darwin's champions became highly influential; for example, T. H. Huxley continued the social revolution by developing scientific education for the working classes. There is hardly an aspect of biological and social sciences that has remained untouched by Darwin's influence.

Martin Angel

BIOGRAPHY
- Charles Robert Darwin.
- Born 12 February 1809 in Shrewsbury, Shropshire, England.
- Enrolled to study medicine at the University of Edinburgh in Scotland in October 1825.
- Abandoned medicine in April 1827 and began to study divinity at Cambridge University in England.
- Appointed naturalist on the HMS *Beagle* on a round-the-world surveying cruise from 1831 to 1836.
- Launched his theory on natural selection to the Linnean Society in 1858.
- Published *On the Origin of Species by Means of Natural Selection* in 1859.
- Died 19 April 1882 in Downe, Kent, England.

SELECTED WRITINGS

Darwin, Charles. *The Voyage of the* Beagle, 1839.

———. *Monograph on the Sun-Class* Cirripedia, *with Figures of All the Species.* Vols. 1 and 2. London: Ray Society, 1851.

———. *Journal of Researches into the Natural History and Geology of Countries Visited During the Voyage Round the World of HMS* Beagle *Under Command of Captain Fitz Roy RN.* London: John Murray, 1912.

———. *The Structure and Distribution of Coral Reefs.* Berkeley, Calif.: University of California Press, 1962. Reprint.

———. *On the Origin of Species by Means of Natural Selection, or the Preservation of Favoured Races in the Struggle for Life.* 1859. Modern edition edited by Greg Suriano. New York: Gramercy Books, 1998.

FURTHER READING

Browne, E. Janet. *Charles Darwin.* London: Jonathan Cape; and New York: Knopf, 1995.

Darwin, Charles. *The Autobiography of Charles Darwin 1809–1882.* Nora Barlow, ed. London: Collins, 1958; reissue, New York: W. W. Norton, 1993.

Keynes, Richard Darwin. *The Beagle Record: Selections from the Original Pictorial Records and Written Accounts of the Voyage of HMS* Beagle. Cambridge and New York: Cambridge University Press, 1979.

Moorehead, Alan. *Darwin and the* Beagle. London: Hamish Hamilton/New York: Harper and Row, 1969.

Weiner, Jonathan. *The Beak of the Finch: A Story of Evolution in Our Time.* New York: Vintage Books, 1995.

RELATED ARTICLES

Coral Atoll; Coral Reef; Galápagos Spreading Center; HMS *Beagle*

DDT

DDT (dichlorodiphenyltrichloroethane) is a chlorinated hydrocarbon insecticide. Introduced in 1939, it is highly toxic to insects (but relatively less so to other animals) and remains active for years. During and after World War II, it was the mainstay of World Health Organization campaigns against insect-borne diseases in Africa and Southeast Asia. In developed countries, DDT was used extensively in agriculture.

DDT is normally applied by aerial spray. DDT enters the marine environment directly by aerial drift, through river runoff and sewage, or by blown dust. Problems with DDT stem from its persistence and its accumulation in the fatty tissues of animals. As a result of biological magnification, predators in the higher trophic levels of food chains may suffer negative effects from DDT bioaccumulation.

Rachel Carson's (1907–64) campaigning book *Silent Spring* (1963) raised awareness about the potential dangers of DDT. By the late 1960s and early 1970s, DDT pollution was being documented in the coastal waters off Los Angeles close to the world's largest manufacturer of DDT. Over two decades, a manufacturing plant had been releasing traces of DDT into the city's sewage system. Elevated levels of DDT (and its derivatives DDE and DDD) were found in tissue samples from local fauna. DDT was linked to the following deleterious effects: impairment of reproduction in local California sea lions, *Zalophus californianus*; catastrophic breeding failure in local populations of the brown pelican, *Pelacanus occidentialis*, due to eggshell thinning; and the death of Californian seagulls and cormorants in the Los Angeles Zoo. In 1969, seabird deaths in Monterey Bay, California, were attributed to runoff of pesticide-rich river water. DDT residue levels as high as 800 parts per million were found in the livers of dead seabirds.

In the northern hemisphere, DDT use was almost entirely phased out in 1972. In developing countries, DDT is still used where it is regarded as comparatively safe for the user applying it, and it is a cheap and effective pesticide. However, in the 1980s, king penguins in Antarctica contained detectable traces of DDT despite being thousands of kilometers from any region where DDT had been applied.

Thomas A. Davies

FURTHER READING
Beyer, W. Nelson, Gary H. Heinz, and Amy W. Redmon-Norwood, eds. *Environmental Contaminants in Wildlife.* Boca Raton, Fla.: Lewis Publishers, 1996.
Clark, R. B., Chris Frid, and Martin Attrill. *Marine Pollution.* Oxford: Clarendon Press/New York: Oxford University Press, 1986; 4th ed., Oxford and New York: Oxford University Press, 1997.
Mellanby, Kenneth. *The DDT Story.* Farnham, Surrey, England: British Crop Protection Council, 1992.

RELATED ARTICLES
Biological Magnification; Carson, Rachel Louise; Food Chain; Food Web; Pollution, Ocean

Deep-Ocean Circulation

The average depth of the oceans on Earth is about 4000 meters (2.5 miles or 13,000 feet). Although water moves much more slowly through the ocean depths than across the surface, deep-ocean circulation plays a vital role in the distribution of oxygen (and thus the maintenance of life) in the oceans and in the regulation of Earth's climate.

Factors Affecting Deep-Ocean Circulation

Heating a pan full of soup on a stove sets up a pattern of circulation throughout the liquid in a continuous loop of warming rising soup and cooling sinking soup known as a *convection current.* It was once supposed that such a process causes the circulation of water between the ocean surface and depths. German climatologist and traveler Alexander von Humboldt (1769–1859) suggested a convection model of ocean circulation in 1814. In his theory, waters near the equator are warmed, become less dense, rise to the surface, and are moved as surface currents toward the poles. At high latitudes they cool and become denser, plunge to the depths, and flow back along the bottom of the ocean to the equator, where the process continues.

Density changes do indeed drive the circulation of the deep oceans, but not in such a simple way. The circulation of water through the ocean depths is a convection process driven mainly by changes in temperature and salinity (saltiness). For this reason, the process is called *thermohaline circulation* (*thermo* means heat; *haline* means salt). At one end of this process, dense cold water is formed at the surface of the oceans near the polar regions. Its higher density causes it to sink and flow slowly toward the equator at depths greater than 2000 meters (6500 feet). The waters retain their temperature and salinity by which oceanographers trace this flow. Cold and sinking oxygen-rich water supplies the oxygen that maintains life in the deep sea. For every cubic meter of water that sinks into the deep ocean, another cubic meter must return to the surface elsewhere. The deep water formed in the high-latitude polar regions is returned to the surface through upwelling, which takes place mainly in low-latitude equatorial regions and along the eastern margins of the oceans.

Although fluid motions in the oceans are turbulent and complex, currents in the deep circulation can be regarded as a set of independently moving water layers or *water masses*. The thin, relatively low-density upper surface layer, about 100 to 300 meters (330 to 980 feet) deep, is heated by the Sun. Surface currents are largely wind-driven and move faster than deep currents, typically with speeds of 25 to 250 centimeters per second (0.5 to 5 knots). But the greatest volume of ocean waters exists in the cold depths beneath the surface layer. This region consists of several layers of water sliding past one another. When dense water sinks from the surface, it descends until it reaches a layer of water of the same density. These density layers flow toward the equator, maintaining their salinity and temperature characteristics with limited mixing between them. Thermohaline circulation is much slower than wind-driven circulation (with typical speeds of a few centimeters per second or less). However, the volume of water in the thermohaline circulation is 10 times greater than that in surface currents.

Circulation in the Ocean Basins

Since the comprehensive worldwide oceanographic cruises during the 1920s and 1930s, oceanographers such as Georg Wust (1890–1977) and Harald Sverdrup (1888–1957) showed that deep waters are formed primarily in two areas: the East Greenland Sea in the North Atlantic and the Weddell Sea in the South Atlantic. It is notable that little deep water is formed in the Pacific and Indian Oceans. These oceanographers traced the movement or spreading of water masses based on their salinity and temperature.

The warm salty Gulf Stream waters lose heat to the atmosphere in high latitudes and mix with the cool, lower-salinity waters in the Norwegian Sea. During the winter this water may have a temperature of -1.5°C (29°F) and a salinity of about 35 practical salinity units (grams of salt per kilogram of water). By the time this water mass sinks below 1000 meters (3300 feet) it has mixed with surrounding waters and has a temperature of 3 to 4°C (37 to 39°F) with a salinity of 34.9 psu. This water mass is called the *North Atlantic Deep Water* (NADW) and fills the North Atlantic from 1000 meters (3300 feet) to the bottom. A tremendous volume of NADW water (estimated to be equivalent to around 100 times that of the Amazon River) flows southward through the deep ocean toward the equator at a speed of a few inches per second.

The NADW flow is deflected by the Coriolis force and moves southward along the western side of the Atlantic. Flow of the NADW can be traced to about 35°S latitude. Here it meets water flowing northward from the other main source of deep water, the *Antarctic Bottom Water* (AABW) formed in the Weddell Sea off Antarctica. Deep waters derived from the AABW and NADW flow eastward around Antarctica as a water mass called *Recirculated Deep Water* (RDW). These deep waters are part of the Antarctic Circumpolar Current. This RDW flows northward from the Circumpolar Current into the Indian and Pacific Oceans.

The American oceanographer Henry Stommel (1920–92) showed that the spreading of the ocean's deep waters is affected by the Coriolis force. Water flows along the eastern sides of the deep ocean basins in the Indian and Pacific as well as in the Atlantic. Deepwater flow into the North Pacific is confined to the Samoan Gap, which is a break in the mid-ocean ridge system. Gradually, the deep water returns to the surface by mixing with the warmer, less dense water in the layers above.

Oceanographers identify a number of distinct water masses in the ocean basins, which are characterized by their different salinity, temperature, and oxygen content. In addition to the NADW, AABW, and RDW mentioned earlier, high-salinity outflows from the Mediterranean and Red Seas increase the salinity of the deep waters. The Mediterranean outflow is partially responsible for the high salinity of the NADW. The Red Sea outflow is relatively low in volume and changes the temperature–salinity characteristics of deep Indian Ocean waters only locally. It is notable that the North Pacific has no large source of deep water because of its low surface salinity (less than 33 psu). Deep water flows into the North Pacific only from the RDW.

The Atlantic Ocean provides the main highway between the northern and southern sources of deep water and supplies deep waters and dissolved oxygen to the other ocean basins. Unlike the Atlantic, the Indian and Pacific Oceans have no sources of deep water, and their deep-ocean currents are weaker. Due to the continual respiration of animals and bacteria in the deep sea, the oxygen concentration in the deep Indian Ocean is less than that in the Atlantic, and the oxygen concentration in the North Pacific is lower still.

The Great Conveyor

Although different processes cause deep- and surface-water circulation, they are clearly interrelated. A model proposed by the contemporary U.S. oceanographer Wallace Broecker (1931–) combines both types of circulation into what appears to be a gigantic conveyor belt that twists and turns around the Atlantic, Pacific, and Indian Oceans carrying warm surface water north and cold deep water south. The global conveyor takes a warm surface current from the tip of South Africa up through the Atlantic in the form of the Gulf Stream, which eventually flows into the deepwater source just south of Greenland. There the current becomes saltier and sinks deep into the ocean, flowing as a western boundary current through the North and South Atlantic back to Antarctica. As it flows around Antarctica just to the north of the Antarctic Circle, some of the cold deep current flows into the Indian and Pacific Oceans. There it rises slowly back to the surface before rejoining the loop that flows back around South Africa. The speed of the conveyor belt circulation is of great interest and is the central topic in the World Ocean Circulation Experiment. This speed is related to how well the oceans will absorb carbon dioxide, which is thought to be a major factor in global warming.

Measuring Deep-Ocean Circulation

Deepwater currents move more slowly than those on the surface, and their flow is not measured using current meters. Neutrally buoyant aluminum cylinders, called *Swallow floats* after their British inventor J. C. Swallow (1817–99), float at predetermined depths. The floats emit sound pulses so that shore stations can track them. The changes in their position provide a measure of deep current movement. These floats show that in some instances deepwater current speeds are as fast as surface currents, but the motion is more chaotic, so that the net movement is small.

Radioactive chemical tracers such as carbon-14 and tritium, hydrogen-3, provide an indirect measure of deep-sea currents. By measuring hydrogen-3 concentrations in the North Atlantic, oceanographers have observed over the past 40 years the gradual southward movement of a plume of tritium. Since atomic explosions released tritium over a relatively short time, oceanographers can estimate the deep circulation rate. Estimates of the thermohaline circulation time or *residence time* of deep-ocean waters are not precise. They vary from about 500 years for deep Atlantic waters to perhaps 1000 years for the deep Pacific. This is still a matter of great interest that requires further investigation.

William W. Broenkow

FURTHER READING
Bond, G. C. "Climate and the Conveyor." *Nature*, 5 October 1995, p. 383.
Broecker, Wallace S. "Chaotic Climate." *Scientific American*, November 1995, p. 44.
Broecker, Wallace S., Stewart Sutherland, and Tsung-Hung Peng. "A Possible 20th-Century Slowdown of Southern Ocean Deep Water Formation." *Science*, 5 November 1999, p. 1132.
Calvin, William H. "The Great Climate Flip-Flop." *Atlantic Monthly*, January 1998, p. 47.
King, Cuchlaine. *Introduction to Physical and Biological Oceanography*. London: Edward Arnold, 1975.
Piccard, George L. *Descriptive Physical Oceanography*. Oxford and New York: Pergamon Press, 1964; 5th ed., Oxford and Boston: Butterworth-Heinemann, 1990.
Stewart, R.W. "The Atmosphere and the Oceans." In *Scientific American: The Oceans*. San Francisco: W. H. Freeman, 1969.
Stowe, Keith. *Exploring Ocean Science*. New York: Wiley, 1996.
Woods, J. D. "The World Ocean Circulation Experiment." *Nature*, 11 April 1985, p. 501.

RELATED ARTICLES
Climate Change; Coriolis Effect; Ocean Current; Salinity; Thermohaline Circulation; Upwelling

Deep-Scattering Layers

Deep-scattering layers are layers within bodies of water that strongly reflect sonar sound signals. Water is highly transparent to sound, especially low-frequency sound. Whales use sound both to echolocate and to communicate with other whales over long distances. Low-frequency sounds are used by geologists to explore structures within the seabed, by hydrographers to measure the depth of the ocean, and by oceanographers to measure currents and to control and communicate with instruments deployed in the sea.

Echo sounders were first used to measure the bathymetric depth of the ocean by recording the time it took for a pulse of sound transmitted from a ship to be reflected back from the seabed. As a result, signals sometimes indicated that the seabed was unexpectedly shallow. Therefore, early charts based on echo sounding often indicated dangerous shoals, when in actuality the seabed is thousands of feet deep. It was soon observed that some of the aberrant bottom signals were migrating up and down at dawn and dusk and were probably the result of biological activity. Moreover, when different sound frequencies were used, layers appeared at different depths. These strongly reflecting layers were named *deep-scattering layers* (DSLs).

Any object suspended in the water that has markedly different acoustic properties to the water and is larger than half a wavelength of the sound will scatter and reflect the sound. A frequency commonly used for echo sounding is 10 kilohertz. Sound at this frequency is most efficiently reflected by objects larger than 10 centimeters (4 inches), but high concentrations of smaller objects will also scatter it as a result of interference. Gas bubbles are good reflectors, so during stormy weather when air bubbles are injected deep into the water by breaking waves, the sound signals can be strongly disrupted in the top 30 meters (100 feet) of the water column. The gas-filled swim bladders of fish and the floats of siphonophores are very good acoustic targets, as are dense objects such as the shells of pteropods. Close to the seabed in shallow seas, sediment resuspended by storm waves or strong tidal currents can scatter the sound. Many DSLs result from the sound being reflected by concentrations of fish or siphonophores, and the characteristics of the layers—intensity, depth, and movement—are used to study the ecology of these organisms. Although sounds of higher frequency do not penetrate deep into the ocean, they are more effective at detecting the presence of the smaller organisms. Sound of 70 kilohertz penetrates about 300 meters (1000 feet) and detects 1-centimeter (0.39-inch) animals and therefore detects DSLs at quite different depths. These smaller planktonic animals tend to drift passively with the local water currents, so oceanographers are now measuring the slight changes in frequency caused by particles moving either toward or away from the observer, called the *Doppler shift. Acoustic Doppler current profilers* (ADCPs) are now being used both to measure fine-scale current patterns in the water and to monitor the mean behavior and abundance of the planktonic community in a noninvasive manner. The simultaneous use of several sound frequencies is now employed both by oceanographers and commercial fishermen to locate and characterize fish shoals and different types of seabed.

Martin Angel

FURTHER READING

Greene, Charles H., Timothy K. Stanton, and Kurt M. Fristop, eds. "Bioacoustical Oceanography." *Deep-Sea Research II*, Vol. 45, No. 7 (1998).

Marshall, Norman B. *Developments in Deep-Sea Biology.* Poole, England: Blandford Press, 1979.

USEFUL WEB SITES

"Classroom BATS."
<http://www.coexploration.org/bbsr/classroombats/index.html>.

RELATED ARTICLES

Acoustic Doppler Current Profiler; Acoustic Oceanography; Echolocation; Sonar

Deep Sea

The deep sea is usually considered to be the part of the ocean that lies beyond the edge of the continental slope, where depths suddenly plunge from about 200 meters (650 feet) to far greater depths.

The ocean is the largest single habitat on Earth. Seawater covers 71 percent of the world's surface to an average depth of 3800 meters (12,500 feet). Continental shelf seas between 0 and 200 meters (0 to 650 feet) deep cover about 5 percent of this area. Therefore, the other 66 percent is deep sea. It includes the continental slopes where depths range from 200 to 3000 meters (650 to 9850 feet) and cover 13 percent of Earth's surface, the abyss where depths range from 3000 to 6000 meters (9850 to 19,700 feet) and cover 51 percent of Earth, and hadal depths, which are deeper than 6000 meters (19,700 feet) and cover less than 2 percent. The total volume of the oceans is 1.37 billion cubic kilometers (1 billion is 10^9; 330 million cubic miles), and it provides a living space that has been estimated to be 168 times greater than that of all terrestrial habitats. This immense volume of seawater contributes about 0.24 percent of the total mass of Earth and has a major influence on its climate. Sunlight cannot reach the deep ocean where it is deeper than about 1000 meters (3280 feet); therefore, it is permanently dark. So the most voluminous environment of Earth, encompassing about 75 percent of the biosphere, is totally dark. In this environment many of the environmental factors whose variability generates so much of the ecological and species diversity that is prevalent on land and in shallow waters hardly vary at all in either time or space. For example, temperatures at depths deeper than 1000 meters (3280 feet) in all the major oceans of the world range only from −1.9 to 5°C (28.5 to 41°F). Over the last 30 million years the temperatures of the deep ocean have gradually cooled from about 10°C (50°F).

Thermohaline Circulation

The deep ocean is kept well stirred by the large-scale thermohaline circulation. This is driven by the formation of Bottom Water, which occurs mostly in the Weddell Sea in the Southern Ocean, but until about a decade ago was also taking place off Greenland in the northwest Atlantic. When seawater freezes [at a temperature of about −1.9°C (28.5°F)] the ice is free of salt, so the water left behind unfrozen is not only cold but also saltier. It is then denser than its surroundings and sinks. Since the colder it becomes, the more gas the water will dissolve, this sinking water carries down rich supplies of oxygen. Therefore, the deep ocean is constantly being "ventilated" with fresh supplies of oxygen.

The water that sinks into the deep ocean in these polar regions displaces the deep water in other regions upward, especially in the tropics. This process stirs (or "turns over") the world's ocean completely every 1500 years. This also explains why the oceans get cooler as the depth increases. At the surface the winds constantly drive relatively warm, fresh water toward the poles, predominantly via the vigorous currents that flow poleward along the eastern boundaries of the continents (e.g., the Gulf Stream in the North Atlantic and the Kuroshio off Japan in the North Pacific).

Light in the Deep Sea

Another important ecological property of water is that it scatters and absorbs light. The shorter ultraviolet wavelengths and the longer red wavelengths are absorbed faster than the blue-green wavelengths. So as depth increases, the color balance becomes more monochromatic (blue-green) with depth. In the upper 1000 meters (3280 feet) light plays a major role in the ecology, but this role wanes once daylight is no longer detectable. In the euphotic zone [about the upper 100 meters (328 feet)], sunlight is one of the key factors regulating the rate of photosynthesis, the process whereby the plants (the phytoplankton) use radiant energy from the sun to convert carbon dioxide and water into organic compounds. Pure water scatters light, but this tendency is greatly enhanced as more and more particles are carried in suspension (just as smoke and steam scatter light in the atmosphere); therefore, the higher the particle loading, the more rapidly the intensity of the light is reduced (attenuated) with depth. Profiles of light intensity and the changes in color balance largely determine the ecological zonation of the communities in the upper ocean through adaptations to counter visual predation.

Pressure

As depth increases, the hydrostatic pressure resulting from the weight of the overlying water also increases. At the surface, an organism is subjected to atmospheric pressure; if it descends 10 meters (33 feet), the pressure increases by 1 kilogram per square centimeter (14 pounds per square inch), equivalent to the mean atmospheric pressure. Therefore, at a depth of 1000 meters (3280 feet) an organism is subjected to a pressure about 100 times the average atmospheric pressure, or 100 atmospheres. Seawater is only slightly compressible, and at a depth of 4000 meters (13,120 feet), its volume is reduced by a factor of nearly 1.0485 and it becomes slightly more viscous. In contrast, gases are highly compressible, and a doubling of the pressure decreases a gas's volume approximately in half and doubles its density, therefore reducing the effectiveness of gas bladders as a means of regulating buoyancy. Gases also become far more soluble with increasing pressure. So not only does it become harder to extract oxygen from the water and to secrete gases into a gas bladder, but also calcium carbonate, which is virtually insoluble in shallow water because it has a weak tendency to dissociate into carbon dioxide, dissolves at great depths. Therefore, the sediments that are deposited on the seabed in the North Atlantic at depths of 4000 meters (13,120 feet) are rich in calcium carbonate derived from the skeletons of planktonic organisms, whereas the red clays found in the Pacific at greater depths are entirely lacking in carbonates.

Vertical Gradients

Gradients of ecological parameters are much stronger in the vertical plane than in the horizontal. The temperature difference between the surface and a depth of 1 kilometer (3280 feet), which in the tropics may exceed 20°C (68°F), may be equaled only over distances of thousands of kilometers at the surface. Because the strongest and most predictable gradients are vertical, distributional patterns of species and their morphological and physiological characteristics are often closely controlled by the adaptations needed to ensure survival within limited sectors of these vertical gradients.

The strength and interaction of the vertical gradients result in the pelagic and benthic communities being organized into depth zones inhabited by different species with distinctive morphological and physiological characteristics. The pelagic zones are the epipelagic, mesopelagic, bathypelagic, abyssopelagic, and hadalpelagic, whereas the benthic zones are sublittoral or continental shelf, bathyal, abyssal, and hadal. The boundaries between these zones are rarely sharp discontinuities; rather, they tend to be steep clines extending over tens of meters and also to fluctuate in time and space as the physical factors regulating the zonation fluctuate.

Almost all the food utilized by deep-sea animals is derived from particles sinking under the influence of gravity or carried by water laden with particles, flowing downslope near the bottom. Only about 0.3 percent is derived from chemosynthesis at hydrothermal vents and hydrocarbon seeps. There are no herbivores in deep water, and the feeding guilds are limited to consumers of detritus, scavengers feeding off the carcasses of large animals, and carnivores. It takes a long time for small particles to sink into deep water, so most of their organic matter is either consumed by shallower-living species or is broken down by bacteria. Only about 1 to 3 percent of organic material produced near the surface reaches the seabed at abyssal depths, so the biomass of the deep-living populations is very small and does not support many carnivores. Almost without exception, the species are adapted to conserving energy reserves, so the pace of life in the deep sea is extremely slow.

Most of the fish species that inhabit the near-surface waters of the ocean by day are countershaded. However, below about 250 meters (820 feet) the vertical distribution of light intensity becomes symmetrical; the brightest light comes from vertically overhead and the dimmest is backscattered from below. A mirror hung in the water reflects light of the same intensity and color balance as its background and thus is perfectly camouflaged. The dominant fishes (e.g., lantern and hatchet fish) have black backs, mirror sides, and lines of ventral photophores. The dominant prawn species (e.g., decapod crustaceans) are half red and half transparent. Their red coloration comes from a red carotenoid pigment that can be synthesized only by plants and has to be obtained from their food. As bright as their color appears in daylight, at the depths at which they live it is black because there is no red light to be reflected. The carotenoid has another advantage; it absorbs blue-green light, which is the color not only of the residual daylight but also of most bioluminescence.

At depths of 700 to 1000 meters (2300 to 3280 feet), the mirror-sided fishes are replaced with species that are uniformly black, and the prawns are replaced with species that are uniformly red. These are depths that are permanently dark except for light produced by the organisms themselves.

Martin Angel

FURTHER READING

Angel, Martin V. "What Is the Deep-Sea?" In David J. Randall and Anthony P. Farrell, eds., *Deep-Sea Fishes.* San Diego: Academic Press, 1997; pp. 2–41.

Marshall, Norman B. *Developments in Deep-Sea Biology.* Poole, England: Blandford Press, 1979.

Nybakken, James W. *Marine Biology: An Ecological Approach,* 5th ed. San Francisco: Benjamin Cummings, 2001.

Thurman, Harold V. *Essentials of Oceanography.* Columbus, Ohio: Charles E. Merrill, 1983; 6th ed., with Alan P. Trujillo, Upper Saddle River, N.J.: Prentice Hall, 1999.

RELATED ARTICLES

Benthic Boundary Layer; Bioluminescence; Bottom Water Formation; Chemosynthesis; Continental Shelf; Continental Slope; Euphotic Zone; Gulf Stream; Hydrocarbon Seep; Hydrothermal Vent; Kuroshio; Ocean Current; Pelagic; Photophore; Southern Ocean; Thermohaline Circulation; Weddell Sea

Deep-Sea Channel

Deep-sea channels are products of seafloor sedimentation by debris flows and turbidity currents. Our ability to map these intriguing features has improved immensely with the advent of modern geophysical technology, especially high-resolution seismic-reflection profilers and side-scan sonar. Precise mapping demonstrates that deep-sea channels and large rivers share many things in common. Some channels evolve as individual entities whereas others form parts of larger depositional systems known as submarine fans.

Truly spectacular deep-sea channels stretch for more than 3000 kilometers (1865 miles), farther than the driving distance from Chicago to San Francisco. One such example is the Northwest Atlantic Mid-Ocean Channel, which begins in the Labrador Sea and extends onto Sohm Abyssal Plain. Its channel floor is from 1500 to 7500 meters (4920 to 24,610 feet) wide, and relief from axis to levee crest measures 100 to 200 meters (330 to 660 feet). Another noteworthy example is Cascadia Channel, located in the northeast Pacific Ocean.

There are three basic varieties of deep-sea channel growth, as viewed in cross-sectional profile: depositional, mixed (erosional–depositional), and erosional. The floor of a depositional channel builds up above a succession of flat-lying beds, and constructional levees rise above the adjacent sediment plain on either side of the channel axis (thalweg). Levees on the right-hand side (looking downchannel) in the northern hemisphere are usually higher than those on the left. This distinctive asymmetry develops gradually because of the Coriolis effect, which deflects turbidity currents during transport. Some channels are classified as mixed because they display many of these same features but also show truncation of older strata on channel walls and levees, plus incision of the channel floor into the abyssal plain. With an erosional channel, beds are sharply truncated on both walls, and terraces or benches typically develop within the channel axis. A submarine canyon is a larger version of an erosional channel.

Some deep-sea channels develop sensational patterns of curvature analogous to meander loops around fluvial point bars. A strong correlation seems to exist between channel sinuosity and downstream valley slope. In general, channel sinuosity first increases as valley slope flattens (to a site-specific maximum) but then decreases with further flattening. Worldwide comparisons allow scientists to identify geometric end members (i.e., high-sinuosity/low-gradient versus low-sinuosity/high-gradient), but there are also large amounts of variability across the continuum observed. Several additional parameters, therefore, must influence deep-sea channel shape, including sediment load (i.e., coarse-grained sand and gravel versus fine-grained mud), the physical process of flow (i.e., low-density turbidity current versus viscous debris flow), and basin morphology. The distal end of Cascadia Channel provides a vivid example of how tectonic features can control channel pathways; its route and map-view geometry are restricted by basement relief on the Blanco Fracture Zone.

Coring transects demonstrate that sediment accumulations on channel floors are distinctly different from those on adjacent levees. Thick deposits of poorly sorted sand and gravel typically cover channel floors as products of debris flows and channel-confined high-density turbidity currents. Levee deposits, in contrast, consist of thin rhythmic interbeds of terrigenous silt and hemipelagic mud (biogenic silty clay), with sporadic lenses of silty sand to coarse sand. Levee deposition occurs via spillover of the upper parts of turbidity currents and vertical settling of suspended mud, similar to the behavior of river floodwaters.

On worldwide average, sediment discharge through deep-sea channels increases during times of lowered sea level because lowstand conditions promote efficient bypassing of continental shelves. Practical interest in modern deep-sea channel-levee complexes relates mostly to exploration for hydrocarbons; deeply buried channel sands commonly act as excellent petroleum reservoirs.

Michael B. Underwood

FURTHER READING

Chough, S., and Reinhard Hesse. "Submarine Meandering Thalweg and Turbidity Currents Flowing for 4,000 km in the Northwest Atlantic Mid-Ocean Channel, Labrador Sea." *Geology*, Vol. 4 (1976), pp. 529–533.

Clark, J. D., N. H. Kenyon, and K. T. Pickering. "Quantitative Analysis of the Geometry of Submarine Channels: Implications for the Classification of Submarine Fans." *Geology*, Vol. 20 (1992), pp. 633–636.

Clark, J. D., and K. T. Pickering. "Architectural Elements and Growth Patterns of Submarine Channels: Application to Hydrocarbon Exploration." *American Association of Petroleum Geologists Bulletin*, Vol. 80 (1996), pp. 194–221.

Flood, Roger D., and John E. Damuth. "Quantitative Characteristics of Sinuous Distributary Channels on the Amazon Deep-Sea Fan." *Geological Society of America Bulletin*, Vol. 98 (1987), pp. 728–738.

Gardner, James V., Michael E. Field, and David C. Twichell, eds. *Geology of the United States Seafloor: The View from GLORIA*. New York: Cambridge University Press, 1996.

Griggs, G. B., and L. D. Kulm. "Sedimentation in Cascadia Deep-Sea Channel." *Geological Society of America Bulletin*, Vol. 81 (1970), pp. 1361–1384.

Nelson, C. Hans, and L. D. Kulm. "Submarine Fans and Channels." In *Turbidites and Deep Water Sedimentation*. Los Angeles: Pacific Section Society of Economic Paleontologists and Mineralogists, 1973; pp. 39–78.

RELATED ARTICLES
Cascadia Deep-Sea Channel; Coriolis Effect; Submarine Canyon; Submarine Fan; Turbidity Current

Deep Sea Drilling Project

The Deep Sea Drilling Project (DSDP) was the first program to conduct a worldwide sampling of the sediments and rocks deep beneath the floors of the oceans. The most ambitious Earth science program of its time, DSDP results led to fundamental changes in our understanding of Earth. The operational phase of DSDP began in August 1968 as an 18-month program to explore the central Atlantic and Pacific Oceans. The program immediately produced such novel and exciting findings, however, that it was extended successively. Ultimately, drilling took place in all the major oceans (except the Arctic), as well as the Caribbean and Mediterranean Seas. In the 15 years of DSDP, its drillship, *Glomar Challenger*, occupied 624 sites, operating in water as deep as 6 kilometers (19,700 feet) and collecting 96 kilometers (60 miles) of core material for scientific study.

One of the earliest and most significant scientific results of DSDP was to show that beneath the sediments of the deep-ocean floor the rocks of Earth's crust increase in age with distance from the mid-ocean ridge crest, as required by the process of seafloor spreading. Furthermore, drilling showed that the age of the seafloor corresponds to that predicted from the magnetic anomaly patterns, and no rocks older than Jurassic (205 to 142 million years ago) were found anywhere. These findings provided fundamental evidence for plate tectonics, the theory that has revolutionized our understanding of the solid Earth and its evolution.

DSDP made it possible, for the first time, to sample the entire oceanic sedimentary record, enabling geologists to document the composition and distribution of sediments in space and time, and leading to major advances in deep-sea stratigraphy, micropaleontology, and biostratigraphy. Changes in deep-sea sediment composition and distribution record changes in deep-ocean circulation and chemistry, and the field of paleoceanography has developed as a distinct specialty founded almost entirely on samples and data gathered by ocean drilling.

Many significant discoveries could not have been made without deep-sea drilling. Among these was the startling discovery that near the end of the Miocene (5 to 3 million years ago) the Mediterranean had rapidly dried up and then refilled, more than once! This catastrophe resulted from relatively minor tectonic events affecting the connection between the Atlantic and the Mediterranean. Not only did this discovery completely change our understanding of the history of the Mediterranean region, it also challenged accepted uniformitarian dogma and

Glomar Challenger. (*SIO Archives, UCSD*)

helped foster a new appreciation of the role of rare, catastrophic events in Earth's history.

Given the strong emphasis on scientific discovery, rather than technology development, DSDP basically adapted established oilfield drilling techniques. However, the project made significant innovations in deep-water drill hole reentry, heave compensation (to decouple the drill string from the vertical motion of the ship), and hydraulic piston coring (for sampling soft sediments), which have since been developed further and are now widely used in the offshore industry.

Scripps Institution of Oceanography managed DSDP under a contract from the U.S. National Science Foundation. Joint Oceanographic Institutions for Deep Earth Sampling (JOIDES, a consortium of major oceanographic institutions) provided scientific direction. Although begun as a U.S. endeavor, DSDP was always international in spirit. In 1975 its international character was recognized with the establishment of the International Phase of Ocean Drilling (IPOD). During IPOD (1975–83), France, Germany, Japan, the Soviet Union, and the United Kingdom contributed to the operational costs of the program, and membership in JOIDES was broadened to include representative organizations from all the partner countries. DSDP ended in 1983 with the start of a new endeavor, the Ocean Drilling Program, but the impact of the project continues to reverberate through the Earth sciences.

Trevor Day

FURTHER READING
Detailed scientific results from the Deep Sea Drilling Project can be found in the following series: *Initial Reports of the Deep Sea Drilling Project.* Washington D.C.: U.S. Government Printing Office, 1969–1986; 96 vols.
Hsu, K. J. *The Mediterranean Was a Desert: A Voyage of the* Glomar Challenger. Princeton, N.J.: Princeton University Press, 1983.
Maxwell, A. E. "An Abridged History of Deep Ocean Drilling." *Oceanus*, Vol. 36, No. 4 (1993), pp. 8–12.
Winterer, E. L. "Scientific Ocean Drilling, from AMSOC to COMPOST." In *50 Years of Ocean Discovery: National Science Foundation, 1950–2000.* Washington, D.C.: National Academy Press, 2000; pp. 117–127.

RELATED ARTICLES
Deep-Sea Sediments; Deep-Sea Stratigraphy; *Glomar Challenger*; Magnetic Anomaly; Mediterranean Sea; Paleoceanography; Plate Tectonics; Seafloor Spreading

Deep-Sea Exploration

The oceans occupy over two-thirds of Earth and their deepest point is almost 11 kilometers (7 miles) beneath the surface, so it is perhaps not surprising that only 5 percent of their volume has been surveyed properly. But as oceanographers frequently point out, that achievement seems less impressive given that space scientists have completely surveyed the surface of the Moon. Not surprisingly, the deepest parts of the oceans are the least well understood. Yet although many techniques have been devised for exploring the ocean depths, the benefits of deep-sea exploration are uncertain and the costs have frequently proved prohibitive.

Techniques

Because pressure increases with distance beneath the ocean surface, the ocean depths are a hostile and largely inaccessible environment for human explorers. Recreational scuba divers, for example, seldom dive below depths of around 40 meters (130 feet), and even deep-sea divers have never ventured below 460 meters (1500 feet), which is less than 5 percent of the depth of the Mariana Trench (the deepest known part of the oceans). Geological exploration of the seabed can be carried out using seismic equipment or by drilling ships such as the *Glomar Challenger* and the *JOIDES Resolution*. But geological data are only one kind of information about the deep sea. Ideally, oceanographers need to travel to the deepest parts of the ocean themselves to see and interpret things that may never have been studied before; as one oceanographer put it, the human brain is still "the best portable computer around." This means that to study the ocean depths, researchers must continue to use submarines (large vessels that can remain underwater for long periods), submersibles (smaller vessels designed for voyages of perhaps a few hours), remotely operated vehicles (ROVs) tethered by fiber-optic or other cables to ships or submersibles, or autonomous underwater vehicles (AUVs), robotic machines that explore entirely under computer control.

All of these techniques have been used with great success. In 1999, in its last mission before decommissioning, the nuclear submarine USS *Hawkbill* was used to map uncharted areas of the Arctic seafloor in a U.S. Navy program called Science Ice Expeditions (SCICEX). The veteran submersible *Alvin*, operated by Woods Hole Oceanographic Institution (WHOI), can explore down to 4500 meters (15,000 feet). WHOI's tethered ROV, *Jason*, can reach depths of 6000 meters (20,000 feet). A Japanese ROV, *Kaiko*, came close to equaling the world record for deep-sea exploration (held by the manned vessel *Trieste*) in March 1995. ROVs and AUVs are used increasingly in commercial and scientific applications. It is estimated that around 3000 ROVs were in commercial operation at the start of 2000.

Costs

Whether or not deep-sea exploration is as great a technical challenge as space exploration, it does not come cheap. Now costing around U.S.$2 billion apiece, large submarines are prohibitively expensive for general underwater exploration, although they can be hired for short periods, and some military resources were diverted for scientific research (such as the SCICEX expeditions) at the end of the Cold War. *Alvin* was completed in 1964 at a cost of U.S.$472,517, but the cost of

developing a sophisticated new submersible, such as the world's deepest diving vessel, *Shinkai* 6500, has been estimated at around U.S.$100 million, not including the cost of the base ship, and with running costs probably adding around U.S.$10,000 to $20,000 a day. Submersibles can be built more cheaply, however. Graham Hawkes, designer of a sleek one-person submersible called *Deep Flight I*, estimates that his vessel could be built for just U.S.$5 million.

Submersibles are much less commonly used now than in the early 1970s because AUVs and ROVs can be built and operated more cheaply. Small commercial ROVs cost U.S.$50,000 to $150,000, but the 9.5-tonne (10.5-ton) Japanese ROV *Kaiko* cost U.S.$41.5 million. AUVs typically cost U.S.$50,000 to $100,000, with onboard instruments often costing more than the robotic vehicle itself.

The end of the Cold War brought about drastic reductions in defense spending in some countries and reduced substantially the funds available for deep-sea exploration, but some countries continue to invest heavily. In the late 1990s, the Japan Marine Science and Technology Center (JAMSTEC) received an additional U.S.$100 million funding just to produce AUVs and deep-sea observatories. By contrast, a high-profile 1998 initiative from the Clinton administration called "Exploring the last U.S. frontier" made available just U.S.$12 million to expand two shallow-water observatories, build two deep-water observatories (in the Gulf of Mexico and the Juan de Fuca Ridge), and build new submersibles.

Benefits

Assessing the merits of deep-sea exploration is a matter of balancing fairly certain short-term financial costs against highly uncertain long-term gains. The commercial benefits of discovering petroleum reserves increase almost daily as world production of the mineral approaches a point of inevitable decline. Petroleum companies are now committed to deep-sea exploration, and ROVs and AUVs have proved invaluable for surveying prospective deep-water fields where ship-based surveys become expensive and problematic. Deep-sea mining of polymetallic nodules has long been promoted as a valuable source of metals. But fluctuations in world metal prices, exaggerated estimates of mineral reserves, and economic restrictions imposed by the U.N. Conference on the Law of the Sea (UNCLOS) make commercial feasibility uncertain. The oceans are also the source of important chemicals and medicines (the AIDS treatment drug AZT, for example, is derived from herring), and biotechnology companies are showing increasing interest in deep-sea organisms as a source of new genetic material. Ironically, one of the greatest immediate commercial benefits lies in the construction of equipment for deep-sea exploration, a rapidly growing market already worth hundreds of millions of dollars each year.

Although it is seldom possible to attach a monetary value to greater scientific understanding, the U.S. National Oceanic and Atmospheric Administration (NOAA) has estimated that its comprehensive 1997–98 El Niño forecast was worth around U.S.$250 million to the country's agricultural industry. The NOAA estimates that better climate prediction is worth around U.S.$2.7 billion annually to the United States alone; deep-sea research, such as the climate study conducted by the USS *Hawkbill* in 1999, can make an invaluable contribution to this.

From the books of Jules Verne (1828–1905) to the films of Jacques Cousteau (1910–1997), undersea exploration has long captivated the public interest. Recreational scuba diving generates billions of dollars of tourist income around the world; some believe that deep-sea tourism might one day do the same, earning revenue for important scientific programs. Some 57 submersibles have been built to carry paying passengers, of which 30 are still operating. Tourist trips to the wreck of the *Titanic*, costing U.S.$30,000 a head, have been used to finance further studies of the site.

Sometimes the benefits of deep-sea oceanography pay off in unexpected ways. Many years of deep-sea research led to the U.S. Navy's SOSUS array of underwater hydrophones, constructed between 1949 and 1952 to listen for enemy submarines, initially at a cost of just U.S.$1 million. According to Admiral Paul Gaffney (1950–), Chief of Naval Research, U.S. Navy, the ultimate cost of U.S.$16 billion was "repeatedly justified," not least because it "contributed significantly" to the end of the Cold War. More recently, the SOSUS array has been used to study whale populations and hydrothermal vents through acoustic oceanography.

Is It Worth It?

Opinions differ on whether the cost of deep-sea exploration justifies the expense. Some advocates of deep-sea exploration, such as Bruce Robison of Monterey Bay Aquarium Research Institute, are highly persuasive: "I can guarantee you that the discoveries beneficial to mankind will far outweigh those of the space program over the next couple of decades. If we can get to the abyss regularly, there will be immediate payoffs." Others, such as deep-sea explorer and *Titanic* discoverer Robert Ballard (1942–), disagree: "I believe that the deep sea has very little to offer. I've been there. I've spent a career there. I don't see the future there."

Those convinced of the need to explore the deep-sea debate the merits of investing in different technologies, from new generations of AUVs and ROVs to small and light submersibles such as *Deep Flight*, and proposals to "merge" the Woods Hole *Alvin* and former U.S. Navy *Sea Cliff* submersible to create a vessel capable of diving down to 9000 meters (29,500 feet). Cuts in defense funding have prompted oceanographers to explore new sources of sponsorship, such as the television stations that helped underwrite the construction of the *Deep*

Flight submersibles and the many corporate sponsors who help to finance the Woods Hole *Jason* Project. The future may lie in collaborations, such as the U.S. National Oceanographic Partnership Program (NOPP), in which the NOAA works jointly with 11 other bodies on oceanographic projects, and a mooted European oceanographic agency similar to the European Space Agency. With oceanographers determined to explore the remaining 95 percent of the oceans, the questions are perhaps not "whether" and "why" but "when" and "how" they will do so.

Chris Woodford

FURTHER READING
Ballard, Robert, and Will Hively. *The Eternal Darkness: A Personal History of Deep-Sea Exploration.* Princeton, N.J.: Princeton University Press, 2000.
Britton, Peter, and Dennis Normile. "Undersea Explorers." *Popular Science,* May 1995, p. 39.
Glasby, G. P. "Lessons Learned from Deep-Sea Mining." *Science,* 28 July 2000, p. 551.
Hawkes, Graham. "Microsubs Go to Sea." *Scientific American,* October 1997, p. 100.
Hecht, Jeff. "20,000 Tasks Under the Sea." *New Scientist,* 30 September 1995, p. 40.
Hodges, Glenn. "The New Cold War: Stalking Climate Change by Sub." *National Geographic,* March 2000, p. 30.
Kaharl, Victoria. *Water Baby: The Story of Alvin.* New York: Oxford University Press, 1990.
Kunzig, Robert. *Mapping the Deep: The Extraordinary Story of Ocean Science.* New York: W. W. Norton, 2000.
Lemonick, Michael. "The Last Frontier." *Time,* 14 August 1995, p.52.
Liddle, D., D. Rowsing, and J. Westwood. *The World UUV Report: The Market for Work-Class ROVs and AUVs, 2000–2004.* Canterbury, England: Douglas-Westwood, 2000.
Simpson, Sarah. "Looking for Life Below the Bottom." *Scientific American,* June 2000, p. 76.
Travis, John. "Probing the Unsolved Mysteries of the Deep." *Science,* 19 February 1993, p. 1123.

RELATED ARTICLES
Alvin; Autonomous Underwater Vehicles; Deep Sea; Deep Sea Drilling Project; *Glomar Challenger*; Ocean Drilling Program; Submersible; *Trieste*

Deep-Sea Mining

Deep-sea mining has not yet occurred, but much effort is going into preparations for that eventuality. All marine mining has taken place in shallow- to intermediate-depth waters and includes the extraction of aggregate (sand and gravel), heavy minerals, such as tin deposits off Southeast Asia, diamonds offshore of southwestern Africa, and offshore petroleum. Deep-sea deposit types that may be exploited in the future include (1) cobalt-rich ferromanganese crusts, which would be mined for the metals cobalt and nickel and perhaps also for manganese, titanium, cerium, platinum, molybdenum, tellurium, and copper; (2) manganese nodules, which would be mined for the metals nickel, copper, and cobalt and perhaps also for manganese and molybdenum; (3) polymetallic sulfides, which would be mined in various places for one or more of the metals copper, zinc, gold, and silver; and (4) metalliferous sediments, such as the metal-rich muds that occur in central Red Sea rifts.

Whether a commodity is ultimately mined from the deep sea depends primarily on the global minerals market but can also be influenced by such issues as government subsidies, land-use priorities for potential areas of on-land mining, and environmental concerns. Most coastal nations claim a 371-kilometer (200-nautical-mile) exclusive economic zone (EEZ), where each nation has jurisdiction over the biological and mineral resources in its EEZ and can determine if and how those resources are exploited. The wealth of the rest of the oceans beyond national jurisdictions—in the international waters—is meant to be common heritage and is to be shared with the developing nations of the world. The mineral wealth in international waters is administered by the United Nations through the International Seabed Authority (ISA), which has codified rules under the Law of the Sea Convention (UNCLOS) for the mining of manganese nodules. The ISA is currently developing rules for the mining of crusts and polymetallic sulfides.

Technology has been developed for mining nodules and Red Sea metalliferous muds but not for the other two deposit types. Adaptation of advanced technologies developed for mining diamonds off southern Africa could be applied to the mining of crusts and sulfides.

James R. Hein

FURTHER READING

Cronan, David S. *Marine Minerals in Exclusive Economic Zones.* London: Chapman and Hall, 1992.

Kunzendorf, H., ed. *Marine Mineral Exploration.* Amsterdam and New York: Elsevier, 1986

RELATED ARTICLES

Exclusive Economic Zone; Ocean Floor Resource; Polymetallic Nodules and Crusts

Deep-Sea Sediment

Deep-sea sediment is deposited at depths greater than 500 meters (1640 feet). It forms a relatively thin layer over more than 50 percent of Earth's surface and records such physical and chemical characteristics as ocean temperature, pressure, salinity, currents, upwelling zones, the formation and history of water masses, the occurrence of hydrothermal vents, river floods, chemical variations with depth in the water column, and biological responses to these various attributes.

Scientists observe deep-sea sediment directly on the ocean floor by remote sensing, submersible diving, ROV (remotely operated vehicle) investigations, and photography (video and still). Remote sensing includes the use of sound sources and sensors (generally, hydrophones) such as those utilized by side-scan sonar and various seismic instruments. Sampling is accomplished with a wide variety of corers, dredges, and grab samplers.

Diverse sources, transportation processes, and a wide variety of depositional environments lead to the heterogeneity of deep-sea sediment. Once on the seafloor, and affected by time, compaction, and interstitial fluids, the sediments generally experience *diagenesis*, a process that leads to the formation of new minerals, and to *lithification*, whereby soft sediment is turned into rock.

Sources of Deep-Sea Sediment

The ultimate sources of deep-sea sediment are rivers, glaciers, wind, volcanoes (including volcanic fissures along spreading centers and hydrothermal vents), submarine landslides, space (cosmic), and marine snow.

Rivers are the main source and contribute (1) clastic grains (e.g., sand, silt, and clay) that are mechanically broken from rock outcrops; (2) dissolved ions, elements, and molecules that are mostly related to the chemical weathering and breakdown of rocks; and (3) organic matter that is predominantly the product of terrestrial biological activity.

Glacial sources are especially important where ice caps occur, such as on Antarctica, Greenland, and Iceland. The resulting clastic sediment generally occurs as moraine detritus on the continental shelf and upper slope and as dropstones, boulder to clay in size, that are dropped to the deep ocean floor when icebergs melt. It is estimated that about 20 percent of the ocean floors receive some ice-transported sediment. This source has been much more important in the recent geologic past when parts of some continents were covered several times by ice caps during the last 2 million years.

Wind is both a source and a transporting means for some fine-grained sand, silt, and clay accumulations on the deep seafloor. Most of the sediment is picked up by strong winds over desert areas, such as the Gobi and Sahara deserts, carried into the atmospheric jet streams, and thence transported throughout the world.

Volcanic eruptions emit ash and other volcanic sediment that settle to the ocean floors. The ash layers are volumetrically important near island arcs such as those in the western Pacific Ocean and the Caribbean Sea. When an ash column from a particularly explosive volcano reaches the upper atmosphere, jet streams distribute ash to most parts of Earth. Volcanic sediment also reaches the deep ocean floor through the breakup of lava flows (mostly from islands, seamounts, and spreading ridges) as they come in contact with cool ocean water; the clasts (broken-up rocks) are subsequently distributed by debris flows, turbidity currents, and other ocean bottom currents. Black smokers along spreading centers emit hot water that is rich in metallic elements and oxides, both suspended and in solution, plus gases such as sulfur dioxide that are important for chemosynthesis by bacteria and other organisms.

Submarine landslides contribute large volumes to the deep sea via debris flows and associated turbidity currents. Generally triggered by oversteepening of a heavily sedimented slope and/or by earthquakes, a single landslide event can spread a layer of debris over thousands of square kilometers.

Cosmic dust is presently a small but steady source of particles that reach the deep ocean floor. Micrometeorites and larger meteorites continuously rain down on the ocean surface. In the past, large meteorites, asteroids, and comets have collided with Earth; some caused widespread havoc by spreading dust and other debris over the entire surface of Earth and causing the extinction of most living species.

Marine snow is the name given to a constant barrage of drifting and settling particles that occurs throughout the water column. It is also referred to as *pelagic rain*. Small particles in the top layer of the ocean, with almost negligible sinking rates, are transformed into larger aggregates that thereby gain mass and density and are able to sink to the ocean floor, generally in a few weeks. This pelagic material is usually composed of gelatinous houses constructed by some zooplankton

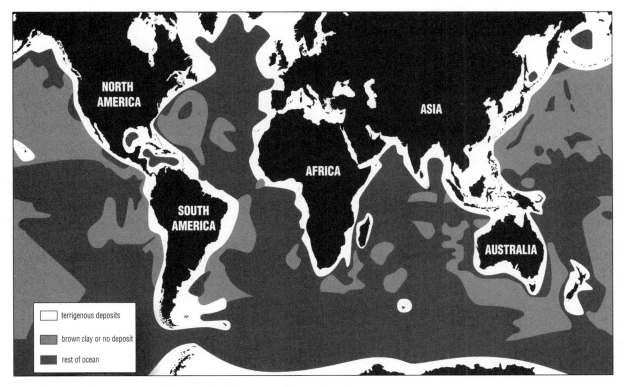

Distribution of terrigenous and brown clay deep-sea sediment deposits.

297

species and mucous feeding webs that are used by others. Additional small particles are feces, aging phytoplankton cells, and zooplankton molts. Once on the ocean floor, the detrital materials are moved about and redeposited by bottom currents, fed upon by benthic biota, and buried by large biota to become part of the deep-sea sediment.

Seawater Composition, Interstitial Water, and Diagenesis

Ocean water contains 35 practical salinity units of dissolved ions and elements, about 86 percent of which is sodium chloride (NaCl), common table salt. Other major constituents are ions of magnesium (Mg), calcium (Ca), potassium (K), and sulfate (SO_4), plus the bicarbonate $NaHCO_3$. River water and volcanic gases are the ultimate sources for most soluble materials. Seawater composition is very different from river water because of solubility characteristics (which concentrate NaCl) and "sinks" that withdraw material such as Ca and CO_2 from seawater. Important "sinks" are for $CaCO_3$ (calcium carbonate) and SiO_2 (silica), which are precipitated in shells (tests) of organisms. Metals are transferred into lattices of authigenic (forms in place) clay minerals, metal oxides (e.g., manganese and iron), and zeolite minerals (particularly phillipsite and clinoptilolite). Sulfur is concentrated in anaerobic (lack of oxygen) sediment, where the mineral pyrite (FeS_2) is a significant component.

Interstitial water, occupying spaces among the sediment components, is important for the process of diagenesis (chemical, physical, and biological changes that occur after deposition and during lithification, the transformation to rock). Ions and other components are concentrated and new minerals form. For example, radiolarian ooze transforms during diagenesis through stages of opal (silica with abundant water) crystallization to form chert (microcrystalline quartz), and foraminiferal ooze converts to chalk and thence to limestone. Mud converts to mudstone, and sand changes to sandstone.

Classification of Deep-Sea Sediment

Deep-sea sediment is classified by origin, composition, and size. These diverse classification schemes lead to some confusion among scientists because of overlaps in processes that form the sediments and compositions. Four major types of deep-sea sediment are distinguished by origin: lithogenous, hydrogenous, biogenous, and cosmogenous. Deep-sea sediment generally falls into the following compositional categories: terrigenous, biogenic, pelagic, hemipelagic (hemiterrigenous), volcanogenic, authigenic, and brown (red) clay. Sediments are also classified by size, particularly if the components are known to have been transported.

CLASSIFICATION OF DEEP-SEA SEDIMENT BY ORIGIN

Lithogenous sediment includes fragments of pre-existing rocks and volcanic ejecta, with transport from land by rivers, wind, and glaciers. The particles are distributed by currents and waves and then settle to the ocean floor to become deposits of sand, silt, clay, and mud. Boulders, cobbles, and pebbles may occur in the deep sea near the mouths of submarine canyons, in deposits formed by submarine landslides, and as dropstones that fall to the ocean floor when icebergs melt. Lithogenous sediments are further divided into terrigenous, volcanogenic, and windblown deposits.

Hydrogenous sediment precipitates from seawater and interstitial (between particles) water that is beneath the ocean floor. Most are authigenic because they form in place. Hydrogenous minerals are zeolites (particularly phillipsite and clinoptilolite), phosphates (more common in shallow water), sulfates (e.g., gypsum, anhydrite, and barite), and halite (NaCl, common table salt). Manganese nodules and iron/manganese crusts are composed mostly of hydrogenous minerals. Clay minerals also can form in place; the best example is the formation of smectite from the alteration of volcanic glass.

Biogenous sediment is the most widespread, covering nearly half of the deep ocean floor. Most is composed of organism remains and consists of calcite and aragonite (carbonates), opal (hydrated silica), and calcium phosphate. The organisms may live on the seafloor (benthic) or float freely in the water column (plankton). As the shells of carbonate plankton settle and drift slowly downward, they pass through increasing pressures and decreasing temperatures, which leads to their dissolution, beginning in the lysocline and proceeding through the carbonate compensation depth (CCD). Biogenous deep-sea sediment is composed mostly of shells of foraminifera, radiolarians, calcareous nannoplankton (platelets of Coccolithophorids and Discoasters), silicoflagellates, and diatoms. Rare shells of larger benthic animals can be included in the sediment, and debris eroded from coral reefs often reaches the deep ocean floor by turbidity current transport.

Cosmogenous sediment has an extraterrestrial source and is the least abundant of all the deep-sea sediment types. These enter the atmosphere as meteorites and fine dust, some of which is composed of micrometeorites [less than about 1 millimeter (0.04 inch) in diameter]. Estimates vary as to how much reaches Earth, but probably between 1 million and 50 million kilograms (2 million and 110 million pounds) per day. Many of the small particles, because they consist of iron, dissolve before reaching the ocean floor. Others are masked by other types of sediment and are not easily recognized.

CLASSIFICATION OF DEEP-SEA SEDIMENT BY COMPOSITION

More commonly, deep-sea sediment is referred to as terrigenous, biogenic, pelagic, hemipelagic, volcanogenic, and authigenic. These can be included in the types described above, and some are included in two or more of them. For example, terrigenous, pelagic, and volcanogenic components all fit within the lithogenous type; biogenous sediment includes biogenic and pelagic components; and hydrogenous sediment is composed of authigenic and pelagic materials.

Terrigenous sediment has a land source and includes particles that are derived directly not only from river input and redistribution but also from turbidites, masswasting (submarine landslides and slumps), channelized processes (canyons, submarine fans, and deep-sea channels), eolian (windblown) fallout, and glacial marine processes.

Biogenic sediment can occur on any part of the seafloor. In deep-sea sediment, however, the biogenic components consist mostly of tests (shells) of microscopic organisms such as foraminifera, radiolarians, diatoms, and calcareous nannoplankton. Shells of benthic organisms also become part of the sediment. Biogenic sediment is greatly affected by the supply (productivity of plants and animals), dissolution as the shells pass through the CCD, dilution by nonbiogenic components such as silt and clay, and diagenetic alteration which converts biogenic ooze to rock.

The term *pelagic sediment* is more or less a relict from the past and is thoroughly lodged in deep-sea sediment terminology. Pelagic sediment includes particles that settle to the deep ocean floor through the water column, no matter where they originate or what their composition. It includes biogenic material, volcanic ash, ice-rafted debris, windblown dust, and extraterrestrial particles.

Hemipelagic (or hemiterrigenous) sediment combines pelagic (mostly biogenic) and terrigenous components. This sediment, common on the continental slopes and abyssal plains, characteristically drapes over the bottom topography in a consistent thickness, rather than filling depressions such as terrigenous sediment. A good example is diatomaceous mud.

Volcanogenic sediment includes windblown volcanic ash, submarine pyroclastic flows, hyaloclastite (fragments of lava flows that break up as they encounter water), and reworked volcanic rocks. This category also includes hydrothermal sediment that is erupted from vents along seafloor spreading ridges such as the Mid-Atlantic Ridge.

Authigenic sediment forms in place either on the seafloor or beneath it within the sediment column. These sediments include zeolites, clay minerals like those of the smectite group, and iron/manganese oxides that precipitate out of solution to form nodules and crusts.

Deep-sea clay, generally referred to as *brown (red) clay* because of its color, covers a large part of the ocean floor. It occurs far from land and in deep water. Brown clay has a broad range of compositions but generally consists of two or more of the following components: silt-sized terrigenous minerals such as quartz, feldspar, and pyroxene; clay minerals; authigenic minerals such as zeolites and Fe/Mn oxides; fish teeth (ichthyoliths); and cosmic debris such as micrometeorites. Four major clay minerals occur in deep-sea sediment: the smectites (montmorillinite, beidellite, and nontronite), which are authigenic products of degraded volcanic materials and of hydrothermal vents; illite, which is very similar to muscovite in crystal structure and composition; kaolinite, a product of intense chemical weathering of rocks on land in a humid climate; and chlorite, which is a common constituent of metamorphic rocks. Clay minerals are brought to the deep sea predominantly by rivers and wind. Smectite, however, commonly forms in situ both on and under the seafloor.

CLASSIFICATION OF DEEP-SEA SEDIMENT BY SIZE

Sediments are classified by size if they have been transported. Size is determined by a number of methods, including sieving, settling, and light transmission. Size classification is the schematic division of continuous ranges of sizes into classes or grades, generally in a geometric manner. The broad divisions commonly used for finer-grained sediments, like most that occur on the deep seafloor, are sand [2.0 to 0.062 millimeter (0.08 to 0.002 inch) in diameter], silt [0.062 to 0.004 millimeter (0.002 to 0.0002 inch)], and clay [less than 0.004 millimeter (0.0002 inch)]. Larger particles include pebbles, cobbles, and boulders. Particles may be terrigenous, biogenic, authigenic, volcanogenic, or a mixture of two or more of these. Deep-sea terrigenous deposits, like those consisting of rock, feldspar, and quartz grains, are named sand, silt, clay, and mud (mixture of silt and clay). However, there may be some confusion with biogenic sediment. For example, a deposit made up entirely of foraminifera between 1 and 2 millimeters (0.04 and 0.08 inch) in size can be named either foraminiferal sand or foraminiferal ooze, depending on whether or not the materials have undergone significant transport since they originally settled.

Deep-Sea Sediment Nomenclature

Relative amounts of each component are calculated by marine geologists to name deep-sea sediment. This system provides other geologists with information about the sediment composition and the oceanographic and seafloor conditions that produced the components. Various microscopic, x-ray diffraction, and chemical methods are used to determine the composition of deep-sea sediment and it is named accordingly, with the least abundant component first and the major component last. For example, if a sediment has 15 percent phillipsite (zeolite), 35 percent calcareous nannoplankton, and 50 percent foraminifera, the sediment might be named a "zeolite-rich nanno foram ooze." If the sediment has 5 percent phillipsite, 20 percent radiolarians, 35 percent foraminifera, and 40 percent calcareous nannoplankton, the sedimentologist might name it a "zeolite-bearing rad-rich foram nanno ooze."

Distribution of Deep-Sea Sediment

The distribution of deep-sea sediment is greatly influenced by proximity to continents, islands, volcanoes, and spreading ridges, to biologic productivity, and to depth. Terrigenous sediment masks most other deep-sea sediment near continents and large islands. Biogenous sediment (e.g., calcareous and siliceous ooze) is important where productivity is high, such as in nutrient-rich zones of upwelling. Brown (red) clay occurs in the older and deeper parts of the oceans. Manganese nodules are concentrated in areas of brown clay accumulation.

Tracy L. Vallier

FURTHER READING

Berger, Wolfgang H. "Deep Sea Sedimentation." In C. A Burk and C. D. Drake, eds., *The Geology of Continental Margins*. New York: Springer-Verlag, 1974.

Duxbury, Alison B., and Alyn C. Duxbury. *Fundamentals of Oceanography*. Dubuque, Iowa: Wm. C. Brown, 1993; 2nd ed., 1996.

Emiliani, Cesare, and John D. Milliman. "Deep Sea Sediments and Their Geologic Record." *Earth Science Reviews*, Vol. 1 (1966), pp. 105–132.

Garrison, Thomas. *Oceanography: An Invitation to Marine Science*. Pacific Grove, Calif.: Brooks/Cole, 2001.

Kennett, James. *Marine Geology*. Englewood Cliffs, N.J.: Prentice Hall, 1982.

Seibold, Eugen, and Wolfgang H. Berger. *The Sea Floor: An Introduction to Marine Geology*. Berlin and New York: Springer-Verlag, 1993; 3rd rev. and updated ed., 1996.

Stow, D. A.V., and David J. W. Piper, eds. *Fine-Grained Sediments: Deep-Water Processes and Facies*. Oxford and Boston: Blackwell Scientific, published for the Geological Society, 1984.

RELATED ARTICLES

Abyssal Plain; Calcium Carbonate Compensation Depth; Clay Mineral; Deep-Sea Stratigraphy; Glacial Marine Processes; Interstitial Water, Chemistry of; Turbidity Current; Upwelling; Windblown Dust, Transport and Deposition of; Zeolite

Deep-Sea Stratigraphy

The term *stratigraphy* encompasses the nature, form, distribution, and succession of rock layers (usually, sedimentary rocks), as well as the interpretation of these observations in terms of geologic history. The principal factors controlling sedimentation in the open ocean are the surface biological productivity, seawater chemistry and circulation, and water depth. The deep-sea stratigraphic record can be understood in terms of the interplay among these factors. By comparison with terrestrial (including lakes and rivers), nearshore, and glacial environments, the deep-sea environment shows limited variability; consequently, the deep-sea record can be interpreted, at least in broad terms, using a relatively simple model referred to as *plate stratigraphy*.

Plate Stratigraphy

Plate tectonics states that new ocean crust is accreted at the crests of mid-ocean ridges (spreading centers) and that in the process, older, preexisting crust is fractured and moved away from ridge crests. The ridges are sites of magmatic intrusion and volcanic activity. They are elevated above the surrounding ocean floor as a result of thermal expansion of the lithosphere. As ocean crust ages and moves away from the hot ridge crest, it cools and subsides. Thus deep-sea sediments accumulate on oceanic crust that is both moving horizontally and, particularly during the first 60 million years after its formation, deepening with time. Plate tectonics states further that ocean crust ultimately returns to Earth's interior through the processes of subduction. This, too, has implications for the deep-sea sedimentary record.

Hydrothermal fluids circulating through the hot ocean crust at or near the ridge crest are rich in various elements, particularly the metals iron and manganese. In some cases hot fluids venting from the seafloor precipitate minerals directly, creating chimneylike structures (black smokers), but these are fragile and rarely preserved in the sedimentary record. More typically, pelagic sediment accumulating on new, young ocean crust simply becomes

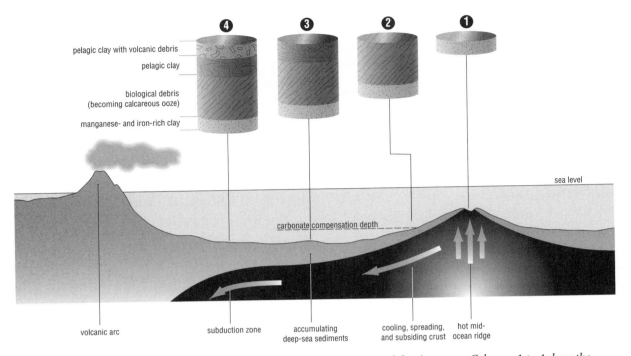

pelagic clay with volcanic debris

pelagic clay

biological debris
(becoming calcareous ooze)

manganese- and iron-rich clay

sea level

carbonate compensation depth

volcanic arc   subduction zone   accumulating deep-sea sediments   cooling, spreading, and subsiding crust   hot mid-ocean ridge

Schematic cross section from a mid-ocean ridge across an ocean basin to a subduction zone. Columns 1 to 4 show the typical stratigraphy expected in four distinct locations, ranging from new, young ocean crust (1) to mature seafloor approaching a subduction zone (4).

highly enriched in iron and manganese, resulting in an iron-enriched layer that forms the base of the sedimentary section, immediately overlying volcanic crustal rocks, oceanwide.

Metal enrichment is rare away from a ridge crest. Biological productivity, the chemistry of seawater, and crustal subsidence become the factors controlling sedimentation. Biological debris begins to dissolve in seawater as soon as the planktonic organisms living in the surface waters die. The accumulation of biological debris (ooze) on the ocean floor is a function of the balance between the production of material in the surface waters and its dissolution in the water column and while exposed on the seafloor before burial. This balance is affected not only by the rates of production and dissolution, but also by the water depth, which determines the length of time sinking debris is exposed to dissolution before reaching the ocean floor. In general, siliceous debris (radiolaria, diatoms) dissolves almost immediately. Consequently, siliceous ooze accumulates

only in regions where siliceous productivity is very high and the supply of skeletal material overwhelms the capacity of the water column to redissolve it. Calcareous debris (foraminifers, coccoliths), on the other hand, dissolves more slowly. Throughout the oceans there is a carbonate compensation depth (CCD) at which the supply of calcareous debris from above is balanced by its removal through dissolution. Above the CCD, calcareous ooze accumulates; below the CCD, all the carbonate is dissolved and only deep-sea pelagic (red) clay accumulates. The depth of the CCD varies from place to place. It is generally deep below areas of high surface productivity and shallower under regions of low productivity, but its depth is also affected by ocean chemistry and circulation. Thus, on the flanks of mid-ocean ridges the metal-enriched basal sediments become buried under calcareous ooze, which continues to accumulate on the ocean floor as long as it remains above the CCD. Once the ocean floor subsides below the CCD, only

302

pelagic clay accumulates, burying the carbonate layer. Accumulation of pelagic clay continues throughout the history of the ocean floor.

The simple tripartite division of the deep-sea stratigraphic record (metal-rich basal sediment, overlain by calcareous ooze, overlain by pelagic clay) is further modified as the ocean floor ages and a given location approaches its ultimate demise in a subduction zone. Subduction zones are typically marked by deep-ocean trenches and, more important from a stratigraphic viewpoint, volcanic island arcs. Thus, as the seafloor approaches a subduction zone, volcanic ash becomes an important contributor to the stratigraphic record. The amount of ash and the distance it travels from its source are strongly influenced by wind patterns. Nevertheless, the appearance of significant amounts of volcanic debris in the deep-sea stratigraphic record, overlying sediments with little or no fresh volcanic component, is a clear indicator of proximity to a volcanic source, usually an island arc associated with a subduction zone.

The interplay among these factors to produce a characteristic deep-sea stratigraphy is summarized in the accompanying figure. Although local conditions produce variations, the basic concept of plate stratigraphy has now been validated in general terms by scientific drilling in all the major oceans.

Applications of Plate Stratigraphy to Earth's History

Beyond its value as a simple descriptive tool, however, plate stratigraphy is a powerful tool for gaining insights into Earth's history. Applying the model and our knowledge of the factors controlling deep-sea sedimentation, it is possible to infer important characteristics of past ocean environments.

At a given location the boundary between calcareous ooze (below) and deep-sea clay (above) marks the time when that location passed below the CCD. Since the water depth can be calculated independently, using simple physical cooling laws with an isostatic correction applied for the weight of accumulated sediment, it is possible to estimate the depth of the CCD at that time. Repeating these calculations in many locations makes it possible to reconstruct the history of variations in the CCD, which in turn gives insights into past oceanographic and productivity conditions.

The central Pacific offers a unique and different application of the plate stratigraphic model. The equatorial high-productivity belt is one place where siliceous productivity is so high that siliceous oozes are accumulating on the ocean floor. Throughout the Cenozoic (past 65 million years) the floor of the Pacific has been moving generally toward the north or northwest. As a result, at locations north of the equator, the passage of the seafloor beneath the equatorial high-productivity belt is recorded as an interval of siliceous ooze within the stratigraphic record. Comparing the times that this has occurred at various locations and the present latitudes of those locations provides an independent estimate of plate motions that can be compared to movements calculated from paleomagnetic reversals and simple plate tectonics.

Finally, looking at the "downstream end" of the system, plate tectonics enables us to estimate the past trajectory of a location and determine its position at times when volcanic debris appears in the stratigraphic record. This position can then be compared with that of nearby subduction zones to make inferences about the magnitude of eruptions at neighboring volcanic island arcs. Further, the number and frequency of ash layers in the sedimentary record allow estimates of the frequency of eruptions.

In summary, the relatively simple model of plate stratigraphy provides not only a straightforward conceptual framework for describing and understanding the stratigraphic record of the deep-sea floor, but also an important predictive tool for reconstructing important elements of past oceanographic and geologic history.

Thomas A. Davies

303

FURTHER READING

Berger, W. H., and E. L. Winterer. "Plate Stratigraphy and the Fluctuating Carbonate Line." In K. J. Hsu and H. C. Jenkyns, eds., *Pelagic Sediments: On Land and under the Sea.* International Association of Sedimentologists, Special Publication 1. Oxford: Blackwell Science, 1974; pp. 11–48.

Broeker, Wallace S. *Chemical Oceanography.* New York: Harcourt Brace Jovanovich, 1974.

Davies, T. A., and D. S. Gorsline. "Oceanic Sediments and Sedimentary Processes" In J. P. Riley and G. Skirrow, eds., *Chemical Oceanography,* Vol. 5. London and New York: Academic Press, 1965; 2nd ed. 1975; pp. 1–80.

Gross, M. Grant. *Oceanography: A View of the Earth.* Englewood Cliffs, N.J.: Prentice Hall, 1972; 7th ed., Upper Saddle River, N.J.: Prentice Hall, 1996.

Kennett, James. *Marine Geology.* Englewood Cliffs, N.J.: Prentice Hall, 1982.

Seibold, Eugen, and Wolfgang H. Berger. *The Sea Floor: An Introduction to Marine Geology.* Berlin and New York: Springer-Verlag, 1982; 3rd rev. and updated ed., 1996.

RELATED ARTICLES

Calcium Carbonate Compensation Depth; Island Arc; Mid-Ocean Ridge; Plate Tectonics; Seafloor Spreading; Subduction Zone

Deep-Sea Vent Water, Chemistry of

In 1977, the discovery of deep-sea hot springs called *hydrothermal vents* (from the Greek *hudor*, water, and *therme*, heat) was to be an opening chapter in some of the most exciting developments in twentieth-century oceanography. The existence of hydrothermal vents had been predicted by higher-than-expected heat flux between underlying rock and the deep ocean near the crests of mid-ocean ridges. However, it was only in 1977, when researchers in the Woods Hole Oceanographic Institution's submersible *Alvin* visited the Galápagos Rift, that hydrothermal vents were observed directly for the first time, together with the astonishing biological communities associated with them.

Since then, three major types of hydrothermal vents have been described, based on temperature characteristics, which, in turn, influence chemical, biological, and other physical features of the vents:

1. Diffuse, clear-water vents at temperatures below 30°C (86°F).
2. White smokers at temperatures between 30°C (86°F) and about 330°C (626°F). The "white smoke" is caused by pale particles of barium sulfate in the hydrothermal fluid. White smokers may develop chimneylike structures several meters tall.
3. Black smokers at temperatures above 350°C (662°F). The "black smoke" is generated by dark particles of sulfides of metals such as iron and copper. Many of these black smokers produce chimneylike structures that can reach several tens of meters tall.

Other ways of classifying hydrothermal vents include those based on geological setting, such as the distinction between sedimented and unsedimented spreading centers. Discoveries such as the basal mound smokers of the East Pacific Rise and Juan de Fuca Ridge and the tall chimneys of the Lost City complex on the Mid-Atlantic Ridge are likely to result in revisions of existing categorizations.

Hydrothermal Circulation

The water that exits through hydrothermal vents originates from the deep ocean. Water seeps downward through fractures in the oceanic crust on or near the flanks of a mid-ocean ridge. In some cases, the water penetrates several kilometers within the crust, where temperatures are well in excess of 400°C (752°F). As the seawater is heated at high pressure, it reacts with the freshly formed basalt crust. Magnesium (Mg^{2+}) and sulfate (SO_4^{2-}) ions—normally abundant in seawater—are extracted from the water. As the water descends and is heated further, reduced metals such as manganese, iron, copper, and zinc, plus silica and sulfide, are leached from the rock. The chemical composition of the seawater is altered substantially. The acid, metal-rich hydrothermal vent fluid now rises rapidly through the crust and seeps or gushes through vents on the seafloor.

When vent fluid mixes with the cool, oxygenated, alkaline seawater of the deep ocean, metal-rich sulfides and oxides precipitate within seconds. Where the exiting vent water is particularly hot [above 350°C (662°F)], most of this precipitation takes place in and around the vent mouth, yielding a slowly building chimney of anhydrite (calcium sulfate) and sulfide deposits, the latter also giving rise to black smoke. At slightly cooler temperatures [below 330°C (626°F)], and where some subsurface mixing with cool seawater has taken place, the vent fluid tends to precipitate more of the metal-rich deposits on the walls of the vent channels leading to the seafloor. The fluid emerging from such vents contains zinc sulfide and oxides and sulfates of minerals, plus silica, generating white smoke.

Low-temperature diffuse seeps produce no "smoke" because metallic sulfides and sulfates have precipitated within the subsurface vent system as a result of mixing with cool seawater. The discharging hydrothermal fluid is, however, rich in reduced manganese and iron that oxidize and settle as insoluble oxides on the nearby seafloor.

Hydrothermal Vent Deposits

The temperature of vent fluids and the longevity of the vents are among the factors that influence the physical and chemical nature of vent deposits. The TAG (Trans-Atlantic Geotraverse) hydrothermal mound at 26°N on the Mid-Atlantic Ridge illustrates the diversity of deposits that can occur in one locality. The mound is about 200 meters (660 feet) in diameter and reaches up to 50 meters (165 feet) high. A network of channels extends through the mound and supplies the vents with hot water. At the center of the mound, black smokers belch hot, acidic fluid at 360°C (680°F) through narrow chimneys

of deposited iron sulfide, copper sulfide, and calcium sulfate. On the upper flanks of the mound, white smokers dominate, spewing water at 300°C (572°F) and producing fat chimneys rich in zinc sulfide. The white smoke contains zinc sulfide, iron sulfide, and silica. The lower flanks release warm water through diffuse vents around which red and orange iron oxides precipitate.

Toward the outer edge of the mound are extinct vents of various ages. Recently active vents—probably blocked by their own mineral deposits—gradually change in color from blue-gray to brown as their constituent iron, copper, and zinc sulfides become oxidized. Recently active hot vents are tinged with blue from deposited calcium sulfate. The blue disappears as the sulfate gradually dissolves. Eventually, the chimneys weaken and collapse and contribute to the rubble that forms the mound. The debris from extinct chimneys and diffuse vents gradually accumulates in the sediment around the flanks of the mound. This sediment is unusually rich in metal-rich sulfide and oxide minerals. The metals in the sediments—up to 45 percent iron, 35 percent copper, and 10 to 15 percent zinc—are a potentially valuable resource if a cost-effective means can be found to harvest them.

In December 2000, scientists onboard Woods Hole Oceanographic Institution's research vessel *Atlantis* discovered a new kind of medium-temperature hydrothermal vent system [temperatures up to 160°C (320°F)] at 30° on the Mid-Atlantic Ridge, an assemblage dubbed "The Lost City." These vents are unusual in that their chimneys are exceptionally tall, up to 60 meters (about 195 feet) high. They are probably composed of carbonate minerals and silica. Their unusual chemistry would be explained by their location on rock uplifted from Earth's mantle.

Wider-Scale Effects

The chemical effects of hydrothermal vent systems are far from purely local. High-temperature vent fluids can rise several hundred meters from the seafloor. They are carried horizontally by prevailing deep-ocean currents. Within an hour of discharge, vent fluid from a TAG black smoker will have been diluted at least 10,000-fold by mixing with ordinary seawater. The novel substances in vent fluids, such as metal oxide and sulfide particles, are readily detectable. In fact, tracing such substances in the water column is a means of detecting hydrothermal vents up to 3 kilometers (about 2 miles) away.

The mid-ocean ridge system extends more than 65,000 kilometers (40,000 miles) through the world's oceans. Estimates from several sources suggest that a volume of water equivalent to the global ocean flows through hydrothermal vents on mid-ocean ridges every 10 million years or so. This being the case, the vents profoundly affect the chemical composition of the world's seawater. For example, they probably control the steady-state concentration of magnesium ions, and by adding calcium, potassium, silicon, and barium, they lower the alkalinity of seawater.

The calculated flux of manganese from ridge crests is large enough to account for all the manganese found in metal-rich deposits and polymetallic nodules. Physical oceanographers now use tracers from hydrothermal vents, such as helium (^{3}He), to monitor the flow of deep-ocean currents.

The Origin of Life

A small but growing community of scientists is championing the proposition that hydrothermal vents may be the sites of the origin of life on Earth. One of the advocates is John B. Corliss, currently of Central European University, one of the first to observe a hydrothermal vent directly.

Reducing conditions are necessary to ensure that simple molecules, such as ammonia and methane, might be combined to form the building blocks (e.g., amino acids) of biochemical polymers (e.g., proteins) rather than be oxidized. Reducing conditions exist in the interior of deep-sea vents. It is feasible that amino acids could be synthesized at high temperature and great pressure inside vent systems and discharged intact into cold seawater at the mouth of a vent and then settle on deposits close by. It can be envisioned that amino acids and other monomers could give rise to polymers that form part of prebiotic assemblages that would eventually evolve to become the first living cells. In favor of this proposition, a deep-sea site offers some protection from the impacts of asteroids and comets that were devastating the early Earth, shallow-water, origin-of-life sites proposed by other theories. The hydrothermal vent origin-of-life scenario is speculation. However, a variety of biochemists, including C. Huber and G. Wächtershäuser of Munich, Germany, are testing whether the kinds of chemical species found in hydrothermal vents today could have functioned as prebiotic catalysts. Could they have catalyzed the formation of organic molecules that would become the building blocks of life?

Trevor Day

FURTHER READING

Crabtree, Robert H. "Where Smokers Rule." *Science*, Vol. 276 (11 April 1997), p. 222.

German, C. R., L. M. Parson, and R. A. Mills. "Mid-ocean Ridges and Hydrothermal Activity." In C. P. Summerhayes and S. A. Thorpe, eds., *Oceanography: An Illustrated Guide*. New York: Wiley, 1996; pp. 152–164.

Humphris, S. E., R. A. Zierenberg, L. S. Mullineaux, and R. E. Thomson, eds. *Physical, Chemical, Biological and Geological Interactions within Hydrothermal Systems*. Geophysical Monograph 91. Washington, D.C.: American Geophysical Union, 1995.

Libes, Susan M. *Marine Biogeochemistry*. New York: Wiley, 1992.

RELATED ARTICLES
Hydrothermal Vent; Mid-Atlantic Ridge

Deep-Water Mass, see Water Mass

Delta

Deltas are deposits of sediment brought to the coast by rivers. Herodotus (c. 484–c. 430 B.C.) introduced the term in the fifth century B.C. to describe the land at the mouth of the Nile River, which had an outline that broadly resembled the Greek capital letter delta with the apex pointing upstream. Deltas can form at all latitudes except at the poles, building out the shorelines of oceans, gulfs, bays, estuaries, and even lakes. Their sedimentary deposits include materials that accumulate subaqueously (below sea level) as well as subaerially (above sea level). Some well-known deltas, such as the Nile, Mississippi, and Ganges–Brahmaputra, can be recognized immediately because of their characteristic shape and large size. Other deltas, such as the Senegal in west Africa and Ord in Australia, have been modified so significantly by marine processes that they are considerably more difficult to recognize as being deltas. Although most deltas have been reworked to some degree by waves, tides, and coastal currents, all deltas share the ability to accumulate sediments more rapidly than they can be dispersed by marine processes.

For centuries, large deltas have been important sites of human habitation, especially in the tropics. People live on deltas because they have fertile soil, provide immediate access to navigable waters, supply fresh seafood, and in some cases, contain vast supplies of coal, oil, and gas in their ancient deposits. Most deltas have luxuriant stands of wetlands that stabilize their sediments and provide nutrients to the surrounding aquatic ecosystems. However, many large marine deltas, perhaps most notably the Mississippi, are now slowly subsiding (sinking) as a result of fluid withdrawal and compaction of the underlying sediments. The effects of subsidence increase when sea level is rising or when the supply of sediments from rivers is diminished.

Delta Variability

Deltas are often classified on the basis of their morphology or shape. The 30 to 35 major marine deltas, as well as the hundreds of smaller deltas of the world, display a wide range of configurations. In many respects, deltas are composite features made up variously of beaches, spits, dune fields, tidal flats, wetlands, and active and abandoned river channels. Whereas some deltas experience low wave energy and negligible tides, others are exposed to continuous and severe wave forces or to tide ranges that may exceed 5 meters (approximately 16 feet). Many deltas, such as the Mississippi, are dominated by silt- and clay-sized particles, whereas others, such as the Burdekin in Australia, are composed almost exclusively of sand and gravel. These differences in sediment reflect the variability from one river drainage basin to another and are determined by factors such as climate, vegetation, and rock type.

The most common delta morphologies are birdsfoot (digitate), lobate (smoothed digitate), cuspate (v-shaped), and arcuate (rounded). These shapes reflect different ratios of sediment supply to energy level; birdsfoot deltas have the highest ratios, arcuate deltas have the lowest ratios, and the other types have intermediate supply-to-energy ratios. Because the river mouth is the point at which sediments are deposited and dispersed, its characteristics, such as water depth and flow speed, have a significant influence on the shape of the delta and the geometry of the sedimentary units that are deposited through time. For convenience, deltas are often simply classified as river dominated, tide dominated, and wave dominated, to reflect the relative contributions of these three energy sources. Regardless of the variability in delta morphology, the basic features of all deltas are distributary (river) channels and an interdistributary (between-channel) framework of sediments.

Processes of Deltaic Sedimentation

When a river enters a larger body of water, such as the ocean, its currents decrease in speed as the flow spreads out upon leaving the confines of the river channel. The decelerating flow allows sediments to begin settling to the bottom, laying down deltaic deposits. The largest particles in the water, which have the fastest settling speeds, settle close to the shore; smaller particles are carried farther into the ocean. Coarse-grained sediments may build a distributary mouth bar, partially blocking or "silting up" the mouth of the river. Sometimes a river will bifurcate (split) in an attempt to move past its own coarse-grained deltaic deposits. Farther offshore, in a region referred to as the *delta front*, intermediate-sized particles are deposited in a halolike pattern that covers an area much larger than that of the distributary mouth bar. Finally, a blanket of very fine-grained sediment is deposited more slowly across a broad region of the continental shelf, well beyond the river mouth. This nearly continuous blanket of muddy sediment is called the *prodelta deposit*.

The seaward growth of a delta allows sediments to build vertically as well as laterally. Vertical growth depends on many factors, such as water depth, sediment supply, and wave and tide processes. As a delta builds seaward over time, the depositional sites for coarse-grained, intermediate, and fine-grained sediments also shift in a seaward direction. Eventually, coarse sediments will be deposited at sites where previously only finer-grained sediments were deposited, creating, at any given location, a coarsening-upward distribution of particle sizes.

Coarsening-upward sequences of sedimentary deposits are used by geologists to help distinguish deltas from other marine and freshwater deposits. Most deltas have more than one distributary, and some deltas, such as the Indus, have many small distributaries and tidal channels. Deltas can thus be very complex depositional systems with interfingering, coarsening-upward sedimentary deposits.

Much of the deposition in a delta occurs during major river floods when sediment loads are high and water levels are elevated. Flood waters that overtop the surface of the delta build the interdistributary framework of the subaerial delta and help to offset natural sea-level rise and subsidence. However, deltas are inherently unstable because they need a continuous supply of river sediments, and most deltas have life cycles that are tied intimately to upstream changes in river course.

Sea-Level Rise, Subsidence, and Loss of Sediments

Many of the world's major marine deltas are threatened by sea-level rise, subsidence, and loss of sediments from upstream river diversions. Although these are natural processes, human activities can increase their magnitude substantially. The combination of global sea-level rise and local subsidence produces a net (relative) sea-level rise that differs considerably from one delta to another. Possible impacts of human-induced climate change (greenhouse effect) on global sea-level rise is a pressing environmental issue, yet deltas often experience subsidence rates that are 10 times the current or projected sea-level rise. Rates of deltaic subsidence can reach an incredible 3 centimeters (approximately 1 inch) per year. Low-lying deltas, where populations tend to be concentrated, are especially at risk. In fact, some of the world's largest cities, including Shanghai, Bangkok, Tokyo, Calcutta, and Bombay, are threatened because they are located at least partly on deltas.

Another threat to deltas is the loss of sediment that occurs during natural river diversions or from upstream engineering projects in the river basins. Sites of deltaic sedimentation can shift periodically as rivers change course. The abandonment of a delta by its river, thus depriving it of sediment, allows inundation of marine waters and usually results in rapid coastal erosion. Engineering projects, such as construction of multipurpose dams, can trap sands upstream and diminish sediment loads to the delta. This, in turn, creates a sediment disparity that prevents a delta from building up or building out at a rate sufficient to keep pace with sea-level rise and subsidence.

John T. Wells

FURTHER READING
Allison, M. A. "Historical Changes in the Ganges–Brahmaputra Delta." *Journal of Coastal Research,* Vol. 14 (1998), pp. 1269–1275.
Stanley, D. J., A. G. Warme, H. R. Davis, M. P. Bernasconi, and Z. Chen. "Nile Delta." *National Geographic Research and Exploration,* Vol. 8 (1992), pp. 22–51.
Wells, John. "Subsidence, Sea-Level Rise, and Wetland Loss in the Lower Mississippi River Delta." In John D. Milliman and Bilal U. Haq, eds., *Sea-Level Rise and Coastal Subsidence: Causes, Consequences, and Strategies.* Dordrecht, the Netherlands, and Boston: Kluwer Academic, 1996.
Wright, L. D., and J. M. Coleman. "Variations in Delta Morphology of Major Deltas as Functions of Ocean Wave and River Discharge Regimes." *American Association of Petroleum Geologists Bulletin,* Vol. 57 (1973), pp. 370–398.
Zhongyuan, Chen, and Daniel Stanley. "Sea-Level Rise on Eastern China's Yangtze Delta." *Journal of Coastal Research* 14 (1998), pp. 360–366.

RELATED ARTICLES
Continental Shelf; Shoreline Morphology; Submarine Fan

Demersal

Demersal is an adjective that describes organisms that live on or near the seafloor or the bed of a lake or river. The word is from *demersus*, which is the past participle of the Latin verb *demergere*, "to submerge."

Many species of demersal fishes are predators that feed on animals that live on the bottom or buried in the bottom sediment. Many demersal species are of great commercial importance. Crabs, lobsters, Norway lobsters (also known as Dublin Bay prawns and scampi), and prawns are among the valuable crustacean species. The fish species include about 60 species of cod, of which the Atlantic cod (*Gadus morhua*) is the best

known, halibut (*Hippoglossus* species), skate (*Raja* species), and the flatfishes, such as sole, turbot, and plaice.

Michael Allaby

FURTHER READING
Marshall, Norman B. *Developments in Deep-Sea Biology.* Poole, England: Blandford Press, 1979.
Nybakken, James W. *Marine Biology: An Ecological Approach,* 5th ed. San Francisco: Benjamin Cummings, 2001.

RELATED ARTICLES
Skate

Deposit Feeder

Deposit feeders are animals that obtain their nutrition by eating large amounts of sediment. A wide variety of phyla are represented, including annelids, echinoderms, and mollusks. They usually live within or on top of marine sediment and range in size from millimeters (e.g., small worms) to meters (e.g., gray whales). Because sediments lie under virtually the entire oceanic water column, these animals are widespread throughout the world's oceans. They are generally limited in abundance by the amount of food delivered to the sediment, so that the greater densities are found under shallower water columns. They are missing from sediments whose overlying water column contains no oxygen for their respiration.

Deposit feeders can process amounts of sediment as great as 100 times their body weight per day. Some can obtain their nutrition from live organisms that are contained in the sediment they swallow; for example, gray whales seek tiny crustaceans living in the sediment, whereas some intertidal snails seek live algae. However, many deposit feeders are sustained largely on dead organic matter in the sediment, with minor nutritive gain from the digestion of microorganisms in the sediment. The nature, origin, and concentrations of this dead organic matter are not well understood, but the available food must be present in very low abundance. Some deposit feeders remain at one spot in the sediments and wait for food to be deposited near them, whereas others move about and forage for food-rich patches. The high feeding rate on sediment deposits causes populations of deposit feeders to mix up the sediment, similar to the action of earthworms in soil on land. Because pollutants are often concentrated in sediment, deposit feeders can suffer unusually high exposure to such contaminants.

Lawrence M. Mayer

FURTHER READING

Barnes, Richard, Peter Calow, and P. Olive. *The Invertebrates: A New Synthesis.* Oxford and Boston: Blackwell Scientific, 1988; 2nd ed., 1993.

Barnes, Richard, and R. Hughes. *An Introduction to Marine Ecology.* Oxford and Boston: Blackwell Scientific, 1982; 3rd ed., Oxford and Malden, Mass.: Blackwell Science, 1999.

Jumars, Peter. *Concepts in Biological Oceanography.* New York: Oxford University Press, 1993.

Levinton, Jeffrey S. *Marine Ecology.* Englewood Cliffs, N.J.: Prentice Hall, 1982.

RELATED ARTICLES

Annelida; Bioturbation; Echinodermata; Mollusca

Desalination

Desalination, or desalinization, is a process by which salt water is *desalted* into fresh water. Only 6 percent of the planet's water supply is fresh water; the remaining 94 percent is seawater. Of the 6 percent that is fresh water, 27 percent is locked in glaciers and 72 percent is underground. As the world's population increases, so does the demand for fresh water. Therefore, desalting becomes an important exercise not only for drinking (or potable) water generation, but also for industrial and agricultural activities.

The first major developments in desalting techniques occurred in the 1940s, during World War II. But it was not until the 1980s that desalination technologies became economically feasible as commercial enterprises. The total desalting capacity currently is 23 billion liters (5 billion gallons) per day, which is spread across 100 countries; however, only 10 countries control 75 percent of that capacity.

A number of processes are utilized to desalt saline water, including thermal processes, membrane processes such as electrodialysis and reverse osmosis, and other developing techniques. The most common desalination process is the thermal, or heat-driven, system. Approximately one-half of the world's desalted water is produced with heat to distill fresh water from saline water. The process, which mimics parts of the natural water cycle, involves heating saline water to the point at which it boils and evaporates into steam (water vapor), and then collecting and cooling that steam into fresh water. To reduce contamination from salts within the saline water, many desalination plants apply pressure to change the boiling point of the water. This procedure, known as *scale control*, is an important development in producing cleaner water while preventing corrosion in desalination plants.

More recent innovations in desalination technology have led to the emergence of membrane

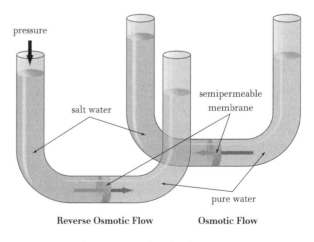

Reverse osmosis process used in desalination.

processes of electrodialysis and reverse osmosis. The former process, introduced commercially in the 1960s, is a voltage-driven procedure in which an electrical potential moves salts selectively through a membrane, leaving behind fresh water. Electrodialysis is most effective in desalting brackish water. Reverse osmosis, a relatively new process from the 1970s, uses a membrane approach similar to that of electrodialysis, but it utilizes pressure to move fresh water through a semipermeable membrane (one that does not allow the passage of salts).

Processes less commonly used are freezing, membrane distillation, solar humidification, and cogeneration. *Freezing* involves the removal of salts from saline water by changing its phase from liquid water to solid ice. *Membrane distillation* is a combination of thermal and membrane processes in which water is boiled and only the steam is allowed to pass through a membrane. *Solar humidification* imitates the natural cycle; saline water is heated by solar panels and the steam is collected and cooled as fresh water. Finally, industrial processes such as *cogeneration* utilize the energy generated from other activities to facilitate thermal desalination.

Desalination holds great promise for the future, as its capital and operating costs have decreased significantly over the years. Also, the emergence of new technologies suggests that these costs may decrease further, providing a secure and affordable freshwater supply to burgeoning populations, thereby reducing the demand on freshwater systems.

Manoj Shivlani

FURTHER READING

Buros, O. K. *The Desalting ABCs.* Topsfield, Mass.: International Desalination Association, 1990.

Heitmann, H., ed. *Saline Water Processing: Desalination and Treatment of Seawater, Brackish Water, and Industrial Waste Water.* New York: VCH, 1990.

Scott, J., ed. *Desalination of Seawater by Reverse Osmosis.* Park Ridge, N.J.: Noyes Data Corporation, 1981.

RELATED ARTICLES

Osmosis; Salinity; Sea Salt; Seawater, Composition of; Water Molecule

Detritus

Detritus is the name given to the solid organic and inorganic trash generated by biological processes. In inshore waters it can be washed or blown in from the land, but in the open ocean it is almost purely marine. It is composed of dead organisms, fecal material, exudates such as mucus, and the products of "dirty feeding."

Detritus is a major food resource, especially in water deeper than the depths at which plants can photosynthesize. The organic content of the detritus is considered to be either labile or refractory, depending on how readily it can be digested by consumers. The labile materials are readily digested and are quickly utilized by detritivores. The refractory material includes many structural components, such as cellulose, lignin, and chitin, which most animals cannot digest; their contents become available to animals only after they have been broken down by bacteria. Where bottom sediments are rich in detritus, the bacterial activity may deplete all the available oxygen and the mud turns anoxic. As the oxygen runs out, aerobic bacteria are replaced by anaerobic bacteria.

In the seabed interface and in the water, detritus is consumed by suspension feeders, which can either actively or passively sieve the particles from the water, trap them on mucous sheets, or, due to their small size, feed directly on the particles. In midwater much of the detritus is in the form of marine snow and can vary considerably in both quality and quantity in time and space.

Martin Angel

FURTHER READING

Alldredge, Alice L., and George A. Jackson, eds. "Aggregation in Marine Systems." *Deep-Sea Research II,* Vol. 42, No. 1 (1995).

Andersen, Tom. *Pelagic Nutrient Cycles: Herbivores as Sources and Sinks.* New York: Springer-Verlag, 1997.

Ittekkot, Venugopalan, et al., eds. *Particle Flux in the Ocean.* Chichester, England, and New York: Wiley, 1996.

Jumars, Peter A. *Concepts in Biological Oceanography.* New York: Oxford University Press, 1993.

RELATED ARTICLES

Anoxia; Marine Snow; Suspension Feeding

Diapir

Diapirs are buoyant materials that rise through the crust as either plastic or crystalline masses. The diapir may be connected to a parent layer or it may be detached. Diapirs most frequently occur as salt domes or as igneous bodies. However, mud diapirs are important features where geologic conditions favor their intrusion along active continental margins. An understanding of salt diapirs and igneous diapirs facilitates interpretations of the sedimentary history in a basin and the melting history of an igneous body.

Salt diapirs are bulb shaped. They rise buoyantly through overlying rocks. For a salt diapir to form, the overlying material must be very thick; the thickness causes the salt to become mobile. Movement of the salt occurs because the overlying thick material causes the salt to behave plastically and ascend through the overlying material. During the ascent of salt it is easily folded and becomes intercalated with the overlying sedimentary pile. If the salt and sediments are porous, oil droplets form in the anticlinal folds. Eventually, an oil deposit may form in the deformed beds or in beds adjacent to the salt dome.

Water temperatures in excess of 250°C (480° F) at over 5800 meters (19,000 feet) are found in some Gulf coast wells. This superheated steam and water indicate that a geothermal energy potential exists at depth on the Gulf coast.

Mud diapirs have been identified in all major oceans, but they generally occur where a thick sequence of sediments has accumulated along an active continental margin. Good examples occur in the fore-arc regions of volcanic arcs. Highly pressurized mud and gas formed by the decomposition of organic matter from below the seafloor are forced into fractures and faults that cut the margins during active tectonism, thereby forming the diapirs.

Diapirs from igneous sources originate from the asthenosphere. These diapirs are often referred to as *hotspots* or *mantle plumes* and are often used as examples of intraplate volcanism. Igneous diapirs rise upward through the asthenosphere into the lithosphere. This occurs because they are less dense than the surrounding rocks (similar to salt domes). The rising diapir begins melting at depths of about 135 kilometers (84 miles), where the solidus is first encountered. The diapir will rise another 35 kilometers (22 miles), where melting is about 30 volume percent. The total amount of liquid available to the systems is controlled by the pressure gradient, and the liquid becomes more plentiful toward the surface.

The source region for igneous diapirs is not understood completely but may be the stagnant regions in the center of the convection cells, or it may be below the region of the mantle that is stirred by convection currents. Some scientists suggest that the source may be the core–mantle interface. As the mantle plume moves upward, the increased temperature feeds hotspot volcanism. The hotspots cover up to 10 percent of Earth's surface and average 200 kilometers (124 miles) in diameter. These are found on continents as well as on the ocean floor. Diapirs move upward into the base of the lithosphere by melting material above it. The magma generated by this process reaches the surface and erupts, creating new islands and seamounts.

Igneous diapirs bring molten mantle material to the surface, including diamond and other mantle xenoliths, allowing investigations of the material that composes the mantle. Diapirs are found at the ocean spreading ridges; back-arc spreading centers; intraplate volcanism, such as the Hawaiian Islands; and on the continents, such as the Yellowstone track.

David L. White

FURTHER READING

Barker, Daniel. *Igneous Rocks.* Englewood Cliffs, N.J.: Prentice Hall, 1983.

Erickson, Jon. *Plate Tectonics: Unraveling the Mysteries of the Earth.* New York: Facts On File, 1992.

Pickering, K. T., R. N. Hiscott, and F. J. Hein. *Deep Marine Environments.* London and Boston: Unwin Hyman, 1989.

Sullivan, Walter. *Continents in Motion: The New Earth Debate.* New York: McGraw-Hill, 1974; 2nd ed., New York: American Institute of Physics, 1991.

RELATED ARTICLES

Hotspot; Mantle Plume; Seamount

Diatom

The diatoms, single-celled organisms with silica walls, are probably the most numerous of all organisms whose cells have nuclei that live in water. Diatoms dominate the phytoplankton in cold, nutrient-rich ocean waters. They can also be found growing on the ocean bottom (benthic), on plants (epiphytic), on animals (epizoic), or within other organisms (endozoic). Where beaches are exposed to heavy wave action, diatoms can be so numerous as to color the surf water brown. They are also found in fresh water and even in moist habitats on land. About 12,000 species in 285 genera have been described. A million or more diatom species may remain undescribed at this time.

Diatoms are among the most important photosynthetic organisms in aquatic environments and make a significant contribution to global primary productivity. Large numbers of diatoms, known as *blooms*, are more likely to be found in waters polluted with excessive amounts of nitrogen-containing compounds.

The most striking characteristic of this group of organisms in the phylum *Ochrophyta* is their cell wall. It is composed of silica, which makes it resistant to attack by enzymes. This resistance allows walls of dead diatoms to accumulate in thick sedimentary deposits known as *diatom ooze*. Their cell walls, or frustules, are composed of two halves that fit together like a box and lid. The type and degree of ornamentation of the frustule is used to help classify the diatoms. Those that appear round in shape from a surface or "valve" view are called *centric*. The earliest fossil diatoms were centric and appeared in the Early Cretaceous Period. The other basic shape is pennate, named because many of its frustules show feathery patterns of grooves and pores. Some of the pennate diatoms have a slit in the frustule called a *raphe*. Raphes and their associated structures enable pennate diatoms to glide rapidly. The living diatom cell contains two to several discoid chloroplasts that contain chlorophyll *a* and *c* and the brownish pigment fucoxanthin. As food reserves, diatoms produce the carbohydrate chrysolaminarin and various lipids.

Vegetative or nonreproductive diatom cells contain two complete sets of chromosomes, the diploid condition. Gametes, the reproductive cells that must fuse with other such cells to continue the life cycle, are produced by meiosis, which reduces them to the haploid state, containing one complete set of chromosomes. Centric diatoms produce one or two egg cells from one parent cell and 4 to 128 sperm from the other. The sperm are flagellate but much reduced from the usual heterokont condition of the other ochrophyte groups. Each sperm has a single flagellum with two rows of hairs that divide into three near the tip. The second smooth flagellum found in most other members of the phylum is missing. Pennate diatoms almost always produce two gametes, similar in size, known as *isogametes*,

Several jewel-like examples of diatoms. (© Lester V. Bergman/Corbis)

neither of which has a flagellum. In both patterns of reproduction, fusion of the gametes results in a large diploid auxospore, which produces a new, two-part silica wall when it divides.

Diatoms are often found in areas of low light and fairly high amounts of dissolved organic materials, such as polar sea ice. When light levels drop, a number of diatoms can switch from phototrophy, using light energy to produce food, to osmotrophy, using absorbed organic materials for basic cell activities. Some species can actually grow faster by osmotrophy than by phototrophy. Since many diatoms living in deep ocean waters migrate between the deep, lightless, but nutrient-rich depths and the lighted shallower waters where nutrients are less available, they make good use of both environments.

Several diatoms can have harmful effects. Some species of *Pseudo-nitzschia* produce a neurotoxin called *domoic acid*, which can cause amnesiac shellfish poisoning in humans and marine mammals. This condition results in memory loss when vertebrates eat filter-feeding shellfish such as mussels that feed on these diatoms and concentrate the toxin in their tissues. A few species of *Chaetoceros* cause fish kills but do not harm humans.

Bette H. Nybakken

FURTHER READING

Bold, H. C., and M. J. Wynne. *Introduction to the Algae,* 2nd ed. Englewood Cliffs, N.J.: Prentice Hall, 1985.

Round, F. E., R. M. Crawford, and D. G. Mann. *The Diatoms: Biology and Morphology of the Genera.* Cambridge and New York: Cambridge University Press, 1990.

Tomas, C. R., ed. *Identifying Marine Phytoplankton.* San Diego: Academic Press, 1997.

RELATED ARTICLES

Benthos; Epiphytic; Epizoic; Ochrophyta; Photosynthesis; Phytoplankton

Dietz, Robert Sinclair

1914–1995

Marine, Terrestrial, and Extraterrestial Geologist

In Robert Dietz's remarkable and varied career, he was the major force behind the record-breaking voyage to the deepest part of the world's ocean, joint developer of the concept of seafloor spreading, and helped establish the importance of terrestrial impacts in Earth's continuing evolution.

Robert Sinclair Dietz was born in Westfield, New Jersey, in 1914. Driven by a childhood interest in mineralogy, Robert opted to study geology at the University of Illinois, starting in 1933. There he was strongly influenced by pioneering marine geologist Francis P. Shepard (1897–1985), who had recently begun investigating the submarine canyons off California. By 1941, Dietz had been awarded an M.S. and a Ph.D. in geology at Illinois, completing most of his doctoral work at Scripps Institution of Oceanography (SIO), where Shepard was also a faculty member. Shepard and Dietz, together with Illinois graduate K. O. Emery (1914–98), were the first to describe the submarine phosphorites off California.

During World War II, Dietz joined the U.S. Army Air Corps, serving as a pilot on missions in South America. In 1946, Dietz was asked to organize a Sea Floor Studies group at the Naval Electronics Laboratory (NEL) in San Diego. In the late 1940s and early 1950s he participated in several joint NEL–SIO cruises during which important features of the Pacific basin were mapped, some detailed for the first time: for example, the Cape Mendocino submarine scarp and the deep-sea fan at the mouth of Monterey Submarine Canyon.

Exploring the underwater world firsthand was an important theme in Dietz's career. Scientists in Dietz's laboratory, including Dietz himself, were among the first to use aqualung equipment to survey the seabed. During much of Dietz's time at NEL (until 1963) he was also adjunct professor at the Scripps Institution of Oceanography (1950–63) and traveled widely. In 1953, Dietz served as a Fulbright Scholar at the University of Tokyo. From 1954 to 1958 he served with the U.S. Office of Naval Research (ONR) in London. While stationed there he met Jacques Piccard (1922–), and Dietz was influential in arranging ONR support for a bathyscaphe that was to become the record-breaking *Trieste*. On 23 January 1960, the *Trieste*, piloted by Piccard and Lt. Donald Walsh (USN), made the deepest dive in history, reaching 10,912 meters (35,800 feet) below sea level in the Challenger Deep of the Pacific. Piccard and Dietz described this feat in their 1960 book *Seven Miles Down*.

During the 1950s, Dietz had been toying with the notion of seafloor movement. In 1953, during lunch with a colleague, he speculated that some process must be carrying the Emperor Seamounts (a submerged chain of extinct Pacific volcanoes) northward like a conveyor belt. Dietz was a strong proponent of continental drift, and he was interested in fitting seafloor movement into the overall pattern of plate tectonics theory. In so doing, he proposed the concept that he named *seafloor spreading*. In a 1960 paper "Continent and Ocean Basin Evolution by Spreading of the Sea Floor," published in *Nature*, he named and described this process. In essence, it stated that new seafloor is created along mid-ocean ridges and gradually moves laterally away from the ridge. Apparently independently, Harry H. Hess (1906–69) of Princeton University had suggested the same idea. In 1960, Hess circulated a preprint paper of the idea but had yet to publish it. The concept of seafloor spreading as proposed by Hess and Dietz was soon adopted as an important piece in the jigsaw of what was to become the paradigm of plate tectonics that emerged during the 1960s.

As a graduate student at Illinois in the late 1930s, Dietz believed the Kentland Structure in nearby Indiana to be a feature of a meteoritic impact site rather than of volcanic origin. His advisers steered him away from investigating this feature for a dissertation. Nevertheless, Dietz harbored a strong interest in terrestrial impact sites, for which he coined the name astroblemes (literally, "star wounds"). By the 1960s he had demonstrated at Kentland and elsewhere that the orientation of shatter cones indicated a fracturing force from above—impact by a cosmic body—rather than a volcanic force from below. In the face of mounting evidence, most geologists have come to accept Dietz's disclosure of impact sites. Dietz had become a pioneering figure in the growing realization that meteorite impacts could be the cause of large-scale extinction events.

In his childhood, Dietz had a burgeoning interest in astronomy. In the 1930s, he wished to make the origin of the Moon's cratered surface the subject of his doctoral thesis but was persuaded otherwise. He returned to this subject and in 1946 published a paper in the *Journal of Geology* on the meteoric impact origin of the Moon's craters, a notion that was very unfashionable at the time but has since been vindicated.

In 1963, Dietz was asked to join and develop the Oceanographic and Geological Studies group within the U.S. Coast and Geodetic Survey team at Washington, D.C. The survey moved to Miami, where it became the Environmental Sciences Administration and was subsumed into the National Oceanic and Atmospheric Administration (NOAA). Between the mid-1960s and mid-1970s, Dietz built a strong team of marine biologists and geophysicists within NOAA of caliber similar to that of the team he had gathered in the Sea Floor Studies group at NEL some 20 years earlier. In addition to managing the research output of this team, Dietz spearheaded the public dissemination of NOAA's role in advancing plate tectonics theory. Dietz retired from NOAA in 1975 and took various visiting professorships from 1974 to 1977, finally accepting a professorship in geology at Arizona State

University in 1977, where he became emeritus professor in 1985. He continued his research, writing, and mentoring. Dietz died in 1995.

Dietz received many distinguished honors during his career, including the Walter H. Bucher Medal of the American Geophysical Union and the Penrose Medal of the Geological Society of America. Dietz labeled himself an *astrogeologist*. He has a Pacific tablemount, an Antarctic mountain, and an asteroid named after him—lasting testaments to the diversity and success of his endeavors.

Trevor Day

BIOGRAPHY
- Robert Sinclair Dietz.
- Born 14 September 1914 in Westfield, New Jersey.
- Educated at the University of Illinois (1933–41), where he recieved B.S., M.S., and Ph.D. degrees in geology.
- Founder and director of the Sea Floor Studies section at the Naval Electronics Laboratory, San Diego (1946–63).
- Headed the Oceanographic and Geological Studies group within the U.S. Coast and Geodetic Survey team (1963–75), which became incorporated within the National Oceanic and Atmospheric Administration (NOAA).
- In 1960, he published *Seven Miles Down* (with Jacques Piccard).
- In 1961, he introduced the concept of seafloor spreading.
- Dietz died at his home in Tempe, Arizona, on 19 May 1995.

SELECTED WRITINGS
Dietz, R. S. "Continent and Ocean Basin Evolution by Spreading of the Sea Floor." *Nature*, Vol. 190 (1961), pp. 854–857.

———. "Earth, Sea and Sky: Life and Times of a Journeyman Geologist." *Annual Review of Earth and Planetary Science*, Vol. 22 (1994), pp. 1–32.

Dietz, R. S., R. V. Lewis, and A. B. Rechnitzer. "The Bathyscaph." *Scientific American*, Vol. 198 (1958), pp. 27–33.

Piccard, Jacques, and R. S. Dietz. *Seven Miles Down: The Story of the Bathyscaph* Trieste. New York: G.P. Putnam, 1960; 2nd ed., London and New York: Longmans, 1962.

FURTHER READING

Anderson, Roger N. *Marine Geology*. New York: Wiley, 1986; 2nd ed., 1988.

Menard, H. W. *The Ocean of Truth: A Personal History of Global Tectonics*. Princeton, N.J.: Princeton University Press, 1986.

Schlee, Susan. *The Edge of an Unfamiliar World: A History of Oceanography*. New York: Dutton, 1973; London: Hale, 1975.

RELATED ARTICLES

Bathyscaphe; Emery, Kenneth O.; Marine Geology; Mass Extinction; Piccard, Auguste; Plate Tectonics; Seafloor Spreading; Shepard, Francis Parker; *Trieste*

Dinoflagellate

The dinoflagellates, members of the phylum *Dinophyta*, are extremely complex single-celled organisms. They form an important link in aquatic food chains, cause harmful algal blooms (called *red tides*), are essential to the existence of coral reefs, and have a major impact on carbon cycling.

The dinoflagellate cell is characterized by a series of vesicles found just beneath the plasma membrane of the cell. In many species, these vesicles each contain a cellulose plate. Species with these plates are called *armored* or *thecate*. Those species whose vesicles lack plates are called *unarmored* or *nonthecate*.

Most dinoflagellates have two distinctive flagella. The position of the flagella divides the dinoflagellates into two cell types. In the small group of species comprising the first type, two dissimilar flagella emerge from the cell apex, the part of the cell that moves through the water first. The vast majority of dinoflagellates have two dissimilar flagella coming out on the side of the cell. One, the transverse flagellum, lies in a groove that encircles the cell called the *cingulum* or *girdle*. The other longitudinal flagellum is found in the sulcus, a smaller groove that extends posteriorly and at

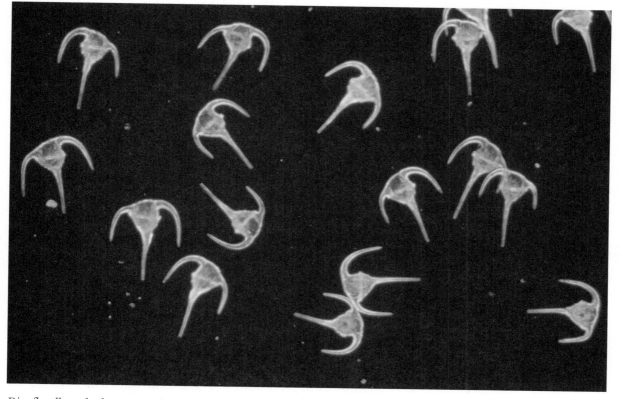

Dinoflagellate plankton magnified twenty times. (© Frank Lane Picture Agency/Corbis)

right angles to the cingulum. Even those species that form filaments or flat disks have reproductive cells with these characteristic flagella.

The motion of these two flagella makes dinoflagellates the best swimmers among the flagellate algae and causes their characteristic rotation as they move through the water. They can sense and swim toward light. A few have eyespots so complex as to resemble miniature versions of the eyes of multicellular animals.

The photosynthetic dinoflagellates use chlorophyll a and c_2 and contain the unique accessory pigment peridinin. This pigment, plus other carotenoids, gives the chloroplast-containing cells a golden-brown color similar to that found in the brown algae and their relatives.

Half of the species of dinoflagellates described cannot carry on photosynthesis because they lack chloroplasts and are heterotrophic. Some small heterotrophic species may be able to survive by osmotrophy, the taking in of dissolved organic carbon-containing molecules. The larger free-living cells must supplement this activity by phagotrophy, feeding on particles of organic material. This process is probably responsible for the great internal complexity of these cells with their wide range of *endosymbionts*, organisms that live within the dinoflagellate cells without causing harm. In addition, a number of dinoflagellates are parasites, living within the cells of fish, invertebrates, and filamentous algae.

The chromosomes and patterns of cell division in dinoflagellates are unlike those found in most cells with nuclei. Dinoflagellate chromosomes, lacking histone proteins found in plants and animals, are coiled at all times except when their DNA is replicating. Their nuclear envelope remains intact throughout cell division. The microtubules, which attach to the chromosomes and move them around inside the cell, never penetrate the nuclear envelope, but pass through tunnels in the nucleus.

Sexual reproduction has been observed in such dinoflagellates as *Pfiesteria*, which has at least 24 stages in its life cycle. In some species, meiosis, the cell division that reduces the chromosome number in the cell by half, occurs quickly. In others, the cell resulting from fertilization, known as the *zygote*, resembles a resting cyst. Resting cysts allow survival of the species in poor environmental conditions. These cysts can be transported long distances by water currents or in ship ballast water. When the ballast water is pumped out at a new port, the cysts germinate and cause a new algal bloom. Human-generated nitrogen pollution may increase the chances of these blooms.

More blooms mean a higher possibility that dinoflagellates producing toxins dangerous to humans and other vertebrates will increase. In 1987, 14 humpback whales died on the Cape Cod coast in Massachusetts from eating mackerel that had fed on a bloom of the dinoflagellate *Alexandrium* and concentrated the saxitoxin they produced. Saxitoxins from other dinoflagellates are responsible for paralytic shellfish poisoning in humans when eaten during quarantine periods. *Pfiesteria* attacks fish, causing open sores and massive fish kills as well as memory loss and learning deficits in humans.

Bette H. Nybakken

FURTHER READING
Bold, H. C., and M. J. Wynne. *Introduction to the Algae*, 2nd ed. Englewood Cliffs, N.J.: Prentice Hall, 1985.
Taylor, F. J. R., ed. *The Biology of Dinoflagellates*. Oxford and Boston: Blackwell Scientific, 1987.
Tomas, C. R., ed. *Identifying Marine Phytoplankton*. San Diego: Academic Press, 1997.

RELATED ARTICLES
Heterotrophic; Phytoplankton

Dipnoi

The Dipnoi (also called Dipneusti), as assigned in Joseph S. Nelson's *Fishes of the World* (1994), is an infraclass within the class Sarcopterygii (lobe- or fleshy-finned fishes). The Dipnoi contains the six living species of lungfishes, all of which inhabit fresh water, but the fossil record for Dipnoi contains over 60 described genera of lungfishes, at least some of which populated the marine environment. Lungfishes appear to have reached their greatest diversity and abundance during the Devonian period (408.5 to 362.5 million years ago).

As their name implies, the lungfishes possess lungs. These highly vascularized structures, derived from the fish's swim bladder, enable lungfishes to breathe air. All living species are bottom dwellers and have characteristically flattened tooth plates that they use for crushing shellfish and small fishes.

The two extant lungfish genera with more derived features—the African *Protopterus* (four species) and the South American *Lepidosiren* (one species)—have paired lungs and lack fully functional gills, although the gills may remain important for carbon dioxide excretion. These lungfishes can survive drought conditions by full or partial *aestivation*, lowering their metabolic activity and remaining more or less dormant during the dry season. The lungfishes aestivate in their own mucous-lined chambers at the bottom of dry lakes or river beds. The Australian lungfish, *Neoceratodus forsteri*, has functional gills and uses its single lung only when the oxygen levels in water are too low for gill respiration or when the gills become clogged with mud. The Australian lungfish does not aestivate.

All extant species are egg-layers. A female produces a batch of between 50 and 5000 eggs, depending on the species. The larvae of African and South American lungfishes have external gills and undergo metamorphosis to become adults. Australian lungfish larvae lack external gills and exchange respiratory gases across their skin and internal gills.

Trevor Day

FURTHER READING

Bemis, W. E., W. W. Burggren, and N. E. Kemp, eds. *The Biology and Evolution of Lungfishes.* New York: Alan R. Liss, 1987.

Helfman, Gene S., Bruce B. Collette, and Douglas E. Facey. *The Diversity of Fishes,* 3rd ed. Malden, Mass.: Blackwell Science, 1997.

Moyle, Peter B., and Joseph J. Cech, Jr. *Fishes: An Introduction to Ichthyology,* 4th ed. Upper Saddle River, N.J.: Prentice Hall, 1999.

Nelson, Joseph S. *Fishes of the World,* 3rd ed. New York: Wiley, 1994.

Paxton, John R., and William N. Eschmeyer, eds. *Encyclopedia of Fishes,* 2nd ed. San Diego, Calif.: Academic Press, 1998.

Pough, F. Harvey, Christine M. Janis, and John B. Heiser. *Vertebrate Life,* 5th ed. Upper Saddle River, N.J.: Prentice Hall, 1999.

RELATED ARTICLES

Acanthodii; Actinopterygii; Coelacanth; Sarcopterygii; Swim Bladder

Dissolved Organic Matter

Dissolved organic matter (DOM) is usually defined as the fraction of organic matter in seawater that passes through a glass fiber filter with a nominal pore size of 0.4 micrometers (0.000016 inch). It is an operational definition, since the effectiveness of filtration varies with the conditions under which it is carried out and the nature of the medium being filtered. The components in DOM range from the simplest organic molecules (amino acids, amines, sugars) to complex macromolecules (polysaccharides, polypeptides, and nucleic acids) and even viruses. Some of the larger components are of a colloidal or even particulate nature, rather than truly dissolved.

Given the complexity and diversity of chemical species in dissolved organic matter (DOM), the concentration of DOM is commonly measured as dissolved organic carbon (DOC). Initially, the seawater sample is treated with acid and purged of carbon dioxide to remove the dissolved inorganic carbon (DIC) fraction, often more than 98 percent of the total dissolved carbon in seawater. The organic carbon is determined by the further release of carbon dioxide by combustion or using one of several other oxidation methods.

In surface waters, DOM originates predominantly from the consumption or decay of phytoplankton or from the release of their excretory products. Recent estimates give one-half of oceanic primary production as being channeled via the consumption of DOM by bacteria in the microbial loop.

DOM influences important physical and chemical processes as well as biological ones. For example, the buildup of DOM at the air–water boundary alters seawater's surface tension. This, in turn, may modify wind wave generation, air–sea gas exchange rates, and the transmission of light.

Although concentrations of DOC in the oceans are low, current estimates give the total mass of DOC in the oceans as 600 to 800 gigatonnes (660 to 880 gigatons), a mass of carbon similar to that found in the carbon dioxide of the atmosphere.

Trevor Day

FURTHER READING

Azam, Farooq. "Microbial Control of Oceanic Carbon Flux: The Plot Thickens." *Science*, Vol. 280 (1 May 1998), pp. 694–696.

Libes, Susan M. *Marine Biogeochemistry*. New York: Wiley, 1992.

Millero, Frank J. *Chemical Oceanography*. Boca Raton, Fla.: CRC Press, 1992; 2nd ed., 1996.

RELATED ARTICLES

Biogeochemical Cycle; Carbon Cycle; Microbial Loop; Particulate Organic Carbon; Phytoplankton

Diurnal and Semidiurnal Tide

In the context of tides, *diurnal* means once per lunar day of 24 hours 50 minutes, and *semidiurnal* means twice per lunar day. The tide-raising forces are a mixture of diurnal and semidiurnal frequencies, in roughly equal proportions. Because they are forced motions, the tides in the oceans have the same frequencies, but not necessarily in the same proportions. The two extremes of oceanic response are the diurnal regime, where the diurnal tide has more than three times the amplitude of the semidiurnal, and the semidiurnal regime, where the semidiurnal tide has more than four times the amplitude of the diurnal. Lying between these are two types of mixed tide: mixed mainly diurnal and mixed mainly semidiurnal.

Semidiurnal tides are found in the North Atlantic Ocean, around parts of the coasts of Australia and New Zealand, and in many other places. The semidiurnal tide is well described by four harmonic constituents: M_2, which allows for the mean motion of the Moon; S_2, which allows for the mean motion of the Sun; N_2, which allows for the variation in the Moon's distance in its elliptical orbit; and K_2, which causes a biannual variation such that the semidiurnal tides at the equinoxes are more extreme than those at the solstices.

Between them, M_2 and S_2 produce the well-known phenomena of spring and neap tides, whereby the range of the semidiurnal tide varies with a period of 14.76 days. Spring tides do not occur exactly at syzygy (i.e., full or new Moon); neither do neaps occur exactly at quadrature (i.e., first and last quarter). There is a delay known as the *age of the semidiurnal tide*, whose value commonly is within the range 36 to 60 hours (1.5 to 2.5 days). This is a measure of the effects of inertia or inertial forces and friction in the real ocean; in the equilibrium tide, the age of the semidiurnal tide would be zero.

The fraction of the world's ocean with a diurnal tidal regime is considerably less than that where the regime is semidiurnal. The best known location is perhaps the coast of South Vietnam; others are found in the Sea of Okhotsk, the Gulf of Carpentaria, and the Gulf of Mexico.

Much of the diurnal tidal variation is explained by just three harmonic constituents: K_1, which, being due to both the Moon and the Sun, is termed *lunisolar*; O_1, which allows for part of the variation in lunar declination (i.e., the Moon's angular distance north or south of the celestial equator); and P_1, which allows for part of the variation in solar declination.

K_1 and O_1 together cause a fortnightly variation, rather like springs and neaps, but having a period of 13.66 days instead of 14.76 days; the diurnal tides of greatest range in this variation are called *tropic tides*.

Ken George

FURTHER READING

Defant, Albert. *Physical Oceanography*, Vol. 2. New York: Pergamon Press, 1961.

Doodson, Arthur Thomas, and H. D. Warburg. *Admiralty Manual of Tides.* London: His Majesty's Stationery Office, 1941.

RELATED ARTICLES

Mixed Tide; Neap Tide; Spring Tide; Sun and Moon, Tidal Effect of; Tide

Divergence

Divergence occurs in the oceans when waters move away from a common line or point. Circulation in the oceans occurs at a number of spatial scales, ranging from microturbulence to basin-scale circulation characterized by the ocean gyres. Correspondingly, circulation processes such as divergence occur over a wide range of spatial and temporal scales and occur both in the deep ocean and in coastal regions.

Divergence in the Deep Ocean

Divergence can occur over large spatial scales in the deep ocean. In these regions of divergence, large volumes of ocean water are moving slowly away from one another. This divergence occurs primarily in the upper layers of the oceans and often results in deeper, cooler, nutrient-rich waters being brought to the surface in a process known as *upwelling*. Examples of large-scale divergences in the deep oceans are the equatorial divergences that occur particularly in the equatorial eastern Pacific Ocean and less so in the equatorial Atlantic Ocean. In these regions the divergence in the surface ocean circulation is a result of Ekman transport forced by the prevailing westerly trade winds. Large-scale divergences are less common in the equatorial Indian Ocean because the winds associated with the monsoon overcome the prevailing trade winds that blow across the Pacific and Atlantic Oceans.

Divergences and convergences occur at the surface or within the interior of the oceans at boundaries between parallel currents flowing in opposite directions. Consider two currents flowing past one-another in the northern hemisphere. In the northern hemisphere the Coriolis force acts to deflect both currents to the right and therefore, depending on the direction that the currents are flowing, either a region of divergence or a region of convergence will be present. For example, there is a zone of divergence between the North Equatorial Current and the North Equatorial Countercurrent in the northern hemisphere.

Mesoscale eddies are a found in the surface layers of all the ocean basins, particularly within Western Boundary Currents such as the Gulf Stream. These eddies rotate either cyclonically (anticlockwise in the northern hemisphere and clockwise in the southern hemisphere) or anticyclonically.

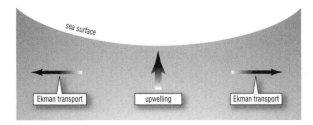

Forces that produce divergence.

Divergence and upwelling occur within cyclonic eddies and convergence occurs within anticyclonic eddies.

Divergence in the Coastal Ocean

Divergence also occurs in the coastal oceans, and similar to the deep oceans, there are a number of different ways in which regions of divergence can be created in the coastal ocean. For example, prevailing winds can blow in different directions in coastal regions. This is often associated with terrestrial features such as mountain ranges or even coastal headlands and inlets. Differences in the wind direction over even relatively small distances can lead to divergences and convergences in the coastal oceans, just like in the deep ocean far from landmasses.

Divergences and convergences also occur within fronts in the oceans. Fronts are commonplace in the coastal ocean and occur where waters with different physical characteristics meet. For example, salinity and temperature fronts often occur at the edge of river plumes where fresher estuarine waters meet more saline coastal waters. Divergences, convergences, and fronts are also commonly associated with recirculation in the coastal ocean. Recirculating flows consisting of individual or groups (sheets) of eddies can occur in the coastal ocean in places where the regular flowing currents are interrupted, particularly by reefs or protruding headlands.

The presence of a straight, featureless coast can lead to divergence. For example, consider the western coast of the North American continent. Under the influence of a persistent northerly wind (wind blowing from the north), the surface waters near the coast set in motion by the wind will be deflected offshore by the Coriolis force associated with the rotation of Earth. If the wind is relatively persistent, the surface waters of the coastal ocean will diverge to the right and away from the coast. In this case deeper nutrient-rich waters will be transported up into the surface layers to replace the water transported offshore. This process, known as *coastal wind-forced upwelling*, has very important biological consequences. Many of the most biologically productive coastal regions are in areas where persistent seasonal upwelling and coastal divergence occur. Coastal wind-forced upwelling also causes the water temperature along some coasts to remain cool even during the summer season. For example, off the Iberian coast of Spain and Portugal the summer season is characterized by regular upwelling that heralds cold water and also supports the important sardine fishery.

Divergence over Small Scales

Small-scale divergences and convergences are a feature of all the oceans. These may be associated with turbulence from microscales to more significant eddies with length scales of a few to tens of meters. Unlike their large-scale counterparts, these eddies may occur in both horizontal and vertical planes. A good example of these types of circulation patterns are Langmuir circulation cells, which form at the sea surface during windy conditions. These cells are formed by corkscrewlike motions that are aligned with the wind blowing over the sea surface. These motions have spatial scales of a few meters, and alternate cells or horizontal helicals (corkscrews) rotate in opposite directions. Between each cell is either a region of convergence or a region of divergence. These convergences in particular are often noticeable as lines of foam and other floating material aligned in the wind direction and are sometimes called *windrows*.

Mark T. Gibbs

FURTHER READING
Cushman-Roisin, Benoit. *Introduction to Geophysical Fluid Dynamics.* Englewood Cliffs, N.J.: Prentice Hall, 1994.
Pickard, George L. *Descriptive Physical Oceanography.* Oxford and New York: Pergamon Press, 1964; 5th enl. ed., Oxford and Boston: Butterworth-Heinemann, 1995.

Pinet, Paul R. *Invitation to Oceanography.* Minneapolis/St. Paul, Minn.: West Publishing, 1996; 2nd ed., Sudbury, Mass.: Jones and Bartlett, 1998.

Pond, Stephen, and George Pickard. *Introductory Dynamical Oceanography.* Oxford: Pergamon Press, 1979; 2nd ed., Oxford: Butterworth-Heinemann, 2000.

Segar, Douglas A. *Introduction to Ocean Sciences.* Belmont, Calif.: Wadsworth, 1998.

RELATED ARTICLES

Convergence; Coriolis Effect; Earth, Rotation of; Eddy; Ekman Transport; Gyre; Langmuir Circulation; Ocean Current

Divergent Plate Boundary

Divergent plate boundaries are regions of Earth where tectonic extension is opening up new ocean basins and pushing continental blocks apart. They are the reason for continental drift. The most dramatic topographic manifestation of this type of boundary is the global mid-ocean ridge system, whose initial recognition drove the development of plate tectonic theory. Most divergent plate boundaries begin life as continental rift zones formed either because of regional extensional stresses, for example, related to adjacent subduction systems, or because of the initiation of a deep-seated mantle plume.

Volcanism at Divergent Margins

Plume initiation is believed to drive the opening of several ocean basins, for example the northeastern Atlantic between Greenland and northwestern Europe, as well as the South Atlantic between Brazil and southwestern Africa. The nature of extension in this earliest phase depends on the rate and mechanical strength of the plate, the latter being strongly governed by the age of the crust. Extension in old, cold, strong plates often results in deep, narrow rift zones (e.g., east Africa), whereas rifting of younger, warmer crust results in broad zones of extension, such as the Basin and Range Province in the western United

States. Some divergent plate boundaries fail before reaching the stage of full seafloor spreading, resulting in a simple sedimentary basin within the continental crust. However, once extension has proceeded beyond a factor of 4 to 5 (i.e., the crust is four to five times thinner after extension than before), extension will proceed until all the continental crust is removed and the mantle is able to upwell into the rift zone, melting at the same time and forming normal, basaltic oceanic crust. If the rift-spreading transition occurs in the presence of a mantle plume, the higher mantle temperatures result in more melting and a massive outpouring of basaltic lavas, together with the underplating of gabbros to the base of the thinned continental crust. The first oceanic crust can be approximately 20 kilometers (12.5 miles) thick in such places (e.g., East Greenland, Eastern North America), far more than the normal 6 to 7 kilometers (3.7 to 4.3 miles). The boundary between continental and oceanic crust is very sharp.

Nonvolcanic Margins

In contrast, when there is no mantle thermal anomaly, magmatism can be very limited or absent completely. In these cases the continental margin is very wide, 100 to 200 kilometers (62 to 124 miles) and is characterized by multiple tilted fault blocks that often overlie subhorizontal extensional detachment faults. Just prior to the emplacement of the first oceanic crust, which is typically thinner than normal, extension culminates in the exposure of continental lower crust and mantle. This phenomenon is best known from the margin of Iberia, where ridges of serpentinized peridotite (ultramafic peridotite rock that has been altered at low temperatures by reaction with seawater) have been recognized.

Transition to Seafloor Spreading

Once extension has culminated in seafloor spreading, the upwelling of the upper mantle, which is typically passive and driven by the separation of the two plates, results in the generation of a relatively uniform oceanic crust of 6 to 7 kilometers (3.7 to 4.3 miles) thickness globally. Extension on mid-ocean ridges is usually strongly focused in a narrow zone along the ridge crest. This is because mantle material decompresses during its ascent, liberating heat and allowing melting to occur. As the lavas reach the seafloor and are chilled, the magnetic minerals within them are set in the orientation of Earth's magnetic field at the time. Because the magnetic field reverses over geologic time scales, the magnetic patterns frozen into the seafloor will also vary away from the axis, depending on the age of eruption. Magnetic anomalies around spreading ridges thus tend to be symmetrical about the ridge crest, a fact that first alerted marine geophysicists to the possibility of seafloor spreading. Because magnetic reversals have been dated, the marine magnetic anomaly pattern can be used to reconstruct the rates of extension in any given ocean basin. Only in equatorial regions is this impossible because Earth's field is subhorizontal, and consequently, reversals do not significantly change the vertical direction (up or down) of the anomaly, which is the factor measured by geophysicists.

Rift and Ridge Segmentation

The mid-ocean ridges are segmented, with each section divided from its neighbor by transform faults that offset the axis by up to 1400 kilometers (870 miles), although typically less. Gravity data suggest that each ridge segment is underlain by its own upwelling region of mantle, centered on the segment center. Because melt is preferentially generated in the center of the upwelling region and then delivered to the crust at that point, the igneous crust at oceanic divergent margins is usually thicker in the middle of a segment and thinner toward the ends. This is especially true of the magma chambers that underlie the ridge and freeze to form gabbros in the lower crust.

Consequently, the crust at segment ends tends to comprise mostly basalt and have little gabbro.

In addition to the transform offsets, short offsets in spreading ridge segments have been recognized. Occasionally, these may even overlap temporarily. Ridge segments are not always stationary through time and can migrate along the ridge crest by propagation of the segment end at the expense of the adjacent ridge segment. Normally, ridge segments tend to migrate toward cooler regions of mantle, away from hotter ones affected by plumes. This migration can be rapid and results in a V-shape pattern in the magnetic and topographic signature of the seafloor, charting the passage of the elongating spreading segment. Ridge migration is most common and rapid in fast-spreading ridges, especially in unstable spreading environments in backarc basins.

At the slowest rates of extension, conductive cooling inhibits melting sufficiently to reduce greatly the total crustal thickness. The best examples of this are in the Arctic, south of Australia, and on the southwestern Indian Ridge. In these settings, extension can often be nonmagmatic for significant periods. In a normal ridge environment, extension is matched by magmatism to create a uniform oceanic crust. However, if magmatism fails in slow spreading regions or toward the ends of spreading ridge segments, extension must be accommodated by brittle faulting, much as it is in the continental examples during the rift phase. In the Basin and Range Province, extension on low-angle faults has brought deep-level rocks to the surface in *metamorphic core complexes*. In practice, the same process can be seen in the ocean basins, where gabbro crops out in such structures, known as *megamullions*. The best known of these lie in the central Atlantic and on the southwestern Indian Ridge. In some cases extension can proceed to the point of exposing the oceanic mantle itself (i.e., with no igneous crust at all).

Peter Clift

FURTHER READING

Buck, W. R. "Modes of Continental Lithospheric Extension." *Journal of Geophysical Research*, B, *Solid Earth and Planets*, Vol. 96, No. 12 (1991), pp. 20,161–20,178.

Dean, S. M., T. A. Minshull, R. B. Whitmarsh, and K. E. Louden. "Deep Structure of the Ocean–Continent Transition in the Southern Iberia Abyssal Plain from Seismic Refraction Profiles: The IAM-9 Transect at 40 degrees 20′N." *Journal of Geophysical Research*, B, *Solid Earth and Planets*, Vol. 105, No. 3 (2001), pp. 5859–5885.

Horsefield, S. J., R. B. Whitmarsh, R. S. White, and Sibuet, J.-C. "Crustal Structure of the Goban Spur Rifted Continental Margin, NE Atlantic." *Geophysical Journal International*, Vol. 119, No. 1 (1994), pp. 1–19.

Skogseid, J., T. Pedersen, O. Eldholm, and B. T. Larsen. "Tectonism and Magmatism during NE Atlantic Continental Break-up: The Voring Margin." In B. C. Storey, T. Alabaster, and R. J. Pankhurst, eds., *Magmatism and the Causes of Continental Break-up.* London: Geological Society, 1992; pp. 305–320.

Taylor, B., A. M. Goodliffe, and F. Martinez. "How Continents Break Up: Insights from Papua New Guinea." *Journal of Geophysical Research*, B, *Solid Earth and Planets*, Vol. 104, No. 4 (1999), pp. 7497–7512.

RELATED ARTICLES

Gabbro; Magnetic Anomaly; Mantle Plume; Plate Tectonics; Seafloor Spreading

Doldrums

The doldrums are geographical regions in which the winds are almost always light and variable, and often from the east. Sometimes there is no wind at all. The name refers to the places where they occur, not to the wind itself or the lack of it. Their location varies and their extent changes considerably with the seasons. At times they can extend the full width of the tropical Atlantic, which means that ships crossing from one hemisphere to the other cannot avoid them. Prior to the introduction of modern meteorological monitoring it was difficult for captains to predict the location of doldrums, even at times of year when they are less extensive. Sailing ships could be becalmed in the doldrums and the lack of sufficient wind to shift the vessel was a very real hazard, because stores of food and drinking water could run low. Until modern times, sailors had no means of rendering seawater drinkable.

The doldrums are located in the Intertropical Convergence Zone (ITCZ), which is the region where the northeasterly trade winds of the northern hemisphere meet the southeasterly trade winds of the southern hemisphere. That is where converging air rises, producing a belt of low surface atmospheric pressure, the equatorial trough. The ITCZ extends all the way around the world, but it is most pronounced over the central Pacific. Elsewhere the convergence is not continuous either geographically or through the year. Although conditions in the doldrums are usually calm, from time to time these regions experience violent tropical squalls generated by the unstable, very moist, rising air.

There are three principal doldrum zones, in the eastern North Pacific in the latitude of Central America, the western North and South Pacific, and the eastern North and South Atlantic. From July to September the eastern Pacific doldrums extend westward as a tongue reaching about halfway across the Pacific. The zone in the western Pacific lies north of Australia and in the vicinity of Indonesia, and in the Indian Ocean. Its area increases from October to December, but it reaches its maximum extent in March and April, when it extends for about 16,000 kilometers (10,000 miles) from about Fiji, at 178°E longitude, all the way to the coast of East Africa. The third doldrum zone is in the eastern Atlantic. For most of the year the Atlantic doldrums extend for only a short distance from the African coast and are confined to the North Atlantic, but from July to September they reach Brazil.

The origin of the word *doldrums* is obscure, but it is probably derived from *dol*, an Old

English word that meant "dull" or "stupid." By early in the nineteenth century a *doldrum* was a dull or stupid person and *the doldrums* came to mean "low spirits." It was not until the middle of the century that the doldrums came to be associated with a geographical locality noted for its sultry, depressing monotony. Despite its association with the days of sailing ships, giving an impression of antiquity, in its geographical sense *doldrums* is a fairly recent word.

Michael Allaby

FURTHER READING

Allaby, Michael. *Encyclopedia of Weather and Climate.* New York: Facts On File, 2002.

Barry, Roger G., and Richard J. Chorley. *Atmosphere, Weather and Climate.* London: Methuen, 1968; 7th ed., London and New York: Routledge, 1998.

Henderson-Sellers, Ann, and Peter J. Robinson. *Contemporary Climatology.* London: Longman Scientific/New York: Wiley, 1986; 2nd ed., Harlow, England: Addison-Wesley, 1999.

RELATED ARTICLES

Hadley Cell; Intertropical Convergence Zone

Dredge

There are two types of dredges in use in the marine environment. One is a large ship or barge that houses equipment that removes bottom sedimentary materials from harbors, canals, bays, and so on. The second type is a small sampling device that is deployed from a surface vessel for the purpose of collecting a sample of the bottom for geological or biological analysis.

The first type of dredge includes some combination of mechanical and hydraulic techniques. In the open ocean, vessels dragging pipes behind them that pump large volumes of water off the bottom accomplish dredging. Dredges may be dippers that operate at the end of a flexible arm (which allows operation at variable depths) or buckets that grab bottom materials that are brought up to the sea surface via a cable. A continuous feed or ladder design is a line of buckets that bring material to the surface. Typical hydraulic dredges are large pumps attached to a barge surface. As sand is liquefied via the pumping process, it is moved through large pipes and eventually pumped to the surface.

The process of dredging is commonly used to obtain material needed for construction or landfill purposes, to retrieve valuable mineral deposits, or to remove sediment from canals, rivers, and harbors used for navigation. Dredges can also be used for salvage or to acquire valuable materials from the sea bottom, including mineral deposits such as gold, tin, chromium, and titanium. Dredge-fill operations have resulted in extensive losses of tidal seagrass communities and of coral reef habitats by direct impact and subsequent releases of sediment.

The second type of dredge is usually a fairly small device. A dredging net made of metal chain or nylon mesh with one end opened by a rigid frame is towed behind the vessel at the desired water depth. Some drawbacks to this method of sample collecting include difficulty in obtaining small or fragile specimens and problems determining a specific sampling location and community structure due to mixing of the samples within the dredge.

Anne Beesley

FURTHER READING

Burchett, Michael, Marc Dando, and Geoffrey Waller. *Sealife: A Complete Guide to the Marine Environment.* Washington, D.C.: Smithsonian Institution Press, 1996.

Dawes, Clinton. *Marine Botany.* New York: Wiley, 1981; 2nd ed., 1998.

Gross, M. Grant. *Oceanography: A View of the Earth.* Englewood Cliffs, N.J.: Prentice Hall, 1972; 7th ed., Upper Saddle River, N.J.: Prentice Hall, 1996.

Holme, N. A., and A. D. McIntyre, eds. *Methods for the Study of Marine Benthos.* Oxford: Blackwell Scientific, 1971; 2nd ed., Oxford and Boston, 1984.

Ingmanson, D. E., and William J. Wallace. *Oceanography: An Introduction.* Belmont, Calif.: Wadsworth, 1973; 5th ed., 1995.

Schlieper, C., ed. *Research Methods in Marine Biology.* Seattle: University of Washington Press, 1972.

RELATED ARTICLES
Grab Sampler; Trawl

Drift Net

A drift net is a modification of a gill net, a net with a relatively wide weave that allows small fish to swim through but catches larger fish, such as salmon and tuna, by their gills. A drift net is essentially several gill nets attached together, with weights on the bottom and buoys, or floats on the top that cause the net to drift underwater at a set depth. Drift nets are used to catch fish that swim at intermediate ocean depths, neither near the surface of the water nor near the ocean floor.

Drift nets can be very large, with some as long as 50 kilometers (31 miles). They are made of very fine plastic filaments that are almost invisible when under water and are often equipped with radio beacons so that the fishermen who set them can find them again. Drift-net fishing is extremely efficient. A fishing boat with a small staff can set and retrieve several large drift nets during a single trip out to the ocean. Consequently, drift nets often contribute to overfishing.

Drift nets also entangle and drown large, air-breathing sea animals such as dolphins, whales, and sea turtles, as well as birds. Such indiscriminate catches have led environmentalist groups to dub drift nets "curtains of death" and to agitate for bans on their use. Although some progress has been made in designing drift nets outfitted with devices that warn sea mammals of their location or allow them to escape the net, concerns about bycatches and overfishing led to drift nets being largely banned in international waters in the 1990s. Enforcement of the ban has been inconsistent, however; also in many coastal regions, drift net fishing is still legal, although the size of the net is usually strictly limited.

Mary Sisson

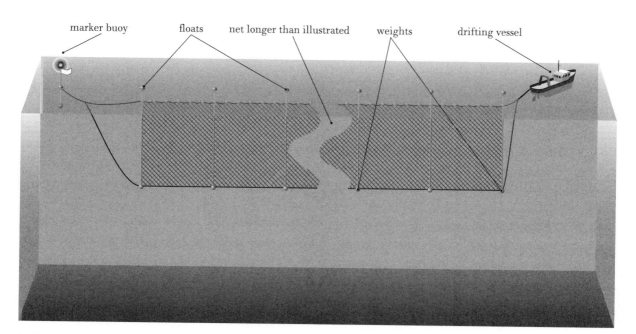

Drift net. The break in the net indicates that drift nets are generally very long, extending for miles.

FURTHER READING

Berrill, Michael. *The Plundered Seas: Can the World's Fish Be Saved?* San Francisco: Sierra Club Books, 1997.

Travis, John. "Acoustic Pingers Protect Porpoises." *Science News*, Vol. 148, No. 26/27 (1995), p. 423.

RELATED ARTICLES
Fisheries

Dysphotic Zone

The dysphotic zone comprises the twilight depths of the ocean, where daylight is detectable but is insufficiently bright to enable photosynthesis to occur. Thus it underlies the euphotic zone, and its upper level is the photosynthetic compensation depth at which the rate of production of organic matter by the phytoplankton exactly balances the rate of respiration of the phytoplankton. Hence the autotrophic phytoplankton cells that rely on sunlight as the source of energy to fuel their growth and metabolism are unable to persist. Therefore, all life, both within and below the dysphotic zone, has either to swim up into the euphotic zone to feed or to rely on organic material transported down from the euphotic zone by sinking particles or migrating animals.

Water absorbs and scatters light of varying colors differentially. Red light is absorbed first and blue-green light penetrates to the greatest depths. So not only does the intensity of daylight decline with depth, but also its color balance changes so that it becomes progressively more monochromatic. Thus the majority of animals inhabiting these twilight depths need to see only monochromatically. In sunlight, many of the crustaceans look bright scarlet. They are colored by carotenoid pigments that will reflect red light, but where there is no red light they look black.

The lower depth of the dysphotic zone, the maximum depth at which daylight is detectable, is generally about 1000 meters (3280 feet). However, below the clearest oceanic (low-productivity, eutrophic) water, such as in the Sargasso, eastern Mediterranean, and Red Seas, daylight is detectable to depths of nearly 1250 meters (4100 feet). This marks the boundary between the dysphotic and aphotic zones. Where the surface waters are productive, indicating that there are many more particles suspended in the water, the light is absorbed and scattered more rapidly, so the dysphotic zone is much shallower.

Another important feature is that below depths of around 250 meters (820 feet) the light becomes so scattered that it is no longer possible to detect where the sun is positioned in the sky. The vertical distribution of light intensity becomes totally symmetrical, with the brightest light coming from directly overhead and the dimmest being backscattered from vertically below. So if a mirror is hung in the water, it reflects exactly the same color and intensity of light as the background and is impossible to see. As a result, many animals, particularly fishes, have evolved mirrorlike sides as a form of camouflage (or cryptic coloration). Their sides are interference mirrors made up of minute platelets of white pigment and guanine that are arranged in a precise and regular pattern. These pigment layers reflect the light by the same mechanism that makes a film of oil on the surface of water reflect the colors of the rainbow.

Thus down throughout the dysphotic zone, daylight continues to play an important role in the ecology and adaptive characteristics of the inhabitants and is one of the important factors contributing to the vertical zonation of species in oceanic water columns. The zone overlaps the lower part of the epipelagic zone and the whole of the mesopelagic zone, so the species composition of the communities changes dramatically and their standing crop declines by 90 percent.

Martin Angel

Further Reading

Angel, Martin V. "Pelagic Biodiversity." In Rupert F. G. Ormond, John D. Gage, and Martin V. Angel, eds., *Marine Biodiversity: Patterns and Processes.* Cambridge and New York: Cambridge University Press, 1997; pp. 35–68.

Cox, C. Barry, and Peter D. Moore. *Biogeography: An Ecological and Evolutionary Approach.* New York, Wiley, 1973; 6th ed., Oxford and Malden, Mass.: Blackwell Science, 2000.

Denton, Eric J. "On the Organization of Reflecting Surfaces in Some Marine Animals." *Philosophical Transactions of the Royal Society of London Series B,* No. 258 (1970), pp. 285–313.

Herring, Peter J., Anthony K. Campbell, Michael Whitfield, and Linda Maddock, eds. *Light and Life in the Sea.* Cambridge and New York: Cambridge University Press. 1990.

Lalli, Carol M., and Timothy R. Parsons. *Biological Oceanography: An Introduction.* Oxford and New York: Pergamon Press, 1993; 2nd ed., Oxford: Butterworth-Heinemann, 1997.

Related Articles

Aphotic Zone; Compensation Depth; Epipelagic Zone; Euphotic Zone; Mesopelagic Zone; Photosynthesis; Phytoplankton

E

Earth, Rotation of

The daily rotation of Earth causes day and night, a basic rhythm for life, as well as the basis for reckoning time. Earth's rotation, combined with the gravitational attraction of the Moon and Sun, causes ocean and Earth tides. The rotation of Earth also produces an apparent or fake force on particles moving across its surface. This force is named the *Coriolis force* after a nineteenth-century French engineer, Gaspard Gustave de Coriolis (1792–1843), who studied problems of rotating machinery. Understanding the effects of Earth's rotation is often key to understanding the motion of the atmosphere and the ocean.

Coriolis Force

Distant stars determine the reference frame for motion. Consider the path of a missile fired southward along the Greenwich meridian (0°E) from the North Pole with a velocity of 100 meters (328 feet) per second, striking Earth two hours later. During the period of the flight, Earth will rotate to the east 30°, so the missile will land 720 kilometers (447 miles) south of the North Pole at 30°W. To the observer in space, the motion of the missile will appear as a straight line. To the observer on Earth, the missile will appear to be deflected to the right of its intended path.

Next consider the path of a missile that is fired northward from the equator along the Greenwich meridian with a velocity of 100 meters (328 feet)

per second with respect to Earth. In this case, it is necessary to consider the fact that the equator is moving 465,000 meters (1,525,590 feet) per second eastward and that this eastward speed is imparted to the missile. As the missile moves northward away from the equator along surface of Earth, the surface of Earth underneath the missile has a slower eastward speed than the missile because it is closer to the axis of rotation of Earth [at 40°N, the eastward speed of Earth is 356,000 meters (1,168,000 feet) per second and at the North Pole, it is 0] than at the equator. In this case the missile will land to the east of the Greenwich meridian, again appearing to an Earth observer to be deflected to the right of its initial path.

A Foucault pendulum provides another illustration of the rotation of Earth. Imagine a pendulum at the North Pole. The plane of motion of the pendulum is fixed with respect to the stars so that Earth appears to rotate counterclockwise beneath the pendulum. If the plane of motion of the pendulum is initially aligned with the Greenwich meridian, in 12 hours Earth will have rotated 180° and the plane of motion of the pendulum will again be aligned with the Greenwich meridian. Note that if the pendulum were at the South Pole, Earth would appear to rotate clockwise beneath the pendulum. Finally, if the pendulum were on the equator and was moving in an east–west direction, as Earth rotated the motion of the pendulum would remain in the same direction. The time in hours that is required for the pendulum to rotate 180° so that it is in the original plane of motion is equal to 12 divided by the sine of the latitude.

Oceanographers and meteorologists have a choice when they are studying motion on the surface of Earth. They can include the tangential velocities of Earth in their calculations or they can include an artificial force. The former approach would unnecessarily complicate matters, so the latter has been adopted. The artificial force is called the *Coriolis force*. The magnitude of the Coriolis force is fv, where v is the speed of a parcel of water and $f = 2\Omega\sin\theta$, and Ω is the angular velocity of Earth, $2\pi/($length of a sidereal day $= 86,164$ seconds ~ 24 hours$) = 7.29 \times 10^{-5}$ per second, and θ is latitude. The magnitude of the Coriolis force increases from zero at the equator to a maximum at the poles. As illustrated in the missile examples above, the Coriolis force acts at right angles to the direction of motion, causing deflection to the right in the northern hemisphere and to the left in the southern hemisphere.

Variations of Rotation Rate

Neither the length of day (the rate of rotation of Earth) nor the location of the poles is fixed. The length of day is measured accurately with an atomic clock, and variations of length of day and the location of the pole are determined by a variety of modern navigation techniques, including very long baseline radio interferometry, lunar and satellite laser ranging, Doppler orbitography by radiopositioning integrated on satellite, and the global positioning system. The International Earth Rotation Service (IERS) provides results of these measurements to the scientific community. IERS measurements are important for the astronomy, geodetic, and geophysical communities.

The length of day is increasing. This is because the ocean tides apply a braking force on the rotation of Earth. Examples of this breaking force are bottom friction, induced by tidal currents flowing across the seabed, and the scattering of tidal waves into oceanic internal waves. The rate of increase of the length of day can be determined from modern IERS measurements as well as by comparing the observations of eclipses of the Sun and Moon by the Babylonians, Greeks, Arabs, and Chinese with computed eclipses using a constant length of day. Fossils and paleomagnetic data can also be used to determine the changes in the length of day over millennia of Earth's history. These data all show that the rotation period of Earth is slowing at a rate of about 2 milliseconds per day. The length of day was 18 hours 900 million years ago.

Beginning in 1972, seconds have been added to the atomic clock to keep differences with the rotation rate of Earth to less than 0.9 second. IERS decides when to do this, but first preference is given to the end of December or June. Because this is similar to inserting February 29 into a leap year, these are called *leap seconds*. To date, there have been 13 leap seconds.

Modern measurements have also made it possible to study seasonal, daily, and subdaily variations in rotation rate. Diurnal and semidiurnal variations of ±40 microseconds are observed. These are related to ocean tides. The moment of inertia of Earth is changed as tides move water around Earth. Tidal currents also exchange angular momentum with Earth as they accelerate. The latter is more important for rotation rate variations, while both contribute about equally to polar motion variations. Seasonal variations of rotation rate are a few milliseconds. Other oceanographic process such as El Niño or meanders of major ocean currents can also affect the rotation rate of Earth by changing the distribution of mass (and hence the moment of inertia) of Earth.

To understand how changes in the moment of inertia of Earth affect the length of day, consider a spinning ice skater. The closer ice skaters hold their arms to their bodies, the faster they spin. This is due to the conservation of angular momentum. Ocean (and air) currents move millions of tonnes per second. If the net motion is directed toward the poles, it will decrease the distance from Earth's axis and result in a decrease in the moment of inertia of Earth. To conserve angular momentum, the length of day would decrease. Conversely, if the net motion is directed toward the equator, it will increase the distance from the earth's axis and result in an increase in the moment of inertia of Earth. The length of day would increase.

Curtis A. Collins

FURTHER READING

Munk, W. "Once Again: Tidal Friction." *Progress in Oceanography,* Vol. 40 (1997).

Munk, W. H., and G. J. F. MacDonald. *The Rotation of the Earth: A Geophysical Discussion.* Cambridge: Cambridge University Press, 1960.

Ray, R. D., D. J. Steinberg, B. F. Chao, and D. E. Cartwright. "Diurnal and Semidiurnal Variations in the Earth's Rotation Rate Induced by Oceanic Tides." *Science,* Vol. 264 (1994).

RELATED ARTICLES

Coriolis Effect; Sun and Moon, Tidal Effect of

Earth Observing System

The U.S. National Aeronautic and Space Administration's (NASA) Earth Observing System (EOS) is a program of remote sensing satellites that, along with other experimental programs, make up the U.S. space agency's Earth Science Enterprise (ESE).

The aim of EOS is to improve our understanding of the interaction between humans and the environment—studying how earth, sea, and air interact with each other, how human activity may be changing the climate, and how climate change in turn affects life. The program was conceived in 1990, although its origins can be traced back to the early 1980s. It is composed of a total of 21 satellite launches, supported by space shuttle and space station missions. Although the satellites themselves are built in the United States and NASA also controls the program, many of the

instruments carried on board have been provided by international collaborators such as Canada, Japan, and Brazil.

Unlike most other satellite programs, which usually have the same satellite design and often the same instruments for all their missions, each EOS spacecraft has been specially built and fitted out for very specific scientific goals. EOS missions of particular interest to oceanographers include SeaWiFS (sea-viewing wide-field-of-view sensor), designed to provide data on the color and other optical qualities of the ocean, and QuikScat, a specialized radar scatterometer for measuring wind speeds at the sea surface. Jason-1, a joint U.S.–French mission to study global ocean circulation, was designed to follow on from the hugely successful venture, *TOPEX/Poseidon.*

Although these smaller missions carry just a few instruments designed to investigate specific questions, the EOS program also includes three major satellites, *Terra, Aqua,* and *Aura.* These spacecraft are equipped with a battery of instruments to gather a wide range of data about the

Images of phytoplankton blooms in the United Kingdom and Ireland captured by SeaWiFS, part of NASA's Earth Observing System (EOS). (The SeaWiFS Project, NASA/Goddard Space Flight Center, and ORBIMAGE)

land, seas, and atmosphere, respectively. The very range of data collected by the EOS missions could make it difficult for scientists to fit the pieces together and identify previously unseen connections, so the EOS satellites are only one element of the overall system. Equally important is an advanced computer network that NASA has developed to improve the exchange and sharing of data between groups of scientists working all around the world.

As well as providing long-term monitoring of the environment to improve scientific theories, information from the EOS satellites can be put to more direct use. For instance, shortly after its launch, *Terra* observed a depletion in snowfall in the midwestern United States during the spring of 2000, an indicator of potential drought conditions to come that allowed scientists to foresee, although not avert, the huge wildfires that swept the region that following summer.

Giles Sparrow

FURTHER READING

Asrar, Ghassem, and Jeff Dozier. *EOS: Science Strategy for the Earth Observing System.* New York: American Institute of Physics, 1994.

Inglis, Andrew F., and Arch C. Luther. *Satellite Technology: An Introduction,* 2nd ed. Boston: Focal Press, 1997.

Rees, Gareth. *The Remote Sensing Data Book.* Cambridge and New York: Cambridge University Press, 1999.

RELATED ARTICLES
TOPEX/Poseidon

East China Sea

The East China Sea is located between China in the west, Taiwan in the south, Kyūshū and the Ryukyu Islands in the east, and Cheju Island in the northeast. It merges with the Yellow Sea in the north. The boundary between the East China and Yellow Seas is somewhat arbitrary and runs from Cheju Island to the Yangtze River mouth.

The East China Sea area is 752,000 square kilometers (290,300 square miles). It extends from 25 to 34°N latitude and from 120 to 130°E longitude. The sea is mostly shallow, less than 150 meters (492 feet). The only deep basin is the Okinawa Trough, west of the Ryukyu Islands, where the depth exceeds 2000 meters (6562 feet). Together with the adjacent Yellow and Bohai Seas, the East China Sea Shelf forms the largest shelf in the Pacific, one of the largest in the world, with a total area of 900,000 square kilometers (347,500 square miles).

The sea's oceanographic regime is shaped by the monsoons that determine the winter and summer circulation patterns, and also by huge runoff and strong tidal currents. In winter, the Siberian cold air outbreaks mix the shelf water completely, decreasing its temperature below 10°C (50°F). The summer monsoon brings about warming, up to 28°C (82°F) at the sea surface. The sea receives an enormous amount of fresh water, 819 billion tonnes (903 billion tons) per year, from the Yangtze River (Changjiang), the fifth-largest runoff in the world. This influx brings down the sea's salinity below 30 parts per thousand off the Yangtze mouth; given the sea's shallowness, the river runoff is volumetrically more important than anywhere else in the World Ocean. The Yangtze River also discharges 432 million tonnes (476 million tons) of sediments per year, the fifth-largest discharge in the world.

The general circulation of the sea is cyclonic (counterclockwise). The sea receives relatively salty and warm water from the South China Sea via Taiwan Strait. This water mixes with the Yangtze River discharge and flows via Tsushima (Korea) Strait to the Japan (East) Sea. It also penetrates the Yellow and Bohai Seas. The Kuroshio extends along the shelf break and exits the sea via Tokara Strait south of Kyushu. The sea features various oceanographic fronts: Kuroshio front; Yangtze River discharge front; tidal fronts; and coastal upwelling fronts. The fronts emerge each year during the same season and are best defined in winter. The sea abounds with fish. The most important fishery ground is associated with coastal upwelling off Zhejiang Province (southeastern China).

Igor M. Belkin

FURTHER READING

Hickox, R., I. M. Belkin, P. Cornillon, and Z. Shan. "Climatology and Seasonal Variability of Ocean Fronts in the East China, Yellow and Bohai Seas from Satellite SST Data." *Geophysical Research Letters* Vol. 27, No. 18 (2000), pp. 2945–2948.

Su, J. "Circulation Dynamics of the China Seas North of 18°N." In A. R. Robinson and K. H. Brink, eds., *The Global Coastal Ocean*, Vol. 11, *Regional Studies and Syntheses*. New York: Wiley, 1998; pp. 483–505.

Zhou, D., Y.-B. Liang, and C.-K. Zeng (C. K. Tseng), eds. *Oceanology of China Seas*, Vols. 1 and 2. Dordrecht, the Netherlands, and Boston: Kluwer Academic,1994.

RELATED ARTICLES

Kuroshio; Monsoon; South China Sea; Upwelling; Yellow Sea.

Eastern Boundary Current

The large-scale circulation of the Atlantic and Pacific Oceans is dominated by major anticyclonic patterns of flow called *gyres* (the term *anticyclonic* implies clockwise rotation in the northern hemisphere and counterclockwise rotation in the southern hemisphere). These current gyres are driven by anticyclonic torque provided by the prevailing surface winds. At midlatitudes (about 30 to 60°N and 30 to 60°S), the westerly winds contribute to this torque, whereas at lower latitudes, the northeast trade winds in the northern hemisphere (about 0 to 30°N) contribute, and their counterpart, the southeast trade winds, contribute in the southern hemisphere (about 0 to 30°S). On the western sides of these subtropical gyres the flow is generally toward the poles and concentrated along the western boundaries, whereas on the eastern sides, the flow is generally toward the equator but spread broadly from the continental boundaries toward the centers of the gyres. Currents that are located along the western boundaries of the gyres (i.e., off the eastern boundaries of the continents) are referred to as *western boundary currents*; conversely, currents located along the eastern boundaries of the gyres (i.e., off the western boundaries of the continents) are referred to as *eastern boundary currents*. Eastern boundary currents tend to be weak, broad, and shallow compared to western boundary currents, which tend to be swift, narrow, and deep. The width of eastern boundary currents, for example, may be 1000 kilometers or more (greater than 600 miles), with maximum speeds of only a few tens of centimeters per second. The asymmetric behavior of the world's major boundary currents is related to several factors, including Earth's rotation, the influence of frictional drag along the coastal boundaries, and the stress imparted by the surface wind. At latitudes below about 45°, winds along the eastern boundaries of the oceans are predominantly toward the equator and the currents tend to follow in the same direction. Examples of major eastern boundary currents include the California Current off the U.S. west coast, the Peru Current off the west coast of South America, and the Benguela Current off the west coast of South Africa.

The physical and biological characteristics of eastern boundary currents at midlatitudes are quite different from those associated with western boundary currents. Eastern boundary currents are preferred locations where coastal upwelling occurs. Through the process of coastal upwelling, deep, cold, nutrient-rich waters are brought to the surface under the influence of the local equatorward winds and Earth's rotation. Coastal upwelling has a major impact on local currents, water temperature, abundance of marine life, and weather along the adjacent coast. Although the flow is generally weak in eastern boundary currents, narrow, jetlike flows associated with coastal upwelling often occur that are embedded within the overall pattern of weak, equatorward flow. Upwelled waters are some of the most biologically productive waters to be found in the world's oceans. Almost 90 percent of the world's fish are caught in 10 percent of the world's oceans, and they are caught primarily in areas of coastal upwelling, areas that are located primarily in eastern boundary currents. In addition to coastal upwelling, eastern boundary currents often contain countercurrents next to the coast that may be seasonal in nature, and undercurrents that flow in opposition to the surface flow and are located next to the continental shelf and slope.

Laurence C. Breaker

FURTHER READING

Gill, A. E. *Atmosphere–Ocean Dynamics.* International Geophysics Series, Vol. 30. New York: Academic Press,1982.

Knauss, John A. *Introduction to Physical Oceanography.* Englewood Cliffs, N.J.: Prentice Hall, 1978; 2nd ed. rev., Upper Saddle River, N.J.: Prentice Hall, 2000.

Richards, F. A., ed. *Coastal Upwelling.* Washington, D.C.: American Geophysical Union, 1981.

Wooster, W. S., and J. L. Reid, Jr. *Eastern Boundary Currents.* In M. N. Hill., ed., *The Sea,* Vol. 2. New York: Interscience Publishers, 1963; pp. 253–276.

RELATED ARTICLES

Ekman Transport; Equatorial Undercurrent; Front; Upwelling; Western Boundary Current

Echinodermata

Familiar sea stars and sea urchins make the echinoderms (phylum Echinodermata) one of the best known groups of marine *invertebrates* (animals without backbones). The name *echinoderm* comes from the Greek word for "spiny skin," since most have a tough outer covering of bumps, spikes, or spines to ward off potential predators. Another feature they share is their distinctive shape. Whereas most animals have a front and rear and left and right sides (bilateral symmetry), echinoderms do not fit this pattern. Instead, the adult echinoderm body, typified by sea stars, has

what is known as *radial symmetry*. It can be divided into equal parts arranged around a central disc. As a result, echinoderms are both headless and brainless as adults.

Diversity

There are around 6000 living species of echinoderms and a further 13,000 or so known only from the fossil record. Scientists divide the living species into six classes: Asteroidea (sea stars), Ophiuroidea (brittlestars), Crinoidea (sea lilies and feather stars), Echinoidea (sea urchins and sand dollars), Holothuroidea (sea cucumbers), and Concentricycloidea (sea daisies). All echinoderms are exclusively marine and most live on the seafloor, but they vary widely in lifestyle and appearance. Some are roving predators that slowly creep around in search of prey, others burrow in sediment, and still others live anchored to the seafloor by a stalk.

Anatomy

Echinoderms range in size from brittlestars 1 centimeter (0.4 inch) wide to sea cucumbers 2 meters (79 inches) long. Because they lack a front or a back end, scientists distinguish between the surface bearing the mouth (oral) and the surface without a mouth (aboral). In most species the mouth is located in the center of the bottom surface, and in some species it serves not only as a mouth but also as an anus. In many echinoderms the mouth is surrounded by a number of arms, usually a multiple of five. Sea stars and brittlestars typically have 5 to 25 arms, but sea lilies may have several hundred. Sea urchins, sea cucumbers, and sand dollars have globular bodies lacking arms.

Echinoderms have a well-developed internal skeleton made up primarily of calcium carbonate, and the skin is stretched over this skeleton. In most species the skeleton consists of plates held together by connective tissue and muscle that move separately to allow the animal to move. In sea urchins and sand dollars the skeletal plates are

Sea urchin on a reef. Sea urchins belong to the Echinoidea species, part of the phylum Echinodermata. (© Stephen Frink/Corbis)

fused into a rigid, hollow skeleton or *test*. As well as giving the body support, the skeleton provides spikes or spines needed for defense. Often, these are blunt, but some sea stars and sea urchins have painfully sharp spines laced with venom.

All echinoderms have a special network of fluid-filled tubes running through the body, the water vascular system. The liquid inside the water vascular system is similar to seawater and helps to distribute oxygen and nutrients around the body, as well as eliminating waste products. In many species the water vascular system also plays a vital role in movement.

Movement

The tubes of the water vascular system end in many tiny, blind extensions that poke through perforations in the skeleton or between skeletal elements on the body. In sea stars, sea urchins, and brittlestars, these fluid-filled extensions serve as feet. When fluid is forced into them they stretch out and touch the surface below, gripping like suckers, thanks to sticky secretions on their tips. Muscles inside the tubes then contract and pull the animal up to the anchored tube feet. The pattern is repeated, creating a forward motion. Sea stars have hundreds of tube feet that extend and contract in coordinated waves, allowing these animals to move slowly along the seafloor.

Not all echinoderms use their feet for walking. Sea cucumbers wave their feathery feet (set around their mouth) through the water to catch drifting particles of food while additional tube feet are employed to stick them to rocks or the seafloor. Other echinoderms have different means of moving around. Feather stars walk gracefully on the tips of their long arms, or they swim by beating their arms rhythmically through the water; sea cucumbers use their flexible, muscular bodies to wriggle into mud; and sea lilies have no need to move as they live anchored to the seafloor by a stalk.

Feeding

The echinoderms show a great variety of feeding strategies. Sea stars are typically predators or scavengers that feed with the mouth facing downward. When a sea star finds a meal on the seafloor, it crawls on top of it and takes the prey in whole or extrudes its stomach out through the mouth and onto the food. The stomach then secretes digestive juices and absorbs the resulting soup of nutrients. Some sea stars prey on oysters and clams, using their tube feet to grip shells and then inserting the stomach into the bivalve and digesting the victim. The crown-of-thorns sea star (*Acanthaster planci*) is a voracious predator of coral polyps and has devastated parts of Australia's Great Barrier Reef.

Sea urchins typically feed by *grazing*, using large teeth (which are part of a complex organ system known as Aristotle's lantern) to rasp away at algae or animal matter; sand dollars burrow through mud and extract edible particles from the water. Unlike most other echinoderms, sea lilies and feather stars feed with their mouths facing upward. With their arms spread out, they use their feathery tube feet to catch microorganisms and larvae drifting through the water. The food is then moved along grooves running toward the mouth by hundreds of microscopic beating hairs, or cilia. Sea cucumbers also catch food from the water with sticky, feathery feet, which they wipe periodically across the mouth.

Reproduction

Most species reproduce by releasing their sperm and egg cells into the water and allowing the sex cells to fuse at random and drift away. Others brood the developing embryos, keeping them trapped within the parent's body until mature enough to release as free-swimming larvae or as juveniles. The tiny larvae bear little resemblance to the adults. Like most animals, they are bilaterally symmetrical, with distinct front and rear ends, and they are covered with bands of tiny beating cilia to help them swim. Eventually, they undergo metamorphosis and sink to the seafloor to begin their adult lives.

Some sea stars have another means of reproduction, albeit an unintentional one; they are capable of regenerating arms broken off by predators; brittlestars sometimes deliberately shed limbs to escape being eaten. But sea stars of the genus *Linckia* can go one step further—severed limbs of these echinoderms can grow into whole animals, provided that they include a portion of the central disk from the "parent" sea star.

Ben Morgan

FURTHER READING

Banister, Keith, and Andrew Campbell. *The Encyclopaedia of Underwater Life.* London: Allen and Unwin, 1985.

Barnes, Robert. *Invertebrate Zoology.* Philadelphia: Saunders, 1963; 6th ed., by Edward Ruppert, Fort Worth, Texas: Saunders, 1994.

Brusca, Richard C., and Gary J. Brusca. *Invertebrates.* Sunderland, Mass.: Sinauer, 1990.

Fish, J. *A Student's Guide to the Seashore.* London and Boston: Unwin Hyman, 1989; 2nd ed., Cambridge: Cambridge University Press, 1996.

Nybakken, James W. *Marine Biology: An Ecological Approach,* 5th ed. San Francisco: Benjamin Cummings, 2001.

Pechenik, Jan A. *Biology of the Invertebrates.* Boston: Prindle, Weber and Schmidt, 1985; 4th ed., Boston: McGraw-Hill, 2000.

Postlethwait, John. *The Nature of Life.* New York: McGraw-Hill, 1989; 3rd ed., 1995.

Purves, William, et al. *Life: The Science of Biology.* New York: Sinauer/Boston: Grant Press, 1983; 5th ed., Sunderland, Mass.: Sinauer, 1998.

RELATED ARTICLES

Asteroidea; Concentricycloidea; Crinoidea; Echinoidea; Holothuroidea; Ophiuroidea

Echinoidea

Echinoids are spherical to flattened animals that occur in all marine habitats from the intertidal to the deep sea. Many have profound impacts on communities through grazing on algae or burrowing in soft substrates, and in turn, they are eaten by many other animals. Some species form important fisheries, and their beautiful skeletons are popular ornaments.

The approximately 900 species are often divided into two groups: rounded "regular" echinoids that occur generally on hard surfaces (sea urchins) and flattened or heart-shaped "irregular" echinoids that occur on or within soft substrates (sand dollars, cake urchins, heart urchins). They belong to the class Echinoidea (phylum Echinodermata), which is divided into two subclasses: Perischoechinoidea, an ancient stock of sea urchins with dead spines, which includes only the order Cidaroidea living mainly in the tropics, deep sea, and Antarctic; and Euechinoidea, which includes all other living echinoids in 14 orders, including the more familiar sea urchins and all irregular echinoids.

All echinoids are encased in an interlocking endoskeleton of calcareous plates. Tube feet extend through perforated plates, the *ambulacral plates*, arranged in five paired columns curving from the mouth on the oral surface to the opposite, aboral surface. On one side of each ambulacral column is a column of interambulacral plates. Together the 20 columns of ambulacral and interambulacral plates form a rigid skeleton (the *test*) bearing movable spines and pedicellariae (tiny pincers used for defense and to capture food).

Most echinoids have an intricate jaw apparatus, *Aristotle's lantern*, holding five continuously growing teeth that protrude through the mouth. The aboral side of the animal carries an apical ring of small plates, including the genital plates, with pores (gonopores) for releasing the gametes, and a single sieve plate (madreporite) that leads to water canals operating the tube feet. In sea urchins these plates surround the anus. In sand dollars and heart urchins, the anus is shifted to one side, forming a posterior end; in heart urchins the mouth is also shifted, but to the opposite, anterior end of the animal, so that it has a bilateral symmetry. Heart urchins are also exceptional because they have no teeth or jaw apparatus.

Grazing by some species of sea urchins can lead to large algal-free barren areas. Sand dollars often occur in dense beds on sandy shores, where they catch small particles brought to them by the waves, whereas heart urchins burrow in and feed on soft substrates, often causing extensive bioturbation. Predators of echinoids include sea anemones, sea stars, crabs, lobsters, fishes, sea otters, and humans.

All echinoids normally have separate sexes. Eggs and sperm are spawned into the surrounding seawater, where fertilization occurs. In most species, embryos develop within free-floating eggs and hatch out as swimming balls of cells (blastulae). These develop further into plutei, exquisite, bilateral, swimming larvae that feed on phytoplankton. Plutei grow and eventually settle on the bottom, where they undergo catastrophic metamorphosis, lose their bilateral symmetry, and become more-or-less spherical juveniles. Some species of echinoids do not have feeding larvae, but instead produce large, yolky eggs that develop in the plankton before settling or are held as embryos by the parent until they leave as juveniles. Growth is both by plate enlargement and by the addition of new plates aborally, slowing with age; animals can reach 100 years or more. Mortality is from disease, predators, or physical stress; senility does not seem to occur.

Sea urchins are the basis of important fisheries in many parts of the world. The large, nutrient-packed gonads that nearly fill the test are eaten raw, as sushi, or in sauces and condiments. As wild sea urchin stocks are depleted, mariculture of sea urchins has become economically more feasible and will probably replace the fishery in coming years.

John Pearse

FURTHER READING

Hyman, L. H. *The Invertebrates,* Vol. 4, *Echinodermata.* New York and London: McGraw-Hill, 1955.

Kalvass, P. E., and J. M. Hendrix. "The California Red Sea Urchin, *Strongylocentrotus franciscanus,* Fishery: Catch, Effort, and Management Trends." *Marine Fishery Review,* Vol. 59 (1997), pp. 1–17.

Lawrence, John M. "On the Relationship between Marine Plants and Sea Urchins." *Oceanography and Marine Biology, Annual Reviews,* Vol. 13 (1975), pp. 213–286.

Nichols, David. *Echinoderms.* London: Hutchinson, 1962; 4th rev. ed., 1969.

Pearse, John S., and R. Andrew Cameron. "Echinodermata: Echinoidea." In A. C. Giese, J. S. Pearse, and V. B. Pearse, eds., *Reproduction of Marine Invertebrates,* Vol. VI, *Echinoderms and Lophophorates.* Pacific Grove, Calif.: Boxwood Press, 1991; pp. 513–662

Pearse, Vicki, et al. *Living Invertebrates.* Palo Alto, Calif.: Boxwood Press, 1987.

Smith, Andrew B. *Echinoid Palaeobiology.* London and Boston: Allen and Unwin, 1984.

RELATED ARTICLES

Asteroidea; Brittlestar; Concentrocycloidea; Crinoidea; Echinodermata; Holothuroidea; Mariculture; Ophiuroidea; Sand Dollar; Sea Lily

Echiura

Members of the invertebrate phylum Echiura are better known as *spoon worms.* These small soft-bodied animals live in U-shaped burrows in sand or mud (or, more rarely, in rock crevices) on the seafloor. About 140 species are known. Most of these are shallow-water species, but others live up to 10,000 meters (33,000 feet) deep.

Spoon worms vary from a few millimeters to 1 meter (3.3 feet) in length. They have plump, rounded bodies; rough, knobbly skin; and a long, mobile proboscis (snout) at the front end. The proboscis is highly flexible. In some species it can extend up to 25 times the length of the body. If attacked by a predator, a spoon worm can shed its proboscis and later grow a new one. Spoon worms feed by extending the proboscis out of the burrow and picking up detrital particles from the substrate. The food particles stick to a mucus-covered groove that runs the length of the proboscis. Tiny hairs (cilia) sweep the food down the groove and toward the mouth, which is located at the base of the proboscis. The food is then digested within a long, convoluted intestine, and any undigested residue passes out of an anus at the base of the trunk.

The sexes are separate, and reproduction takes place by release of sex cells into the sea, where fertilization occurs. The fertilized egg cells grow into larvae that drift away in the plankton and eventually metamorphose into adults. In most species the sexes look similar, but members of the genus *Bonellia* are a notable exception. In these spoon worms the males are only 1 millimeter (0.039 inch) long and live as parasites inside the much larger females, which grow up to 1 meter (3.3 feet) in length (including the proboscis).

Ben Morgan

FURTHER READING

Barnes, Robert. *Invertebrate Zoology.* Philadelphia: W. B. Saunders, 1963; 6th ed., by Edward Ruppert, Fort Worth, Texas: Saunders College Publishing, 1994.

Brusca, Richard C., and Gary J. Brusca. *Invertebrates.* Sunderland, Mass.: Sinauer Associates, 1990.

Margulis, Lynn. *Five Kingdoms: An Illustrated Guide to the Phyla of Life on Earth.* San Francisco: W. H. Freeman, 1982; 3rd ed., New York, 1998.

Pechenik, Jan A. *Biology of the Invertebrates.* Boston: Prindle, Weber and Schmidt, 1985; 4th ed., Boston: McGraw-Hill, 2000.

RELATED ARTICLES

Commensalism; Intertidal

Echolocation

The toothed whales (suborder Odontoceti) apparently have the ability to echolocate, a feature similar to echolocation by bats. Basically, echolocation is the ability to sense surrounding objects using sound. Sound travels about four times faster in water than in air, can generally travel farther in water (because the increased density of water transmits the energy better than air), and can be used when it is dark (such as at night and at depth). These features make sound the preferred means of sensing things underwater. Vision is impaired in the oceans because the water can be murky (turbid) from particles, light is reflected at the water's surface and absorbed with depth so the deeper waters are darker, and seeing in air and in water require different forms of accommodation.

The sonar or echolocation system of toothed whales can be divided into three categories: the sending, receiving, and processing components. The general process is that the toothed whale produces a sound that travels away until it hits an object (e.g., prey item, sea bottom, other whales) that has a density different from that of water. It then bounces off the object and the toothed whale receives the sound pressure wave. The toothed whales can use this information to determine the distance to the object (based on the time the signal was generated and the time it returns), which is similar to the way echosounders on ships determine bottom depth. The signal that bounces off the object and returns to toothed whales can also tell them something about the characteristics of the object, such as density, surface texture, size, and shape. Higher-frequency sound is used at short range to determine greater detail of an object, whereas lower frequencies travel farther but provide fewer details about an object. In this way the toothed whales can use echolocation to "visualize" their surroundings without actually seeing them. It is a highly evolved system that allows toothed whales to produce a complicated signal of many frequencies that generally is projected forward of the animal, with the returning signal being processed in milliseconds. The toothed whales have evolved a sophisticated sonar system that rivals anything produced by humans.

There is still some controversy about where the echolocation signals are produced in toothed whales. Most recent work indicates that acoustic signals are generated either at the nasal plugs or the dorsal bursae (projections of the melon), structures that exist along the air passage that goes from the blowhole through the skull and into the lungs. Using sophisticated instruments (e.g., x-ray computer tomography and magnetic resonance imaging), we know that echolocation signals are produced in front of the skull. The shape and consistency of the melon helps to direct sounds slightly forward of the animal; however, most focusing of sounds to the front of an echolocating odontocete occurs because of the bony skull and jaw and the various air sacs in the head. These structures generally reflect sound so that the main projection of acoustic energy is directed forward. The air sacs hold air during a dive so that a toothed whale can echolocate by passing air back and forth to the air sacs through the sound production areas without expelling air in the process. For echolocation, toothed whales produce a pulsed, broadband signal called a *click* [frequencies of 1 to 200 kilohertz, duration of 40 to 200 milliseconds, usually with many clicks in a series (a click train)]. They will change the interval between clicks depending on the distance and characteristics of the target. The main objective of using echolocation involves the detection, localization, discrimination, and recognition of targets of interest. Toothed whales can do this very well. For instance, using only echolocation (i.e., blindfolded), they can detect a 2.54-centimeter (1-inch)-diameter steel ball at a distance of 113 meters (371 feet); they can determine that two objects differ in size when they differ by only millimeters in diameter; and they can recognize differences in the thickness of walls of objects. Toothed whales also produce vocalizations used for communication among individuals; these signals differ in frequency and intensity from echolocation signals.

The ability to receive acoustic signals has been tested with many odontocetes, but the main experimental animal has been the bottlenosed dolphin. Unlike terrestrial mammals, toothed whales do not have ear flaps (pinnae). Instead, they have a small pinhole in the side of the head, and the ear canal (external auditory meatus) is small and filled with fibrous tissue. These characteristics indicated that sound reception probably was not by means of an ear canal similar to that used by humans and other terrestrial mammals. Researchers found that the lower jaw of odontocetes had a region of thin bone (pan bone) acting as an acoustic window that allows sound to pass through the jaw. Specialized fat (*acoustic fat*) transmits sound without much absorption and may actually intensify the sound as it travels posteriorly toward the middle ear. Sound travels down the acoustic fat in the lower jaw to the three middle ear ossicles contained within the bony auditory bulla, where the sound is transmitted along the middle ear bones from the malleus to the incus to the stapes. The bulla and middle ear bones are not firmly attached to the skull, basically allowing the middle ear bones to be acoustically isolated from the skeleton. Acoustic energy is then passed from the stapes to the oval window. The oval window separates the middle ear from the cochlea, which is a spiral tube containing auditory nerve endings. Acoustic energy causes deflection of the oval window, creating vibration of the basilar membrane within the cochlea, which deforms the receptor cells on the basilar membrane. In this way, mechanical energy is converted into electrical energy that can be sent via nerves to the brain for processing. The stiffness, dimensions, and number of receptor cells of the basilar membrane provide some clues as to the frequencies and sound levels that can be discriminated by toothed whales. Although these whales can detect signals from 75 hertz to 150 kilohertz, their best hearing is from 3 to 100 kilohertz, depending on the species.

This elaborate and well-developed system gives toothed whales the ability to sense their environment with a great deal of accuracy and precision. They can detect prey from a distance before the prey can see the whales, they can use echolocation to determine the seafloor depth and type of structures on the seafloor, and it has been proposed that odontocetes can use their acoustic signals to stun their prey while foraging. All these traits are necessary for animals that feed in deep water [such as sperm whales finding squid at 1000 meters (3281 feet) depth] or in very murky water (such as river dolphins finding prey where there is zero visibility), or when their prey may flee rapidly (such as killer whales detecting their marine mammal prey at some distance).

Jim Harvey

FURTHER READING
Au, Whitlow W. L. *The Sonar of Dolphins.* New York: Springer-Verlag, 1993.
Berta, A., and J. L. Sumich. *Marine Mammals: Evolutionary Biology.* San Diego: Academic Press, 1999.
Leatherwood, Stephen, and Randall R. Reeves. *The Sierra Club Handbook of Whales and Dolphins.* San Francisco: Sierra Club Books, 1983.
Purves, P. E., and G. E. Pilleri. *Echolocation in Whales and Dolphins.* London and New York: Academic Press, 1983.
Slijper, E. J. *Whales.* Translated by A. J. Pomerans. New York: Basic Books, 1962.

RELATED ARTICLES
Odontoceti

Ecological Succession

Ecological succession is defined by marine ecologist James W. Nybakken (1936–) as "an orderly process of community change controlled through modification of the physical (and chemical) environment."

The structure and composition of biological communities—natural assemblages of plants, animals, and microbes—change with season and over longer periods of time. The term *ecological succession* was devised by the North American botanist F. E. Clements (1874–1945) in the 1910s and applied to terrestrial vegetation. Since then, the term has been adopted widely to encompass sequential changes in the structure of aquatic communities.

Classical Ecological Succession

Two main forms of succession are recognized. *Primary succession* occurs where life forms establish themselves in a previously lifeless habitat, as in colonization of the shores of a newly emerged volcanic island. *Secondary succession* occurs in areas where a community that previously existed has been eliminated, for example, where storm waves have removed sessile intertidal organisms from a rocky shore, leaving a "bare" patch.

In the classical form of ecological succession proposed by Clements and applied to terrestrial vegetation, the community changes in an orderly fashion through a recognizable series of transitional steps called *seral stages*. Eventually, as determined by climate and soil type, a final stage—the *climax community*—establishes itself. This community persists provided that there are no climatic changes or other major forms of disturbance. The orderly progression of community change is brought about by modification of the physical and chemical environment by the biological communities themselves. Each community modifies the environment, making it suitable for the next community, in a process called *facilitation*.

At first sight, the *classical model* of succession appears to apply to mangrove communities at the edge of the sea. J. H. Davis working in Florida in the 1930s suggested that the zonation of mangrove species, from shallow water to inland, was equivalent to the seral stages in classical succession. In this scheme the seaward zone of red mangroves is the starting point, with black-and-white mangrove zones as seral stages, leading eventually to the development of inland terrestrial communities. However, research carried out in the 1970s

and 1980s suggests that this ecological succession may be more apparent than real. Transplantation experiments show that various species from one mangrove zone can grow well in another. Also, the different zones appear to reach an equilibrium state, and left undisturbed, they do not "progress" from one zone to another over time. The zonation appears to be a response to external physical factors rather than being facilitated by the mangroves themselves.

Succession in temperate salt marshes appears to be a more clear-cut phenomenon. On the seaward side of estuarine shorelines, true marine species—brown or green algae—predominate. The low salt marsh community, whose roots are inundated by seawater at most stages of the tidal cycle, includes salt-tolerant eelgrasses (*Zostera* spp.) and cordgrasses (*Spartina* spp.). As they grow, they consolidate the mud and raise the soil level, allowing less salt-tolerant species to invade, first sea aster (*Aster* sp.) and sea lavender (*Limonium* sp.) and then rushes (*Juncus* spp.). In the United Kingdom the grass fescue (*Festuca*) grows in drier, salt-rich soils, and grazing by sheep halts the succession at this stage. If the succession is allowed to continue, shrubs may invade the consolidating soil, which is gradually flushed of salt by rainfall and runoff, and eventually a climax community of forest trees may be established.

As a general rule, early seral stages in a succession are dominated by *opportunistic* (*r*-selected) species. They propagate and grow rapidly and disperse in abundance. They tend to have high mortalities and short life spans. Later seral stages and the climax community itself are dominated by *equilibrium* (*K*-selected) species. These are longer-lived and reach reproductive maturity more slowly. They tend to be larger than early colonizers and gradually outcompete and replace them.

Succession on Temperate Rocky Shores

The intertidal zone of a rocky shore, particularly in temperate seas, shows a vertical zonation, or banding, with various communities of plants and animals at different heights on the seashore. Superimposed on this overall pattern is a patchiness, indicating areas where organisms are temporarily sparse or where less characteristic species dominate. Both physical and biological factors promote patchiness.

Storm damage may create open spaces in the carpet of flora and fauna, and the bare patches become available for recolonization. Secondary succession in the temperate rocky intertidal does not follow the facilitation model in a straightforward manner. Succession here is best explained by incorporating elements from other, later ecological models.

According to the *inhibition model* of succession, originally proposed by F. E. Egler (1911–96) in 1954, whichever species colonizes the site first is able to exclude other species, at least temporarily. It may do so by eating other potential colonizers, by removing food resources, or by actively excluding competitors using chemicals or aggressive behavior. The course of succession, in this case, may depend upon precedence—which species got there first.

The *tolerance model* of ecological succession, proposed by J. H. Connell and R. O. Slayter (1923–) in 1977, is intermediate between the classical (facilitation) and inhibition models. The colonizing species neither inhibits other would-be colonizers nor promotes their establishment. Any colonizing species can start the succession, which then proceeds as determined by the life history features and competitive abilities of other colonists.

In 1980, on the Pacific coast of North America, W. Sousa showed the green alga *Ulva* to be an early colonist of a rocky shore. Healthy *Ulva* inhibited colonization by red algae (e.g., *Gelidium, Gracilaria, Endocladia*), but algal grazing by the crab *Pachygraspus crassipes* broke this inhibition, enabling succession to proceed to a community of red algae. Eventually, the red alga, *Gigartina canaliculata*, with better resistance to desiccation

and overgrowing than that of other red algae, would dominate that region of the intertidal zone.

On Pacific coast, rocky shores of temperate North America, clearance of a space in a mussel bed may produce a "classical" succession, with a film of bacteria and microscopic algae such as diatoms, followed by seaweeds such as *Fucus* spp., then barnacles, and finally, mussels, the dominant competitor. However, this pattern may deviate in a variety of ways. Grazers such as limpets and chitons moving into the space early may remove seaweed spores and consume newly settled invertebrate larvae. A bacterial and algal film may perpetuate. Or if barnacle larvae settle before seaweed spores, the seaweed stage of the succession may be missed entirely. The climax of the succession—a dense mat of mussels—may never be reached in the presence of predators such as sea stars. With sea stars present and able to reach and consume young mussels in the middle intertidal zone, a much more diverse community is established, containing a mixture of barnacles, seaweeds, and mussels as a stable climax community.

In conclusion, parts of the rocky intertidal in temperate locations can be envisaged as a mosaic of patches that were cleared at different times and have entered different stages of a succession that may lead to more than one form of climax community. The species composition of the patches depends on chance factors, such as which spores or larvae settle first, plus other factors, such as the degree of physical disturbance and predation.

Seasonal Succession in Phytoplankton

Seasonal succession occurs in the open ocean, where one or more species of phytoplankton dominates for a period of weeks or months and is then replaced by other species. With a given geographic locality, this pattern is repeated annually. Seasonal succession is cyclical, which means that an endpoint or climax is not reached.

Various factors have been suggested as the cause of seasonal succession in phytoplankton.

Temperature is an obvious candidate—succession is most marked in temperate seas. Temperature is a major contributory factor, but changes in dominant species occur quite abruptly, with the same species becoming dominant at different times and at different temperatures, so other factors are undoubtedly involved. *Biological conditioning*—changes in water quality brought about by the release of metabolites by phytoplankton—has been shown experimentally to affect phytoplankton growth. Such metabolites can promote or inhibit the growth of other plankton, including the very species releasing the chemicals. Planktonic herbivores—in particular, copepods and invertebrate larvae—are selective grazers and can change the species composition of phytoplankton blooms. The availability of nutrients for phytoplankton growth is another contributory factor.

Evidence from computer simulations, field trials, and laboratory investigations suggests that temperature, growth inhibition, and promotion by metabolites, grazing, and nutrient availability are all factors that contribute to seasonal succession. They do so in a complex manner that varies with locality, season, and the species involved.

Trevor Day

FURTHER READING
Connell, J. H., and R. O. Slayter. "Mechanisms of Succession in Natural Communities and Their Role in Community Stability and Organization." *American Naturalist,* Vol. 111 (1977), pp. 1119–1144.
Dayton, P. "Competition, Disturbance and Community Organization: The Provision and Subsequent Utilization of Space in a Rocky Intertidal Community." *Ecological Monographs,* Vol. 41 (1971), pp. 351–359.
Egler, F. E. "Vegetation Science Concepts. I. Initial Floristic Composition—A Factor in Old Field Vegetation Development." *Vegetatio,* Vol. 4 (1954), pp. 412–417.
Nybakken, James W. *Marine Biology: An Ecological Approach,* 5th ed. San Francisco: Benjamin Cummings, 2001.
Ricklefs, Robert E. *Ecology.* Newton, Mass.: Chiron Press, 1973; 4th ed., New York: W. H. Freeman, 1999.
Sommer, U. "Competition and Coexistence." *Nature,* Vol. 402 (25 November 1999), pp. 366–367.
Sousa, W. "Experimental Investigations of Disturbance and Ecological Succession in a Rocky Intertidal Algal Community." *Ecological Monographs,* Vol. 49 (1980), pp. 227–254.
Winston, J. E. "Intertidal Space Wars." *Sea Frontiers,* Vol. 36, No. 1 (January/February 1990), pp. 46–51.

USEFUL WEB SITES
"Rocky Intertidal Habitats." <http://bonita.mbnms.nos.noaa.gov/sitechar/rocky.html>.

RELATED ARTICLES
Biological Conditioning; Diatom; Intertidal; Mangrove Forest; Phytoplankton; Salt Marsh

Ecology

Ecology is the science that seeks to understand the spectrum of relationships that exist between living organisms and their physical and chemical environments, and the relationships that exist among groups of different and similar organisms existing in the same environment. Sometimes ecology is defined as environmental science or environmental biology. The term *ecology* is derived from the Greek word meaning "house" and thus literally can be defined as the study of houses (= environments). A more succinct definition of ecology is that it is the science of the structure and function of nature. Regardless of how one defines ecology, it is one of the most significant of the several basic divisions of the broad field of biology. The importance of ecology has increased as the deleterious effects of humans on the world's ecosystems has become more widespread and pervasive, leading to concerns about the future of the planet and its ability to sustain life. One has only to open a newspaper or magazine, listen to the radio, or watch television to be aware of serious problems such as global warming, desertification, destruction of the rainforests and coral reefs, and burgeoning human populations, all of which have their basis in the science of ecology. Therefore, it is imperative that people have a basic understanding of the principles of ecology so that they may make intelligent decisions concerning the future of the planet.

Ecology is an extremely complex science that employs principles from many other sciences, such as physics and chemistry, as well as from the field of mathematics. At the same time a basic understanding of ecology is possible without an extensive background in science and mathematics. The simplest way to explain ecology is to consider the science as composed of a number of levels of organization, with each successive level being more complex. Within ecology there are considered to be usually four levels of organization: populations, communities, ecosystems, and the biosphere.

The lowest level in ecology, the population, refers to a group of individuals of any one kind of organism usually inhabiting a given area. This is the least complex level in ecology and therefore the one that has been most often studied by ecologists. The population level has a number of attributes not shared by the next levels in ecology. This includes density, a birth rate, a death rate, an age distribution, and a growth rate. The population of a species shifts not only due to changes in the previously mentioned attributes but also due to interactions with the physical and chemical environment in which it is found, as well as interactions with other species. To understand fully the ecology of a species, we must understand the factors that influence the aforementioned population attributes and how the environment and other species affect these attributes. Among the interactions with other species the most significant factors for populations are competition and predation. Interspecific competition for resources in short supply can limit populations or even drive them to extinction. Similarly, predation by other species can control the size of populations.

A final interaction that can limit the size of populations is parasitism.

The next organizational level in ecology is that of the community, sometimes called the *biotic community*. The community in ecology includes all of the populations within a given area. In contrast to the population level, the community includes a number of different species so that we can speak of the species diversity of the community. Communities vary considerably in their species diversity, but a very characteristic and consistent feature is that they contain a comparatively few species that are abundant and a larger number that are uncommon or rare. The few common species are often called *dominants* and are used to name the communities. Since this level considers all of the populations in a given area, a community has different *trophic levels*. The lowest trophic level, the *producer level,* contains populations of organisms that have chlorophyll and produce energy-rich organic compounds from carbon dioxide and water using the energy of sunlight. (In some portions of the deep sea the lowest trophic level are composed of bacteria, which synthesize energy-rich organic compounds using the energy in reduced inorganic compounds.) These organisms are the primary producers of the community.

The next trophic level includes those organisms that obtain energy by consuming the organisms of the first trophic level. Usually, these are called *herbivores*. All subsequent levels obtain food from the level below them and are generally called *predators*. An important ecological principle is that at each transfer of energy from one trophic level to the next a large part of the energy is lost as required by the second law of thermodynamics. The amount lost varies but is commonly 90 percent. A final trophic level includes all those organisms that break down the dead remains of organisms, called *decomposers*, and recreate the inorganic nutrients. Within a given community there are several routes of the transfer of energy from the photo-synthetic organisms through a series of organisms to the final predator. Each of these is termed a *food chain,* and the entire series of food chains is considered a *food web.* In the marine environment it is important to note that there are often communities, such as in the deep sea, that lack the autotrophic component and are dependent on energy-rich compounds that are produced in the lighted zone of the ocean and are transported by various mechanisms to the deep sea.

The third level of ecology is the *ecosystem.* An ecosytem comprises the community and the nonliving environment. This is a comprehensive level that takes into account the movement of both energy and materials. It is at this level that ecologists consider biogeochemical cycles, which refer to the cycling back and forth between organisms and the physical environment of chemical elements and compounds that are necessary to continued maintenance and life in the ecosystem. The most significant of these are the cycles involving carbon, nitrogen, and phosphorus in the marine environment.

The final level of ecology is the *biosphere.* This level is essentially the portion of Earth in which the ecosystems occur, the thin layer of soil, water, and atmosphere inhabited by living organisms.

James W. Nybakken

FURTHER READING

Krebs, Charles J. *Ecology: The Experimental Analysis of Distribution and Abundance.* New York: Harper and Row, 1972; 5th ed., San Francisco: Benjamin Cummings, 2001.

Nybakken, James W. *Marine Biology: An Ecological Approach,* 5th ed. San Francisco: Benjamin Cummings, 2001.

Odum, Eugene P. *Ecology.* New York: Holt, Rinehart and Winston, 1963.

RELATED ARTICLES

Biogeochemical Cycle; Competitive Exclusion; Competitive Interference; Ecological Succession; Food Chain; Food Web; Keystone Species; Primary Productivity

Ecotone

Ecotones are transitional zones located between different biological communities and associations. They tend to develop where environmental gradients are gradual, so no definitive line can be drawn between the communities. Within the ecotone there tends be a mixture of species derived from the two associations.

Associations of species tend to form mosaics in which the patches are inhabited by assemblages of different species or by species in varying proportions. Within the patches the key ecological processes, such as primary productivity, nutrient cycling, and food web structure, tend to be consistent but may change radically across the ecotones at the boundaries. On the bottom of the sea, the geological character of the seabed may create abrupt changes from rock to soft sediment, but elsewhere, mosaic patterns occur, often reflecting the history of environmental disturbance and recovery. The disturbances may be caused by biological processes, such as a mass settlement or mortality, or physical processes, such as a change in current or a turbidity event. The factors controlling the occurrences of biological assemblages are often dynamic, so ecotones reflect the advances and retreats of species' ranges and the ecological successions that determine the progression of the character of the communities.

In the oceans, vertical gradients tend to be steep, whereas horizontal gradients are extremely shallow. Thus the change in water temperature encountered between the surface and a depth of 1000 meters (3280 feet) may be encountered horizontally only by moving more than 1000 times laterally. So the ecotones that occur at the boundaries between the epipelagic and mesopelagic zones are spatially more restricted then those that occur laterally between temperate and subtropical plankton assemblages.

Martin Angel

FURTHER READING

Cox, C. Barry, and Peter D. Moore. *Biogeography: An Ecological and Evolutionary Approach*. New York: Wiley, 1973; Oxford, and Malden, Mass.: Blackwell Science, 2000.

Harris, Roger, et al. *ICES Zooplankton Methodology Manual*. San Diego and London: Academic Press, 2000.

RELATED ARTICLES
Epipelagic Zone; Food Web; Mesopelagic Zone

Ecotourism

Ecotourism (sometimes called *nature tourism*) is the fastest-growing sector of the tourist industry with an estimated annual growth rate of 25 to 30 percent. Broadly defined, it refers to tourism that treats the environment (including indigenous people and their cultures) with greater respect. As a way to reconcile the demands of Earth's increasingly mobile population with the increasing fragility of its environment, ecotourism is certain to become much more significant during the twenty-first century. But while supporters emphasize the need for tourism to be more environmentally friendly, critics believe ecotourism can sometimes be as damaging as traditional tourism and question whether there can ever be such a thing as "sustainable tourism" that meets the demands of today's tourists without compromising the needs of future generations.

Problems of Traditional Tourism

Despite its many social, cultural, and economic benefits, traditional tourism has long been recognized as a major threat to the marine (particularly the coastal) environment. Since the age of cheap air travel began in the 1950s, mass tourism has systematically replaced the diversity of some of the world's most extraordinary natural wonders with a "monocultural" beach experience that varies little from California to Florida or from Thailand to the Caribbean. Within a few years, mass tourism can transform the tourist's "unspoiled paradise" with massive transport infrastructure, such as airports, highways, and harbors, and equally massive resort complexes often obliterating sensitive areas of the coastal environment. The Philippines is estimated to have lost 90 percent of its mangrove swamps, partly to resort development. Quickly constructed to earn foreign revenue, resorts have frequently neglected such important considerations as proper sewage treatment facilities and have created environmental problems such as red tides and waterborne diseases. Meanwhile, recreational activities such as boating and scuba diving may damage highly sensitive parts of the marine environment such as coral reefs. Swamped by an influx of foreign tourists, local people also suffer. Indigenous cultures may disappear as resorts literally try to make tourists feel at home. Most of the money paid by tourists goes to foreign travel companies (a phenomenon known as *leakage*); sometimes only 30 percent or less is fed into the local economy and, in developing countries with pressing social needs, only a fraction of this fraction remains for environmental protection. Local people experience all the problems of mass tourism with few of the benefits, and tourists can inadvertently destroy the very qualities that initially made a place worth visiting.

Coral reefs illustrate some of these problems. It is estimated that over 100 nations could develop viable tourist industries from the spectacular marine life of their reefs. Each year, about 100 million people visit the Caribbean, and it is estimated that this region alone will earn around U.S.$1.2 billion from scuba diving by the year 2005. But the tourists who provide such economic benefits also damage the environment that attracts them. Some scientists believe that the coral-destroying crown-of-thorns starfish (*Acanthaster planci*)

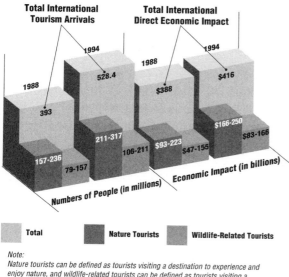

Total International Tourism Arrivals

Total International Direct Economic Impact

1994

1988

1994

1988

528.4

$388

$416

1988

393

211-317

$93-223

$166-250

$83-166

157-236

79-157

106-211

$47-155

Numbers of People (in millions)

Economic Impact (in billions)

Total   Nature Tourists   Wildlife-Related Tourists

Note:
Nature tourists can be defined as tourists visiting a destination to experience and enjoy nature, and wildlife-related tourists can be defined as tourists visiting a destination to observe wildlife.
Source:
International Ecotourism Society. Ecotourism Statistical Fact Sheet. Accessed from http://www.ecotourism.org/textfiles/stats.txt on 4/20/01.

Trends in ecotourism.

has proliferated because scuba divers have removed its predator, the Triton mollusk (*Charonia tritonis*), from coral reefs. Apart from the direct damage wreaked by souvenir-hunting divers and their boats, reefs are harmed by pollution from hotels and cruise liners and overharvesting of marine life to supply tourists. Around 60 percent of Earth's remaining reefs are estimated to be at high or medium risk from human disturbance.

Vision of Ecotourism

Ecotourism offers a different vision in which tourists interact more sympathetically with the environment they have chosen to visit. Some tour operators define ecotourism as a tourist experience that includes any kind of involvement with nature, such as a whale-watching trip. At the opposite end of the scale, environmentalists might define ecotourism as conservation work, such as mangrove replanting, that brings positive benefits to the environment and the local community that manages it. Although there is no generally agreed upon definition of the term,

ecotourism is generally understood to mean a tourist experience that is centered on and mindful of conserving the value of the local environment, which requires much less transport and resort infrastructure, respects native people and their cultures, and provides greater benefits to the local community.

Recognizing long-term environmental and economic benefits, many nations have established successful ecotourism projects since the concept first became fashionable in the 1980s. The Seychelles in the western Indian Ocean, which saw a tenfold growth in tourist capacity between 1970 and 1975, is held up as one model of how mass tourism can be made more sustainable. Hotels are now built only on certain islands and only in small groups no higher than the palm trees that surround them. State-of-the-art sewage treatment protects water quality and the marine environment. Other islands are managed as wildlife refuges and local people who used to hunt endangered wildlife, such as sea turtles, have now been retrained to earn their income elsewhere.

If the Seychelles is an example of the greening of mass tourism, other projects represent more of an environmental ideal and aim to attract visitors purely on the basis of providing conservation benefits to threatened habitats or species. A U.S. organization called the Mangrove Replenishment Project works with volunteers to plant, monitor, and nurture mangrove seedlings in areas such as Florida and the Virgin Islands. Since its inception in 1976, the Caribbean Coral Reef Ecosystems (CCRE) project has brought thousands of volunteers to help oceanographers study the barrier reefs of Belize. Often, ecotourism is used to counter a specific environmental threat. Researchers monitoring the few remaining Komodo dragons in the Indonesian islands believe that this remarkable species can be saved only by safeguarding its habitat, and for this, ecotourism will be the key.

Uncertain Benefits

In environmental terms, ecotourism may be less damaging than mass tourism, but critics point out that the concept is not without its flaws. One concern is that in the absence of an agreed upon definition, some tour operators use ecotourism to sell holidays with questionable environmental benefits, just as some chemical companies abuse the term *environmentally friendly*. But even ecotourists, who may view themselves as environmentally superior to mass tourists, cause damage. The Annapurna region of Nepal, one of the first popular ecotourism destinations, has been plagued by excessive numbers of visitors causing litter and sewage contamination and deforestation of virgin forests to provide wood fuel. Today's backpacker experience becomes tomorrow's tourist resort; as more people discover a new area, the ecotourists lose interest and move on to new places, which succumb in their turn to mass tourism. Local people may be the first to suffer. Ecotourism packages sold in affluent countries do little to solve the problem of leakage and may provide too little compensation to local people to give up unsustainable practices such as overharvesting of threatened habitats and species.

Wildlife protection policies may exclude the local community from areas that once provided their home or livelihood, whereas prohibitive tourist prices may prevent them traveling elsewhere in their country. Meanwhile, organizations such as the World Bank have helped developing nations to finance large-scale infrastructure projects to support traditional tourism in developing countries, but often at the expense both of the environment and the basic needs of their own people. Truly sustainable ecotourism projects, such as conservation volunteer holidays, represent only a tiny fraction of the global travel industry and in no way compensate for the damage of the whole. Finally, even if ecotourism could help to protect marine habitats such as coral reefs by making scuba divers more sensitive to the damage they can cause, it would do little, directly, to address wider threats to the reefs, such as cyanide farming and global warming.

Making Ecotourism Work

Such an assessment of ecotourism may be more realistic than pessimistic, and although ecotourism is still a relatively new concept, there are now numerous model, grassroots-driven ecotourism projects around the world for other nations to copy. Global environmental initiatives such as the United Nations' Agenda 21, national environmental legislation, full participation from the local community, and increasing tourist education can help to address the major problems. For all the difficulties, it seems certain that ecotourism must play an increasingly important role in safeguarding both the marine environment and the planet as a whole in the twenty-first century.

Chris Woodford

Further Reading

Coral Reefs and Tourism: The Threat and the Potential. Bureau of Oceans and International Environmental and Scientific Affairs Fact Sheet. Washington, D.C.: U.S. Department of State, 19 October 1998.

Doggart, Caroline, and Nike Doggart. "Environmental Impacts of Tourism in Developing Countries." *Travel & Tourism Analyst,* Vol. 2 (1996).

France, Lesley, ed. *The Earthscan Reader in Sustainable Tourism.* London: Earthscan, 1997.

Hall, C. Michael, and Alan Lew, eds. *Sustainable Tourism: A Geographical Perspective.* Harlow, England: Longman, 1998.

Pleuramom, Anita. "The Political Economy of Tourism." *The Ecologist,* Vol. 24, No. 4 (July/August 1994), p. 142.

Swarbrooke, John. *Sustainable Tourism Management.* Wallingford, England, and New York: CABI Publishing, 1999.

Related Articles

Biodiversity; Coral Reef; Mangrove Forest; Pollution, Ocean; Red Tide; Scuba

Ectoprocta, see Bryozoa

Eddy

Eddies are self-contained, rotating bodies of water of limited dimensions that are found throughout the world's oceans. The larger rotating patterns of circulation around the major ocean basins are called *gyres*. Eddies take on the form of closed cylinders that rotate vertically either clockwise or counterclockwise, depending on how they are formed. With the availability of satellite data since the early 1970s, it has been possible to observe eddies as they appear at the ocean surface on a global basis. Many types of eddies have been identified. However, a typical eddy found in mid-ocean may have a diameter of 100 kilometers (62 miles) and a lifetime of several months. The existence of eddies was suspected for over a century, but their occurrence has been confirmed only within the past 70 years or so. Because the physical, chemical, and biological properties of eddies are usually very different from those of the surrounding waters, they are of interest to a wide range of marine scientists. Although eddies often have diameters of 100 kilometers or more, they can be as small as 10 kilometers (6.2 miles) in diameter. It may take an eddy from 10 to 30 days to make one complete revolution. Vertically, eddies can extend all the way to ocean bottom. Although eddies typically last for several months, some have lasted for several years before they lost their distinctive characteristics and were absorbed into the surrounding waters.

Eddies are found throughout the world's oceans. Weakly flowing eastern boundary currents such as the California Current and the Peru–Chile Current are populated by dozens of eddies at any one time. They are common near intense boundary currents such as the Gulf Stream off the U.S. east coast and the Kuroshio off Japan. Gulf Stream eddies are often called *rings* because of their distinctive circular shape. Rings or eddies spawned by the Gulf Stream have been particularly well observed. Gulf Stream rings develop from oscillations or meanders that grow in amplitude and eventually break off to become separate features of the circulation. Rings can occur on either side of the Gulf Stream, depending on how the meanders form. Looking downstream, a meander that grows in amplitude to the right of the Gulf Stream will entrain waters from the left side, forming a ring that will contain waters that are characteristic of those to the left of the Gulf Stream. Conversely, a meander that grows in amplitude to the left will entrain waters from the right, forming a ring that will contain waters that are characteristic of those to the right of the Gulf Stream. Finally, although eddy formation is often associated with strong ocean currents, they can also be formed through the action of the wind on the ocean surface.

Laurence C. Breaker

FURTHER READING
MacLeish, William H., ed. *Ocean Eddies*. Woods Hole, Mass.: Woods Hole Oceanographic Institute, 1976.
Robinson, Allan R., ed. *Eddies in Marine Science*. Berlin and New York: Springer-Verlag, 1983.

RELATED ARTICLES
Boundary Current; Gulf Stream Meander; Kuroshio; Ocean Current

Edge Wave

Edge waves are water waves that are trapped at the shoreline. When you stand on the beach and look seaward, the wind-generated waves that you see are approaching the beach with their crests more or less parallel to the beach. Edge waves are perpendicular to these waves; their crests are perpendicular to the beach, and they propagate alongshore. They are also longer than the waves that you see approaching the beach, typically hundreds of meters between their crests. As you move seaward from the beach, the amplitude of the edge waves decreases exponentially with distance from shore. Edge waves can have an important role in surf zone dynamics, contributing to the formation of rip currents and cusps along what would otherwise be a straight shoreline.

Edge waves are not dissipated by wave breaking in the surf zone. Their phase speed is that of a deepwater wave modified by the slope of the sea bottom. Since bottom slopes are so small, the speeds are much less than those for deepwater waves. As a consequence, edge waves have periods (the time taken in seconds for a wave to travel a distance equal to one wavelength) of 30 to 300 seconds, longer than that of the wind-generated sea and swell. Waves with these periods are classified as *infragravity waves*. Alongshore wavenumber spectra of infragravity motions in a few meters depth indicate that a significant fraction of the seaward radiated infragravity energy is refractively trapped as edge waves within a few hundred meters of the shoreline. Edge waves are believed to be generated nonlinearly by groups of incoming wind waves but can also be generated by atmospheric fronts as they pass over the shoreline.

Edge waves can dominate inner surf zone velocities and sea-surface fluctuations, with heights exceeding 1 meter (3.3 feet). Observations from a range of coastal settings suggest that the energy levels on the continental shelf depend not only on conditions in nearby surf zones, but also on the general geographic surroundings. For example, more edge wave energy is trapped on a steep narrow shelf than on a gently sloping wide shelf. The existence of energetic bar-trapped edge waves suggests that trapping may also occur at other depth perturbations, such as submarine canyons and offshore shoals.

Curtis A. Collins

FURTHER READING

Holman, Rob. "Nearshore Processes." U.S. National Report to the International Union of Geodesy and Geophysics, 1991–1994. *Reviews of Geophysics,* Supplement, 1995, pp. 1237–1247.

RELATED ARTICLES

Surf Zone; Wave

Ekman, Vagn Walfrid
1874–1954
Physical Oceanographer and Mathematician

Swedish scientist and mathematician Vagn Walfrid Ekman is best known for his practical and theoretical contributions to physical oceanography, ranging from his ocean current meter and water-sampling bottle to his highly influential descriptions of water movement: the Ekman spiral, Ekman layer, and Ekman transport.

Vagn Walfrid Ekman was born in Stockholm, Sweden, in 1874, the youngest son of a Swedish physical oceanographer, Fredrik Laurentz Ekman. Walfrid was schooled in Stockholm and then majored in physics at the University of Uppsala. After attending lectures on hydrodynamics given by the pioneer oceanographer and meteorologist Vilhelm Bjerknes (1862–1951), Ekman's interest turned, like that of his father, to physical oceanography.

While still a student at Uppsala, Ekman made a major contribution to physical oceanography by devising a mathematical description of the effect of wind on water. During the famous Arctic voyage of the *Fram* (1893–96), Fridtjof Nansen (1861–1930) had noticed that sea ice drifted 20 to 40° to the right of the prevailing wind direction. Nansen suggested that Ekman investigate this phenomenon. Ekman showed that wind-induced motion in the water column is the result of the interaction between the force of the wind on the water surface, the turning effect due to Earth's rotation (the Coriolis effect), and frictional forces between layers of water. The resulting description, called the *Ekman spiral,* was to become a fundamental model in fluid dynamics.

Ekman graduated from Uppsala in 1902, the same year in which he published a short paper on the "wind spiral." He joined the staff of the International Laboratory for Oceanographic Research in Christiania (now Oslo) in 1902, remaining there until 1909. During these and later years, he showed himself to be a skilled inventor and experimenter as well as a consummate theoretician. The simple and reliable Ekman current meter, which he developed for measuring sea current velocity and direction over prolonged periods, has been used in various forms for most of the twentieth century. The Ekman reversing water bottle, for sampling water and measuring temperature at a predetermined depth, has had a similarly long working life.

A paper by Ekman, "On the Influence of the Earth's Rotation on Ocean Currents," published in 1905, had a major impact in the oceanographic world. This paper and later work established several mathematical descriptions with which his name is now associated: the Ekman spiral (the descending spiral that describes water movement induced by a surface wind), Ekman transport (net movement of surface water at 90° to wind direction), and the Ekman layer (the depth over which the Ekman spiral extends). Ekman transport, in which water

Vagn Walfrid Ekman. (Courtesy, Lund University Library, Sweden)

moves offshore, accounts for cold-water coastal upwelling off coasts such as Peru and California. Ekman's mathematical descriptions were starting points for modern theories of oceanic circulation. They are fundamental to much theoretical and experimental work on rotating fluids.

Ekman also examined several other physical oceanographic phenomena. His investigation of the "dead-water" phenomenon highlighted both his experimental and theoretical talents. *Dead water* is the effect that some vessels experience when traveling through Arctic waters and fjords. The propulsive force of the vessel is lost, and the ship seems to wallow. Ekman's experiments in wave tanks showed that this feature was caused by a boundary layer between waters of different densities, such as brackish water floating on more saline water, that absorbed energy to produce internal waves.

Between 1910 and 1939, Ekman worked as professor of mechanics and mathematical physics at the University of Lund, Sweden. He continued his interest in physical oceanography and in 1923 published a highly influential paper on the mathematical theory behind wind-driven circulation in ocean basins. His work was far ahead of its time, and it took more than 20 years for a new generation of theoretical oceanographers to build on his ideas. He was one of the first oceanographers to analyze the fluid dynamics of the Gulf Stream and to begin to dissect the knotty problem of ocean turbulence.

One of Ekman's greatest contributions to oceanography was his empirical formula for the mean compressibility of seawater as a function of temperature and pressure. This formula is still used to calculate the density of deep-ocean water under hydrostatic pressure from the water column.

From 1922 to 1929, Ekman made several cruises with a Norwegian colleague, Bjørn Helland-Hensen (1877–1957), to test prolonged operation of Ekman's current meter. In 1930, Ekman cruised to the trade wind belt off northwestern Africa to take average current readings at various depths in the water column. He published some of the findings, but the remainder were not released until 1953, when Ekman was 79 years old. Part of the delay was caused by the loss of some data during World War II, but it also reflected the great care that Ekman took in perfecting his work.

Although he appeared cool and reserved to acquaintances (Ekman rarely attended international conferences), he was perceived as a kindly, warm, and thoughtful man by his mentors and close colleagues. During his career, Ekman published more than 100 scientific papers as well as several articles on religious and philosophical matters. He was engaged in research on turbid currents up to a few days before his death in March 1954. Ekman's theoretical explanations of water movement remain a foundation for modern physical oceanographers' understanding of surface and near-surface currents.

Trevor Day

BIOGRAPHY

- Vagn Walfrid Ekman.
- Born 3 May 1874 in Stockholm, Sweden.
- In 1902, he graduated in physics from the University of Uppsala and was on the staff of the International Laboratory for Oceanographic Research, Oslo, from 1902 to 1909.
- He published an influential paper, "On the Influence of the Earth's Rotation on Ocean Currents," in 1905.
- He was a professor of mechanics and mathematical physics at the University of Lund, Sweden, from 1910 to 1939.
- Died 9 March 1954 in Gostad, Sweden.

SELECTED WRITINGS

Ekman, V. Walfrid. "On the Influence of the Earth's Rotation on Ocean Currents." *Arkiv foer Matematik, Astronomi och Fysik*, Vol. 2, No. 11 (1905), reprinted 1963. Stockholm: Royal Swedish Academy of Sciences.

———. "On Dead-Water." In F. Nansen, ed., *Norwegian North Polar Expedition, 1893–1896: Scientific Results*, New York: Greenwood Press, 1969.

FURTHER READING

Gillispie, C. C., ed. *Dictionary of Scientific Biography*, Vol. 4. New York: Scribner's, 1971; pp. 344–345.

McConnell, Anita. *No Sea Too Deep: The History of Oceanographic Instruments.* Bristol, Gloucestershire, England: Adam Hilger, 1982.

Sears, M., and D. Merriman, eds. *Oceanography: The Past.* New York: Springer-Verlag, 1980.

RELATED ARTICLES

Coriolis Effect; Ekman Current; Ekman Layer; Ekman Transport; *Fram*; Helland-Hansen, Bjørn; Internal Wave; Nansen, Fridtjof

Ekman Current

Ocean currents result from the interaction of several forces, among them surface wind stress, turbulent friction in the water column, lunar and solar tides, bottom friction, and the slope of the sea surface. The study of complex ocean currents has evolved by simplifying the equations that describe fluid flow. Ekman currents are an example of such currents.

During Norwegian explorer Fridtjof Nansen's (1861–1930) year-long drift across the Arctic Ocean in the *Fram*, he observed that ice floes in which the *Fram* was trapped did not drift directly downwind, but moved 20 to 40° to the right of the wind. He remarked about this curious fact to a Swedish scientist, Vagn Walfrid Ekman (1874–1954). In 1905, Ekman developed a mathematical theory that considered three forces. The primary force that sets the ice (or surface waters) moving is wind stress at the ocean surface. Water friction within the water column is a secondary force that retards the flow. The Coriolis force produced by Earth's rotation causes slow-moving ocean currents to veer to the right of the applied force in the northern hemisphere and to the left in the southern hemisphere.

This mathematical description of Ekman currents (with simple models of fluid friction in the water column) leads to a number of features of Ekman currents (see figure). First, the surface flow does not move downwind; rather, it moves 45° to the right of the wind in the northern hemisphere and 45° to the left in the southern. Second, the speed of the wind-driven current is greatest at the surface and decreases exponentially downward through the water. Third, the direction of flow also changes with depth and spirals clockwise in the northern hemisphere and counterclockwise in the southern hemisphere. Finally, the Ekman depth is the depth at which the current flow matches exactly the direction of the surface current. At this depth the flow is reduced to a small fraction of the surface flow.

The average direction of flow in the Ekman layer is perpendicular to the wind. If in the northern hemisphere, the wind blows toward the east, the average Ekman flow or Ekman transport is toward the south. This rule applies to all directions: The Ekman flow is perpendicular to the wind no matter in which direction the wind blows.

Although oceanographers believe in the fundamental principles of Ekman theory, no well-defined Ekman current such as that shown in the illustration has been observed using current meters. However, meteorologists have observed the Ekman spiral in near-surface winds, and laboratory models also show the expected spiral. This is not to say that Ekman currents do not exist in the ocean; simple Ekman theory depends on steady winds blowing in a constant direction and on constant fluid drag in the water column. The second issue is the main difficulty.

The surface current speed increases directly with increases in wind speed and on the latitude that changes the Coriolis force. The Ekman depth of frictional resistance depends on both the Coriolis force and on friction: Higher friction causes a deeper Ekman depth. The Ekman depth varies from about 50 to 200 meters (165 to 655 feet). Because it depends on latitude, the Ekman depth is greatest at low latitudes; the depth at 10° latitude is 5 times that at 80°.

Ekman currents are important in our understanding of upwelling processes that bring waters from the base of the Ekman layer to the surface.

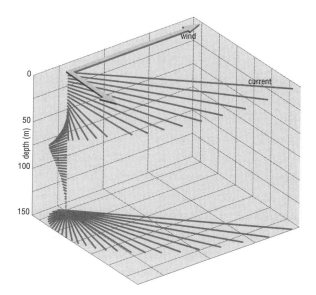

Computer model of a theoretical, northern hemisphere, Ekman current. The direction of the surface flow is 45° to the right of the wind. The current direction changes in a clockwise sense as depths increase. At the same time, the current speed decreases. The projection of the current arrows on the bottom plane shows the speed and direction changing.

Wind-driven upwelling is caused by winds blowing parallel along straight coastlines. The northern hemisphere California Current and the southern hemisphere Peru–Chile Current are areas where seasonal winds blow equatorward. According to the Ekman theory, wind-driven surface current moves water away from the coastline in both regions. Surface waters in these upwelling areas, as well as many others in the ocean, exhibit properties of deep waters [no greater than about 200 meters (655 feet)] brought to the surface: cooler surface temperature, higher plant nutrient concentrations (phosphate, nitrate, silicate); and lower dissolved oxygen concentrations. Depending on the locality of the upwelling region, coastal upwelling may produce surface salinities that are either higher or lower than those of the non-upwelled surface water. The supply of nutrients causes phytoplankton blooms, which are fed upon by zooplankton, which in turn attract fish. The major fisheries in the world are concentrated in upwelling regions.

Ekman currents also occur in the open ocean. The North Atlantic Equatorial and North Pacific Equatorial Currents flow under the northeast trade winds. These winds do not blow directly from east to west, but converge along the equator. The surface currents in these areas, however, flow generally from east to west. The directional difference between the trade winds and equatorial currents is consistent with Ekman theory. In several ocean areas, wind systems blow parallel to one another; this happens at the equator between the north and south trade winds. Because the average Ekman flow is directed to the right in the northern hemisphere and to the left in the southern hemisphere, surface waters diverge. Upwelled water must replace this surface divergence. Consequently, nutrient levels and phytoplankton-abundant fisheries stocks are relatively high along this equatorial band.

In other areas, such as between the westerly winds and the southeast trade winds near 30°S latitude, the predominant wind directions are opposite. Surface Ekman flow causes a movement of water under both wind regimes toward about 30° latitude. This is a convergence, and these areas are warm, poor in nutrients, and support low phytoplankton abundance.

William W. Broenkow

FURTHER READING

Gross, M. Grant. *Oceanography: A View of the Earth.* Englewood Cliffs, N.J.: Prentice Hall, 1972; 7th ed., Upper Saddle River, N.J.: Prentice Hall, 1996.

Pickard, George L. *Descriptive Physical Oceanography.* Oxford and New York: Pergamon Press, 1964; 5th enl. ed., Oxford and Boston: Butterworth-Heinemann, 1995.

Pond, Stephen, and George L. Pickard. *Introductory Dynamical Oceanography.* Oxford and New York: Pergamon Press, 1978; 2nd ed., Oxford: Butterworth-Heinemann, 2000.

RELATED ARTICLES

Boundary Current; Coriolis Effect; Ekman, Vagn Walfrid; Ekman Transport; Upwelling

Ekman Layer

Winds over the ocean impart a tangential stress to the ocean surface that sets the water in motion, producing currents. The wind stress is equal to the product of the density of the overlying air, a constant that essentially quantifies the ability of the wind to move the surface waters below, and the square of the wind speed. In the form of a simple equation, the wind stress, τ, can be expressed as $\tau = \rho_{air} C_D W^2$, where Rho_{air} is the density of air, C_D is the drag coefficient representing the effect of friction at the ocean surface, and W is the wind speed. Vagn Walfrid Ekman (1874–1954) developed a simple model in 1905 to explain how water moves in response to wind stress in the open ocean away from coastal boundaries. Initially, the wind produces surface flow. The surface waters, once in motion, are deflected by Earth's rotation (the Coriolis effect). In the northern hemisphere, this deflection is 45° to the right of the wind (and 45° to the left of the wind in the southern hemisphere). As the surface waters move obliquely with respect to the wind, the waters just below the surface are further deflected and their speed reduced through internal friction. This process continues vertically layer by layer, forming a spiral of currents, called the *Ekman spiral,* whose direction eventually becomes opposite to the direction of flow at the surface. If we average all the currents that make up the Ekman spiral, the net water motion is 90° to the right of the wind in the northern hemisphere (or 90° to the left in the southern hemisphere). The net transport of water 90° to the right (or left) of the wind is referred to as *Ekman transport.* Finally, the layer between the surface and the bottom of the Ekman spiral is called the *Ekman layer.* Typical values for the depth of the Ekman layer vary from a few tens of meters to perhaps 100 meters (approximately 328 feet). In practice, however, it has been difficult to identify the Ekman spiral as a unique phenomenon because of other processes that occur simultaneously.

Laurence C. Breaker

FURTHER READING

Duxbury, Alyn C. *The Earth and Its Oceans.* Reading, Mass.: Addison-Wesley, 1971.

Ekman, V. Walfrid. "On the Influence of the Earth's Rotation on Ocean Currents." *Arkiv foer Matematik, Astronomi och Fysik,* Vol. 2, No. 11 (1905), reprinted 1963. Stockholm: Royal Swedish Academy of Sciences.

Knauss, John A. *Introduction to Physical Oceanography.* Englewood Cliffs, N.J.: Prentice Hall, 1978; 2nd ed., Upper Saddle River, N.J.: Prentice Hall, 2000.

RELATED ARTICLES

Coriolis Effect; Earth, Rotation of; Ekman, Vagn Walfrid; Ekman Current; Ekman Transport

Ekman Transport

Ekman transport, a part of the Ekman theory of wind-driven currents, gives the total volume of water from the sea surface to the bottom of the Ekman layer moving under the influence of the wind. The Ekman current is strongest at the surface, decreases rapidly, and changes direction with increasing depth. Ekman transport may be thought of as the vertically averaged Ekman current. Its units are given as volume transport per meter width of the current. Ekman transport can be calculated from a simple formula; $T_E = \tau/f$, where T_E is the Ekman transport, τ the wind stress, and f the Coriolis parameter. The transport is directed at 90° to the right of the wind in the northern hemisphere and 90° to the left in the southern hemisphere. Because the Coriolis parameter, for a given wind stress, depends on the latitude, the transport is largest at low latitudes and weakest at high latitudes. The wind stress is proportional to the square of the wind speed.

Winds blowing parallel along straight coastlines cause wind-driven upwelling. Because

Ekman transport is perpendicular to the wind direction, the transport is directed away from the coastline. This causes a 10– to 20-centimeter (4- to 8-inch) drop in the sea-surface elevation along the coast and an upwelling of water to replace that transported offshore.

The California Current in the northern hemisphere and the Peru–Chile Current in the southern hemisphere are two locations where strong coastal upwelling occurs. These are areas where winds blow equatorward seasonally. Upwelling areas exhibit properties of deep [about 200 meters (656 feet)] waters brought to the surface: cooler surface temperature, higher plant nutrient concentrations (phosphate, nitrate, silicate), and lower dissolved oxygen concentrations. Depending on the locality of the upwelling region, coastal upwelling may produce surface salinities that are either higher or lower than those of the non-upwelled surface water. The supply of nutrients causes phytoplankton blooms, which are fed upon by zooplankton, which in turn attract fish. The major fisheries in the world are concentrated in upwelling regions. The U.S. National Marine Fisheries Service uses the Ekman transport formula to publish an upwelling index based on maps of large-scale wind stress.

In several open ocean areas, wind systems blow parallel to one another; this happens at the equator between the north and south trade winds. Because Ekman transport is directed to the right of the wind in the northern hemisphere and to the left in the southern hemisphere, surface waters diverge; that is, they are pushed away from the equator. Upwelled water must replace this surface divergence. Consequently, nutrient levels and phytoplankton abundance are high along this equatorial band.

In offshore areas such as between the westerly winds and the southeast trade winds near 30°S latitude, the predominant wind directions are opposite. Under both wind regimes, surface

Ekman flow causes a movement of water toward about 30° latitude. This is a convergence, and these areas are warm, poor in nutrients, and support low phytoplankton abundance.

William W. Broenkow

FURTHER READING

Gross, M. Grant. *Oceanography: A View of the Earth.* Englewood Cliffs, N.J.: Prentice Hall, 1972; 7th ed., Upper Saddle River, N.J.: Prentice Hall, 1996.

Pickard, George L. *Descriptive Physical Oceanography.* Oxford and New York: Pergamon Press, 1964; 5th enl. ed., Oxford and Boston: Butterworth-Heinemann, 1995.

Pond, Stephen, and George L. Pickard. *Introductory Dynamical Oceanography.* Oxford: Butterworth-Heinemann, 1983; 2nd ed., 2000.

RELATED ARTICLES

Coriolis Effect; Ekman, Vagn Walfrid; Ekman Current; Upwelling

Elasmobranchii

The class Chondrichthyes (cartilaginous fishes) is divided into two subclasses, the Holocephali (chimaeras) and Elasmobranchii (sharks, skates, and rays). Although often portrayed as primitive, modern elasmobranchs are highly derived and specialized fishes that differ dramatically from the abundant and diverse elasmobranchs that dominated marine habitats through much of the upper Paleozoic and Mesozoic Eras (400 to 65 million years ago). The translation of the Greek name, *strap gills*, refers to the five to seven gill slits present in this group. Other distinguishing characteristics include cartilaginous skeletons, toothlike placoid scales, internal fertilization and the presence of copulatory organs (*claspers*) in males, fin rays stiffened by horny rays called *ceratotrichia*, no gas bladder, rows of replacement dentition, and a spiral valve intestine.

The first definitive elasmobranch fossils appear in the Devonian Period (408.5 to 362.5 million years ago), although fragmentary remains suggest that their origins may date back to the Silurian or even into the Ordovician Period (up to 450 million years ago). The cartilaginous skeletons of these fishes do not often fossilize, and taxonomic distinctions are based primarily on morphology of teeth, spines, or scales. The interrelationships within this subclass are therefore fraught with controversy, and many divergent classifications have been proposed. It is clear that the first known elasmobranchs, the cladoselachian sharks (order Cladoselachiformes), had ancestral characteristics of more primitive fishes. They were, however, well equipped as predators, with sharp, multicusped (cladodont) teeth and sizes of up to 2 meters (approximately 6.5 feet). The overall evolutionary trend in this group has been toward steady improvements in the basic anatomical plan already evident in cladoselachians. While cladoselachians were diversifying in marine environments, the xenacanth sharks (order Xenacanthiformes) were becoming common in fresh water. These forms resembled lobe-finned fishes (class Sarcopterygii) in some ways and disappeared during the Triassic Period (247.5 to 205.7 million years ago), possibly due to competition with emerging bony fishes (Osteichthyes). During the Permian Period (290 to 248.2 million years ago), the cladoselachians were replaced by the hybodont sharks (order Hybodontiformes), which developed a more advanced and protrusible jaw structure and a more variable dentition. Modern elasmobranchs probably evolved from hybodont ancestors during the Jurassic Period (205.7 to 144.2 million years ago).

Modern elasmobranchs are an extremely diverse and specialized group of fishes that are primarily large, apex predators in marine systems. Elasmobranchs have good osmoregulatory capabilities and, although overwhelmingly marine, are often found in estuaries and even some freshwater systems. The number of orders and families are high compared to teleosts, although the total number of species (approximately 400 sharks, more than 280 rays, and more than 210 skates) is rather low. Thus, most elasmobranchs, although superficially similar, are actually quite different taxonomically. Rays are believed to be derived from sharks, although the actual lineage and interrelationships are unclear. Among the sharks, the requiem or ground sharks (order Carcharhiniformes) comprise more than half of the shark species and are diverse in tropical and subtropical nearshore habitats. The rays and skates (*batoids*) are distinguished from sharks primarily by pectoral fins fused to the sides of the head and ventral rather than lateral gill slits. Rays are most commonly encountered in tropical inshore waters, whereas skates are most abundant in deep water and at high latitudes. Some distinctive characteristics of modern elasmobranchs that have undoubtedly contributed to their success are large size, high mobility, predatory feeding habits, reliance on nonvisual senses (especially keen are olfactory and electroreception), and well-developed young. Their basic lifestyle of long life, slow growth, late ages at maturity, low reproductive rates, and high survival rates make them especially vulnerable to overfishing, habitat destruction, and ecosystem alterations. As a consequence, their numbers and diversity are rapidly declining, and many of these species are becoming increasingly rare and endangered. Since elasmobranchs are apex predators in many marine ecosystems, declines in their abundance may have unpredictable cascading effects on other species.

Joseph J. Bizzarro

FURTHER READING
Bond, Carl E. *Biology of Fishes.* Philadelphia: W. B. Saunders, 1979; 2nd ed., Fort Worth, Texas: Saunders College Publishing, 1996.
Carroll, R. L. *Vertebrate Paleontology and Evolution.* New York: W. H. Freeman, 1988.
Hamlett, William C., ed. *Sharks, Skates, and Rays: The Biology of Elasmobranch Fishes.* Baltimore: Johns Hopkins University Press, 1999.
Helfman, Gene S., Bruce B. Collette, and Douglas E. Facey. *The Diversity of Fishes.* Malden, Mass.: Blackwell Science, 1997.
Moyle, Peter B., and Joseph J. Cech. *Fishes: An Introduction to Ichthyology.* Englewood Cliffs, N.J.: Prentice Hall, 1982; 4th ed., Upper Saddle River, N.J.: Prentice Hall, 2000.
Nelson, Joseph S. *Fishes of the World,* 3rd ed. New York: Wiley, 1994.
Taylor, Leighton R., Jr., et al., eds. *Sharks and Rays.* Alexandria, Va.: Time-Life Books, 1999.

RELATED ARTICLES
Chondrichthyes; Holocephali; Ray; Sarcopterygii; Shark; Skate

Electrical Conductivity

The electrical conductivity of seawater is a measure of its electrical current-carrying capacity by charged particles. These are the seawater major constituent cations and anions (Na^+, K^+, Mg^{2+}, Cl^-, Br^-, SO_4^{2+}, etc.). At first the electrical conductance of seawater appears straightforward: the greater the concentration of charge-carrying ions, the easier it is for seawater to conduct an electric charge. However, the actual process by which this is accomplished is a very difficult problem in physical chemistry. The specific conductance of the various ions depends on their hydration state: that is, the degree of complexation between the ions and the polarized water molecule.

The importance of electrical conductivity of seawater is related to fact that the specific conductance of an electrolyte increases almost linearly with the concentration of the electrolyte and almost linearly with an increase in temperature. These facts led to the development in the 1960s of salinometers, which use the measured electrical conductivity to compute the seawater salinity. Seawater salinity is numerically equal to the grams of sea salt in 1 kilogram (2.2 pounds) of seawater. Before the electrical conductivity method, oceanographers used the laborious Knudsen chemical titration to determine the concentration of Cl⁻ and Br⁻ from which salinity was calculated.

The development of the electrical conductivity method allows very precise determination of salinity by laboratory salinometers in which a small sample of seawater is introduced into a conductivity cell. An electric field is established across some length (several millimeters to centimeters) of the seawater sample using platinized platinum electrodes, and the minute electric current is measured precisely. Because the cell constant of the conductivity cell is affected by the condition of the electrodes, the platinum cells must be kept scrupulously clean. As the conductivity is measured, laboratory salinometers must either measure the sample temperature or control it precisely. For example, a seawater sample having a salinity of 35 practical salinity units (psu) has an electrical conductivity of 4.79 siemens per meter at 208°C (about 406°F) and 4.89 siemens per meter at 218°C (about 424°F). The conductivity of 36-psu seawater at 208°C is 4.91 siemens per meter. A 18°C (64°F) increase in temperature causes nearly the same increase in conductivity as a 1-psu increase in salinity. The siemens is the unit for conductivity, the reciprocal of electrical resistance

Following the introduction of laboratory salinometers, *conductivity–temperature–depth* (CTD) *profilers* were developed to measure these properties continuously without the need to take water samples and perform laboratory analyses. The early CTDs used induction conductivity measurements rather than platinum conductivity cells. Induction cells have the advantage that fouling of the platinum surface is avoided and that the induction head is less fragile than the conductivity cell. Most precision CTD profilers now use small [5 centimeters (2 inches) long] platinum conductivity cells. Modern CTD instruments are lowered over the side of oceanographic vessels by electrical conducting cable. Electrical conductivity, temperature, and pressure signals are transmitted to the ship at rates of 24 samples per second. From this, computers use complex equations to transform conductivity, temperature, and pressure values into salinity and density, which are the basic seawater properties by which oceanographers understand ocean circulation and mixing processes.

In 1978 the *Practical Salinity Scale* was defined in terms of the precisely measured relationship between the Knudsen titration and measurements of electrical conductivity, temperature, and pressure. Under the best circumstances, laboratory electrical conductivity measurements now yield salinity measurements with a precision of 60.0002 psu, and CTD profilers yield a precision of 60.002 psu.

William W. Broenkow

FURTHER READING

Horne, Ralph. *Marine Chemistry.* New York: Wiley-Interscience, 1969.

Millero, Frank J. *Chemical Oceanography.* Boca Raton, Fla.: CRC Press, 1992; 2nd ed., 1996.

Wallace, William J. *The Development of the Chlorinity/Salinity Concept in Oceanography.* Amsterdam and New York: Elsevier Scientific, 1974.

Whitfield, M. "Seawater as an Electrolytic Solution." In J. P. Riley, ed., *Chemical Oceanography.* London: Academic Press, 1965; 2nd ed., 1975; pp. 43–171.

RELATED ARTICLES
CTD Profiler; Salinity

El Niño

Nothing illustrates the close coupling of the atmosphere and the oceans more acutely than El Niño, a reversal of normal weather and oceanographic conditions in the Pacific region that occurs every few years. Meteorologists now recognize that El Niño is related to abnormal weather across much of the world. El Niño was first noticed as a warm ocean current off the coast of South America that arrived every few years around Christmas (hence the name, which means "the boy child" in Spanish). During the twentieth century, climatologists realized that El Niño was part of a large-scale climate reversal called the Southern Oscillation, and the term *El Niño–Southern Oscillation* (ENSO) is now generally used to describe the phenomenon. Although the causes are still unknown, careful monitoring of recent ENSO events has given scientists a better understanding of the mechanism by which El Niño produces changes in the world's weather and will help people prepare more thoroughly for future ENSO events.

Brief History of El Niño

Only in the last few years has El Niño seized the popular imagination, but climatologists believe that the phenomenon may have been happening for anything from a few thousand to hundreds of thousands of years. It was not until the sixteenth century that El Niño was named, when Peruvian fishermen noticed an abnormally warm water current off their shores that increased rainfall and plant growth in barren regions but decimated marine life in the eastern Pacific. During the 1920s British meteorologist Sir Gilbert Walker realized that these abnormal weather events in the eastern Pacific were closely related to opposite weather events happening at the same time in Australia and Indonesia. He coined the term *Southern Oscillation* because these weather patterns are related to a shift in the center of low pressure in the western Pacific. In the 1960s, a Norwegian-born professor at the University of California named Jacob Bjerknes (1897–1975) explained how a close coupling of the atmosphere and the oceans across the Pacific produced both Walker's Southern Oscillation and El Niño, which are really two parts of the same phenomenon.

How El Niño Occurs

The circulation of the Pacific Ocean is dominated by two large subtropical gyres: The North Pacific gyre rotates clockwise; the South Pacific gyre rotates counterclockwise. Between them lie the westward-flowing North and South Pacific equatorial currents. The most important driving mechanism for this gyral circulation is the trade wind system, which drags water away from Central America and South America toward Australia and the western Pacific islands. El Niño is a disruption of the trade wind system, during which the trade winds weaken or even reverse direction, due to shifts of the atmospheric high- and low-pressure cells. (A strengthening of the trade winds produces weather effects opposite to those of an El Niño through a phenomenon called *La Niña.*)

Normally, the trade winds cause the sea surface to slope upward nearly 1 meter (3.3 feet) from the coast of South America to the Indonesian Archipelago. At the same time the thermocline (the boundary layer between the warmer, upper ocean and the cooler depths) slopes downward from 30 meters (100 feet) in the eastern Pacific to 100 meters (330 feet) in the western Pacific. Surface temperatures in the equatorial western Pacific are normally 8°C (14°F) higher than along the South American coast. The overall effect is a "mound" of warm water, thicker in the western Pacific than in the eastern Pacific. When the winds slacken, this mound of water moves eastward along the equator as a Kelvin wave at speeds of about 100 kilometers (62 miles) per day. The sea level falls on equatorial islands and the sea level rises along the eastern Pacific coast. At the same time, sea surface temperatures rise in the eastern Pacific and the thermocline sinks. The Kelvin wave sweeps southward along the Peru–Chile coast and northward along the central American coast. Warm waters and higher-than-normal sea level along the coast cause a displacement of cool water fishes and reduce coastal upwelling. Both of these effects have major impacts on local fisheries. The high sea level, coupled with more intense winter storms and their attendant storm waves, may cause coastal flooding and erosion, and sometimes disastrous stream flooding.

The oceanographic changes are related to meteorological changes. Normally, low pressure over the western Pacific causes rising warm air and plentiful rain around Indonesia and Australia, while high pressure over South America produces cool, descending air and comparatively dry conditions. The difference between the low-pressure western and high-pressure eastern regions means that trade winds flow from the east to west near the ocean surface and back from the west to east high above it, producing a clockwise atmospheric conveyor called a *Walker circulation cell* (named for Sir Gilbert Walker). The Walker circulation cell causes increased rainfall and flooding in the eastern Pacific and droughts or forest fires in the west. In a strong ENSO event, the effects can be much more widespread.

Effects of El Niño

El Niño—once thought of simply as a warm current arriving off the coast of Peru—is now known to be so powerful and far reaching that it can drastically alter weather throughout much of the world.

In the western Pacific, El Niño spells torrential rain for the west coast of South and Central America [around 2.5 meters (100 inches) of rain is estimated to have fallen during the six months of the very severe 1982–83 ENSO event] and heavy rain in California, while the east coast of North America experiences milder winters and fewer hurricanes. The middle and eastern Pacific warms so much that it kills off coral around Tahiti [many corals die at temperatures above 30°C (86°F)]. The deepening of the thermocline

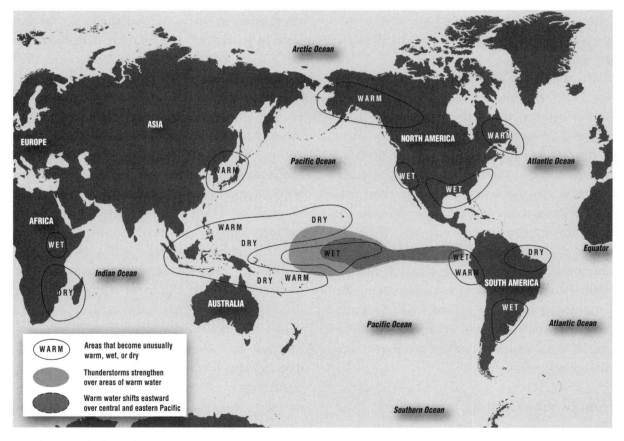

Conditions and effects of El Niño.

and warming of surface waters off Peru cuts off the upwelling supply of plant nutrients, reduces phytoplankton productivity, and displaces cool-water fish species. For example, the abundant population of anchovies around Peru fell from 20 million to just 2 million during the 1972 ENSO. The severe 1982–83 ENSO is estimated to have reduced marine life around Peru by around 25 percent overall. Higher sea level caused partially by warming and partially by a relaxation in winds resulted in increased coastal erosion. California experienced sea-level rises of around 20 centimeters (8 inches) during 1982–83. Meanwhile, precisely the opposite events happen in the eastern Pacific. Australia, Indonesia, and India experience droughts or forest fires. Hawaii and Tahiti see an increase in cyclones and tropical storms.

Although the effects depend on the strength of an ENSO, during particularly severe events they have been experienced even in Antarctica, some 6000 kilometers (3700 miles) away, as a major reduction in seal births. El Niño is also known to contribute to droughts in southern Africa that cause famines. Scientists have found that they can accurately predict corn harvests in Zimbabwe from the previous year's temperatures in the Pacific.

Causes of El Niño

Although El Niño is now much better understood than in preceding decades, climate scientists still do not know what actually causes an ENSO event in the first place. Some scientists believe that ENSO is simply a random occurrence systematically magnified by the atmosphere–ocean coupling. There may be no single trigger that switches on El Niño, because it involves a complex cycle of events in both the ocean and the atmosphere.

Future of El Niño

With strong evidence to suggest that El Niño has been a prominent feature of Earth's climate for thousands of years, there is every reason to suppose that it will be equally significant in the future. Although ENSO events occur every few years, their severity varies from one event to the next. The very severe 1982–83 ENSO had at least one positive effect. With an estimated $8 billion damage and thousands of lives lost, scientists at the National Oceanic and Atmospheric Administration (NOAA) launched a 10-year Tropical Ocean-Global Atmosphere (TOGA) program to better understand the phenomenon. They now use the Tropical Atmosphere/Ocean Array (TAO), a line of 70 moored buoys packed with scientific instruments stretching from Peru to Australia, and the *TOPEX/Poseidon* satellite system, to monitor changes in the Pacific Ocean that could signal the start of an ENSO event.

Future research will provide not just a better understanding of El Niño and how to prepare for it (such as when to plant crops in Peru or Zimbabwe), but how it relates to other phenomena, such as global warming. Some scientists believe that global warming may intensify El Niño; others point out that computer models are not yet comprehensive enough to take both phenomena into account. But with very severe ENSO events occurring as much as 50 years apart, it may be a century or more before scientists fully understand what effect El Niño will have in the future.

Chris Woodford

FURTHER READING:
Broecker, Wallace S. "The Great Ocean Conveyor." *Oceanography*, Vol. 4 (1991), p. 79.
———. "Chaotic Climate." *Scientific American*, November 1995, p. 44.
Cane, Mark A. "Oceanographic Events During El Niño." *Science*, December 1983, p. 1189.
Diaz, Henry F., and Vera Markgraf. *El Niño: Historical and Paleoclimatic Aspects of the Southern Oscillation.* Cambridge and New York: Cambridge University Press, 1992.

Fagen, Brian. *Floods, Famines, and Emperors: El Niño and the Fate of Civilizations*. New York: Basic Books, 1999.

Gannon, Robert. "Solving the Puzzle of El Niño." *Popular Science*, September 1986, p. 118.

Glantz, Michael H. *Currents of Change: El Nino's Impact on Climate and Society*. Cambridge and New York: Cambridge University Press, 1996.

Philander, S. George. *El Niño, La Niña and the Southern Oscillation*. San Diego: Academic Press, 1990.

Rasmusson, E. M., and J. M. Wallace. "Meteorological Aspects of the El Niño/Southern Oscillation." *Science*, Vol. 222 (1983), p. 1195.

Suplee, Curt. "El Niño/La Niña." *National Geographic*, March 1999, p. 72.

RELATED ARTICLES
Air-Sea Interaction; Gyre; La Niña; Ocean Current; Upwelling

Elopomorpha

The subdivision Elopomorpha is composed of a diverse group of fishes within the division Teleostei. The taxonomy of this group is highly debated because many of the morphological characteristics of fishes in this group are dissimilar, with body shape ranging from tarpon to that of eels. A reduction in the number of uroneural bones (modified neural arches of the terminal vertebrae) in the caudal fin and the development of epipleural (dorsal) ribs distinguish this group from Osteoglossamorpha. However, the presence of leptocephalus larvae is the main characteristic that classifies this group of fishes as elopomorphs. Leptocephalus larvae (from the Greek *lepto*, thin, and *cephalus*, head) are a planktonic life stage distinguished by an extremely compressed body, commonly described as leaflike. Leptocephali may be large and shrink during transition to the juvenile phase. Based on the classification scheme proposed by Joseph S. Nelson in *Fishes of the World* (1994), there is one extinct and four extant orders of Elopomorpha.

The earliest fossil records of elopomorphs possibly extend to the Jurassic (205.7 to 144.2 million years ago). However, the dominant fossil record of the extinct marine order Crossognathiformes dates to the Cretaceous (135 million years ago) and extends into the Eocene (56.5 to 35.4 million years ago). The order Elopiformes consists of tenpounders and tarpon, which are marine fishes living in tropical and subtropical waters. Some scientists consider orders Elopiformes and Albuliformes to be one group because they are morphologically similar. Bonefishes, halosaurs, and spiny eels constitute the three families of Albuliformes. Bonefishes occur in tropical marine waters, but halosaurs and spiny eels are found around the world in the deep sea. The order Anguilliformes is the most diverse group and includes moray eels, snake eels, worm eels, snipe eels, and conger eels. Anguilliformes are true eels, lacking pelvic fins with confluent dorsal, anal, and caudal fins. These fishes are marine, except the catadromous family Anguillidae. The most derived order, Saccopharyngiformes, is characterized by the absence of opercular bones, branchiostegal rays, scales, pelvic fins, ribs, and swim bladder. This order includes many species of swallower and gulper eels, located in the deep waters of the Atlantic, Pacific, and Indian Oceans.

Jeffrey M. Field

FURTHER READING
Long, J. A. *The Rise of Fishes: 500 Million Years of Evolution*. Baltimore: Johns Hopkins University Press, 1995.

Moyle, P. B., and J. J. Cech, Jr. *Fishes: An Introduction to Ichthyology*, 4th ed. Upper Saddle River, N.J.: Prentice Hall, 1996.

Nelson, Joseph S. *Fishes of the World*. Upper Saddle River, N.J.: Prentice Hall, 1982; 4th ed., 2000.

RELATED ARTICLES
Clupeomorpha; Deep Sea; Euteleostei; Osteoglossomorpha; Teleostei

Emery, Kenneth O.

1914–1998

Marine Geologist and Geophysicist

American marine geologist Kenneth O. Emery encouraged collaborative research between U.S. oceanographic institutions and between scientists from different nations and different disciplines. Among his major contributions were his geological surveys of the California coastal margin and his collaborative surveys of the east and west margins of the Atlantic Ocean.

Kenneth O. Emery, or "K.O." as he was known to his colleagues, was born in 1914 in Swift Current, Saskatchewan, Canada, but grew up in Texas. He studied engineering at North Texas Agricultural College and graduated in geology from the University of Illinois in 1935. His research life started there under his mentor, Francis P. Shepard (1897–1985), considered by many U.S. marine geologists to be the "father" of their discipline. From Illinois, in 1939, Emery gained his M.S. in geology, and in 1941 his doctorate; the latter was based on his research of the continental margins of California as a guest of the Scripps Institution of Oceanography.

Between 1943 and 1945, Emery worked for the Division of War Research at the University of California, San Diego, where he produced maps of sediment types based on survey data from a wide variety of sources. These maps were used for interpreting acoustic signals in submarine warfare. Emery and others later used the maps of sediment distributions to shed light on geological processes on continental margins.

In 1946, Emery participated in a U.S. Geological Survey study of Bikini Atoll prior to the atomic bomb tests. The study supported Charles Darwin's sinking seamount hypothesis for atoll formation—that subsiding volcanic islands gave rise to ring-shaped coral formations. Much later—with increasing concern about global warming and sea-level rise—Emery was to question the use of tide gauges on coral atolls and volcanic islands. For instance, in the 1991 book *Sea Levels, Land Levels, and Tide Gauges,* Emery and his coauthor, David G. Aubrey, argued that oceanic islands are typically moving laterally and are subsiding, rebounding, or tilting, and so, over time, make unreliable sea-level indicators unless these factors are taken into account.

After World War II, Emery continued his research on the California continental margin in his 16-year career as assistant professor and later professor at the University of Southern California. In 1960 he published the influential volume *The Sea Off Southern California: A Modern Habitat of Petroleum,* and this and his other work on oil- and gas-bearing geological structures, such as in the east and south China Sea, were of great interest to petroleum geologists from U.S. oil companies.

In 1962, Emery joined the Woods Hole Oceanographic Institution (WHOI), where he assembled a team of young marine geologists from a wide range of U.S. oceanographic institutions to participate in the USGS/WHOI study of the continental margin of the U.S. east coast. This work was part of a field program that was to extend across the continental margins of the east and west Atlantic using a wide variety of techniques: predominantly echo sounding and low-frequency seismic profiling, but also gravity, magnetics, and suspended particle analysis. Many of the findings from this program were incorporated in a book (coauthored with Elazar Uchupi), *Geology of the Atlantic Ocean.* This work demonstrated Emery's great capacity for synthesis, relating findings from different sources and disciplines—a skill that he considered to be among the most important qualities of a scientist. As a practical geologist he was fond of saying, "Geophysics is just another hammer," implying that, for him, its greatest usefulness was in techniques that shed new light on geology.

Emery's interests were broad, yet focused. His abiding interest in geology extended beyond Earth, as demonstrated in a book, written with Elazar Uchupi, *Morphology of the Rocky Members of the Solar System*. He lived for many years at Oyster Pond, Massachusetts, where he surveyed the coastal pool by rowboat, producing a classic account of a small-scale study, *A Coastal Pond Studied by Oceanographic Methods*. When Hurricane Gloria passed through the region in fall 1985, Emery, at the age of 71, was in his yard taking meteorological measurements. He was able to document the snuffing out of the hurricane by cold air from a front approaching from the west.

During his years at WHOI, to retirement and beyond, Emery took various posts, including first dean of the WHOI/Massachusetts Institute of Technology doctorate program (appointed 1968), Henry Bryant Bigelow Oceanographer (1975–79), and scientist emeritus (1979). Among his list of awards and honors were the Prince Albert de Monaco Medal (1971) and the American Geophysical Union's Maurice Ewing Award (1985). To the end, Emery remained enthusiastic about generating and testing new ideas and acting as a mentor to students. Many years after his official retirement, he continued to work at WHOI, doing so almost every week until shortly before his death in 1998.

During his career, Emery reported his discoveries and syntheses in 15 books and about 290 articles. He gained a well-deserved reputation for great rigor and enthusiasm in all stages of the research process, from planning, to working with others on practical aspects, to analysis of data and publication of results. Among his outstanding qualities was his enthusiasm for collaborating with people from many nationalities. After World War II, working with Hiroshi Niino, he was influential in helping establish Japanese marine geology. Later, his collaborations with Elazar Uchupi and other African scientists helped further marine geology on that continent. Less a high-profile figurehead than a highly productive manager, mentor, scientist, and collaborator behind the scenes, his drive to involve others in "getting the job done" inspired many oceanographers of different disciplines and nationalities to work together.

Trevor Day

BIOGRAPHY

- Kenneth O. Emery.
- Born 6 June 1914 in Swift Current, Saskatchewan, Canada. Raised in Texas.
- Studied engineering at North Texas Agricultural College.
- Geology degree from University of Illinois in 1935, where he also took his M.S. (1939) and Ph.D. (1941).
- Worked in the Division of War Research, University of California, San Diego, producing sediment maps from 1943 to 1945.
- Assistant professor and then professor in geology at the University of Southern California (1946–62).
- Part of the Woods Hole Oceanographic Institution's marine geology group, joining as senior scientist and retiring as scientist emeritus (1962–79).
- Known for his international collaborations and major syntheses in books, such as *Geology of the Atlantic Ocean* (with Elazar Uchupi).
- Died 12 April 1998, in Milton, Massachusetts.

SELECTED WRITINGS

Emery, K. O. *The Sea off Southern California: A Modern Habitat of Petroleum*. London and New York: Wiley, 1960.

———. "Organic Transportation of Marine Sediments." In M. N. Hill, ed., *The Sea*, Vol. 3. New York: Wiley–Interscience, 1963; pp. 776–793.

———. *A Coastal Pond Studied by Oceanographic Methods*. Oyster Pond, Mass.: Oyster Pond Environmental Trust, 1997.

Emery, K. O., and David G. Aubrey. *Sea Levels, Land Levels, and the Tide Gauges*. New York: Springer–Verlag, 1991.

Emery, K. O., and C. O. Iselin. "Human Food from the Ocean." *Science*, Vol. 57, No. 3894 (1969), pp. 1279–1281.

Emery, K. O., and E. Uchupi. *Geology of the Atlantic Ocean*. New York: Springer-Verlag, 1984.

Uchupi, E., and K. O. Emery. *Morphology of the Rocky Members of the Solar System*. New York and Berlin: Springer-Verlag, 1993.

FURTHER READING

Schlee, S. *The Edge of an Unfamiliar World: A History of Oceanography.* New York: E. P. Dutton, 1973.

Stevenson, R. E. "Maurice Ewing Medalist: K. O. Emery." *EOS: Transactions American Geophysical Union,* Vol. 67, No. 3 (1986), pp. 31–32.

Williams, A. J., and D. A. Ross. "Kenneth O. Emery (1914–1998)." *EOS: Transactions American Geophysical Union,* Vol. 79 No. 29 (1998), pp. 347–349.

RELATED ARTICLES

Continental Margin; Dietz, Robert Sinclair; Iselin, Columbus O'Donnell; Seismic Profiling; Shepard, Francis Parker

Emperor Seamounts

The Emperor Seamounts are part of the Hawaiian–Emperor chain of seamounts, guyots, and volcanic islands that have formed over the past 80 million years as a result of a hotspot over the Pacific Ocean Plate. The seamounts provide evidence for a hotspot that forms volcanoes as the ocean floor moves over it. The Emperor Seamounts have been an important key to understanding Pacific Plate motion. Recognition of their successively older ages, from south to north, unlocked answers to questions related to the entire vector (velocity and direction) of motion between about 80 million and 43 million years ago.

Origin of the Emperor Seamounts: The Hotspot Theory

The Emperor Seamounts were named by Robert Sinclair Dietz (1914–95), a geologist from the Scripps Institution of Oceanography who studied the submarine geology of the northwest Pacific basin in the 1950s. The mechanism by which the seamounts and the Hawaiian chain were formed was not determined until 1963, when Canadian geophysicist J. Tuzo Wilson (1908–93) proposed the *hotspot theory.* He suggested that in areas that show a sustained level of volcanism, there might

be small, long-lasting, and very hot regions that provide the energy (or thermal plumes) to sustain that volcanic activity. Wilson suggested that the linear shape of the Hawaiian–Emperor chain may be a result of the Pacific Plate moving over a deep, stationary hotspot in the deeper part of Earth's mantle (that part of Earth below the lithosphere). The hotspot melts part of the Pacific Plate and pushes up the molten rock (magma), creating an active underwater volcano (known as a *seamount*). Over time, eruptions lead to the seamount rising above sea level, where it forms an island volcano. When the plate moves the island beyond the hotspot, the volcanism ceases. But then the adjacent part of the plate is heated up by the hotspot, creating another seamount, and the cycle is renewed.

Evidence for this theory is partially substantiated by the age of the oldest rock on the islands and seamounts. The Emperor Seamounts have rocks that are much older than those found on the Hawaiian Islands, and within the latter chain, the volcanically active island of Hawaii contains the youngest rocks (0.7 million years old). The hotspot is currently forming a seamount that will someday grow into the youngest island of the Hawaiian chain. Loihi Seamount is located 35 kilometers (21.7 miles) off the southern coast of Hawaii and

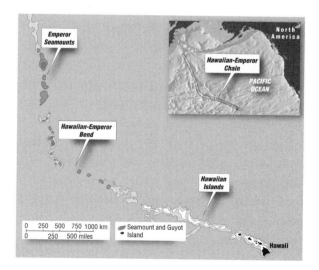

Emperor Seamounts.

has risen 3 kilometers (1.9 miles) above the seafloor to reach within a kilometer of the surface; it is estimated that this next Hawaiian island will break the water's surface within 1 million years.

Emperor Seamounts and Hawaiian Islands Chain

The Hawaiian–Emperor chain extends almost 6000 kilometers (3800 miles) from the island of Hawaii to the Kurile Trench, near the junction of the Kurile and Aleutian Trenches in the far northwestern Pacific Ocean. The amount of lava erupted to form the entire chain is estimated at 750,000 cubic kilometers (180,000 cubic miles). A sharp bend in the chain, which occurred at about 43 million years ago and demarcates the Emperor Seamounts from the Hawaiian Chain, represents a bend in the motion of the Pacific Plate from its northerly movement to a more northwestern track. However, there is more recent research that suggests that it may be the orientation of the hotspot, rather than the movement of the Pacific Plate, that caused the change in direction of the forming seamounts. The Emperor Seamounts extend 2327 kilometers (1445 miles) from Daikakuji Seamount to Meiji Seamount. Meiji, which is the oldest seamount, is between 75 and 80 million years old. Older seamounts of the Emperor chain apparently collided with Russia along the inner wall of the Kurile Trench and either were subducted or became attached (accreted) to the fore-arc region of the Kurile island arc. Some scientists believe that the subducted seamounts influence the spatial distribution of volcanoes on the Kamchatka Peninsula.

Volcanoes, Seamounts, and Guyots

The Hawaiian–Emperor chain is also called an *aseismic ridge,* as it is formed by volcanism over a hotspot and is composed of coalescing volcanoes, but only where volcanism is current at the end of the ridge. The Emperor Seamount chain also contains a number of *guyots,* which are flat-topped seamounts that have had their tops planed off by wave action, and like seamounts, have subsided below sea level. Subsidence occurs when the heated and expanded plate over a hotspot cools and contracts; when combined with the weight of the seamount it carries, the result is a depression in the mantle that gradually carries the seamount below the ocean surface. There are roughly 13 volcanoes per 1000 kilometers (625 miles) on the Emperor Seamounts, compared to 18 volcanoes per 1000 kilometers on the Hawaiian chain.

Manoj Shivlani

FURTHER READING

Kious, W. J., and R. I. Tilling. *This Dynamic Earth: The Story of Plate Tectonics.* Washington, D.C.: U.S. Geological Survey, 1996.

Seibold, Eugen, and Wolfgang H. Berger. *The Sea Floor: An Introduction to Marine Geology,* 2nd rev. and updated ed. Berlin and New York: Springer-Verlag, 1993.

Sullivan, Walter. *Continents in Motion: The New Earth Debate.* New York: McGraw-Hill, 1974; 2nd ed., New York: American Institute of Physics, 1991.

Tarduno. J. A., and R. D. Cottrell. "Paleomagnetic Evidence for Motion of the Hawaiian Hotspot During Formation of the Emperor Seamounts." *Earth and Planetary Science Letters,* Vol. 153, No. 3/4 (1997) pp. 171–180.

Tilling, R. I., C. Heliker, and T. L. Wright. *Eruption of Hawaiian Volcanoes: Past, Present, and Future.* Washington, D.C.: U.S. Government Printing Office, 1987.

RELATED ARTICLES

Dietz, Robert Sinclair; Guyot; Hawaiian–Emperor Bend; Hotspot; Pacific Plate; Seamount

Endothermic

Endothermic organisms are capable of maintaining body temperature above environmental temperatures. Homeothermic organisms such as birds and mammals maintain their elevated body temperatures within a narrow range. The body temperature of most mammals ranges from 37 to 40°C (98.6 to 104°F), and birds' temperatures range from 37 to 41°C (98.6 to 105.8°F).

Much of the ocean environment is cold, and many marine mammals have insulation in the form of subcutaneous fat underneath the skin to help maintain their body temperature. Such blubber is an effective insulator. Very little blood flows throughout and thereby reduces the amount of heat that would be released if blood were present at the surface of the body. In cetaceans, the outer layer of blubber is about the same temperature as the surrounding water. If the blubber had a higher temperature, the heat would be transferred into the water and lost.

Another mechanism to conserve heat is *countercurrent heat exchange,* which functions by directing the flow of blood either toward or away from the skin, depending on the temperature of the environment. In cold environments, blood is directed away from the skin to conserve heat; in warmer environments, blood is directed toward the skin so that it releases heat and more closely matches external temperatures. Dolphins and whales do not have insulation in their flippers and flukes because the layer of blubber or fat would prohibit effective locomotion. Blood is still needed in these areas, but flippers and flukes have a high surface area and are prone to heat loss. To prevent heat loss, warm arterial blood flowing from the center of the organism passes next to cold venous blood flowing back to the heart from the limbs and other extremities. As the arteries and veins direct the blood, the warmer arterial blood transfers heat to the cooler venous blood. The arterial blood becomes cooler as it approaches the extremities, and when it arrives in the limbs, it is only a few degrees warmer than the surrounding water. Similarly, the venous blood becomes warmer as it nears the center of the body and maximizes the amount of heat retained in the body.

Erin O'Donnell

FURTHER READING
Eckert, Roger, and David Randall. *Animal Physiology: Mechanisms and Adaptations.* San Francisco: Freeman, 1978; 2nd ed., New York: W. H. Freeman, 1983.
Solomon, Eldra P., Linda R. Berg, Diana W. Martin, and Claude Ville. *Biology.* Philadelphia: Saunders, 1985; 5th ed., Fort Worth, Texas: 1999.

RELATED ARTICLES
Blubber; Flipper

Energy from the Sea

Although most of the energy used by humans comes ultimately from the Sun, future generations may believe that it is the sea that meets much of the energy needs of Earth's growing and ever more demanding population. It is the sea that offers the hope of finding new fossil fuels (reserves of petroleum and gas hydrates—methane gas trapped inside ice) and of developing environmentally benign, renewable sources of energy such as wave power, tidal power, and offshore wind power. Harnessing the vast energy potential of the seas is much more problematic, however. New fossil fuel reserves are increasingly difficult to find and increasingly expensive to extract and carry hidden environmental costs, such as their contribution to global warming and acid rain. But the long-term vision needed to develop renewable energy sources, such as tidal *barrages* (barriers that stretch across estuaries), requires ever greater investment and can create other kinds of environmental problems.

Energy on Earth
Most of Earth's energy comes from the Sun, the exceptions being geothermal energy and tidal energy. *Geothermal energy* is ultimately created by nuclear reactions inside Earth's core and released at Earth's surface in a variety of ways, from the geysers of Yellowstone National Park and the steaming springs of Iceland to the volcanic "ring

of fire" in the Pacific Basin and the hydrothermal vents of the mid-ocean ridges. *Tidal energy,* the ebb and flow of the tides, comes from the gravitational attraction between the Moon and Earth, but even this includes a contribution from the Sun; the relative positions of the Sun and Moon produce the fortnightly spring and neap tides.

Of the energy transmitted by the Sun, about 30 percent is reflected straight back into space by Earth's atmosphere and never reaches our planet's surface. Fifty percent of the energy is absorbed by Earth, causing it to heat up and radiate the heat back into space. The remaining 20 percent provides our useful energy, driving winds and ocean waves, fueling green plants through photosynthesis, and causing the evaporation and precipitation that constantly cycles water between oceans and inland waters and the atmosphere.

Humankind's energy needs are vast and ever increasing. The current annual energy demand of everyone on Earth is estimated to be roughly 10,000 gigawatts (GW; 1 GW = 1 billion watts). To put this huge figure into perspective, the biggest hydroelectric plant in the United States, the Grand Coulee Dam in Washington, can generate about 6.5 GW of power, so approximately 1500 Grand Coulee Dams would be needed to meet Earth's entire energy needs.

World energy consumption is forecast to rise by 60 percent from 1997 to 2020. It will continue to increase significantly both as the global population rises to its projected maximum of about 11.5 billion (sometime after 2050) and as people in developing nations demand the level of affluence of people in more industrialized nations. (Around the year 2015, the combined energy consumption of China and India will exceed that of the rest of the world put together.) Yet despite our vast collective energy consumption, Earth's potential energy supplies are still much greater. The total solar energy arriving at Earth's surface is about 1000 times greater than total human energy consumption. Thermal energy stored in the oceans alone is estimated to be at least as great as total human power demands.

Fossil Fuels

Although environmental problems such as global warming and pollution have created enormous interest in renewable energy sources, *fossil fuels* (those which trap energy once produced by photosynthesis in hydrocarbons, such as coal, oil, and natural gas) still meet about 75 to 80 percent of human energy needs. Reserves of some fossil fuels (such as coal) are still relatively abundant and could theoretically last for hundreds of years, but reserves of petroleum are much more limited. The real concern is the huge disparity between the average time that reserves of fossil fuels have taken to accumulate (about 350 million years) and the time that humans have taken to deplete them. (Estimates suggest that 80 percent of Earth's total fossil reserves will have been consumed in just the 60 years between 1960 and 2020.)

Ever-increasing demand for petroleum has forced oil companies to explore in ever-deeper and more extreme regions of the ocean using increasingly sophisticated and expensive offshore oil technology. Considerable interest is now being shown in exploiting other types of hydrocarbon fuels present in the sea, notably methane gas hydrates. Sometimes known as *clathrates* (derived from a Latin word meaning "locked behind bars"), methane hydrates are methane molecules effectively locked inside lattices (crystalline structures) of ice. In the United States alone, large deposits of methane hydrates have been located off the coasts of Alaska, the west coast of California, the east coast, and in the Gulf of Mexico. Worldwide reserves of methane hydrates are estimated at 11.3 million trillion cubic meters (400 million trillion cubic feet), compared to known gas reserves of 141 trillion cubic meters (5000 trillion cubic feet). Exploiting these vast reserves will be problematic, however, because methane is 20 times more potent as a greenhouse gas than carbon dioxide, the gas considered to be most responsible for global warming.

Concerns such as this lead many scientists and environmentalists to believe that future energy needs must be met not through fossil fuels but through a variety of renewable energy sources. Yet renewables are expected to meet only about 8 percent of the world's energy needs between 1997 and 2020, and most of this will come from hydroelectric plants on rivers; renewable energy from the sea will contribute only a tiny fraction of the total.

Tidal Power

Harnessing the energy of the tides could provide roughly 10 to 100 GW of the world's energy needs. The basic principle of tidal systems is to capture the potential energy stored in a high tide and release it at low tide. Unlike a fossil-fuel power plant, in which the cost is split between the upfront cost of construction and the ongoing cost of the fuel, a tidal plant requires much greater upfront investment and has much lower running costs. This offers a large disincentive to potential investors and explains why so few tidal plants have been constructed so far. The world's best-known tidal plant, at La Rance River estuary in France, has been operating successfully since 1966 and generates about 240 megawatts (MW) of power. Numerous schemes to construct a massive tidal barrage across the Severn Estuary in England have been proposed since the 1920s, but the enormous investment required (estimated at £10 billion or U.S.$1.5 billion) and environmental concerns have delayed the project repeatedly.

Wave Power

A typical wave about 2 to 3 meters (6.6 to 10 feet) high can provide about 40 to 100 kilowatts (kW) of energy per meter (3.3 feet) of its length, enough energy to run about 1000 conventional lamp bulbs. Although all the coastal wave power on Earth combined could provide roughly 10 GW, wave electricity generators have been deployed even less successfully than tidal plants. Ironically, the need to site wave generators in places where waves are vigorous and wave energy is plentiful (usually in the windy high latitudes) also makes it necessary to develop extremely robust equipment. Several promising wave energy prototypes have been destroyed by heavy seas during testing.

The energy crises of the 1970s prompted considerable research into wave devices, notably in countries such as the United Kingdom, but few working wave plants have been constructed. Exceptions include a small (60-kW) oscillating water column (OWC) plant, which operates on the Scottish island of Islay, and a 1000-kW OWC built into a cliffside at Toftestallen in Norway in 1985 and destroyed by storm waves three years later. In November 2000, the wave power generator on Islay became the first in the world to feed into a national power distribution system (the U.K. national grid).

Ocean Thermal Energy

Temperature differences between the surface of the ocean and the ocean depths offer another means of extracting energy using a technique called *ocean thermal energy conversion* (OTEC). Thermal energy reserves in the world's oceans are estimated to be very roughly 10,000 GW, or roughly the same as current world energy consumption. Recovering just 0.1 percent of this would meet current U.S. energy demands 20 times over. Because OTEC is the type of device known as a *heat engine* (it converts heat into another form of energy), it is governed by basic principles of physics known as the *laws of thermodynamics*. These set an upper limit on the efficiency of an OTEC device, which turns out to be about 4 percent; actual efficiency might be only half this figure. In practice, this means that OTEC devices generating even small amounts of electricity need extremely large water flows of the same order as a very large hydroelectric power plant.

Offshore Wind Turbines

Estimates suggest that Earth's wind power provides roughly 1000 GW, yet only about 1 percent of this capacity is currently harnessed. Wind energy became one of the fastest-growing sources of renewable energy in the 1980s, when tax concessions led to the development of vast wind farms in areas such as California. (Another boom occurred in the late 1990s with U.S.$1 billion of wind-generating equipment installed in the United States alone.) But the growth of wind power has sometimes been frustrated by environmental objections, notably the noise and the visual intrusion caused by turbines sited in prominent positions on the tops of hills. In countries such as the United Kingdom, where wind turbines proposed in scenic landscapes have been defeated by strident objections, both governments and private energy companies have shown interest in developing offshore wind farms.

Following the successful development of a semi-offshore wind farm in 1992, in which nine turbines were installed on a harbor wall at Blyth in Northumberland, construction of the first U.K. offshore wind farm began at Blyth in June 2000. Two 2-MW wind turbines, powerful enough to supply electricity for 3000 households, were sited 200 meters (656 feet) apart in about 8 meters (26 feet) of water and approximately 1 kilometer (0.6 mile) offshore. Each three-blade turbine has a diameter of 66 meters (217 feet) and turns at 21.3 revolutions per minute in wind speeds from 14 to 90 kilometers (9 to 56 miles) per hour. These are the first turbines to be deployed in the harsh conditions of the North Sea and the largest ever mounted offshore. If the project is successful, a flood of similar projects could follow. Future wind farms are expected to feature clusters of turbines generating about 2 GW, or roughly the same power as the very largest conventional power plants. The U.K. government has estimated that the country could eventually invest £6 billion (U.S.$9 billion) in offshore wind turbines.

Offshore wind turbines may also have other uses. In 1999, an offshore wind farm was proposed for Cape Cod, Massachusetts, featuring both a collection of wind turbines and a mariculture farm. The farm was expected to provide energy for 10,000 people and contribute to the growing need for farmed fish.

Biomass

Photosynthesis (the process by which green plants turn sunlight into hydrocarbons) provides a potential power supply roughly 100,000 GW in marine plants alone, which is roughly 10 times more than Earth's combined energy needs. Some species can accumulate biomass very quickly; types of grasses and algae may produce 124 tonnes (136 tons) per hectare (2.47 acres) per year. Following the energy crises of the 1970s, U.S. government and commercial organizations launched a research program called the Ocean Food and Energy Farm (OFEF), whose aim was to produce biomass that could be used both as a source of food (through mariculture) and energy (natural gas). Although the research program ended in 1986, interest has been renewed following concerns over global warming; biomass grown in this way absorbs carbon dioxide during its growth, so no net carbon dioxide is produced when it is subsequently harvested for energy.

Other Sources of Energy from the Sea

Several other methods of generating energy have also been proposed. Ocean currents have an estimated energy potential of roughly 0.1 GW. Vast, fast-moving currents such as the Gulf Stream could, in theory, be used to drive tethered underwater turbines either connected to the shore or generating hydrogen gas in situ that could be piped or shipped onshore. In 1995, U.S. engineering professor Alexander Gorlov patented an underwater turbine shaped like the double helix of DNA, initially for power generation in tidal estuaries where conventional hydroelectric techniques such as barrages have proved too expensive. The twisted-turbine design ensures rotation at a continuous speed no matter how the current direction changes. Only experimental devices of this kind have been developed so far, and it remains unclear how feasible the idea is in practice.

Geothermal activity under the sea offers another potential energy source. In theory, it should be possible to harness the power of underwater geothermal sources just as they are harnessed on land. Hydrothermal vents, which produce a steady stream of superheated water [water that remains a liquid even at temperatures of 350°C (662°F) because it is under high pressure], might be tapped for their energy. However, because vents are sited along mid-ocean ridges at considerable depths, transmitting that energy back to shore would be problematic.

The continental shelves of the oceans also contain large quantities of uranium, the seed material for the nuclear fission power plants that currently meet 16 percent of world power generation capacity (nine countries generate over 40 percent of their energy in this way). Although there is no shortage of uranium, environmental concerns about nuclear power and the disposal of nuclear waste, and the proliferation of nuclear weapons, make the long-term prospects for nuclear power uncertain.

Future of Energy from the Sea

Earth's increasing population, ever-increasing energy demands, declining reserves of fossil fuels, and environmental problems such as global warming and pollution make the development of renewable energy a necessity. The potential of using moving water as an energy source is not in question; hydroelectric power (from dammed rivers) currently provides about 8 percent of the world's energy needs, and 24 countries produce more than 90 percent of their power in this way.

Riverine dams are expensive and controversial, yet harnessing the power of the sea may prove equally problematic, and it is unclear to what extent the potential of the ocean's energy, however vast, can actually be tapped.

In the short term, the ocean will continue to meet a significant proportion of world petroleum needs. In the medium term, it may offer new sources of hydrocarbon fuel, such as methane hydrates. In the longer term, however, it must seek to offer truly renewable forms of energy, but how quickly and effectively the vast reserves of energy trapped in the ocean can be harnessed is unclear. Small-scale, well-established technologies, such as offshore wind turbines, seem to have a bright future, yet even if all the world's wind power could be tapped, it would still meet only a fraction of total human energy needs. More sophisticated forms of power generation, such as tidal barrages or OTEC plants, offer the potential to develop vastly greater quantities of energy, but their development may continue to be defeated by the sheer scale of the investment required and the associated environmental drawbacks.

Chris Woodford

FURTHER READING
BP Amoco. *Statistical Review of World Energy.* London: BP Amoco, 1999.
Elliott, David. *Energy, Society and Environment: Technology for a Sustainable Future.* London and New York: Routledge, 1997.
Foley, Gerald. *The Energy Question.* London: Penguin Books/New York: Viking Penguin, 1987.
Haq, Bilal. "Methane in the Deep Blue Sea." *Science,* 23 July 1999, p. 543.
Leggett, Jeremy. *The Carbon War: Dispatches from the End of the Oil Century.* London: Allen Lane, 1999.
Ramage, Janet. *Energy: A Guidebook,* 2nd ed. Oxford and New York: Oxford University Press, 1997.
Ross, David. *Power from the Waves.* Oxford and New York: Oxford University Press, 1995.
Scientific American. *Energy for Planet Earth: Readings from* Scientific American *Magazine.* New York: W. H. Freeman, 1991.

USEFUL WEB SITES
Energy Information Administration. *International Energy Outlook 2002*. Washington, D.C.: U.S. Department of Energy, 2002. <http://www.eia.doe.gov/oiaf/ieo/index.html>.

RELATED ARTICLES
Gas Hydrate; Ocean Thermal Energy Conversion; Petroleum; Photosynthesis; Tidal Energy; Tide; Wave; Wave Energy

Entoprocta

Entoprocts are tiny, stalked marine animals, about 0.5 centimeters (0.2 inch) tall, that live attached to rocks, shells, or other objects. Some are *epizoites*, animals that live attached to other animals without causing harm. Entoprocts may be solitary or colonial. Colonial forms sometimes reproduce in such numbers that the colony forms a living "mat" on the seafloor. There are about 150 known species of entoprocts. These were once classified as members of the phylum Bryozoa but are now assigned their own distinct phylum, Entoprocta, although there is still controversy about this classification. No entoproct species has a common name.

Entoprocts live attached to a solid object by means of a thin stalk. At the top of the stalk is the main part of the body—a translucent, cup-shaped structure called the *calyx*. The calyx contains a U-shaped digestive tract and reproductive organs. Around the upper margin of the calyx is a crown of tentacles, which are used to filter microscopic algae from the water. The algal cells stick to a layer of mucus covering the tentacles, and this mucus is conducted down to the mouth by tiny hairs (cilia). The tentacles can bend and contract, but unlike the tentacles of cnidarians (such as sea anemones), they cannot be withdrawn into the body.

Due to their small size, entoprocts have no need for hearts, gills, or circulatory vessels. They simply absorb oxygen from the water through their skin and allow waste carbon dioxide to diffuse out. A simple nervous system controls the muscle cells in the stalk, calyx, and tentacles, but there is no brain. There are no specialized sense organs either, but entoprocts are thought to possess sensory cells that respond to light, movement, and certain chemicals. Most species are unable to move about, but some can creep along by bending over.

Entoprocts can reproduce asexually. The parent animal produces genetically identical "daughters" from buds on the side of the body. As a result, a single individual can quickly give rise to a colony of hundreds. In shallow waters entoproct colonies sometimes form "animal mats" on the seafloor. The individuals in a colony stay attached to each other by horizontal branches called *stolons*, which connect the base of each stalk. Entoprocts can also reproduce sexually. They are *hermaphrodites*, which means that each individual can produce both male and female sex cells. Once fertilized, the female egg cells are brooded in a special pouch in the calyx, while the embryos grow into larvae. The cilia-covered larvae are then released to swim away in the plankton and establish new colonies elsewhere.

Ben Morgan

FURTHER READING
Brusca, Richard C., and Gary J. Brusca. *Invertebrates*. Sunderland, Mass.: Sinauer, 1990.
Margulis, Lynn. *Five Kingdoms: An Illustrated Guide to the Phyla of Life on Earth*. San Francisco: W. H. Freeman, 1982; 3rd ed., New York, 1998.

RELATED ARTICLES
Filter Feeder

Epibenthic

Epibenthic describes organisms that live on the surface of the seafloor. In contrast, infaunal organisms live in or burrow through the sediment. *Epibenthic* is a general term and can be used to modify more specific descriptors. For example, epibenthic organisms can be large (e.g., epibenthic megafauna) or small (e.g., epibenthic macrofauna), and they can be mobile (e.g., sea stars) or sessile (e.g., anemones). Some epibenthic organisms live on hard substrate (e.g., rocks, coral reefs, plants, and other animals), whereas others live on the sediment surface (e.g., continental slope, abyssal plain). Epibenthic fauna (also called *epifauna*) can be found from the shallowest waters to the deepest trenches, and most invertebrate phyla and some protozoan groups have epibenthic representatives. Epifauna can play an important role in establishing community structure through competition, predation, and grazing (e.g., sea urchins in kelp forests). In addition, mobile deposit-feeding epibenthic organisms can affect the chemical composition of sediments through sediment mixing (e.g., sea urchins in the deep sea).

Epibenthic organisms inhabit most marine environments, but composition of the epibenthic fauna varies from habitat to habitat. For example, reef-building hermatypic corals are unique to the highly diverse and species-rich coral reef habitat, as are the giant clams that inhabit certain tropical locales. Sea urchins, sea stars, lobster, gastropods, and octopus commonly inhabit kelp beds. Epibenthic sponges, sea pens, sea pansies, anemones, corals, bivalves, snails, octopus, polychaetes, crustaceans, sea stars, brittlestars, crinoids, sea urchins, sea cucumbers, tunicates, brachiopods, and bryozoans all can be found living on the sediments of the continental slope. Most of the deep seafloor is composed of soft sediment, and taxa similar to those found on the continental slope can be found in the deep sea. Glass sponges, echinoderms, decapod crustaceans, sea spiders, and polychaetes are particularly conspicuous epibenthic deep-sea fauna. Manganese nodules and seamounts provide oases of hard substrate in the deep sea on which epifauna live. Hydrothermal vents and cold seeps harbor their

own unique epibenthic fauna, which includes clams, crabs, limpets, and tube worms.

The sampling gear that researchers use to study epibenthic fauna depends on the environment in question. The intertidal zone is readily accessible and requires little in the way of sophisticated equipment. For habitats within diving depth, researchers use scuba to observe and collect epifauna. Studying the epibenthic fauna in deep water requires oceanographic research vessels and sampling equipment such as grabs, trawls, dredges, epibenthic sleds, remote operated vehicles (ROVs), or submersibles. Researchers also study abundance, dispersion, and behavior of deep-water epibenthic megafauna using time-lapse, still, and video photography.

Lynn L. Lauerman

FURTHER READING
Gage, J. D., and P. A. Tyler. *Deep-Sea Biology: A Natural History of Organisms at the Deep-Sea Floor.* Cambridge and New York: Cambridge University Press, 1991.
Nybakken, James W. *Marine Biology: An Ecological Approach,* 5th ed. San Francisco: Benjamin Cummings, 2001.

RELATED ARTICLES
Benthos; Infauna; Macrofauna

Epifauna

Epifauna are plants, animals, and bacteria that are attached to the benthos, move over the substrate, or are found on top of the substrate. Typically, epifauna organisms are most common on hard-bottom habitats, especially in rocky areas and coral reefs. Epifauna make up most of the organisms living on or attached to the seafloor; up to 80 percent of all benthic animals are epifauna. These include corals, barnacles, echinoderms, and sponges. Animals that are associated with the seafloor but occasionally swim above it, such as crustaceans or benthic vertebrates, also fall into this category. Epifauna protozoans include unicellular organisms such as foraminiferans and ciliates. Sponges are sessile epifauna that are found attached to hard and soft substrates. They are obligate filter feeders, ingesting detritus and plankton. Other epifauna include members of the phylum Cnidaria, such as hydroids, sea anemones, and corals (including stony corals that are responsible for coral reefs). Like sponges, most epifauna cnidarians are sessile and suspension feeders. Benthic worms belonging to a variety of invertebrate phyla are very common in the benthos; although a majority is infaunal, many species occur as epifauna. Others, such as the tube worms of the phylum Pogonophora, are sessile and live in tubes that are partially buried in the substrate. Some Pogonophorans have developed a symbiotic relationship with bacteria for their nutrition, as they lack a digestive tract as adults. Other, more motile epifauna include mollusks, echinoderms, and crustaceans, all of which occupy a variety of habitats on the benthos. A few molluscan species can bore into hard subtrates, but most reside as epifauna; these include snails, clams, and other shelled mollusks, as well as octopi and nudibranchs. Echinoderm epifauna include a variety of sea urchins, starfish, feather stars, brittlestars, and sea cucumbers. Crustacean representatives range from motile, decapod crustaceans (such as crabs, shrimps, and lobsters) to the sessile barnacles.

As do other benthic organisms, epifauna play a major role in marine food webs. By feeding on detritus and other suspended organic material, epifauna assist in the recycling of pelagic organic matter. Moreover, many epifauna species serve as prey or act as predators in pelagic–benthic food webs. Finally, a majority of epifauna release their larvae into the marine environment, thus both proliferating epifauna species and providing a planktonic food source for the pelagic food web.

Manoj Shivlani

FURTHER READING

Barnes, R. S. K., and R. N. Hughes. *An Introduction to Marine Ecology.* Oxford and Boston: Blackwell Scientific/St. Louis, Mo.: Blackwell Mosby Books, distributor, 1982; 3rd ed., Oxford, and Malden, Mass.: Blackwell Science, 1999.

Lalli, Carol M., and Timothy R. Parsons. *Biological Oceanography: An Introduction.* Oxford and New York: Pergamon Press, 1993; 2nd ed., Oxford: Butterworth-Heinemann, 1997.

Levy, J., M. Chiappone, and K. M. Sullivan. *Invertebrate Infauna and Epifauna of the Florida Keys and Florida Bay.* Zenda, Wis.: The Preserver, 1996.

Little, Colin. *The Biology of Soft Shores and Estuaries.* Oxford: Oxford University Press, 2000.

Nybakken, James W. *Marine Biology: An Ecological Approach,* 5th ed. San Francisco: Benjamin Cummings, 2001.

Sumich, J. L. *An Introduction to the Biology of Marine Life.* Dubuque, Iowa: Wm. C. Brown, 1976; 6th ed., 1996.

RELATED ARTICLES

Benthos; Cnidaria; Crustacea; Echinodermata; Foraminifera; Infauna; Mollusca; Symbiosis

Epipelagic Zone

The epipelagic zone is the ecological zone usually encompassing the top 200 to 250 meters (655 to 820 feet) of the water column. It includes the euphotic zone in which photosynthesis occurs, the seasonal thermocline (when it is present), and the uppermost levels of the dysphotic zone.

The extent of the zone is determined by the characteristics and composition of the zooplanktonic inhabitants, particularly those that are there during the day. The majority of these permanent animal inhabitants are tiny, partly because the plant cells on which most graze are microscopic and partly because the smaller they are, the harder it is for visually hunting predators to see them. The vast majority of the larger organisms are either transparent or translucent. During the day as much as 25 percent of the entire standing crop of pelagic organisms throughout the total water column occurs in the epipelagic. At night this proportion may double as vertical migrants swim up at dusk to feed in the zone, but they swim back down as dawn approaches. A large proportion of the animals are herbivores, feeding on the phytoplankton either by sieving the plant cells out of the water using fine combs, entrapping them on sticky sheets of mucus, or feeding directly on individual cells. Direct feeding is carried out mainly by very tiny protozoan animals and is one of the main ways that the smallest phytoplankton cells, the *picoplankton,* can be consumed. However, many physiological processes show size-related (*allometric*) relationships; the smaller an animal is, the faster its physiological processes go. So the predominant small animals tend to have shorter life spans, faster relative metabolic rates, and much faster turnover times. This means that the buildup of large stocks of organisms that are a familiar phenomenon in terrestrial environments are exceptional in both the epipelagic zone and in the oceans in general.

Martin Angel

FURTHER READING
Marshall, Norman B. *Developments in Deep-Sea Biology.* Poole, England: Blandford Press, 1979.
Nybakken, James W. *Marine Biology: An Ecological Approach,* 5th ed. San Francisco: Benjamin Cummings, 2001.

RELATED ARTICLES
Dysphotic Zone; Pelagic; Thermocline

Epiphytic

Epiphytic in the marine environment refers to an autotrophic organism that lives on another, usually larger, autotrophic organism but is not parasitic on the larger organism. The organism that supports epiphytic organisms is usually called the *host.* Epiphytes can be very common in some marine communities. For example, sea grasses often have numerous small algae, diatoms, and other photosynthetic microorganisms on their blades. Similarly, many of the larger algae will have other smaller algae epiphytic on them. Although the epiphytes are not parasitic and do not extract material from the host, they can interfere with the photosynthetic process in the host simply by intercepting the light, thereby reducing the light available to the host. Heavy infestations of epiphytes may also weigh down the blades of the host autotroph, further reducing productivity.

James W. Nybakken

FURTHER READING
Krebs, Charles J. *Ecology: The Experimental Analysis of Distribution and Abundance.* New York: Harper and Row, 1972; 5th ed. San Francisco: Benjamin Cummings, 2001.
Nybakken, James W. *Marine Biology: An Ecological Approach,* 5th ed. San Francisco: Benjamin Cummings, 2001.
Odum, Eugene P. *Ecology.* New York: Holt, Rinehart and Winston, 1963.

RELATED ARTICLES
Autotrophic; Photosynthesis

Epizoic

Epizoic animals are those that live on the external surfaces of other animals: on their epithelia, skin, carapaces, and shells, depending on which provides a suitable site. Epizoic animals were first observed by Antonie van Leeuwenhoek (1632–1723) just over three centuries ago living on the freshwater *Hydra*, and later described as the ciliate *Korona.* Many of those living on the external surfaces of soft-bodied animals are epizoite *ectoparasites*, damaging their hosts directly, as copepod parasites do on fish gills, whereas *epibionts* merely use the host as an attachment site at no apparent cost to the host. Some hosts actively seek epibionts, such as the crabs, which camouflage and protect themselves by attaching seaweed and actinians to their claws and carapaces. Such mutualistic associations between hosts and epibionts benefit both parties. They may involve very considerable specializations of the epibiont. For instance, the brittlestar *Asteroschema tenue* is only found wrapped around the whiplike gorgonian *Ellisella barbadensis*, where its extremely elongate arms are held parallel to the gorgonian stem except for anchoring twists around the stem at intervals. Both partners are suspension feeders, and it seems possible that current flow around the "double" hydrozoan/cnidarian stems is beneficial to both.

Host specificity here and between a number of other ophiuroids and gorgonians strongly suggests a long period of coevolution. Sometimes, however, the association (beneficial to both) requires no specializations and perhaps occurs at an earlier stage. For example, where the sponge epibiont *Halichondria* overgrows the shell of the scallop *Chlamys*, the mollusk is protected by the sponge against the attacks of starfish, and the sponge gains an increased supply of suspended nutrients from the inhalant current of the scallop. Neither host nor epibiont are specialized for each other.

These mutualistic relations between epibionts and hosts are perhaps more rare than those where the epibiont simply utilizes the host as a substrate, without providing any benefit. However, this may be simply that the benefits of the association to either side are not obvious to us. The special bacteria that live on the epidermis of the mud-burrowing *Priapulus*, or at the apical pole of scaphopod eggs, may possibly benefit their hosts—although in what way is hard to imagine. Nevertheless, the discovery that bacterial epibionts living on the skin of fast-swimming fishes can reduce their hydrodynamic drag shows that relations between epiobiont and host may be far from self-evident.

There are instances where the host is simply a transport mechanism, a phoretic situation like that of some barnacles carried around on whales. The whale–barnacle association is of particular scientific interest for it has been shown that the oxygen isotope compositions of barnacles attached to the Californian gray whale *Eschrichtius robustus* record changing ocean temperatures as the whales migrate between arctic and subtropical waters. Thus it is possible from the barnacles not only to track the migrations of the whales, but also to work out the recent movements of stranded whales. Whales are hosts to the largest epizoic parasite, the copepod *Pennella*, which rooted in a triangular holdfast may be 25 centimeters (9.84 inches) or so long but does little harm to its gigantic host.

Many adult sessile benthic animals such as hydroids and bryozoa are normally found on rocks and other inert, hard substrates such as pier pilings, which are typical settlement sites for the pelagic larvae of most sessile or semisessile benthic invertebrates. But such sites are often a limiting resource for which competition is intense. It is scarcely surprising that a wide range of marine invertebrate phyla have epizoic members, ranging from cnidaria to echinoderms and tunicates, for benthic animals with hard shells and carapaces represent similar sites, and so attract larval settlement. Common fouling organisms such as bryozoans are often found not only on rocks but also on mollusk shells, crustacea, and even on mobile nektonic animals such as turtles and sea snakes. Like most larvae, bryozoan larvae settlement seems not to be on any hard substrate at random, but is triggered by a particular array of microflora. The occasional settlement on such substrates as turtle shells or sea snake scales may simply imply that the larvae were at the end of their larval life and thus not so selective. Curiously, there are some epibionts, such as the barnacle *Stolidobalanus*, that are always epibionts, for their larvae never settle on rocks, only on animal surfaces.

The costs and benefits of the epizoic life for both epibionts and hosts have been discussed many times, particularly with reference to mobile hosts. Probably the epibionts primarily benefit the most, and their hosts are even, if slightly, disadvantaged.

Quentin Bone

FURTHER READING

Key, M. M., W. B. Jefferies, H. K. Voris, and C. M. Yang. "Epizoic Bryozoans, Horseshoe Crabs, and Other Mobile Benthic Substrates." *Bulletin of Marine Science,* Vol. 58 (1996) pp. 368–384.

Nybakken, James W. *Marine Biology: An Ecological Approach,* 5th ed. San Francisco: Benjamin Cummings, 2001.

Whal, M. "Marine Epibiosis: I. Fouling and Antifouling: Some Basic Aspects." *Marine Ecology Progress Series,* Vol. 58, 1989, pp. 175–189.

RELATED ARTICLES

Parasitism

Equator

Earth's equatorial zone is a region of great oceanographic interest and importance. The equator is a great circle perpendicular to the polar axis. The equator, defined as 0° latitude, separates the northern hemisphere from the southern hemisphere. Equatorial oceanographic processes are based on two facts: First, the Sun's rays heat the equatorial zone to a greater extent than at higher latitudes, and second, the Coriolis force changes direction as one crosses the equator.

The equatorial region supplies the Sun's energy to drive atmospheric and oceanographic circulation by the differential heating of Earth. This heat is moved poleward by western boundary currents fed by the equatorial currents in the Atlantic, Pacific, and Indian Ocean basins. The atmosphere distributes this heat by vertical convection and cyclonic storms generated in the Intertropical Convergence Zone (ITCZ). In the northern hemisphere the largest of these storms, the hurricanes, move hot, humid air westward as they extract heat from the ocean surface. They usually curve north away from the tropics, carrying sensible heat and latent heat in the form of water vapor. The Northeastern and Southeastern Trade Winds owe their existence to a low-pressure band in ITCZ toward which they converge. The ITCZ is located on the *meteorological* equator a few degrees north of the geographic equator. With the prospect of global warming, the atmospheric and oceanic heat transport mechanism is currently of great interest to meteorologists and oceanographers.

The Coriolis effect, which accounts for the characteristics of a number of oceanographic processes (geostrophic currents, Ekman currents, hurricanes), causes moving objects to veer to the right of the direction of motion in the northern hemisphere and left in the southern hemisphere. At the equator the Coriolis effect vanishes (because its magnitude is proportional to the sine of the latitude). Because of this change in direction, westward-flowing currents, such as the North Equatorial and South Equatorial Currents, are "steered away" from the equator. This creates a divergence at the surface and results in equatorial upwelling. The fishing industry has long known about the effects of upwelling, which brings cool, nutrient-rich waters to the surface, and in turn results in increased productivity in the food web and good fishing.

The westward-flowing equatorial currents lying directly on the equator exhibit an interesting wavelike behavior. The currents do not move steadily westward but undulate: first northward, then westward, then southward, and at times even eastward in opposition to the trade winds. This periodic movement has a cycle time of 3 weeks and is an example of Rossby waves. Satellites images show this ribbon of current centered on the equator as a cool band that wiggles north and south.

Another oddity of equatorial oceanography is the eastward-flowing Equatorial Undercurrent, which owes its existence to the fact that the

Coriolis effect acts toward the right of the flow direction in the northern hemisphere and toward the left in the southern. Eastward flow just to the north or south of the equator causes a convergence of flow toward the equator. This results in the fast (154 centimeters per second; 3 knots), deep (50 to 250 meters; 165 to 820 feet), and narrow (50 kilometers; 31 miles) subsurface flow, centered in the thermocline (the region where the vertical temperature change is greatest). This is one of nature's strangest hydrodynamic processes, one that is not yet completely understood by oceanographers.

An interesting current is found along the meteorological equator (ITCZ), where the trade winds converge. Here in the doldrums, winds are light and variable. The trade winds blowing toward the western side of the ocean basins create a slight upslope of the sea surface (about 1 meter or 3.3 feet) toward the west. Because in the absence of other forces, water tends to flow downhill, a reverse surface flow, the North Equatorial Countercurrent, flows eastward at the latitude of the doldrums, where the wind stress is nearly absent.

An important process of the equatorial ocean concerns El Niño, the periodic warming of water in the eastern Pacific off Peru, Mexico, and California. This phenomenon occurs (often in December) when the trade winds weaken or even change direction. The meteorological cause is a shift in the western Pacific low-pressure center from its position near Indonesia south toward Australia. The combined oceano-graphic–meteorological process is called the *El Niño Southern Oscillation* (ENSO). When the trade winds stop, El Niño events are first noticed as a rise in sea level along the equator when the east-to-west tilt relaxes. This results in a wave that moves slowly over several months toward Central and South America. The rise in sea level causes warm, nutrient-poor offshore water to overlay cool, nutrient-rich coastal waters. This wavelike disturbance (a Kelvin wave) eventually propagates away from the equator to the north and south. During El Niño events, fish catches decrease and weather patterns change to produce torrential rains in some areas and drought in others.

William W. Broenkow

FURTHER READING

Knauss, John A. *Introduction to Physical Oceanography.* 2nd ed. Upper Saddle River, N.J.: Prentice Hall, 1997.

Open University. *Ocean Circulation,* Vol 3. Oxford: Pergamon Press, 1989.

RELATED ARTICLES
Coriolis Effect; Doldrums; El Niño; Equatorial Countercurrent; Equatorial Currents, North and South; Equatorial Undercurrent; Intertropical Convergence Zone; Trade Winds

Equatorial Countercurrent

The Equatorial Countercurrent is a surface ocean current that flows from west to east, parallel to the equator, between approximately 5° N and 10° S latitude. It is found in the Atlantic, Pacific, and Indian Oceans but is most strongly developed in the Atlantic and Pacific. The current is about 300 to 500 kilometers (185 to 310 miles) wide and extends to a depth of 100 to 200 meters (330 to 660 feet). It is located just north of the equator in the Atlantic and Pacific and just south of it in the Indian Ocean. The countercurrents return some of the water that is carried from east to west by the Equatorial Currents.

The Equatorial Counterurrent lies within the Intertropical Convergence Zone (ITCZ) in areas called the *doldrums,* where the winds are light and variable. They are driven by the trade winds. These push warm, surface water toward the west, where it accumulates, so the sea level is normally slightly higher around Indonesia than it is off the Pacific coast of South America (a situation that changes during El Niño episodes). The trade winds exert no pressure on surface waters inside the ITCZ, however. This allows water to flow back in the opposite direction.

A current flowing in an easterly direction at the equator is inherently stable. This is because the magnitude of the Coriolis effect is zero at the equator. Consequently, the Equatorial Countercurrent follows the pressure gradient from the raised level in the west to the lower level in the east. Should the current swing away from the equator, the Coriolis effect will begin to influence it, deflecting the moving water to the right in the northern hemisphere and to the left in the southern hemisphere. This moves the current back toward the equator in both hemispheres.

The Equatorial Countercurrent crosses the North Atlantic and North Pacific Oceans. It moves northward in the summer, following the seasonal movement of the ITCZ, and is strongest in July and August. In the Atlantic the countercurrent is most pronounced off the coast of Ghana, where it is known as the Guinea Current. In winter the countercurrent weakens as it returns to a lower latitude. In late winter it sometimes disappears in parts of the eastern North Pacific. The Equatorial Countercurrent is less marked in the Indian Ocean, where it is confined by the equator to its north and the South Equatorial Current to its south, at about 4°S.

Michael Allaby

FURTHER READING

King, Cuchlaine A. M. *Introduction to Physical and Biological Oceanography.* London: Edward Arnold/New York: Crane, Russak, 1975.

Knauss, John A. *Introduction to Physical Oceanography.* Englewood Cliffs, N.J.: Prentice Hall, 1978; 2nd ed. rev., Upper Saddle River, N.J.: Prentice Hall, 2000.

RELATED ARTICLES

Coriolis Effect; Doldrums; Equatorial Currents, North and South; Equatorial Undercurrent; Intertropical Convergence Zone; Trade Winds

Equatorial Currents, North and South

The Equatorial Currents are surface ocean currents that flow from east to west across the Atlantic, Pacific, and Indian Oceans, forming part of the anticyclonic gyre in each of these oceans. The currents are located on either side of the equator and parallel to it at approximately 12°N and 5°S latitude. The currents are confined mainly to the upper 500 meters (1640 feet) of the ocean, are about 1000 kilometers (620 miles) wide, and move fairly slowly, at 30 to 100 centimeters per second (0.5 to 2.1 knots). At greater depths, below the thermocline, the currents move much more slowly.

Between the two Equatorial Currents, the Equatorial Countercurrent is a narrow surface current that flows from west to east just to the north of the equator in the Atlantic and Pacific Oceans and just south of it in the Indian Ocean. At the equator the Equatorial Undercurrent (sometimes called the Cromwell Current in the Pacific) flows from west to east along the thermocline at about 140 centimeters per second (2.7 knots).

The currents in the northern and southern hemispheres are known as the North Equatorial Current and South Equatorial Current, respectively. The same name is used for the currents in all three oceans. There are, therefore, two North Equatorial Currents and two South Equatorial Currents, the current through the Indian Ocean being continuous with the current that crosses the South Pacific.

The North Equatorial Current also crosses the Arabian Sea, but only in winter. It does not flow precisely parallel to the equator because it is deflected before reaching the sea by its passage through the Strait of Malacca and then by the Indian subcontinent. This turns the current first to the right, then to the left around Sri Lanka, and to the right again in the Arabian Sea, where it

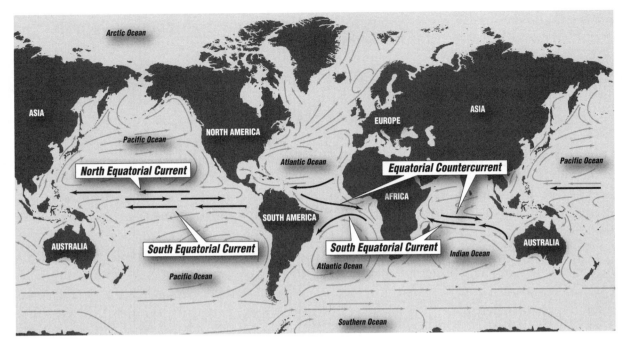

Equatorial Currents.

reaches about latitude 12°N before turning to the left and flowing parallel to the East African coast before joining the Equatorial Countercurrent. In summer, the current crosses the Arabian Sea farther to the north, as the Monsoon Drift.

The Equatorial Currents are driven by the prevailing winds. These are the trade winds, blowing from the northeast in the northern hemisphere and from the southeast in the southern hemisphere. In accordance with the Ekman theory, the currents flow at an angle of about 45° to the wind direction, due to the effect of friction between the surface current and the layer of water beneath it. In the northern hemisphere this deflection is to the right of the wind direction and is to the left in the southern hemisphere. This results in a track that runs parallel to the equator in both hemispheres.

At the equator, the magnitude of the Coriolis effect is zero. Consequently, the Equatorial Currents flow parallel to the pressure gradient rather than circling a pressure center as a geostrophic flow. As they approach the continents on the western borders of the oceans,

however, the currents turn away from the equator. The Coriolis effect then deflects them farther away from the equator. They enter higher latitudes and become western boundary currents, which comprise the next stage in the ocean gyre.

The Equatorial Currents are separated by the Equatorial Countercurrents. These flow in the opposite direction just north of the equator in the Atlantic and Pacific and just south of it in the Indian Ocean. There are also Equatorial Undercurrents. These flow from west to east between 50 and 150 meters (165 to 500 feet) below the surface, at about 5 kilometers (3 miles) per hour.

Michael Allaby

FURTHER READING

Knauss, John A. *Introduction to Physical Oceanography.* Englewood Cliffs, N.J.: Prentice Hall, 1978; 2nd ed. rev., Upper Saddle River, N.J.: Prentice Hall, 2000.

USEFUL WEB SITES

Chamberlin, Sean. "Whirlpools in Your Bathtub." *The Remarkable Ocean World.* 1999. <http://www.oceansonline.com/whirl.htm>.

Equatorial Undercurrent

The Cromwell Current, which is the name given to the Equatorial Undercurrent in the Pacific, flows beneath the surface of the equatorial Pacific Ocean between 1.5°N and 1.5°S latitude. Other ocean currents change their locations periodically, but the Cromwell Current is always centered on the equator. It is about 300 kilometers (190 miles) away from the Equatorial Countercurrent. The undercurrent was discovered during a research expedition in the 1950s by the oceanographer Townsend Cromwell, for whom it is named.

The upper surface of the Cromwell Current lies below the surface at a depth of about 50 meters (165 feet) in the east and about 200 meters (650 feet) in the west. The current is about 200 meters (656 feet) thick. This makes it much thinner than most of the major surface currents. It is about 300 kilometers (190 miles) wide. The Cromwell Current is fast, flowing at up to 150 centimeters per second (3.4 miles per hour).

The North and South Equatorial Currents are driven by the trade winds and carry warm surface water toward the west (from South America in the direction of Indonesia). Because of the reliability of the trade winds, the currents flow fairly constantly, pushing surface water in a westerly direction. This water forms a deep pool around Indonesia and the accumulation of water raises the sea level. Consequently, there is pressure for water to flow in the opposite direction, from west to east, but at the surface the prevailing winds exert greater pressure. Beneath the surface the effect of the winds diminishes, but the pressure from the accumulation of water in the west remains.

Water in the deep pool in the western Pacific is well mixed as a result of the action of the winds

and currents. This depresses the thermocline, so it is deeper in the western Pacific than in the east. The pycnocline (where water density increases rapidly with depth) slopes upward from west to east, following the thermocline. The Cromwell Current, driven by the difference in pressure between the two sides of the ocean but following the pycnocline, therefore flows uphill.

Air or water that moves as a wind or current over a long distance is deflected by the Coriolis effect (CorF). In the absence of friction, winds and currents follow paths determined by the balance of the pressure-gradient force (PGF) and CorF. The resultant flow is said to be *geostrophic* and is at right angles to the PGF. At the equator, however, the magnitude of the CorF is zero. Therefore, the Cromwell Current, flowing very close to the equator, is not deflected. It flows across the pressure gradient but is nevertheless in geostrophic balance.

Michael Allaby

Further Reading
Knauss, John A. *Introduction to Physical Oceanography.* Englewood Cliffs, N.J.: Prentice Hall, 1978; 2nd ed. rev., Upper Saddle River, N.J.: Prentice Hall, 2000.
Marshall, Norman B. *Developments in Deep-Sea Biology.* Poole, England: Blandford Press, 1979.
Talley, Lynne D., Gerard Fryer, and Rick Lumpkin. "Physical Oceanography of the Tropical Pacific." In M. Rapaport, ed., *The Pacific Islands: Environment and Society.* Honolulu, Hawaii: Bess Press, 1999.

Estuarine Circulation

Estuaries are frequently referred to as bays, sounds, inlets, lagoons, firths, or fjords, but usually represent locations where river outflows meet waters from the coastal ocean. Many estuaries are essentially drowned river mouths that entered the sea thousands of years ago, much farther offshore than they do today. According to Donald Pritchard (1967), an *estuary* is a semienclosed coastal body of water that has a free connection with the open sea and within which seawater is measurably diluted with fresh water derived from land drainage. In estuaries, fresh water of terrestrial origin is often prevented from streaming into the open ocean by the surrounding mainland, peninsulas, barrier islands, or fringing salt marshes. This transition zone where fresh and salt waters mix creates a coastal environment that contains an abundance of essential nutrients that support rich and diverse ecosystems.

Classification of Estuaries

To discuss estuarine circulation, it is useful first to consider how estuaries are classified. Estuaries can be classified in a number of ways, but two criteria that are frequently used are topography and salinity structure. Based on topography, estuaries can be classified as coastal plain, fjord, or bar-built. *Coastal plain estuaries* tend to become deeper and widen toward their mouths, although they are usually shallow overall. Often, the bottom is composed of recently deposited sediments. Coastal plain estuaries generally occur in temperate latitudes, and the river flow is generally small compared to the volume of tidal waters that are exchanged. The Chesapeake Bay is an example of a coastal plain estuary. *Fjords* were originally ice-covered. In preexisting river valleys, the ice caused the estuary to form and become deeper and broader over time. As the ice retreated, shallow bars or sills were often left near the mouth of the fjord. In some cases these sills are only a few meters deep and their presence often restricts water movement into and out of the estuary. Alberni Inlet in British Columbia is an example of a fjord. *Bar-built estuaries* often occur along somewhat uniform coastlines where freshwater input is derived primarily from drainage off lowlands adjacent to the coast. Through the deposition of sediment over long

periods, bars are often formed across their mouth. In bar-built estuaries the tidal range is usually restricted and they tend to be shallow but are often extensive. Bar-built estuaries occur off the east and Gulf coasts of the United States.

Based on their salinity structure, estuaries are classified as salt wedge, fjord, partially mixed, or homogeneous. In a *salt wedge estuary* the incoming tide causes a saltwater wedge to intrude below the lighter outflowing fresh water in the region of the mouth. Such estuaries are thus highly stratified. Frictional effects along the boundary that separates the incoming saltwater from the river outflow cause turbulence that helps to mix the salt water and the surface outflow. As the tidal volume increases and the wedge of saltwater intrudes farther into the estuary, the tidal inflow can far exceed the river outflow. The surface outflow becomes comparable to the tidal inflow, and both are considerably larger than the river outflow itself. Also, the effect of Earth's rotation may cause the cross-channel surface to become inclined, influencing the circulation inside the estuary. The mouth of the Mississippi River is an example of a salt wedge estuary.

Fjord-type estuaries are also highly stratified, with fresh water on top and tidally driven salt water below. However, fjord-type estuaries are often deep and the presence of a sill at the mouth can restrict the exchange of water between the estuary and the coastal ocean. As a result, circulation inside the fjord may be quite different from the water movements near the sill and beyond.

A *partially mixed estuary* occurs when tides are introduced inside the estuary. The tides produce greater mixing and so reduce the density differences between the fresh water above and the salt water below. This causes the near-surface salinity to increase, enhancing outflow near the surface and inflow near the bottom. Thus, a distinct two-layer system of circulation is produced. The James River in Virginia is an example of a partially mixed estuary.

In *homogeneous estuaries,* the mixing is strong enough to mix the entire water column from the surface to the bottom. In these estuaries the tidal flow will be much larger than the river flow. If a homogeneous estuary is sufficiently wide, the effect of Earth's rotation may cause seaward flow to occur on the right-hand side (in the northern hemisphere) and compensating landward flow on the left. The lower reaches of the Delaware River provide an example of a homogeneous estuary.

Circulation in Estuaries

It is clear that the circulation within an estuary depends to a large extent on the type of estuary involved. In certain simple cases the type of circulation that occurs can be inferred. In cases where the river outflow is much greater than the tidally induced inflow, circulation within the estuary can be dominated completely by the freshwater outflow. As river flow decreases, the importance of tidally induced inflow increases. In a highly stratified narrow estuary, with fresh water above and salt water below, water in the surface layer flows seaward and water in the bottom layer flows into the estuary. The subsurface salt water generally forms a wedge that points upstream. As frictional drag between the salt wedge and surface water increases, the two water types tend to mix. Increased mixing leads to greater upstream flow in the subsurface layer. If the estuary becomes wide enough, Earth's rotation may cause opposing flows to occur on each side of the estuary. Tides tend to dominate the circulation in most estuaries. Over one tidal cycle, the upstream and downstream tidal flows tend to cancel each other out, leaving a residual estuarine flow that is independent of the tide. In fjords, the circulation tends to be more complicated because they are deeper. The deeper waters inside the fjord may be completely isolated from freshwater flows at the surface and the waters beyond the entrance due to sills that are often present. In these cases, the circulation is determined primarily by density differences in the water column.

In reality, most estuaries are complex physical systems that do not fit any of the simple types that have been described. Consequently, to determine the circulation in most estuaries, detailed hydrographic measurements are required. Also, hydrodynamic models are often used to predict the circulation. These models solve the governing equations of motion, continuity, conservation, and state on a numerical grid that is tailored to the geometry (shape and depth) of the estuary in question.

Laurence C. Breaker

FURTHER READING
Dyer, Keith R. *Estuaries: A Physical Introduction.* London and New York: Wiley, 1973; 2nd ed., Chichester, England, and New York: Wiley, 1997.
Gross, M. Grant. *Oceanography: A View of the Earth.* Englewood Cliffs, N.J.: Prentice Hall, 1972; 7th ed., Upper Saddle River, N.J.: Prentice Hall, 1996.
Pritchard, D. W. "What Is an Estuary?" In G. H. Lauff, ed., *Estuaries.* Publication 83. Washington, D.C.: American Academy for the Advancement of Science, 1967.

RELATED ARTICLES
Bay; Estuarine Sedimentation; Estuary; Lagoon; Salinity

Estuarine Sedimentation

Estuaries can be sites of significant sediment accumulation along the coast. Estuaries typically occur as drowned river valleys, glaciated river valleys (fjords), or structural valleys that are created by tectonic activity within Earth's crust. Because estuaries are located at or near the mouths of rivers, they exhibit exceedingly diverse sedimentary deposits worldwide and in many cases are gradually filling with sediments. Thus estuaries can conveniently be considered the "filter" through which dissolved and particulate fluvial (river) material, both organic and inorganic, must pass along the route to the ocean.

The water and sediments in an estuary are part of a coupled system where exchange processes take place. That is, the water and sediments interact continually, exchanging and redistributing particles and solutes so as to affect the operation of the entire estuarine system, including its biology. Although much of a river's sediment load may ultimately be trapped within its estuary, these exchange processes ensure that there will be much recycling prior to final deposition of material on the bottom. Understanding the recycling and redistribution of estuarine sediments is especially important because they play a critical role in transporting pollutants, modulating productivity (by altering the penetration of light), and releasing nutrients through resuspension.

Numerous factors influence estuarine sedimentation: sediment source, physical processes that move water, chemical processes that alter particles, and biological processes that stabilize and destabilize the bottom. Human impacts in the watershed, such as deforestation or construction of dams and reservoirs, can also be important because of their impact on the quantity of sediments delivered to the estuary.

Sources and Composition of Sediments

Estuarine sediments are derived from rivers, the oceans, shoreline erosion, biologic production, and occasionally from transport of windblown materials. Although there is much variability from one estuary to another, rivers and streams are the primary source of sediments to most estuaries. Coarse particles of sand and gravel are carried into estuaries by bedload transport, a process wherein the sediments are rolling or sliding along the bottom. Finer particles of silt and clay are carried into estuaries by suspended load transport, wherein the sediments are kept suspended in the water by turbulence. Organisms contribute to estuarine sediments by producing skeletal material (shell) and by ingesting estuarine mud, which is later excreted as sand-sized pellets. Most estuaries contain significant quantities of organic-rich mud. Detritus from decaying marsh or mangrove vegetation along the estuarine shorelines, together with plant debris from upstream, contribute most of the organic material. Thick deposits of very soft organic-rich silt and clay are referred to as *fluid mud*. This yogurt-like material, which is especially common in low-latitude coastal plain estuaries, is an important biological habitat and can temporarily sequester rich stores of nutrients. Fluid mud also creates a hazard to navigation by reducing channel depths. Whereas average rates of estuarine sediment accumulation are on the order of 0.1 to 1.0 centimeter (0.04 to 0.4 inch) per year, fluid mud can accumulate at rates exceeding 1 meter (3.3 feet) per year.

Mechanisms for Trapping Sediments

Estuaries are natural sediment traps because of their shape and their characteristic circulation processes. Because estuaries usually have a funnel shape, the flow in a river, upon reaching the estuarine funnel, will decelerate, allowing the coarser sedimentary particles to be deposited. The product of this deposition will be a submerged estuarine delta or, if fluvial discharge is extremely high, a delta that extends vertically above sea level. The finer-grained particles that settle more slowly will continue to be transported downstream through the estuary; however, the gravitational circulation that is common in most estuaries will eventually transport these particles back upstream in the lower layers of the water column, into which they eventually will have settled. The convergence of river flow and the landward estuarine circulation near the bottom can create a turbidity maximum. This region of very high suspended sediment concentration often serves as a focal point for sediments in the estuary and a region where fluid mud deposits tend to dominate the bottom sediments.

Estuaries also trap sediments because of a process called *flocculation*. Flocculated or aggregated sediments are composed of very fine-grained particles that are bound together by organic (mucus) secretions or by molecular forces, increasing their size 10 to 100 times, and thus their settling speed. Particles that settle faster have a greater chance of being retained in an estuary. Although flocculation from organic secretions occurs throughout the estuary, flocculation from molecular forces depends on water salinity and occurs only in the upper reaches of estuaries where fresh and salt water begin to mix. Flocculated particles that settle along shallow estuarine shorelines can be trapped by wetlands vegetation, and estuaries are often observed to fill in from their margins.

Formation of Sedimentary Deposits

Deposition of sediments over time produces stratigraphic sequences. In an estuary these deposits are extremely variable. This is due in part to the character of the source sediment but also to the circulation patterns of estuarine water. Estuarine (gravitational) circulation, which influences the morphology and distribution of stratigraphic sequences, is controlled by the relative amount of fluvial, tidal, and to a lesser degree, wave energy. In estuaries where there is an approximate balance between fluvial and tidal energy (referred to as partially mixed estuaries), the sandy deposits occur near the head and near the mouth of the estuary; these deposits reflect the strong influence of the river and ocean, respectively. The central section, or *estuarine funnel*, is dominated by muddy sediments that are trapped by the same circulation patterns that produce the turbidity maximum.

In estuaries where fluvial discharge is high and tide range is low (referred to as *highly stratified estuaries*), sedimentary deposits will build a delta that usually extends above sea level. Upstream estuarine circulation will be poorly developed and virtually all of the sediments supplied by the river will progressively be transported downstream. The stratigraphic sequences will

contain coarse-grained sediment close to the head of the estuary and finer-grained sediment farther downstream. Fluvially dominated estuaries are usually characterized by fine-grained sediments since the sediment load in most large coastal plain rivers is dominated by suspended sediments. Through time, deltas usually build seaward.

In estuaries where fluvial discharge is low and tide range is high (referred to as *well-mixed estuaries*), sedimentary deposits tend to have coarser grain sizes. Tidal currents are strong, and much sand can be transported in from the ocean or bay. Sandbars form throughout the estuary with an orientation parallel to the estuarine axis as a result of the back-and-forth motion of the tides. Because of the physical effects of the exaggerated funnel shape in high-tide-range estuaries, rising tides are usually stronger than falling tides, resulting in upstream bedload transport throughout much of the estuary. Although present in tide-dominated estuaries, fluid mud deposits are usually small.

Large floods, which can deliver in a few days the same amount of sediment that an estuary typically receives in a few years, can shift coarse sediment deposition farther downstream and flush fine-grained sediments into the ocean, where they can be seen from satellite imagery as turbid plumes. The rate at which an estuary fills with sediments and forms stratigraphic sequences depends on the amount of sediment it receives from upstream and offshore, its trapping efficiency, and the rate of relative sea-level rise.

John T. Wells

FURTHER READING
Bokuniewicz, Henry. "Sedimentary Systems of Coastal-Plain Estuaries." In G. M. E. Perillo, ed., *Geomorphology and Sedimentology of Estuaries.* Amsterdam and New York: Elsevier Science, 1996.
Nichols, Maynard, and Robert Biggs. "Estuaries." In R. A. Davis, ed., *Coastal Sedimentary Environments.* New York: Springer-Verlag, 1978; 2nd ed., 1985.

Nichols, M. M., G. H. Johnson, and P. C. Peebles. "Modern Sediments and Facies Model for a Microtidal Coastal Plain Estuary, the James Estuary, Virginia." *Journal of Sedimentary Petrology*, Vol. 61 (1991) pp. 881–899.

Riggs, Stanley. "Sediment Evolution and Habitat Function of Organic-Rich Muds within the Albemarle Estuarine System, North Carolina." *Estuaries*, Vol. 19 (1996) pp. 169–185.

Schubel, J. R., and H. H. Carter. "The Estuary as a Filter for Fine-Grained Suspended Sediment." In V. S. Kennedy, ed., *The Estuary as a Filter*. Orlando, Fla.: Academic Press, 1984.

RELATED ARTICLES
Bay; Coastal Morphology; Estuarine Circulation; Estuary; Lagoon

Estuary

An estuary is a partially enclosed coastal embayment in which fresh and salt water mix. This means that an estuary has a free connection with the sea and a freshwater source for at least part of a year. However, there are quite a number of geomorphological features of coastlines called by other names that fall under this definition and are discussed below.

Types of Estuaries

There are several different types of estuaries in the world, depending on the geomorphology of the area, the geological history of the area, and the prevailing climatic conditions. The best known and most common type of estuary is the coastal plain estuary. This type of estuary dates from the end of the last ice age when the rising sea level invaded coastal plain river valleys. Examples of this type of estuary include most of the estuaries of the east coast of North America, such as Chesapeake Bay, and the mouths of the larger rivers, such as the Delaware and Hudson. Similar estuaries are also common in Great Britain and northwestern Europe. A second type of estuary is the tectonic estuary. This estuary is formed when the sea invades the land following a subsidence of the land due to earthquake activity. Perhaps the best example of this type is San Francisco Bay. The semienclosed bay or lagoon is the third type of estuary. This type of estuary arises along low-lying coasts where sandbars build up parallel to the coast, partially cutting off the water behind them from the open sea, thus creating shallow lagoons. The lagoons collect freshwater runoff from the surrounding land and permit the entrance of salt water through the openings to the sea. Such lagoons vary in salinity depending on the prevailing local climatic conditions, whether there is a river flowing into it, and the extent of the opening to the sea. Estuaries of this type are common along the Gulf of Mexico coast in North America and in northwestern Europe and parts of Australia. The fjord is the final category of estuary. A fjord is a deep valley that has been carved out by glacial action and is subsequently reinvaded by the sea. A characteristic feature of fjords is a shallow sill at the mouth that restricts the interchange of seawater to the shallow surface water, leaving the deeper water stagnant. Fjords are abundant along the coasts of Norway, Chile, New Zealand, and British Columbia.

Classification of Estuaries

Estuaries are classified according to the way that the salinity gradients form. In most estuaries, regardless of their type, there is usually a gradient in salinity from pure fresh water in the upper reaches where rivers or streams enter to full salt water at the mouth. Since fresh water is less dense than salt water, the fresh water will float on the more dense salt water unless other factors act to mix them together. The amount of mixing varies with a number of factors, including the geomorphology of the basin, the tide, the amount of river flow, the season, and the amount and occurrence of rainfall. In a salt wedge or positive estuary there is usually substantial freshwater outflow and reduced evaporation such that the fresh water moves out at the surface of the estuary and mixes with the salt water only to a limited extent near the surface, thus leaving the deeper waters more saline. At any given point in such an estuary a vertical cross section of the estuary would reveal the lowest salinity at the surface and the highest salinity at the bottom; this is also called a *stratified estuary*. Such estuaries actually form a continuum, from those that show little mixing and very prominent stratification to those with more and more mixing or less freshwater flow, such that complete mixing and equal salinities occur from the surface to the bottom. The latter estuaries are often called *homogeneous* or *neutral estuaries*. In very hot climates and deserts where the amount of fresh water that flows into the estuary is small and the rate of evaporation is high, a negative estuary may occur. In a negative estuary there is so little fresh water and the evaporation rate is so high that the incoming surface seawater is increased in salinity above the salinity of the underlying seawater and becomes more dense. This hypersaline water then sinks to the bottom and flows out of the estuary as a bottom current. In this situation the vertical salinity profile is the reverse of that in a positive estuary. In climates where there is a marked wet and dry season, often called a *Mediterranean climate*, estuaries may be seasonal or intermittent. In such estuaries during the rainy season they act like positive estuaries, but in the dry season there is no freshwater input and they may become dry or stagnant. Salinity in these estuaries varies seasonally.

Factors Affecting Organisms in Estuaries

Estuaries appear to be stressful environments for most organisms. The variation in salinity on

Mawddach Estuary, Wales, at low tide, showing a pattern of tidal creeks. (© Heather Angel)

a daily or seasonal basis is probably the most significant environmental factor that acts to restrict the ability of organisms to inhabit estuaries. Other environmental factors affecting organisms include the wide variation in temperature, the lack of oxygen in the predominantly fine muddy substrate, and the high turbidity in the water column. As a result of the stressful conditions, estuaries tend to have low numbers of species, particularly in those parts of the estuary that are subject to the greatest range of environmental conditions. Estuaries tend to have three groups of organisms present: freshwater, marine, and true estuarine. Penetration into the estuary is greatest among the marine organisms and includes two subgroups. Those marine organisms that are either unable or barely able to tolerate changes in salinity from full seawater are generally restricted to the mouths of the estuary, where the salinity remains above 25 practical salinity units (psu). These organisms are called *stenohaline*. The second subgroup includes marine organisms that are able to tolerate a limited amount of salinity reduction, down to perhaps 15 to 18 psu. These organisms are termed *euryhaline*. The true estuarine species are the smallest in number and are found in the middle reaches of the estuary, where the salinity ranges from 5 to 18 psu. Finally, the freshwater organisms are restricted to the uppermost reaches of the estuary, where the salinity does not go above 5 psu.

The most significant adaptation for organisms to live in estuarine habitats is the ability to maintain the ionic balance of their body fluids. This ability is called *osmoregulation* and is found in relatively few organisms. Organisms that lack the ability to osmoregulate are called *osmoconformers*. Most estuarine organisms are either osmoregulators or are able to function as osmoconformers with fluctuating internal salt concentrations.

James W. Nybakken

FURTHER READING

Barnes, R. S. K. *Estuarine Biology.* London: Edward Arnold, 1974; 2nd ed., London and Baltimore: Edward Arnold, 1984.

Day, J. W., C. A. Hall, W. M. Kemp, and Alejandro Yanez-Arancibia. *Estuarine Ecology.* New York: Wiley, 1989.

Green, J. *The Biology of Estuarine Animals.* Seattle, Wash.: University of Washington Press, 1968.

McLusky, Donald S. *The Estuarine Ecosystem.* Glasgow, Scotland: Blackie, 1981; 2nd ed., 1989.

Nybakken, James W. *Marine Biology: An Ecological Approach,* 5th ed. San Francisco: Benjamin Cummings, 2001.

RELATED ARTICLES

Coastal Morphology; Estuarine Circulation; Estuarine Sedimentation; Euryhaline; Fjord; Salinity

Euphotic Zone

The euphotic zone is the uppermost zone of the sea that is brightly illuminated by sunlight. It is the only zone where photosynthesis occurs. Its lower boundary is the critical depth (*compensation depth*) at which the rate of production of organic material exactly balances the rate at which it is used up. Water both absorbs and scatters light, so even in the clearest of oceanic water the maximum depth of the euphotic zone is about 150 meters (about 490 feet). In coastal seas where there are large populations of phytoplankton and suspended sediment, the light is cut out much faster and may penetrate less than 10 meters (33 feet).

The zone coincides with the wind-mixed layer, which is the layer in which the temperature and salinity of seawater is kept uniform by the stirring effects of wind and wave. It overlies the *thermocline*, which is the zone across which there is a sharp drop in water temperature that inhibits the mixing of the upper water with the deeper water. This stratification is important because while it benefits the suspended phytoplankton by keeping it within the euphotic zone, it also cuts off the deepwater source for the resupply of nutrients, nitrates, phosphates, and silicates that the photosynthetic cells need for survival.

The turbidity (cloudiness) of the water also fluctuates and increases with the number of outflows from a river into the sea or sewage or industrial wastes discharged into the sea. Another factor that affects the compensation depth in all parts of the ocean is season. As the Sun's track across the sky changes, the angle at which its radiation intercepts the sea surface changes. As this angle becomes more acute, more light is reflected from the surface so that the compensation depth shoals.

In the open ocean, photosynthesis by the phytoplankton in the euphotic zone supports the total food web throughout the rest of the water column and most of life on the seabed as well. Chemosynthesis at hydrothermal vents provides only an estimated 0.3 percent of the organic production needed to support life in the oceans. So the ecological integrity and health of the euphotic zone is essential not only to all ocean life, but also to the role played by the ocean in maintaining the habitability of global systems.

Martin Angel

FURTHER READING
Dawes, C. J. *Marine Botany.* New York: Wiley, 1981; 2nd ed., 1998.
Lalli, Carol M., and Timothy R. Parsons. *Biological Oceanography: An Introduction.* Oxford and New York: Pergamon Press, 1993; 2nd ed., Oxford: Butterworth-Heinemann, 1997.
Longhurst, Alan R. *Ecological Geography of the Sea.* San Diego: Academic Press, 1998.
Nybakken, James W. *Marine Biology: An Ecological Approach,* 5th ed. San Francisco: Benjamin Cummings, 2001.

RELATED ARTICLES
Chemosynthesis; Compensation Depth; Food Web; Hydrothermal Vent; Photosynthesis; Phytoplankton

Euryhaline

Euryhaline organisms are organisms that can withstand wide limits of salinity. In an aquatic environment, organisms are subject to salt and water loss or gain, depending on the ambient salinity. In freshwater conditions, most organisms are more saline than is the water around them. Therefore, water flows into the organisms and salts diffuse out. The opposite is true in marine conditions where organisms are generally less saline than the water around them. In this case, salts diffuse in and water flows out. Most organisms have adjusted to fresh- and saltwater conditions by either allowing their internal salinity to match that of the external environment (osmoconformers) or by actively maintaining an internal salinity level (osmoregulators). However, this adjustment is usually specific to the salinity (or salinity range) of the environment, and most organisms—referred to as *stenohaline*—that are introduced to different salinity conditions do not survive. However, euryhaline organisms can and do adjust to varying salinity conditions, utilizing the ability to perform a variety of functions and behaviors, such as feeding, seeking shelter, breeding, and spawning.

Organisms have two different mechanisms by which they accomplish osmoregulation, either by blocking passage to the environment or by actively maintaining internal salinity conditions. The former mechanism is a physical method employed by mostly invertebrates, and it consists of shells and other barriers that restrict input from the medium. The latter mechanism, that of actively maintaining internal salinity conditions, is performed mostly by vertebrates. When a euryhaline fish enters higher-salinity water, it must combat losing water to the environment, so it shuts off kidney function to conserve water, makes the kidney tubules permeable to water to allow for greater water retention, ceases active uptake of salts through the gills, and produces enzymes to secrete excess salts from its blood. Conversely, when a euryhaline fish enters less saline water, it must combat losing salts to the environment, so it changes kidney function, producing dilute and frequent urine, and its gills begin actively uptaking salts. Fish typically switch their physiology as they move from fresh water to salt water and back, and the change occurs primarily in brackish water such as bays and estuaries.

Euryhaline species include anadromous and catadromous fish as well as several estuarine fish. Many salmon species are euryhaline only twice in their lifetimes, during their initial migration to the ocean as juveniles and then on their final return to their home streams for spawning. Marine fish that enter fresh water to spawn are referred to as *anadromous*. Freshwater fish that spawn in seawater (e.g., eels) are called *catadromous* species. They also are euryhaline only during certain phases of their life histories. Many estuarine species, although not able to osmoregulate in either full seawater or fresh water, can adapt to changing, brackish salinities. Other species, such as striped bass and tilapia, are more generalized in their adaptations, and they can exist as either marine or freshwater fish and do not rely on specific life stages or intermediate salinity conditions.

Manoj Shivlani

FURTHER READING

Evans, D. H., ed. *The Physiology of Fishes.* Boca Raton, Fla.: CRC Press, 1993; 2nd ed., 1998.

Horn, Michael H., Karen L. M. Martin, and Michael A. Chotkowski, eds. *Intertidal Fishes: Life in Two Worlds.* San Diego: Academic Press, 1999.

Schmidt-Neilsen, Knut. *Animal Physiology: Adaptation and Environment.* Cambridge and New York: Cambridge University Press, 1975; 5th ed., 1997.

RELATED ARTICLES
Stenohaline

Eustatic Sea Level

Eustatic sea level is the worldwide elevation of the sea surface. Eustatic sea level changes when processes that affect the entire ocean change the volume of seawater or the shape of its basins (a much slower process). Sea level affects the coast in many ways, including the distribution and type of coastal landforms, the extent of habitats, the intensity of coastal erosion (a rise in sea level will cause more coastal erosion), and coastal flooding. Eustatic sea level is rising today 10 to 20 centimeters (4 to 8 inches) per century. This rate is known from tide gauge measurements in stable areas made during the past several hundred years. Although this rise seems slow and insignificant, it causes coastal erosion by allowing waves and currents to move farther inland than in the past.

Sea level has been drastically different in the past and will continue to change in the future. During the past 1 million years, for example, eustatic sea level has alternated between lows and highs dozens of times. The last low stand of sea level was 18,000 years ago. Sea level was approximately 130 meters (425 feet) lower than it is today and the continental shelf (the broad underwater platform bordering the coast) was exposed. Mammal bones and Native American ruins found underwater on the continental shelf today are evidence of this lower sea level.

The primary cause of these fluctuations is the exchange of water between the oceans and glaciers. During cold periods (glacial periods), more water is taken from the ocean to form ice in glaciers. As a result, sea level is lower. During warm periods (interglacial periods), glaciers melt, filling the ocean and raising sea level. Glaciers today contain vast quantities of water and cover much of the poles and high latitudes. If all the glaciers melted, which is highly unlikely, sea level would rise by about 70 to 80 meters (230 to 260 feet).

Another cause for changes in eustatic sea level is a cooling or warming of the ocean's water.

Cooling seawater causes it to contract, lowering sea level. Warming seawater causes it to expand, thereby raising sea level. The changes in sea level from cooling and heating of seawater are much smaller, on the order of meters (about 3.3 feet) or tens of meters (about 33 feet), than changes caused by glaciers growing or shrinking.

Change in glaciers is caused by variations in the amount of solar energy striking Earth. Changes in Earth's orbit around the Sun and the tilt of its axis cause these variations. Orbital and tilt cycles are very predictable and repeat every 21,000 to 90,000 years. The combination of these cycles results in a pattern called *Milanchovich cycles*, which correspond with glacial and interglacial periods, resulting in lowering and raising of eustatic sea level.

On longer time scales, tectonics modify the shape of the oceans and their capacity to hold water. Sediment accumulating in ocean basins, also a slow process, causes a rise in eustatic sea level. The change in the sizes of ocean basins results in a lowering (when the basins decrease in size) or raising (when basins increase in size) of sea level.

Currently, we are at the end of a glacial period, and sea level is gradually rising. However, human activities may accelerate this rise. Global warming is predicted to increase sea level by about 50 centimeters (1.6 feet) during the next 100 years. This rise in sea level will cause increased coastal erosion and flooding.

Bruce E. Jaffe

FURTHER READING
Bird, Eric. *Submerging Coasts: The Effects of a Rising Sea Level on Coastal Environments.* New York: Wiley, 1993.
Douglas, Bruce C., Michael S. Kearney, and Stephen P. Leatherman. *Sea Level Rise: History and Consequences.* San Diego: Academic Press, 2000.
Kennet, James. *Marine Geology.* Englewood Cliffs, N.J.: Prentice Hall, 1982.
Komar, Paul. *Beach Processes and Sedimentation,* 2nd ed. Upper Saddle River, N.J.: Prentice Hall, 1998.

RELATED ARTICLES
Climate Change; Glacial Marine Processes

Euteleostei

The teleosts (division Teleostei) are by far the dominant group of extant fishes, accounting for about 96 percent of the approximately 25,000 extant fish species. Functional improvements that have contributed to teleostean success include reduction in bony elements, repositioning and elaboration of the dorsal fin, alterations in the placement and function of paired fins, and improvements in the jaw mechanism. Teleosts arose in the early Mesozoic Era (approximately 200 million years ago) and underwent four or five major radiations, although the relationships within and between lineages is a matter of considerable debate. The first three subdivisions of teleosts are the Osteoglossomorpha (bony-tongues and mooneyes), Elopomorpha (tarpons, ladyfishes, true eels, and spiny eels), and Clupeomorpha (e.g., herring, anchovies). The fourth subdivision, Euteleostei, is the primary line of teleost evolution.

The Greek word *euteleost* ("true perfect bone") refers to the elevated evolutionary position of this group as the most advanced of the bony fishes (Osteichthyes). This taxon is incredibly diverse and speciose, containing 9 superorders, 32 orders, 391 families, 3795 genera, and over 22,000 species. The five largest families, Cyprinidae (minnows and carps), Gobiidae (gobies), Cichlidae (cichlids), Characidae (e.g., tetras, piranhas), and Labridae (wrasses), comprise almost 30 percent of all euteleosts. Although unified taxonomically, the Euteleostei is very poorly characterized. *Adipose* (fleshy) fins, nuptial tubercles, and unique characteristics in the structure of specific tailbones (*uroneurals*) are present only in euteleost fishes. However, there is no strong evidence that the euteleosts are *monophyletic* (derived from a common ancestor), and there are no known unifying characters exhibited by all species.

The most primitive of the nine superorders of euteleosts is the Ostariophysi, a group of predominantly freshwater fishes such as minnows, suckers, loaches, and catfishes. Modified anterior vertebrae that aid in hearing (*Weberian ossicles*) and alarm pheremones (*Schreckstoff*) characterize ostariophysans. Schreckstoff, released when a fish is severely stressed or wounded, may be species-specific or more generally recognized by other ostariophysans. It has been debated that the Ostariophysi should be considered a fifth line of teleostean evolution rather than grouped with the Euteleostei.

A second primitive superorder of euteleosts is the Protacanthopterygii. Protacanthopterygyans are a group of loosely related marine, freshwater, and diadromous fishes that include pikes, smelt, and salmon. Although there is wide debate as to whether this taxon is *paraphyletic* (derived from more than one ancestor), no widely accepted alternative grouping has been proposed.

The remaining seven, more advanced superorders of euteleosts are known as *neoteleosts* ("new perfect bones"). These groups are united due to similar advancements in skull and jaw morphology. The first three superorders of neoteleosts are mainly deep-sea or pelagic fishes. They include the Stenopterygii (e.g., bristlemouths, hatchet fishes), the Cyclosquamata (e.g., telescope fishes, lizard fishes), and the Scopelomorpha (e.g., lantern fishes).

The next three superorders, the acanthomorphs, are distinguished by the presence of true fin spines and improved vertebral structure and jaw protrusibility. The Lampridiomorphs (e.g., tube-eyes, oarfishes) are almost all pelagic, oceanic fishes with unusual body and fin proportions, while the Polymixiiomorphs (beard fishes such as brotulas) exhibit a confusing combination of primitive, advanced, and unique traits that complicate determinations of their taxonomic relationships. The

final superorder of acanthomorph euteleosts is the Paracanthopterygii (e.g., cods, angler fishes, toadfishes), which consists primarily of marine, benthic fishes, most of which are nocturnal.

The final superorder of euteleosts, Acanthopterygii, contains approximately 250 families and 13,500 species. These fishes have highly protrusible jaws, a complex pharyngeal apparatus (tooth-bearing throat bones), two dorsal fins, and spines in the first dorsal, anal, and pelvic fins. Three groups of these fishes are recognized. The Mugilomorpha consists of marine and freshwater mullets. Atherinomorphs (e.g., flying fishes, silversides, needlefishes) are shallow-water, surface-oriented fishes found in both marine and freshwater environments. The remaining fishes are of the superorder Percomorpha, a diverse and varied clade consisting of over 12,000 species of primarily marine families, although several successful freshwater families are also contained within this group. Percomorphs typically have an anterior spine and five rays in their pelvic fins, although more primitive taxa may exhibit additional rays. The largest percomorph order, the Perciformes, contains approximately 150 families and 9000 species and includes most marine and freshwater fishes of the littoral zones (e.g., basses, jacks, snappers, croakers). The most derived of the percomorphs are the Pleuronectiformes (flatfishes) and Tetraodontiformes (e.g., trigger fishes, puffers, porcupine fishes). These fishes exhibit morphologies that are highly modified from the basic fusiform acanthopterygiian body plan.

Joseph J. Bizzarro

FURTHER READING

Bond, Carl E. *Biology of Fishes*. Philadelphia: W. B. Saunders, 1979; 2nd ed., Fort Worth, Texas: Saunders College Publishing, 1996.

Carroll, R. L. *Vertebrate Paleontology and Evolution*. New York: W. H. Freeman, 1988.

Helfman, Gene S., Bruce B. Collette, and Douglas E. Facey. *The Diversity of Fishes*. Malden, Mass.: Blackwell Science, 1997.

Moyle, Peter B., and Joseph J. Cech. *Fishes: An Introduction to Ichthyology.* Englewood Cliffs, N.J.: Prentice Hall, 1982; 4th ed., Upper Saddle River, N.J.: Prentice Hall, 2000.

Nelson, Joseph S. *Fishes of the World.* New York: Wiley, 1976; 4th ed., Upper Saddle River, N.J.: Prentice Hall, 2000.

RELATED ARTICLES
Actinopterygii; Benthos; Clupeomorpha; Elopomorpha; Osteichthyes; Osteoglossomorpha; Pelagic; Teleostei

Eutrophic

Environments that are richly productive are described as being *eutrophic*, as opposed to those that are *oligotrophic* where productivity is low. The enhanced productivity results from the greater-than-normal supplies of the nutrients required for plant growth reaching the ecosystem. As a result, the standing crops of both plants and animals build up to high levels. In these conditions the assemblages tend to be dominated by very few species, so that diversity tends to decline. Moreover, if the ratio between the available nitrogen and phosphorus is unusually high, nuisance and toxic algae tend to bloom. These blooms not only disrupt the dynamics of the food web but can also make human consumption of shellfish a real danger. The high living biomass creates a high demand for oxygen, especially where water temperatures are high. No oxygen remains in the bottom sediments; they turn black and smell of hydrogen sulfide (similar to the smell of bad eggs). Under extreme conditions all the oxygen in the water is used up, and buildup of the highly toxic sulfide ions causes mass mortalities of fish and other organisms. If these conditions persist, for example as a result of pollution, dead zones may be created in which no species that require oxygen can survive.

Eutrophication is the process in which human activity causes environments to become more eutrophic because of the organic enrichment that occurs as a result of discharges of sewage and excessive runoff of agricultural fertilizers. There is a general global trend toward eutrophication. In order to grow more food to feed the burgeoning population, we are more than doubling the amounts of nitrogen available in the environment by fixing atmospheric nitrogen in the manufacturing of fertilizers, by growing more and more leguminous crops, and by polluting the air through car emission.

Martin Angel

FURTHER READING
Evans, L. T. *Feeding the Ten Billion: Plants and Population Growth.* Cambridge and New York: Cambridge University Press, 1998.

Jorgensen, B. B., and K. Richardson, eds. "Eutrophication in Coastal Marine Waters." *Coastal and Estuarine Studies,* Vol. 52. Washington, D.C.: American Geophysical Union, 1996.

Pearl, H. W. "Coastal Eutrophication and Harmful Algal Blooms: Importance of Atmospheric Deposition on Groundwater as 'New' Nitrogen and Other Nitrogen Sources." *Limnology and Oceanography,* Vol. 45, No. 2 (1997) pp. 1154–1164.

USEFUL WEB SITES
"Understanding Lake Ecology: Trophic Status." <http://wow.nrri.umn.edu/wow/under/primer/page16.html>.

RELATED ARTICLES
Oligotrophic; Standing Crop

Evaporite

Evaporite rocks form by the chemical precipitation of minerals from a brine (a highly concentrated water solution of salt). This process usually occurs in a closed or restricted basin where evaporation exceeds the influx of fresh water. Evaporation produces gypsum, anhydrite, and halite; chert may be precipitated from a silica gel. Although thick evaporite deposits occur in the geologic record, they represent only about

3 percent of the rock record. From a tectonic perspective, evaporites generally characterize the early stages of continental rift formation.

Evaporite deposits are found in both marine and terrestrial environments. Marine settings include lagoons, inland lakes, margins of seas, and isolated marine basins. Playas and alkali lakes are the main environments for terrestrial evaporite deposits. Marine and terrestrial evaporite deposits may grade into each other and often form interbedded deposits. These are recognized within red beds of Devonian (409 to 362 million years ago), Permian (290 to 248 million years ago), and Triassic (248 to 206 million years ago) age.

Terrestrial salt deposits form in basins of interior drainage with high surface evaporation rates. The Dead Sea was originally a Pliocene (5.2 to 1.64 million years ago) marine embayment along the Great Rift Valley and became landlocked by Pleistocene (1.64 million years ago) time. The River Jordan flows through salt deposits and empties into the Dead Sea, increasing its salinity. *Playas*, also called *salinas*, are shallow lakes with interior drainage and high evaporation rates. Death Valley is an example of a playa; borax is associated with halite, gypsum, and anhydrite minerals. *Alkali lakes* are similar to playas but are longer in length and remain highly alkaline throughout repeated drying and replenishing periods.

Marine salt deposits are forming today. Examples include small enclosed lagoons and basins in the Bahamas and parts of Cyprus where strong summer evaporation produces salt precipitation. Along the coastal area of the Persian Gulf limestone is forming. This area is dominated by deposition of aragonite and calcite, and algal mats are common. Salt deposits are mixed with and replace the carbonate rocks. These coastal Sabkha deposits are similar to ancient deposits that were once interpreted as lagoonal deposits. Other examples where evaporite deposits are forming include shallow estuaries in Peru and along the Caspian Sea.

Ancient examples of evaporite deposits include the salt diapirs that are found in the Gulf of Mexico and the Kavir Desert of Iran. Beneath the Mediterranean Sea a sequence of evaporite deposits are found. These deposits formed when water filled the basin, on a cyclical basis, and was unable to escape. High evaporation rates formed minerals that were deposited on the basin floor. This sequence or cycle of flooding, evaporation, mineral formation, and deposition was repeated numerous times. These regularly spaced alternating beds are termed *varves*. Analysis of varves helps determine the number of flooding events that occurred.

When salts become concentrated, they tend to precipitate along paths of solution chemistry. The mineral sequence starts with carbonates and sulfates and continues through the chlorides, terminating with the bittern salts. This order is subject to change based on the seasonal variations and differences in evaporation rates. The general order of precipitation as evidenced by the evaporation of present-day seawater is: carbonate precipitation when the concentration is four times normal; sulfate precipitation when the concentration is 12 times normal; halite precipitation when the concentration is more that 64 times normal; magnesium–potassium salt precipitation when concentration is more than 120 times normal; and finally, bischofite (a magnesium chloride) precipitation.

Three general and overlapping models explain the formation of evaporite deposits. The first is the deepwater–deep basin model, where thick deposits form in topographic lows; examples are the deposits of New York State and the deposits of Europe. The second, the shallow-water/shallow basin model, accounts for shallow platform or subaerial-deposited evaporites and includes Sabkha-type deposits. The third, the shallow-water/deep basin model, includes the Mediterranean deposits, where new water enters the basin periodically to resupply the evaporite materials.

David L. White

FURTHER READING

Condie, Kent C. *Plate Tectonics and Crustal Evolution.* New York: Pergamon Press, 1976; 4th ed., Oxford and Boston: Butterworth-Heinemann, 1997.

Hatch, F. H., and R. H. Rastall. *The Petrology of the Sedimentary Rocks.* London: Allen, 1913; 7th ed., by J. T. Greensmith, London and Boston: Unwin Hyman, 1989.

Montgomery, Carla W. *Physical Geology.* Dubuque, Iowa: Wm. C. Brown, 1987; 3rd ed., 1993.

Tarbuck, Edward J., and Frederick K. Lutgens. *Earth.* Columbus, Ohio: Charles E. Merrill, 1984; 8th ed., Upper Saddle River, N.J.: Prentice Hall, 1997.

RELATED ARTICLES

Sea Salt

Ewing, William Maurice

1906–1974

Marine Geologist and Geophysicist

William Maurice Ewing was the first director of the Lamont–Doherty Geological Observatory and was highly influential in the reexamination of Alfred Wegener's (1880–1930) continental drift theory in the 1950s and 1960s. Among a long list of achievements, he was responsible for the first reflection and refraction seismic traverses across a continental shelf (1935) and took the first deep-sea photographs (1939). Ewing and his coworkers made important contributions in the development of plate tectonics theory and the seafloor spreading concept.

Born in Lockney, Texas, in 1906, William Maurice Ewing—he chose to be called simply Maurice Ewing—was the oldest of seven children. As a child he showed exceptional ability in constructing electrical and mechanical devices with whatever cast-off items he could muster. Maurice graduated from Lockney High School at 15 and was accepted into the Rice Institute (later Rice University) in Houston. He was elected Hohenthal Scholar in 1923 and graduated from Rice with a B.S. in mathematics and physics in 1926. He stayed on under a fellowship to complete

an M.A. in 1927 and then a doctorate in 1931. His doctoral thesis was titled "Calculation of Ray Paths from Seismic Time Curves." At this time he was also an instructor in physics at the University of Pittsburgh (1929–30), and then at Lehigh University he became an instructor (1930–36), assistant professor of physics (1936–40), and associate professor of geology (1940–44).

At Lehigh, colleagues introduced Ewing to the challenges of ocean geophysics. By the mid-1930s, Ewing had focused his attention on the nature of the submarine crust and its transition from continental to oceanic forms at continental margins. He used all the latest techniques at his disposal and developed new ones. By the late-1930s he was detonating controlled explosions at sea and taking seismic measurements with automatic recording devices on the seafloor.

In 1940, Ewing took a leave of absence from Lehigh and moved his research group to the Woods Hole Oceanographic Institute (WHOI). There he worked with Columbus Iselin (1904–71) on the problems of submarine detection, especially those resulting from sound transmission as affected by vertical temperature gradients. Ewing,

William Maurice Ewing. (From the collections of the Library of Congress)

Iselin, and J. Lamar Worzel produced an invaluable WHOI training manual for naval officers called *Sound Transmission in Sea Water*. Iselin and Chaim Pekeris recognized the properties of the *sofar* (sound fixing and ranging) *channel*, the feature that "traps" sound waves and is associated with the thermocline. They demonstrated how this layer acted as a sound-wave guide. When they detonated a small explosion in the eastern Atlantic, its sound waves were picked up on hydrophones in the sofar channel of the western Atlantic.

In 1946, Ewing and part of his research group moved to Columbia University, where in 1949 they established the Lamont (later Lamont–Doherty) Geological Observatory. During Ewing's 23 years as its director, the observatory moved to the international forefront of marine research. Under Ewing's guidance, a series of sophisticated surveying methods were developed for improving the precision of marine geological and geophysical surveys. These included seismic refraction readings using hydrophones rather than bottom instruments, continuous reflection profiling with air-gun sources rather than intermittent profiling with explosives, and the use of towed magnetometers, precision depth recorders, and gravity measurers. He also improved methods for taking seafloor cores and coupled them with taking in situ heat-flow measurements. The application of these methods vastly improved knowledge of the surface contours and subsurface structure of the ocean floor, and thereby provided evidence to develop and test theories for ocean basin evolution.

With Bruce Heezen (1924–77), Ewing confirmed earlier suggestions that turbidity currents were a major cause of erosion in submarine canyons. Ewing was among the first to appreciate the great importance of turbidity currents in sedimentary processes, such as deposition on abyssal plains. Ewing, Wenceslas Jardetzky, and Frank Press (1924–) together launched a new age in seismology in which they explained many hitherto misunderstood aspects of seismograms.

Their book *Elastic Waves in Layered Media* (1957) became the standard textbook for a budding generation of seismologists.

At Columbia during his Lamont directorship, Ewing served as associate and then full professor of geology (1947–59) and Higgins Professor (1959–72). From the mid-1950s, Ewing favored the initiation of a deep-sea drilling program to penetrate the deep-sea floor and reach the Mohorovicic discontinuity (boundary between crust and mantle). The project was shelved, and it was not until 1968 that the drilling vessel *Glomar Challenger*, as part of the Joint Oceanographic Institution's Deep Earth Sampling (JOIDES) project, carried out the kind of drillings that Ewing had been advocating. Ewing headed the first part of the JOIDES expedition, which ultimately sampled 31 sites in the Atlantic and 53 in the Pacific. The drill cores resoundingly confirmed the seafloor spreading hypothesis—sediment layers were younger and thinner close to the mid-ocean ridge, and thicker and older farther away.

During the 1950s and 1960s, Ewing and his colleagues at Lamont–Doherty, such as Bruce Heezen and Marie Tharp, made profound advances in developing the seafloor spreading concept and plate tectonics theory. They identified the comparative thinness of the oceanic crust [5 to 8 kilometers (3 to 5 miles) thick] as compared to the continental crust [about 40 kilometers (25 miles) thick]. Most notably, they identified the continuous mid-ocean ridge system, where seafloor spreading was later confirmed.

Ewing left Lamont in 1972 over his concerns regarding the university's funding practices and moved to Texas, where he became Green Professor in Geological Sciences at the University of Texas, Galveston. During his long and fruitful career as researcher and teacher, Ewing wrote or contributed to more than 300 research papers, and he helped train more than 200 graduate students. Among his many honors were the Distinguished Public Service Award of the U.S.

Navy (1955), the Agassiz Medal (1955), and the National Medal of Science (1973).

A tireless worker, Ewing would often work 18-hour days at sea and would take part in operations whatever the weather. Some of his colleagues claimed that he took no vacation for 30 years. Ewing died in 1974, aged 67, working to the last. In 1976, the U.S. Navy and the American Geophysical Union jointly established the Maurice Ewing Medal for "significant original contributions to understanding physical, geophysical and geological processes in the oceans; and/or significant original contributions to scientific ocean engineering, technology, and instrumentation; and/or outstanding service to marine sciences"—a fitting tribute and reminder of Ewing's immense contribution to marine physics, geology, and geophysics.

Trevor Day

BIOGRAPHY

- William Maurice Ewing.
- Born 12 May 1904 in Lockney, Texas.
- Educated at the Rice Institute (now Rice University), where he gained a B.A. (1926), an M.A. (1927), and a Ph.D. (1931).
- Taught physics at the University of Pittsburgh (1929–30); physics, geology, and geophysics at Lehigh University (1930–44); and geology at Columbia University (1944–71).
- At Columbia, he was professor of geology (1947–59) and then Higgins Professor (1959–72), and was research associate at the Woods Hole Oceanographic Institute (1940–46).
- He served, most influentially, as the first director of Columbia University's Lamont (later Lamont–Doherty) Geological Observatory (1949–72).
- Died in Galveston, Texas, on 4 May 1974.

SELECTED WRITINGS

Ewing, J., and M. Ewing. "Sediment Distribution on the Mid-ocean Ridges with Respect to Spreading of the Sea-Floor." *Science*, Vol. 156 (1967) pp. 1590–1592.

Ewing, M., and L. Engel. "Seismic Shooting at Sea." *Scientific American*, Vol. 206, No. 5 (1961) pp. 116–127.

Ewing, M., W. S. Jardetzky, and F. Press. *Elastic Waves in Layered Media*. New York: McGraw-Hill, 1957.

Heezen, B. C., and M. Ewing. "The Mid-Oceanic Ridge." In M. N. Hill, ed., *The Sea*, Vol. 3. New York: Wiley-Interscience, 1963; pp. 388–410.

Heezen, B. C., M. Tharp, and M. Ewing. "The Floors of the Oceans: I. The North Atlantic." *Geological Society of America Special Paper 65* (1959), p.125.

FURTHER READING

Anderson, R. N. *Marine Geology: A Planet Earth Perspective*. New York: Wiley, 1988.

Bullard, E. C. "William Maurice Ewing." *Biographical Memoirs of Fellows of the Royal Society*, Vol. 21 (1975) pp. 269–311.

Menard, H.W. *The Ocean of Truth: A Personal History of Global Tectonics*. Princeton, N.J.: Princeton University Press, 1986.

Schlee, S. *The Edge of an Unfamiliar World: A History of Oceanography*. London: Hale, 1975.

RELATED ARTICLES

Heezen, Bruce Charles; Iselin, Columbus O'Donnell; Marine Geology; Plate Tectonics; Seafloor Spreading; Sofar; Submarine Canyon; Turbidity Current

Exclusive Economic Zone

The Exclusive Economic Zone (EEZ) is a legally defined marine area that extends the boundaries of coastal states from their coastlines to a maximum limit of 370.6 kilometers (200 nautical miles). Within the EEZ, coastal states enjoy sovereign rights over natural resources and economic exploration and exploitation; however, the freedoms of other states exercising overflight, navigation, and the laying of cables and pipelines are not affected.

The EEZ has its origins in the nineteenth century, when western South American nations such as Chile and Peru claimed 200 nautical miles as their patrimonial rights. Other nations, including much of Europe and the United States, used the "cannon-shot" rule of a 5.6-kilometer (3-nautical-mile) territorial sea. Under this system, the farthest length that a cannonball could reach defined a nation's territorial claim to the marine environment. However, as technology progressed, countries began claiming more of the coastal zone, and by the 1950s, most nations had expanded their territorial sea claims to 22.2 kilometers (12 nautical miles). In 1945, the United States—under the Truman Proclamation on the Continental Shelf—asserted jurisdiction over the natural resources of subsoil and seabed of the continental shelf contiguous to its coasts. The *continental shelf regime* expanded the U.S. right (and those of the U.S. coastal states, which followed with similar assertions) to its continental shelf to a maximum of 183 meters (600 feet), thereby providing exclusive access to petroleum and benthic natural resources. The 1958 United Nations Convention on the Continental Shelf incorporated the Truman Proclamation, establishing a depth [200-meter (656-feet) isobath] or exploitability criterion for the jurisdiction of coastal states over their continental shelf. However, the continental shelf regime did not provide exclusive access to pelagic natural resources, namely fisheries, and it did not prevent foreign states from utilizing the coastal state waters directly above the continental shelf for other economic purposes.

To address these and other coastal state concerns, the United Nations 3rd Convention on the United Nations Law of the Sea (UNCLOS III) formalized the continental shelf regime. The convention was completed in 1982 but did not enter into force until 1994. Described in Part V (Articles 55 to 75) of the convention, the EEZ is defined as a zone that extends to a distance of 200 nautical miles from the baseline from which the breadth of the territorial sea is measured and where the coastal state has sovereign rights to exploring, exploiting, conserving, and managing living and nonliving resources of the seabed and subsoil and the superjacent (overlying) waters, and has jurisdiction over the establishment and use of artificial islands and other structures for economic purposes. The convention provides for management responsibilities for anadromous, catadromous, and highly migratory species that traverse EEZs, and it also calls on coastal states to share resources with geographically disadvantaged and landlocked states. Importantly, the convention lays the framework to resolve EEZ disputes, claims between adjacent and neighboring coastal states, and boundary discrepancies.

The United States, which has not yet ratified UNCLOS III, asserted its own EEZ claim through the 1983 Reagan Proclamation. However, U.S. fishery interests were protected prior to the Reagan Proclamation. In 1976, the U.S. Congress passed the Fishery Conservation and Management Act (FCMA), more commonly known as the Magnuson–Stevens Act. This act created a fishery conservation zone extending 200 nautical miles in which U.S. fishing vessels would enjoy exclusive access to all fishery resources. The United States has sovereign rights over 7.6 million square kilometers (2.93 million square miles) of marine area, giving it the second largest EEZ in the world after France, which has an EEZ of almost 10 million square kilometers (3.86 million square miles).

Manoj Shivlani

FURTHER READING

Burke, William T. *The New International Law of Fisheries: UNCLOS 1982 and Beyond.* Oxford: Clarendon Press/New York: Oxford University Press, 1994.

Churchill, R. R., and A. V. Lowe. *The Law of the Sea.* Manchester, and Dover, N.H.: Manchester University Press, 1983; 3rd ed., Manchester: Manchester University Press/Yonkers, N.Y.: Juris, 1999.

Galdorisi, George V., and Kevin R. Vienna. *Beyond the Law of the Sea: New Directions for U.S. Oceans Policy.* Westport, Conn.: Praeger, 1997.

Reagan, R. Proclamation 5030. "Exclusive Economic Zone of the United States of America." 10 March 1983.

RELATED ARTICLES

Ocean Floor Resource

Expendable Bathythermograph

The expendable bathythermograph (XBT) is used by oceanographers to measure the temperature structure of oceans while a ship is under way and without interference of normal ship routine. The launcher, the recorder, and the expendable probe are the three major components of the XBT. The expendable probe consists of a ballistically shaped device containing a calibrated thermistor placed in a canister. A very fine conducting wire is wrapped around a spool in the probe and another spool inside the canister. The canister is placed in the launcher and the probe is released from the launcher by removing a launch pin. The fine wire from the probe unwinds as it sinks beneath the sea surface, and the fine wire on the canister spool unwinds as the ship moves ahead. This allows the probe to free-fall through the water at a nearly constant rate. As the probe descends, the electrical resistance of the thermistor changes with water temperature, and the temperature and depth are recorded on the surface. When all the fine wire is let out, the wire breaks, and the probe drops to the seafloor. The XBT is launched as far aft on the ship as possible and on its leeward side. This minimizes the chance that the fine wire will scrape the ship's hull and cause the wire to break. The XBT can be recorded digitally, can be used on surface ships moving at speeds up to about 25 knots, can be launched in relatively rough seas [wave heights of about 4 to 8 meters (13 to 26 feet)], and is capable of providing temperature measurements in water depths up to about 1500 to 2000 meters (4900 to 6600 feet). These are major advantages over the original, now obsolete mechanical bathythermograph. XBT results are recorded on a standard bathythermograph log and may be transmitted in real time from ship to shore via satellite. The XBT is a reliable instrument requiring little maintenance.

XBT temperature profiles are collected internationally by oceanographic research vessels and voluntary observing ships in support of global oceanographic and climate studies. For example, international research programs such as the World Ocean Circulation Experiment (WOCE) and the Tropical Ocean Global Atmosphere (TOGA) program use XBT data to monitor the ocean, validate models, and increase understanding of climatically important ocean processes.

Philip Rabinowitz

FURTHER READING

Daneshzadeh, Y. C., J. F. Festa, and S. M. Minton. "Procedures Used at NOAA-AOML to Quality Control Real Time XBT Data Collected in the Atlantic Ocean." *NOAA Tech. Memo. ERL AOML-78*, NOAA Atlantic Oceanographic and Meteorological Laboratory, 1994, p. 44.

U.S. Naval Oceanographic Office. *Instruction Manual for Obtaining Oceanographic Data*, Publication 607, 3rd ed., Washington D.C.: U.S. Government Printing Office, 1968; pp. C-1 to C-12.

RELATED ARTICLES

Bathythermograph

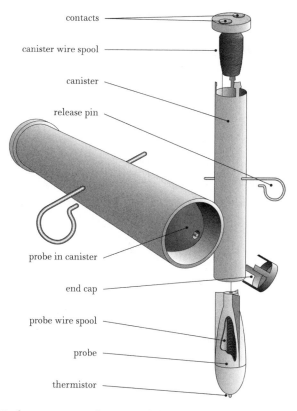

Probe component of an expendable bathythermograph.

Exploitive Competition

Competition describes an ecological interaction between individuals or species in response to the need for a common resource such as space or food. Because competition can occur via different mechanisms, ecologists have subdivided the concept of competition to describe different ways in which organisms interact in pursuit of shared resources. Historically, ecologists have divided competitive interactions into two forms: exploitive and interference.

Exploitive (also called *exploitative*) *competition* describes an interaction in which one individual or species is more efficient than another individual or species at exploiting a resource and therefore affects the fitness of the other competitor by depriving it of that resource. Unlike *interference competition*, in which organisms directly interact via physical or chemical means, exploitive competition is a passive phenomenon; it occurs indirectly via depletion of a shared resource rather than by direct interaction (e.g., physical or chemical harm). An example of exploitive competition in the marine environment can be found in coral reef communities. Some types of upright branching corals grow more rapidly than do encrusting or massive corals. In some cases, species in the former group grow over species in the latter group, thereby depriving the slow growers of light and water movement (both resources are required for coral survival).

Many ecologists who study competition have found that observed interactions among organisms do not fit neatly into the exploitive versus interference classification scheme. Therefore, while the term *exploitive competition* remains widely used in the ecological literature, it has been supplemented with numerous other subdivisions to describe specific mechanisms of competition.

Lynn L. Lauerman

FURTHER READING

Nybakken, James W. *Marine Biology: An Ecological Approach*, 5th ed. San Francisco: Benjamin Cummings, 2001.

Park, Thomas. "Beetles, Competition, and Populations." *Science*, Vol. 138, No. 3548 (1962), pp. 1369–1375.

RELATED ARTICLES
Coral Reef

Explorer Plate

The Explorer Plate is a fragment of a plate fragment and may not even be a true plate. This microplate (or plate sliver) is the northwestern tip of the larger Juan de Fuca Plate, which is located offshore of California, Oregon, Washington, and British Columbia. It occurs at a triple junction, where three plates (Pacific, North American, and Juan de Fuca) come together. The Explorer Plate has an area of approximately 30,000 square kilometers (11,600 square miles) and is situated off the northwestern end of Vancouver Island.

To visualize this tiny plate, one can imagine a dipper (like the constellation, the Little Dipper) with its handle on the left (west) and that side tilted upward at a 45° angle. The top of the dipper is a 230-kilometer (143-mile) segment of the Cascadia Subduction Zone, north of which is the continental margin of British Columbia. At its southernmost point, the dipper seems balanced on the northern end of the Juan de Fuca Ridge. The eastern side of the dipper bowl is formed by the Nootka Fault, a transform fault that connects the tip of the Juan de Fuca Ridge with the Cascadia Subduction Zone and separates the Explorer Plate from the Juan de Fuca Plate to the southeast. On its west side, the Explorer Plate is bounded by mid-ocean ridge segments and two transform faults that offset them. These transform faults trend northwest, with the Sovanco Fracture Zone forming the base of the dipper bowl and the Revere–Dellwood Fracture Zone defining the bottom of the dipper handle. In between these two faults is the Explorer Ridge, which trends northeast. At its northern end, the ridge may split into two active, overlapping spreading segments. Similarly, to the north of the Revere–Dellwood Fracture Zone, two volcanic lineaments, the Tuzo Wilson Knolls and Dellwood Knolls, may represent overlapping, diffuse spreading centers that connect the fracture zone with the trench.

The Explorer Plate probably formed about 4 million years ago as the small Juan de Fuca Plate fragmented while being subducted in the Cascadia Subduction Zone. The Juan de Fuca Plate itself is a fragment of the erstwhile Farallon Plate, which once covered most of the eastern Pacific Ocean. As the Juan de Fuca Plate became smaller, the stresses caused by subduction began to tear off its ends, the Explorer Plate on the north side and the Gorda Plate on the south side. Because the Explorer Plate is so small, it may be undergoing internal deformation, bending rather than acting as a rigid microplate. For that reason the term plate may be inappropriate in its strictest sense. One effect of this behavior is that the plate boundaries that surround the Explorer Plate are more diffuse than usual: for example, the apparently overlapping spreading segments of the Explorer Ridge as well as the Tuzo Wilson and Dellwood knolls volcanic zones.

William W. Sager

FURTHER READING

Govers, Rob, and Paul Th. Meijer. "On the Dynamics of the Juan de Fuca Plate." *Earth and Planetary Science Letters*, Vol. 189 (15 July 2001), pp. 115–131.

Riddihough, Robin. "Recent Movements of the Juan de Fuca Plate System." *Journal of Geophysical Research*, Vol. 89 (10 August 1984), pp. 6980–6994.

Riddihough, Robin, and Roy D. Hyndman. "Queen Charlotte Islands Margin." In Edward L. Wineterer, Donald L. Hussong, and Robert W. Decker, eds., *The Eastern Pacific Ocean and Hawaii, Decade of North American Geology*, Vol. N. Boulder, Colo.: Geological Society of America, 1989; pp. 403–411.

Wilson, Douglas S. "Tectonic History of the Juan de Fuca Ridge over the Last 40 Million Years." *Journal of Geophysical Research*, Vol. 93 (10 October 1988), pp. 11,863–11,876.

RELATED ARTICLES

Cascadia; Convergent Plate Boundary; Farallon Plate; Gorda Plate; Juan de Fuca Plate; Juan de Fuca Ridge; Mid-Ocean Ridge; Plate Tectonics; Subduction Zone; Transform Fault

F

~

Farallon Plate

Today, most of the Pacific ocean floor is part of the Pacific Plate, Earth's largest plate. Not long ago in geologic time, about 200 million years, there was no Pacific Plate. Instead, the Pacific basin floor consisted of at least three large plates: Izanagi, Farallon, and Phoenix. The three plates met at a triple junction where three spreading ridges, separating the three plates, came together. The Farallon Plate took up much of the eastern Pacific, with the Izanagi Plate in the west and the Phoenix Plate in the south. Today only a few remnants of the once-vast Farallon Plate remain, up against the eastern edges of North and South America. The rest disappeared, consumed by the convergent plate boundaries in the northern and eastern Pacific.

Geophysical Evidence of a Lost Plate

The story of the Farallon Plate is revealed in linear magnetic anomalies preserved within the Pacific Plate crust. Recorded at the spreading ridge by magnetic minerals in newly formed, cooling crust, the linear magnetic anomalies result from quasi-periodic reversals of geomagnetic field direction. These magnetic stripes are isochrons showing past locations of the spreading ridges that once bounded the Pacific Plate. Western Pacific plate magnetic lineations range in age from anomaly M29 (158 million years ago) to M0 (124 million years ago), whereas eastern Pacific lineations

span anomaly C33 (83 million years ago) to C0 (present day). A gap of 41 million years occurs in between the two lineation groups in the central Pacific because the geomagnetic field did not reverse between M0 and C33 (called the *Cretaceous Quiet Period*). In the western Pacific, three groups of magnetic lineations form a triangle, evidence of the birth of the Pacific Plate as a small plate. Each side of the triangle formed at a spreading ridge separating the Pacific Plate from one of the three plates surrounding it. As the Pacific Plate slowly grew in size, the spreading ridges on its borders did the same. In the western Pacific, the northwest-trending Hawaiian lineations record the growth of the Pacific–Farallon ridge. By the end of the Cretaceous Quiet Period, the Pacific–Farallon ridge was over 6700 kilometers (4160 miles) in length, as shown by north–south magnetic lineations in the eastern Pacific that stretch from near the Aleutian Trench past the equator into the south Pacific. Among the features left behind by this spreading ridge is a set of long fracture zones that range across most of the Pacific basin. These fracture zones are scars left behind by transform fault offsets on the Pacific–Farallon Ridge. The longest is the Mendocino Fracture Zone, which begins in the western Pacific, south of Shatsky Rise, and stretches to the California coast, ending near Cape Mendocino. Moving south from the Mendocino, the other great fracture zones are Pioneer, Murray, Molokai, Clarion, and Clipperton.

History of the Farallon Plate

Knowledge of the origin and growth of the Farallon Plate is lost forever, having been recorded in predecessor ocean plates long since consumed by subduction at convergent plate boundaries surrounding the Pacific Basin. Western Pacific magnetic lineations record only the part of the Farallon Plate that was adjacent to the Pacific Plate, which began to form about 180 million years ago. These lineations indicate that the Farallon was a large plate, located to the east of the growing Pacific. How far it stretched eastward and what its boundaries were like will never be known. At some point it came into contact with the convergent plate boundaries on the western margins of North and South America, sealing its eventual fate.

By about 100 million years ago, the Pacific Plate had become a large plate. At about this time, it became engaged in western Pacific convergent plate boundaries. With the Pacific Plate pulled toward the western Pacific trenches and the Farallon Plate drawn toward the eastern Pacific trenches, the two plates were rapidly pulled apart, forming ocean lithosphere at a high rate at the Pacific–Farallon Ridge. During the Cretaceous Quiet Period, when no magnetic lineations were recorded, a tectonic shift changed the plate configuration in the Pacific basin. The lack of lineations was like turning the lights out on plate history; when the lights came on again, one player had exited and another entered. Gone was the Izanagi Plate, probably consumed at the trenches bordering the northwest Pacific. In its place, the Kula Plate appeared in the north. Many geophysicists think the Kula Plate actually began its existence as a piece of Farallon Plate that was torn off when the Aleutian Trench was formed.

Formation of the Kula Plate foreshadowed the future for the Farallon Plate. As the Farallon Plate subducted toward eastern Pacific convergent plate boundaries, the divergent stresses ripped it apart, little by little. The next great tear occurred about 55 million years ago, when the Farallon fragmented into northern and southern pieces. The northern piece became the Vancouver Plate and was mostly consumed beneath North America. Today, only a small remnant remains as the Juan de Fuca and Gorda Plates offshore between Queen Charlotte Island in southern British Columbia and Cape Mendocino in California. The southern Farallon Plate also fragmented. At about 25 million years ago, it split into two large pieces, which became the Cocos and Nazca Plates. Bits of those two plates were sliced off by an eastward jump of the East Pacific Rise about 10 million years ago, further reducing the area of the Farallon's descendants. Today, the Cocos Plate is being consumed at the Middle America Trench on the western margin of Central America, whereas the Nazca Plate is subducting in the Peru–Chile Trench, which occupies most of the western margin of South America. A tiny fragment of the Farallon and Cocos Plates, the Rivera Plate, subducts into the northern Middle America Trench at the mouth of the Gulf of California.

How Farallon Got Its Name

Farallon in Spanish means "cliff" and is a common part of many island names bestowed by Spanish explorers. The Farallon Plate was named in 1969 by geophysicists Dan P. McKenzie and W. Jason Morgan in one of the first scientific articles that laid out plate tectonics theory. They gave the plate that had largely disappeared beneath western North America the name of the Farallon Islands, located offshore of central California.

William W. Sager

FURTHER READING

Atwater, Tanya. "Plate Tectonic History of the Northeast Pacific and Western North America." In *The Geology of North America*, Vol. N, *The Eastern Pacific Ocean and Hawaii*. Boulder, Colo.: Geological Society of America, 1989.

Engebretson, David C., Allan Cox, and Richard G. Gordon. *Relative Motions between Oceanic and Continental Plates in the Pacific Basin.* Special Paper 206. Boulder, Colo.: Geological Society of America, 1985.

Kennett, James. *Marine Geology.* Englewood Cliffs, N.J.: Prentice Hall, 1982.

Mayes, Catherine L., Lawrence A. Lawver, and David T. Sandwell. "Tectonic History and New Isochron Chart of the South Pacific." *Journal of Geophysical Research,* Vol. 95 (10 June 1990), pp. 8543–8567.

McKenzie, Dan P., and W. Jason Morgan. "Evolution of Triple Junctions." *Nature,* Vol. 224 (1969), pp.125–133.

Rosa, José W. C., and Peter Molnar. "Uncertainties in Reconstructions of the Pacific, Farallon, Vancouver, and Kula Plates and Constraints on the Rigidity of the Pacific and Farallon (and Vancouver) Plates between 72 and 35 Ma." *Journal of Geophysical Research,*Vol. 93 (10 April 1988), pp. 2997–3008.

RELATED ARTICLES
Cocos Plate; Gorda Plate; Juan de Fuca Plate; Kula Plate; Nazca Plate; Pacific Plate; Plate Tectonics; Seafloor Spreading; Subduction Zone

Feather Star, see Crinoidea

Femtoplankton

The term *plankton* describes the diverse assemblage of small organisms that live in the water column. Oceanographers often group planktonic organisms into categories based on size. Femtoplankton is composed of the smallest planktonic organisms; this size category includes all organisms smaller than 0.20 micrometer (0.0000079 inch). Femtoplankton (a term used synonymously with *viroplankton*) comprises marine viruses. Marine viruses are too small to collect with plankton nets. Instead, oceanographers take a water sample and then centrifuge the sample to concentrate the organisms, allow the organisms to settle onto a substrate, or pump the sample through very fine meshed filters that retain the organisms.

Marine viruses were discovered in the 1960s, but the role that viruses play in the oceanic ecosystem is still unclear. Viruses are extremely abundant in the ocean—1 milliliter (0.03 ounce) of seawater can contain more than 10 million virus particles—and they probably play an important role in the microbial loop. Scientists think that viruses primarily infect bacteria and phytoplankton cells, both of which are intimately linked in oceanic food webs. By infecting these hosts, viruses may help control their population growth.

Lynn L. Lauerman

FURTHER READING
Cochlan, William P., Johan Wikner, Grieg F. Steward, David C. Smith, and Farooq Azam. "Spatial Distribution of Viruses, Bacteria and Chlorophyll a in Neritic, Oceanic and Estuarine Environments." *Marine Ecology Progress Series,* Vol. 92 (1993), pp. 77–87.

Kirchman, David L., ed. *Microbial Ecology of the Oceans.* New York: Wiley, 2000.

RELATED ARTICLES
Microbial Loop; Plankton

Filter Feeder

Filter or *suspension feeders* are organisms that rely for their nutrition upon small organic particles suspended in the water column, consisting largely of planktonic organisms. Filtering of water occurs either passively, by positioning in a water current, or actively, by ciliary or muscular pumping. Filter feeding is the primary method of food collection in several higher taxa of marine invertebrates, including the phylum Porifera (sponges); the lophophorates, consisting of the phyla Brachiopoda, Phoronida, and Ectoprocta (Bryozoa); the Entoprocta; the hemichordate class Pterobranchia; and the invertebrate chordate classes, which include the sea squirts (Ascidiaceae), salps (Thaliaceae), and

Larvaceae. Filter feeding has also evolved independently in members of many other marine taxa, including the polychaetes, mollusks, crustaceans, and echinoderms.

The collection of food is accomplished in a variety of ways. In sponges, specialized cells called *choanocytes* line the internal cavities; each has a single flagellum that acts in concert to create a feeding current through the sponge, and a collar of microvilli surrounding the flagellum functions in food capture. The lophophorates, pterobranchs, and many filter-feeding polychaetes have a crown of tentacles covered in cilia that either create a feeding current or aid an existing, natural one; particles are captured on the tentacle and moved to the mouth with the help of mucous secretions and ciliary tracts. Other polychaetes, some mollusks, and the invertebrate chordates secrete mucous nets, either held passively into water currents exterior to the body or within secreted shelters (e.g., tubes) with active pumping. Some organisms have adapted other ciliated body parts for the purpose of filter feeding, such as the gills or ctenidia in bivalve mollusks. Other organisms, which might otherwise deposit feed, undertake suspension feeding by orientation of their body in a way that maximizes surface area exposure to a water current, thereby enhancing particle capture, as in certain sand dollars (echinoid echinoderms). Filter-feeding crustaceans, which do not possess cilia, capture particles with the fine setae of specialized appendages, although small organisms simply ingest packets of water directed to the mouth with appendages. Finally, many planktonic larvae feed by ciliary bands surrounding the larval body, also a type of filter feeding.

Other adaptations to filter feeding include special features in the gut to process the particulate material and management of feeding currents so that water that has been filtered is not reprocessed.

Patrick D. Reynolds

FURTHER READING

Barnes, Robert. *Invertebrate Zoology.* Philadelphia: W. B. Saunders, 1963; 6th ed., by Edward Ruppert, Fort Worth, Texas: Saunders College Publishing, 1994.

Brusca, Richard C., and Gary J. Brusca. *Invertebrates.* Sunderland, Mass.: Sinauer, 1990.

Pechenik, Jan A. *Biology of the Invertebrates.* Boston: Prindle, Weber and Schmidt, 1985; 4th ed., Boston: McGraw-Hill, 2000.

RELATED ARTICLES

Brachiopoda; Bryozoa; Crustacea; Echinodermata; Entoprocta; Larvacean; Mollusca; Phoronida; Polychaeta; Porifera

Fins

Fins are structures used by aquatic organisms for locomotion. Fish have a variety of fins, which serve various functions. Median fins, one of the two general types of fins, are vertical fins and found along the midline of the animal, which includes the dorsal, caudal (tail), and anal fins. Paired fins, such as the pelvic and pectoral fins, are located on the sides of the animal. In fishes, fins are used for stability, steering, and braking and in some fishes for locomotion. Caudal fins transmit the thrusting power from the body muscles.

Bony fish use the dorsal and anal fins as rudders to keep them from rolling over. The pectoral and pelvic fins are useful in turning, breaking, and balancing, while the caudal fin transmits the thrusting power from the body muscles to drive the fish through the water. Although the function of fins is primarily for movement and coordinating movement, some fish have adapted their fins for different lifestyles. For example, batfish and sea robins use their pectoral fins to walk along the ocean floor. Flying fish have greatly enlarged winglike pectoral fins, enabling them to glide through the air for up to 90 meters (295 feet).

The cartilaginous fishes—the sharks, skates, and rays—use fins for swimming, maneuvering, and for lift. Skates and rays use their greatly enlarged pectoral fins for moving through the water. Sharks have a stiff dorsal fin that maintains stability. The paired pectoral and pelvic fins help provide lift, as they do not possess a swim bladder to prevent them from sinking. The stiff heterocercal caudal fin provides great thrusting power.

Erin O'Donnell

FURTHER READING
Campbell, Neil A. *Biology.* Menlo Park, Calif.: Benjamin Cummings, 1987; 5th ed., 1999.
Cousteau, Jacques. *The Ocean World.* New York: Abrams, 1979.
Nybakken, James W. *Marine Biology: An Ecological Approach,* 5th ed. San Francisco: Benjamin Cummings, 2001.

RELATED ARTICLES
Fish Propulsion; Ray; Shark; Skate

Fisheries

As a concept, fisheries are concerned with the relationships between humans and marine organisms harvested commercially and recreationally. Each fishery is composed of the marine organisms, their environment, and the humans that harvest the organisms and influence the condition of their environment. Included in the interaction are increasingly important factors such as conservation and management. Moreover, fisheries are multidisciplinary in nature, as they contain natural (physical, biological, and ecological), economic, cultural, social, and political components that interact with each other continually. Biological factors such as growth rates and recruitment control the standing stocks and growth potential of populations and stocks. Ecological conditions affect the directionality of population growth, either enhancing or contracting the stocks available for harvest. Political and economic environments and frameworks influence harvesting capacity, rates, and efficiency, whereas cultural and social norms create and reinforce attitudes toward policies and economies. Collectively, these interactive matrices define the fisheries dynamic, itself a changing paradigm. To better understand how fisheries are organized and have evolved, it is important to describe the concepts behind fisheries science and assessment, and fishing methods and regulatory controls, and provide a historical review of the world's major fisheries and their current conditions.

Fisheries Science and Assessment

Fisheries are dynamic, subject to physical factors, such as temperature, currents, and salinity, among others, and biological conditions and interactions, including prey availability, predators, and competition. Other, larger events, such as the El Niño Southern Oscillation (ENSO) and global warming, also affect the status of fisheries.

Trawlers on the Massachusetts coast in the 1930s. This region has been a traditional center for commercial fleets that often fish the Grand Banks and other North Atlantic fisheries. (From the collections of the Library of Congress)

Fishery scientists have developed an analytical system, termed *stock assessment*, to determine sustainable harvest levels. By determining the capacity of a fishery stock to replace the total lost to harvest, scientists attempt to predict how the stock will change over time (often predicted at various levels of fishing effort). Two important variables in the change of stock size over time are recruitment and growth rates of populations. *Recruitment* is the process of adding new individuals via reproduction and dispersal minus mortality to the stock size. *Growth rates* refer to the speed at which a fishery stock increases, and the rates affect how rapidly the harvested stock is replenished.

The general concept applied for sustainable management is that of *maximum sustainable yield* (MSY). Based on the general premise that fishery stocks maintained at a density roughly half their maximum population should yield the greatest replacement per harvest, the MSY (or Schaefer) model represents the surplus fishery stock that can theoretically be removed and replaced by new recruits for the next harvest (known as *surplus production*). Thus, under MSY conditions, if half the fishery stock is removed by fishing, it is replaced back to its original condition for the next harvest cycle. If more than half of the stock is removed, it may provide short-term gains (i.e., larger harvest levels); however, these would not be sustained, leading to reduced population sizes and lower future harvest. Therefore, MSY is the biologically optimal state, and it is the benchmark most often used to develop sustainable fishery plans. However, MSY is not the only concept utilized to determine efficient harvest levels in fisheries, which, as noted above, consist of both natural and human components. Also, MSY is very difficult to assess in many fisheries.

Fishery economists and managers also derive two related concepts, *maximum economic yield* (MEY) and *optimum yield* (OY), to determine acceptable harvest levels. MEY refers to a harvest level that generates the greatest economic benefits (or maximum resource rent), as defined by the maximum difference between total revenues and total costs of exploiting a fish stock. Importantly, MEY is generally realized at harvest levels lower than those that produce MSY. OY is a social concept that is based on MSY as modified by social, economic, and ecological factors.

Fishing Methods and Controls

The biological, economic, and social concepts used to estimate fishery harvest levels must function with a number of regulatory controls that circumscribe the working environment of fisheries operations, referred to broadly as conservation and management. Regulatory controls supervise the types of fishery resource users, harvesting methods, and the fishery resources.

There are three basic user types in fisheries: commercial users, recreational anglers, and subsistence fishers. Commercial users account for most of the fish stocks harvested, and they utilize their catch for commercial (sale) purposes. In 1999, U.S. commercial fishery landings were approximately 4.2 million tonnes (4.6 tons), worth U.S.$3.5 billion. Total U.S. aquaculture exceeded 380,000 tonnes (418,000 tons) and was worth almost U.S.$990 million. By contrast, global harvest totals that year exceeded 92 million tonnes (101.2 tons), and aquaculture reached 33 million tonnes (36 tons). Recreational anglers, the largest of the three groups, fish more for enjoyment than for subsistence or income. In 1999, over 7.8 million people in the United States participated in recreational fishing, taking almost 57 million trips. Subsistence fishers are a dwindling group who rely on the harvest for food and as part of their cultural heritage. Subsistence fisheries are most prevalent in developing countries. Although not within the scope of this discussion, it is important to note that allocation issues (or how and in what quantities the fisheries are divided among different user groups) play a major role in the interactions and conflicts within and between user groups in fisheries. Also, indirect users such as nongovernmental organizations (NGOs) have begun taking a more active approach, demanding that allocations be given not only to user groups, but also to the environment (for preservation and ecotourism purposes).

Fisheries utilize a variety of harvesting methods to capture target (and, in many fisheries, bycatch) species. Harvesting methods are divided into the different types of gear: hook and line gear, active entrapment gear, passive entrapment gear, and entanglement gear. Hook and line gear includes individual pole or handlines and longlines. Pole and handlines are used individually, are labor-intensive, and are utilized in specialized fisheries. Longlines are baited hooks that are attached to cables or rope and left in the water to fish. Longline is the typical gear used in pelagic fisheries, such as those for swordfish, tuna, and sharks (although many of these species are now captured using other gear as well). Active entrapment gear consists mostly of nets that are pulled through the water column or bottom. These include trawls and dredges, both gear types that, unless modified, result in bycatch. Shrimp trawls, for instance, are now required to include openings, called *turtle excluder devices* (TEDs), to allow marine turtles to escape from the nets. Seines are mesh nets that are used to encircle schooling fish, and a modified version called a *purse seine* is utilized in the major tuna fisheries (and dolphin bycatch). Passive entrapment gear includes trap (funnel-shaped) nets and pots and traps. Trap nets create barriers that guide passing fish into a funnel-shaped net, where they are harvested. Pots and traps are rigid or mesh frames that have openings through which fish and invertebrates are captured. The American and spiny

lobster fisheries, as well as many crab fisheries, are pot- and trap-based. Finally, entanglement gear, which refers to gill, trammel, and other entangling nets, consists of fixed netting in the water column that is used to capture fish by entrapping them around the head or other body parts. A modified version, called a *driftnet*, is used in open waters. Used most extensively in the Pacific Ocean, in the 1980s fishing fleets began using driftnets that reached 60 kilometers (about 37 miles) in width. As with other entangling nets, driftnets trapped large amounts of bycatch (sharks, turtles, cetaceans, and others). By the late 1980s, various nations began calling for the end of driftnet fishing. In 1991, the United Nations General Assembly agreed on a resolution calling for a ban on driftnet fishing on all high seas starting in 1993.

A variety of regulatory controls employed by councils, fishery agencies, governments, and international organizations exist to achieve conservation and management goals. Most important, these controls generally attempt to achieve sustainability, in terms not only of MSY, but also MEY and OY. Controls are most commonly placed on the harvest, effort, and gear. Harvest controls include size limits (such as minimum size, maximum size, and intermediate size limits), daily catch limits, catch-and-release requirements, quotas, and closures. Closures can be temporary, seasonal, or permanent. Marine reserves are an example of a permanent (spatial) closure, where a part of a fishing ground is excluded from harvest. Effort controls consist of restricting the number of fishing units allowed per user, limiting entry into a fishery, and establishing individual transferable quotas (ITQs). This latter form of effort control creates a number of quotas that are distributed among users, who are then free to trade the ITQs on the free market. Finally, gear restrictions regulate gear efficiency, prohibit the use of gear, and modify gear (as in the above-discussed case of TEDs).

These regulatory controls do not represent an exhaustive list, and one type of control is often used in conjunction with others to achieve conservation and management goals. But, as described later, these controls and the aforementioned fishery concepts have not prevented overfishing; instead, most stocks in the world are overfished. Property-rights proponents may point to the veracity of Garrett Hardin's 1968 "Tragedy of the Commons" article, in which he argued that open access leads to overexploitation, and because most fisheries are shared by many people and nations, that the end result will always lead to resource depletion because too many users take them collectively. Others counter that the reason for the collapse of many fisheries has not been the ineffectiveness of regulatory controls; rather, it has been the result of inconsistent execution and contradictory approaches on the part of decision-making bodies, due in part to scientific uncertainty, perverse capacity-building incentives, and other counterproductive policies. These include not utilizing the precautionary principle in protecting poorly understood stocks, providing financial incentives for entering fishers without considering the capacity that the fishery may hold, and maintaining a fishery artificially by subsidizing users.

Review of the World's Major Fisheries

In 1999, the world's total fishery production reached 125 million tonnes (137.5 million tons). Over a quarter of that total, 33 million tonnes, was realized from aquaculture. Important farm-raised species include finfish such as tilapia and salmon, along with shrimp, mollusks, and seaweed. Seen as a sustainable alternative to wild harvests, aquaculture may very well represent the future of fisheries. However, aquaculture presents its own problems as well. These include pollutants that are generated from aquacultural practices (ranging from animal waste to chemical additives), increased incidences of diseases within cultured organisms, and conversion of coastal systems into aquaculture facilities or plots.

The remainder of the catch, realized from wild harvests, is divided among relatively few species groups. Most fisheries, constituting about 90 percent of the catch, are located in the continental shelves and overlying waters, a region constituting less than 10 percent of the world's ocean area. Coastal upwelling regions are especially productive and can account for up to half of total landings. These fisheries dominate the world catch. Among the largest fisheries in the world is the anchoveta fishery of Peru and Chile. The fishery is affected negatively by the warm waters generated by the El Niño Southern Oscillation (ENSO) phenomenon, and it crashes during ENSO years. In 1996, catch totals neared 8.16 million tonnes (9 million tons). However, catch dropped to less than 1.8 million tonnes (2 million tons) in 1998, an ENSO year. Other members of the group, menhaden and herrings, also form significant fisheries in Asia and the North Atlantic Ocean.

Another of the largest groups consists of the gadoids, which include the prolific Alaska pollock fishery in Alaska. Alaska pollock production exceeded 3.4 million tonnes (3.7 million tons) in the late 1990s. The gadoid group also includes the cod, haddock, and hake, all part of the groundfish complex that collapsed in the Grand Banks in the early 1990s.

The third largest group includes mackerel, or scombroid, fishes. Together with their close relatives the tunas, these fishes comprise an important food source that is highly prized and actively targeted. Among their representatives is the overfished bluefin tuna, which is among the most lucrative species in the world. Other important groups include the flatfishes, rockfishes, and salmonids. The most important crustacean species are shrimp, followed by krill and lobsters. Mollusk species that are targeted include oysters, mussels, and clams.

Marine mammals constituted an important, albeit minor in terms of landings, fishery prior to the commercial extinction of whaling in the 1940s, followed by preservation measures taken by the International Whaling Commission (IWC) in the 1980s and 1990s, as well as the influential U.S. Marine Mammal Protection Act of 1972 (MMPA), which have effectively barred the reintroduction of whaling. Although Japan continues "scientific whaling" and Norway resumed hunting minke whales, whaling has not reemerged as a dominant fishery.

History of Fisheries: Exploitation and Depletion

Humans have fished since prehistoric times. Middle Eastern fleets developed in parts of the Persian Gulf as early as 2300 B.C., and Egyptians harvested fish more than 3400 years ago. The Chinese have practiced aquaculture, or fish farming, since 2000 B.C. Native Americans harvest nearshore fishes and living resources such as shellfish and salmon. As the European settlement of the New World occurred in the fifteenth century and beyond, fisheries played a major role as a food source and then for commercial gain. The discovery of whale stocks and the Grand Banks in the North Atlantic and salmon populations in the Pacific Northwest facilitated colonization of early North America and the western United States, respectively. As navigational technology improved, humans began exploiting most of the continental shelf, as well as the high seas (areas beyond the continental shelf), for pelagic resources, especially cetaceans. By the end of the nineteenth century, fleets routinely fished remote areas such as the Antarctic Convergence Zone, the South Pacific, and the Indian Ocean. Importantly, there were few to no controls on fisheries, as most resource experts of the era believed that fisheries were inexhaustible. Thomas H. Huxley (1825–95), a famed British naturalist, is quoted as saying in 1883 in relation to the then-current modes of fishing that "a number of the most important fisheries . . . are inexhaustible." He based his statement on the grounds that catch was relatively insignificant in comparison to the number of fish and that fishermen could not increase the death rate of fishes.

But as fishery capacity and technology advanced in the twentieth century, scientists and fishery managers realized that fish stocks could be depleted. In fact, in less than 30 years after Huxley's statement, scientists already found evidence for depletions in demersal (bottom) fish stocks in the northeastern Atlantic Ocean. However, fisheries were often treated as a panacea for populations suffering from low protein nutrition and world hunger, and governments and international organizations assisted in the development of increased fishery capacity. Between 1948 and 1968, fishery landings increased at a rate of 7 percent per year, from 20 million tonnes (22 million tons) to 60 million tonnes (66 million tons). In 1976, the U.S. Congress passed the Fisheries Conservation and Management Act (amended in 1996 as the Sustainable Fisheries Act). The act created a fishery conservation zone extending out to 370.6 kilometers (200 nautical miles), in which the United States would exercise rights over all fishery resources. Other nations followed suit, but extended ownership of marine resources did not result in more sustainable management. Between 1980 and 1989, catch totals rose more slowly, and then in 1990, the global fish harvest declined for the first time ever, and the United Nations Food and Agriculture Organization (FAO) announced that increased fishing efforts would not yield higher landings in most traditional fisheries.

Total fishery production did increase in the 1990s, including 122 million tonnes (134.2 million tons) in 1997, 117 million tonnes (128.7 million tons) in 1998, and 125 million tonnes (137.5 million tons) in 1999; however, aquaculture accounted for 29 million, 31 million, and 33 million tonnes (31.9, 34.1, and 36.3 million tons) of production for those years, respectively. Therefore, wild harvest rates, which had increased since the end of World War II, leveled off in the 1990s. More important, stock conditions worsened in the 1990s. The FAO found that an estimated 50 percent of all stocks were fully exploited, or near their limit, with no scope for further expansion. Approximately 15 percent were overfished, meaning that unless more restrictive measures are taken, there is a likelihood that catches may decrease. About 7 percent were depleted, resulting in a loss of total production (or the closure of those fisheries), and 2 percent were improving slowly. Only 25 percent of the once perceived "inexhaustible" resource was projected to produce higher yields, and this included mostly small pelagic stocks. The report added that the proportion of stocks that had been exploited beyond their maximum sustainable yield increased in the past 25 years. The crash in fish stocks was evidenced in several fisheries around the world in the 1990s, most noticeably with the closure of the Grand Banks groundfish fishery, the depletion of wild salmon stocks in the Pacific Northwest, and the lowered catches of large pelagic species such as swordfish and bluefin tuna. Subject to a variety of political, social, and economic pressures, these and other fisheries succumbed to unsustainable harvest levels, to the detriment of both the natural resource and the humans involved.

Moreover, as the twentieth century progressed, factors other than overfishing led to declines in fisheries. Unsustainable activities such as dynamite and cyanide fishing destroyed essential fish habitats, sedimentation from logging and other deforestation practices smothered nearshore areas, pollutants altered major estuarine environments that serve as juvenile and larval grounds for many commercially important species, and dams and other human constructions decreased or altered natural flows on which many anadromous and catadromous species depend. Yet other poorly understood changes, either natural phenomena such as ENSO or anthropogenic inputs resulting in global warming and sea-level rise, may lead to decadal or entire regime shifts in species. Unless these and other problems facing fisheries are viewed as more than an over-exploitation issue, other nonfishery factors will result in equally destructive effects on fishery resources and, eventually, on the human component.

Manoj Shivlani

FURTHER READING

Anderson, L. G. *The Economics of Fisheries Management.* Baltimore: Johns Hopkins University Press, 1986.

Casey, J. M., and R. A. Myers. "Near Extinction of a Large, Widely Distributed Fish." *Science*, Vol. 281, No. 5377, pp. 690–692.

Doeringer, P. B., and D. G. Terkla. *Troubled Waters: Economic Structure, Regulatory Reform, and Fisheries Trade.* Toronto: University of Toronto Press, 1995.

Gulland, J. A., ed. *Fish Population Dynamics: The Implications for Management,* 2nd ed. New York: Wiley, 1988.

Gunderson, D. R. *Surveys of Fisheries Resources.* New York: Wiley, 1993.

Hardin, G. "The Tragedy of the Commons." *Science*, Vol. 162, No. 3859 (1968), pp. 1243–1248.

Hilborn, R., and C. J. Walters. *Quantitative Fisheries Stock Assessment: Choice, Dynamics, and Uncertainty.* New York: Chapman and Hall, 1992.

H. John Heinz III Center for Science, Economics, and the Environment. *Fishing Grounds: Defining a New Era for American Fisheries Management.* Washington, D.C.: Island Press, 2000.

Iudicello, S., M. Weber, and R. Wieland. *Fish, Markets and Fishermen: The Economics of Overfishing.* Washington, D.C.: Island Press, 1999.

National Marine Fisheries Service. *Our Living Oceans. Report on the Status of U.S. Living Marine Resources, 1999.* U.S. Department of Commerce, NOAA Technical Memorandum NMFS-F/SPO-41. Washington, D.C.: 1999.

O'Bannon, B. K. *Fisheries of the United States, 2000.* Silver Spring, Md.: NMFS/NOAA, 2001.

Ross, M. R. *Fisheries Conservation and Management.* Upper Saddle River, N.J.: Prentice Hall, 1997.

Tait, R. V., and F. A. Dipper. *Principles of Marine Ecology,* 4th ed. Woburn, Mass.: Butterworth-Heinemann, 1998.

Tietenberg, T. H. *Environmental and Natural Resource Economics,* 5th ed. Reading, Mass.: Addison-Wesley, 2000.

United Nations Food and Agricultural Organization, Marine Resources Service, Fishery Resources Division. *Review of the State of World Fishery Resources: Marine Fisheries.* Fisheries Circular 920. Rome: FAO, 1997.

USEFUL WEB SITES

National Marine Fisheries Service home page. <http://www.nmfs.noaa.gov>.

Seaweb home page. <http://www.seaweb.org>.

United Nations Food and Agricultural Organization. *The State of World Fisheries and Aquaculture, 2000.* <http://www.fao.org/DOCREP/003/X8002E/X8002E00.htm>.

RELATED ARTICLES

Anchoveta; Bycatch; Cetacea; Clupeomorpha; Crustacea; Drift Net; El Niño; Krill; Mariculture; Marine Mammal Protection Act; Mollusca; Pelagic; Purse Seine; Trawl; Upwelling

Fish Propulsion

Being 800 times denser than air, water presents fishes with several problems—high viscosity, hydrostatic pressure, friction, and pressure drag—that produce turbulence around the body and eddies in its wake. To overcome these obstacles to efficient swimming and to cope with their own density, fishes have evolved hydrodynamic spindle-shaped bodies and devised various means to achieve relative weightlessness. As a result, they expend less energy on maintaining propulsion through the water. Most teleosts (bony ray-finned fishes) have swim bladders to help them maintain buoyancy; sharks are denser than water but use their fat-filled liver partly to offset the weight of their musculature and cartilage to approach neutral buoyancy.

Body Shape

A typical "fish" swims in a sinuous S-shaped (carangiform) motion with a torpedo-shaped (fusiform) body containing paired side (pectoral and pelvic) fins, fins on the back and underside (dorsal and anal), and a vertical (caudal) tail. A fish's elongate, undulating body can be pressed against the relatively solid medium of water to provide forward movement by a sculling motion. The oscillation of tail fin and body surfaces across the line of motion exerts backward thrust, which propels the fish forward.

Shapes have been selected that give fishes the least possible drag at any given speed. Speeds vary depending on size and muscle power, and swimming muscles comprise 40 to 65 percent of body weight. From tiny larval fishes to the 12-meter (about 39-foot) whale sharks, these fishes operate over a very wide Reynolds number (Re), a dimensionless ratio relating momentum (inertia) and viscosity used to describe the motion of an object in water that is either turbulent or laminar. Inertial forces must be larger than the viscous forces of the surrounding water in order for a fish to initiate or maintain movement. Most trout- or herring-sized fishes cruise at around two body lengths per second. In cross section, fish are usually rounded or ovoid with V- or more advanced W- shaped musculature, supported by numerous small bones, which contract against a strong backbone. Some are equipped with red muscle for prolonged swimming and "fast" white muscle for burst swimming, turns of speed, and feats such as jumping and darting.

The shapes are strongly determined by the mode of locomotion in the fluid environment. Fast-swimming fishes, tuna, mackerel, moonfish, and sharks such as oceanic whitetips and makos have a hydrodynamic bullet-shaped body. When traveling at high speeds, their body stiffens and ceases to undulate, and the powerful muscles contained in a firm skin pull on a sickle-shaped tail to provide thrusting oscillations. Long, slender eel-like (anguilliform) fishes have sacrificed fins for an undulatory snakelike motion with side-to-side contractions. Rays (such as *Manta* and *Mobula*) propel themselves with the aid of enlarged pectoral fins. The sea horse, *Hippocampus*, also uses its pectoral fins to help it glide through the water. Long-distance ocean goers, oarfish, ribbonfish, and frilled sharks are long and thin with sail-like fins. Slow-moving plankton eaters (e.g., whale, basking, and megamouth sharks) are all relatively rounded, with large tails. Fish flattened top to bottom (e.g., halibut or whale sharks) or side to side (e.g., angelfish or sunfish) and boxlike pufferfish are much less streamlined and are therefore not well equipped for efficient and prolonged locomotion. Ostracoform swimming produced by sculling action of the tail and simple alternate contraction of muscle blocks allows a fairly rigid-bodied fish such as a pufferfish to move in a series of arcs through the water.

Tail Shape

The tail is the main source of propulsion in most fishes, with fixed hydrofoil (most sharks) or more flexible fins providing maneuverability. Fish have experimented with different tails over the millennia. Early fishes, which often had no paired fins, sported a downturned vertebral column and a long lower lobe. Lateral movement of this *hypocercal tail* depresses it and effects raising of the head. Other fishes, including most sharks, had the opposite *heterocercal tail*. Most teleosts retain an internally upturned vertebral column within an expanding symmetrical (*homocercal*) tail fin. Extremes are seen where all singular fins and the tail join together or the tail is reduced to a whip or grasping device.

Strong tail musculature alone is enough to provide efficient propulsion in many fishes; others, like Scarids, use mainly pectoral fins. The semicircular lunate (*crescentic*) tail plays a significant role for all fast-swimming fish. The rare lobed-fin coelacanth, *Latimeria*, has an unusual rounded tail with an extra midlobe, the gentle undulations of which some think help it maintain close swimming formation when sleeping in caves.

Fins and Fin Spines

The possession of fins typifies "fishes." Only rarely, as in some pipefishes, do they seem completely absent. Fins form cutwaters and hydrofoils to prevent pitching and yawing as well as to increase hydrodynamic stability. Undulating pectoral fins can produce lift as in *Manta* rays, which can beat their "wings," then use the large mobile surfaces like gliders to conserve energy. Many bottom-living fishes move either by undulating horizontally or vertically or by beating the pectoral fins. Some fish even walk on "limbs" (e.g., climbing perch, Tasmanian handfish), usually modifications of the rays (*lepidotrichia*) of the pectoral fins.

Classical ideas about sharks using pectoral fins to generate lift that balances the moment produced by the oscillating tail are not true for all fishes. Leopard shark pectoral fins initiate maneuvering but provide little lift in horizontal swimming.

Squamation

Most fish have scales as an external shinglelike covering (squamation) over the body and embedded in the skin to help reduce friction. Bony fishes have lightened their scales over time, teleosts now having thin, rounded, growing scales of bone. *Ruvettus* (castor oil fish) and others have ctenoid (comblike) scales with high, sharply pointed spines that act as vortex generators to stabilize the boundary layer.

Sharks are renowned for their ability to move fast. In recent years it was discovered that their tiny skin (placoid) scales, which form just like our teeth, also contribute to propulsion. Their scales grow along vector fields on the outer surface of the skin, influencing movement of water over the body and adding to efficient laminar flow at the boundary layer (i.e., helping maintain a better Reynolds number). Slower-moving plankton-eating sharks have widespread large-hooked denticles, whereas fast-swimming great white, hammerhead, and mako sharks have overlapping microscopic flattened scales with complex patterns of microsculpture that help reduce drag. This attribute has inspired the design of Airbus cladding and has recently been applied to the astonishing "shark skin" suits of Olympic swimmers.

Susan Turner

FURTHER READING
Alexander, R. McNeil. *Functional Design in Fishes.* London: Hutchinson, 1967; 3rd ed., 1974.
Blake, R. W. *Fish Locomotion.* Cambridge and New York: Cambridge University Press, 1983.
Bone, Quentin, and N. B. Marshall. *Biology of Fishes.* Glasgow, Scotland: Blackie, 1982; 2nd ed., with J. H. S. Baxter, London and New York: Chapman and Hall, 1995.
Reif, Wolf-Ernst. *Squamation and Ecology of Sharks.* Courier Forschungsinstitut Senckenberg 78. Frankfurt, Germany: Senckenbergische Naturforschende Gesellschaft, 1985.

RELATED ARTICLES
Coelacanth; Fins; Form Resistance; Shark; Swim Bladder

Fjord

A fjord, or fiord, is one category of estuary that serves as a transition zone between fresh- and saltwater aquatic ecosystems. A fjord is a narrow, deep, steep-sided, U-shaped inlet or waterway that was formed either by the submergence of a rocky or mountainous coast or by the sea entering a deeply carved glacial trough after a glacier has melted.

Fjords generally result from the movement of glaciers through valleys that had previously been cut by streams. Fjords have sheer, parallel walls, which often branch and extend a great distance below the surface of the water. Typically, fjords are shallow near their mouth, with a sill of rock and/or gravel (often a moraine) near the entrance, but several hundred meters deep and farther inland. The shallow sill at the mouth of a fjord greatly restricts water exchange between the fjord and the sea; thus, fresh water remains at the surface, overlying more saline waters. Because mixing is generally limited to surface layers due to restricted tidal forcing, wind stress, and wave motion, deeper water is often stagnant due to lack of circulation. Organic matter is typically supplied to fjords via rivers and products of photosynthesis that have seasonal and spatial patterns of productivity (e.g., phytoplankton). After nutrients enter the water column by means of these routes, they eventually settle on the sediment layer. Due to restricted circulation in the water column, oxygen is quickly depleted in the sediment layer.

Fjords are common in both hemispheres where there has been glacial activity and are exceptionally spectacular on subduction-related coasts (coasts on the leading edges of convergent plate margins). Fjords are characteristic of the coastlines of Chile, Norway, Scotland, Greenland, British Columbia, Antarctica, southern New Zealand, and Alaska. Sognafjord, one of the most notably grandiose and picturesque fjords, is located off the coast of Norway and is 1220 meters (3950 feet) deep and over 160 kilometers (100 miles) long.

Anne Beesley

FURTHER READING
Burchett, Michael, Marc Dando, and Geoffrey Waller. *Sealife: A Complete Guide to the Marine Environment.* Washington, D.C.: Smithsonian Institution Press, 1996.
Day, J. W., C. A. Hall, W. M. Kemp, and Alejandro Yanez-Arancibia. *Estuarine Ecology.* New York: Wiley, 1989.
Ingmanson, D. E., and William J. Wallace. *Oceanography: An Introduction.* Belmont, Calif.: Wadsworth, 1973; 5th ed., 1995.
Nybakken, James W. *Marine Biology: An Ecological Approach,* 5th ed. San Francisco: Benjamin Cummings, 2001.

RELATED ARTICLES
Anoxic Basin; Estuarine Circulation; Estuary

Flagellate

The flagellates (subphylum Mastigophora) are a diverse group of single-celled organisms that possess, at some stage in their life cycle, a hairlike structure called a *flagellum*, which is used for movement. Flagellates are extremely common members of the marine plankton and therefore comprise an important part of the ocean food chain.

There are about 8500 recognized species of flagellates, and these can be divided into two groups: phytoflagellates and zooflagellates. *Phytoflagellates* obtain food as plants do, using sunlight to build energy-rich carbohydrate molecules by photosynthesis. Like plants, they contain green photosynthetic structures called *chloroplasts*. As a result, botanists sometimes describe phytoflagellates as algae, although zoologists often disagree with this classification. *Zooflagellates* obtain food as animals do: by ingesting other organisms or particles of organic matter. However, unlike animals, zooflagellates do not have mouths or digestive systems. They take food particles into tiny bubbles (*vacuoles*) inside the cell, and then secrete digestive juices into the bubbles to break the food down. The resulting soup of nutrients is absorbed by the cell and the undigested residue is expelled back into the sea. Some flagellates, such as the euglenids, can both photosynthesize and take in food particles, blurring the distinction between the phytoflagellates and the zooflagellates.

Flagellates range in size from 0.005 to 2 millimeters (0.0002 to 0.08 inch), but the vast majority are microscopic and invisible to the naked eye. As well as possessing one or more flagella, flagellates often have a stiff outer jacket called a *pellicle*, which gives the cell a definite shape. Some types of flagellates, such as dinoflagellates, have an armored surface bearing long spikes that makes it difficult for other microorganisms to eat them. Dinoflagellates are among the most common of the marine phytoplankton and are largely responsible for the faint glow of bioluminescence seen in breaking waves at night. They occasionally build up in huge numbers, causing toxic red tides that kill fish and other animals.

The hairlike flagella of the flagellates are similar to the tails of sperm cells, but they produce movement in a surprising variety of ways. Some species swim like sperm, propelled by waves of movement passing along the flagellum from the base to the tip. Others swim backward, pulled by waves of movement passing from the tip of the flagellum to the base. In yet other species the flagellum swings from side to side, rowing the cell through the water; or it flicks backward with a complex looping action; or whirls around in a helical pattern; or its tip may spin around like a tiny propeller. Flagellates can move up to 1.2 centimeters (0.5 inch) per second, much faster than the single-celled organism amoeba, which moves by changing the shape of its cell.

The extraordinary diversity and abundance of flagellates make them likely candidates for the origin of multicelled plants and animals. Indeed, one group of zooflagellates—the choanoflagellida–shows striking similarities to the cells of sponges, suggesting that sponges evolved from choanoflagellid cells that became colonial.

As well as being common in the oceans, flagellates abound in freshwater habitats and many are parasites of animals, including humans. One parasitic species causes the unpleasant disease giardia, characterized by chronic diarrhea. Another species, transmitted by the bite of the tsetse fly, causes the deadly disease African trypanosomiasis or sleeping sickness. Some flagellates live not as parasites but as symbionts. For example, termites are able to eat wood because of a symbiotic flagellate that lives in their intestines.

Ben Morgan

FURTHER READING

Brusca, Richard C., and Gary J. Brusca. *Invertebrates.* Sunderland, Mass.: Sinauer, 1990.

Margulis, Lynn. *Five Kingdoms: An Illustrated Guide to the Phyla of Life on Earth.* San Francisco: W. H. Freeman, 1982; 3rd ed., New York, 1998.

Pechenik, Jan A. *Biology of the Invertebrates.* Boston: Prindle, Weber and Schmidt, 1985; 4th ed., Boston: McGraw-Hill, 2000.

Postlethwait, John. *The Nature of Life.* New York: McGraw-Hill, 1989; 3rd ed., 1995.

Purves, William, et al. *Life: The Science of Biology.* Sunderland, Mass.: Sinauer/Boston: Grant Press, 1983; 5th ed., Sunderland, Mass.: Sinauer, 1998.

RELATED ARTICLES

Dinoflagellate; Phytoplankton; Sarcomastigophora; Zooplankton

FLIP

FLIP is an acronym for *floating instrument platform,* a unique 108-meter (355-foot)-long platform used for oceanographic research. The acronym also describes the platform's ability to flip from the horizontal to the vertical position when on station, thereby creating a stable platform from which a variety of oceanographic measurements can be made; FLIP is the only research platform in the world with this ability. FLIP is nonpropelled and must be towed to the research site in the horizontal position. Once on station, FLIP is flipped to the stable vertical position by flooding the ballast tanks with seawater, leaving 17 meters (55 feet) of the platform above water. Researchers then can deploy equipment such as vertical arrays of oceanographic or acoustic sensors and make measurements via instruments attached to the hull. FLIP can drift freely or can be moored, depending on the research being conducted, and it can operate in shallow or deep water. Since it was launched in 1962, FLIP has been used by the U.S. Navy and other organizations to support a host of research projects; scientific uses include studies of acoustics (such as ambient noise and sound propagation), geophysics, internal waves, laser communication, meteorology, ocean–atmosphere interactions, and ocean waves.

FLIP is owned by the U.S. Navy and is operated by the Marine Physical Laboratory of the Scripps Institution of Oceanography (SIO) in San Diego, California. FLIP's home port is the SIO Nimitz Marine Facility in San Diego. The platform is most often used in the eastern Pacific, but it has been used for projects in the Gulf of Alaska and in the Caribbean. At full capacity, FLIP carries five crew members and 11 scientists; it can operate for 30 days without replenishment.

Lynn L. Lauerman

FURTHER READING

Bronson, Earl D., and Larry R. Glosten. *FLIP: Floating Instrument Platform.* San Diego, Calif.: Marine Physical Laboratory of the Scripps Institution of Oceanography, 1985.

Edson, James B. "Improving Weather Forecasts with Better Marine Measurements." *Oceanus,* Vol. 39, No. 1 (Spring/Summer 1996).

USEFUL WEBSITES

Marine Physical Laboratory of the Scripps Institution of Oceanography, University of California, San Diego, Calif.: <http://www.mpl.ucsd.edu>.

RELATED ARTICLES

Oceanographic Research Vessel

Flipper

Marine mammals and sea turtles have their four limbs modified into flippers, which are flattened structures similar to the pectoral fins in fish. Penguins, though, have their wings modified as flippers. Cetaceans (whales, dolphins, and porpoises), seals, sea lions, turtles, and walruses all use flippers for various locomotive functions. Flippers of all marine mammals and turtles have bones similar to the bones found in human hands, wrists, and fingers. The flippers function as rudders, allowing the animals to avoid obstacles, to make turns, and to steer. Walruses, seals, sea lions, and turtles use their front and hind flippers to propel themselves forward.

True seals propel themselves through the water by means of the hind flippers. Hind flippers of true seals cannot be rotated to support their weight on land and are dragged behind them. Fur seals and sea lions use their powerful front flippers to propel them through the ocean. With their long, thin front flippers, they are extremely maneuverable. Unlike the true seals, they can walk on land with their hind flippers by rotating them forward.

Flippers can also function in temperature regulation in marine mammals. To maintain flexibility, flippers cannot be insulated heavily with blubber or other fat deposits. Because they are not as insulated as other body areas, they are susceptible to heat loss. The mechanism known as *countercurrent heat exchange* enables the animals to prevent heat loss and also functions to regulate body temperature. Arteries and veins are located next to each other in the body, and as the arterial blood travels away from the heart, it transfers heat to the cooler venous blood moving toward the heart. When the arterial blood reaches the flippers, it differs by only a few degrees from the environmental temperature, and conversely, the venous blood is warmed by the time it reaches the warm core of the animal. Seals also use flippers to keep cool as they lay on hot rocks, by extending them into the air.

Erin O'Donnell

FURTHER READING
Cousteau, Jacques. *The Ocean World.* New York: Abrams, 1979.
Duxbury, Alison B., and Alyn C. Duxbury. *Fundamentals of Oceanography.* Dubuque, Iowa: Brown, 1993; 2nd ed., 1996.
Nybakken, James W. *Marine Biology: An Ecological Approach,* 5th ed. San Francisco: Benjamin Cummings, 2001.
Orr, Robert T. *Vertebrate Biology.* Philadelphia: Saunders, 1961; 5th ed., 1982.

RELATED ARTICLES
Endothermic; Pinnipedia

Florida Bay

Part of the Everglades system, Florida Bay is a shallow, lagoonal estuary bordered on the north by the Florida peninsula, the south and east by the Florida Keys, and on the west by the Gulf of Mexico. The bay, which developed into its present-day form 2000 years ago following the last deglaciation period, extends almost 2200 square kilometers (850 square miles) in total area but has an average depth of only 1 meter (3.3 feet). Actually, the geologic processes that formed much of the present bay began as early as 125,000 years ago (in the Pleistocene Epoch). During that period of time, deglaciation led to sea-level rise, flooding the bay and supporting large populations of bryozoans and calcareous worms. When glaciation recurred about 28,000 years ago, Florida Bay was exposed, first into a swamp and then into dry land. Then, between 15,000 and 11,000 years ago, another intense deglaciation period occurred, resulting in water covering the bay again. By 2000 years ago, the estuary was almost completely formed, with increases in sea level occurring until the present time.

The bay is fed by the Everglades system sheet flow, which results in fresh water entering the bay from the many prairies and creeks in the lower Everglades. Florida Bay is generally divided into two main environments: the upper bay, which is more subject to freshwater conditions; and the lower bay, which is characterized by tidal (or ocean) regimes. These environments are further divided into four subenvironments: northern, interior, Atlantic, and Gulf. The northern subenvironment is subject to freshwater runoff and is located near the mangrove fringe. The interior subenvironment is characterized by restrictive, shallow mudbanks that result in limited circulation and wide ranges of salinity. The Atlantic and Gulf subenvironments are both well-circulated oceanic areas that experience marine salinity conditions.

The primary vegetation in Florida Bay is seagrass, which covered more than 80 percent of the bottom until the seagrass die-offs that began in 1987. Mangrove fringes and small islands cover less than 2 percent of the bay. Hard-bottom areas, characterized by calcium carbonate, are most common in the southern portions of the bay and contain sponges, octocorals, and macroalgae. Due to the variety of habitats and salinity conditions, Florida Bay serves as an ideal nursery and juvenile ground for a variety of marine species, including at least 22 species of commercially and recreationally harvested fishes and invertebrates (such as pink shrimp, spiny lobster, and stone crab). The bay also supports an important recreational guide fishery (bonefish, pompano, and snook), as well as commercial fishing activities. Finally, Florida Bay also serves as a home for many bird and endangered marine species, such as the American crocodile and Florida manatee.

Since the 1987 seagrass die-offs, Florida Bay has suffered several massive phytoplankton blooms, which in turn have increased nutrient levels while reducing oxygen concentrations. These blooms have led to the decline of the bay, including losses in seagrass habitat, sponge mortality, and declines in economically important species and birds. Although there is disagreement over the causes of these problems, scientists and managers generally agree that the system must be restored to its natural conditions. An estimated 69 to 90 percent of all fresh water that used to enter the Everglades has been diverted via 1400 miles of canals (mostly to drain the Everglades to allow for urban development in flood zones) into the Atlantic Ocean and the Gulf of Mexico. Water that now enters the bay is not necessarily timed or distributed in a natural fashion, and there are additional concerns over the quality of that water (especially due to upland agricultural inputs). Since the 1990s, various government agencies have begun the task of restoring the bay and the Everglades in joint initiatives, including the Governor's Commission for a Sustainable South Florida and the South Florida Ecosystem Restoration Task Force.

Manoj Shivlani

FURTHER READING

Cantillo, A. Y., L. Pikula, J. Beattie, E. Collins, K. Hale, and T. Schmidt. "Natural and Anthropogenic Events Impacting Florida Bay, 1910–1994: A Time Line." *NOAA Technical Memorandum* 90. Silver Spring, Md.: Ocean Resources Conservation and Assessment/National Ocean Service/National Oceanic and Atmospheric Administration, 1995.

Chiappone, M. *Site Characterization for the Florida Keys National Marine Sanctuary and Environs,* Vol. 1, *Geology and Paleontology of the Florida Keys and Florida Bay.* Zenda, Wis.: The Preserver, 1996.

Chiappone, M. *Site Characterization for the Florida Keys National Marine Sanctuary and Environs,* Vol. 4, *Marine Benthic Communities of the Florida Keys.* Zenda, Wis.: The Preserver, 1996.

McIvor, C. C., J. A. Ley, and R. D. Bjork. "Changes in Freshwater Inflow from the Everglades to Florida Bay Including Effects on Biota and Biotic Processes: A Review." In S. M. Davis and J. C. Ogden, eds., *Everglades: The Ecosystem and Its Restoration.* Delray Beach, Fla.: St. Lucie Press, 1994.

Tilmant, J. T. "A History and an Overview of Recent Trends in the Fisheries of Florida Bay." *Bulletin of Marine Science,* Vol. 44 (1989), pp. 3–22.

RELATED ARTICLES
Estuary; Gulf of Mexico; Lagoon

Florida Escarpment

The Florida Escarpment is located along the west coast of Florida and separates the Gulf of Mexico from the Florida Platform. This is the transition from the continental slope to the deep water of the Gulf of Mexico.

The escarpment is about 1.6 kilometers (1 mile) high and separates the Florida Platform carbonate from the basin. This structure is extremely steep compared with the very gentle nature of most continental slopes. Buried strata of the Florida Platform crop out at the base of the Florida Escarpment and indicate that the platform has subsided about 2 kilometers (1.2 miles) since about 130 to 110 million years ago in the Early Cretaceous. The ocean floor in front of the escarpment is composed of skeletal limestone that forms a gently sloping ramp to the escarpment. Dome structures are associated with the Florida Escarpment. Many of these are Early Cretaceous reef structures that nearly encircle the gulf.

A hypersaline seep exists near the base of the Florida Escarpment. Located at a depth in excess of 3000 meters (9850 feet), the salinity value is 46.2 practical salinity units (psu), although the temperature is normal. Some scientists have suggested that the source of these hypersaline waters is from salt diapirs in the area. These hypersaline waters seep through the fractured limestone of the Florida Platform at the base of the escarpment. The limestone is dissolved by the hypersaline water and allows the overlying material to collapse. Eroded material does not accumulate at the base of the escarpment and is apparently carried away by the strong currents that keep the base of the escarpment clear. Highly adapted biocommunities have developed at this seep and derive their energy through chemosynthesis.

David L. White

FURTHER READING

Rezak, Richard, and Vernon J. Henry. *Contributions on the Geological and Geophysical Oceanography of the Gulf of Mexico.* Houston, Texas: Gulf Publishing, 1972.

Thurman, Harold V. *Essentials of Oceanography.* Columbus, Ohio: Charles E. Merrill, 1983; 6th ed., with Alan P. Trujillo, Upper Saddle River, N.J.: Prentice Hall, 1999.

RELATED ARTICLES
Chemosynthesis; Diapir; Salinity

Flushing Time

Flushing time, sometimes called *residence time,* provides a measure of how long it takes to replace one volume of water with another. It can be estimated by taking the total volume of water in question and dividing it by the rate of flow into that volume. If Q represents the total volume and the inflow rate is represented by R, the flushing time T is given by the equation $T = Q/R$. For a total volume given in cubic meters and an inflow rate given in cubic meters per hour, the flushing time would be given in hours. In applying this formula it is assumed that the total volume remains fixed and so the same amount of water that flows into the volume must flow out. Although the concept is rather simple, problems often arise in trying to estimate the volume, the rate of inflow, or both. This replacement time can be estimated for oceanic waters that reside within a given ocean basin, for example, or for bays, rivers, and estuaries.

Flushing times are important because they provide an indication of how long it takes for a given body of water to rid or cleanse itself of pollutants that may have been released into it. The residence time of water in the major ocean basins is an important quantity that oceanographers have tried to determine since the beginning of the twentieth century and during the 1990s in the World Ocean Experiment. The flushing time for the Atlantic Ocean is roughly 500 to 700 years, whereas the flushing time for the Pacific Ocean is somewhat less than 1000 years. For the Mediterranean Sea, the flushing time is roughly 70 years, due to its restricted access to the Atlantic Ocean and the vigorous sinking of dense salty water caused by a high rate of evaporation. For Monterey Bay, the flushing time is somewhere between 5 and 12 days, due to its broad exposure to, and direct contact with, the open sea. For the Bay of Fundy in the northern Gulf of Maine, the flushing time is approximately 76 days.

Laurence C. Breaker

FURTHER READING
Knauss, John A. *Introduction to Physical Oceanography.* Englewood Cliffs, N.J.: Prentice Hall, 1978.
Officer, Charles B. *Physical Oceanography of Estuaries (and Associated Coastal Waters).* New York: Wiley, 1976.

RELATED ARTICLES
Residence Time

Food Chain

A food chain is an ecological concept used to describe the linkages between organisms at different (usually increasingly) trophic, or energy, levels. The chain begins at the producer level and progresses through several consumer levels, and the total number of levels (or links) determines the complexity of the food chain. A food web is the combination of all food chains in a particular community or ecosystem. The study of food chains and webs is called *trophodynamics*; it examines the relationships and factors that affect energy transfer between trophic levels.

Food Chain Components

Producers, or autotrophs, are organisms that derive energy from an outside source, usually the Sun but occasionally from reduced chemical compounds. The most common types of producers are photosynthesizing plants, bacteria, and algae, which use special pigments to trap the energy in sunlight. Other producers, such as some bacteria, capture chemical energy in a process known as *chemosynthesis*. All producers provide the basis of their respective food chains, and they use inorganic elements such as nitrogen,

carbon, and phosphorus to form energy-rich organic components. The energy that is stored in the organic compounds serves as a source of energy for the producers themselves and for the subsequent levels of organisms in the food chain. Organisms in all subsequent levels, beyond the producer level, are known collectively as *consumers*, or *heterotrophs*. They are differentiated into the level, or order, to which they belong. For instance, consumers that feed directly on producers are called *first-order* (or *primary) consumers*. First-order consumers are also known as *herbivores*, since they feed on plants and/or algae. Second-order consumers feed on first-order consumers, and they are more commonly known as *carnivores*. Third-order consumers, also carnivores, feed on all types of carnivores. The food chain stratification is not rigid, however, as certain organisms can occupy several orders. Omnivores are animals that feed on all types of organisms, including producers. Other consumers change their order during their life history stages (such as certain fish and crustacean larvae that start out as first- or second-order consumers and then mature into higher-order predators). Two consumers that do not fit into the linear food chain scheme are detritivores and decomposers. Both are essentially consumers, but they do not occupy any of the aforementioned orders. Detritivores, also known as scavengers, feed on dead or decomposing organic material, and decomposers break down organic matter. Both play an essential role in the recycling of nutrients necessary to drive the food chain.

As organisms are arranged in various trophic levels throughout the food chain, energy captured and stored by producers is transferred to primary-order consumers (herbivores and omnivores) that graze on the producers, then to second-order consumers, and so on. However, as energy is passed from level to level, most of it is lost via heat and metabolic use. The amount lost ranges from 80 to 90 percent, and the loss is lowest during transfer from producers to first-order consumers; thus, only 1/10 to 1/20 of the energy is passed from one level to the next. For instance, within a food chain with six links, an original kilogram of producer biomass equals only 0.00001 kilogram (0.00002 pound) of a fifth-level consumer biomass. Such energy relationships demonstrate why producers and lower-order consumers are more abundant in food chains than higher-order, or apex, carnivores. Graphs called *trophic pyramids* are used to show the vertical (or higher-order) diminution of energy and biomass in food chains.

Terrestrial ecosystems generally have three links in their food chains, from a producer to a first-order consumer to a second-order consumer, as when an antelope eats grass and a lion eats the antelope. Marine ecosystems, however, are more complex, containing an average of five links. Also, unlike terrestrial food chains, marine food chains are often less linear. Several marine organisms, particularly filter feeders, feed on both autotrophic and heterotrophic organisms. The description below of several ocean food chains illustrates the diversity in feeding strategies and strata in the marine environment.

Examples of Marine Food Chains

Among the simplest oceanic food chains are those encountered in the oceans' most productive regions, upwelling areas. The chains generally consist of three levels: one producer level and two consumer levels. Phytoplankton serve as the producers, and they serve as prey for consumers such as planktivorous fish and zooplankton. Piscivorous fish and baleen whales, which are secondary consumers, feed on the smaller fish and zooplankton. Certain upwelling areas, such as the highly productive Antarctic Ocean, support tertiary and quarternary consumers. Tertiary consumers include birds and small-toothed whales that feed on piscivorous fish.

Finally, quarternary consumers consist of larger-toothed whales and pinnipeds that feed on both secondary and tertiary consumers.

Another productive region, the continental shelf, has food chains that consist generally of four levels. Within the benthic subdivision, phytoplankton (producers) are fed upon by benthic grazers or herbivores, which are then eaten by benthic, second-order consumers, and piscivorous fish (third-order consumers) feed on the benthic carnivores. In the pelagic subdivision, zooplankton graze on the phytoplankton. Zooplanktivorous fish, second-order consumers, feed on the zooplankton. Finally, piscivorous fish as in the benthic subdivision feed on the second-order, zooplanktivorous fish.

Open ocean food chains are among the most complex food chains, containing five or more levels. Also, open oceans (and other oligotrophic systems) include a parallel, coupled microbial food chain, called the *microbial loop*, that has been better understood in recent decades. Within the classical food chain, the order of ingestion is from microplankton to mesoplankton to macroplankton. Planktivorous fish feed on macroplankton, and piscivorous fish and squid feed on the planktivorous fish. The microbial loop begins at the bacterial level, where heterotrophic bacteria feed by absorbing dissolved organic carbon, and autotrophic bacteria serve as primary producers. These bacteria (and other photosynthetic picoplankton and nanoplankton) are eaten by micrograzers, including nanoplankton such as ciliates and flagellates. The loop is completed when these grazers (and the other components of the microbial loop) die and are recycled; however, the loop is also coupled with the classical food chain. This is accomplished via net zooplankton that ingest the micrograzers.

Threats to Marine Food Chains

The two major threats facing marine food chains today are overfishing and pollution.

Overfishing has developed into a more serious problem as the fishing sector has scaled up its effort and updated its technology in finding and capturing fish. As higher-order consumer fish have been exhausted, such as tuna and whales, the commercial industry has begun targeting lower-order species. The effects of removing a link within the food chain can be disastrous, especially in ecosystems where there is no substitute species at that link (or order). Governments specifically recognized the risk of overfishing in the Antarctic ecosystem, where factory ships began harvesting krill in the 1970s; in 1982, the Convention for the Conservation of Antarctic Marine Living Resources (CCAMLR) entered into force, creating a management and regulatory structure for the krill and fishery resources of the region. Krill is an integral part of the Antarctic food chain, feeding on producers and serving as prey for secondary consumers such as baleen whales and planktivorous fish and invertebrates. Larger seabirds and marine mammals all rely on species that feed on krill.

Pollution also presents a major threat to marine food chains. Many classes of chemical pollutants result in widespread mortalities throughout the food chain. Other chemical pollutants have a more insidious effect, known as *biomagnification*. Biomagnification occurs with an increase in the concentration of a pollutant from one link in a food chain to another, although it may be present in much lower quantities in the environment. Among the best examples of biomagnification is the case of DDT (dichlorodiphenyltrichloroethane), a chlorinated hydrocarbon formerly used as a pesticide in the United States. A producer may absorb DDT, and as the producer is eaten, it passes the DDT over to the primary consumer. However, DDT is not metabolized by the consumer; it is long-lived, and it is biologically active. Therefore, it builds up in the tissues of subsequent consumers as it moves up the food chain. By the time DDT reaches higher-order consumers, it can attain concentrations about 10 million times that of the ambient environment. This is what occurred within several bird species, especially raptors, which suffered from DDT biomagnification in the 1950s and 1960s. As higher-order consumers, they accumulated large concentrations of DDT, which they passed on to their offspring. Specifically, the DDT concentrations resulted in fragile eggshells that cracked prior to chick hatchings, leading to catastrophic chick mortality rates. By the early 1960s, Rachel Carson wrote her seminal book, *Silent Spring*, on the effects of DDT on wildlife, leading to the eventual ban of the pesticide in the United States in 1973. Other biomagnifying substances include polyaromatic hydrocarbons (PAHs), polychlorinated biphenyls (PCBs), and heavy metals.

Manoj Shivlani

FURTHER READING

Barnes, R. S. K., and R. N. Hughes. *An Introduction to Marine Ecology.* London and Boston: Blackwell Scientific, 1982; 3rd ed., Oxford and Malden, Mass.: Blackwell Science, 1999.

Carson, Rachel. *Silent Spring.* New York: Houghton Mifflin, 1962.

Loeb, V., V. Siegel, O. Holm-Hansen, R. Hewitt, W. Fraser, W. Trivelpiece, and S. Trivelpiece. "Effects of Sea-Ice Extent and Krill or Salp Dominance on the Antarctic Food Web." *Nature*, Vol. 387 (26 June 1997), pp. 897–900.

Longhurst, Alan R., and Daniel Pauly. *Ecology of Tropical Oceans.* San Diego: Academic Press, 1987.

Post, D. M., M. L. Pace, and N. G. Hairston. "Ecosystem Size Determines Food-Chain Length in Lakes." *Nature*, Vol. 405 (29 June 2000), pp. 1047–1049.

Waller, Geoffrey. *Sealife: A Complete Guide to the Marine Environment.* Washington, D.C.: Smithsonian Institution Press, 1996.

RELATED ARTICLES

Autotrophic; Benthos; Food Web; Heterotrophic; Krill; Phytoplankton; Plankton

Food Web

A food web summarizes all the trophic pathways within a community or ecosystem. It encompasses a hierarchy of trophic levels, starting with the primary producers, which photosynthetically convert carbon dioxide and water into the organic building blocks that are the basis for all other life. A special case in the deep ocean are the bacteria that chemically synthesize organic material using the energy provided by the oxidation of reduced sulfide compounds, but considering the oceans as a whole, chemosynthesis is estimated to contribute less than 0.3 percent to the total quantity of organic material produced. The primary producers are grazed by herbivores or secondary consumers, which in turn are consumed by a series of tertiary consumers. An important but often neglected role is played by the detritivores, which recycle the waste organic material that results from the incomplete consumption and ingestion of food, any deaths of organisms other than by predation, and organic wastes such as fecal pellets that are excreted. In terrestrial ecosystems trophic relationships tend to be better organized because species seldom change their trophic level more than once, if at all. However, in marine ecosystems a species may change trophic level several times; consequently, food webs tend to be very complex. For example, when a fish like a sardine first hatches, it may feed directly on large phytoplankton. At this early stage it may be eaten by planktonic predators such as chaetognaths and ctenophores. As it grows, the larval fish starts to eat zooplankton, small copepods that it hunts visually, and eventually it reaches the stage where it will even eat the same chaetognaths that early in its life cycle it was in danger of falling prey to. Another complexity results from shifts in an animal's diet that may result from changes in the availability of certain prey that occurs either with season or spatially because the environment is patchy.

Ecological Efficiency

If everything an organism consumes were to be converted into new growth and reproductive products, its ecological efficiency would be 100 percent. However, trophic links can never be that efficient. First, not all the organic matter that is consumed is digested. Some organic substances, such as the cellulose of the cell walls of plants, are very resistant to the digestive enzymes of many animals. In addition, when food is plentiful, digestive efficiency often declines; thus a higher proportion of the organic matter consumed may be voided as feces. Some of the energy (or biomass) that is absorbed by the gut is used in keeping the organism's basal metabolism and all its tissues functioning. Some is expended either in foraging for the next meal or in finding a mate. The percentage of the energy or biomass taken up that is eventually converted into new tissue (growth) or used in the production of reproductive products is the ecological efficiency, and this can be as low as 10 percent. Thus the links or food chain within a food web along which energy and organic carbon are flowing are leaky and inefficient. This results in the development of ecological pyramids, in which only about 10 percent of the productivity of the primary producers is converted into herbivore biomass and only about 1 percent into primary carnivores. Thus the maximum potential productivity of a commercial fish like a cod, which occupies a niche at the end of an extended food chain, is far less than that of an anchoveta, which can graze directly on phytoplankton. However, only the organic carbon (and energy) lost through respiration is lost from the ecosystem because all the other losses feed into the detrital branches of the food web.

Microbial Food Web

In many pelagic environments primary production is dominated by picoplankton, tiny plant cells less than 2 micrometers (0.00008 inch) in length. In low-productivity, oligotrophic conditions, these tiny cells may be responsible for over 80 percent of photosynthetic production. They are so small that they cannot be grazed by the majority of suspension feeders that sieve the cells from the water. Instead, they are grazed by ciliate protozoans that are little bigger than the plant they are feeding on and so small that neither they nor their waste products will sink under the influence of gravity. The efficiency of the trophic link between picoplankton and protozoans is unusually high, sometimes exceeding 50 percent. Even so, most of the energy fixed by the picoplankton does not flow into the pelagic food web that supports the production of fish, but is lost through the respiration and metabolism of the protozoans. Moreover, the majority of carbon dioxide fixed by the picoplankton is recycled within the euphotic zone and neither supports life in the deep ocean nor helps to lower carbon dioxide concentrations in the atmosphere.

Martin Angel

FURTHER READING

Alldredge, Alice L., and Mary W. Silver. "Characteristics, Dynamics and Significance of Marine Snow." *Progress in Oceanography,* Vol. 20 (1988), pp. 41–82.

Hopkins, T. L., T. T. Sutton, and T. M. Lancraft. "The Trophic Structure and Predation Impact of a Low Latitude Midwater Fish Assemblage." *Progress in Oceanography,* Vol. 38 (1996), pp. 95–153.

Nybakken, James W. *Marine Biology: An Ecological Approach,* 5th ed. San Francisco: Benjamin Cummings, 2001.

Rowe, Gilbert T., and Vita Pariente, eds. *Deep-Sea Food Chains and the Global Carbon Cycle.* Dordrecht, the Netherlands, and Boston: Kluwer Academic, 1992.

RELATED ARTICLES

Chemosynthesis; Pelagic; Picoplankton; Primary Productivity

Foraminifera

Foraminiferans, or *forams* as they are known informally, are single-celled marine organisms closely related to freshwater amoebas. Unlike the free-flowing amoebas familiar to biology students, foraminiferan cells are enclosed by a protective shell called a *test*. Most species live on the seafloor among sand particles and organic detritus or attached to other organisms. However, some species are planktonic, and these form an important component of the marine zooplankton on which many other organisms depend.

Most foraminiferans are tiny, but some can grow to more than 5 centimeters (2 inches) wide, and fossilized species up to 15 centimeters (6 inches) wide are known. The test is usually multichambered and consists of organic materials reinforced with minerals such as calcium carbonate (chalk) or embedded with sand grains. Tiny pores in the test of most species allow extensions of the cell, called *podia*, to reach into the water. However, some foraminiferan tests have no perforations, and the living protoplasm emerges from a single aperture. The podia are similar to the pseudopodia that freshwater amoebas use to engulf food particles, but in foraminiferans they are much finer. In some species they form a network of thin, interconnected branches, called *reticulopodia*. The podia may be used for swimming, crawling on the seafloor, and gathering materials for the test, but their primary function is to catch particles of food. These include microscopic algae, other protists, bacteria, fungi, and decaying organic matter. Some foraminiferans also house symbiotic algae to supplement their food supply.

The life cycles of foraminiferans are varied and complex. In many species a sexual stage alternates with an asexual stage. The asexual form reproduces by dividing into multiple daughter cells, whereas the sexual form produces sex cells called *gametes*, which fuse together to form a new asexual cell.

Over millions of years the tests of dead foraminiferans have accumulated on the seafloor and become compressed to form limestone rock. Blackboard chalk consists largely of foraminiferan remains, as do the pyramids of Egypt. By identifying the fossil species present in sedimentary rocks, geologists can locate rock strata that are likely to cover oil deposits.

Scientists classify foraminiferans as members of the order Foraminiferida, within the phylum Sarcomastigophora (kingdom Protista).

Ben Morgan

FURTHER READING
Banister, Keith, and Andrew Campbell. *The Encyclopaedia of Underwater Life*. London: Allen and Unwin, 1985.
Margulis, Lynn. *Five Kingdoms: An Illustrated Guide to the Phyla of Life on Earth*. San Francisco: W. H. Freeman, 1982; 3rd ed., New York, 1998.

RELATED ARTICLES
Protozoa; Sarcomastigophora; Zooplankton

Form Resistance

Form resistance is the resistance to movement through the water that is proportional to the cross-sectional area of the object in contact with the water. The least amount of form resistance would be found in an object that was long and thin, such as a piece of wire or a very thin cylinder. Conversely, the greatest amount of form resistance would be generated by a spherical object. The significance of form resistance is seen in the shape of various swimming animals. If an animal is to be a fast swimmer, it needs to reduce the form resistance, hence fast-swimming fishes tend to have bodies that are narrow or thin in cross section, often with tapered anterior and posterior ends. However, no fast-swimming animal has a shape like a wire, due to the fact that to be a fast swimmer also requires the muscle mass to propel the animal, which takes up a lot of cross-sectional area.

James W. Nybakken

FURTHER READING
Nybakken, James W. *Marine Biology: An Ecological Approach*, 5th ed. San Francisco: Benjamin Cummings, 2001.

RELATED ARTICLES
Fish Propulsion

Fracture Zone

The ocean floor is scarred by a large number of long linear features that have formed at right angles to the mid-ocean spreading ridge. These features, called *fracture zones*, encircle large parts of Earth, similar to the mid-ocean ridge system. Fracture zones are long linear zones of weakness on the ocean floor and cover extensive distances. Found in many places on the ocean floor, fracture zones are aseismic extensions of active transform faults along the spreading axes. Fracture zones are very large features. They may be several thousand kilometers in length, hundreds of kilometers wide, and tens of kilometers deep. Ridge offset from fracture zones is variable but may be as much as 40 kilometers (25 miles).

Fracture zones have an implied mobility. These zones represent parts of the ocean floor that have been in motion for long periods of time but at varying velocities. Fracture zones are curved and small segments are approximately parallel to the direction of plate movement when the fracture zone developed. Fracture zones are ancient fault scars in the lithospheric plate and are generally considered to be the fossil remnants of former spreading axes and transform faults. The Atlantic Ocean hosts more fracture zones than the Pacific Ocean and they are more regularly spaced because the Mid-Atlantic Ridge moves slower than the East Pacific Rise. In the Atlantic, fracture zones are relatively simple features and appear about every 55 kilometers (34 miles). In the Pacific, however, fracture zones are complex

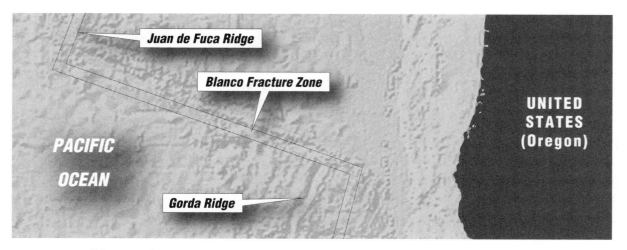

Fracture zone off the coast of Oregon, in the northwest part of United States.

systems of ridges and basins that occur less frequently but with larger offsets.

A fracture zone may be considered as being a single feature composed of three distinct sections. The central portion of the fracture zone contains the spreading ridge that is offset by, and includes, a transform fault. The spreading axis is displaced along the fracture zone and has movement that is in opposite direction to the movement across the transform fault. Active transforms lie between two offset oceanic spreading ridges, which slowly grind past each other along the transform fault. Beyond the ridge crests the fracture zone continues away from the spreading axis in both directions and is essentially inactive or has only minor amounts of seismic activity. It is the scar of an extinct transform fault.

Fracture zones and transform faults are distinguished by the following differences. A fracture zone has movement in the same direction across the feature, whereas a transform fault moves in opposite directions; a fracture zone is an intraplate feature, whereas a transform fault is an actual plate boundary; fracture zones have only minor seismic activity; fracture zones occur outside or away from the mid-ocean ridge segment, whereas transform faults are confined to the mid-ocean ridge segment; fracture zones show evidence of past transform fault activity; and transform faults are a part of the overall fracture zone.

David L. White

FURTHER READING

Condie, Kent C. *Plate Tectonics and Crustal Evolution.* New York: Pergamon Press, 1976; 4th ed., Oxford and Boston: Butterworth-Heinemann, 1997.

Sullivan, Walter. *Continents in Motion: The New Earth Debate.* New York, McGraw-Hill, 1974; 2nd ed., New York: American Institute of Physics, 1991.

Tarbuck, Edward J., and Frederick K. Lutgens. *Earth: An Introduction to Physical Geology.* Columbus, Ohio: Charles E. Merrill, 1984; 8th ed., Upper Saddle River, N.J.: Prentice Hall, 1997.

Thurman, Harold V. *Essentials of Oceanography.* Columbus, Ohio: Charles E. Merrill, 1983; 6th ed., with Alan P. Trujillo, Upper Saddle River, N.J.: Prentice Hall, 1999.

RELATED ARTICLES
Mid-Atlantic Ridge; Transform Fault

Fram

The *Fram* (Norwegian for "forward") is the ship in which the Norwegian explorer Fridtjof Nansen (1861–1930) drifted across the Arctic Ocean in the 1890s. This expedition was an attempt to reach the North Pole and determine the nature of the extreme Arctic—whether made of land, sea, or ice. The *Fram* was a three-masted schooner built to Nansen's own specifications. A key feature was the ship's smooth, rounded steel hull, which was designed to rise above encroaching pack ice rather than be crushed by it.

In the summer of 1893, Nansen with the *Fram*'s crew of 12, embarked from Oslo, Norway, with provisions for five years. Nansen's intention was to lock the *Fram* in pack ice and drift over or near the North Pole. This would prove that the Arctic was a frozen polar ocean, not an ice-covered continent as in the case of Antarctica. In September 1893, the *Fram* became locked in sea ice north of Siberia and drifted with the pack ice for nearly three years—at one point coming to within 400 kilometers (248 miles) of the North Pole—before being released near Spitsbergen, Norway. Nansen and a companion attempted to reach the North Pole on skis and reached as far as 86°14′N before being forced to turn back.

During the voyage, Nansen and his crew made numerous observations and took systematic readings of temperature and other physical parameters above and below the water surface. Several discoveries during the voyage led to important scientific developments. For example, Nansen's observations of surface currents led Vagn Walfrid Ekman (1874–1954) to develop the mathematical model, the Ekman spiral, relating wind to subsurface currents. In 1911, the Norwegian explorer Roald Amundsen (1872–1928) took the *Fram* to the Bay of Whales, Antarctica, on his attempt to be the first to reach the South Pole. Amundsen's expedition arrived at latitude 90°S on 14 December 1911, completing its mission successfully. The *Fram* is being preserved in a museum in Oslo.

Trevor Day

FURTHER READING

Nansen, Fridtjof. *Farthest North*. New York: Modern Library, 1999.

Nansen, Fridtjof, ed. *The Norwegian North Polar Expedition, 1893–1896*. London and New York: Longmans, Green and Fridtjof Nansen Fund for the Advancement of Science, 1900–06; New York: Greenwood Press, 1969.

USEFUL WEB SITES

"Fridtjof Nansen—Scientist, Diplomat and Humanist." <http://www.nrsc.no/nansen/fritjof_nansen.html>.

"The Northern Lights Route: With Nansen to the North Pole." <http://www.ub.uit.no/northernlights/eng/nansen.htm>.

RELATED ARTICLES

Amundsen, Roald; Nansen, Fridtjof; Oceanographic Research Vessel

Frictional Resistance

Oceanographers can spend their entire career studying ocean currents and eddies and never worry about friction. This is because the forces that govern motion in the deep ocean for horizontal scales greater than 10 to 100 kilometers (about 6 to 60 miles) are much greater than the frictional forces. On the other hand, frictional resistance is important when studying smaller-scale phenomena such as acoustic or capillary waves or motions with scales of centimeters to meters. Friction is due to the viscosity of water and is caused by molecular forces. Viscosity (or friction) converts kinetic energy due to motion into heat.

Viscosity is determined by measuring the tangential stress and dividing by the rate of change of velocity with distance. The molecular viscosity of seawater at the sea surface for 10°C, S = 35 practical salinity units, is 1.39×10^{-3} newton per square meter. Molecular viscosity decreases as temperature rises but increases with salinity and pressure. Within the ocean, the molecular viscosity can change by a factor of 2 due to temperature changes, but changes associated with salinity and pressure variability are only about 10 percent.

Energy cascades from large-scale motions to smaller-scale motions. When examining the balance of forces for larger scales, it is unnecessary and impractical to consider all possible smaller scales, so the loss of energy to smaller scales is modeled by a single frictionlike term that includes a parameter called the *eddy viscosity.* The eddy viscosity is much larger than the molecular viscosity. Typical values depend upon the scale of the motion that is being modeled and range from 0.1 to 10 newtons per square meter for vertical eddy viscosity and from 10^5 to 10^8 newtons per square meter for horizontal eddy viscosity. The difference between the vertical eddy viscosity and the horizontal eddy viscosity reflects the extent to which mixing occurs in the ocean. Mixing in the vertical direction must overcome buoyancy forces caused by stable stratification, so that much less mixing occurs in the vertical direction than in the horizontal.

Frictional boundary layers exist at the surface and bottom of the ocean where water comes into contact with air and seafloor, respectively. These layers are usually called *Ekman layers,* in honor of V. Walfrid Ekman (1874–1954), who published the correct physical model for these layers in 1905. Ekman developed this theory to explain Fridtjof Nansen's (1861–1930) observation that Arctic ice consistently moved 20 to 40° to the right of the wind direction. Ekman balanced the wind stress on the surface of the ocean with the effect of the rotation of Earth and frictional forces. His solution yielded a current spiral in the upper ocean, but more important, he determined that the transport in the frictional surface layer is directed to the right (left) of the wind stress in the northern (southern) hemisphere. The depth of the Ekman layer is the depth at which the current is opposite to that at the surface and is called the *depth of frictional influence.* The depth of frictional influence varies with latitude, from 45 meters (about 145 feet) near the pole to 100 meters (about 325 feet) near the equator. This frictional upper layer effectively isolates the interior of the ocean from the stresses caused by wind.

A similar situation occurs at the bottom of the ocean, where the current must decrease to zero at the interface between water and sediment. If the ocean currents are steady, the model developed by Ekman for the surface layer works for the bottom layer as well. This layer is called the *benthic boundary layer* or *Ekman bottom layer.* An interesting interaction between the currents and the ocean bottom can develop if the currents are strong enough to move or to suspend the sand or sediment in the water.

Curtis A. Collins

FURTHER READING
Cushman-Roisin, B. *Introduction to Geophysical Fluid Dynamics.* Englewood Cliffs, N.J.: Prentice Hall, 1994.
Knauss, J. A. *Introduction to Physical Oceanography.* Englewood Cliffs, N.J.: Prentice Hall, 1978; 2nd ed. Upper Saddle River, N.J.: Prentice Hall, 1997.
Pedlosky, J. *Geophysical Fluid Dynamics.* New York: Springer-Verlag, 1979; 2nd ed., 1982.

RELATED ARTICLES
Eddy; Ekman Layer

Fringing Reef

A fringing reef is a coral reef that closely follows the shoreline of an island or continent. The body of water (lagoon) between reef and land is narrow—hundreds of meters wide at most—and shallow. This distinguishes fringing reefs from barrier reefs, which develop farther from the shore and have lagoons that may be tens of kilometers wide, as in the case of the Great Barrier Reef, and deep enough to allow the passage of ocean liners. The third coral-reef type, an atoll, is a horseshoe- or ring-shaped reef enclosing a near-circular lagoon. Charles Darwin (1809–82) documented these distinctions between coral-reef types in 1842. He also proposed—correctly, as was later confirmed—that a fringing reef can be the first stage in the development of a coral atoll, with a barrier reef as an intermediate stage.

Fringing reefs and other coral-reef types develop where the combination of environmental factors encourages reef-building (*hermatypic*) coral polyps to grow profusely. These features are shallow water, water temperatures in the range 18 to 30°C (64 to 86°F), near-normal seawater salinity, and water of low turbidity. Clear water and high light levels are necessary for photosynthesis by the algae that grow symbiotically inside reef-building coral polyps. The algae give coral reef systems their enormously high productivity despite being found in nutrient-sparse waters. To grow well, coral polyps need to be immersed in seawater for all or most of the time, but not in water that is too deep for strong sunlight to reach.

In the warm Indo-Pacific region, a newly emerged volcanic island may develop a fringing reef alongside its shore. As the island subsides, the reef grows upward some distance away from the shore to form a barrier reef. In the final stage of coral-reef development, the original island submerges entirely and the reef system becomes an atoll. Elsewhere, fringing reefs and barrier reefs are not part of a developmental sequence leading to atoll formation but stable endpoints in themselves.

Fringing reefs grow best where the subtidal surface for larval settlement is suitable and where the freshwater runoff is minimal. Because fringing reefs occur close to shore, they are readily damaged by land-based human activities. Coastal developments that increase freshwater runoff, sedimentation, and agricultural, industrial, or domestic pollution will affect reefs adversely. With easy access for shore-based tourism, many fringing reefs are subject to physical damage from swimming, diving, and boat activities. The world's longest system of fringing reefs extends some 4000 kilometers (2500 miles) along the coast of the Red Sea, from the Gulf of Aden to the Gulfs of Suez and Aqaba. Other well-developed fringing reefs are found along the shores of East Africa and around many Indo-Pacific islands. Fringing reefs are the most common reef type in the Caribbean Sea.

The shoreward side of the fringing reef typically slopes gently and may be partly exposed at low tide. If a lagoon is present, its floor may be interspersed with clumps of coral and sandy areas formed from reef debris. The highest point of the reef, the reef crest, is subject to heavy, breaking surf and often features a growth of red encrusting coralline algae. Beyond the reef crest, the reef slope typically falls away to a depth of 100 meters (330 feet) or more, with growth of reef-forming coral most abundant in the top 50 meters (165 feet). On the reef slope, vertical zonation produces a community of corals, algae, and associated reef animals that is among the most luxuriant and diverse assemblages in the ocean.

Trevor Day

FURTHER READING

Birkeland, Charles, ed. *Life and Death of Coral Reefs.* New York: Chapman and Hall, 1997.

Dubinsky, Z., ed. *Coral Reefs,* Vol. 25. Amsterdam and New York: Elsevier, 1990. Series title: *Ecosystems of the World.*

Gray, William. *Coral Reefs and Islands: The Natural History of a Threatened Paradise.* Newton Abbot, England: David and Charles Publishers, 1993.

Kaplan, Eugene H. *A Field Guide to Coral Reefs of the Caribbean and Florida: A Guide to the Common Invertebrates and Fishes of Bermuda, the Bahamas, Southern Florida, the West Indies, and the Caribbean Coast of Central and South America.* Boston: Houghton Mifflin, 1982.

Karlson, Ronald H. *Dynamics of Coral Communities.* Boston: Kluwer Academic, 1999.

Wood, Rachel. *Reef Evolution.* Oxford and New York: Oxford University Press, 1999.

RELATED ARTICLES
Barrier Reef; Coral Atoll; Coral Reef

Front

A front is a relatively narrow zone of enhanced horizontal gradients of physical, chemical, and biological properties (temperature, salinity, nutrients, etc.) that separates broader areas of different vertical structure (stratification). Fronts occur on a variety of scales, from several hundred meters up to many thousand kilometers. Some of them are short-lived, but most are quasistationary and seasonally persistent: They emerge and disappear at the same locations during the same season, year after year. The most prominent fronts are present year-around. The temperature and salinity ranges (differences) across the strongest fronts could be as high as 10 to 15°C (50 to 59°F) and 2 to 3 practical salinity units (psu), although somewhat smaller figures [5°C (41°F) and 1 psu] are much more common. The width of fronts varies widely; sometimes the frontal interface is very narrow, less than 100 meters (330 feet), but some major fronts are 50 to 200 kilometers (31 to 124 miles) wide. Vertically, many fronts extend several hundred meters in depth; major fronts extend as deep as 2000 meters (over 6500 feet). Fronts are crucial in various processes that evolve in the ocean and at the ocean interfaces with the atmosphere, sea ice, and ocean bottom.

1. Fronts are associated with current jets, so that any frontal pattern represents a circulation pattern.
2. The along-frontal current jets are accountable for the bulk of water/heat/salt transport.
3. Fronts separate different water masses and spawn rings responsible for the bulk of cross-frontal and meridional transport of water, heat, and salt.
4. Fronts usually coincide with major biogeographical boundaries associated with zones of enhanced bioproductivity, including fisheries grounds.
5. The surface heat fluxes, wind stress, and other meteorological parameters may differ drastically between the warm and cold sides of a front. Fronts strongly interact with the marine atmospheric boundary layer and separate regions with different responses to atmospheric forcing, so they are crucial for weather forecasting and climate monitoring.
6. Some high-latitude fronts are directly related to sea ice conditions, so the front locations are determined by the maximum extent of the sea ice cover.
7. Fronts profoundly influence acoustic environment, so that solving any sound propagation problem requires knowledge of the fronts' locations and characteristics.
8. Ocean sedimentation regimes are largely determined by the circulation (hence frontal) pattern; therefore, the interpretation of paleoceanographic and paleoclimatic information recorded in marine sediments requires a priori knowledge of the modern frontal situation.
9. Because fronts are associated with convergent currents, oceanic and riverine pollutants can be concentrated thousands of times on fronts, thus endangering the fish, seabirds, and marine mammals that inhabit the frontal zones.

Basic Types of Fronts

Fronts are formed by various processes; accordingly, there are several major frontal types, described below.

Estuarine fronts. These fronts form as interfaces between the freshwater river outflow (plume) and the ambient seawater. Consequently, they are mainly salinity fronts, although in most cases there is a temperature gradient as well across the principal salinity front. Since most rivers carry substantial amounts of sediments (silt), most estuarine fronts are turbidity fronts as well and therefore could easily be observed from space, owing to the distinct color/transparency gradients across these fronts. Some examples are the

433

Amazon River, Rio de la Plata, Chesapeake Bay, Yangtze River, and Ganges plume fronts.

Shelf fronts. These fronts are observed over the mid-shelf areas, well inshore of the shelf-break. Their origin is sometimes related to the opposing currents over the shelf, with the offshore current typically flowing north (in the northern hemisphere) and the inshore current flowing south (e.g., the South Atlantic Bight). Some examples are the Bering Sea, Middle Atlantic Bight, and eastern China seas (Bohai, Yellow, and East China) shelf fronts. Some shelf fronts are apparently related to the shelf's geomorphology, specifically, submerged terraces (paleoshorelines; e.g, in the Bering Sea).

Tidal mixing fronts. In some shallow areas tides dissipate a tremendous amount of energy through bottom friction. In such areas the water column might be completely mixed by the tides. Typically, the maximum depth where it happens is approximately 100 meters (330 feet), whereas the average depth is 50 meters (165 feet). Consequently, a front forms between the completely mixed water column over the shallow depths and the stratified water column over the deeper bottom. Such fronts are observed over many shelves (e.g., in the North, Celtic, Bering, East China, Yellow, and Okhotsk Seas). The tidal mixing fronts also form around banks (e.g., Georges Bank), islands (e.g., Pribilof Islands in the Bering Sea), and peninsulas (e.g., Shandong Peninsula, Yellow Sea or Península Valdés, Patagonian Shelf).

Shelfbreak fronts. This is the most common frontal type; such fronts are aligned with the shelfbreak and separate the on-shelf water from the off-shelf (oceanic) water. The shelfbreak fronts are water mass fronts because they separate two distinct water masses, onshore and offshore (this is not the case, for example, with the tidal mixing fronts described above). There is always a well-defined current along the shelfbreak fronts.

Some examples are the Mid-Atlantic Bight and Bay of Biscay.

Coastal upwelling fronts. Any upwelling (wind-induced, topographic, or tidal) brings the subsurface water to the surface. Because the subsurface water is usually colder than the surface layer, a front emerges between the cold, upwelled water inshore and the warmer water offshore. Such fronts are observed off Washington–Oregon–California, Peru–Chile, northwestern Africa, Angola–Namibia–South Africa, and the Yucatán Peninsula, among others.

Equatorial upwelling fronts. The Coriolis force causes equatorial divergence, with the surface waters moving away from the equator in both hemispheres. The colder subsurface water comes to the surface to create a temperature (and salinity) gradient at the contact with the warm surface water. Such fronts are prominent in the central and eastern Pacific Ocean and in the Atlantic Ocean. The landmass asymmetry of the Indian Ocean boundaries might be the main reason why equatorial upwelling fronts are not prominent in the Indian Ocean.

Western boundary current fronts. Fronts associated with the Gulf Stream, Kuroshio, Agulhas Current, Brazil, and East Australia Currents are the world's strongest in terms of the cross-frontal ranges of oceanographic properties, vertical extent, along-front current speed and transport, and other characteristics. These fronts could be traced into the open ocean for many thousand kilometers. In winter, two fronts are distinct on both sides of the western boundary current because each current carries tropical water that is warmer then the ambient waters inshore and off-shore of the currents.

Subtropical convergence fronts. These fronts form because of the Ekman wind convergence, which brings together waters of different temperature (because of the north–south large-scale temperature gradient in the ocean) and maintains the emerging front. Such fronts are observed in the North Atlantic (Sargasso Sea) and North Pacific and in the southern parts of the Atlantic, Indian, and Pacific Oceans.

Marginal ice zone fronts. These fronts are associated with the sea ice edge and very specific processes that operate within this zone. During sea ice formation, the brine rejection (salt release) causes haline convection. During sea ice melting, the surface freshening creates a local salinity front between the low-salinity meltwater and the ambient water. In spring, as the meltwater absorbs solar radiation, a temperature gradient (thermal front) develops across the initial salinity front. Some examples are the Labrador, Greenland, Barents, and Bering Seas and the Southern Ocean.

Southern Ocean fronts. This is the only ocean with truly circumpolar fronts, the Subantarctic, Polar, and Southern Antarctic Circumpolar Current Fronts; the Southern Subtropical Front is nearly circumpolar. The origin of these fronts is related to the dynamics of the Antarctic Circumpolar Current. The Antarctic Slope Front forms between the shelf water near the Antarctic continent and the offshore oceanic water; therefore, it could be considered as one of the shelf-break fronts. However, its structure and dynamics are different from those of other shelfbreak fronts. Katabatic winds from the Antarctic continent help maintain the westward current over the Antarctic shelf, thus playing a role in the Antarctic Slope Front maintenance.

Societal Importance and Applications of Fronts

Fronts are important in the following applications:

1. *Marine transportation.* Frontal locations and their characteristics are used to optimize ship routing depending on area and season and the observed long-term (interannual and decadal) variability of ocean fronts and associated currents.

2. *Fishing industry.* Many important fishery grounds, including some underexploited fish stocks, are located along fronts.

3. *Climate change monitoring and prediction.* These require adaptive strategy for the global ocean observing system, based on all available information about the location and variability of major ocean currents (i.e., fronts) to optimize construction, deployment, and utilization of observational platforms.

4. *Marine mining, including oil and gas industry.* Marine mining uses information on the pattern and persistence of ocean currents (hence fronts and frontal eddies, including rings) that directly affects drilling operations and production cycle on offshore platforms.

5. *Pollution control, waste disposal, and hazards mitigation.* These benefit from knowledge of the current (i.e., frontal) pattern and its variability, especially in the regions influenced by strong frontal currents and rings (e.g., the U.S. east coast and the Gulf of Mexico).

6. *Integrated coastal zone management.* This is dependent on exact knowledge of the potential vulnerability of managed areas to nature hazards (hurricanes, storms, floods, tornados) whose frequency and spatial pattern are dependent on the large-scale ocean circulation/frontal system.

7. *Submarine navigation.* This is facilitated by incorporation into computer acoustic and circulation models of detailed information on the locations and characteristics of fronts.

Igor M. Belkin

FURTHER READING

Bowman, M. J., and W. E. Esaias, eds. *Oceanic Fronts in Coastal Processes: Proceedings of a Workshop Held at the Marine Sciences Research Center, May 25–27, 1977.* Berlin and New York: Springer-Verlag, 1978.

Fedorov, K. N. *The Physical Nature and Structure of Oceanic Fronts.* Berlin and New York: Springer-Verlag, 1986.

IOC (International Oceanographic Commission). *Oceanic Fronts and Related Phenomena: Proceedings of Konstantin Fedorov International Memorial Symposium, Pushkin, St. Petersburg, Russia, 18–22 May 1998.* IOC Workshop Report 159. Paris: UNESCO, 2000.

Longhurst, A. *Ecological Geography of the Sea.* San Diego: Academic Press, 1998.

Mann, K. H., and J. R. N. Lazier. *Dynamics of Marine Ecosystems: Biological–Physical Interactions in the Oceans.* Cambridge, Mass.: Blackwell Scientific, 1991; 2nd ed., Blackwell Science, 1996.

Pickard, G. L., and W. J. Emery. *Descriptive Physical Oceanography: An Introduction.* Oxford: Pergamon Press, 1964; 5th ed., 1990.

Siedler, G., J. Church, and J. Gould, eds. *Ocean Circulation and Climate: Observing and Modelling the Global Ocean.* San Diego: Academic Press, 2001.

Tchernia, P. *Descriptive Regional Oceanography.* New York: Pergamon Press, 1980.

Tomczak, M., and J. S. Godfrey. *Regional Oceanography: An Introduction.* New York: Pergamon Press, 1994.

RELATED ARTICLES
Antarctic Circumpolar Current; Coriolis Effect; Salinity; Temperature, Distribution of; Upwelling; Water Mass; Western Boundary Current